HMH SCIENCE DIMENSIONS™

Earth & Space Science

Houghton Mifflin Harcourt™

Michael R. Heithaus, PhD

Dean of the College of Art, Sciences & Education
Florida International University
Miami, Florida

Mike Heithaus joined the Florida International University Biology Department in 2003, where he has served as director of the Marine Sciences Program and executive director of the School of Environment, Arts, and Society, which brings together the natural and social sciences and humanities to develop solutions to today's environmental challenges. He now serves as dean of the College of Arts, Sciences & Education. His research focuses on predator-prey interactions and the ecological importance of large marine species.

Michael J. Passow, PhD

Adjunct Associate Research Scientist
Lamont-Doherty Earth Observatory
Palisades, New York

Mike Passow taught 44 years in middle school, high school, and college classrooms, finally retiring from Dwight Morrow High School in his hometown of Englewood, New Jersey. Dr. Passow continues to provide professional development for science teachers. He is the founder and organizer of the Earth2Class workshops for teachers at the Lamont-Doherty Earth Observatory of Columbia University. Dr. Passow is also active in many professional earth science societies, serving multiple terms as president of the National Earth Science Teachers Association and National Association of Geoscience Teachers-Eastern Section.

Acknowledgments
Cover Credits
iron-nickel meteorite ©Breck P. Kent/Animals Animals/Earth Scenes; *meteor crater* ©Stephen Alvarez/National Geographic Stock; (bg) *topographic pattern* ©Perfect Vectors/Shutterstock

Printed in the U.S.A.

ISBN 978-0-544-86181-7

10 11 0029 26 25 24 23 22

4500853114   A B C D E F G

Image Credits: © HMH

ENGINEERING CONSULTANT

Cary I. Sneider, PhD
Associate Research Professor
Portland State University
Portland, Oregon

PROGRAM ADVISORS

Paul D. Asimow, PhD
Professor of Geology and Geochemistry
California Institute of Technology
Pasadena, California

Eileen Cashman, PhD
Professor of Environmental Resources
  Engineering
Humboldt State University
Arcata, California

Mark B. Moldwin, PhD
Professor of Space Sciences and
  Engineering
University of Michigan
Ann Arbor, Michigan

John Nielsen-Gammon, PhD
Regents Professor of Atmospheric
  Sciences
Texas A&M University
College Station, Texas

Sten Odenwald, PhD
Astronomer
NASA Goddard Spaceflight Center
Greenbelt, Maryland

CLASSROOM REVIEWERS

Scot F. Abel, PhD
Science Curriculum Coordinator
DC Everest School District
Weston, Wisconsin

Nine Dodge
Lead Teacher/Guide
Coulee Montessori Adolescent Program
La Crosse, Wisconsin

Eric Garber
Secondary Science TOSA
Twin Rivers Unified School District
Sacramento, California

Kit Keane
Teacher on Special Assignment –
  Instructional Support in Science
  and Math
Twin Rivers Unified School District
Sacramento, California

Christine Pratt
Science Coordinator
Kenosha Unified School District
Kenosha, Wisconsin

Justin Siering
Science Teacher
Jackson Liberty High School
Jackson, New Jersey

Ted K. Werner
Teacher AP Environmental/AP Physics
Jackson Liberty High School
Jackson, New Jersey

Chad Wilkinson
Science Teacher
La Crosse Central High School
La Crosse, Wisconsin

HMH SCIENCE **DIMENSIONS** # Earth & Space Science

WILL SPARK YOUR CURIOSITY

and prepare you for next year, college, a career, and life!

Where do you see yourself in
10 YEARS?

Be a Scientist.
DO SCIENCE.

Have fun with science and approach it as a real scientist would!

Explore

Gather Evidence

Be an Engineer.
SOLVE PROBLEMS.

Design

Test

Refine
Solutions

Be Inquisitive.
ASK QUESTIONS.

The solution starts with a question. What is your question?

Think Critically

Investigate

Overcome Challenges

Your Answer.
YOUR EVIDENCE.

HMH Science Dimensions puts you in charge of your own learning.

Work in Teams

Develop Explanations

Defend Your Answer

YOUR Program

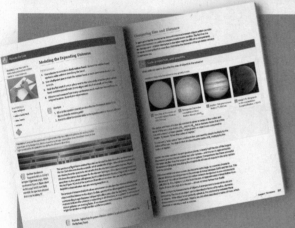

YOUR BOOK
- A brand-new and innovative textbook that will guide you through your next generation earth & space science curriculum, including your lab program

Tools to help you be successful as you learn science:

SCIENCE AND ENGINEERING PRACTICES
Online Handbook

CROSS-CUTTING CONCEPTS
Online Handbook

ENGLISH LANGUAGE ARTS
Online Handbook

MATH
Online Handbook

THING EXPLAINER features that explain complex science using drawings and simple language.

HMH SCIENCE **DIMENSIONS** Earth & Space Science

INTERACTIVE ONLINE STUDENT EDITION
- A complete online version of your textbook enriched with videos, interactivities, animations, simulations, and room to enter data, draw, and store your work

Contents in Brief

Earth can be studied as a singular system or a collection of smaller systems.

Introduction to Earth and Space   **2**

The structure and characteristics of minerals are determined by the matter that makes them up.

Image Credits: ©Scenics & Science/Alamy

Cities are complex systems that are created and sustained through the use of natural resources.

Image Credits: ©exzozis/Fotolia

UNIT 4

Earth in the Solar System   174

While Earth can be studied as a collection of smaller systems, it is also part of a larger solar system.

Image Credits: ©NASA Johnson Space Center

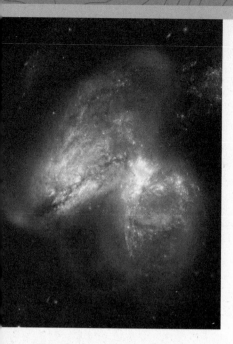

The study of matter in space requires an understanding of how light behaves when it is absorbed or emitted by elements.

Image Credits: ©Science Source

Volcanic eruptions frequently occur at the boundaries between Earth's tectonic plates.

Features on Earth's surface are shaped by the geosphere's interactions with Earth's other spheres.

UNIT 8
Earth's Water 452

Water is an essential resource for living things as well as an important agent of change for Earth's surface.

Image Credits: ©jorisvo/Fotolia

Conditions in Earth's atmosphere are reflected in climate and weather.

Image Credits: ©krasyuk/Fotolia

Changes in Earth's spheres take place over a wide range of timescales.

Image Credits: ©Hermes Images/AGF Srl/Alamy

UNIT 11

Human Activity and Earth

618

Human activity has a major effect on Earth systems, which in turn affect human activity.

Image Credits: ©rabbit75_fot/Fotolia

Lab Safety

Before you work in the laboratory, read these safety rules. Ask your teacher to explain any rules that you do not completely understand. Refer to these rules later on if you have questions about safety in the science classroom.

Directions

- Know where the fire extinguisher, fire blanket, shower, and eyewash station are located in your classroom.

- Read all directions and make sure that you understand them before starting an investigation or lab activity. If you do not understand how to do a procedure or how to use a piece of equipment, ask your teacher.

- Do not begin any investigation or touch any equipment until your teacher has told you to start.

- Never experiment on your own. If you want to try a procedure that the directions do not call for, ask your teacher for permission first.

- If you are hurt or injured in any way, tell your teacher immediately.

Dress Code

- Wear goggles when using glassware, sharp objects, or chemicals; heating an object; or working with anything that can easily fly up into the air and hurt someone's eye.

- Tie back long hair or hair that hangs in front of your eyes.

- Remove any article of clothing—such as a loose sweater or a scarf—that hangs down and may touch a flame, chemical, or piece of equipment.

- Observe all safety icons calling for the wearing of eye protection, gloves, and aprons.

Heating and Fire Safety

- Keep your work area neat, clean, and free of extra materials.

- Use only borosilicate glass for heating substances.

- Never reach over a flame or heat source.

- Point objects being heated away from you and others.

- Never heat a substance or an object in a closed container.

- Use oven mitts, clamps, tongs, or a test tube holder to hold heated items.

- Never touch an object that has been heated. If you are unsure whether something is hot, treat it as though it is.

- After heating test tubes, place them in a test tube rack.

- Do not throw hot substances into the trash. Wait for them to cool, and dispose of them in the container provided by your teacher.

Chemical Safety

- Always wear goggles when working with any type of chemical, even household items such as baking soda.

- Stand when you are working with chemicals. Pour them over a sink or your work area, not over the floor. If you spill a chemical or get it on your skin, tell your teacher right away.

- If you get a chemical in your eye, use the eyewash station immediately.

- Never touch, taste, or sniff any chemicals in the lab. If you need to determine odor, waft. To waft, hold the chemical in its container 15 cm (6 in.) away from your nose, and use your fingers to bring fumes from the container to your nose.

- Keep lids on all chemicals you are not using.

- Use materials only from properly labeled containers.

- Never use more chemicals than the procedure calls for.

- When diluting acid with water, always add acid to water.

- Never put unused chemicals back into the original containers. Dispose of extra chemicals in the container provided by your teacher.

- Always wash your hands after handling chemicals.

Electrical Safety

- Never use lamps or other electrical equipment with frayed cords.

- Make sure no cord is lying on the floor where someone can trip over it.

- Do not let a cord hang over the side of a counter or table so that the equipment can easily be pulled or knocked to the floor.

- Never let cords hang into sinks or other places where water can be found.

- Turn off all power switches before plugging an appliance into an outlet.

- Never touch electrical equipment with wet hands.

- Never try to fix electrical problems. Immediately inform your teacher of any problems.

- Unplug an electrical cord by pulling on the plug, not the cord.

Glassware and Sharp-Object Safety

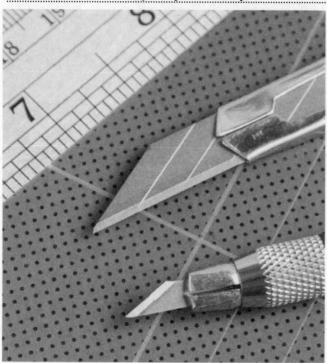

- Use only clean glassware that is free of chips and cracks.

- If you break glassware, tell your teacher right away.

- If you use a microscope that has a mirror, do not aim the mirror directly at the sun, as you can damage your eyes.

- Use knives and other cutting instruments carefully. Always wear eye protection and cut away from yourself.

- Clean glassware according to your teacher's instructions after you use it.

- Use an appropriately sized test tube for the quantity of chemicals you are using, and store test tubes in a test tube rack.

Safety in the Field

- Be sure you understand the goal of your fieldwork and the proper way to carry out the investigation before you begin fieldwork.

- Use proper safety equipment and personal protective equipment, such as eye protection, that suits the terrain and the weather.

- Follow directions, including appropriate safety procedures as provided by your teacher.

- Do not approach or touch wild animals. Do not touch plants unless instructed by your teacher to do so. Leave natural areas as you found them.

- Stay with your group.

- Use proper accident procedures, and let your teacher know about a hazard in the environment or an accident immediately, even if the hazard or accident seems minor.

Cleanup

- Follow your teacher's instructions for the disposal or storage of supplies.

- Clean your work area and pick up anything that has dropped to the floor.

- Wash your hands.

Safety Symbols

Safety is the priority in the science classroom. In all of the activities in this textbook, safety symbols are used to alert you to materials, procedures, or situations that could be potentially hazardous if the safety guidelines are not followed. Learn what you need to do when you see these icons, and read all lab procedures before coming to the lab so you are prepared. Always ask your teacher if you have questions.

 ANIMAL SAFETY Never injure an animal. Follow your teacher's instructions for handling specific animals or preserved specimens. Wash your hands with soap and water when finished handling animals or preserved specimens.

 APRON Wear an apron when using any substance that could cause harm if spilled on you. Stand whenever possible to avoid spilling in your lap.

 BREAKAGE Use caution when handling items that may break, such as glassware and thermometers. Always store test tubes in a test tube rack.

 CHEMICAL SAFETY Always wear goggles when working with chemicals. Stand whenever possible when working with chemicals to avoid spilling on your lap. Tell your teacher immediately if you spill chemicals on yourself, the table, or floor. Never taste any substance or chemical in the lab. Always wash your hands after working with chemicals.

 DISPOSAL Follow your teacher's instructions for disposing of all waste materials, including chemicals, specimens, or broken glass.

 ELECTRICAL SAFETY Keep electrical cords away from water to avoid shock. Do not use cords with frayed edges. Unplug all equipment when done.

 FIRE SAFETY Put on safety goggles before lighting flames. Remove loose clothing and tie back hair. Never leave a lit object unattended. Extinguish flames as soon as you finish heating.

 FUMES Always work in a well-ventilated area. Bring fumes up to your nose by wafting with your fingers instead of sniffing.

 GLOVES Always wear gloves to protect your skin from possible injury when working with substances that may be harmful or when working with animals.

 HAND WASHING Wash your hands with soap and water after working with soil, chemicals, animals, or preserved specimens.

 HEATING SAFETY Wear goggles and never leave any substance while it is being heated. Use tongs, hot pads, or test tube holders to hold hot objects. Point any materials being heated away from you and others. Place hot objects such as test tubes in test tube racks while cooling. Always wear gloves such as oven mitts when handling larger hot materials.

 PLANT SAFETY Do not eat any part of a plant. Do not pick any wild plants unless your teacher instructs you to do so. Wash your hands after handling any plant.

 POISON Never touch, taste, or inhale chemicals. Most chemicals are toxic in high concentrations. Wear goggles and wash your hands.

 SAFETY GOGGLES Always wear safety goggles when working with chemicals, heating any substance, or using a sharp object or any material that could fly up and injure you or others.

 SHARP OBJECTS Use scissors, knives, or razor tools with care. Wear goggles when cutting something with scalpels, knives, or razor tools. Always cut away from yourself.

Using Your
Evidence Notebook

Throughout the units and lessons of **HMH ScienceDimensions Earth & Space Science**, you will see notebook icons that highlight important places for you to stop and reflect. These Evidence Notebook prompts signal opportunities for you to record observations and evidence, analyze data, and make explanations for phenomena.

The Evidence Notebook is your location to gather evidence and record your thinking as you make your way through each lesson. Your teacher may determine a specific format for you to use, such as a digital or paper notebook. Whatever the format, you will record here the evidence you gather throughout the lesson to support your response to the Can You Explain It? challenge. You will also record significant information from the lesson to use as a study tool and to build your own study guide at the end of the lesson.

The following pages from one of the lessons in the book will familiarize you with the main types of Evidence Notebook prompts you will see throughout the course.

Gather Evidence Record observations or other evidence you've collected throughout the lesson. A Gather Evidence prompt on the first page of each lesson reminds you to record evidence you can use to support the claim you will make about the Can You Explain It? challenge.

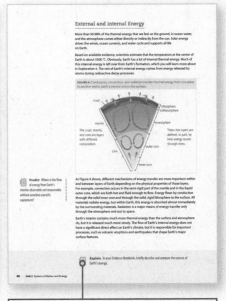

Predict Make a prediction or record your initial thoughts about a question you will return to later in the lesson.

Model Draw or create another model to help you interpret and understand information.

Explain Synthesize information from evidence, analysis, models, and other information gathered over the course of an exploration.

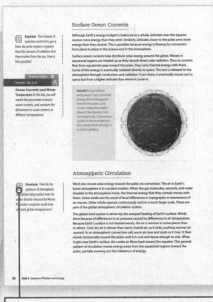

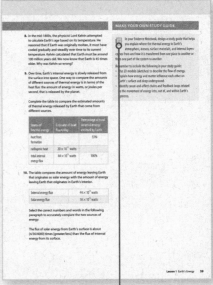

Analyze Interpret data or observations you have made about the text or visuals.

At the end of each lesson, you will also be prompted to use the notes from your Evidence Notebook to construct an explanation and to make your own study guide for the main ideas from the lesson.

Introduction to Earth and Space

Earth and the surface of the moon, as seen from the Lunar Reconnaissance Orbiter in 2015

FIGURE 1: A global relief map of Earth

Scientists use maps of Earth and other planets to display and communicate data and as tools for analyzing data. A relief map displays information about elevations of different points on Earth's surface. The map helps us understand features like high mountains, deep valleys, and flat plains in a way that a photograph of Earth cannot. A map is a type of model: it represents some but not all aspects of the real object. Like all models, a map is accurate in some ways but inaccurate in others.

 Predict How do you think the data used to create this relief map were collected?

DRIVING QUESTIONS

As you move through the unit, gather evidence to help you answer the following questions. In your Evidence Notebook, record what you already know about these topics and any questions you have about them.

1. How do scientists use a systems approach to construct an understanding of Earth and space?

2. How do scientists use patterns and models to explain processes and make predictions about Earth systems?

3. How do scientists study the interactions and flow of matter and energy within and between Earth's spheres?

UNIT PROJECT

Map Your School

 Go online to download the Unit Project Worksheet to help plan your project.

What types of information can be communicated on a map? How is that information communicated? Make a map or set of maps of your school or school grounds. Decide what aspects of the school you want to communicate or analyze using the map. For example, a map could use different colors to indicate different flooring and surface materials or different ways that spaces inside and outside the building are used. What questions can your maps help answer?

Studying Earth

Land, oceans, and clouds are visible from satellites orbiting Earth.

CAN YOU EXPLAIN IT?

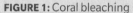
FIGURE 1: Coral bleaching

Gather Evidence
Record observations on how scientists study and think about Earth. As you explore the lesson, gather evidence to help explain what systems are made of and how they work.

Coral reefs are found in the clear, shallow tropical and subtropical regions of the world's oceans. They are an important part of the ocean environment. Coral reefs help support many species of marine organisms, providing them shelter and sources of food. During coastal storms, coral reefs help prevent beach erosion from strong ocean waves.

Healthy coral reefs are typically colorful. The color comes from microscopic organisms that live within the corals and use sunlight, much like plants, to make their own food.

Biologists are concerned about the health of the world's coral reefs, including problems such as coral bleaching—this happens when corals lose their colors. Earth scientists are helping to understand this problem by studying how changing conditions in the oceans and atmosphere are affecting coral reefs.

 Predict How might knowledge from Earth science help explain coral bleaching?

Exploring Patterns and Systems on Earth

Earth scientists study all the different parts of our planet, from global to local environments, to understand how these parts interact and to find solutions to problems such as coral bleaching.

Exploring the Earth System

What part or parts of Earth would you study to understand the problem of coral bleaching? Would you study the whole ocean or just the parts where coral reefs are found? When studying phenomena—observable events or circumstances—scientists often start by defining a system. A system is a part of the universe, made up of interacting components, that can be studied independently. To explore coral bleaching, for example, scientists could define a system as a single coral and the ocean water around it. They could also define the system as entire coral reefs and oceans.

Systems can be defined in many ways depending on what you want to figure out. What if you wanted to know what happens to solar energy that reaches Earth? How would you define that system?

Explain The figure on this page shows energy moving in and out of the Earth system. What everyday experiences would you cite as evidence to support the claim that there is a balance in energy coming in and out of Earth?

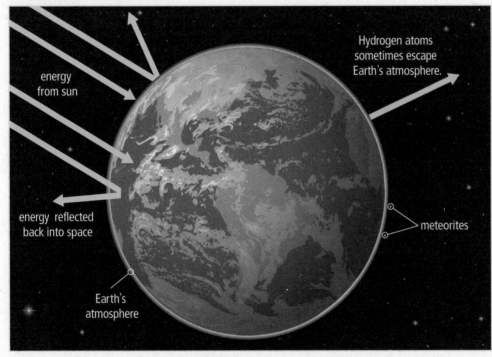

energy from sun

Hydrogen atoms sometimes escape Earth's atmosphere.

energy reflected back into space

meteorites

Earth's atmosphere

FIGURE 2: The whole Earth can be thought of as a system. Energy can flow in and out of the Earth system, while matter remains mostly the same.

Our thinking about Earth changed significantly in the late 20th century. Scientists, who until then had studied Earth as a collection of separate parts, such as the atmosphere, geosphere, hydrosphere, and biosphere, began to think of it as a system of interconnected parts and processes. Around this time, scientists discovered strong evidence suggesting that changes in one part of Earth could affect conditions in several other parts. Scientists, for example, found that the amount of carbon dioxide in the atmosphere and Earth's temperature were related. They learned that when one of these variables goes up, the other one follows. Thinking of Earth as a system helps scientists make connections between seemingly unrelated events.

Predict What parts of Earth do you think would be the most affected by a significantly warmer Earth? Use evidence and reasoning to support your claims.

Systems in Earth's Atmosphere and Oceans

If you think of Earth's spheres as systems within the larger Earth system, you could then ask, how are Earth's systems interconnected? And how do these systems interact? Earth's systems are interconnected and interact through matter and energy. Earth's atmosphere and oceans, for example, interact through processes in the water cycle. Recall that water moves from the oceans to the atmosphere and back through the water cycle. Energy also moves between these systems as air and water particles interact.

Earth scientists understand that interactions between the atmosphere and oceans greatly affect Earth's weather and climate patterns. For instance, global wind patterns in the Pacific Ocean near the equator, known as trade winds, help develop surface ocean currents that, under normal conditions, move warm water westward, from the western coast of South America to the eastern coast of Asia and Australia.

Analyze Interactions between the atmosphere and oceans affect weather and climate. Think about how the atmosphere and oceans (hydrosphere) may interact with another Earth system. Use evidence and facts to describe such an interaction.

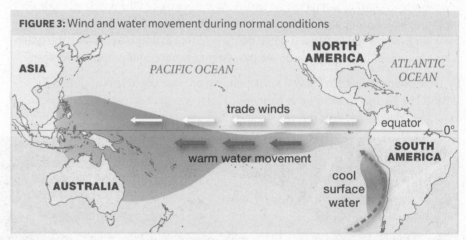

FIGURE 3: Wind and water movement during normal conditions

Every two to seven years, however, the trade winds weaken, and warm surface water pools in the middle of the Pacific Ocean and off the west coast of South America. This phenomenon is known as an El Niño event.

Predict The oceans can affect the temperature and moisture of air that moves over them. In the map showing normal conditions in the Pacific Ocean (Figure 3), cool surface water is found off the western coast of South America. What can you predict about the characteristics of air moving over this part of the ocean?

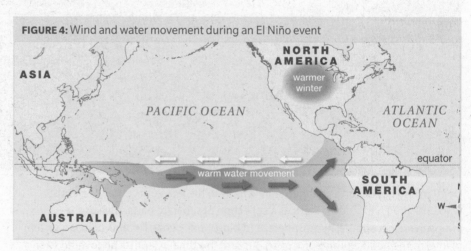

FIGURE 4: Wind and water movement during an El Niño event

An El Niño event affects the normal weather patterns in regions around the Pacific Ocean. During an El Niño, the weather on the west coast of South America is much warmer and wetter than usual. In the western Pacific region, near Australia and Asia, dry weather conditions prevail.

System Components and Processes

What factors cause the trade winds to weaken, the ocean water to warm up, and traditional weather patterns to change during an El Niño event? These questions are about cause-and-effect relationships. To begin to answer questions like these, scientists often identify the parts, or components, of systems and make observations about how these components change and interact through different processes.

Matter and energy are the basic components in natural systems. Matter components in the system where El Niño events originate include air and water. The energy components in this system include heat, or thermal energy, and air and water currents.

The components in systems interact through processes. Water evaporation is a common process that involves water particles and heat. Heating and cooling of the atmosphere and ocean and the movement of air and water are processes in the system related to El Niño events.

Once the components and processes of a system are identified, scientists can ask more specific questions about the system. They can decide what data they need to better understand the system and what tools are best to collect and analyze that data. As scientists explore and understand cause-and-effect relationships in systems, they can make predictions and draw conclusions about them.

Collaborate Although scientists know that El Niño is related to complex interactions between the ocean and the atmosphere, they are not sure what triggers an El Niño event or what causes conditions to return back to normal. What would you expect the data to show just before conditions in the area where El Niño originates return to normal? Hint: Think about the process(es) in the system that are known to change during an El Niño event.

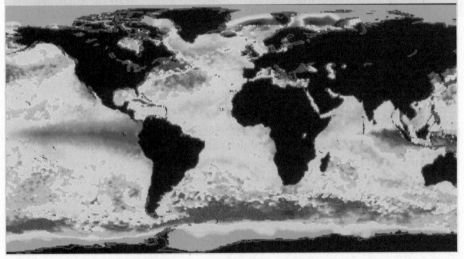

FIGURE 5: Surface water temperature. Regions in red show the highest increase.

Analyze Examine the surface water temperature map. The highest recorded temperature increase is off the western coast of South America. What can you infer about the strength of the trade winds in this area at the time the data were recorded?

Scale of Systems and Events

How significant are the effects of El Niño on regional and global weather and climate patterns? The significance of events like El Niño can be difficult to study—especially because their effects are often not the same everywhere. One way to study complex systems or events is to consider their scales.

Scale refers to the size, time, and energy characteristics of a system or event. Scientists can use information about scales to identify patterns and to describe, compare, and evaluate the significance of systems and events. For example, scientists know that El Niño originates in a relatively small region of Earth. They monitor and compare the conditions in this region over time and look for patterns in their data to accurately make predictions about the duration and strength of a possible El Niño event.

Explore Online ▶

Hands-On Lab

Observing the Sky Design, test, and revise a method for observing an aspect of the sky, such as weather or astronomical objects.

Orders of Magnitude of Systems

Image Credits: (l) ©L. Clarke/Corbis (r) ©NASA, ESA, and the Hubble Heritage Team/STScI/AURA/A. Riess

Collaborate
Describe the relative size order of magnitude of systems found in the Milky Way galaxy. Use reasoning and evidence to support your description.

The systems and events that are important in Earth and space science differ in size, duration, and energy. They can be as small as an atom or as large as the universe. These systems and events can exist and occur in time periods shorter than a second to longer than billions of years. They may involve little or vast amounts of energy. Comparing the size, duration, and energy of systems and events allows us to understand how systems relate to each other. The Milky Way galaxy, and Earth's place in it, is a familiar example of size order of magnitude.

FIGURE 6: Earth is part of the larger solar system, which itself is part of an even larger system of billions of stars and planets.

a Earth b Solar system c Milky Way galaxy

The significance of events on Earth is often dependent on their scale. The size, duration, and energy of these events determines their effects on systems. For example, although El Niño originates in a relatively small region of Earth it has global effects. The map in Figure 7 shows climate conditions observed during an El Niño event. Because surface water temperature affects the characteristics of the air above it, ocean currents have a strong effect on weather. Because air moves and interacts with air around the globe, changes in the Pacific Ocean can cause changes in weather and climate around the world.

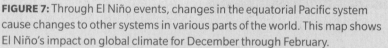

FIGURE 7: Through El Niño events, changes in the equatorial Pacific system cause changes to other systems in various parts of the world. This map shows El Niño's impact on global climate for December through February.

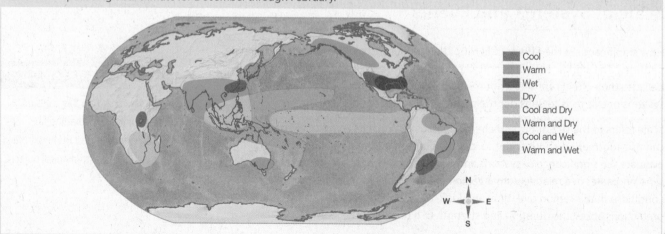

Cool
Warm
Wet
Dry
Cool and Dry
Warm and Dry
Cool and Wet
Warm and Wet

Data Analysis

Analyzing Monthly Sea Surface Temperatures

To study El Niño, scientists measure water and air temperatures, air pressure, wind, and ocean currents over time in the eastern Pacific Ocean, near the equator. The data in Figure 8 shows a pattern of increasing and decreasing water temperature over many months for three years when El Niño events occurred. El Niño gives way to La Niña conditions, and global climate and weather patterns shift again.

Monthly Sea Surface Temperature in the Eastern Equatorial Pacific

FIGURE 8: Sea surface temperatures in the equatorial Pacific fluctuate naturally over time. The x-axis is marked at every 2 months, beginning with July.

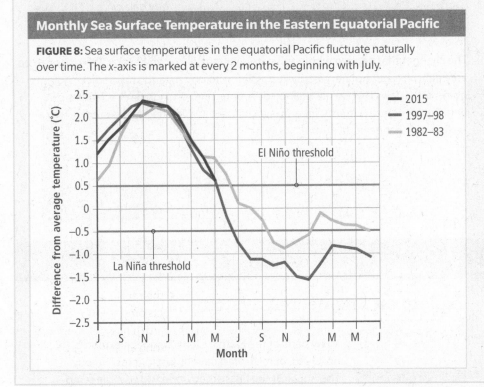

Analyze Examine the graph in Figure 8. What time of year are the conditions in the system most likely to develop into an El Niño event? A La Niña event?

The energy conditions of systems can help scientists identify patterns. For example, during the year, air temperature data show a rising and falling pattern related to seasons. Similarly, in the El Niño system, surface water temperature data show a heating and cooling pattern. The observed heating pattern can result in an El Niño event if the surface water temperature remains 0.5 °C above average for more than six months. A cooling pattern can result in a La Niña event if the surface water temperature remains 0.5 °C below average for more than six months.

La Niña is the opposite effect of El Niño. It is characterized by unusually cold ocean temperatures in the middle and eastern Pacific Ocean. The impact of La Niña on global climate and weather tends to be opposite that of El Niño. Dry and drought conditions can occur in western South America, while wetter than average conditions can be observed in Asia and Australia.

Explore Online ▶

FIGURE 9: Earth is a dynamic system. Thunderstorms can form and dissipate in just a few hours.

a Developing thunderstorm

b Mature thunderstorm

Dynamic Systems

Some systems are very stable and do not change very quickly. For example, without an atmosphere or surface water, rocks exposed on the moon's surface change very little over long periods of time. Earth is a dynamic system. Different parts of Earth interact with each other in complex ways that cause Earth to change over both short and long periods of time.

Thunderstorms can form in just a few hours in response to instability in the atmosphere caused by matter and energy interactions. They can dissipate just as quickly once the storm's energy decreases. Volcanic eruptions and earthquakes are other examples of events that can happen very quickly. However, these events can have immediate, long-lasting effects on Earth's systems.

The changes that happen within a dynamic system with many interacting parts can be very difficult—but not necessarily impossible—to understand and predict. Systems obey natural laws that do not change over time. With enough data, scientists can begin to recognize patterns, identify specific causes and effects, and predict how a system will change in the future.

Engineering

Explore an Engineered System

FIGURE 10: Aquarius Reef Base

Many parts of the Earth system cannot be explored, observed, or measured directly without technology. The Aquarius Reef Base is an underwater engineered system—a system designed by people—used by researchers to study the ocean, the coral reef, and other marine organisms in the Florida Keys.

The Aquarius Reef Base is designed to provide researchers a safe place to explore the underwater environment. Like Earth, this complex system consists of several smaller systems. As you would expect, some of the Aquarius systems—the main chamber where researchers live and work and the wet porch used to access the water—are below the surface of the ocean. But perhaps the most important system, the life support system, is up on the surface. This system is made of the electric generators, air compressors, and data connections that make life and work possible in the chambers below.

Explain In the Aquarius Reef Base, researchers find everything they need to survive and conduct their research. Explain how this engineered system is like the Earth system.

Connecting El Niño and Coral Bleaching

Thinking of Earth as a system of interconnected systems helps us see how sometimes change in one system is related to change in another system. To understand the relationship between coral bleaching and sea temperature, scientists plotted bleaching events in Tahiti, an island near the equator and in the middle of the Pacific Ocean, on a graph showing weekly average water temperature in the region (Figure 11). They were able to use these data to determine the bleaching threshold—the temperature at which bleaching is likely to occur—for the area.

The graph shows that in the years the observations were made, coral bleaching events were reported when the sea temperature exceeded 29 °C. During these years, El Niño conditions were also observed.

Bleaching Events over Time

FIGURE 11: Comparison of surface water temperature and coral bleaching events

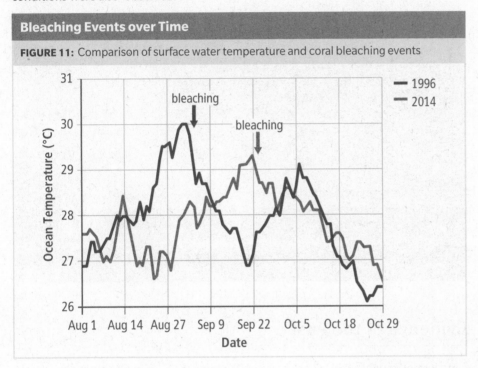

The Systems Approach

When they took to the road, these drivers in Southern California didn't expect to be trapped by tons of rock and mud. After a long dry spell, heavy rains in the area produced the flash floods and mudslides that buried these vehicles. Scientists associate weather extremes like this in California with El Niño events. They know that in the Earth system, changes in one system can affect other systems hundreds or even thousands of miles away.

FIGURE 12: Mudslide on a California highway

Explain What are the advantages and disadvantages of viewing Earth as a collection of individual, isolated systems?

Evidence of Changes in Systems

Some scientists study very small parts of Earth's system, such as mineral crystals; others study large mountain ranges. Some collect and analyze data to understand processes that occur very quickly, such as earthquakes and landslides, whereas others develop models—simplified representations— to understand how Earth's atmosphere, oceans, and interior and surface features have changed over the past 4.5 billion years.

Gather Evidence
As you read through this exploration, gather evidence to describe one way in which Earth has changed since it formed more than 4.5 billion years ago.

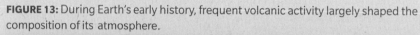

FIGURE 13: During Earth's early history, frequent volcanic activity largely shaped the composition of its atmosphere.

Evidence of the Past

Earth formed roughly 4.56 billion years ago, but humans have been keeping historical records for only about the past 5000 years. To understand what Earth was like in the distant past, we need to make inferences based on evidence that we can examine today and on our understanding of how Earth systems operate today. Where does the evidence we examine come from? Rock.

FIGURE 14: Banded iron formations provide evidence of long-term global changes in Earth's systems.

For example, the banded iron formation was deposited in shallow water more than 2.5 billion years ago. It provides evidence that Earth's atmosphere and oceans once contained much less oxygen—and many fewer oxygen-producing organisms—than it does today.

How do scientists arrive at this conclusion? They think that the iron in these rocks was originally present in other rocks. As the original rocks weathered, or broke apart, the iron was dissolved by water and transported to the ocean. Tiny grains of magnetite, a mineral, formed when the dissolved iron combined with oxygen produced by algae in the ocean. The magnetite grains settled out of the water and formed layers on the seafloor.

Today, iron that weathers from rocks combines with oxygen in the air almost immediately and thus cannot be dissolved in water. This suggests that at some point after the banded iron rocks formed, there was a global change in the characteristics and interaction between the land, ocean, air, and living systems. What was the nature of this change? We know that plants—and plant-like organisms—produce much of the oxygen present in the air and water today. An increase in the population of oxygen-producing organisms must have been a factor in the oxygenation of the Earth system.

Explain Assuming scientists' interpretation of banded iron formation is correct, how does it demonstrate ways in which Earth's systems of rock, oceans, atmosphere, and living things are interconnected?

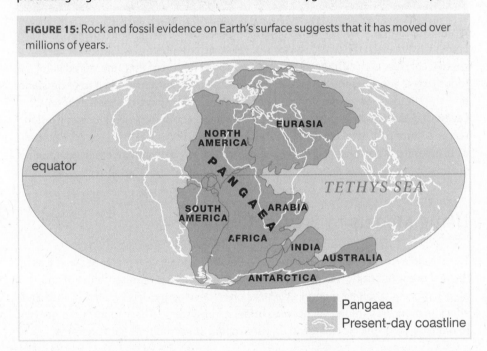

FIGURE 15: Rock and fossil evidence on Earth's surface suggests that it has moved over millions of years.

Infer How might changes in the position of continents and oceans change other Earth systems? What would be the timescale of these changes? Use evidence and reasoning to support your answers.

Scientists can observe over a few months or years the interactions between systems that result or are caused by El Niño, but they need to make inferences from evidence to consider changes that occurred over millions to billions of years.

There is evidence that the size, shape, and position of Earth's continents and oceans have changed over the past 200 million years. These changes have affected not only the distribution of landmasses, but also ocean currents, wind patterns, climate, ecosystems, and life itself.

Evidence from rocks, fossils, and surface structures, such as mountains, suggest that large pieces of Earth's surface moved great distances over millions of years. Approximately 210 millions years ago, all of Earth's landmasses were together and formed a supercontinent. Since then, a slow process known as *plate tectonics* that originates deep within Earth has moved the continents, opening and closing oceans.

Patterns in Systems

Using technology such as satellite, weather buoys, and land weather stations, scientists monitor conditions in the equatorial Pacific during late winter, spring, and summer months in order to predict the likelihood of an El Niño event later in the year. Scientists look for patterns in order to understand the systems they study.

Gather Evidence

How can analyzing ice from Antarctica help us understand processes occurring on a distant continent thousands of years ago?

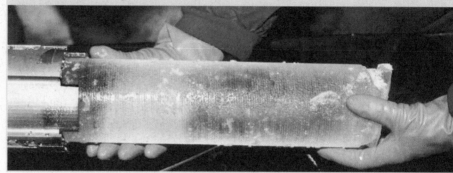

FIGURE 16: Scientists drill into the ice sheet in arctic regions to understand how Earth's atmosphere has changed over time.

While rocks like banded iron formations provide evidence for general changes in Earth's systems over millions or billions of years, ice cores record evidence for very specific changes in the atmosphere over a narrower period of time, measured in thousands of years. Scientists analyze the ice and the gases trapped in it to understand how the composition and temperature of the atmosphere have changed over time. Layers of dust and ash in the ice provide information about forest fires, desertification, volcanic eruptions, wind patterns, and, more recently, human activity. Ice cores allow us to investigate patterns of change due to interactions between different subsystems of Earth over seasons, years, centuries, and even hundreds of thousands of years.

Explore Online

Hands-On Lab

What's Before Your Eyes?
Make and record observations about multiple samples of salt solution.

Using Models to Predict Changes

The El Niño event of 1997 and 1998 was one of the strongest ever recorded and was the first predicted using a mathematical model. A model is a representation of an object, process, or phenomenon. Scientists often develop models based on cause-and-effect relationships among variables to understand systems. These models can be used to predict how a specific change in a system could affect multiple Earth systems.

FIGURE 17: The GEOS-5 computer model shows how the concentration of carbon dioxide in the atmosphere changes from season to season.

Explore Online

a Summer

b Winter

Image Credits: (t) ©Vin Morgan/AFP/Getty Images (bl) ©NASA Goddard Space Flight Center (br) ©NASA Goddard Space Flight Center

The GEOS-5 is a computer-simulation model used to predict how carbon dioxide levels might change throughout the year. In Figure 17, the model's red hues show increasing levels of carbon dioxide in the atmosphere in the Northern Hemisphere during fall and winter. Decreasing levels in the spring and summer are shown by the gray hues. Models like this are made using measurements of carbon dioxide levels in the atmosphere from stations on the ground and from satellites orbiting Earth.

Analyze The simulation shows seasonal patterns observed in the concentration of carbon dioxide levels in the atmosphere. What are some seasonal changes that can account for this increase?

Evidence, Patterns, and Predictions

Scientists collect and analyze data to describe what Earth is like at a given time. They compare the data over time to understand how Earth is changing. They also look for patterns of change, which helps them better understand how different parts of Earth's systems are related.

FIGURE 18: Map showing risk of coral bleaching during an El Niño on September 12, 2016.

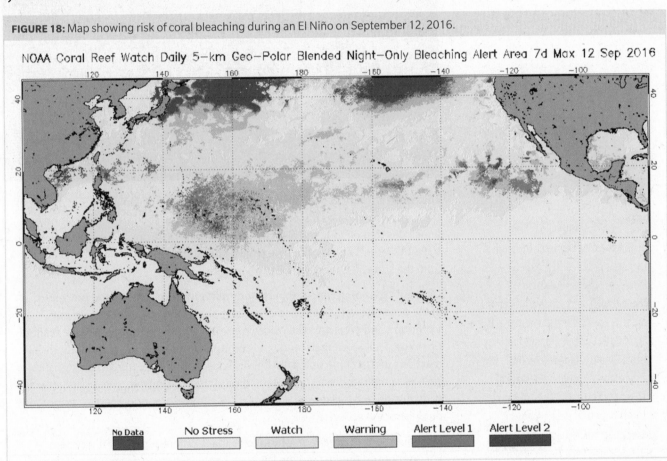

Scientists combine their understandings of the many components of the system to prepare bleaching alert maps. Both El Niño, which is part of a natural cycle, and global climate change, which is linked to human activities, affect the temperature of seawater. Scientists monitor the changes in sea surface temperatures during the year and also from year to year. These maps help people prepare for bleaching events. With careful planning, people are able to minimize the effects of bleaching by controlling factors that can harm the reef, such as tourism and pollution.

Analyze The Hawaiian islands and their coral reefs are located 20° North of the equator, in the central Pacific. What is the risk of bleaching of the Hawaiian coral reefs during an El Niño? Why?

Explain How can gathering data and analyzing patterns help us explain phenomena and also predict future conditions or events? Use evidence and reason to support your claim.

Careers in Science

Oceanographer

FIGURE 19: Oceanographer studying the properties of seawater

Collaborate

Understanding natural phenomena often requires the work of many scientists in different fields, such as biology, geology, meteorology, oceanography, and astronomy. Climate change is one of these phenomena. If you are trying to understand how and why Earth's climate changes over time, why is it important to consider the work of different types of scientists? What types of contributions could be made by oceanographers? Geologists? Meteorologists? Astronomers? Biologists?

The ocean is a very large system that includes not only ocean water, but also all of the minerals and gases dissolved in the water and the solid particles floating in it. It includes the seafloor and all of the living organisms, from single-celled plankton to Earth's largest animal, the blue whale. The oceans also contain energy absorbed from the sun and energy from Earth's interior.

Different types of oceanographers study different components and processes in the ocean system. Geological oceanographers study the rocks, sediments, landforms, and processes like volcanic eruptions and earthquakes on the seafloor. Chemical oceanographers study the components of seawater and the chemical reactions that occur in seawater. Physical oceanographers study characteristics such as temperature and pressure and ways that ocean water moves and interacts with outside forces like wind and gravity. Biological oceanographers study marine organisms and ecosystems.

Most questions in oceanography involve many different parts of the system. For example, to understand the living and nonliving systems around scalding hot springs on the deep ocean floor, different oceanographers work together to measure populations of different organisms, collect and examine the organisms, measure the temperature and pressure of the seawater, and analyze the chemistry of the rocks on the seafloor and the water flowing out from beneath the seafloor.

Analyze What are three questions that a physical oceanographer might try to answer in an investigation of El Niño?

| USING THE PRESENT TO UNDERSTAND THE PAST | CLASSIFYING EVENTS IN EARTH SYSTEMS | Go online to choose one of these other paths. |

Lesson Self-Check

CAN YOU EXPLAIN IT?

FIGURE 20: Coral reef bleaching

Thinking of a coral reef as a system that is part of the larger Earth system might help you to understand and find solutions to the coral reef bleaching problem. Coral reefs are marine ecosystems that include living organisms like coral, fish, and grasses, and nonliving components such as rock and seawater, and forms of energy such as sunlight and heat.

Scientists think that coral bleaching is caused by changes in the reef environment. Bleaching can occur in a small area as a result of things like the concentration of small particles in the water, changes in salinity, pollution, and too much sunlight. Disease can also cause bleaching. When bleaching occurs on a regional or global scale, however, it is known as mass bleaching.

Mass bleaching cannot be explained by local factors such as pollution. By comparing patterns of coral bleaching to patterns of change in environmental conditions, scientists have determined that mass bleaching is caused by an increase in seawater temperature. Studying patterns related to events like El Niño and global climate change allows scientists to understand the causes of mass bleaching and predict and prepare for future events.

 Explain How would scientists' understanding of the causes of coral bleaching and their ability to predict bleaching events be different if they studied only the body system of the coral and not the larger ocean-atmosphere system?

Image Credits: ©AP Television/AP Archive

CHECKPOINTS

Check Your Understanding

1. A system consists of components of matter and energy and the processes that involve the matter and energy. Sort the items in the list as components of matter, energy, or processes in a system.

   a. chemical reaction

   b. gas

   c. heat

   d. lava

   e. light

   f. melting

   g. motion

   h. rock

   i. water

2. Which of the following questions can best be answered by thinking of Earth as a system of interconnected parts? Choose all that apply.

   a. How is heat transported from the equator to the poles?

   b. How much water in Earth's hydrosphere may have come from comets?

   c. What was the role of Earth's early life forms in the evolution of Earth's atmosphere?

   d. Where can the effects of changes in global wind patterns be observed?

3. Explain why some Earth science questions can't be answered without thinking of Earth as a system.

4. Natural systems vary in scale in terms of both size and time. Put the systems below in order from smallest to largest.

   a. the Atlantic Ocean

   b. the Mississippi River

   c. Earth's atmosphere

   d. a pond

   e. an oyster

   f. the Grand Canyon

5. The map shows the regions that are studied to predict El Niño events.

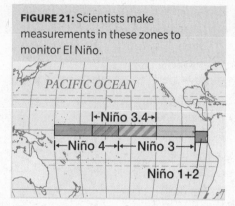

FIGURE 21: Scientists make measurements in these zones to monitor El Niño.

Which best describes the purpose of the map?

   a. It defines the systems where El Niño originates.

   b. It identifies processes in the Pacific Ocean.

   c. It shows how the atmosphere and ocean interact.

   d. It shows where seawater temperature is the warmest.

6. Which is an inference that can be made about the characteristics of the early Earth system based on evidence from the study of the banded iron formation?

   a. Earth's early surface was almost entirely made of rock lacking iron-bearing minerals.

   b. Iron-bearing rocks exposed to the atmosphere combined very quickly with oxygen.

   c. Oxygen levels in the air and water were as high during the early Earth as those observed in today.

   d. Free oxygen was concentrated mainly in the ocean where it was produced by algae.

7. The significance of systems and phenomena can be described in terms of their size, duration (time), and energy (strength) scales. Think about a phenomenon such as a thunderstorm. Then describe it in terms of its scales.

8. The evidence supporting the Earth system approach for studying the planet came from several discoveries including the relationship between carbon dioxide in the atmosphere and temperature. Explain how an increase in carbon dioxide in the atmosphere could affect other systems.

9. Which of the following are principles that scientists use to study, explain, and predict natural phenomena? Choose all that apply.

   a. Patterns can be used to predict future changes.

   b. Although energy does not move within Earth's systems, matter does move.

   c. Small systems of matter and energy operate independently of other systems.

   d. Earth system is closed and therefore stable and basically unchanging over time.

   e. The natural laws that describe how matter and energy interact were the same in the past as they are today.

   f. The processes that move matter from place to place within Earth's systems in the past are very similar or the same as the processes that operate today.

 In your Evidence Notebook, design a study guide that supports the main ideas from this lesson:

- A system is a group of parts—components of matter and energy—that interact with each other. Dynamic systems interact with other systems and change over time.
- Scientists can understand and predict how Earth changes over time by thinking of it as a dynamic system composed of many smaller subsystems that interact with each other.
- Earth is also part of larger systems such as the Earth–sun system, the solar system, the Milky Way Galaxy, and the universe.
- Scientists study Earth using a variety of tools, practices, and ways of thinking.

Remember to include the following in your study guide:

- Support main ideas with details and specific examples, such as those related to studies of coral bleaching, El Niño, and global climate change.
- Describe causes and effects of the phenomena you investigated.
- Describe how modeling patterns can be used to understand phenomena.

Earth's Systems

Connections between users of a social media platform

CAN YOU EXPLAIN IT?

FIGURE 1: The concentration of ozone in the stratosphere above Antarctica fluctuates throughout the year. Blue and purple indicate the least ozone, whereas yellow and red are where there is more ozone.

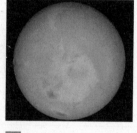  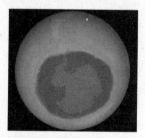

 July 2015   b August 2015   c October 2015

Gather Evidence

Record observations about Earth's systems and the ways scientists use models to understand Earth. As you explore the lesson, gather evidence to help describe and explain

- the major subsystems or spheres of Earth.

- how models such as graphs, diagrams, maps, and animations are used to describe, understand, and communicate characteristics and processes of Earth's systems.

One of the most important components of Earth's atmosphere is oxygen. About 21% of Earth's atmosphere consists of oxygen gas, which plants produce and animals need in order to survive. In addition, a very small portion of the atmosphere is another form of oxygen called ozone. Most of the ozone is concentrated in a thin layer of the stratosphere, between about 10 and 25 km above the surface. The rest is in the troposphere, the bottom layer of the atmosphere, near the ground. Unlike ground-level ozone, which is a pollutant that can cause respiratory problems, stratospheric ozone is vital to life on Earth. Ozone absorbs ultraviolet radiation from the sun. Ultraviolet radiation can cause skin cancer, cataracts, and can cause damage to DNA in all living organisms.

 Explain The maps in Figure 1 were made using enormous numbers of individual ozone measurements. What do the maps show? What are the advantages of displaying data visually as a series of maps? What are some other ways that data about ozone in the atmosphere could be presented and analyzed?

Image Credits: (t) ©Karen Bleier/AFP/Getty Images; (cl) (c) (cr) ©NASA

Modeling Earth's Systems

FIGURE 2: Earth's geosphere, hydrosphere, atmosphere, and biosphere are visible from space.

The Earth's system includes all of the solids, liquids, and gases, living and nonliving things, and all of the different forms of energy on Earth. For the purposes of studying and better understanding Earth, the system is often divided into smaller systems, or subsystems.

Earth's Spheres

Earth can be described as being composed of four main subsystems, also called spheres: the geosphere, atmosphere, hydrosphere, and biosphere. Like all systems, each sphere is made of components of matter and energy that interact with each other. Each of Earth's spheres has a unique composition and set of characteristics and processes. Although the spheres overlap and interact, thinking about Earth as a set of different subsystems helps scientists make sense of Earth as a whole.

Explain What are some ways to separate Earth into different subsystems? What are the boundaries of those systems? Do they overlap or interact?

The Geosphere

The geosphere includes all of the solid and liquid rock on Earth, from the surface to the core. It includes all of the mountain ranges, volcanoes, lava, river and beach sediments, soils on land, and all of the rock, sand, gravel, and mud on the ocean floor. The geosphere also includes all of the solid rock and magma below the surface in the crust and mantle and the liquid and solid metal in Earth's core. Glaciers and ice sheets, fossilized plants that make up coal, and the skeletons of corals and other marine animals can also be considered part of the geosphere.

Gather Evidence Look carefully at the photographs. In what ways does the geosphere interact with the hydrosphere, atmosphere, and biosphere?

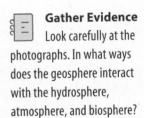

FIGURE 3: The geosphere includes all of the solid and liquid rock on Earth. The geosphere includes the solid rock of the crust, as seen here in the Dolomite mountains of Italy, and on the ocean floor near the Revillagigedo Islands. The geosphere also includes all of the solid and liquid rock and metal far beneath Earth's surface.

The Atmosphere

Gather Evidence What evidence is there to support the claim that the atmosphere interacts with other parts of Earth?

Earth's atmosphere is the layer of gases and particles that surrounds the planet. Most of the atmosphere is within 100 km of the ground. It is composed primarily of air, a mixture of of nitrogen (N_2) and oxygen (O_2), with small amounts of water vapor, argon, carbon dioxide, and other gases. Clouds, which are made of ice crystals and water droplets, dust, and other solid particles called *aerosols,* are also part of the atmosphere.

FIGURE 4: Earth's atmosphere is the layer of gases and small particles that float between Earth's surface and outer space.

The Hydrosphere

Gather Evidence The hydrosphere interacts with the geosphere, atmosphere, and biosphere. What are some examples of interactions between the hydrosphere and other Earth systems?

The hydrosphere includes all of the liquid, solid, and gaseous water on Earth's surface, in the atmosphere, and underground. The salty water of the oceans makes up most of the hydrosphere. The remainder is found in glaciers, ice sheets, rivers, streams, lakes, ponds, and groundwater in sediments in the crust. Water, ice crystals, and water vapor in the air can be considered part of the hydrosphere as well as part of the atmosphere. Sometimes, the water within molten rock and even within mineral crystals deep underground is considered to be part of the hydrosphere, as well as part of the geosphere. Sometimes, the water within living things is included in the hydrosphere.

FIGURE 5: About 97% of the water on Earth is found in the oceans. The energy and motion of surface water is influenced primarily by energy and motion in the atmosphere.

The Biosphere

The biosphere includes all of the living things on Earth, from the largest blue whale to the tiniest single-celled bacterium. The biosphere includes all plants, animals, fungi, protists, bacteria, and archaea on Earth's surface, in the oceans, floating or flying in the atmosphere, in the rocks and sediments underground, and in the bodies of other organisms. Sometimes the hard skeletons and fossilized and decomposed parts of once-living organisms are also included as part of the biosphere as well as part of the geosphere. Aerosols made of tiny organisms or parts of living things may be considered part of the biosphere as well as part of the atmosphere.

FIGURE 6: A rainforest is a subsystem of the biosphere. Rainforests are said to have great biodiversity because they include a wide variety of living organisms.

Gather Evidence The biosphere is not a closed system: Matter moves in and out of the biosphere from the other three spheres. Provide at least three pieces of evidence (examples)—one for each sphere, to support this claim.

FIGURE 7: In January 2016, winter storm Jonas buried Washington, Baltimore, and New York in more than two feet of snow.

Explore Online

Hands-On Lab

GPS and Earth's Circumference Use angles obtained from GPS measurements to estimate Earth's size.

Scientists may define the geosphere, atmosphere, hydrosphere, and biosphere slightly differently, depending on the purpose of their study. For example, the frozen portion of the hydrosphere—including glaciers, ice sheets, and loose snow—is sometimes separated out as the cryosphere. The portion of Earth that has been constructed or modified by humans—including cities, farms, mines, reservoirs, landfills, and pollutants—is sometimes referred to as the anthroposphere.

Collaborate The biosphere includes human beings and their activities. How are Earth's atmosphere, hydrosphere, and geosphere affected by the human part of the biosphere?

Image Credits: (t, b) ©NASA

FIGURE 8: Snow falls in the Sierra Nevada during the winter months and begins to melt at the beginning of April. The amount of snowpack depends on both precipitation levels and temperature. Snowpack levels are lower when the weather is dry and when precipitation is in the form of rain instead of snow.

 Explain What do the arrows in the water cycle model represent?

Modeling Earth Systems Interactions

Many Earth scientists focus on the matter, energy, and processes in one Earth sphere. At the same time, there are many scientists who study very large-scale systems that can only be understood by studying the interactions between Earth's spheres.

Explain What causes the change in snowpack levels in the Sierra Nevada from year to year? What are the effects of those changes? Explain the causes and effects in terms of interactions between the hydrosphere, geosphere, atmosphere, and biosphere.

On average, about 30% of California's freshwater supply comes from snow that fell on the Sierra Nevada Mountains during the winter and then melted in the summer and fall. This meltwater is particularly important during months when there is little rainfall to replenish surface and groundwater supplies.

After several years of drought, the snowpack levels in 2015 were among the lowest ever recorded. Based on satellite and ground measurements and on data gathered from ancient tree rings, scientists concluded that the snowpack in 2015 was the lowest it has been in the past 500 years. By April 2016, it had returned to 86% of normal levels, thanks in part to an El Niño, which brought wet weather to the region.

FIGURE 9: The water cycle consists of a series of processes that move water and energy to different places within the hydrosphere. The water cycle also includes parts of the biosphere, atmosphere, and geosphere, and is affected by the anthroposphere.

Many factors influence weather in the Sierra Nevada. One of these is the temperature of the ocean water in the eastern Pacific. One way to understand how the Pacific Ocean can affect snowpack in the Sierra Nevada is to use the water cycle model. The water cycle describes the movement of matter (water molecules) and energy (thermal energy, or heat) between the hydrosphere, atmosphere, geosphere, and biosphere.

When the water in the eastern Pacific is warmer, as it is during an El Nino year, the air is also warmer and can hold more water vapor. Humid air masses move eastward from oceans over land, cooling as they rise up over the mountains. When they cool off enough, they and drop water as snow and rain on the mountains.

 Explain Briefly compare Earth's four main systems and summarize how they are related to each other physically (where they are, where their boundaries are, and how they overlap) and in terms of the matter and energy they are composed of.

Visualizing Data

Ozone (O_3) is made up of 3 oxygen atoms. It forms in the stratosphere when ultraviolet light breaks apart an oxygen (O_2) molecule. Each oxygen atom combines with another O_2 molecule to form O_3. Ozone molecules break apart when they absorb ultraviolet radiation. These molecules form and break apart rapidly in an ever-changing balance.

FIGURE 10: The ozone layer is located between 15 and 25 km above Earth's surface. In a regular photograph, ozone cannot be distinguished from other gases in the atmosphere.

Because ozone is invisible, it is not possible to estimate ozone concentrations or watch concentrations change over time just by looking. To understand how ozone is distributed with altitude and how it is distributed around the globe, scientists must make careful measurements using instruments on the ground, in airplanes, in weather balloons, and on satellites. These measurements can then be used to create visual models of ozone that are easier to interpret and analyze than raw data.

Graphing the Ozone Layer

Scientists have been measuring ozone concentrations in the stratosphere over Antarctica daily for more than 50 years. This adds up to thousands of data points every day. Imagine trying to analyze a data table with many thousands of rows.

One of the simplest ways to present data is to plot them on a graph. Graphs can be used to analyze how different variables are related to each other and how variables change over time.

Analyze Describe the change in ozone concentration over Antarctica from 1979 to 1994. When did the concentration start to change significantly? Would the data be as easy to analyze in table form?

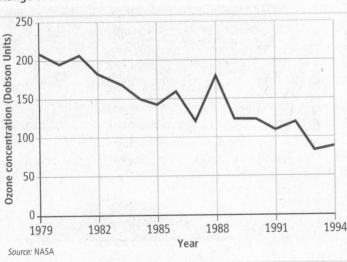

Ozone Depletion Over Antarctica

FIGURE 11: A graph of average ozone concentration with altitude over the South Pole helps us visualize the ozone layer.

Image Credits: ©Detlev van Ravenswaay/Science Source

From the graph in Figure 11, it is clear to see that ozone levels decreased significantly between the mid-1970s and the mid-1990s. In 1984, measurements showed that an ozone "hole" had developed over Antarctica: the concentration of ozone was less than 50% of what it was in the 1950s.

Not only is a graph easier to interpret than a table of data, it is also more effective for communicating to other scientists and to the public. Graphs are used not only to describe the past changes, but also to predict future changes. By the mid-1980s, it was clear from the graphs that if the trends continued, life on Earth would be in great danger.

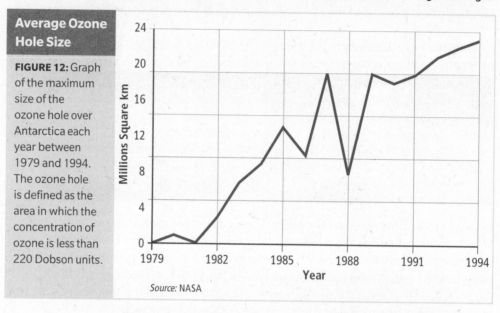

Average Ozone Hole Size

FIGURE 12: Graph of the maximum size of the ozone hole over Antarctica each year between 1979 and 1994. The ozone hole is defined as the area in which the concentration of ozone is less than 220 Dobson units.

Source: NASA

Analyze Based on the data, what do you think happened to the size of the ozone hole in 1995? in 2000?

Using Diagrams to Explain Ozone

Analyze How does the release of CFCs into the atmosphere affect the amount of UV-B radiation that reaches Earth's surface?

Scientists had been studying chemical reactions between pollutants and ozone for many years. They were quickly able to link the development of the ozone hole to the buildup of pollutants, particularly chlorofluorocarbons (CFCs), in the atmosphere.

FIGURE 13: Ozone in the stratosphere is destroyed when chlorine atoms from pollution react with ozone molecules, breaking them apart.

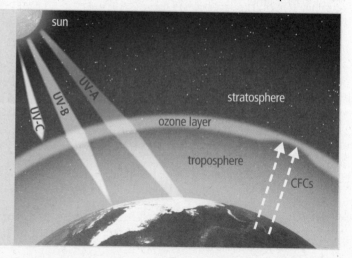

Collaborate It is always important to protect your skin from sunlight, either with clothing or with sunscreen. Why is this even more important today than it was in the 1950s?

Ground-level ozone is a pollutant that can cause respiratory problems, but stratospheric ozone is vital to life on Earth. Ozone absorbs ultraviolet radiation (UV) from the sun. While small amounts of UV are important for the production of vitamin D in humans, too much UV can cause skin cancer, cataracts, and other health problems.

Scientists predict that the thinning of the ozone layer will result in a 10% increase in the incidence of skin cancer in the United States by 2050.

Mapping the Ozone Hole

It can be difficult to understand what someone means when they refer to "the ozone hole." Although graphs like the one in Figure 11 clearly show the decrease in ozone over time in a specific location and altitude, they are less useful for understanding geographic variation—variation over a large area. Is the ozone hole a long narrow tube right over the South Pole or does it cover the entire Earth? A set of thousands of graphs from different locations would include the data needed to understand the extent of the ozone hole, but would be impossible to understand and analyze quickly.

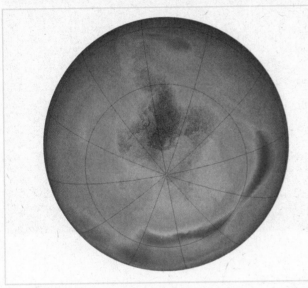

FIGURE 14: The ozone hole over Antarctica on September 17, 1979. The map is in false color: Colors correspond to the concentration of ozone in the atmosphere, not to the actual color of the atmosphere.

FIGURE 15: Antarctic ozone in 1985 and 1990

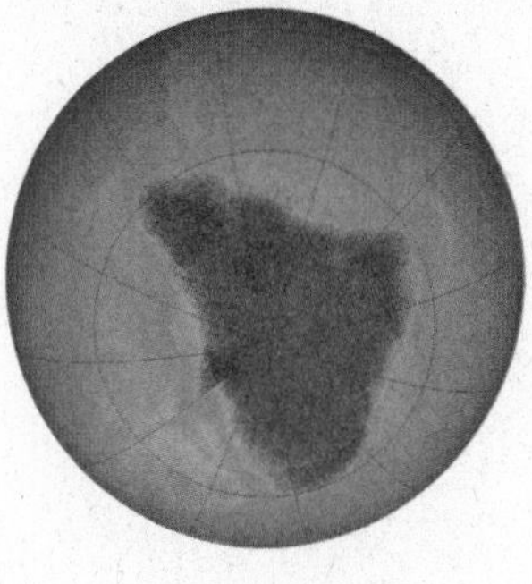

a October 25, 1985

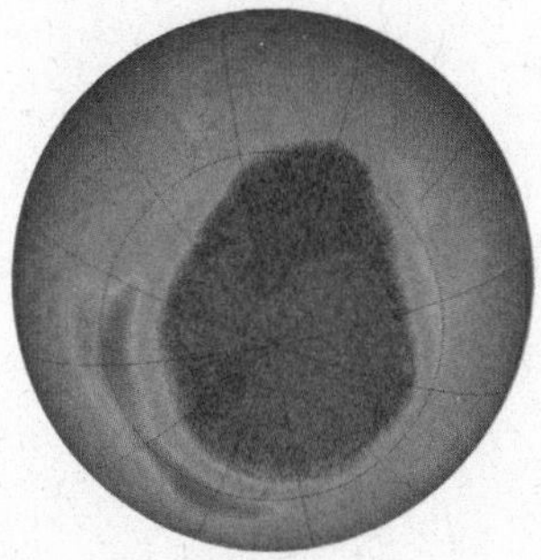

b October 5, 1990

Maps of the ozone hole, such as the one shown in Figure 14, are much more effective visual models of conditions on Earth at a specific time. Individual maps can also be combined in quick succession to create an animation. An animation can serve as a model that allows us to easily understand how conditions change over both space and time.

Visual models like these graphs, maps, and conceptual diagrams were instrumental in communicating the reality and severity of ozone depletion, not just to other scientists, but also to health professionals, politicians, and the general public. As a result of effective communication, the Montreal Protocol, an international treaty to ban CFCs, was signed in 1987. Although the ozone hole still forms in Antarctica around September, scientists think it will disappear by 2070.

Collaborate Compare the map of ozone levels in 1979 to the map from 1990. What was the cause of the difference? What do you think the map in 1990 would look like if CFCs had never been emitted? What might it look like if CFC emissions had increased?

 Explain Maps like those in Figure 15 and graphs like the one in Figure 12 can both be used to analyze and communicate changes in ozone concentrations over time. How are they similar and different? What are some advantages and disadvantages of each type of model?

Viewing Earth from Above

In 2013, Canadian astronaut Chris Hadfield looked out the window of the International Space Station, 350 km above Earth's surface, to see the night lights of Berlin, Germany. Hadfield was immediately struck by a stark contrast in the brightness and color of the lights below. While the west side of the city gave off a bright white glow, the east side was dimmer and yellower.

FIGURE 16: Berlin, Germany as seen from the International Space Station in 2013.

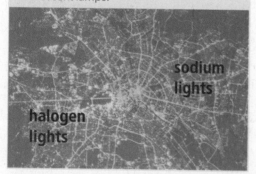

FIGURE 17: Berlin, Germany: Sodium-vapor lamps give off a softer, yellower light than fluorescent lamps.

Cities from Space

What is the cause of the differences in brightness and color? What else can we observe and infer from the photograph? What *can't* be understood by looking at the photograph alone?

It is clear that the lights in Berlin are artificial city lights. We can infer from experience that they are brightest where there are more lights and more activity, for example in the center of the city where there are offices, shops, theaters, and restaurants. We can infer that the long strips of lights are major roads and that large dark areas are probably parks. But with the photograph alone, it is almost impossible to know why the lights on the east side of the city are yellower than those on the west side.

To understand the difference in lighting between the east and west side of Berlin, we must look to other sources of information, such as street maps and historical maps. We must also do some ground-truthing: making direct observations on the ground. If you go to Berlin, you will find that the western part of the city is lit mostly by fluorescent lights, which give off a bluish white glow, while the eastern part of the city is lit with sodium-vapor lamps, which give off a yellow glow.

While ground-truthing helps explain why the colors of lights are different, the historical map in Figure 18 helps explain why the lights on different sides of the city are different and why there is a distinct difference in color.

As can be seen in Figure 18, Germany consisted of two separate countries between 1945 and 1990, with the city of Berlin divided into two parts. West Berlin was part of West Germany, while East Berlin was part of East Germany. Because of their differences in government and economy, the two halves of the city developed very differently.

While West Germany slowly converted from old-style sodium lamps to more modern energy efficient fluorescent lamps, East Germany did not have access to the same resources to do this. Although Germany has been unified since 1990, the two sides of the city are still very different. This subtle trend wasn't obvious from the ground and could only be shown through the unique aerial perspective that maps provide.

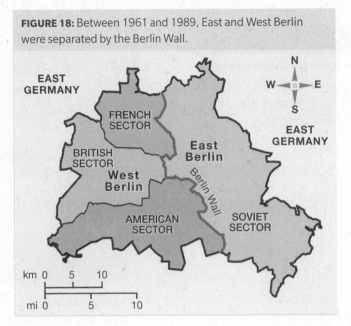

FIGURE 18: Between 1961 and 1989, East and West Berlin were separated by the Berlin Wall.

Mapping Earth's Systems

Maps are some of the most useful types of models for describing, communicating, and analyzing Earth's systems. While the map of Berlin in Figure 18 describes part of the anthroposphere, maps that Earth scientists use generally describe natural parts of the system.

FIGURE 19: A simple map of Earth's surface may model parts of the geosphere, hydrosphere, and biosphere.

Analyze Can you tell which way the river is flowing based on the map in Figure 19? Can you tell from this map why the lakes formed? What additional information would be useful to understand why the river is located where it is and how the lakes formed?

The map in Figure 19 provides some information about Earth's surface. We can see that the river runs between the northwest and southeast, and we can see that it cuts through different types of vegetation. But we can't tell for sure in which direction it is flowing. We can infer that it must be flowing downhill (all water flows downhill under the pull of gravity), but it is not possible to tell whether it is flowing down a very steep slope or a very gentle slope. Because the rock formations are not mapped, we can't tell if there is any relationship between the rocks and the river. Because no human-made features are shown, we can't tell if the lakes are natural or artificial.

Explore Online ▶

Hands-On Lab

Contour Maps; Island Construction Create a model based on information from a topographic map.

FIGURE 20: A topographic map includes contour lines. Each contour line connects points of equal elevation. Slopes are steeper where lines are closer together.

Topographic maps, such as the one shown in Figure 20, are useful tools for describing, analyzing, and understanding landforms. By showing the elevation, or height, they show the topography—the sizes and shapes of the surface features. Most topographic maps also depict water and other information, such as forests and human-made structures. They do not include direct information about other aspects of the area such as soil types, weather and climate, rock types, wildlife populations, air quality, or how the landscape has changed over time. Including all information available about a place on one map would be very confusing. Part of the purpose of a map or other model is to simplify a system, focusing on only a few aspects of the system.

Systems and System Models

FIGURE 21: Radar map of a storm moving through the United States.

There are many cases in which scientists want to analyze many different characteristics of an area to find out how they are all related. Showing all characteristics of an area on one map would be so confusing that it would not be useful. One way to present and analyze many different data sets from an area is by using map layers. Each map layer includes just one or two sets of data.

For example, a resource to help people understand weather might include a base map showing landforms, cities, and roads. Different types of meteorological data, such as air temperature, air pressure, humidity, wind speed, pollen concentration, and pollution levels, would be plotted on different map layers. Layers can be viewed separately or can be placed on top of each other to analyze relationships.

If you have ever opened a map on the Internet and clicked on "roads" or "terrain" or "restaurants" to see different views of the same place, you have worked with map layers.

 Language Arts Connection A wide variety of interactive maps are available online. Go to the Internet to find maps of places and topics that are of interest. Use search terms such as *interactive map* and *map layers,* along with terms to describe what you are interested in (e.g., earthquakes, volcanoes, oceans, forests, or any other aspect of Earth's geosphere, atmosphere, biosphere, or atmosphere). Use the maps to explore relationships between different characteristics of the area that is mapped.

Mapping Data

The maps in Figures 18–20 are models of Earth's physical surface, including natural and human-made features that can actually be seen in photographs or in person on the ground. Many maps that scientists use, however, present characteristics of Earth's systems—for example, surface temperature, population density, earthquake magnitude, gravitational pull, and ozone concentration—that cannot actually be observed directly in a photograph of a single instant in time. These data are plotted on maps in order to analyze or communicate the relationships between these characteristics and latitude, longitude, topography, and other characteristics of Earth's surface.

Explore Online ▶

🧪 **Hands-On Lab**

Remote Sensing Model a landscape and create a map with information gathered using a probe.

FIGURE 22: Scientific maps are used to show the relationships between Earth's surface and specific characteristics of its geosphere, hydrosphere, atmosphere, and biosphere.

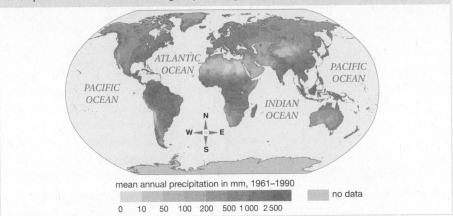

You may have noticed that the maps in Figures 22 and 23 look similar to topographic maps. This is because the data are presented in a similar way, using contour lines to connect measurements of equal value. Colors are used to emphasize the differences in values of average rainfall and biodiversity—the variety of organisms within an area.

FIGURE 23: The biodiversity of vascular plants across Earth's surface

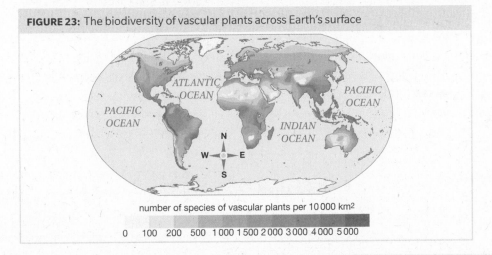

Collaborate Analyze the information shown in the two maps. What can you infer about the relationship between biodiversity and rainfall? How does viewing these maps together help you better understand one or both of the data sets better than viewing the maps on their own? What questions about biodiversity and rainfall do these map layers *not* answer?

Explain The maps in Figures 22 and 23 were made based on data collected in thousands of locations around the world. Suppose you only had access to the raw data: tables of rainfall measurements in different areas and scientists' field notes with lists of vascular plants found in different areas. Describe the advantages and disadvantages of raw data versus summaries of data displayed on maps.

Guided Research

Map Projections

You may have noticed that different maps represent the relative sizes, shapes, and orientations of the continents differently. This is not because some maps represent the surface accurately and some don't, but rather because Earth is spherical, not flat. When a spherical surface is modeled as a flat plane, it gets distorted.

There are many different ways of projecting a spherical or curved surface onto a flat plane. Each type of map project distorts the surface in different ways. Some projections distort distances; some distort shapes; some distort areas; and some distort directions. The type of map projection that a scientist chooses to plot their data depends on the exact location and size of the area, and the purpose of the map. For example, a Mercator projection is useful for navigation because all straight lines on the map are lines of constant compass direction. A Mercator projection is not useful for estimating distances, however, because the scale is not the same everywhere on the map.

Conduct additional research to find out about different map projections: ways that they accurately represent Earth's surface, ways that they distort Earth's surface, and when each type is best to use. Create a table that helps you organize your research and summarize what you find for others.

FIGURE 24: The size, shape, and locations of continents look different in different map projections.

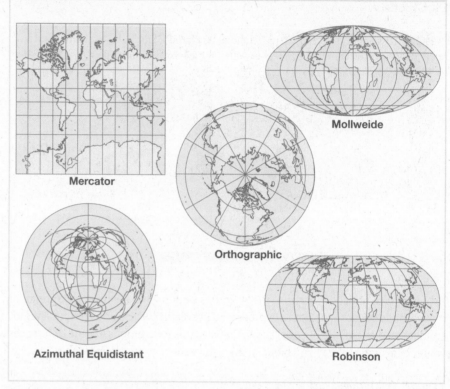

Mercator

Mollweide

Orthographic

Azimuthal Equidistant

Robinson

Collaborate Work with a partner to find examples of different types of map projections. What types of data are mapped? Why do you think the people who made the maps decided to use those projections?

HUMAN EFFECTS ON EARTH'S SYSTEMS   CROSS-SECTIONS AND BLOCK DIAGRAMS   Go online to choose one of these other paths.

Lesson Self-Check

CAN YOU EXPLAIN IT?

FIGURE 25: The concentration of ozone in the stratosphere above Antarctica fluctuates throughout the year. Blue and purple indicate the least ozone, whereas yellow and red are where there is more ozone.

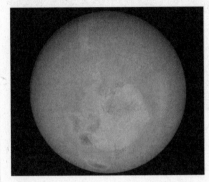
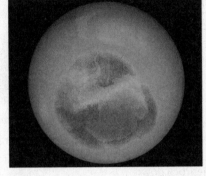
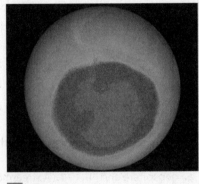

a July 2015

b August 2015

c October 2015

Every year since 1985, an ozone "hole" has developed over Antarctica between July and October. This hole is not a topographic hole like a hole in the ground. Nor is it a complete absence of ozone in the atmosphere. Rather, it is a region of the atmosphere where the concentration of ozone is exceedingly low. The ozone hole develops as a result of both pollution and weather. During the Antarctic winter, a strong, cold west-to-east wind forms, circling Antarctica. This system is known as the polar vortex. During the winter, the temperatures drop so low that high stratospheric clouds form. Chemical reactions release chlorine in the clouds, which then reacts with the ozone molecules in the atmosphere, transforming them into other molecules.

Although the main chemicals that reduce ozone levels were banned in the late 1980s, these chemicals stay in the atmosphere for around 80 years. Scientists think that the ozone holes that form will be smaller and less severe over time, but it will take several decades for the hole to "heal" completely.

Analyze Refer to the notes in your Evidence Notebook to explain the visualization of the ozone layer.

Explain The maps were made using enormous numbers of individual ozone measurements. What do the maps show? What are the advantages of displaying data visually as a series of maps? What are some other ways that data about ozone in the atmosphere could be presented and analyzed?

Image Credits: (d) (c) (cr) ©NASA

CHECKPOINTS

Check Your Understanding

1. Match each component or process to the sphere or spheres of Earth that it is part of.

   a. dirt road
   b. evaporation
   c. glaciers
   d. groundwater
   e. ocean
   f. ozone
   g. people
   h. plants
   i. rock
   j. volcanic eruption

   1. anthroposphere
   2. atmosphere
   3. biosphere
   4. cryosphere
   5. geosphere
   6. hydrosphere

2. Match each sphere interaction with the process that best exemplifies it.

   a. geosphere and atmosphere
   b. geosphere and hydrosphere
   c. geosphere and biosphere
   d. atmosphere and hydrosphere
   e. atmosphere and biosphere
   f. hydrosphere and biosphere

   1. A stream carries rock down a mountainside.
   2. A tree root breaks apart a rock.
   3. A volcano erupts, emitting sulfur dioxide into the air.
   4. Animals breathe in oxygen and breathe out carbon dioxide.
   5. Water condenses out of the air as dew on the ground.
   6. Plants take in water through their roots.

3. Which type of model is best used to show how a variable differs from place to place over Earth's surface?

   a. map
   b. graph
   c. data table
   d. chemical equation

4. The map below shows the ozone hole in 2015. What do the colors represent?

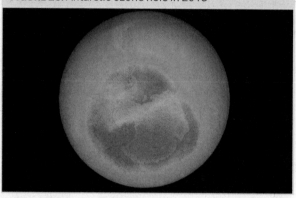

FIGURE 26: Antarctic ozone hole in 2015

   a. the topography of Earth's surface
   b. the temperature of the atmosphere
   c. the color of ozone as seen from space
   d. the concentration of ozone molecules in the atmosphere

5. In 2015, the ozone hole was one of the largest on record. How do scientists explain this observation?

   a. CFCs do not cause the ozone hole after all.
   b. CFCs stay in the atmosphere for many years after they are released.
   c. Countries have not actually complied with the international ban on CFCs.
   d. The satellite making the ozone observations must not have been operating properly.

6. Match each question to the type of model that can be used to answer the question.

   a. What was the extent of the snowpack in the Sierra Nevada during a major drought?
   b. How did the amount of snow in the Sierra Nevadas change over time?
   c. What caused the increase in snowpack between 2015 and 2016?

   1. Animation showing changes in the Sierra Nevada snowpack from 2010–2016
   2. Computer model showing the effects of El Niño on weather
   3. Map of the Sierra Nevada snowpack in 2015

7. Which of the following inferences can be made based on the maps below? Choose all that apply.

FIGURE 27: Rainfall and biodiversity maps

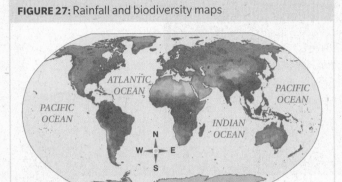

mean annual precipitation in mm, 1961–1990

0   10   50   100   200   500 1000 2500   no data

a   Average rainfall world map

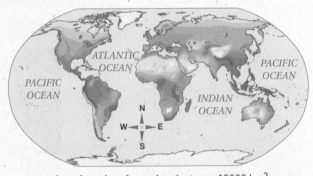

number of species of vascular plants per 10000 km²

0   100   200   500   1000 1500 2000 3000 4000 5000

b   Plant biodiversity world map

a. Biodiversity might depend on rainfall.

b. There were 40 inches of rain in New York last year.

c. There are 50 species of vascular plants in Antarctica.

d. Rainfall is greater in ocean water closer to the equator.

e. Rainfall increases in a region when biodiversity increases.

f. Biodiversity is greater on land closer to the equator.

A BOOK EXPLAINING
COMPLEX IDEAS USING
ONLY THE 1,000 MOST
COMMON WORDS

SHARED SPACE HOUSE
A work place that travels around Earth

In our efforts to study space, we have developed many technologies, from simple telescopes to the International Space Station. Here's a look at the parts of the space station, a research laboratory that orbits Earth.

RANDALL MUNROE
XKCD.COM

THE STORY OF LIVING IN SPACE

THIS BUILDING FLIES THROUGH SPACE JUST ABOVE THE AIR. PEOPLE FROM DIFFERENT COUNTRIES BUILT IT AND FLY UP TO VISIT IT IN SPACE BOATS.

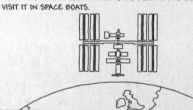

BECAUSE THE HOUSE IS FALLING AROUND THE EARTH, THINGS INSIDE IT HANG IN THE AIR INSTEAD OF DROPPING TO THE FLOOR.

INSIDE THE HOUSE, NORMAL THINGS LIKE WATER ACT VERY STRANGE, AND YOU CAN FLY AROUND BY KICKING OFF THE WALLS. EVERYONE SAYS IT'S A LOT OF FUN.

THE PEOPLE IN THE HOUSE SPEND THEIR TIME WORKING, PLAYING, AND TAKING PICTURES OF EARTH.

THEY DO WORK FOR PEOPLE ON THE GROUND, HELPING TO LEARN HOW THINGS LIKE FLOWERS AND MACHINES WORK IN SPACE.

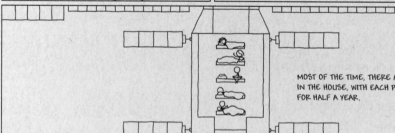

MOST OF THE TIME, THERE ARE SIX PEOPLE IN THE HOUSE, WITH EACH PERSON STAYING FOR HALF A YEAR.

A BIG REASON WE BUILT THE SPACE HOUSE WAS SO WE COULD LEARN TO KEEP PEOPLE ALIVE AND STRONG IN SPACE FOR MONTHS OR YEARS WITHOUT GETTING SICK. WE'LL NEED TO BE GOOD AT THAT IF WE EVER WANT TO TRAVEL TO OTHER WORLDS.

HEY, LOOKS LIKE SPACE IS REALLY WORKING OUT FOR YOU!

TO BUILD THE SPACE HOUSE, WE TOOK EACH PIECE UP IN A BOAT, PUSHED IT UNTIL IT WENT REALLY FAST, THEN CAUGHT UP TO THE HOUSE, AND STUCK THE PART TO THE HOUSE.

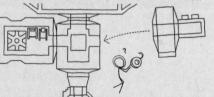

VISITORS

These space boats have flown up to the space house, bringing food, water, parts, and visitors.

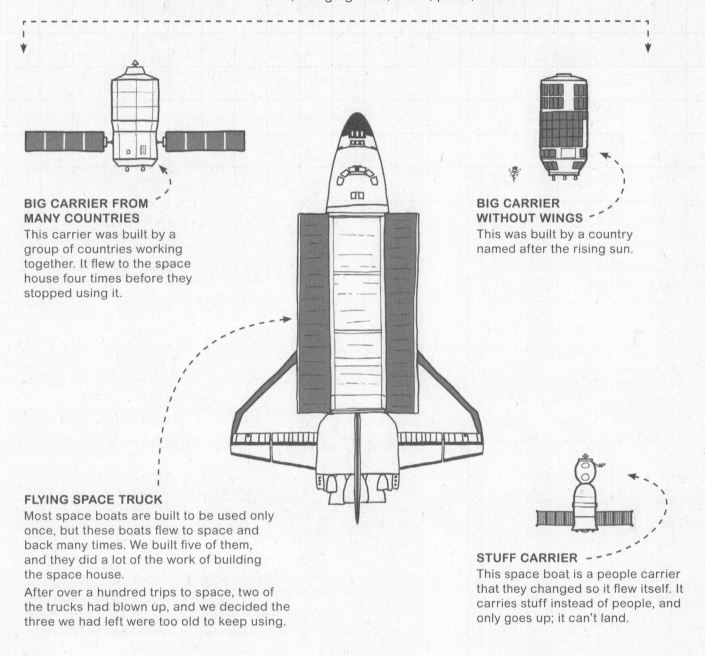

BIG CARRIER FROM MANY COUNTRIES

This carrier was built by a group of countries working together. It flew to the space house four times before they stopped using it.

BIG CARRIER WITHOUT WINGS

This was built by a country named after the rising sun.

FLYING SPACE TRUCK

Most space boats are built to be used only once, but these boats flew to space and back many times. We built five of them, and they did a lot of the work of building the space house.

After over a hundred trips to space, two of the trucks had blown up, and we decided the three we had left were too old to keep using.

STUFF CARRIER

This space boat is a people carrier that they changed so it flew itself. It carries stuff instead of people, and only goes up; it can't land.

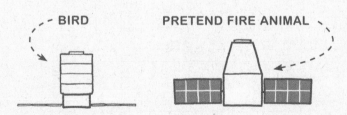

BIRD   PRETEND FIRE ANIMAL

The other space boats here, even when they were built by companies, were owned by big countries or groups of countries. These two, which are newer, were built and flown by companies, and countries pay them to carry stuff to the space house.

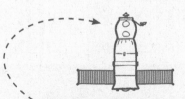

PEOPLE CARRIER

This is an old and simple space boat that works very well. Once we stopped using the truck with wings, it became the only space boat that could carry people to the space house.

SHARED SPACE HOUSE

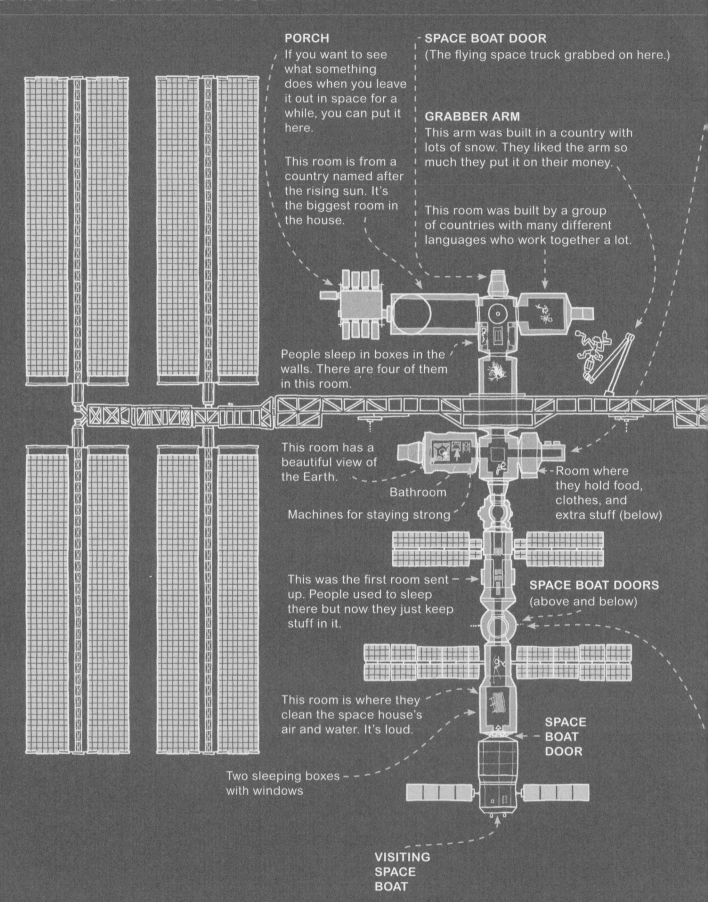

PORCH
If you want to see what something does when you leave it out in space for a while, you can put it here.

This room is from a country named after the rising sun. It's the biggest room in the house.

SPACE BOAT DOOR
(The flying space truck grabbed on here.)

GRABBER ARM
This arm was built in a country with lots of snow. They liked the arm so much they put it on their money.

This room was built by a group of countries with many different languages who work together a lot.

People sleep in boxes in the walls. There are four of them in this room.

This room has a beautiful view of the Earth.

Bathroom

Machines for staying strong

Room where they hold food, clothes, and extra stuff (below)

This was the first room sent up. People used to sleep there but now they just keep stuff in it.

SPACE BOAT DOORS
(above and below)

This room is where they clean the space house's air and water. It's loud.

SPACE BOAT DOOR

Two sleeping boxes with windows

VISITING SPACE BOAT

PEOPLE DOOR
(Put on space clothes before going through, or you'll die.)

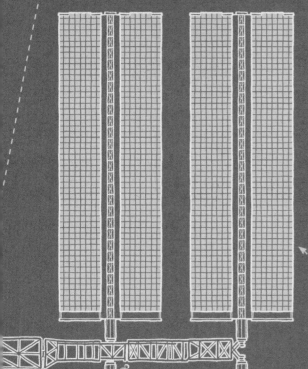

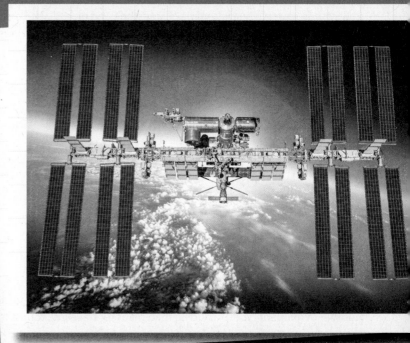

POWER WINGS
These wings turn the Sun's light into the power that runs the machines on the space house.

PART HOLDER
This part has no air in it. It holds the wings and other pieces of the house.

PROBLEM BOATS
We keep extra boats stuck to these doors for people to use if there's a problem that makes them not want to be in space anymore, but no one will come get them.

Engineering Connection

Building Designs Bermuda is a group of islands in the Atlantic Ocean known for its tropical climate, pink sand beaches, and clear blue water. Nearly all of the houses in Bermuda have white roofs made of limestone and mortar, with distinct steps. The roofs are specially designed for two purposes: to resist high winds and to help collect rainwater.

Using Internet resources, research the location, climate, and geology of Bermuda. Why is it important for roofs to be able to resist high winds? Why is it so important that the roofs be able to collect rainwater? Make a sketch pointing out the aspects of the design that help roofs meet these criteria. How is the design of buildings influenced by climate, topography, geology, and other natural aspects of the region where you live?

FIGURE 1: Roofs in Bermuda must be designed to withstand powerful winds and to help collect rainwater.

Social Studies Connection

Regional Maps If you search for a map of your state or city, you are likely to find a number of different types, including road maps for traveling; tourist maps showing the locations of museums, parks, and shops; and historical maps showing what the area was like in the past. How many different types of maps can you find of your area? What can you learn about where you live based on these maps?

Create an online catalog of maps of your area. The catalog can be a simple webpage that includes a thumbnail (a small image) of each map, a description of what the map shows and how it can be used, and a link to the original webpage.

FIGURE 2: Map of average annual precipitation in Oregon

Art Connection

Landscape Paintings In the 1860s, the American painter Albert Bierstadt traveled out west, across the Sierra Nevada mountains of California. When he returned, he transformed his sketches and memories into huge spectacular landscape paintings designed to wow audiences with the natural splendor of the American West. Landscapes paintings like Bierstadt's depict the flow of matter and energy within and between Earth's systems, including the atmosphere, hydrosphere, geosphere, and biosphere.

Identify specific aspects of Earth's spheres and examples of interactions or flows of energy and matter within and between different parts of Earth that are depicted in the painting *Among the Sierra Nevada, California*. Communicate your analysis with a "gallery label," a short essay that could be posted next to the painting in a museum. You may also wish to include a line sketch with specific aspects of the painting pointed out.

FIGURE 3: *Among the Sierra Nevada, California* by Albert Bierstadt, 1868

SYNTHESIZE THE UNIT

In your Evidence Notebook, create a concept map, graphic organizer, or outline using the Study Guides you created for each lesson in this unit. Be sure to use evidence to support your claims.

When synthesizing individual information, remember to follow these general steps:

- Find the central idea of each piece of information.
- Think about the relationships among the central ideas.
- Combine the ideas to come up with a new understanding.

Go online to access detailed lesson summaries for this unit.

DRIVING QUESTIONS

Look back to the Driving Questions from the opening section of this unit. In your Evidence Notebook, review and revise your previous answers to those questions. Use the evidence you gathered and other observations you made throughout the unit to support your claims.

PRACTICE AND REVIEW

1. Which of the following statements about Earth's living systems is true?

   a. Corals are unique in that they are affected not only by changes in the water but also by changes in the atmosphere.

   b. Corals are typical of most other marine organisms in that they live best in water that is clear and warm but not hot.

   c. Corals are unique in that they are affected not only by changes to water and atmosphere but also by changes to other living things.

   d. Corals are typical of other living things in that they can be affected by changes to the hydrosphere, atmosphere, and geosphere.

2. Which of the following statements about systems are accurate? Select all correct responses.

   a. A system is a group of components that interact with each other but not with anything outside the system.

   b. A system can be almost any size, from as small as a subatomic particle to as big as the universe.

   c. A system can be described by components, processes, inputs, outputs, and boundaries.

   d. All scientists define any given system in the same way.

   e. Earth and the sun together can be considered a system, but Earth and the moon cannot.

   f. Any given component can be part of only one system.

3. Match each example with the aspect of a system that it best represents.

   a. Air
   b. Ocean water
   c. Thermal energy
   d. Wind pushes warm water westward, pulling up cold water in the eastern Pacific.
   e. The effects of the increasing wind strength cause the wind to increase even more.

   1. Component
   2. Feedback
   3. Process

4. Two groups of scientists are using systems model approaches to study El Niño. Each defines the system in a different way.

Group	Components of the System	Boundaries of the System
A	Pacific Ocean water	Top: Surface of the Pacific Ocean Bottom: Floor of the Pacific Ocean
B	Pacific Ocean water, air above Pacific Ocean	Top: Top of the troposphere Bottom: Floor of the Pacific Ocean

Briefly explain why both ways of defining the system are valid.

5. The graph at the right shows the pattern of ocean temperature change in the equatorial Pacific. What can be inferred directly from this pattern alone? Select all correct responses.

 a. Each year, the temperature of the equatorial Pacific changes from hot to cold or cold to hot.

 b. The temperature in the equatorial Pacific fluctuates over a period of multiple years.

 c. The pattern of temperature change is related to coral bleaching.

 d. Changes in the size of the ozone hole are linked to this pattern of temperature change.

 e. A difference in temperature of 1–2 degrees Celsius from year to year is to be expected.

 f. The pattern of temperature change is a result of human activities.

6. Which of the following are principles that scientists use to study, explain, and predict natural phenomena? Select all correct responses.

 a. Patterns of past change are not useful for predicting future change.

 b. Matter and energy travel together through Earth's systems.

 c. Earth can be thought of as a complex system of interacting subsystems.

 d. Earth's system is dynamic and changes on different scales of space and time.

 e. The natural laws that describe how matter and energy interact have evolved and changed over time.

 f. Earth changes slowly from day to day but overall is basically the same today as it was soon after it formed 4.5 billion years ago.

7. Is Earth an open, closed, or isolated system? Explain your answer.

8. For each process described, identify the spheres of Earth that are described as interacting.

 a. An increase in air temperature causes snow to melt in the Sierra Nevadas.

 b. An increase in air temperature along with melting snow causes plants to grow.

 c. Runoff from heavy rains carries particles of sediment downhill into streams and rivers.

 d. Sediments carried by streams and rivers block sunlight in a pond, causing plants to die.

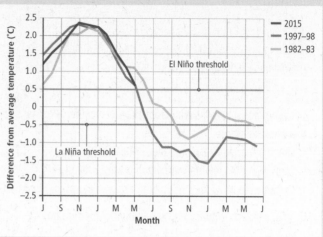

FIGURE 4: Sea surface temperature (*x*-axis marked every 2 months, beginning with July)

9. The water cycle involves interactions among Earth's spheres. Describe an example of a process for each pair of spheres: (a) hydrosphere and atmosphere; (b) hydrosphere and geosphere; (c) hydrosphere and biosphere; and (d) biosphere and atmosphere.

10. For each model described, write a scientific question that could be answered using the model.

 a. Graph of ozone concentration at McMurdo Station, Antarctica between December 1978 and December 2004

 b. Map of ozone concentration in the southern hemisphere in December 2004

 c. Animation of the ozone hole from December 1978 to December 2004

MAP YOUR SCHOOL

Return to your unit project. Finalize your map, including a title, a key, and a scale bar if appropriate. When presenting your map, explain what it shows, how you collected the data, and how the data are displayed. Also be prepared to evaluate your map in terms of how clearly it displays the information and how it can be used by others.

Remember these tips while evaluating:

- Does the title clearly convey what the map is supposed to show?

- Does the key include all symbols, colors, patterns, and other map elements?

- Is the map to scale? If not, is it still clear where everything is in relation to everything else?

- What can the map be used for?

Using Maps to Assess Problems

A company is planning to build a complex of offices, workshops, and warehouses along the Mississippi River. The land is inexpensive, and the location along the river will be ideal for shipping materials to and from the complex. The owners of the company have been warned that the river periodically floods, but they are not sure why that would happen or what the effects could be. They are not sure whether or not they should be worried or if there is any way they could prevent flooding or its effects.

FIGURE 5: The company plans to build the new complex just west of the Mississippi River, somewhere in the area marked in white.

1. DEFINE THE PROBLEM

With your group, look carefully at the map showing where the company wants to build. Does it look like the area is at risk of flooding or not? What makes you think so? Brainstorm the possible problems the company could have if they build in the area shown along the river. Make a chart that describes possible causes of each problem and the specific effects of each problem on the new business development.

2. CONDUCT RESEARCH

With your team, add to what you already know by researching the causes and effects of flooding on a river like the Mississippi. Then research the ways that engineers try to prevent or deal with flooding and its effects. Can these solutions cause other problems to people or to other living or non-living parts of the ecosystem?

3. ANALYZE DATA

On your own, analyze the company's situation. What specific risks do they face by building in this location? What evidence and reasoning supports your claim that they are at risk? What can the company do to minimize these risks? What would you recommend?

4. IDENTIFY AND RECOMMEND A SOLUTION

Present your suggested solution to your team, with reasoning to back it up. Listen to others' solutions. As a team, weigh the pros and cons of each solution. Come to a consensus on which solution you recommend as a team.

5. COMMUNICATE

Present a brief report to the company explaining the problem, its causes, and the solution your recommend. Be sure to include the reasoning behind your recommendation.

 **CHECK YOUR WORK**

A complete report should include the following information:

- A clear description of the problems that the business could have if they were to build the new complex in this area.
- Evidence that supports the claims.
- A recommendation for preventing the predicted problems.
- Reasoning to support the recommendation.

Systems of Matter and Energy

This micrograph of conglomerate rock reveals the variety of minerals inside.

Image Credits: ©Scenics & Science/Alamy

Earth systems are incredibly dynamic. Whether we observe systems at a global scale or at the microscopic level, we can see the results of the flow of matter and energy within and between systems. At a microscopic scale, for example, thin sections of rock like the ones you see here reveal the internal structures that result from the processes of rock formation. On the global scale, satellites monitor the flow of matter and energy within and between the atmosphere and oceans.

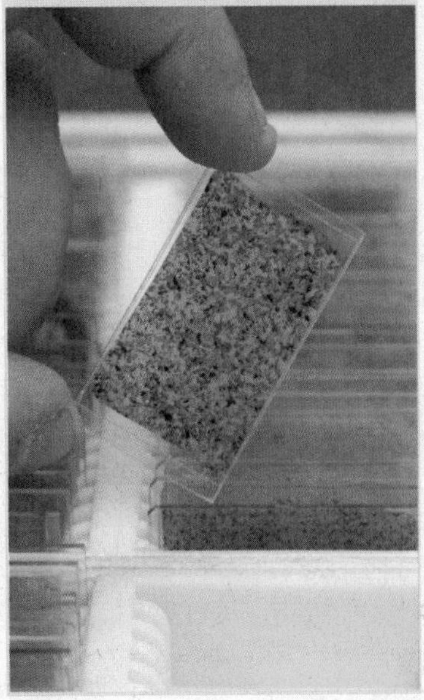

Scientists develop and use a wide range of models to study matter and energy in Earth's systems. The most basic models include diagrams of processes such as the rock cycle and carbon cycles, as well as maps of changes on Earth's surface. Among the most sophisticated models are the computer and computational models used to predict future changes to Earth's oceans and climate.

 Predict What are some of the processes involved in the flow of matter and energy among Earth's geosphere, hydrosphere, atmosphere, and biosphere?

FIGURE 1: A thin section of rock

DRIVING QUESTIONS

As you move through the unit, gather evidence to help you answer the following questions. In your Evidence Notebook, record what you already know about these topics and any questions you have about them.

1. How does Earth receive energy? How does energy move around the planet?
2. What are the primary characteristics used to distinguish minerals?
3. What processes change rock from one type to another? In what ways do these processes involve inputs and outputs of matter and energy?
4. How do essential elements such as carbon, nitrogen, and phosphorus cycle through the living and nonliving components of Earth's systems?

UNIT PROJECT

Developing a Convection Model

How do materials of different densities interact within Earth's systems? In this project, you will research various ways of modeling density and convection, and then develop and observe your own physical model of convection.

Go online to download the Unit Project Worksheet to help plan your project.

Earth's Energy

Superheated water erupts from the Strokkur Geyser in Iceland.

CAN YOU EXPLAIN IT?

FIGURE 1: Mount Pinatubo, Philippines On June 15, 1991, Mount Pinatubo erupted violently, sending ash and gas 40 km into the atmosphere. The ash and gas spread out in all directions with the wind, forming a cloud hundreds of kilometers across.

Gather Evidence As you explore the lesson, gather evidence to help explain the origin of Earth's surface and internal energy. Note how energy flow affects Earth's systems.

The 1991 eruption of Mount Pinatubo was the second-largest volcanic eruption in the twentieth century. The eruption not only had a devastating effect on hundreds of thousands of people living in the area, but it also caused a 0.5 °C drop in average global temperature that lasted about two years.

Pinatubo was not the only eruption to have had this effect on global climate. For example, after the massive eruption of Laki in Iceland in 1783, Europe experienced an extremely severe winter, with temperatures nearly 5 °C lower than average. The 1883 eruption of Krakatoa in Indonesia had similar cooling effects around the world.

Predict Why do you think eruptions of volcanoes like Mount Pinatubo might have a cooling effect on Earth's surface?

Energy Sources and Flows

All processes within Earth as well as on its surface involve the flow of energy and the cycling of matter. The energy that Earth emits into space comes from the surface, which is heated by the sun, and from hot rock and metal underground.

Energy Flow

Energy moves through Earth's systems in three different ways—by radiation, conduction, and convection. Energy from the sun reaches Earth through radiation, the movement of energy as visible light, ultraviolet rays, and other types of electromagnetic waves. Unlike conduction and convection, radiation does not require a medium. Thus, radiation is the only way that energy can travel through outer space.

Model Make a sketch that shows three possible paths of energy as it moves from the sun, to Earth, and back to space.

FIGURE 2: More than 99.98% of the energy that Earth emits to space originally comes from the sun. Solar energy is reflected and absorbed and then reemitted back out to space.

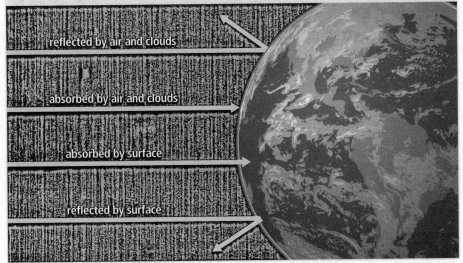

reflected by air and clouds

absorbed by air and clouds

absorbed by surface

reflected by surface

Explore Online ▶

🧪 **Hands-On Lab**

Energy Transfer
Measure the results of conduction between metal and water.

Conduction is the transfer of heat energy through collisions of the atoms or molecules of a substance. When you walk barefoot on hot ground, for example, heat moves by conduction from the ground to the soles of your feet. Air touching warm ground also is heated by conduction.

Convection is the movement of matter caused by differences in density. Recall that density is the ratio of the mass to volume of a substance. Convection often moves thermal energy through a liquid or gas. For example, in a pot of simmering water, the water at the bottom of the pot is heated by conduction and becomes less dense. Because it is less dense, it rises and is replaced by downward-flowing water that is colder and denser. Energy is transferred by convection both within Earth's atmosphere and oceans and within Earth's interior.

FIGURE 3: Energy moves out of this hot steel bar into the surrounding air via radiation, into the air touching it by conduction, and by convection as air circulates around it.

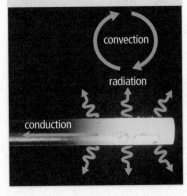

convection

radiation

conduction

Gather Evidence Note the ways in which you think the eruption of Mount Pinatubo might have interfered with the flow of energy on and above Earth's surface.

External and Internal Energy

More than 99.98% of the thermal energy that we feel on the ground, in ocean water, and the atmosphere comes either directly or indirectly from the sun. Solar energy drives the winds, ocean currents, and water cycle and supports all life on Earth.

Based on available evidence, scientists estimate that the temperature at the center of Earth is about 5500 °C. Obviously, Earth has a lot of internal thermal energy. Much of this internal energy is left over from Earth's formation, which you will learn more about in Exploration 4. The rest of Earth's internal energy comes from energy released by atoms during radioactive decay processes.

FIGURE 4: Conduction, convection, and radiation transfer thermal energy from one place to another within Earth's interior and on the surface.

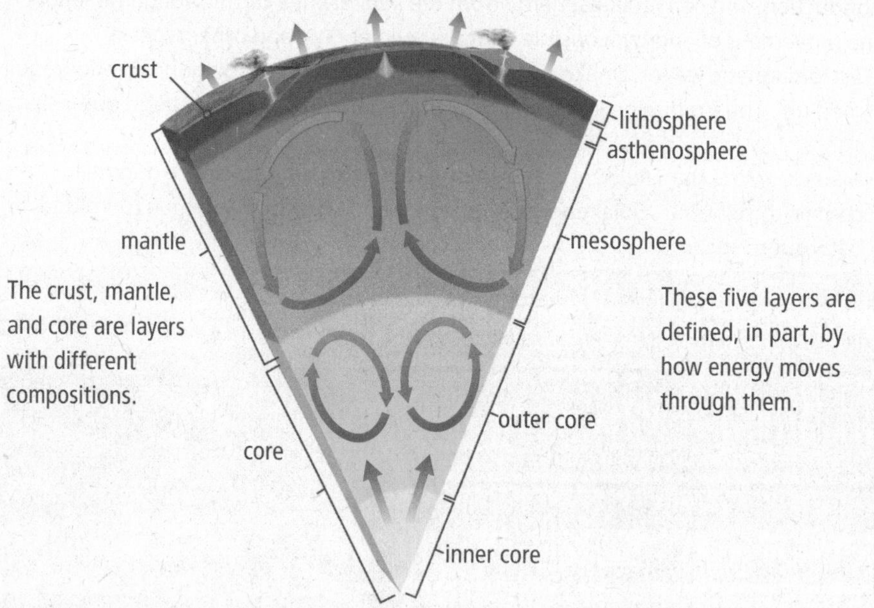

crust

lithosphere
asthenosphere

mantle

mesosphere

The crust, mantle, and core are layers with different compositions.

These five layers are defined, in part, by how energy moves through them.

outer core

core

inner core

Predict Where is the flow of energy from Earth's interior observable and measurable without sensitive scientific equipment?

As Figure 4 shows, different mechanisms of energy transfer are more important within and between layers of Earth depending on the physical properties of those layers. For example, convection occurs in the semi-rigid part of the mantle and in the liquid outer core, which are both hot and fluid enough to flow. Energy flows by conduction through the solid inner core and through the solid, rigid lithosphere to the surface. All materials radiate energy, but within Earth, this energy is absorbed almost immediately by the surrounding materials. Radiation is a major means of energy transfer only through the atmosphere and out to space.

Earth's interior contains much more thermal energy than the surface and atmosphere do, but it is released much more slowly. The flow of Earth's internal energy does not have a significant direct effect on Earth's climate, but it is responsible for important processes, such as volcanic eruptions and earthquakes that shape Earth's major surface features.

Explain In your Evidence Notebook, briefly describe and compare the sources of Earth's energy.

Earth's External Energy

Earth is a relatively warm planet, with an average surface air temperature of about 15 °C (59 °F). How is it that Earth's surface is so warm and stays so warm? It is because most of the thermal energy we can feel and measure on Earth's surface comes from the sun and flows through the atmosphere and oceans.

Income Equals Outgo

Solar energy is constantly reaching the top of Earth's atmosphere. On average, the same amount of energy leaves Earth's surface and atmosphere each second and moves out into space.

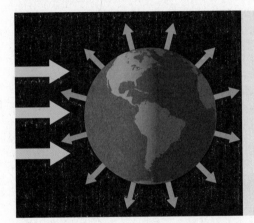

FIGURE 5: The incoming energy from the sun is in the form of visible light, as well as ultraviolet light and infrared radiation, which we can not see. Most of the outgoing radiation is in the form of invisible infrared radiation. The amount of energy that Earth receives from the sun is balanced by the amount of energy that is reflected and emitted by Earth back out into space.

In order for Earth's surface temperature to remain stable, the total amount of incoming and outgoing radiation must be balanced. The balance of incoming and outgoing energy is known as Earth's energy budget. Figure 5 shows a simplified view of energy flow into and out of the Earth system. In Unit 4 you will learn more about the details of energy flow within and between Earth systems, including the role of some gases in keeping Earth warmer than it otherwise would be.

Reflection and Absorption

About 45% of the sunlight that reaches Earth from space is reflected and absorbed by gas molecules, dust, other small particles, called *aerosols*, and water droplets in the atmosphere. When sunlight reaches rock, plants, oceans, and ice on Earth's surface, some of it is reflected while the rest is absorbed. Albedo is a measure of the percentage of light that a particular surface will reflect. Ice has a high albedo—more light is reflected than is absorbed. Forests have a low albedo—more energy is absorbed than is reflected. You can tell whether a surface has a high or low albedo just by looking at it. Surfaces with a high albedo are light or bright colored, because they reflect a relatively high percentage of light. Surfaces with a low albedo are dark, because they reflect relatively little light.

Predict What happens to Earth's surface temperature when the amount of incoming and outgoing energy is not equal?

Explore Online ⏵

Hands-On Lab

Energy of the Sun
Estimate the sun's energy output and evaluate the differences between known values and experimental values.

Predict The Mount Pinatubo eruption released nearly 20 million tons of sulfur dioxide, which formed tiny droplets of sulfuric acid that floated high in the atmosphere. How do you think this might have affected Earth's energy budget?

Clouds also reflect and absorb solar energy. Some clouds have a high albedo and appear white from above, while others absorb more light and are grayer in color. Smoke absorbs more light than it reflects, giving it a low albedo.

Temperature Changes

As long as the amount of radiation entering Earth's system and the amount leaving Earth's system are equal, Earth's surface air temperature remains stable. Surface air temperature differs from place to place and changes over the course of the day and from season to season, but the average annual global temperature does not change.

What happens if the amounts of incoming and outgoing solar energy are not balanced? If Earth emits more energy than it absorbs, its temperature will decrease. In contrast, if Earth absorbs more energy than it emits, its temperature slowly rises.

Albedo has an important effect on both local and global climate. Surfaces with low albedo generally warm up more easily than those with high albedo. On a local scale, asphalt and other building materials with low albedo contribute to urban heat islands, city areas that have warmer temperatures than surrounding rural areas.

On the global scale, changes in the amount of Earth's surface covered by ice can cause corresponding changes in global temperatures. For example, as temperatures increase today because of global climate change, many glaciers and large areas of the polar ice caps are melting. This melting reduces the surface area covered by ice and thus decreases Earth's overall albedo. This decrease in albedo in turn leads to a further increase in global temperatures.

Stability and Change

Analyze A drop in temperature can lead to an increase in ice. How would the added ice affect the temperature? Would the ice reinforce or counteract the change in temperature?

The effect of albedo on climate shows how a change in a system can lead to further change—a process called *feedback*. For example, higher temperatures cause melting and reduced albedo, which in turn leads to further warming. This is called positive feedback because the change leads to further change of the same type. An increase (+) leads to further increase (+). In contrast, negative feedback occurs when a process counteracts a change, slowing the change or moving the system back toward its previous state. In this way, negative feedback helps to maintain the stability of a system.

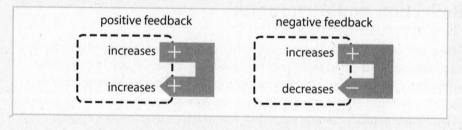

Analyze What other factors might affect Earth's albedo? For each, note whether it depends on temperature.

Distribution of Sunlight

The amounts of incoming and outgoing energy differ during the day and from place to place on Earth. Although Earth's energy budget is balanced as a whole, some places have more energy coming in than going out, while others have more going out than coming in. Energy moves not only between the surface and atmosphere but also from place to place *within* the atmosphere and oceans.

Latitude and Sunlight

The amount of radiation that any specific region of Earth receives depends on the angle of the sun in the sky. The higher the sun is in the sky, the more radiation that reaches each square meter of the surface and atmosphere in that region. For this reason, the concentration of solar energy reaching the ground varies throughout the day as Earth rotates. It is greatest when the sun is highest in the sky and is least at night, when the surface is facing away from the sun.

Because Earth is a sphere, the amount of radiation falling on the surface at any given time also differs with latitude. As Figure 6 shows, this occurs because the lower the sun is in the sky, the more the solar energy is spread out on the surface. For this reason, the amount of incoming radiation is greatest in the equatorial regions, where the sun shines more directly, and is least in the polar regions, where the sun is lower in the sky.

Finally, the amount of daily radiation any single square meter receives varies from season to season. Earth's axis is not perpendicular to its orbit around the sun, but rather is tilted at an angle of about 23.5 degrees. As a result, each point on Earth's surface receives more direct radiation and experiences longer days during the summer months than during the winter months. These seasonal variations are greatest at the poles and diminish as you get closer to the equator.

Gather Evidence
Make a list of variables that affect the concentration of solar energy reaching a particular place on Earth's surface.

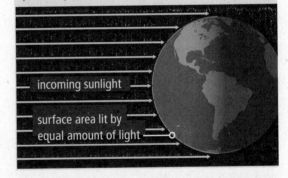

FIGURE 6: Because Earth is a sphere, the amount of energy that strikes the surface differs from place to place.

incoming sunlight

surface area lit by equal amount of light

 Hands-On Activity

Light and Latitude

PROCEDURE

1. Hold a **flashlight** so that the beam shines directly down on a **white piece of paper.** Use a **pencil** to trace the outline of the beam of light.

2. Move the flashlight so that the light shines on the paper at an angle. Trace the outline of the beam of light.

ANALYSIS

1. How does the area of the direct beam differ from the area of the angled beam?

2. How does this lab illustrate the way latitude affects incoming solar radiation?

MATERIALS
- flashlight
- paper, white
- pencil

Surface Ocean Currents

Explain The amount of radiation emitted to space from the polar regions is greater than the amount of radiation that they receive from the sun. How is this possible?

Explore Online ▶

Hands-On Lab 🧪

Density Currents
Model the movement of a fluid, such as ocean water, due to differences in density.

Although Earth's energy budget is balanced as a whole, latitudes near the equator receive more energy than they emit. Similarly, latitudes closer to the poles emit more energy than they receive. This is possible because energy is flowing by convection from place to place in the oceans and in the atmosphere.

Surface ocean currents help distribute solar energy around the globe. Waters in equatorial regions are heated up as they absorb direct solar radiation. Thus as currents flow from equatorial areas toward the poles, they carry thermal energy with them. Some of this energy is eventually radiated directly to space. The rest is released to the atmosphere through conduction and radiation. From there, it eventually moves out to space but from a higher latitude than where it came in.

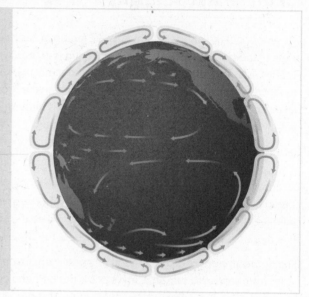

FIGURE 7: Currents of warm water carry thermal energy from the equator toward the poles, and cooler waters flow back toward the equator and are rewarmed. Convection cycles in the atmosphere also redistribute energy in a similar pattern.

Atmospheric Circulation

Analyze How do the patterns of atmospheric circulation help explain how the sulfur dioxide released by Mount Pinatubo's eruption could have affected global temperatures?

Wind also moves solar energy toward the poles via convection. The air in Earth's lower atmosphere is in constant motion. When the gas molecules, aerosols, and water droplets in the atmosphere move, the thermal energy that they contain moves with them. Some winds are the result of local differences in topography or movements of air masses. Other winds operate continuously and on a much larger scale. These are part of the global atmospheric circulation system.

The global wind system is driven by the unequal heating of Earth's surface. Winds blow because of differences in air pressure caused by differences in air temperature. Because Earth's surface is not heated evenly, the air is warmer in some places than in others. Cool, dry air is denser than warm, humid air, so it sinks, pushing warmer air upward. In an atmospheric convection cell, warm air rises and cools as it rises. It then travels horizontally toward the poles until it is cool and dense enough to sink. When it gets near Earth's surface, the cooler air flows back toward the equator. This general pattern of circulation moves energy away from the equatorial regions toward the poles, partially evening out the imbalance of energy.

Redistribution of Energy

Ocean water holds much more energy than the air. For this reason, most of the transfer of energy between the equator and poles takes place through the movement of water. However, the winds and ocean currents are very closely linked. Air over the oceans is heated by energy that moves from the oceans via conduction, evaporation, and radiation. Differences in heating cause the air to move. At the same time, the movement of the air helps drive the surface ocean currents.

Over time, the flow of air and water redistribute solar energy over Earth's surface. This process decreases the difference in temperature between the equator and the poles.

Predict How might surface temperatures on Earth be different if there were no oceans and no wind?

Modeling Circulation

The circulation of water in the oceans and air in the atmosphere can be represented simply with two-dimensional maps. But to better understand how Earth's surface energy moves over space and time, we need a more complex model.

A Three-Dimensional Climate Model

FIGURE 8: A three-dimensional General Circulation Model (GCM) can be used to study a variety of variables that are part of the global climate.

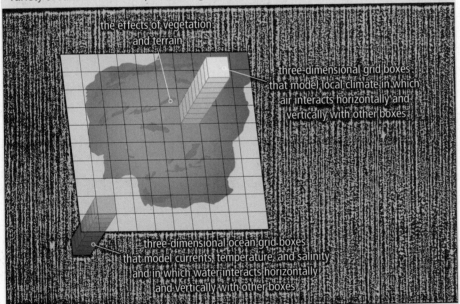

the effects of vegetation and terrain

three-dimensional grid boxes that model local climate in which air interacts horizontally and vertically with other boxes

three-dimensional ocean grid boxes that model currents, temperature, and salinity and in which water interacts horizontally and vertically with other boxes

A General Circulation Model (GCM) is designed to describe and predict how energy moves with the atmosphere and oceans in three dimensions over time. A GCM is used to see how different variables, such as topography, vegetation, and the composition of the atmosphere, affect how solar energy is redistributed over the globe. GCMs are valuable tools for predicting weather over the short term and climate changes over the long term.

Gather Evidence Make notes about ways in which the atmosphere and oceans help to redistribute solar energy on a global scale. What are some key patterns that you notice?

Earth's Internal Energy

In a deep gold mine 3 km below the surface, the rocks can be hotter than 60 °C (140 °F). At a depth of 10 km, the temperature could be 200 °C to 300 °C. The temperature in the core is greater than 5500 °C. Earth's interior clearly contains an enormous amount of thermal energy. This energy comes from two main sources: energy that is left over from Earth's formation, and energy that is still released today as a result of radioactive decay.

Collisional Heating

Based on the best available evidence, scientists infer that much of Earth's internal energy is a result of the way the planet formed. The widely accepted model of the formation of the solar system indicates that Earth formed through accretion, or gradual build up, as smaller rocky bodies in space collided. You will learn more about this process in Unit 4.

Recall that every moving object has kinetic energy. The greater the object's mass and velocity, the more kinetic energy it has. When an object collides with another object, some of the kinetic energy is transformed into thermal energy. This thermal energy then heats up the colliding objects. If they carry enough kinetic energy, the objects could melt or vaporize.

With every collision that occurred as Earth formed, its thermal energy increased. At some point the materials got so hot that they melted. As a result, the early Earth was completely molten and has gradually cooled over time.

Predict Do you think collisional heating can still occur on Earth today? Why or why not?

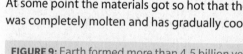

FIGURE 9: Earth formed more than 4.5 billion years ago through the process of accretion of smaller solid rocky objects in space.

Explore Online ▶

Image Credits: ©Joe Tucciarone/SPL/Science Source

Contraction and Settling

As more material was added to Earth during accretion, its mass increased. Earth's gravitational pull also increased, because gravitational force is directly related to mass. This increase in force then caused Earth to contract as materials moved closer toward Earth's center. When an object falls or moves toward Earth's center, it loses a form of energy known as gravitational potential energy. Just as kinetic energy can be converted into thermal energy, so can gravitational potential energy. In this way, contraction caused further heating of Earth's interior.

Once Earth was molten, iron and other heavy elements sank toward the center and formed the core. Their gravitational potential energy was also converted into thermal energy, further heating Earth.

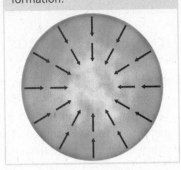

FIGURE 10: Earth's internal thermal energy increased through contraction and core formation.

Radioactive Decay

The other major source of Earth's internal thermal energy is radioactive decay of isotopes—atoms of the same element that have different numbers of neutrons. The rock of the crust and mantle both contain small portions of radioactive isotopes, which break down. When they decay, they release energy. This energy is absorbed by the surrounding atoms and molecules in the rock, causing it to heat up. This process is known as radiogenic heating.

Three elements are responsible for most of the radiogenic heating that occurs today: potassium (K), uranium (U), and thorium (Th). The concentration of radioactive isotopes is greater in the crust, but the mantle makes up a much greater volume of Earth, so most of Earth's radiogenic heat is generated there.

Most of the radioactive isotopes responsible for radiogenic heating decay very slowly. As a result, Earth still has much of its original radioactive heat sources. Radiogenic heating will continue to keep Earth's interior hot for billions of years to come.

Explain How would Earth's mantle and crust be different if they did not contain radioactive isotopes?

Stability and Change

Uranium-Lead Decay

About 40% of Earth's radiogenic heat comes from uranium-238 (U-238), which decays to form lead-206 (Pb-206). U-238 has 92 protons and 146 neutrons. Pb-206 has 82 protons and 124 neutrons. U-238 becomes Pb-206 through a complex chain of reactions.

Uranium-238 has a half-life of about 4.5 billion years. The half-life is the time required for half of the isotopes present in a sample to decay. That means that half of the U-238 isotopes that were present at the very beginning of Earth have now decayed to Pb-206.

FIGURE 11: Radioactive decay heats the mantle and crust.

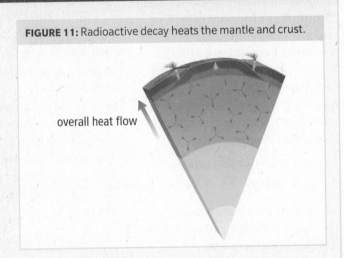

overall heat flow

Analyze Describe and compare the sources of Earth's internal energy.

Engineering

Urban Heat Islands

Urban heat islands are city areas where average temperatures are significantly higher than in the surrounding region. According to the Environmental Protection Agency (EPA), the annual mean temperature of a large city may be 1–3 °C (1.8–5.4 °F) warmer than in nearby rural areas.

A number of factors can contribute to the heat island effect. Most importantly, the low albedo of dark rooftops and surface paving materials reduces the amount of solar radiation reflected back to space. The increased amount of radiation absorbed raises the temperature of these surfaces, which in turn increases the air temperature.

The negative effects of heat islands are most obvious in summer. The hotter city temperatures lead to increased electricity use for air conditioning, increased air pollution, and a higher rate of heat-related illnesses and deaths.

Engineers use scientific knowledge to design solutions to real-world problems such as urban heat islands. The first step in the engineering design process is to define the problem clearly, including defining the criteria that a successful solution to the problem must meet. Some of the more promising solutions for reducing the impact of heat islands include:

1. cool roofs designed to reflect more sunlight

2. green roofs, which replace traditional roofing materials with trees and other plants

3. planting large areas with trees and other vegetation

FIGURE 12: Rooftop gardens are one way to reduce the effects of urban heat islands.

One noteworthy example of a green roof is the rooftop of Chicago's City Hall. Built as part of the EPA's Urban Heat Island Pilot Project, the City Hall rooftop garden was developed to demonstrate the benefits of green roofs in reducing summer temperatures. The green roof also has had other benefits, including reducing the amount of runoff from storms and increasing biodiversity in the city.

Language Arts Connection

Use Internet and library resources to learn more about one solution to the problem of urban heat islands. Then prepare a presentation about your chosen solution. Be sure to include:

- the criteria that the solution must meet
- the costs and benefits of the solution
- other positive effects of the solution

To find detailed guidance on preparing a presentation, see the Learning Resources for this lesson.

COMPARING WORLDS

ICE AGES

Go online to choose one of these other paths.

Image Credits: ©yuk8691/E+/Getty Images

Lesson Self-Check

CAN YOU EXPLAIN IT?

FIGURE 13: Mount Pinatubo, Philippines The thick cloud of gas and dust that erupted from Mount Pinatubo in 1991 rose 40 km into the atmosphere and spread out around the globe.

The eruption of Mount Pinatubo in 1991 was one of the largest volcanic eruptions in recent history. From 1992 to 1994, the average global surface temperature was an average of 0.5 °C lower than normal. Think about what you have learned about Earth's external energy and energy budget as you explain the cause-and-effect relationship between these two phenomena.

 Explain Refer to the notes in your Evidence Notebook to explain how the eruption of Mount Pinatubo led to a drop in average temperatures worldwide. Use the Claims, Evidence, Reasoning format to construct your argument.

Claim: Make a clearly stated claim about the cause-and-effect relationship between the eruption and temperature change.

Evidence: Identify the important evidence from the lesson that is relevant to your claim.

Reasoning: Clearly explain how the evidence supports your claim.

CHECKPOINTS

Check Your Understanding

1. Which of the following statements about Earth's energy budget are true?

   a. Most energy reaches Earth from space as visible light.

   b. Most of the energy that leaves Earth travels in the form of visible light.

   c. More than 99% of Earth's outgoing energy comes from energy brought to Earth's surface in volcanic eruptions.

   d. Energy leaves Earth's system only during the daytime.

   e. The thermal energy (heat) that you feel when you put your hand on the ground originates from the sun.

2. Energy moves through and out of Earth through conduction, convection, and radiation. Match each region of Earth to the process by which most thermal energy flows.

   a. from Earth's surface directly to space

   b. through the lithosphere to surface

   c. within the mantle, below lithosphere

   d. within the outer core

   e. from the inner core to outer core

   f. within the inner core

   1. Conduction
   2. Convection
   3. Radiation

3. "Cool roofs" are roofs that are painted or covered in a very reflective material with a high albedo. They are designed to prevent houses from heating up so much during the day, especially in the summertime. Cool roofs also can decrease the air temperature above a house. Explain the principle behind a cool roof.

4. Many scientists are concerned that the melting of Earth's sea ice will increase Earth's surface temperature. Make a sketch that explains this phenomenon in terms of a feedback loop.

5. Over the past 150 years, the concentration of greenhouse gases, such as carbon dioxide, in Earth's atmosphere has been increasing. Greenhouse gases absorb infrared radiation emitted by the ground. The greater the concentration of greenhouse gases, the more energy is absorbed by the atmosphere and the greater the air temperature. If the concentration of greenhouse gases leveled off (stopped increasing), what would happen to the air temperature?

   a. Less energy would be absorbed by the atmosphere, causing air temperature to decrease back to the level it was 150 years ago.

   b. The amount of energy being absorbed would exceed the amount emitted to space, causing air temperature to rise indefinitely.

   c. Air temperature would continue to rise but only until the amount of energy emitted by the atmosphere balances the amount absorbed by it.

6. Why does sunshine feel warmer in the middle of the day during the summer months and in places closer to the equator?

   a. Earth's albedo is lower.

   b. Earth's surface is closer to the sun.

   c. Earth's surface faces the sun more directly.

   d. Earth's atmosphere absorbs more infrared radiation.

7. Complete the paragraph below to summarize Earth's original sources of internal energy.

   The initial source of Earth's internal thermal energy was _____. The _____ energy of the objects that collided to form Earth was converted into thermal energy. As Earth gained mass, its _____ also increased, causing it to _____. This caused further heating, as gravitational potential energy was transformed into _____ energy. Once Earth was molten, iron and other _____ elements sank toward the center to form the _____. Their _____ potential energy was also converted into thermal energy. Over time, the core and other layers began to _____, releasing additional thermal energy.

8. In the mid-1800s, the physicist Lord Kelvin attempted to calculate Earth's age based on its temperature. He reasoned that if Earth was originally molten, it must have cooled gradually and steadily over time to its current temperature. Kelvin calculated that Earth must be around 100 million years old. We now know that Earth is 45 times older. Why was Kelvin so wrong?

9. Over time, Earth's internal energy is slowly released from the surface into space. One way to compare the amounts of different sources of thermal energy is in terms of the heat flux: the amount of energy in watts, or joules per second, that is released by the planet.

Complete the table to compare the estimated amounts of thermal energy released by Earth that come from different sources.

Source of internal energy	Estimate of heat flux today	Percentage of total internal energy emitted by Earth
heat from formation		55%
radiogenic heat	20×10^{12} watts	
total internal energy flux	44×10^{12} watts	100%

10. The table compares the amount of energy leaving Earth that originates as solar energy with the amount of energy leaving Earth that originates in Earth's interior.

Internal energy flux	44×10^{12} watts
Solar energy flux	18×10^{16} watts

Select the correct numbers and words in the following paragraph to accurately compare the two sources of energy:

The flux of solar energy from Earth's surface is about [4/30/4000] times [greater/less] than the flux of internal energy from its surface.

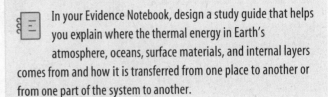

In your Evidence Notebook, design a study guide that helps you explain where the thermal energy in Earth's atmosphere, oceans, surface materials, and internal layers comes from and how it is transferred from one place to another or from one part of the system to another.

Remember to include the following in your study guide:
- Use 2D models (sketches) to describe the flow of energy.
- Explain how energy and matter influence each other on Earth's surface and deep underground.
- Identify cause-and-effect chains and feedback loops related to the movement of energy into, out of, and within Earth's systems.

2.2

Minerals

Calcium, sulfur, oxygen, and hydrogen atoms came together to form these giant crystals of gypsum found in a cave in Mexico in 2000.

CAN YOU EXPLAIN IT?

Observe: Record observations about mineral properties, composition, and structure. As you explore the lesson, gather evidence to help explain the physical properties of minerals.

The shapes of crystals come from their structure. A crystal is a solid whose atoms or other components appear in a regular, repeating pattern.

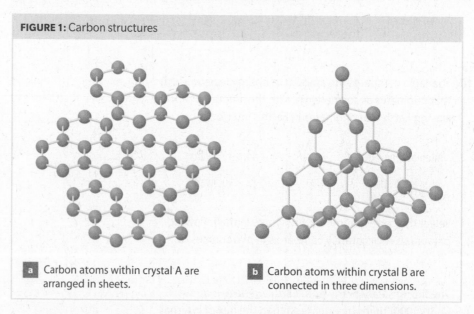

FIGURE 1: Carbon structures

a Carbon atoms within crystal A are arranged in sheets.

b Carbon atoms within crystal B are connected in three dimensions.

Crystals A and B are two different substances composed of pure carbon. In each crystal the carbon atoms are arranged in a specific pattern. This pattern gives each crystal its structure.

Predict Compare the structures of the two crystals. Which mineral do you think might be harder? What makes you think so?

Introducing Minerals

The matter around you is made of atoms of various elements. An element is a substance that cannot be broken into simpler substances by chemical means. The most common elements in Earth's crust are listed in Figure 2. Atoms combine to make more complex structures such as molecules and crystals. Molecules and crystals may be of one element or of more than one element.

What Is a Mineral?

The term *mineral* is often used in a very loose way. We hear that breakfast cereals are "full of vitamins and minerals" and that potting soil "includes important minerals." In Earth science, a mineral is a substance that has specific characteristics. It is a solid substance that has a characteristic chemical composition—it is made of the same material throughout. It has an orderly internal structure. In other words, it is in the form of crystals, though the crystals may be too small to see. Because minerals have specific chemical compositions and definite crystal structures, they also have characteristic physical and chemical properties. For example, they have different colors and textures. Geologists use these properties to identify and classify minerals.

Minerals make up the rock that forms Earth's crust. The properties of each type of rock depend, in part, on the properties of its minerals. On Mars and many other bodies in space, the temperature is so low that carbon dioxide and other gases freeze into crystals and become minerals. The resulting rock can have different properties than rock on Earth.

FIGURE 2: Element abundances in Earth's crust

Name	Element symbol	Percent by mass
oxygen	O	46.6
silicon	Si	27.7
aluminum	Al	8.1
iron	Fe	5.0
calcium	Ca	3.6
sodium	Na	2.8
potassium	K	2.6
magnesium	Mg	2.1
other		1.5

Explain Why are quartz, ice, and calcite considered to be minerals, while coal, sugar, and glass are not?

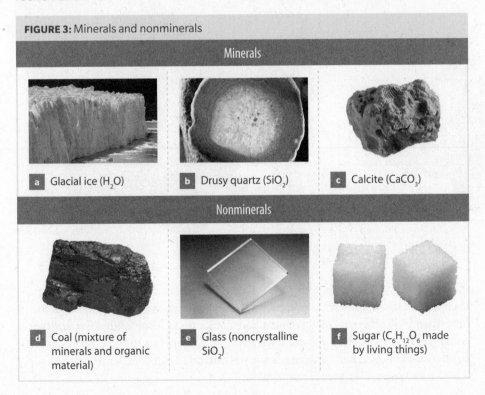

FIGURE 3: Minerals and nonminerals

Minerals

a Glacial ice (H_2O)

b Drusy quartz (SiO_2)

c Calcite ($CaCO_3$)

Nonminerals

d Coal (mixture of minerals and organic material)

e Glass (noncrystalline SiO_2)

f Sugar ($C_6H_{12}O_6$ made by living things)

FIGURE 4: Criteria that define a mineral

Criteria	Explanation and example
occurs naturally	All minerals can be found in nature. Although diamonds can be made in a lab, they are still minerals because they also occur naturally.
inorganic	If a compound forms only through biological processes, then it is not a mineral. Calcite often forms through biological processes, such as the formation of shells. However, it is a mineral because it can also form as a result of chemical processes.
solid	Although ice is a mineral, liquid water is not.
has a specific chemical composition	Minerals are elements or compounds. You can write a chemical formula to describe their composition. Most rocks, on the other hand, are mixtures of minerals. You can't write a single chemical formula for a rock.
has a definite crystalline structure	The atoms in a mineral are arranged in a specific and repeating pattern. Opal has a similar composition to quartz, but its atoms are not arranged in a specific, repeating pattern, so it is not considered to be a true mineral.

Elements and Compounds

Explain Why are most minerals compounds rather than elements?

All minerals have a specific chemical composition. That is, every mineral can be described by a chemical formula. Some minerals, called *native elements*, are crystals of a single element. Gold, silver, copper, sulfur, and carbon all exist in mineral form on Earth's surface. Of the 92 naturally occurring elements on Earth, only about 19 exist as native element minerals.

FIGURE 5: Elements and compounds

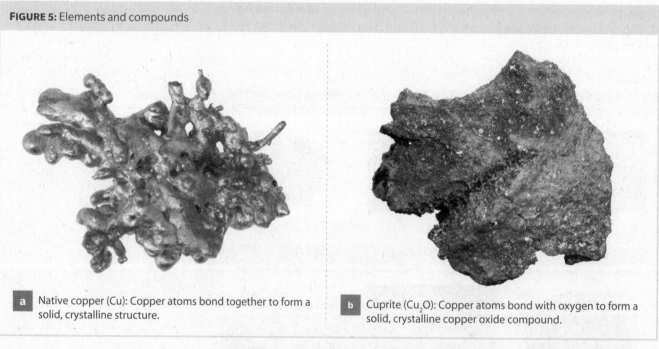

a Native copper (Cu): Copper atoms bond together to form a solid, crystalline structure.

b Cuprite (Cu_2O): Copper atoms bond with oxygen to form a solid, crystalline copper oxide compound.

On the other hand, there are countless ways that elements can combine. Most of the more than 5000 different known minerals are compounds. A compound is a substance composed of atoms of two or more different types of elements that are held together by chemical bonds. Common minerals such as quartz (SiO_2), halite (NaCl), calcite ($CaCO_3$), and pyrite (FeS_2) are all compounds.

Minerals in Earth's Crust

Elements on Earth do not exist in equal amounts, nor are they distributed evenly. Only eight elements make up most of the mass of Earth's rocky crust. Oxygen and silicon have the greatest abundance, or relative amount. The most abundant minerals in the crust are compounds rich in silicon and oxygen called *silicates*. The other most common elements in Earth's crust shown in Figure 6 combine with silica (SiO_2) to form a wide variety of minerals. Some minerals do not contain silica.

Data Analysis

Interpreting Graphs of Composition

The chemical formula for silicate (SiO_2) indicates a 2:1 ratio of oxygen to silicon—two atoms of oxygen for every atom of silicon. This might seem to suggest that there is twice the amount of oxygen as there is silicon in Earth's crust. Yet in Figure 6, the amount of silicon is more than half the amount of oxygen.

When you study graphs or tables that describe composition, look for information about whether they represent mass, volume, numbers of atoms, or other quantities. The graph in Figure 6 represents 100% of the mass of Earth's crust. However, chemical formulas give the relative number of atoms rather than the relative masses. To convert between these quantities, you can use the atomic masses found in a periodic table of the elements. How many atoms of aluminum would you expect for each atom of oxygen?

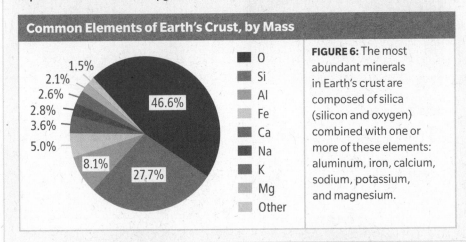

Common Elements of Earth's Crust, by Mass

1.5%
2.1%
2.6%
2.8%
3.6%
5.0%
8.1%
27.7%
46.6%

O
Si
Al
Fe
Ca
Na
K
Mg
Other

FIGURE 6: The most abundant minerals in Earth's crust are composed of silica (silicon and oxygen) combined with one or more of these elements: aluminum, iron, calcium, sodium, potassium, and magnesium.

Analyze Look at the graph of common elements of Earth's crust. What are some familiar elements that are not shown in this table? Is it surprising to you that they are not shown? Why or why not?

Explain What is the common state of matter for each of the most common elements found in minerals? Describe the pattern you see, and note any important variations from the pattern. What might you consider unusual in the pattern?

Properties of Minerals

Every mineral has a set of characteristic properties by which it can be identified. Some can be seen easily, such as shape or color. Other properties, like hardness and density, can only be determined through tests and measurements. In some cases, a mineral can be identified by unique properties such as magnetism, seeing how the mineral appears under different lighting, and seeing how it reacts with other substances.

Looking at Minerals

When trying to identify a mineral, the first step is to simply look at it. What color is it? How does it reflect and transmit light? What shape is it?

Color, Luster, and Transparency

Color, transparency, and luster are all related to the way light interacts with a mineral. Color is a function of the wavelengths of light that the mineral reflects. Luster is a description of the way the mineral reflects light. Transparency is a measure of the amount of light that the mineral absorbs or allows to pass through.

Analyze Describe the color, luster, and transparency of three other mineral samples shown in this lesson.

Explore Online ▶

Hands-On Lab 🧪

Growing Crystals
Grow ammonium alum crystals.

FIGURE 7: Color, luster, and transparency are related to the way light interacts with a mineral.

a Halite comes in a range of colors and has a waxy to glassy luster. It is translucent—it allows some light to pass through.

b Long, fibrous crystals give tremolite a silky luster.

c Pyrite is an opaque mineral with a brassy color and metallic luster.

d Quartz is a transparent mineral with a luster similar to that of broken glass.

The size, shape, and arrangement of crystals also affect the way a mineral looks. While some mineral samples consist of a single crystal, others are masses of many crystals. The pyrite cubes are large, well-formed crystals with flat faces that can easily reflect light. The pyrolusite consists of microscopic crystals oriented in different directions. Light is scattered in all different directions, giving it a dull, earthy luster.

In some cases, the combination of color, transparency, and luster provides strong clues as to the identity of the mineral. For example, sulfur has a distinctive bright yellow color. Gold has a distinctive gold-yellow color and metallic luster. Diamond is transparent and has a particularly bright and brilliant luster.

In most cases, however, none of these properties are definitive. There is more than one type of mineral with the same color, luster, or transparency. In addition, different samples of the same mineral can come in different colors, transparencies, and lusters. Hematite, for example, is an iron oxide mineral that can be black, gray, or red, with a luster that is metallic, specular (sparkling with many reflective surfaces), or earthy, depending on the size and arrangement of its crystals.

Explain Why might one sample of sulfur have a glassy luster while another has a dull, earthy luster?

Shape

Another property that is easy to examine is a mineral's overall shape and how it normally appears in nature.

FIGURE 8: Some mineral shapes

a Needle-like crystals of barite

b Bladed crystals of gypsum

c Pyrolusite with a branched or treelike shape

d Native copper with an open, poorly defined shape

e Cinnabar with a massive, poorly defined shape

f Malachite with a bumpy shape

For example, pyrite crystals have a distinctive cubic shape. Garnet typically forms nearly spherical 12-sided crystals. Groups of parallel fibers make tremolite look fibrous. A mineral sample is described as having a massive shape if it is not an easily describable shape. Minerals more commonly appear like this and not in distinct crystals.

Like color, transparency, and luster, shape may not be useful in identifying a mineral. Some minerals take on a very distinctive shape that few others do. Others can have the same shape as many other mineral samples or can exist in many different forms. For example, there are more than 300 different shapes and appearances of the mineral calcite. The particular shape that a mineral takes depends on the way that the atoms within it are organized, the way it forms, and the environment that it forms in.

Tests for Identifying Minerals

Many minerals can be identifed through simple tests that can be done in the field or lab with a basic set of tools.

How Minerals Break

The external appearance of a mineral displays important properties of the mineral. In some cases, what is visible is the fresh face of a crystal. In others, it is a broken surface. When geologists are out in the field, they often use rock hammers to break off pieces of rock and examine the minerals. Cleavage and fracture both describe the way a mineral breaks.

FIGURE 9: Cleavage and fracture

a Halite breaks apart in perfect cubes. You can see the structure in the upper left corner.

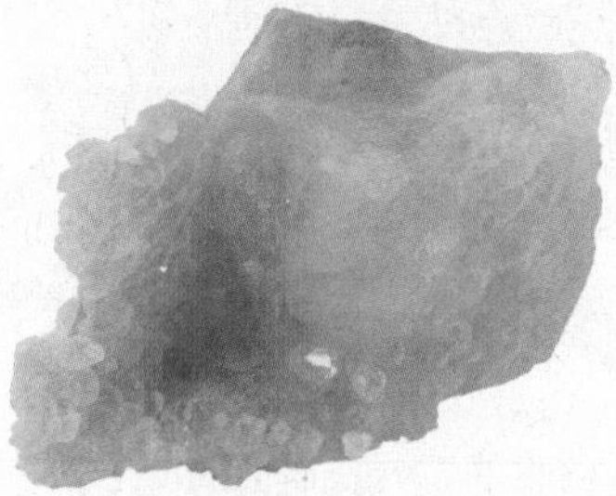

b Quartz crystals such as this can break like glass, forming smooth, curved surfaces.

Explain How might you use fracture to distinguish halite from quartz?

How a mineral breaks and what the small pieces look like after it is broken can be important in helping to identify the mineral. For example, calcite and halite crystals can both be clear and glassy, but calcite breaks apart into small, regularly shaped pieces. The sides of the pieces do not meet at right angles. Halite breaks apart into perfect cubes. Calcite and quartz can look very similar, but quartz breaks to form smooth, curved surfaces. Copper and pyrite can be a similar color, but pyrite breaks to form smooth, curved surfaces, while copper has a jagged fracture.

Color and Streak

As you know, many minerals come in a number of different colors, so color alone is not a good identifying characteristic. However, the color of a mineral in its powdered form—its streak—can help to identify the mineral. Geologists often perform streak tests by rubbing the sample across an unglazed ceramic surface called a *streak plate*.

Predict Compare the color of each mineral to its streak. What would the streak color of a sample of pink quartz be? What would the streak of a dark black sample of hematite be?

FIGURE 10: The streak of different minerals

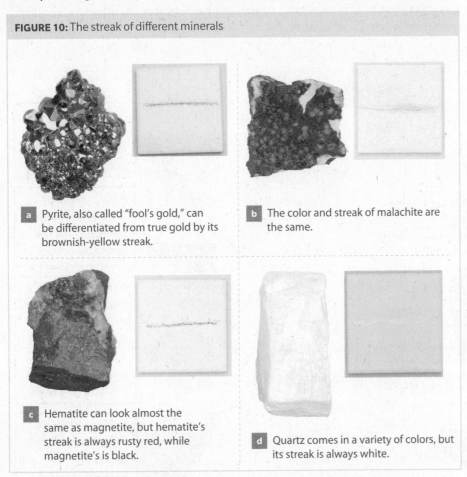

a Pyrite, also called "fool's gold," can be differentiated from true gold by its brownish-yellow streak.

b The color and streak of malachite are the same.

c Hematite can look almost the same as magnetite, but hematite's streak is always rusty red, while magnetite's is black.

d Quartz comes in a variety of colors, but its streak is always white.

Although each mineral has a definite chemical composition, it may contain small quantities of other elements or compounds scattered throughout. Amethyst, the purple variety of quartz, gets its color from iron ions. Ruby, the red variety of corundum, is red because of the presence of chromium. Some crystals even contain tiny crystals of other minerals, which change the color of the main crystal.

These impurities can change the color of the mineral by affecting the way the crystal transmits, absorbs, reflects, or refracts light. As a result, a single type of mineral can exist in a variety of colors, and a single crystal can vary in color throughout. Crystals of watermelon tourmaline, for example, are green on the outside and pink on the inside.

When the mineral is in powder form, however, most of these variations are no longer visible. Streak can be a more useful property than color for mineral identification because it does not differ significantly from sample to sample. All samples of calcite—whether they are pink, yellow, white, brown, or clear—have a white streak.

Mineral Hardness

If you use a streak plate to test the streak of a mineral, you may notice that some minerals are easier to test than others. Some rub off on a streak plate with almost no effort, while others are impossible to turn into powder, no matter how hard you press down (in fact, these minerals will scratch the streak plate). The same is true if you try to scratch the face of a crystal—some scratch easily with almost any object, while others are almost impossible to scratch.

FIGURE 11: Mohs hardness scale

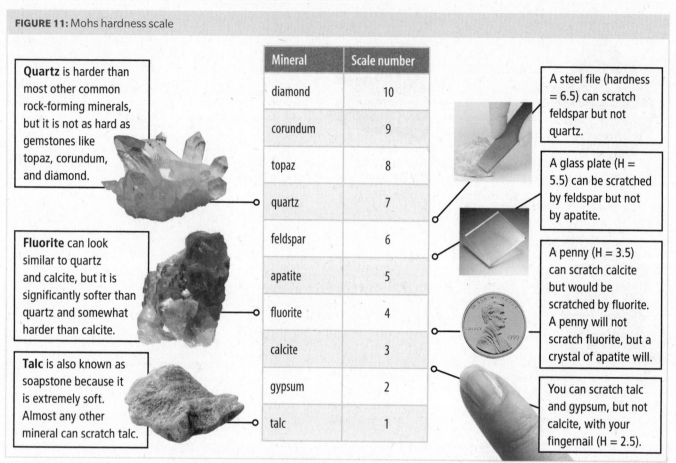

Quartz is harder than most other common rock-forming minerals, but it is not as hard as gemstones like topaz, corundum, and diamond.

Fluorite can look similar to quartz and calcite, but it is significantly softer than quartz and somewhat harder than calcite.

Talc is also known as soapstone because it is extremely soft. Almost any other mineral can scratch talc.

Mineral	Scale number
diamond	10
corundum	9
topaz	8
quartz	7
feldspar	6
apatite	5
fluorite	4
calcite	3
gypsum	2
talc	1

A steel file (hardness = 6.5) can scratch feldspar but not quartz.

A glass plate (H = 5.5) can be scratched by feldspar but not by apatite.

A penny (H = 3.5) can scratch calcite but would be scratched by fluorite. A penny will not scratch fluorite, but a crystal of apatite will.

You can scratch talc and gypsum, but not calcite, with your fingernail (H = 2.5).

The Mohs hardness scale is used to describe the relative hardness of a mineral crystal, or its resistance to being scratched. All minerals fall somewhere on this scale between 1 and 10. A mineral can scratch the face of any mineral with a lower value, and it can be scratched by any mineral with a higher value. Two minerals that have the same hardness can scratch each other.

Like cleavage, hardness is related to the strength of the bonds between atoms within the crystal. Because the bonds are the same in every sample of a mineral, hardness does not vary significantly from sample to sample. Geologists often test hardness to distinguish minerals that look very similar.

Hardness is not the same as resistance to breaking. Diamond is the hardest mineral known, but that does not mean it won't break. In fact, diamond breaks fairly easily along its cleavage planes. Jewelers use this ability to break easily along some planes to shape the diamonds they put into rings and other jewelry.

Explain Why is it important to describe a variety of properties when examining an unknown mineral? Use specific examples to support your answer.

Image Credits: (tl) ©Siede Preis/Photodisc/Getty Images; (cl) ©Editorial Image, LLC/Alamy; (bl) ©Houghton Mifflin Harcourt; (tr) ©Houghton Mifflin Harcourt; (tcr) ©Horiyan/Shutterstock; (bcr) ©Houghton Mifflin Harcourt; (br) ©Guy Jarvis/Houghton Mifflin Harcourt

Hands-On Lab

Mineral Identification

A mineral identification key can be used to compare the properties of minerals so that unknown mineral samples can be identified. Mineral properties in mineral identification keys include color, hardness, streak, luster, cleavage, and fracture. Hardness is determined by a scratch test. The Mohs hardness scale classifies minerals from 1 (softest) to 10 (hardest). Streak is the color of a mineral in a finely powdered form. The luster of a mineral can be classified as either metallic (having an appearance of metals) or nonmetallic. Cleavage is the tendency of a mineral to split along a flat plane. Minerals can cleave in one or more directions or can have no cleavage. Minerals can also break, or *fracture*, along irregular surfaces. In this lab, you will use these properties to identify several mineral samples.

PROCEDURE

1. Make a table with columns for sample number, color/luster, hardness, streak, cleavage/fracture, and mineral name.

Sample number	Color/luster	Hardness	Streak	Cleavage/ fracture	Mineral name
1.					

2. Examine and record the color of each mineral sample in your table. Note whether the luster of each mineral is metallic or nonmetallic.

3. Using a fingernail, copper penny, glass square, and steel file, test each mineral to determine its hardness based on the Mohs hardness scale. Arrange the minerals in order of hardness. Record your observations in your table.

4. Rub each mineral against the streak plate, and determine the color of the mineral's streak. Record your observations.

5. Determine whether the surface of each mineral displays cleavage and/or fracture. Record your observations.

6. Use online mineral databases to help you identify the mineral samples. Remember that properties of the same mineral can vary somewhat from sample to sample.

ANALYZE

Did you find any properties that were especially useful or especially not useful in identifying each sample? If you had to write a manual to explain, step by step, how to identify minerals, in what order would you test different properties? Explain your reasoning.

MATERIALS

- file, steel
- hand lens
- mineral samples (5)
- penny, copper
- square, glass
- streak plate

 Engineering

If you are asked to show quantitative or technical information (such as the results of a lab activity) in a visual format, keep this tip in mind: use the rows and columns of a table to show how facts are related to one another.

| GROWING CRYSTALS | MINERAL RESEARCH | Go online to choose one of these other paths. |

Lesson Self-Check

CAN YOU EXPLAIN IT?

FIGURE 12: Carbon mineral structures

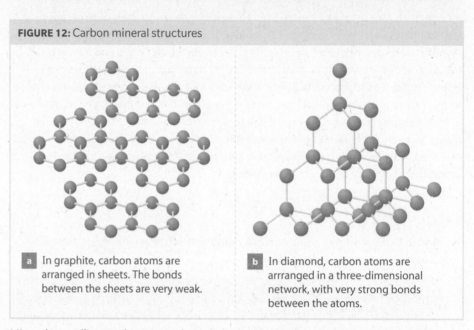

a In graphite, carbon atoms are arranged in sheets. The bonds between the sheets are very weak.

b In diamond, carbon atoms are arrranged in a three-dimensional network, with very strong bonds between the atoms.

 Explain Refer to the notes in your Evidence Notebook to explain how the chemical composition and arrangement of atoms and molecules affects a mineral's properties.

Minerals are all around us: not only in the solid and broken rock that make up Earth's surface and interior, but also in the natural and synthetic materials that we use every day. Both graphite and diamond are minerals with properties that make them useful for many purposes.

Graphite and diamond are both composed of pure carbon. In both minerals, the carbon atoms are arranged in a specific pattern. This pattern gives each mineral its distinct crystal structure. Compare the crystal structures of the two minerals.

The difference in crystal structure between diamond and graphite makes the two minerals useful for different purposes. Diamond is prized as a gemstone because of its transparency, colors, brilliant luster, and resistance to being scratched. Because it breaks evenly and easily along four different planes, it is relatively easy to fashion into various shapes for jewelry. Diamond's extreme hardness also makes it useful in industry. Saw blades and drill bits used for cutting rock, cement, steel, and other hard substances have diamond dust embedded in them.

Because graphite is soft and slippery, it is very useful as a lubricant. (The layers of carbon slide easily past one another.) Graphite is useful in pencils because it is a dark-gray color and soft enough to rub off on paper. Graphite is also a source of carbon used to make carbon steel. Its high melting point makes it useful in engines and other places where a lubricant is needed that won't break down under high temperatures.

Model Compare the structures of the two crystals. Which do you think is harder? Test your prediction by modeling the structures.

Check Your Understanding

1. Which of the following statements describe the properties of a mineral?

    a. Atoms in a mineral are arranged in a specific and repeating pattern.

    b. Not all minerals occur in nature; some minerals can be produced in laboratories.

    c. Minerals can occur in both a solid or liquid form.

    d. Because all minerals are elements or compounds, a chemical formula can be written for a mineral to describe its composition.

    e. If a compound forms only through biological processes, then it is not a mineral.

2. Scientists use a variety of properties to identify minerals. Identify the description that best matches each property.

Description	Property
a. Light reflects evenly off a galena crystal, giving its surfaces a mirrorlike appearance.	**1.** cleavage
	2. luster
b. Halite crystals break evenly along three planes oriented at 90 degrees to each other.	**3.** shape
	4. hardness
c. Native copper can have a treelike form.	**5.** streak
	6. transparency
d. Black hematite crystals produce a red powder.	
e. Light is absorbed by magnetite crystals and does not pass through it.	
f. The face of a diamond crystal can be scratched only by another diamond.	

3. A geologist examines the properties of an unknown sample. The results are shown in the table.

Measurements and Test Results
• is transparent and slightly pink
• breaks into regularly shaped pieces
• has a glassy luster
• has a white streak
• can be scratched by a penny but not by a fingernail

Based on the observable properties, what is the mineral most likely to be?

4. Use the pictures of the minerals in this lesson to determine which properties of minerals you would use to distinguish between these mineral pairs or groups:

    • feldspar and quartz

    • halite, calcite, and quartz

    • pyrite and hematite

    • native copper and cuprite

    • malachite, fluorite, and halite

Support your claims with evidence from the text, and give your reasons for why the tests you selected may be the most effective.

MAKE YOUR OWN STUDY GUIDE

In your Evidence Notebook, design a study guide that helps you explain the observations that scientists need to make to determine the identity of a mineral.

Remember to include the following in your study guide:

• Explain the physical properties of minerals.

• Explain the chemical composition of minerals.

• Explain the internal structure of minerals.

The Rock Cycle

Flowing water can cause dramatic and subtle changes to the rock on Earth's surface over short and long periods of time.

CAN YOU EXPLAIN IT?

It may appear that the rock on Earth's surface is stable and unchanging. However, if you look carefully, you will notice some small changes occurring over time. You might also have observed more dramatic events. Other changes happen underground or occur too slowly to see. Over millions of years, all of the rock on Earth changes in subtle and dramatic ways as it passes through the different stages in the rock cycle.

FIGURE 1: This fossiliferous limestone includes visible shells of marine animals.

Observe Record observations about what rock is made of and evidence for how rock forms. As you explore the lesson, gather evidence to help explain how and why rock changes over time.

The processes that form and change rock occur in all four Earth systems—the atmosphere, biosphere, geosphere, and hydrosphere. For example, rock may change as it combines with oxygen from the atmosphere. In the rock in Figure 1, there are visible pieces of shells from the biosphere.

Predict The gray material between the shells in Figure 1 is rich in carbon, an important element in many of Earth's processes. Which of Earth's spheres might be the source of this material? What type of evidence would be needed to check or support your claim?

Rock and the Rock Cycle

Conglomerate is a type of rock that forms when pieces of rock are broken, transported by water or ice, and then deposited hundreds or thousands of kilometers from where they formed. Scientists can infer how conglomerate formed based on its observable properties. Conglomerate consists of large, rounded pieces of other rock, called *clasts*, with much smaller particles, or matrix, in between. Sharp edges of the clasts were broken off when they collided with the riverbed and with other rocks as they tumbled downstream. The rounded shape of the clasts is evidence that they spent a significant amount of time being transported, most likely by water. The clasts might have been deposited on a beach, where they were rounded and smoothed even more by wave action.

Stability and Change

FIGURE 2: The sedimentary rock conglomerate contains rounded grains of different sizes and composition.

Analyze We can infer some aspects of the history of a rock from its observable properties. Identify some properties that are easy to examine. What can these properties tell us about the history of a rock?

Rock Properties and Rock Types

Rock is natural, solid, nonliving material that makes up Earth's crust, mantle, and core. Most rock is composed of combinations of one or more minerals. Properties of a particular type of rock, such as color, texture, and mineral composition, are a result of how the rock forms and changes over time. Properties can be used to identify and classify rock, and to infer how it formed.

If you compare different types of rock, you will notice that they have different textures. The size, shape, and arrangement of the particles (mineral crystals or smaller rock) differ from rock to rock.

Texture is one property that is used to identify and classify rock. Texture is the size, shape, and positions of the grains that make up a rock. Texture also provides clues as to how the rock formed and changed. Texture can help answer questions such as:

- Did the rock form on Earth's surface or deep underground?
- Did the rock form quickly or slowly?
- Were the particles carried by wind, water, or ice?

FIGURE 3: Texture can be used to classify rock and infer how it formed.

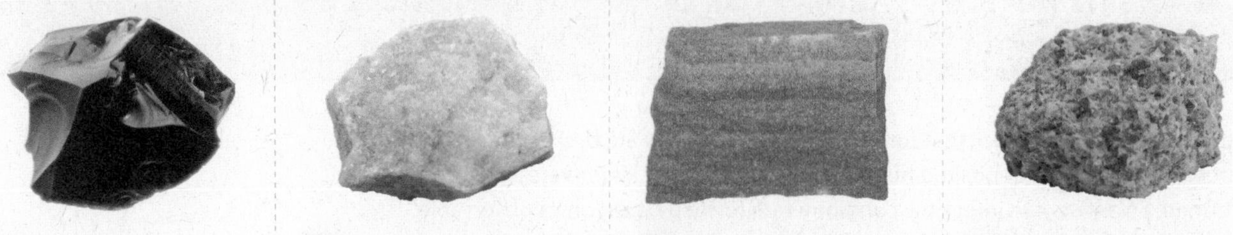

| a Glassy texture | b Crystalline texture | c Fine-grained texture | d Coarse-grained texture |

Analyze Compare the textures of the rocks shown in Figure 3. Which has large rounded grains? small rounded grains? interlocking crystals? no visible grains or crystals at all?

Geologists classify rock into three main groups based on how it forms. However, because it is usually not possible to actually observe rock forming, we must infer how it formed based on observable characteristics such as texture and mineral composition.

FIGURE 4: Sedimentary rock—sandstone

FIGURE 5: Igneous rock—granite

FIGURE 6: Metamorphic rock—marble

Classification of Rocks
Compare and contrast characteristics of the three types of rock.

Sedimentary Rock

Sedimentary rock forms when particles of preexisting rock are transported by water, wind, or gravity and accumulate to form layers of material called sediment on Earth's solid surface. These layers become solid sedimentary rock that can be uplifted to form new land surfaces. Individual grains can be observed in many types of sedimentary rock.

Igneous Rock

Igneous rock forms when other rock partially melts underground. This molten rock then separates from the solid "parent" rock and moves upward toward Earth's surface. This hot fluid mixture, called magma when below the surface and *lava* above the surface, eventually solidifies, forming new rock. The minerals grow together from the magma, forming a texture that is characteristic of most types of igneous rock.

Metamorphic Rock

Metamorphic rock forms when rock is subjected to extreme heat, extreme pressure, or both. Metamorphic rock generally forms when rock is buried deep underground. Heat from Earth's interior and pressure from surrounding rock cause the atoms and molecules in the original solid rock to rearrange. While the rock is still solid, new minerals form as the atoms and molecules rearrange themselves. The new rock has the same composition of elements as the original "parent" rock, but the minerals and textures are different.

Processes in the Rock Cycle

The three types of rock, and the processes that form rock and transform it from one type into another, are all part of the rock cycle.

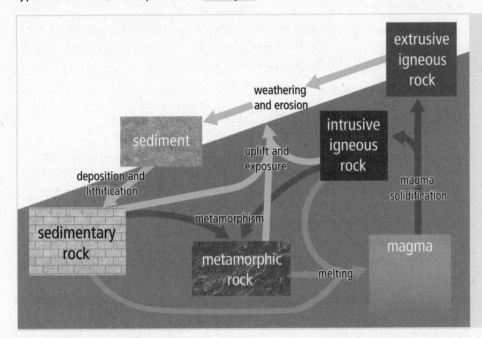

FIGURE 7: The rock cycle can be modeled as a system. Matter moves continually among the parts of the system, which are shown as boxes in this diagram. Each type of matter—rock, magma, and sediment—moves out of one part of the system into another part of the system. These outputs and inputs connect the parts of a system. They are shown in the diagram as arrows that connect the boxes.

A more complex model includes the processes that move and change matter. For example, melting can change each of the three types of rock into magma.

Melting and Solidifying

Heating, changes in pressure, and the addition of water can all cause rock to partially melt. The resulting magma is a mixture of crystals, liquid, and gases. It can move away from the parent rock—the rock from which it formed. Cooling and changes in pressure can then cause the magma to solidify, forming igneous rock underground (intrusive) or on Earth's surface (extrusive).

Explain Describe the role of water in the processes of the rock cycle.

Breaking Down and Forming

Gravity, changes in temperature, and the growth of tree roots break rock apart. Interactions with water, air, and living things affect minerals in rock on and near Earth's surface. Minerals in the rock break down and new minerals may form. These changes break down the parent rock and are called *weathering*.

Running water, flowing ice, wind, and gravity move the pieces from one place to another over Earth's surface—a process called *erosion*. Particles of rock settle out of air and water and accumulate as sediments on Earth's surface—a process called *deposition*. Over time, sediments are buried and compressed. Water moving through pores between the grains of sediment deposits chemicals, such as calcium carbonate, that act as cement. The processes that produce sedimentary rock are called *lithification*.

Changing Form

Rock is buried by other layers of rock. Heat from Earth's interior and from nearby bodies of magma flows into the rock while the forces due to gravity and motions of Earth's crust exert pressure on the rock. Over millions of years, the heat and pressure cause the atoms and molecules in the solid rock to rearrange, forming new crystals, new minerals, and new textures—a process called metamorphism. The presence of fluids helps to speed up the chemical transformation of metamorphic rock.

Over time, any of the three types of rock can be transformed into any other type. A model of the rock cycle illustrates the possible sequence of changes that a rock can go through over time. These changes occur both on Earth's surface and underground, and they are driven by solar energy, thermal energy from Earth's interior, gravity, and chemical reactions.

The rock cycle spans all four of Earth's systems as the rock that makes up the geosphere interacts with the gases of the atmosphere, the living things of the biosphere, and the water and ice of the hydrosphere.

The Rock Cycle as a System

The rock cycle can be modeled as a system of inputs, outputs, and processes. In this model of the rock cycle, the inputs into each part of the system include matter, such as rock, magma, and sediment. Inputs also include energy, such as heat, and forces, such as gravity. The output of each part of the system is the new rock, magma, lava, or sediment. Outputs can also include energy. Processes such as melting, solidification, erosion, and metamorphism transform the input into the output. The parts of the system are all connected; the output of rock, magma, or sediment of one part of the system is the input—the parent rock or starting material—of another part.

The rock cycle is not a definite sequence like a life cycle. There are many possible paths that matter can take through the cycle. For example, material may be repeatedly weathered, eroded, deposited, and lithified into sedimentary rock before going through any of the other processes.

Engineering

FIGURE 8: One part of the rock cycle

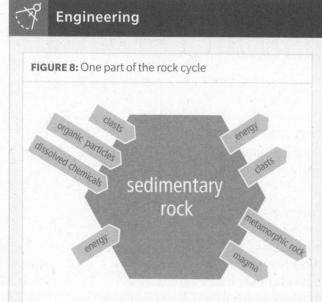

Parts of a System

Sedimentary rock can be modeled as part of the rock cycle. The input materials include clasts (pieces of rock), particles from organisms, and chemicals dissolved in water. These materials become sedimentary rock. The outputs show how sedimentary rock changes into other types of material.

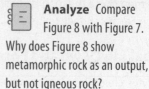 **Analyze** Compare Figure 8 with Figure 7. Why does Figure 8 show metamorphic rock as an output, but not igneous rock?

 Explain Sketch a simple model of the rock cycle from memory. Then check your model against Figure 7. Did you forget or mislabel any components?

Sedimentary Rock

Over time, the rock on Earth's surface is broken down by physical forces and chemical reactions. Pieces of rock are transported elsewhere by wind, water, ice, and gravity. After they settle, the sediments are slowly transformed into new sedimentary rock.

Characteristics of Sedimentary Rock

Compare the characteristics of the three types of sediments shown below. What types of sedimentary rock will these sediments become?

FIGURE 9: Different types of sediment form different types of sedimentary rock.

a Particles of rock that have eroded from other rocks are known as clastic sediments.

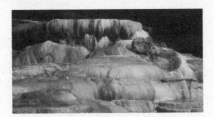

b Chemical sediments are made of crystals that precipitate from water.

c Shells and shell fragments are organic sediments that were originally formed by living organisms.

The loose, rounded grains of quartz sand will become sandstone. The hot spring water contains calcium carbonate that has dissolved, or passed into a solution. The mineral will precipitate, or pass out of the solution, to form different layers of travertine. The shells will accumulate on the sea floor and become part of limestone. The differences between the types of rock that form will be related to the composition of the sediments and to the processes that form them.

There are three main types of sedimentary rock: clastic, chemical, and organic.

- *Clastic sedimentary rock* is made of pieces of preexisting rock.
- *Chemical sedimentary rock* forms when minerals dissolved in water precipitate back out of the water.
- *Organic sedimentary rock* (sometimes called *biological sedimentary rock*) is made of organic material such as leaves or shells.

Analyze Think about the rock cycle. Where might each of the sediments, or the chemical components that make up the sediments, have originally come from?

Clastic Rock

Clastic sedimentary rock is made of pieces of preexisting rock and can be classified based on the size and shape of the clasts or particles they are made of. The differences between clastic rock such as conglomerate, sandstone, breccia, and shale are a result of the way that they form. Sediments are transported and then deposited. The way they are transported and the amount of time they spend moving affects the size and shape of the pieces.

Image Credits: (l) ©Anthony Buckingham/Alamy Images; (c) ©Corbis; (r) ©Annett/Shutterstock

FIGURE 10: Types of clastic sedimentary rock

a **Conglomerate** Conglomerate clasts were once loose gravels. Pieces of gravel are large and therefore heavy, likely transported by a powerful agent such as fast-running water. The rounded shape of the clasts is evidence that they spent time in a high-energy environment—a river or a beach—where they were constantly being picked up and knocked against other rocks.

c **Sandstone** The particles in sandstone are rounded and are much smaller than those in conglomerate but are still visible. Sand particles are small enough to be carried by relatively slow-moving water and by strong wind.

b **Breccia** The large size and angular shape of the clasts in a breccia indicate that they have not traveled far from their parent rock. They are too large to have been carried by wind and were therefore either pushed by glacial ice or simply pulled downhill by gravity. It is unlikely that they spent much time being carried by water, otherwise their sharp edges would be worn down more. Breccia clasts can look like freshly broken rock fragments.

d **Shale** Silt particles are not visible without a magnifying glass, but they are large enough that they feel slightly gritty. Silt particles can be carried by very slow-moving water and by wind.

e **Siltstone/mudstone** The clay particles that make up shale are too small to feel as individual grains. Clayey sediments feel soft and slippery. Clay particles can be carried by very slow-moving water and by light winds.

Explain What can the size of a clast or particle in a clastic rock tell you about the environment where the sediments were deposited?

The size of a clast or particle affects where it tends to be deposited. Large particles can settle out of fast-moving water, but smaller particles cannot. As a result, different types of sediments are deposited in different environments. Rivers generally decrease in speed from the mountains toward the ocean. Large, heavy rock fragments and gravels can settle out of fast-moving river water upstream. Smaller sand and silt particles cannot settle out until the water has slowed down farther downstream. The smallest particles generally don't settle out until they reach calm, deep ocean water.

Evaporation and Chemistry

Have you ever left a drink out and returned a few days later to find that it had evaporated? Unless you are drinking pure water, if you leave a drink out, a residue will be left on the glass after all of the water in it evaporates. Some of this residue consists of particles (such as orange juice pulp and coffee grounds) that simply settled out of the drink. These are similar to the sand, silt, and clay particles that settle out of river water. But some of the residue is made of substances that were originally dissolved in the water. These residues form in a similar way to another type of sediment called a *chemical sediment*.

Explain Rock salt, which is known as halite, is a chemical sedimentary rock that forms in hot, dry climates as water evaporates. In what form do the components of salt exist before it is deposited?

Rock that forms through the precipitation of minerals from water is known as chemical sedimentary rock. Evaporation of water is just one cause of precipitation. Minerals like calcite can precipitate from water as a result of a change in temperature of the water or a change in the chemistry of the water. This is how travertine limestone forms in caves and is one way that limestone forms on the ocean floor.

Sediments from Organisms

Organic sedimentary rock forms when the remains of plants, shells, and other living things are deposited and then buried. Coal, for example, is made of the remains of swamp plants. Chalk is composed of the skeletons of microscopic sea animals.

FIGURE 11: Coal is an organic sedimentary rock that is burned for fuel. The "rank" of coal that forms depends on how deep and how long the sediments are buried.

a Peat is a soft sediment made of partially decomposed plant matter. Peat has the highest water content and the lowest carbon content of the different ranks of coal. Peat is found at Earth's surface.

b Lignite is a relatively soft, brown-colored form of coal. Some of the original leaves, stems, and other plant matter may still be present in lignite. Lignite has a higher carbon content and lower water content than peat.

c Bituminous coal is harder and more compact than lignite, but not as hard or dense as anthracite. The carbon content of bituminous coal is higher than lignite but lower than anthracite.

d Anthracite is the darkest, densest form of coal. The plant matter is no longer recognizable. Anthracite coal can consist of more than 95% carbon by weight and almost no water.

Sedimentary Environments

Different types of sedimentary rock form in different environments. For example, chemical sedimentary rock, like salt, can be found in evaporated lake beds. Travertine forms in caves and around hot springs. Limestone forms in warm, shallow ocean water. In river deltas, particles of sand, silt, and clay settle out to form clastic sediments, while bodies of marine plants and animals settle out to form organic sediments.

Analyze Over time, peat can be transformed into anthracite. How can this happen? How does peat change as it is transformed into anthracite?

FIGURE 12: The type of sedimentary rock that forms depends on factors such as climate, topography, and sediment source.

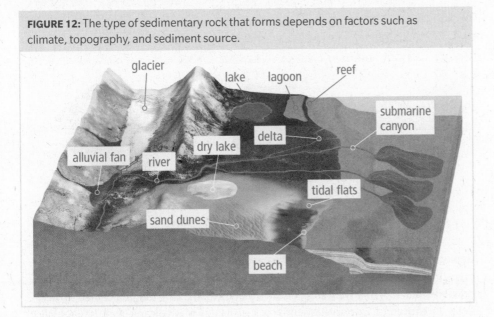

 Analyze How can the characteristics of a sedimentary rock be used to infer how it formed and what Earth was like at the time and place where it formed? Use examples to support your claims.

Igneous Rock

Igneous rock forms when molten rock solidifies underground or on Earth's surface. Igneous rock is classified by observable properties, such as texture, measureable properties, such as composition, and by the environment in which it forms.

Characteristics of Igneous Rock

One way geologists classify igneous rock is by the size of the crystals, which typically range from microscopic to several centimeters across. Grain size in an igneous rock is generally a result of the rate at which the molten rock solidified. If a magma solidifies very slowly, crystals have time to grow relatively large. If a lava solidifies quickly, the crystals are smaller because they have less time to grow. If lava turns solid instantly, crystals do not have time to form at all.

FIGURE 13: Geologists examine grain size to classify igneous rock as intrusive or extrusive.

Intrusive Igneous Rocks

Intrusive rock forms deep underground, where magma cools very slowly and crystals have a long time to grow. The crystals in an intrusive rock are large enough to see.

a Granite has visible crystals of quartz, feldspar, and mica.

b Gabbro has visible crystals of feldspar and pyroxene.

Extrusive Igneous Rocks

Extrusive rock forms when magma erupts on the surface and turns solid very quickly. Most of the crystals in extrusive rock are too small to see without a microscope.

c Most of the quartz, mica, and feldspar crystals in rhyolite are microscopic.

d Basalt contains mostly small crystals.

e Obsidian is a glass with no real crystals.

Explain Granite and rhyolite are both igneous rock made of feldspar, quartz, and mica crystals. Why are they classified into two different groups?

Geologists can use texture to infer whether an igneous rock formed underground or on Earth's surface. Intrusive igneous rock, also called *plutonic rock*, is generally coarse grained—made of relatively large crystals that formed as the magma cooled slowly deep underground. Extrusive igneous rock, also known as volcanic rock, is generally fine-grained—made of microscopic crystals or glass that formed as the lava cooled quickly on the surface.

Composition of Igneous Rock

Igneous rock can also be classified based on chemical composition—specifically silica content. Most types of igneous rock are composed primarily of silicate minerals. All silicates contain silica (silicon dioxide, SiO_2), but some contain more silica than others. Mafic rock is made of minerals that are relatively low in silica and high in iron and magnesium. Felsic rock is high in silica and low in iron and magnesium. The percentages of silica, iron, and magnesium of intermediate rock are in between those of mafic and felsic.

FIGURE 14: Geologists use mineral content and color to classify igneous rocks by composition.

Basalt and gabbro are mafic rocks composed of dark-colored minerals, such as pyroxene and olivine, which are rich in iron and magnesium but poor in silica.

Andesite and diorite are intermediate rocks composed of a mixture of light-colored minerals such as feldspar, and dark-colored minerals such as amphibole.

Rhyolite and granite are felsic rocks composed of light-colored minerals, such as quartz and feldspar, which are rich in silica but poor in iron and magnesium.

a Basalt

b Andesite

c Rhyolite

Dark-colored mafic 50% SiO_2 ←— intermediate —→ Light-colored felsic 70% SiO_2

d Gabbro

e Diorite

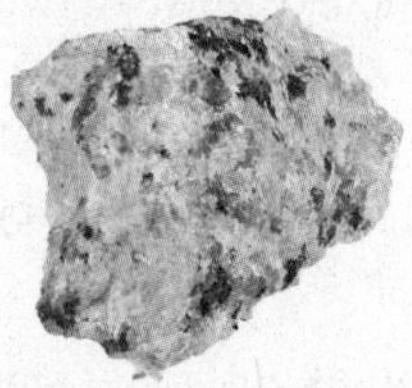

f Granite

Explain How can a geologist use the color of a fine-grained igneous rock to infer its composition?

It can be difficult to identify individual mineral grains in an igneous rock, but the color of the rock can provide important clues about its composition. The color of an igneous rock depends on the color of the minerals that compose it. Minerals that are rich in silica and poor in iron and magnesium are generally light in color. Minerals that are poor in silica but rich in iron and magnesium are generally dark in color. Intermediate rock tends to be gray or a fairly even mixture of light and dark minerals.

Math Connection

Analyze Compare the compositions of mafic and felsic rocks. How are they similar? How do they differ?

Igneous Environments

Analyze Basalt can form underground in sills and dikes. How is this possible?

Igneous rock can form a variety of structures in different geological environments.

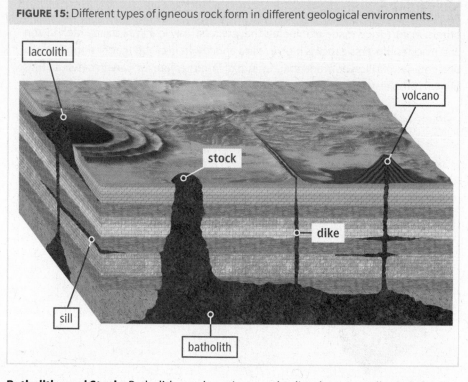

FIGURE 15: Different types of igneous rock form in different geological environments.

laccolith

volcano

stock

dike

sill

batholith

Batholiths and Stocks Batholiths are large igneous bodies that generally cool slowly deep underground. Granite batholiths are common on the continents. Stocks are similar to batholiths but smaller.

Sills, Laccoliths, and Dikes As molten rock rises toward the surface, it may flow between layers of sedimentary rock. Because the magma is just a thin layer sandwiched between two cool layers of rock, it can cool quickly, forming fine-grained rock such as basalt. A laccolith is a lens- or dome-shaped intrusion that forms between layers of sedimentary rock. Laccoliths can cause the rocks above to dome upward. A dike is similar to a sill, but it cuts across the layers that it intrudes rather than between them.

Volcanoes Volcanoes are places where molten rock erupts onto Earth's surface. A volcano can just be a hole in the ground (a vent), or it can be a structure made of layers of extrusive igneous rock. The shape of a volcano is related to the composition of the magma and the way the volcano erupts.

 Explain Granite is a coarse-grained intrusive igneous rock that forms deep underground. How is it possible that large bodies of granite are found on Earth's surface?

Metamorphic Rock

When rock is exposed to extreme heat or pressure, the atoms and molecules within it rearrange to form new minerals. The changes that a rock undergoes during metamorphism happen while the rock is still solid and generally without any atoms being added or removed.

Metamorphic rock can be classified based on specific observable characteristics. These characteristics can then be used to determine the parent rock, how hot the rock was, how much pressure was applied to it, and the depth at which it formed. The foliation, or banding, of metamorphic rock can also be used to infer the direction tectonic plates were moving tens to hundreds of millions of years ago.

Explain How is the chemical composition of a metamorphic rock related to its parent rock?

Characteristics of Metamorphic Rock

Geologists classify metamorphic rock based on observable characteristics, such as texture and mineral content. Metamorphic rock can also be classified based on the parent rock—the rock from which it formed—as well as the environment in which the rock formed.

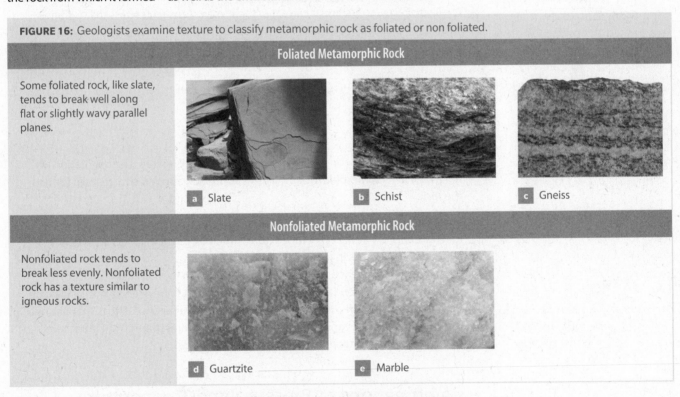

FIGURE 16: Geologists examine texture to classify metamorphic rock as foliated or non foliated.

Foliated Metamorphic Rock

Some foliated rock, like slate, tends to break well along flat or slightly wavy parallel planes.

a Slate

b Schist

c Gneiss

Nonfoliated Metamorphic Rock

Nonfoliated rock tends to break less evenly. Nonfoliated rock has a texture similar to igneous rocks.

d Guartzite

e Marble

Foliation can look a lot like sedimentary layering, but it forms in a different way. During metamorphism, rock is subject to pressure from the weight of the rock above it and the motion of tectonic plates. In many cases, the forces affecting the rock are greater in one direction than another. As a result, the existing crystals in the rock rotate, and new crystals grow perpendicular to the direction of force. Rock rich in elements that can form platy minerals, such as micas, can form strong foliation. Foliation also occurs as minerals that have different compositions separate to produce a series of alternating light and dark bands.

Nonfoliated rock can form if the pressure affecting the rock is the same from all directions. When this happens, the crystals can grow or remain oriented in many different directions. Some rock is nonfoliated simply because it is made of minerals like quartz and calcite, which don't form flat crystals.

Directed Stress

Predict Why would metamorphic rock such as marble withstand weathering better than sedimentary rock such as limestone?

Pressure

foliation

Pressure

The agents that cause rock to undergo metamorphism are temperature, pressure, chemically active fluids, and directed stress. When one of these conditions changes in the environment, the minerals in a rock move from a stable state to an unstable state. This instability causes the rock to change, or metamorphose, to reach a more stable state in the new conditions.

Stress is the amount of force per unit area. Stress can be caused by fluids that are trapped in rock or by the load of overlying and surrounding rock. At about 3 km below the surface of Earth's crust, the pressure of overlying rock is great enough to metamorphose rock.

In general, stress affects rock equally in all directions. However, sometimes stresses acting in particular directions exceed the mean stress on the rock. This type of stress is called *directed stress*, and it can act in three ways. Tension is stress that expands the rock or pulls the rock apart. Compression is stress that squeezes the rock. Shear stress is stress that pushes different parts of a body of rock in different directions.

Foliation planes are perpendicular to the direction of pressure. The orientation of foliation in a metamorphic rock provides information about the forces that formed the rock.

Foliation is typical of rock that has undergone regional metamorphism. Regional metamorphism is a change in the texture, structure, or chemical composition of a rock due to changes in temperature and pressure over a large area, generally as a result of tectonic forces. Rock that has undergone metamorphism as a result of burial by sediments (burial metamorphism) tends not to develop as strong foliation because the forces affecting them are the same in all directions. A rock that has been metamorphosed through the action of hot fluids flowing through it (hydrothermal metamorphism) also tends not to show foliation.

Combinations of Pressure and Temperature

Analyze Make a simple graph showing temperature on the *x*-axis and pressure on the *y*-axis. Plot each of the three types of metamorphic rock shown in Figure 17 on the graph.

As pressure and temperature increase, rock progresses through a sequence of changes in mineral composition to become different metamorphic rock types. Each change in mineral composition makes the rock stable at the higher temperatures and pressures that increase with burial.

FIGURE 17: With increasing pressure and temperature, slate is transformed into gneiss.

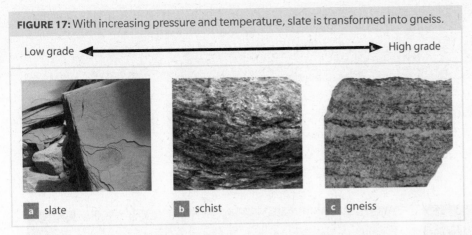

Low grade ←――――――――――――――――――→ High grade

a slate   **b** schist   **c** gneiss

Analyze How is the size of the mineral crystals in a foliated metamorphic rock related to metamorphic grade?

The extent to which a rock has been metamorphosed is known as metamorphic grade. Rocks that have been subjected to less or more pressure and temperature are known as low-grade or high-grade metamorphic rocks, respectively. High-grade metamorphic rocks, such as gneiss, show evidence of being buried to greater depths than low-grade rocks, such as slate, do.

Metamorphic Environments

The type of metamorphic rock that forms depends on the parent rock and the geological environment of metamorphism.

FIGURE 18: Different types of metamorphism occur in different metamorphic environments.

Hydrothermal Metamorphism
Hot fluids flow through rock, transforming it into nonfoliated metamorphic rock.

Regional Metamorphism
Tectonic plates collide, burying rock to great depth, where it is transformed into foliated metamorphic rock.

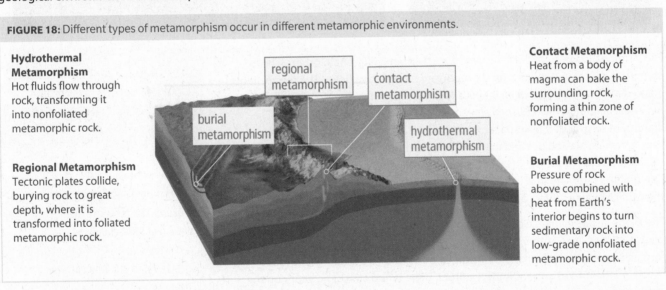

regional metamorphism

contact metamorphism

burial metamorphism

hydrothermal metamorphism

Contact Metamorphism
Heat from a body of magma can bake the surrounding rock, forming a thin zone of nonfoliated rock.

Burial Metamorphism
Pressure of rock above combined with heat from Earth's interior begins to turn sedimentary rock into low-grade nonfoliated metamorphic rock.

Explain Quartzite forms when sandstone is metamorphosed. Which type of metamorphism is most likely to form a thick quartzite formation?

Guided Research

The Rock Cycle on the Moon

FIGURE 19: The colors and shapes visible on the surface of the moon reflect the rock it is made of and the geological processes that have affected it.

Earth's moon is similar to Earth in some ways, but very different in others. The smooth, dark-colored regions on the moon are basaltic lava flows. The rough, light-colored regions are made of an igneous rock called *anorthosite*. Most of the craters are impact craters, which formed when meteoroids crashed into the moon. The craters are surrounded by impact breccias, which are mixtures of angular broken rock that were blasted out and metamorphosed during the impacts. The surface of the moon is covered in a thin layer of lunar soil called *regolith*. Regolith is made of fine-grained sediment and has formed through the continuous bombardment of the surface by tiny meteoroids.

The moon shows evidence of ancient volcanic activity, but there is no evidence of plate tectonics or any other type of movement of the crust. The mountains are not formed by plate motions like they are on Earth. Most of the mountain ranges on the moon are the rims of ancient impact craters. There is also almost no water on the moon and no evidence that there was ever any running water. Because the moon is so small, its gravitational pull is much weaker than Earth's. Any gases that were released from the moon's interior during volcanic eruptions have escaped to space. The moon has virtually no atmosphere.

 Explain Think about the types of rock found on the moon and the processes that occur and don't occur there. How and why is the rock cycle on the moon similar to and different from the rock cycle on Earth?

Language Arts Connection
Write to Inform Informative/explanatory writing is a well-organized analysis of a topic. This type of writing tells how or why. Be sure to:

- provide an introduction that clearly states the topic and engages readers
- organize your ideas to make important connections and distinctions
- include details that support your ideas
- provide a conclusion that supports your explanation

You can find guidance on writing an informative/explanatory essay in the Learning Resources for this lesson.

 THE ROCK IN YOUR CITY | **CLASSIFICATION OF ROCKS** | Go online to choose one of these other paths.

Lesson Self-Check

CAN YOU EXPLAIN IT?

FIGURE 20: Coquina is a sedimentary rock made of the shells of marine animals.

As rock forms and transforms from one type into another, the atoms that make up the minerals within the rock rearrange. Although most of the atoms themselves do not change significantly, their arrangement (the molecules they form), the physical state they are in (solid, liquid, or gas), and their locations change.

For example, molecules of silica (SiO_2) exist as liquid in magma and then combine to form crystals of feldspar as the magma cools and forms igneous rock. The silica molecules are uplifted with the feldspar in the igneous rock to Earth's surface. They then react with air and water, recombining with other elements to form clay. As microscopic clay crystals, the silica molecules are transported down rivers and to the ocean, where they are deposited. The silica molecules are buried with the rest of the sediment and slowly become part of a solid rock. They are buried further, heated and squeezed, and then recombine to form part of a mica and then garnet in a metamorphic rock. If the rock gets hot enough, the minerals they are part of may melt, and the silica molecules become part of a liquid once more.

Analyze: Refer to the notes in your Evidence Notebook to explain how rock forms and transforms over time.

Explain Carbon also exists in different forms on Earth: in minerals, in living things, dissolved in water, and in gases in magmas and in the atmosphere. Like silica, carbon can be traced through the rock cycle.

Describe a possible path that carbon atoms in shell fragments could have taken through Earth's spheres before they reached the shells. Where could they go in the future?

CHECKPOINTS

Check Your Understanding

1. A geologist receives a call from a friend asking for help identifying the type of rock that a large boulder is made of. Which questions could the geologist ask to help narrow down which type of rock it is?

   a. How big is the boulder?

   b. Is the rock hot or cold?

   c. What color or colors is it?

   d. What shape are the crystals or grains?

   e. How far from the river is the boulder?

   f. Are there crystals or grains large enough to see?

   g. Do you see anything that looks like layers in the boulder?

2. In the rock cycle, one type of rock is transformed into another type of rock. For each transformation, identify the processes likely to be involved in forming the new rock.

Transformation:	Process:
sedimentary to igneous	burial
sedimentary to metamorphic	deposition
sedimentary to sedimentary	erosion
	heating
	lithification
	melting
	recrystallization
	solidification
	weathering

3. Water is an important part of the rock cycle. How would the rock cycle be different if there were no water on Earth?

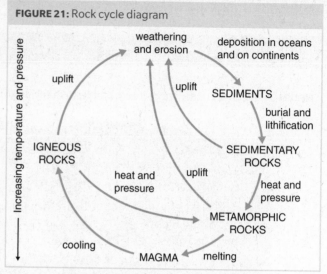

FIGURE 21: Rock cycle diagram

4. Explain the parts of the rock cycle where thermal energy plays a role.

5. Glacial ice forms as snow accumulates over time. As the snowflakes are buried, they are compacted. As they are buried deeper and deeper, they recrystallize and form a dense mass of interlocking crystals. With enough weight from above, the crystals become elongated and flattened. What type of rock is this glacial ice classified as?

   a. felsic igneous rock

   b. extrusive igneous rock

   c. clastic sedimentary rock

   d. chemical sedimentary rock

   e. contact metamorphic rock

   f. foliated metamorphic rock

6. Limestone is any sedimentary rock composed primarily of the mineral calcite. Limestone can be classified as clastic, chemical, or organic, depending on how it forms. Explain how each of these types of limestone could form.

7. How might a piece of rock be transformed from an angular fragment into a gravel, then sand, then silt, and finally clay? Which process of the rock cycle is this part of?

8. The color of an igneous rock can be used to infer its composition. Complete the statements.

   Dark-colored igneous rock is likely to have a ___ composition, with ____ silica and ___ iron and magnesium. Lighter colored igneous rock is more likely to have a ___ composition, with ____ silica and ___ iron and magnesium.

9. Porphyry is a type of igneous rock that consists of a mixture of large well-formed crystals and fine-grained, microscopic crystals. Which is the best interpretation for how this rock formed?

   a. A rock was buried deep underground. Pressure from rock aboveground changed some of the minerals into tiny pieces.

   b. Water from a volcanic hot spring flowed out onto the surface. As the water evaporated, large and small crystals grew and settled out of the water.

   c. Magma cooled slowly underground, forming large crystals. While it was still partially liquid, the magma rose quickly toward the surface, causing the rest of the liquid to turn solid quickly.

   d. An igneous rock weathered and eroded, forming a mixture of large and small pieces that were then transported by water and deposited. The sediment was buried by other sediments and slowly turned to solid rock.

10. If basalt comes in contact with a hot body of magma or lava, it can undergo contact metamorphism. The metamorphic rock that forms is a nonfoliated rock called hornfels. Why would contact metamorphism result in a nonfoliated rock?

11. Because certain rocks form under certain geological conditions, rocks can be used as evidence for what a particular place on Earth was like in the past. Match each rock to the inference that can be made based on the rock.

   a. schist (foliated metamorphic rock)

   b. granite batholith (intrusive igneous rock)

   c. layer of rock salt (chemical sediment)

   1. This rock crystallized several kilometers underground, but it is at the surface now. Therefore, several kilometers of rock must have been eroded.

   2. When this rock formed, this area had a hot, dry climate.

   3. The orientation of mica crystals in this rock is evidence for compression from the east and west.

In your Evidence Notebook, design a study guide that helps you understand how scientists use observable characteristics to describe, classify, and understand the origins of different types of rock, and how rock changes from one form into another over time.

Remember to include the following in your study guide:

• Support main ideas with details and specific examples.

• Record explanations for the phenomena you investigated.

• Use the crosscutting concept that matter is neither created nor destroyed to explain the rock cycle.

Cycles and Cycle Models

Earth's systems exchange matter.

CAN YOU EXPLAIN IT?

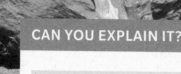

FIGURE 1: Muddy water in Lake Nyos, Cameroon, at the time of the disaster

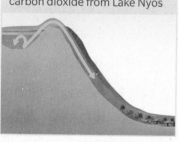

FIGURE 2: The movement of carbon dioxide from Lake Nyos

On August 21, 1986, more than 1700 people and 3500 cattle living near Lake Nyos, a volcanic crater lake in Cameroon, died suddenly. The killer was silent and invisible—carbon dioxide (CO_2) gas that came from the bottom of the lake and flowed over the mountains and down into the villages in the valley.

Carbon dioxide is not poisonous at the low concentrations that are generally in our atmosphere. However, if there is too much carbon dioxide in one place, it pushes away the air, including oxygen, which we need to stay alive. Carbon dioxide is denser than the normal mixture of gases in air, so it collects in low-lying areas. At Lake Nyos, about one cubic kilometer of carbon dioxide came out of the lake and flowed like a river 50 m deep, suffocating all oxygen-breathing organisms in its path.

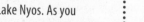

Gather Evidence: Record evidence about the disaster of Lake Nyos. As you explore the lesson, gather evidence to help you use a system model to explain the phenomenon.

 Predict Where do you think the carbon dioxide in the bottom of Lake Nyos might have originally come from?

Carbon in Earth's Systems

Carbon occurs in many different forms in Earth's systems. It is found in solid form in the black soot on a tree struck by lightning or the diamonds on a saw blade, dissolved in seawater and acid rain, and in gaseous form in the air that we breathe in and out.

FIGURE 3: Carbon can be found as atoms, molecules, or ions—atoms or molecules that have an electrical charge.

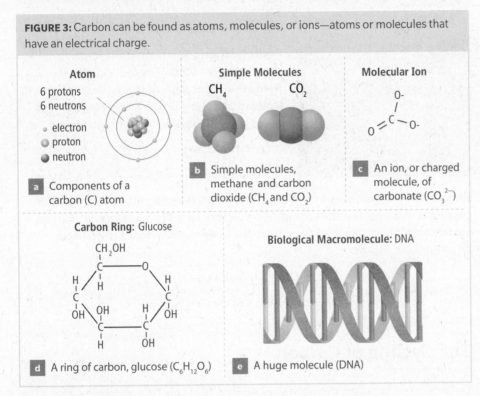

Atom

6 protons
6 neutrons

- electron
- proton
- neutron

a Components of a carbon (C) atom

Simple Molecules

CH_4 CO_2

b Simple molecules, methane and carbon dioxide (CH_4 and CO_2)

Molecular Ion

c An ion, or charged molecule, of carbonate (CO_3^{2-})

Carbon Ring: Glucose

CH_2OH

d A ring of carbon, glucose ($C_6H_{12}O_6$)

Biological Macromolecule: DNA

e A huge molecule (DNA)

Explore Online ▶

FIGURE 4: Carbon is used by organisms for energy and growth. Some of the carbon becomes part of a coral reef.

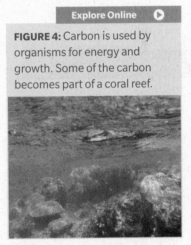

The Many Roles of Carbon

The element carbon is only a small part of Earth's mass. It makes up no more than 0.03% of the crust, 0.05% of the atmosphere, and 0.01% of the ocean. In spite of this, carbon is very important in Earth's systems.

Carbon in the Atmosphere Most of the carbon in the atmosphere is in the form of invisible gas called carbon dioxide (CO_2). Carbon in the atmosphere helps plants and other organisms grow. It is a greenhouse gas that helps keep Earth's surface warm.

Carbon in the Biosphere Almost all living things on Earth are carbon-based—made up of molecules that contain carbon. Some organisms remove carbon directly from the atmosphere, while others get carbon from eating other organisms.

Carbon in the Hydrosphere Carbon dioxide gas dissolves in water. It moves from air into cloud droplets and raindrops. It moves from air into seawater at the ocean's surface. The carbon dissolved in water is used in photosynthesis by microorganisms near the ocean's surface. Some of the carbon becomes part of the shells and skeletons of animals that live in the ocean, such as coral.

Collaborate With a partner, brainstorm the ways in which people use natural carbon-based substances. For each substance, identify the ways in which carbon moves or changes forms as people use it.

Explain Think about the carbon that makes up a coral reef. Where might it have come from—which sphere? Which sphere might the carbon go to next?

Photosynthesis and Respiration

Every year, billions of tons of carbon move back and forth between Earth's organisms and other spheres through photosynthesis and respiration. As you read the equation for photosynthesis, imagine a carbon atom being removed from carbon dioxide (CO_2) to leave oxygen gas (O_2). The carbon remains in the organism.

Photosynthesis Plants and other organisms use energy from sunlight. They cause carbon dioxide from the air or ocean (or other water) to react with water to produce glucose, a form of sugar. They release oxygen gas into the atmosphere or ocean.

$$6CO_2 + 6H_2O \rightarrow C_6H_{12}O_6 + 6O_2$$

carbon dioxide + water $\rightarrow$ glucose + oxygen

Respiration Glucose is used for energy by the organisms that made it and by other organisms that consume them. Respiration is the reverse of photosynthesis. Carbon dioxide moves back into the atmosphere. The same reaction occurs when dead organisms decompose.

$$C_6H_{12}O_6 + 6O_2 \rightarrow 6CO_2 + 6H_2O$$

glucose + oxygen $\rightarrow$ carbon dioxide + water

Explore Online ▶

Hands-On Lab

The Blue-Green Ocean
Predict how the amount of daylight will affect the growth of phytoplankton and the color of water.

The Cycling of Carbon

The movement of carbon through the biosphere, atmosphere, hydrosphere, and geosphere is called the carbon cycle. This cycle can be modeled as a system, in which we can track the movement of carbon through different places where it is stored, or reservoirs.

The geosphere contains more than 99.9% of the carbon on Earth. The oceans and other parts of the hydrosphere contain less carbon, and the atmosphere and biosphere have very small fractions of Earth's total carbon. Although carbon is concentrated in organisms, the total mass of organisms—total biomass—is much less than the mass of air, which is less than the mass of water and much less than the mass of rock.

The processes that move carbon from one reservoir to another work at different scales. Processes that move carbon into or out of the ocean are generally large-scale processes because the ocean covers most of Earth's surface. In contrast, volcanic activity is a small-scale process. Even though a single volcano may release carbon at a high rate, active volcanoes do not make up much of Earth's surface. The total effect of volcanoes is a very small fraction of Earth's carbon cycle.

The importance of the processes that cycle carbon between Earth's systems depend on the timescale and rate at which these processes operate. The natural processes that move carbon between the hydrosphere, atmosphere, and biosphere work at a timescale of a few hundred years; therefore, these processes can have a more immediate impact on Earth system than processes that move carbon in and out of the geosphere. In the biosphere, photosynthesis, respiration, and decomposition are processes that cycle carbon between systems. The ocean and the atmosphere are constantly exchanging gases, including carbon dioxide. The physicochemical exchange and the biological pump mentioned in Figure 6 are processes that move carbon between these two systems.

Predict How would the processes and reservoirs of the carbon cycle change over time if photosynthesis stopped?

FIGURE 6: A different model of carbon, with a focus on the biosphere

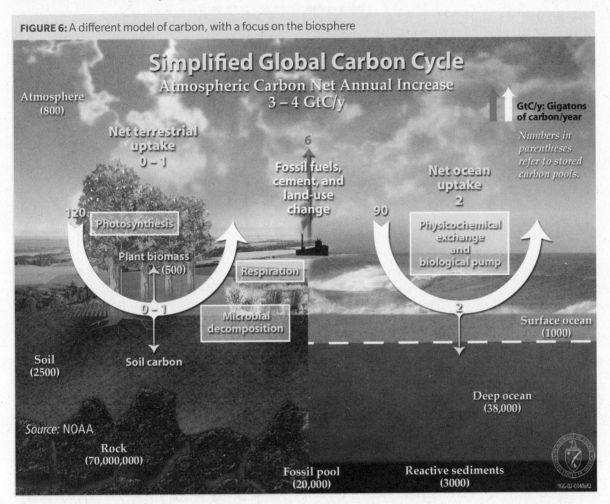

Figure 6 focuses on the biosphere. The large curved arrows show how photosynthesis and respiration roughly balance each other, but move some carbon toward longer-term reservoirs. However, human activities move carbon into the atmosphere from long-term storage in the geosphere. The model shows an additional 6 Gt per year of carbon moving into the atmosphere from human activities.

Measuring Carbon

It is extremely difficult to measure carbon precisely. Different types of measurements give varying results. The amounts also change over time. Numbers in models can also differ because reservoirs can be grouped differently. For example, in some models, soil is included with biomass, while in others, it is included with sediment. Some models show the entire ocean as one reservoir, while others divide it up into two reservoirs: the surface and the deep ocean. Different models can be used together to explain changes and predict future changes.

System Models

Using Models

The numbers in models of the carbon cycle may be inconsistent because models are designed for different purposes. Models may round the numbers, may use different data sources, may group quantities differently, or may use different simplifications. When you compare models, judge whether the important points are similar enough for your purposes.

Explain Compare the concentration of carbon dioxide in different parts of Earth's surface in January with those in June. What process might explain the differences?

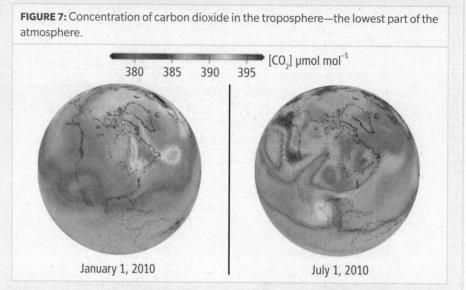

FIGURE 7: Concentration of carbon dioxide in the troposphere—the lowest part of the atmosphere.

$[CO_2]$ µmol mol^{-1}

380   385   390   395

January 1, 2010   July 1, 2010

Figure 7 shows carbon dioxide in the atmosphere, based on frequent measurements of air collected at ground level and by aircraft around the world. The maps show how carbon dioxide varies from place to place and how it changes over the year. Scientists can track the effects of natural events and human activities, such as volcanic eruptions, forest fires, and factory and vehicle emissions. Although the maps focus on only one reservoir, the atmosphere, we can use the general model of the carbon cycle to understand why carbon in the atmosphere is changing and to infer how other reservoirs might be changing at the same time.

Models of Atmospheric Carbon

Although it is a relatively small reservoir of carbon, most research related to the carbon cycle today centers on the atmosphere. About 220 gigatons— billion metric tons— of carbon are added to the atmosphere each year, but only about 215 gigatons are removed. Most of the increase of 5 gigatons per year is in the form of carbon dioxide. Models show that this net increase is directly related to the amount of carbon released from burning fossil fuels and other human activities.

Scientists are concerned with the increase in carbon dioxide because it is a greenhouse gas. An increase in the concentration of greenhouse gases in the atmosphere causes Earth's surface and atmosphere to warm up. The extra energy affects weather, climate, ocean currents, and life on Earth. Scientists are using carbon measurements over time and past observations to model how carbon in the atmosphere is changing and to predict how it will change in the future. These models are used to help understand where carbon is coming from, where it is going, and how different variables such as vehicle emissions and forest growth affect carbon concentrations. The results may help guide choices people make.

Explain How can a simple model of the general carbon cycle (such as Figure 6) help you understand a complex model that shows changes of carbon dioxide concentrations in the atmosphere (Figure 7)?

Image Credits: (l) (r) ©CT2015, http://carbontracker.noaa.gov/NOAA Earth System Research Laboratory/National Oceanic And Atmospheric Administration (NOAA)

System Models

Earth is composed of interacting and overlapping systems that act over different scales of time and space. These systems can be modeled in many different ways. The familiar carbon and water cycles will be used to study a formal system model.

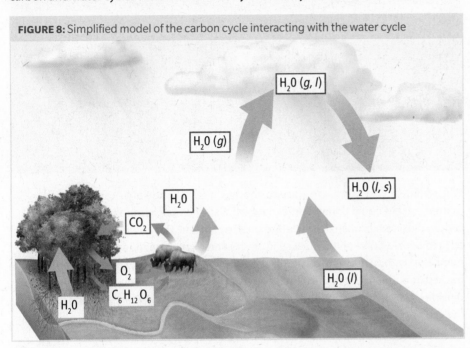

FIGURE 8: Simplified model of the carbon cycle interacting with the water cycle

Analyze Identify where photosynthesis is occuring in the model in Figure 8. Which of Earth's spheres are involved?

Inputs, Outputs, and Boundaries

The simplest system model shows only what moves in and out—the inputs and outputs of the system. It does not describe what happens within the system, such as how water moves and changes within the atmosphere. This type of model is called a *black box* because you can't see what is happening inside.

The choice of a boundary of a system affects the model inputs and outputs. When you define the boundaries of a system, you decide what to model as inside the system and what to model as outside the system. Inputs and outputs cross the boundary. When modeling a cycle such as the carbon cycle, boundaries are often around the reservoirs.

In many cases, the boundary of a system is physical because the whole system is within a single place. For example, the ocean is between the sea floor and the sea surface, which form a continuous boundary around it. In other cases, the system is more conceptual, and so the boundary may not be physical or continuous. For example, the boundary of the hydrosphere is complex because the hydrosphere includes all of the water in different forms and places on Earth.

Models often use simplifications, such as using the ocean rather than the entire hydrosphere in a model of the carbon cycle. Water in the atmosphere would be outside the ocean system. But organisms, dissolved gases, and sediment might or might not be included. Sediment might be an output of the ocean because it crosses the boundary. It becomes an input of another system, the geosphere.

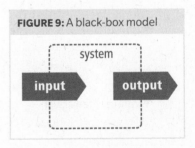

FIGURE 9: A black-box model

Predict Inputs to photosynthesis are H_2O, O_2, and also energy. What are the outputs?

Explain For a model of the cycling of carbon into and out of the ocean, which of the labeled items would you count as part of the ocean system? Why?

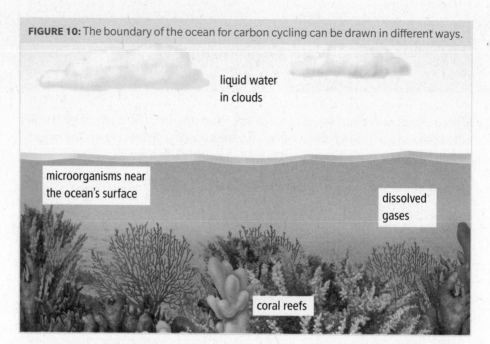

FIGURE 10: The boundary of the ocean for carbon cycling can be drawn in different ways.

liquid water in clouds

microorganisms near the ocean's surface

dissolved gases

coral reefs

When matter cycles from one place to another, it can change physical form, such as from solid to liquid or gas. Some materials also change chemically. For example, carbon dioxide is broken down during photosynthesis. The atoms of carbon and oxygen become part of the glucose ($C_6H_{12}O_6$) and oxygen gas (O_2) that form. The number of carbon atoms is constant throughout these changes, so carbon can be tracked. It is much more difficult to keep track of carbon dioxide because carbon dioxide molecules are continually forming and breaking down. The same is true for molecules of glucose and oxygen gas.

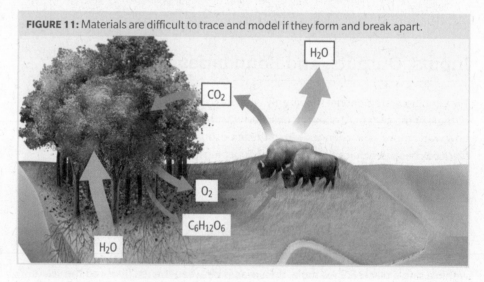

FIGURE 11: Materials are difficult to trace and model if they form and break apart.

H_2O

CO_2

O_2

$C_6H_{12}O_6$

H_2O

Explain The diagram shows parts of the carbon cycle, the oxygen cycle, and the water cycle. Why don't we say that it shows the carbon dioxide cycle?

Modeling Initial Conditions

Models of cycles help scientists describe and predict changes. For example, a model can show the rates at which carbon moves between reservoirs. It can show how the rates and the total amounts of carbon in different reservoirs change over time. But to model such changes, scientists must set the initial, or starting, conditions of the model.

A Simple Model

PROCEDURE

1. On the paper, mark two reservoirs: atmosphere and ocean.

2. Divide the water, represented by the pennies, between the ocean and the atmosphere. Record these initial conditions.

3. Proceed in rounds: one partner moves (evaporates) a fraction of the ocean's water into the atmosphere. One partner moves (precipitates) a fraction of the atmosphere's water into the ocean. Each person should use the same fraction every time. Count the number of rounds it takes to reach a steady state.

4. Repeat steps 2 and 3 at least twice, using different initial conditions.

ANALYZE

1. What choices did you make?

2. How did the initial conditions affect the outcome?

3. What can you learn by combining the class results?

 Collaborate Some models show the movement into and out of part of the system. Other models show the total movement (the amount in minus the amount out). For example, a model of the carbon cycle might show that 220 gigatons (Gt) of carbon move into the atmosphere every year and 215 Gt move out, or it might just show a total movement of 5 Gt into the atmosphere. What are the advantages and disadvantages of showing the total movement in the model?

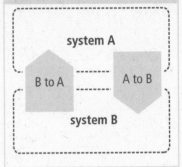

FIGURE 12: Matter moves between two reservoirs.

MATERIALS

- large piece of paper
- marker or pen
- pennies or other small objects

Collaborate How would your results have differed if you moved a certain number of pennies each time rather than a certain fraction? Try it.

System Components and Interactions

If you use a black box model to explore the movement of water into and out of the atmosphere, the model would show water vapor as an input and rain, snow, or other forms of precipitation as outputs. It would not show how water vapor becomes rain. It would not show any of the processes that happen within the atmosphere: transport of water vapor, condensation of water vapor to form droplets, or growth of water droplets.

While a black box model includes only inputs and outputs, a full system model also includes components and interactions that occur inside the boundaries of the system. A full model shows how inputs become outputs.

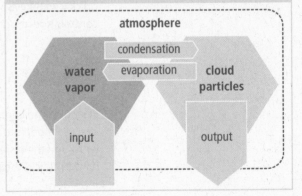

FIGURE 13: Scientists add layers of detail as they build system models.

Predict If you were to model icy cloud particles separately from liquid cloud particles, would that be enough to estimate the amounts of snow and ice? Think about ways to adjust the model that would give you better estimates.

Feedback and Controls

The inputs, outputs, components, and interactions of a system affect one another. An input can change an output. If that output in turn changes the input, the change can produce more change. This type of relationship is called *feedback*. For example, when ice melts and exposes the ground, more sunlight is absorbed, leading to more ice melting. Feedback that increases the original change is known as positive feedback. Because the change keeps going, positive feedback tends to make a system unstable. A small change can lead to a very large effect.

Feedback can cause a system to be stable by decreasing the change. For example, when you get too hot, your body produces sweat, which evaporates and cools you off. Negative feedback decreases the original change.

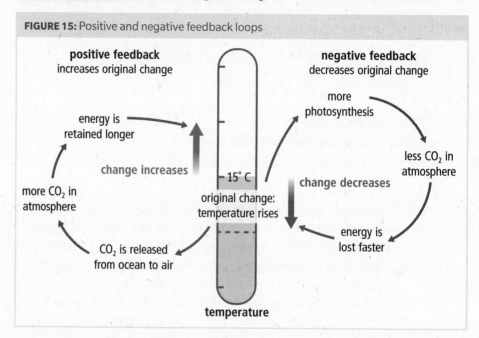

FIGURE 15: Positive and negative feedback loops

positive feedback
increases original change

energy is retained longer

change increases

more CO_2 in atmosphere

CO_2 is released from ocean to air

original change: temperature rises

15° C

temperature

negative feedback
decreases original change

more photosynthesis

less CO_2 in atmosphere

change decreases

energy is lost faster

A model needs to take account of factors that affect a system, even if they are not inputs, outputs, components, or interactions. Factors that change a system or its parts are known as controls. In the atmosphere, temperature is a control that affects how quickly water evaporates, as well as whether it freezes. In the ocean, temperature controls how much carbon dioxide can be dissolved in the water.

Defining a Useful Model

Scientists and engineers choose what to model based on what they wish to learn. They also use models to communicate their understanding to others. They generally begin with something simple, such as a black box model, and then add details until they have achieved their purpose.

 Collaborate To the simple model of the water cycle in the atmosphere, add ocean temperature as a control. Decide how to adjust the inputs, outputs, and processes that should be affected by temperature. For example, evaporation should increase with temperature. How is the amount of water in the atmosphere affected by higher temperature, according to your model results?

Other Chemical Cycles on Earth

You've seen how water and carbon cycle through Earth's systems. Other materials are also important for organisms and for the many ways that Earth's spheres interact.

How Matter Cycles

Matter and energy change form and move within and between different systems, or cycle. Cycle models can be broad, encompassing weather or the entire rock cycle, or be limited, such as to water or carbon. Elements such as carbon interact chemically as they cycle through the geosphere, biosphere, atmosphere, and hydrosphere. The movement of a chemical through the biosphere and geosphere is sometimes called a biogeochemical cycle.

Nitrogen

As an important component of biological molecules such as proteins and DNA, nitrogen is a necessary element for life on Earth. Like carbon, nitrogen occurs in different forms and moves through different reservoirs in all four of Earth's spheres.

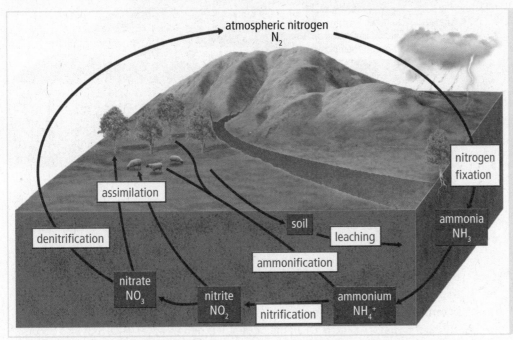

FIGURE 15: Nitrogen moves between the atmosphere, biosphere, hydrosphere, and geosphere by way of many different processes. Bacteria and other organisms change the forms of nitrogen through processes called *nitrogen fixation, ammonification, nitrification, denitrification,* and *assimilation.*

 Gather Evidence Trace an atom of nitrogen as it moves between different reservoirs. Use a simple graphic to record each form and reservoir and the processes by which it moves and changes forms.

Nitrogen, in the form of N_2, makes up most of Earth's atmosphere, which also includes nitric oxide (NO) and nitrous oxide (N_2O). Smaller amounts of nitrogen can be found as dissolved N_2 in the oceans, and in the soil and oceans as ammonia (NH_3), nitrite (NO_2^-), and nitrate (NO_3^-). Nitrogen forms part of biological molecules, but rarely minerals.

Nitrogen is often a limiting factor for plant growth. This is because the N₂, though plentiful, cannot be used directly by most living things. It must first be "fixed," or converted into more usable forms, as shown in Figure 15. Bacteria in the soil and in plant roots fix nitrogen. Other types of bacteria return nitrogen to the atmosphere. The use of ammonia-rich fertilizers heavily affects the nitrogen cycle.

Phosphorus

Phosphorus, like nitrogen, is an important part of biological molecules. But phosphorus forms compounds with different properties and so it cycles differently. Unlike nitrogen, phosphorus is found in significant quantities in the geosphere, in the form of phosphate minerals in rock. At Earth's surface, the rock breaks down. It becomes part of the soil or is moved to other places by running water and deposited as sediment. In this way, phosphorus moves from rock to soil and sediment on the surface. Once in the soil, phosphorus can be absorbed by plants. It becomes part of biological molecules such as DNA. Only very tiny amounts of phosphorus are in the atmosphere—as solid dust particles rather than as gases.

Explore Online ▶

Hands-On Lab 🧪

Modeling a Biogeochemical Cycle
Design a model to show chemical cycling among Earth's spheres.

FIGURE 16: Phosphorus is released from long-term storage in rock by natural processes and human activities. It then cycles mostly among three of Earth's spheres. It can move back into the slower rock cycle as sediment becomes rock.

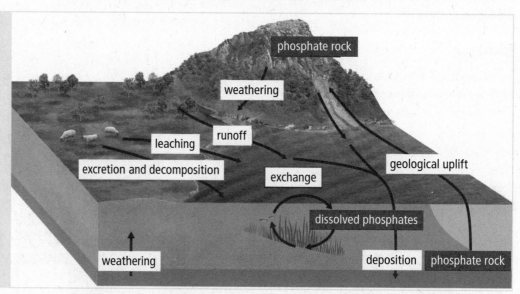

phosphate rock

weathering

runoff

leaching

excretion and decomposition

exchange

geological uplift

dissolved phosphates

weathering

deposition   phosphate rock

Gather Evidence
Trace an atom of oxygen as it cycles between different reservoirs. Record the results as you did for nitrogen.

Oxygen

Most of the oxygen on Earth —more than 99%—is in rock in the crust and mantle. Most of the oxygen cycling, however, occurs in the biosphere, hydrosphere, and atmosphere by way of photosynthesis, respiration, and decomposition. When you think about oxygen, you may tend think about oxygen gas (O₂) in the atmosphere, the form of oxygen that all animals need. Oxygen also is found in the atmosphere as part of carbon dioxide and in very small quantities as other gases such as ozone (O₃) and nitrogen oxides (NO and N₂O). In the oceans, it is part of water (H₂O), but also occurs as dissolved gases such as oxygen and carbon dioxide, and ions such as bicarbonate (HCO₃⁻). Like carbon, oxygen that is taken in by plants and animals is converted into almost every type of biological molecule, including carbohydrates, fats, and proteins. Oxygen can be cycled back into the geosphere as a result of deposition of minerals and burial of minerals and organisms.

Other Elements

Organisms on Earth also use hydrogen (H), sulfur (S), potassium (K), calcium (Ca), and other elements. Hydrogen moves between water (H_2O) and glucose ($C_6H_{12}O_6$) during photosynthesis and respiration. Sulfur cycles in ways similar to nitrogen and phosphorus; it occurs in minerals, and in soil and water as sulfate ions that can form compounds important to living things. Cycles of other elements can also be traced.

In addition to the main elements that are needed for life, scientists are also interested in the cycling of elements that are harmful. For example, mercury is found in rock as native mercury and mercury minerals, in the air in as mercury vapor, and in water as a poisonous substance called methylmercury. The methylmercury gets taken up by plants and microorganisms. It builds up in the food chain. By understanding cycles of harmful materials, people can find ways to protect the environment and themselves.

Explain How do you think human activities such as burning fossil fuels and using nitrogen and phosphorus fertilizers have changed Earth's chemical cycles directly over time?

Interacting and Changing Cycles

Although scientists often model the carbon, nitrogen, phosphorus, and other cycles separately, the cycles overlap and affect one another. Elements cycle within and between the same reservoirs. They often move by the same processes, including the rock cycle and life processes such as photosynthesis. Water, especially, affects other cycles. It covers most of Earth's surface and cycles in large quantities, moving other materials with it. Water also dissolves many materials and affects—usually increases—the rates of chemical reactions. It also affects temperatures around the world, which affect other processes.

Changes in one cycle can have large effects on other cycles, especially where positive feedback occurs. It is important to model the interactions of cycles because human activities can change these cycles. The changes, in turn, can affect the stability of organisms—including humans.

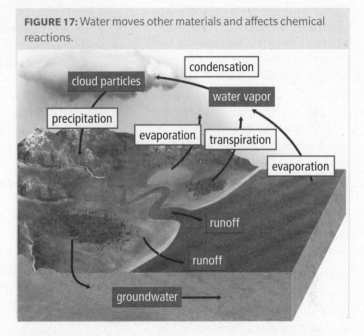

FIGURE 17: Water moves other materials and affects chemical reactions.

Engineering

Fertilizer

Plants need carbon, oxygen, hydrogen, and nitrogen. They obtain nitrogen from soil. They also obtain small amounts of other elements, such as phosphorus and potassium. But soil in many places has too little of these elements. Farming and gardening can remove these elements faster than natural processes supply them. Fertilizers have been researched and developed to add one or more of these three elements: nitrogen, phosphorus, and potassium. Sulfur, magnesium, calcium, and other elements may also be included.

Explain Carbon is almost always a component of fertilizers in some form. Why do you think carbon is not listed as a key nutrient in fertilizer?

Explain How can changes in the carbon cycle affect Earth's albedo—its ability to reflect light? How can the albedo affect the carbon cycle?

Data Analysis

Elements and Plants

Plants get most of their basic components—carbon, oxygen, and hydrogen—from air and water. However, plants need other nutrients to live and grow, such as the elements nitrogen, phosphorus, and potassium.

Nitrogen (N) is a major component of proteins, DNA, and chlorophyll, which is needed for photosynthesis. Phosphorus (P) is used in many processes within plants. It is important for the growth of roots, flowers, seeds, and fruit. Potassium (K) plays a role in photosynthesis, helps transport water and nutrients, and regulates the movement of carbon dioxide, oxygen, and water vapor in and out of the plant. Because potassium is a component of strong plant cell walls, it can increase a plant's resistance to cold weather, wind, and other stresses.

Nitrogen and many other nutrients dissolve in water easily. The dissolved nutrients are easier for plants to use, but can also be washed out of the soil. In contrast, phosphorus may come from rock that contains phosphates (PO_4^{3-}). It tends to remain in the soil. It dissolves mostly when the soil is acidic (pH lower than 7.0). As a result, soil in a particular place can be rich in some nutrients and poor in others.

Functions of Fertilizers

Fertilizers are substances that are rich in forms of nutrients that plants can use. People test the soil and apply fertilizers to restore nutrients or to add extra nutrients for a particular purpose.

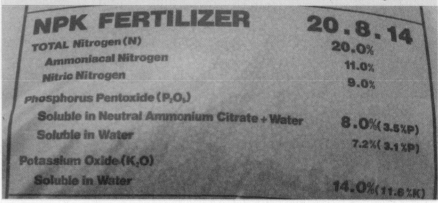

FIGURE 18: Learn how to interpret the three numbers that make up fertilizer grades.

NPK FERTILIZER 20.8.14
TOTAL Nitrogen (N) 20.0%
Ammoniacal Nitrogen 11.0%
Nitric Nitrogen 9.0%
Phosphorus Pentoxide (P_2O_5)
Soluble in Neutral Ammonium Citrate + Water 8.0% (3.5%P)
Soluble in Water 7.2% (3.1%P)
Potassium Oxide (K_2O)
Soluble in Water 14.0% (11.6%K)

Fertilizers have different amounts of nutrients. A fertilizer's grade is given as percentages of nitrogen (N), phosphorus (in the form of P_2O_5), and potassium (in the form of K_2O). A grade of 10-10-10 means 10 percent of each, by weight. You could get the same amounts by using half as much of a fertilizer with a grade of 20-20-20 because the ratios of N, P, and K are the same. But a 20-0-0 fertilizer would give different results. Use your skills with ratios to compare fertilizer grades. You may wish to round the numbers.

Fertilizers have different uses. A fertilizer high in nitrogen may be applied to lawns and other greenery in spring. The extra nitrogen helps leaves grow. In fall, some plants may be strengthened for cold weather by a fertilizer high in potassium. However, it may be unhelpful to encourage plants to grow leaves shortly before winter, so it may be better to apply little or no nitrogen.

Analyze

a. A farmer adds diammonium phosphate (18-46-0) to soil when planting carrots. Which nutrient is being used to increase the carrots' size?

b. A gardening website suggests grades of 15-30-15 for flowering plants and 1-1-1 for general use. Which nutrient should be increased to help produce flowers?

c. Urea (46-0-0) and cow manure (approximately 10-2-1) are both used in agriculture. For each, use the grade to give a reason a farmer might choose that fertilizer.

d. Would you choose a fish-based fertilizer (5-5-5), phosphate rock (0-5-0), or bird manure (12-4-7) to provide extra phosphorus for fruit?

e. Suppose a heavy rain washed away most of the nitrogen from an 8-46-0 fertilzer. Would it be best to apply more of the same fertilizer? Explain your answer.

| CIVIL ENGINEER | USING A COMPUTER MODEL | MODELING A BIOGEOCHEMICAL CYCLE | Go online to choose one of these other paths. |

Lesson Self-Check

CAN YOU EXPLAIN IT?

FIGURE 19: Lake Nyos, Cameroon, at the time of the disaster

FIGURE 20: The movement of carbon dioxide from Lake Nyos

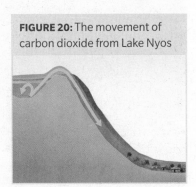

Think back to the event at Lake Nyos in 1986. A river of carbon dioxide gas came out of the lake and flowed down a valley, killing hundreds of people and animals. A similar event had occurred at nearby Lake Monoun two years earlier. Both lakes fill dips in the tops of old volcanoes. Most lakes on Earth never experience an event like these.

Carbon dioxide gradually built up at the bottom of Lake Nyos. Scientists think that a landslide or a small earthquake might have caused the gas to be released in the same way that tapping a glass of soda releases carbon dioxide bubbles from the bottom of the glass. Alternatively, seasonal changes in air pressure and winds might have caused the lake waters to circulate more, releasing the carbon dioxide.

Apply what you have learned about how materials cycle through Earth's biosphere, atmosphere, hydrosphere, and geosphere. Make a claim to explain the source of the carbon dioxide in Lake Nyos. List the evidence. You may wish to include examples of how carbon and other elements can cycle through Earth's spheres. Then explain how the evidence supports your claim.

Explain Which of Earth's spheres supplied the carbon dioxide in the bottom of Lake Nyos? Explain your reasoning.

Analyze Refer to the notes in your Evidence Notebook to explain the source of the carbon dioxide in the bottom of Lake Nyos.

CHECKPOINTS

Check Your Understanding

FIGURE 21: Earth's systems exchange matter.

1. Look at Figure 21. For each cycle listed below, describe one way that matter is moving between spheres. Use evidence from the image along with reasoning to support your claims.
   a. water cycle
   b. carbon cycle
   c. oxygen cycle

2. Give an example of how the carbon or oxygen cycle in Figure 21 would be different if the water cycle did not exist or stopped working.

3. There is about 20 times as much argon in the atmosphere as there is carbon. Why do you think we talk about the carbon cycle, but not "the argon cycle"?

FIGURE 22: Global carbon dioxide

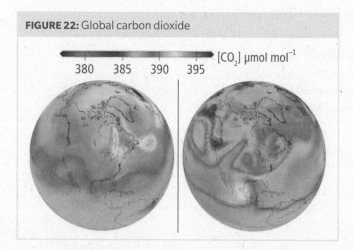

$[CO_2]$ µmol mol^{-1}

380 385 390 395

4. Complete each statement based on Figure 22.
   a. The reservoir being modeled is the [atmosphere/biosphere/geosphere/hydrosphere].
   b. The colors in the image represent different [amounts of water vapor/concentrations of CO_2/species of plants/types of pollution].
   c. The model helps us understand [long-term/short-term/all aspects of] cycling of [carbon/nitrogen/water].
   d. The main differences between the two images are most likely a result of [global warming/ozone destruction/plant growth/plate tectonics/volcanic eruptions].

5. Chemical cycles can be modeled using system models. For each part of the model (a through g), list the best example (1 through 8).

   a. process
   b. control
   c. net movement
   d. reservoir
   e. positive feedback
   f. negative feedback
   g. component of matter
   h. component of energy

   1. sunlight
   2. nitrogen
   3. About 800 Gt of carbon are in the atmosphere.
   4. The acidity of water affects the cycling of nitrogen.
   5. During nitrogen fixation, microbes convert nitrogen from the atmosphere into forms of nitrogen that can be used by plants.
   6. As global temperatures rise, permafrost melts, releasing carbon dioxide and methane into the atmosphere, which causes temperatures to rise.
   7. 0.2 Gt of carbon enter the geosphere each year, while 9.2 Gt leave the geosphere, resulting in a total decrease of 9 Gt of carbon from the geosphere each year.
   8. As carbon dioxide levels rise, more plants grow, causing carbon dioxide levels to drop, causing fewer plants to grow.

6. Figure 23 is a model of the feedback that occurs between the atmosphere and the hydrosphere when carbon dioxide concentrations increase in the atmosphere.

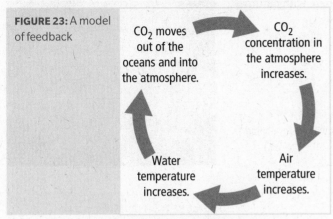

FIGURE 23: A model of feedback

CO₂ moves out of the oceans and into the atmosphere. → CO₂ concentration in the atmosphere increases. → Air temperature increases. → Water temperature increases. →

Which type of feedback loop is this? Why?

a. negative, because the results of global warming are generally negative

b. negative, because carbon dioxide moves out of the oceans

c. positive, because air temperature, water temperature, and carbon dioxide in the atmosphere all increase

d. positive, because the effects of the increase in carbon dioxide in the atmosphere cause further increase of carbon dioxide in the atmosphere

7. Atmospheric carbon dioxide has such a strong effect on Earth's climate that other reservoirs are often classified based on how they affect the atmosphere. A reservoir is called a carbon source if there is a net flow of carbon from it into the atmosphere. A reservoir is called a carbon sink if there is a net flow into it from the atmosphere. A source contributes carbon to the atmosphere while a sink removes it. Use the word "sink" or "source" to complete each statement.

a. Fossil fuels are burned much faster than they form. Fossil fuels are a carbon _____.

b. During cement-making, carbon dioxide is released from limestone millions of times faster than it can form limestone. Limestone used in cement-making is a carbon _____.

c. Scientists are worried that as permafrost melts, it will release stored carbon dioxide and methane (CH_4). They are worried that permafrost is changing from a _____ into a _____ of carbon in the atmosphere.

d. Livestock such as cows, sheep, and goats give off carbon dioxide as they breathe and methane as they digest their food. These animals are a carbon _____.

e. As corals build their skeletons, calcium ions react with bicarbonate ions to form calcium carbonate, water, and carbon dioxide. Although corals remove some carbon from the water, they are considered to be a carbon _____ because they add carbon dioxide to it.

f. During mountain-building, rock is pushed upward. It is exposed to air and water and so breaks down, or weathers, at an increased rate. Weathering uses carbon dioxide from the atmosphere. This process could be a carbon _____.

g. Cool ocean water can hold more dissolved carbon dioxide than warm ocean water. A cooler part of the ocean acts as a carbon _____ while a warmer part can act as a carbon _____.

h. During the spring and summer months, plants take in more carbon dioxide than they give off, and they act as a carbon _____. But during the fall and winter, they are a carbon _____. Overall, plants take in more carbon than they release, thus they act as a carbon _____.

MAKE YOUR OWN STUDY GUIDE

In your Evidence Notebook, design a study guide that supports the main ideas from this lesson:

Many elements, including carbon, oxygen, phosphorus, and nitrogen, cycle between the biosphere, hydrosphere, atmosphere, and biosphere.

- Chemical cycles can be modeled in different ways using system models.
- Chemical cycles change over time as matter moves between reservoirs and as rates of processes change.
- Understanding chemical cycles is important because human activities affect these cycles and so affect other living things.

Remember to include the following in your study guide:

- Support main ideas with details and examples.
- Record explanations for the phenomena you investigated.
- Use system models to describe and explain chemical cycles.

Engineering Connection

Removing CO_2 from the Atmosphere As atmospheric levels of carbon dioxide continue to rise and contribute to global climate change, scientists and engineers are investigating various strategies for removing CO_2 from the atmosphere. One interesting approach involves reacting CO_2 from the atmosphere with naturally occurring minerals to form carbonate minerals. If engineers can design an effective process, mineral carbonation could remove and store billions of tons of CO_2 each year.

> Use Internet resources to learn more about the challenges and benefits of using mineral carbonation to reduce the levels of CO_2 in the atmosphere. Then work with a partner to develop a list of criteria and constraints that engineers must work with in developing an effective and successful process.

FIGURE 1: Magnesite can be produced by reacting CO_2 with the mineral olivine.

Health Connection

Mineralogy of Toothpaste Toothpaste may seem like an afterthought— something you use every day. But toothpaste is a complex mixture of minerals that are used to promote healthy teeth and gums.

> Using library and Internet resources, research the minerals found in toothpaste. Write a blog entry explaining the benefit of the minerals found in toothpaste for promoting healthy teeth and gums. How has the composition of toothpaste changed during the past 100 years?

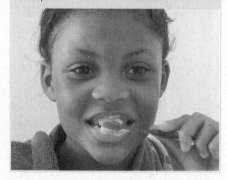

FIGURE 2: Toothpaste contains a complex mixture of minerals.

Art Connection

Minerals and Art You might not realize it, but most of the colors we use today in paints and other art supplies are chemical versions of pigments originally made from crushed minerals. Similarly, mica powders are used to create dichroic (changing color) effects in art glass and ceramics.

> Use library and Internet resources to learn more about the uses of minerals in the visual arts. Then work with a partner to prepare a visual presentation of the uses of minerals as pigments, dichroic effects from mica powders, or another topic of your choice.

FIGURE 3: Mica powders are responsible for the dichroic effect in these handmade glass balls.

SYNTHESIZE THE UNIT

In your Evidence Notebook, create a concept map, graphic organizer, or outline using the Study Guides you created for each lesson in this unit. Be sure to use evidence to support your claims.

When synthesizing individual information, remember to follow these general steps:
- Find the central idea of each piece of information.
- Think about the relationships among the central ideas.
- Combine the ideas to come up with a new understanding.

Go online to access detailed lesson summaries for this unit.

DRIVING QUESTIONS

Look back to the Driving Questions from the opening section of this unit. In your Evidence Notebook, review and revise your previous answers to those questions. Use the evidence you gathered and other observations you made throughout the unit to support your claims.

PRACTICE AND REVIEW

1. Carbon is an important element on Earth. It is found both in organic forms, produced by plants and animals, and in inorganic forms. What are the major processes that move carbon between organic and inorganic forms?

2. Select the statement that describes the relationship between cellular respiration and photosynthesis.

   a. The overall reactants and products produced in photosynthesis are consumed in cellular respiration and vice versa. Photosynthesis uses light energy to build carbon-based molecules and releases oxygen; cellular respiration uses oxygen to break down carbon-based molecules to release energy.

   b. Photosynthesis and cellular respiration consume and produce the same reactants and products. Photosynthesis and carbon dioxide both produce carbon-based molecules that are then broken down to release stored energy.

   c. The processes of storing energy in carbon-based molecules during photosynthesis and breaking down those molecules to release energy during cellular respiration both occur in the same organelle.

   d. All of the energy and matter produced during photosynthesis is consumed during cellular respiration and vice versa.

3. Select all statements that are true about energy flow in and out of Earth systems.

   a. The amount of solar energy that reaches Earth is balanced by the amount that is reflected and emitted back out to space.

   b. Of the total radiation that reaches Earth from the sun, 60% is absorbed by the atmosphere and the surface.

   c. About 30% of the sunlight that reaches Earth from space is reflected back into space.

   d. Most incoming solar radiation is visible light, while most outgoing radiation is longwave radiation.

4. There are 92 naturally occurring elements on Earth, but the most abundant mineral group in Earth's crust is silicates. What does this fact reflect about the relative abundances of elements in the crust?

5. The map shows the concentration of free carbon dioxide (CO_2) in the troposphere in January 2010. How does the concentration of carbon dioxide vary across North America?

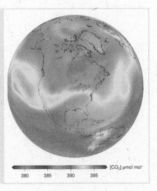

FIGURE 4: Concentration of free carbon dioxide (CO_2) in the troposphere in January, 2010

6. Create a model in your Evidence Notebook to show how carbon is cycled through the different reservoirs on the planet. In your model, include visuals and text to convey the size of each carbon reservoir and the residence time of carbon in each reservoir, as well as the path that carbon from the reservoirs moves along.

7. Which statements support the model of rocks transitioning from one group to another?

   a. Metamorphic rocks generally form when other rocks are buried deep underground.

   b. Sedimentary rocks are composed of sediment clasts that originated from other sedimentary, igneous, or metamorphic rocks.

   c. Igneous rocks solidify from molten rock and exhibit interlocking crystals.

   d. Rocks begin as metamorphic rocks before transitioning between igneous or sedimentary rocks.

8. Describe how the growth of the polar icecaps would likely affect Earth's albedo. Explain how this process could become a positive feedback mechanism affecting the global climate.

9. Which substance is a mineral?

   a. opal

   b. ice

   c. coal

   d. coral

10. In your Evidence Notebook, create a model to represent how nitrogen moves between different reservoirs on the planet.

11. As the planet warms, more and more permafrost, permanently frozen ground in the Arctic, begins to thaw. As the permafrost thaws, it releases methane (CH_4) into the atmosphere. Methane is another component of the carbon cycle. It is a stronger greenhouse gas than carbon dioxide. Explain how the input of methane into the atmosphere will likely affect global climate conditions.

12. Nitrogen makes up 78% of Earth's atmosphere. Despite its abundance, atmospheric nitrogen (N_2) cannot be used directly by living things. Describe the role played by bacteria and other organisms in moving nitrogen between the atmosphere and biosphere.

FIGURE 5: Processes that move oxygen

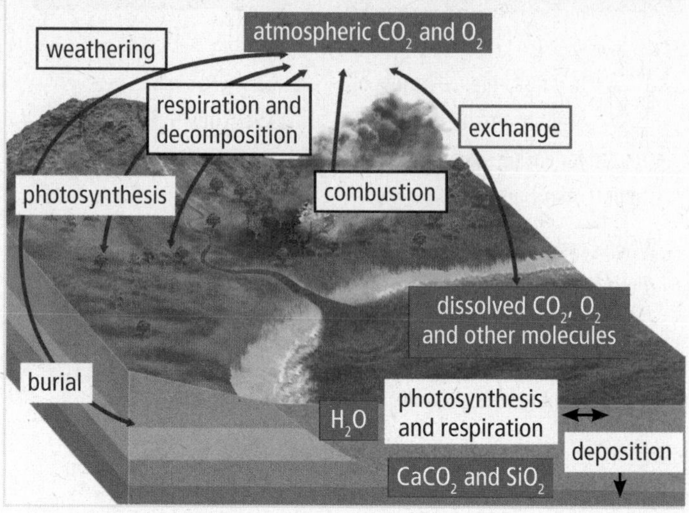

13. Which of the following statements accurately describe processes that move oxygen and carbon dioxide between the atmosphere and living things? Select all correct answers.

   a. Photosynthesis removes carbon dioxide from the atmosphere.

   b. Respiration removes carbon dioxide from the atmosphere.

   c. Decomposition releases carbon dioxide to the atmosphere.

   d. Photosynthesis releases oxygen to the atmosphere.

UNIT PROJECT

Return to your unit project. Prepare your research and materials into a presentation to share with the class. In your final presentation, be sure to include an evaluation of the strengths and limitations of your model. Remember these tips while evaluating:

- Look at the research you did into various ways of modeling convection. Why did you choose to develop the particular physical model you used?

- Consider which aspects of convection are effectively represented by your model.

- Think of changes that you might make to your model to address some of its limitations.

A Carbon Model

In this activity, you will use pennies or other small objects to model how carbon cycles between different reservoirs. You will also observe how a change would affect the cycle.

1. DEFINE THE PROBLEM

Preview the model instructions below. With your team, decide what type of change(s) you will model. Determine what processes to model, and look up any needed information.

2. CONDUCT RESEARCH

With your team, implement your model of the carbon cycle and the change. You may need to refine your model.

1. On a large piece of paper, mark four reservoirs: atmosphere, biosphere, geosphere, and hydrosphere.

2. Divide the water (pennies) among the reservoirs in a way that seems reasonable. These are the initial conditions.

3. Each person should model a process by moving pennies between reservoirs. Decide how you will move the pennies in each round. Record the initial conditions and the processes you have chosen to model.

4. Start the model. Continue the rounds until you have a result that the team agrees upon, such as equilibrium.

5. Choose a change to model, such as a decrease in photosynthesis or a change in temperature. Decide how to model it and what you expect to learn. Set up and start the model with the change.

3. ANALYZE DATA

On your own, analyze the results and the effectiveness of your model.

4. IDENTIFY AND RECOMMEND A SOLUTION

Summarize what your model results tell you about a change in the carbon cycle. Construct an argument about whether the model results are reasonable and, if not, what would need to be improved to produce a reasonable result.

5. COMMUNICATE

Present your argument to the class in a town hall-style meeting. Listen to the arguments of others, and determine whether your ideas about your model results have changed.

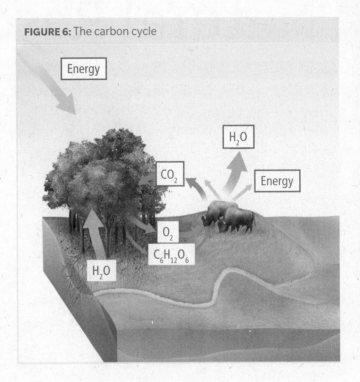

FIGURE 6: The carbon cycle

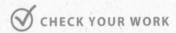 CHECK YOUR WORK

A complete argument should include the following information:

- a summary of your initial and changed model and the results, possibly in the form of a diagram
- an interpretation of the results
- an evaluation of how reasonable or realistic the model results are
- a recommendation of what, if anything, is needed to improve the results

Natural Resources

Rock, mineral, and energy resources affect
almost every aspect of our daily lives.

Image Credit: ©excerts/Fotolia

FIGURE 1: Landfill and an open-pit mine

a Materials that are not recycled can end up in landfills like this one.

b Mineral resources such as copper are mined from Earth's crust.

The availability of natural resources is essential for modern life. However, resource exploration, mining and drilling, processing, and disposal can all have a negative impact on Earth's living and non-living systems.

 Predict What are some ways in which the use of rock, mineral, and energy resources affect other natural resources on Earth?

DRIVING QUESTIONS

As you move through the unit, gather evidence to help you answer the following questions. In your Evidence Notebook, record what you already know about these topics and any questions you have about them.

1. How has human society been influenced by the availability of rock, mineral, and energy resources?

2. What is the impact of developing and using rock, mineral, and energy resources on Earth's living and non-living systems?

3. How can the engineering design process be used to solve environmental, social, and economic problems related to the availability, development, and use of rock, mineral, and energy resources?

UNIT PROJECT

Recycling Resources

What materials can be recycled where you live? How are these materials recycled? Research the recycling system in your area. Evaluate the system in terms of how well it serves your community and how well it protects the environment. Write a proposal to the local government for improving the system. Your proposal should describe the existing system, describe one or more changes you think should be made, and provide reasoning for these changes.

 Go online to download the Unit Project Worksheet to help plan your project.

Designing Solutions to Resource Problems

Aluminum is much more efficient to recycle than to extract from raw materials.

CAN YOU EXPLAIN IT?

FIGURE 1: Plastic and paper bags each have disadvantages.

a Plastic bags don't degrade easily.

b Paper bags can break when wet.

Gather Evidence
As you explore the engineering design process, use it to help you look at the paper-or-plastic choice in new ways and to make informed choices.

Individuals, stores, and communities have often had to choose between paper bags and plastic bags. There are reasons for each choice.

Plastic bags are made from materials extracted from underground, such as oil. Paper bags are made from wood pulp from trees, which can be regrown. Paper may seem to be a better choice for the environment. However, people think about many factors when choosing between paper and plastic bags.

Plastic bags require less energy to produce than paper bags. They are lighter in weight and cost less to ship. Both types of bags can be recycled, but if both are thrown out, then plastic bags take less space in a landfill. However, plastic bags take longer to decompose. People disagree about which bag is more harmful to the environment.

The choice involves more than environmental issues. People have different opinions about which bags are easier or better to use. Plastic bags are not harmed by water but may tear. Paper bags may hold more items—at least, when dry.

Explain Which type of bag—paper or plastic—do you think should be used in stores in your community? Explain your reasoning.

Image Credits: (t) ©moonrise/Fotolia; (bl) ©Jeffrey Phelps/Aurora/Getty Images; (br) ©Diane Collins and Jordan Hollender/The Image Bank/Getty Images

Managing Natural Resources

Many of the objects around you are made of materials that came from the geosphere. Other materials come from the biosphere, hydrosphere, atmosphere, or more than one sphere. Energy comes from Earth's spheres and from sunlight. People—including you—make choices every day that affect the future of these natural resources.

Human Uses of Resources

Energy, materials, and products made from materials are resources, but there are also other types of resources. Space on Earth's surface and in the air above it can be resources, such as rivers used for transportation. For example, the Panama Canal is a resource because it shortens travel and transportation between the Atlantic and Pacific Oceans. Biodiversity, or the variety of organisms, is an important resource. Part of the value of biodiversity comes from the complex ways that organisms interact with other spheres. For example, trees in rainforests remove a lot of carbon dioxide from the air.

FIGURE 2: Rainforests have a wide range of organisms—they are very rich in biodiversity.

Many human activities include the use of natural resources, even when the activity doesn't seem to be about resources. For example, laws, ownership of land, and discussions between countries often involve natural resources. People manage resources to make sure that the resources are available now and in the future. You may already know some actions, such as recycling, that people take to manage resources.

FIGURE 3: People ask some common questions when solving problems. Some of the questions are tied to resources.

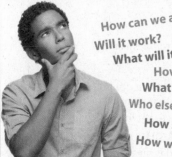

How can we achieve our goal?

Will it work?

What will it cost?

How long will it take?

What else will this solution affect?

Who else will be affected? Should they help make decisions?

How safe will it be?

How well will we like the result?

Collaborate With a partner, use Earth's spheres as a way to try to classify the main resource(s) involved in food, radio communication, tap water, farmland, and nuclear power.

Predict Why else might people think of biodiversity as an important resource?

Image Credits: (t) ©Ammit/Fotolia; (b) ©aldomurillo/ E+/Getty Images

Types of Resources

Resources have different properties. Some resources are nonrenewable—a limited amount of the resource exists, or it is used more quickly than it can form. Other resources are renewable—the resource can be replaced at the rate it is used. For example, sunlight is renewable, while metals from Earth's crust are nonrenewable. However, a resource that is renewable now may become nonrenewable if people use it faster than it can be replenished naturally. People may evaluate whether the use can continue—whether it is sustainable—or whether the resource will be used up. Other properties include whether a resource is found everywhere or only in certain areas and whether it is very limited, such as gold, or plentiful, such as sunlight. Some resources are difficult to transport or store.

Many human activities depend on energy resources. Preparing and using materials usually requires a fuel or other source of energy. Fossil fuels, including coal, oil, and natural gas, formed from organisms that lived long ago. They are nonrenewable and are found only in some places. About 80% of the energy resources used in the United States in 2015 came from fossil fuels. When fossil fuels are burned, they produce pollution and affect human health. In the regions where the fossil fuels are collected, the environment and lives of people can be affected.

Analyzing a Resource

As you saw with the choice of paper or plastic bags, human activities can have many different effects. The effects of an activity occur from the time any raw materials are gathered until the activity ends and any remaining material or waste is in its final storage. This full view is called a *life cycle*. You can use a model of a life cycle, such as that shown in Figure 4, to think through all of the effects of an activity or to compare choices. A life-cycle analysis can be a way to compare the total use of fossil fuels for paper and plastic bags. The analysis can help you make informed choices.

Evaluate Would your choice of paper or plastic bags change if you compared their life cycles? Explain.

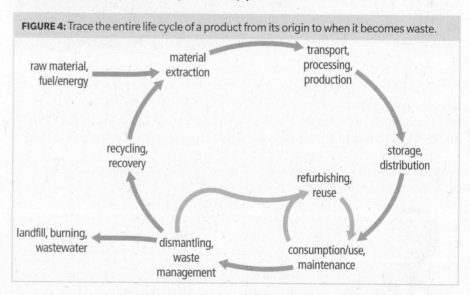

FIGURE 4: Trace the entire life cycle of a product from its origin to when it becomes waste.

Communities and businesses use this type of analysis to help manage natural resources. They may use experts in engineering, science, and business to try to achieve a balance between different needs and wants. These experts may examine a range of factors—physical, economic, legal, political, social, and ethical—to help keep projects within budgets, ensure sustainable use of resources, and protect the environment.

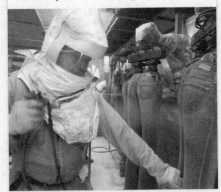

FIGURE 5: Harmful chemicals are used to make jeans look worn.

Costs of Making Jeans

Engineering design involves making choices, which can reflect what a community values. A design with a lower price may have hidden environmental costs. A life-cycle analysis is a tool from engineering design that can reveal these costs. For example, a pair of jeans requires about 3,700 liters of water. Some of this water is used to grow cotton, which is the raw material for jeans. Some water is used whenever the owner washes the jeans. Carbon dioxide is released into the environment in the making, using, and disposing of a pair of jeans. Chemicals from denim processing pollute water and land.

 Analyze What might you do to reduce the negative effects on the environment of buying, using, and disposing of jeans?

The Engineering Design Process

Engineers look at a need or a want as a problem to be solved. They design ways to achieve that goal. The ways that they identify and solve problems are jointly called the engineering design process. A simple model for this process has three phases: defining the problem, designing solutions that can work, and optimizing, or trying to use the best solution. The process can start with any of the phases. Engineers usually go back and forth between the phases many times as they learn about the problem, try possible solutions, and refine a solution.

Collaborate With a partner, list some pros and cons of using paper and plastic bags. Then, discuss how subjectivity came into the process of making the list.

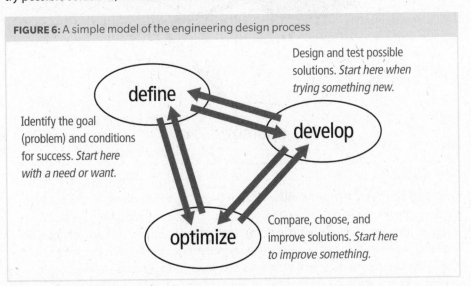

FIGURE 6: A simple model of the engineering design process

define — Identify the goal (problem) and conditions for success. *Start here with a need or want.*

develop — Design and test possible solutions. *Start here when trying something new.*

optimize — Compare, choose, and improve solutions. *Start here to improve something.*

 Analyze Think about some of the choices you make. Identify one choice that involves the use of natural resources. How might the tools of engineering help you to make an informed choice?

Image Credits: ©Don Bartletti/Los Angeles Times/Getty Images

Define a Problem

The engineering design process very often starts with a situation that somebody wants to change. Defining a problem involves stating the want or need clearly and thinking about the characteristics of a successful solution.

Defining a Problem

A clear definition is a good way to start to solve a problem. You might visit other stages of the engineering design process briefly as you define a problem. For example, thinking about possible solutions may help you define a need or want.

Sometimes, you will start a design process with one of the other stages, such as when you recognize a solution that would be useful. However, if you run into difficulties, a clear definition can be helpful. A definition can also help you determine the priority, or relative importance, of related goals. A definition can help you set clear goals and avoid getting distracted by a related problem.

People may disagree about priorities. When a need or want involves several people, defining the problem can help the group work together to meet a shared goal.

Analyze Paper bags and plastic bags are two possible solutions to a problem. What problem—what need or want—is being addressed?

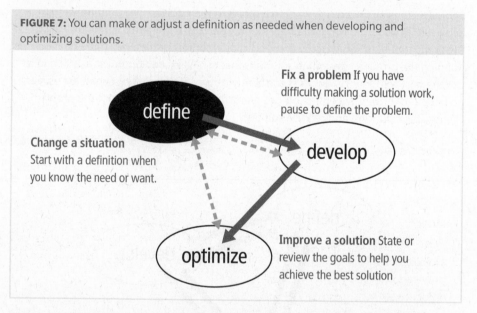

FIGURE 7: You can make or adjust a definition as needed when developing and optimizing solutions.

Fix a problem If you have difficulty making a solution work, pause to define the problem.

Change a situation Start with a definition when you know the need or want.

Improve a solution State or review the goals to help you achieve the best solution

Gather Evidence To make buildings more accessible, engineers consult people with disabilities. How might consultation help define the problem?

Engineers add detail to the definition of a problem. They list properties of a possible solution: the criteria and constraints. Criteria and constraints are usually grouped together, but sometimes looking at them separately can be useful. A constraint is a limitation or restriction on the solution. A proposed solution fails if it does not stay within the constraints. Cost and time are often constraints, because a proposed solution doesn't solve the problem if you can't afford it or if it occurs too late.

Criteria (singular: *criterion*) are the required or desired properties of a solution. Some criteria are more important—higher priority—than others. One way to spell out importance is to determine which criteria are required and which are only desired. In the choice of paper or plastic bags, a required property would be the ability to hold a customer's purchased items. A desired property might be that the bag be attractive. You can also set priorities by ranking the criteria from most to least important. A third approach is to rate each criterion by giving it a relative value, sometimes called a weight. Later, when you evaluate possible solutions, weights can make the job easier.

Gather Evidence
Record an example of a time you had to set priorities to solve a problem. Were you defining the problem?

Example: New Light

Figure 8 shows a dark landing at the top of the first set of stairs in an apartment building. The dark landing is a safety hazard for residents and their visitors. Some people have tripped and fallen when walking from the first set of stairs to the second. The building manager wants to improve this situation.

One resident has asked for a table and a lamp on the landing. Another resident prefers a ceiling light, because a table would make the landing too narrow. A third resident has suggested a new window in one wall to make the landing lighter and more attractive. It may be best to define the problem before choosing a solution. The manager has determined that any solution must cost no more than $300, including the cost of maintenance and energy for the rest of the year.

Explain How would you define this problem?

FIGURE 8: The dark landing at the top of these stairs is a safety hazard. The top few stairs of this set are difficult to see. The bottom few stairs of the second set, beyond the panel on the right, are also dark.

MATERIALS
- pencil
- paper or sticky notes
- spreadsheet application (optional)

New Light: Criteria and Constraints

1. Make an initial table, perhaps by using a computer spreadsheet application. Use these column headers: Criterion or Constraint, Weight. Plan to adjust your table and to add more columns later (for possible solutions).

2. For the new-light problem, list each criterion or constraint (each item) in a separate row or on a separate sticky note. Mark the constraints in some way, such as by underlining them.

3. Compare the importance of the items. Judge the relative importance of the criteria. Assign each criterion a weight between zero and ten, such that the weights add up to ten. Constraints are limitations that must be met for a solution to be acceptable, so leave their weights blank.

4. Put the criteria in order of decreasing importance from the top of the column. Put the constraints below the criteria.

 Analyze

1. Which items involve natural resource issues?
2. Compare your table to that of a classmate. How do your judgements of the importance of items differ?
3. Did the comparison help you improve your table?

Comparing Science and Engineering

 Analyze List at least two ways to measure or describe the growth of a plant. How would you decide which operational definition to use?

Science and engineering share many tools, such as models and math, but they have differences. An awareness of the differences can help you use what you know about science to develop skills in engineering design.

The main focus of science is explaining phenomena. The main focus of engineering is solving problems. It often involves applying scientific knowledge. In science, variables are examined separately, or controlled, whenever possible. Controlling variables is also useful in engineering design, especially when testing ideas. However, a solution often involves a balance between many factors at the same time. A tradeoff is the reduction of one desirable characteristic in order to increase another, usually because the two characteristics can't both be maximized. Tradeoffs are sometimes made when defining a problem, but they are more common in other stages. Exact, complete definitions are often a goal of science. Definitions in engineering may be more practical than exact. Engineers and scientists both use operational definitions, or descriptions of how to measure a concept or variable in a particular situation. Science emphasizes replicating or repeating tests in exactly the same way. Iterating, or repeating with small improvements or variations, is typical of engineering.

 Collaborate With a partner, develop criteria and constraints to further define the problem of the choice of paper or plastic bags.

Develop Solutions

Designing and testing one or more solutions is often the second phase of engineering design. A successful solution meets at least the required criteria while staying within the constraints.

Developing Solutions

A design often begins with sketches of several ideas. A sketch provides a visual representation of, for example, components and processes. It can help you test an idea against the criteria and constraints. It can be a quick way of selecting or thinking through an idea. A sketch or other model can also uncover new limitations or other challenges, such as a space limitation or a part of a solution likely to be costly.

FIGURE 10: A wide range of ideas may be possible—the first idea is not always best. Some people have chosen to earn income through tourism, such as by building ziplines, rather than by cutting down rainforests for wood, grazing land, and farmland.

A common test of cost, for example, is to multiply the price of each component by the number needed or number of times it would need to be replaced. A spreadsheet application can be used to test many possibilities easily. Possible components might be tested until the total cost falls within the limitations. Iterations of testing and adjusting are often needed to develop a solution that meets criteria while staying within constraints.

You will encounter many problems that are difficult to solve. However, you can usually divide a problem into parts and work on one part at a time. Team members may work on different parts at the same time. For example, one person might focus on how best to use a resource while another works out a good way to get the resource. You may need to go back and forth (iterate) so that the parts of the solution work well together. You may even need to go back to adjust the criteria and constraints.

FIGURE 9: To develop a design, you may need to adjust a definition or to optimize some part of a design.

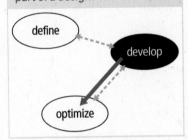

Gather Evidence Make a note of a time you used brainstorming to generate possible ideas to develop into a solution.

Image Credits: ©picaya/Fotolia

FIGURE 11: The solution to this puzzle can help you think about other problems.

Adapting Existing Solutions

Often, there is no need to develop a completely new solution to a problem because one already exists. The solution has already been tested and refined. It is typically much easier and more reliable to adapt such a solution than to start over. For example, the rope systems used to move large canvas sails on ships were adapted to move large pieces of canvas in theaters.

In a classic puzzle, two people are challenged to escape. A rope with a loop on each end connects each person's hands. The wrist loops are loose but must not be removed. The two ropes are linked in a way similar to the center of the puzzle in Figure 11. The solution to either puzzle can be adapted to solve the other puzzle.

Brightness and Color When most light bulbs were incandescent, the amount of energy mostly determined the brightness, temperature, and color of the light. Go online for a lab to compare these properties in modern light bulbs.

Example: New Light

The manager researches ways to make the stairway safer and finds several possibilities. One possible solution is a ceiling light. The manager tries to determine properties of such a fixture needed to solve the problem. The properties include the amount of light or brightness, which is measured in lumens. A lumen is about equal to the amount of light produced by a birthday candle. Energy usage per unit of time is measured in watts and forms part of the ongoing cost. The frequency and cost of replacing light bulbs must be considered, so the expected bulb lifetime is important. The light must shine on the nearest stairs but not shine in people's eyes, so the manager determines the needed spread, or angular width, of the light beam.

The manager finds that the color of the light is sometimes described as warm or cool, because people often describe red and yellow as warm colors and blue as a cool color. Sometimes color is given as an equivalent temperature in kelvin (K), called color temperature. In this measurement, a lower temperature such as 2700 K describes a yellowish light. Higher-color temperatures include more blue light. These temperatures are related to the filaments of incandescent light bulbs and other very hot materials.

FIGURE 12: Color can be expressed as the temperature of a heated material that would produce that color.

 Collaborate With a partner, sketch out one of the possible solutions to the choice of paper or plastic bags. Include information for each criterion or constraint.

Optimize a Solution

The remaining stage of the engineering design process includes choosing or adjusting—optimizing—a solution to give the best possible results. The solution is evaluated against the criteria and constraints.

Optimizing a Solution

A solution is acceptable only if it will meet the criteria and stay within the constraints. When several solutions are acceptable, the criteria can help determine which solution is optimal, or best. A tradeoff matrix is a chart to compare several solutions. When none of the solutions is perfect, some desirable qualities must be traded for others.

Another way to analyze solutions is to look at costs, risks, and benefits. Benefits are the advantages of a solution. Costs include money paid and other disadvantages. Risks are costs that may or may not occur. The costs, risks, and benefits can be a way of looking at criteria and constraints of the problem, but often go beyond the problem itself. A solution can affect other systems, a local community, or even global issues. For example, many solutions affect the management of natural resources. Recall that a life-cycle analysis is one way to look at the total costs of a solution. Models can also be used to estimate risks. Published reviews can show how other people have evaluated possible solutions. Many tools can be used to evaluate solutions.

The chosen solution is tested either in advance or when it is put into use. When a solution fails or isn't good enough, engineers troubleshoot, or attempt to find the cause of the difficulty. A test may reveal flaws in a design or unintended consequences, such as an undesirable effect on something else. The design may need to be adjusted.

Analyze In a design of safety belts in school buses, which of these would you trade for the others: cost, safety, or impact on the environment?

Predict Suppose you change a light bulb to a new type, but it does not turn on. How would you find the problem? Discuss with a partner and come up with a good troubleshooting plan.

FIGURE 12: A solution may introduce a new problem.

A solution can usually be improved. Sometimes, many iterations are needed to optimize a solution. For example, an improvement in safety or effectiveness may increase the price or cause additional harm to the environment. More iterations may help reduce these costs back to acceptable levels.

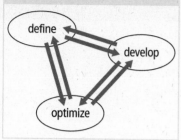

FIGURE 13: Engineering design involves iterating among the stages.

To construct a tradeoff matrix, record a measure of how each solution meets each criterion and constraint. For example, you might add all of the costs to confirm that a design meets a spending limit or addresses a criterion of low price. You might use a scale of zero to five to rate how well a solution meets a criterion. Or, you might simply compare each solution to the current situation. For example, a store considering a change from paper bags might record **+1** for durability if a new solution would break less often (be better) than paper bags, **0** if the new bags would break about as often as paper, and **–1** if the new bags break more often. Subjective items can also be evaluated by rating. Ratings from different people may vary, so an average or an expert's evaluation may help.

You can combine the evaluations to give each solution an overall rating. A typical approach is to use the same rating scale for each criterion, multiply each by the weight assigned to the criterion, and add the results. Each solution then has a numerical score.

Example: New Light

The manager has chosen to look separately at two different parts of a possible solution. One part is the choice of a fixture or lamp. Another part is the choice of bulb.

 Data Analysis

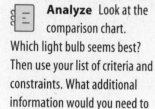 **Analyze** Look at the comparison chart. Which light bulb seems best? Then use your list of criteria and constraints. What additional information would you need to optimize the solution?

Calculating Tradeoffs

Add to your table of criteria and constraints for the new light problem by comparing partial solutions of each of the bulbs below.

FIGURE 14: Use information from this comparison chart in your tradeoff matrix.

BULB TYPE	STANDARD	HALOGEN	CFL	LED
LUMENS				
450	40 W	29 W	9 W	8 W
800	60 W	43 W	14 W	13 W
1100	75 W	53 W	19 W	17 W
1600	100 W	72 W	23 W	20 W
RATED LIFE	1 year	1–3 years	6–10 years	15–25 years

The manager tries a quick test using a borrowed lamp with a standard incandescent bulb of 60 W. The test shows that 800 lumens is enough light. A check of prices shows that the lower-energy bulbs are more expensive. However, any of the four bulb types would be within the cost constraint. The manager chooses the best bulb, then considers the bulb and fixture together to optimize the solution.

 Collaborate Find or prepare a tradeoff matrix for choosing plastic or paper bags. You may want to group some related factors, such as costs or environmental impacts. Compare your results with a partner and discuss how to optimize the solution.

The Use of Iteration

Iteration means to repeat a process, typically with a change. Expect to repeat different parts of the process when designing a solution.

Iterating through a Problem

You've seen how people use the stages of the engineering design process repeatedly. With each pass through the stages, they learn more about the problem and about possible solutions. They apply what they learn to improve the work in other stages. If a test or design fails, they may study the failure to get ideas for an improvement or a different solution. When a problem is broken down, iterations may be used on the separate parts, then on several parts together, and then on the whole solution.

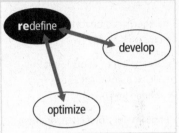

FIGURE 15: Lessons learned during other phases may cause you to redefine the problem.

 Hands-On Activity

Practice Run

Place a coin on the floor just below the edge of a table. Push a second coin off the edge of the table so that it lands as close as possible to the first coin. Then try again with a third coin.

Explain Did the result of your first try help you do better on your second try? How does this show a way iteration can help produce better solutions?

Sometimes a problem is over-constrained—no solution can satisfy all the constraints. In such a case, it can be helpful to look at the need or problem definition in a different way. In the new-light problem, if no lighting fixture stayed within the cost constraint, you might look at other ways to improve safety. Perhaps a mirror, a lighter color of paint, and reflective strips might help. Perhaps an uneven floor is increasing the chance of someone tripping. Or perhaps another expense can be reduced to change the cost constraint of this problem.

Analyze In your notebook, use a diagram similar to Figure 15 to show how you moved between stages while working on the problem of paper or plastic bags.

Collaborate With a partner, review your definition(s) of the problem of paper or plastic bags. If your goals were to minimize cost, make the most efficient use of resources, and minimize environmental impact, how might you redefine the problem?

Even though problems may seem isolated, the solutions are usually human activities that can have other impacts. When you finish solving a problem or have no more opportunities for optimization, it may still be useful to evaluate the solution and its impacts. You may learn something that will help with a later problem.

 Analyze With a partner, discuss what you would do differently the next time you apply the engineering design process and why.

Hands-On Lab

Brightness and Color

MATERIALS

- lamps or sockets, identical (4)
- incandescent light bulbs, 60 W and 100 W
- LED light bulbs, approx. 800 lumens with different colors such as warm white and daylight
- halogen or compact fluorescent bulbs (optional)
- package information about the specific bulbs, such as energy required and price
- photometer, color chart, or other tools (optional)

FIGURE 16: Color temperature is based, in part, on the glowing filament of incandescent light bulbs. In such bulbs, the energy use determines the temperature, which mostly determines both the brightness and the color.

In this investigation, you will compare light bulbs to determine what characteristics to consider. Not all combinations of color and brightness may be available. In some types of bulbs, filters change the color by absorbing some light and wasting energy.

PROCEDURE

1. Take safety precautions. Always unplug the lamps before inserting or removing a bulb. Use insulated gloves to handle bulbs that have been turned on. Handle the bulbs very gently to avoid breaking the glass. Do not touch a halogen bulb with bare skin (the oil in your skin can cause the bulb to break when hot).

2. Insert the bulbs in the lamps. Turn on the lamps.

3. Rank the bulbs from least bright to most bright and then from most red or yellow to most blue or white.

4. Record information about the bulbs, such as price, expected brightness, and energy use.

 Language Arts Connection

Research the effects of various light bulbs on the environment. Government or consumer sources may provide the most reliable information.

 Analyze

1. Are your rankings of the brightnesses and colors consistent with the package information? What might account for any difference?

2. Which of the bulbs gives you the most light per unit of energy?

3. Explain how the properties of the bulbs are related to criteria such as minimizing cost and minimizing the effect on the environment.

| RESOURCE SOLUTIONS | ENGINEERING SPECIALIST | CROP LINES | Go online to choose one of these other three paths. |

Image Credits:©ohsuriya/Fotolia

Lesson Self-Check

CAN YOU EXPLAIN IT?

FIGURE 17: Plastic and paper bags each have advantages and disadvantages.

Analyze Refer to the notes in your Evidence Notebook to help you address the problem of which type of bag to use.

Apply what you have learned about the engineering design process to look again at the choice between plastic bags and paper bags. Present an opinion about which type of bag should be used in stores in your community. Construct an argument to support that opinion.

In your argument, address a range of factors. Take into account the need that is being addressed by the bags, the costs and benefits over the lifetime of the bags, and the effects on the community. For example, if you support plastic bags, consider how you might respond to people who complain about the sight of bags caught in trees, as in Figure 17. Think about other possible reactions, such as how store owners might react to the cost or convenience of your choice.

In your argument, use at least one tool from the engineering design process. For example, you may wish to show the criteria and constraints for choosing bags. You may wish to put the possible solutions into a tradeoff matrix.

Other people have made arguments about the choice between paper and plastic bags. Some arguments have changed over time as technology, costs, and public opinions have changed. You may wish to review these arguments or to gather specific information, such as costs or energy used in making different types of bags. Document any sources you use and evaluate the reliability of your sources, including the date of the information.

 Gather Evidence Based on what you know now, which type of bag do you think should be used in stores in your community? Construct an argument to support your choice.

CHECKPOINTS

Check Your Understanding

1. Which of these are the goal(s) of natural resource management? Choose all that apply.
   a. To stop the extraction and use of natural resources
   b. To reduce the effect of the use of resources on the environment
   c. To preserve nonrenewable natural resources
   d. To come up with solutions that balance costs and benefits
   e. To decrease the use of renewable natural resources

2. Do part of a life-cycle analysis for paper bags. Choose one of the stages shown in Figure 4, such as "refurbishing, reuse." Describe the costs and benefits of paper bags in this stage. You might use relative terms, such as "much less than plastic bags," rather than specific numbers.

3. In engineering, how is a problem typically defined?

4. The design of a solution usually involves iterations. When can a designer stop iterating?

5. What tools might be used to find an optimal solution?

Use the following situation for problems 6–9:

Suppose you are asked to come up with a design for a new mobile phone that uses solar energy as its energy source.

6. Give examples of one criterion and one constraint for this mobile phone.

7. Describe a risk that you would need to address.

8. Which battery would be best to use in the design? Support your answer.
   a. The most common battery used
   b. The least expensive battery
   c. The most efficient battery
   d. The smallest battery

9. What possible tradeoffs do you think you will make in choosing a battery for the design?

Use the following situation for problems 10–13:

Suppose your school is not near your house and walking to school is not practical. You need to select or develop a way to get to and from school.

10. List several possible solutions that might help you to get to school while having the least undesirable effect on the environment.

11. Of the possible criteria and constraints, list several that you would evaluate in your comparison of possible solutions.

12. Compare riding a bike to school with either taking a bus or carpooling. Which of these natural resources would you be helping to conserve by riding a bike? Explain your choice(s).
   a. Fossil fuels
   b. Earth's atmosphere
   c. Biodiversity
   d. Minerals

13. Suppose you decide that riding a bicycle to school is the best solution. How might you further refine, or optimize, this solution?

MAKE YOUR OWN STUDY GUIDE

In your Evidence Notebook, design a study guide that shows how the engineering design process can be used to identify and solve problems, including the management of natural resources.

Remember to include the following in your study guide:
- Support main ideas with details and examples.
- Record ways to apply the skills that you develop.
- Note how the use of natural resources is often part of designed solutions, though sometimes indirectly, such as through the cost of energy.

Use the tools of defining criteria and constraints and of analyzing costs and benefits to help you take into account aspects of design that are not part of science, such as social values and personal preferences.

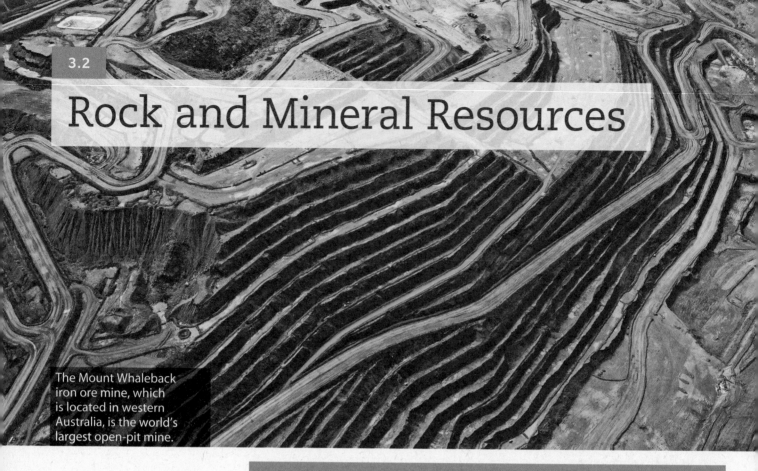

Rock and Mineral Resources

The Mount Whaleback iron ore mine, which is located in western Australia, is the world's largest open-pit mine.

CAN YOU EXPLAIN IT?

For many people, a smartphone has become part of everyday life. Like every other object or material that we use, smartphones are made of elements and compounds.

FIGURE 1: More than 70 different elements are found in the plastic and metal casing, touchscreen, battery, electronics, and circuitry that make up a smartphone.

Gather Evidence
Record evidence about rock and mineral resources. As you explore the lesson, gather evidence to help explain how the use of resources has changed over time, what resources are used today, how resources are mined, and the effects of mining on the environment.

Predict All elements that make up the products we use every day come from living things, like plants and animals, or non-living resources, such as rocks and minerals. Where do you think the elements that make up a smartphone come from? What rocks and minerals are they found in? What parts of the world do they come from?

Image Credits: ©John W Banagan/Photographer's Choice/Getty Images; ©Scanrail/Getty Images

The History of Rock and Mineral Extraction

Mining in the Ancient World

Humans and their ancestors have been using rocks and minerals for more than 2.5 million years. Early humans fashioned stone tools from hard rocks such as flint, quartzite, and obsidian for protection, hunting, and preparing foods. Early humans also used native metals like gold and copper and even native iron from iron meteorites in places where they were available. People used pigments made of compounds such as iron oxide, manganese oxide, and charcoal for painting, salt for flavoring and preserving food, and clay to make durable pottery figures and containers.

Analyze Why do you think people started using rocks, native metals, pigments, and clay much earlier than they started using non-native metals and alloys?

FIGURE 2: Metals such as copper, gold, lead, and mercury, which are relatively easy to extract from rocks, were mined in the ancient world.

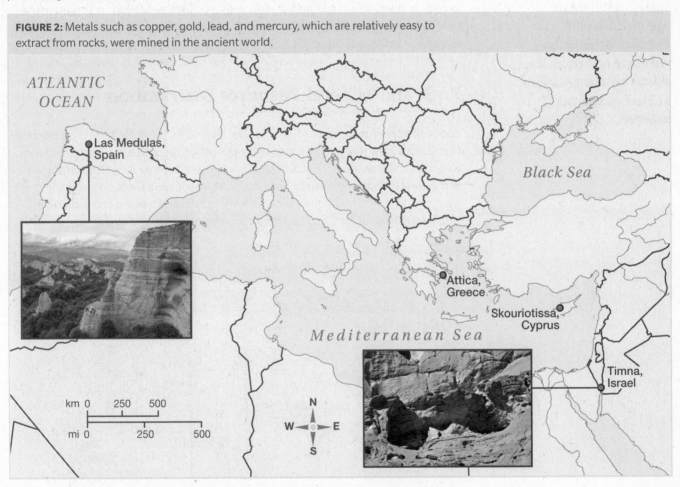

Around 4000 BCE, modern humans began smelting—heating rocks to extract metals such as copper, tin, and lead. They also began making alloys, or mixtures of metals, such as bronze. Bronze is a mixture of copper and tin and is much harder and stronger than either copper or tin alone. By 1500 BCE, people had figured out how to extract iron, a much stronger but much harder-to-work metal, from iron-rich rocks.

Image Credits: (r) ©moris kushelevitch/Alamy; (l) ©NoraDoa/Fotolia

These stone axes were recovered from the Etowah Indian Mounds Historic Site near Cartersville, Georgia and date from approximately 1200 to 1000 CE.

Analyze Compare the properties and uses of materials such as quartzite and flint, coarse-grained igneous cobbles, and native copper. How were the ways that the materials were used related to their properties?

Native American Quarrying and Mining

Thousands of years before Europeans settled in North America, Native Americans were using a wide variety of rock and mineral resources for tools, weapons, pottery, building materials, jewelry, and artwork. As in other parts of the world, the specific materials used depended on what was available locally or through trade, what methods had been developed to extract and use the materials, and what the need was for certain materials with certain properties.

For example, as early as 10 000 years ago, people were quarrying quartzite, a very hard metamorphic rock that breaks into sharp pieces that are ideal for use in knives and spears. Obsidian and flint were also used for weapons. Other types of hard rocks were used for grinding and hammering. Beginning around 7000 years ago, Native Americans mined copper in Michigan from both surface pits and underground shafts. The malleable copper was used for making items like fishhooks, spear points, and jewelry, and was also used for trade. Soft and colorful minerals such as turquoise were used for beads and jewelry. Native Americans also used clays for pottery and mined or extracted salt for cooking.

Rock and Mineral Resource Distribution

Rock and mineral resources include all rocks, sediments, minerals, and native elements from Earth's crust that people use to make things such as structures, tools, medicines, weapons, and artwork. Rock and mineral resources include rocks such as sandstone and granite for building; limestone for making cement; sand for construction, to make glass, and to replenish beaches; salt for flavoring food and melting snow; clays for ceramics; galena for lead; and bauxite for aluminum in cans and airplanes.

FIGURE 4: World Mineral Production from 2005–2009: This map shows the relative amounts of major metals mined in various countries around the world.

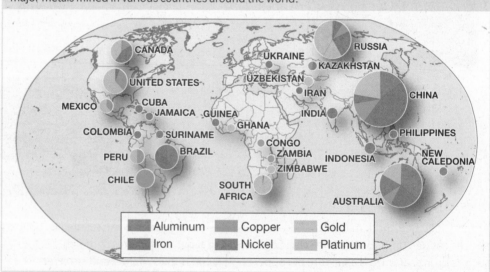

Model If you had maps of resource production for different decades, describe how you could use them to model resource production and use. How could you use them to predict future resource discovery?

Exports/Imports

In early prehistoric times, people were limited to using the rock and mineral resources found nearby. Thus, different populations of people likely used different resources, and different technologies, artwork, and cultures developed as a result. Over time, however, as human populations grew and spread, resources also spread through trade, plunder, and resettlement.

Today, although rock and mineral resources are not evenly distributed, people around the world generally do need or want the same resources. There is now a global market for rock and mineral resources, and unlike thousands of years ago, we now have a complex transportation system that makes trade possible.

United States Net Import Reliance, 2008–2011

FIGURE 5: The United States produces only some of the mineral resources that it uses. It imports the rest from other countries. In 2014, the United States exported $153 billion worth of minerals and metals, but imported $205 billion.

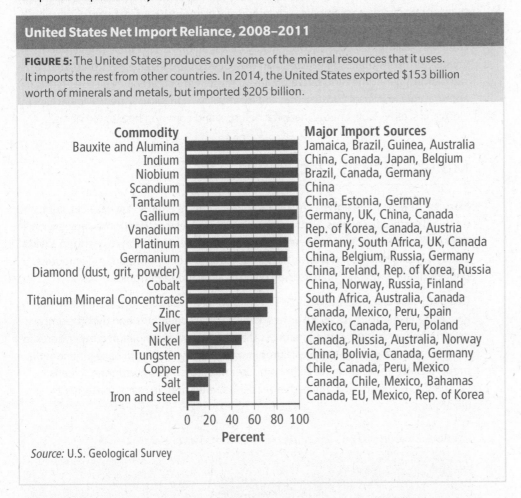

Commodity	Major Import Sources
Bauxite and Alumina	Jamaica, Brazil, Guinea, Australia
Indium	China, Canada, Japan, Belgium
Niobium	Brazil, Canada, Germany
Scandium	China
Tantalum	China, Estonia, Germany
Gallium	Germany, UK, China, Canada
Vanadium	Rep. of Korea, Canada, Austria
Platinum	Germany, South Africa, UK, Canada
Germanium	China, Belgium, Russia, Germany
Diamond (dust, grit, powder)	China, Ireland, Rep. of Korea, Russia
Cobalt	China, Norway, Russia, Finland
Titanium Mineral Concentrates	South Africa, Australia, Canada
Zinc	Canada, Mexico, Peru, Spain
Silver	Mexico, Canada, Peru, Poland
Nickel	Canada, Russia, Australia, Norway
Tungsten	China, Bolivia, Canada, Germany
Copper	Chile, Canada, Peru, Mexico
Salt	Canada, Chile, Mexico, Bahamas
Iron and steel	Canada, EU, Mexico, Rep. of Korea

Percent

Source: U.S. Geological Survey

For any given type of resource, there are countries that produce more of the resource than they use, and those that produce less than they use. Those countries that produce more than they need export to those who produce less. Importing countries rely heavily on exporting countries for raw materials, while exporters rely on importers to buy what they produce.

Explain What natural and human factors have influenced the rock and mineral resources people have used and how resources have been used in different places over time? Use evidence from the lesson and other sources to support your claims.

Minerals for New Technologies

New Uses for Minerals

The use of rock and mineral resources has changed over time as people have discovered new elements and mineral deposits, new properties of elements and compounds, and new ways of extracting and processing materials. It has also changed as the demand for certain materials, products, and capabilities has changed. Minerals that contain rare earth elements—certain heavy elements that react very easily with other elements—make it possible to meet the demand for products like cars that cause less pollution, medical tools that can better diagnose and treat illnesses and injuries, airplanes that can fly faster than the speed of sound, and electronics that can monitor our homes and bodies. Many of these minerals are referred to as "critical and strategic" minerals because they are essential for agriculture, medical devices, electronics, renewable energy, national defense, and common household items.

Mineral Use in Electronics

Electrical devices transform electricity into other forms of energy, such as heat, light, and motion. Toasters, flashlights, and fans are all electrical devices. Electronics, however, are devices that use complex circuits to manipulate the flow of electrons to perform a wide variety of tasks, such as sensing, analyzing, and transmitting information. Computers, phones, digital cameras, and television displays all include electronics.

One of the key components of the electronics we use today are rare earth elements. Rare earth elements (REEs), such as neodymium, praseodymium, and dysprosium, are used to make extremely strong magnets that can also withstand high temperatures in electric motors and wind turbines. Europium, yttrium, and terbium have luminescent properties that make them ideal for computer monitors and smartphone screens. Lanthanum is important in the rechargeable batteries used in many consumer electronics.

Analyze When designing electronics, engineers need to consider the specific physical, chemical, electrical, and magnetic properties of elements. What properties do you think are particularly important for elements used in electronics?

FIGURE 6: The display on a smartwatch uses luminescent rare earth elements.

Image Credits: ©Leo Lintang/Fotolia

Mineral Use in Hybrid Cars

A typical passenger car has a mass of about 1500 kg. More than half that weight is steel, an inexpensive and strong alloy of iron and other elements, such as carbon, manganese, and chromium, which is used to make the frame, doors, and engine. Manufacturing a car also requires resources like aluminum for the wheels and body panels, silica for the glass windows, asbestos used in brake pads, mica used in shock absorbers, copper in the wiring, tungsten for the light bulb filaments, cerium in catalytic converters, gallium for the mirrors, and antimony to make the upholstery fire resistant. Each material is chosen based on its unique set of properties, its availability, and its cost. Aluminum, for example, is lighter and resists impacts and corrosion better than steel, but it is also more expensive. As a result, it is still only used in the frames of expensive cars, while most other cars are still made of steel.

Predict If the demand for cars with smart technology and green technology continues to increase, how will this affect the demand for REEs? How could it affect the supply of REEs? How would it affect the overall abundance of REEs on Earth?

FIGURE 7: This electric car is powered by 102 lithium ion batteries, which give it a range of 340 km and a top speed of 115 km/hr.

Modern cars also include color touchscreens, computer chips, and other electronic components, and thus use many of the same elements as smartphones, including rare earth elements (REEs).

With the increasing concern about the effects of burning gasoline on the environment, more and more people are choosing to buy "green" vehicles like hybrids. Hybrid cars use less gasoline than traditional cars because they run on an electric motor as well as a gasoline engine. The electric motor relies on a battery that is recharged as the car moves and brakes. Hybrid cars require about twice the amount of REEs as a traditional car. The electric motor and generator include neodymium, praseodymium, dysprosium, and terbium, while a hybrid battery uses lanthanum, neodymium, and cerium or lithium, cobalt, and graphite. Although REEs are found around the world, most REE production is currently in China.

Mineral Use in Aerospace Technology

As with cars and electronic devices, the technology of air- and spacecraft has changed significantly over the past 100 years in large part because of the increased availability of resources and the development of new materials and components that have been designed from those resources. The materials that make up aircraft need to be lightweight, strong, flexible, and resistant to temperature extremes. The communication and control systems inside the craft need to be electrically conductive.

Analyze Why do you think materials used to build a plane should be lightweight, strong, flexible, and resistant to extreme temperatures?

Image Credits: ©Paul Rapson/Science Source

FIGURE 8: The F-22 fighter jet is composed of titanium, carbon-fiber composite, aluminum, and thermoplastic. Titanium is used because it is relatively lightweight and strong. Carbon-fiber composites are used for the body frame and for skin panels. Thermoplastics are used for the landing gear and weapons bay doors.

Modern airplane bodies are made mostly of light but strong materials such as aluminum, titanium, carbon fiber, and fiberglass. Engine components require alloys of metals like rhenium, cobalt, nickel, niobium, hafnium, and titanium, which are able to withstand high temperatures. Flight controls include samarium (a rare earth element) and cobalt. Stealth technology uses the rare earth elements samarium and neodymium, as well as cobalt, nickel, and titanium. Modern aircraft also include all of the elements found in everyday electronic displays, communication systems, and computer processors.

 Technology and Society

Carbon Fiber

Carbon fibers are long, thin strands of carbon atoms that can be twisted and woven together into fabric and combined with other materials like resin to make a composite. Like many carbon-based materials, the carbon that makes up carbon fiber generally starts out as petroleum deep underground.

Carbon fiber and carbon-fiber composites have a number of important properties that make them useful for many different types of products, including sporting goods, automobiles, and airplanes. Carbon fiber is resistant to corrosion, expands and contracts very little with changes in temperature, and is very light, rigid, and strong for its weight. Cars made of carbon fiber, for example, can weigh about half as much as cars with steel bodies.

Carbon fiber was first invented in 1958, and by the mid-1960s, engineers had developed a process to manufacture it on a large scale. But manufacturing carbon fiber is still very slow and energy intensive. It is therefore also very expensive. Right now, although they are much more energy efficient, very few carbon-fiber cars are manufactured because very few people can afford them. As a result, engineers are working on improving not only carbon-fiber fabric design, but also the manufacturing process.

Minerals Used in Medical Technology

Numerous elements and compounds derived from rocks and minerals are used to make the wide variety of medical devices that are used to diagnose and treat illnesses and injuries. For example, stainless steel (an alloy of iron and chromium) is used in numerous surgical devices and in implants. Gold is used in life-support devices, pacemakers, and heart stents. Together with silver, gold is used in CAT scan devices. Lithium is widely used in pacemakers, defibrillator machines, and other types of portable electronic equipment. Other metals, such as aluminum, nickel, titanium, and cobalt, are used in joint replacement, and rare earth elements are used to produce powerful magnetic fields used in medical imaging devices such as MRIs.

Collaborate With a partner, try to identify elements and compounds that are used in medical devices that you are familiar with.

FIGURE 9: Medical devices contain elements such as rare earth elements and lithium.

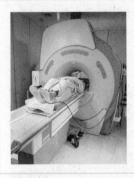

a MRIs enable doctors to diagnose illnesses and injuries that otherwise would be harder to detect.

b A defibrillator is an electronic device that sends an electric shock to the heart to stop an irregular heartbeat.

Rare Earth Elements in Technology

Although rare earth elements are not truly rare, they are generally not concentrated enough to be mined profitably. When they are concentrated, they form minerals that contain REEs, such as bastnäsite and monazite, which are found in relatively rare types of igneous rocks in the continental crust. Until recently, it has been difficult to extract and separate REEs from the rocks and minerals and from each other.

FIGURE 10: Rare earth elements

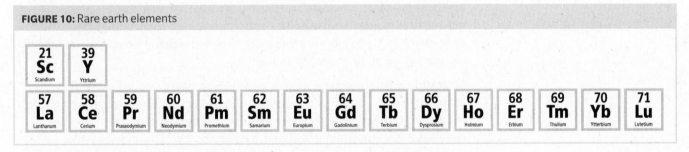

Small deposits of REEs are found throughout the world, but the vast majority of REE production is currently in China. Because REEs have become essential in so many important applications, from everyday consumer electronics to medical, renewable energy, and defense technology, the United States considers the rare earth minerals to be critical and strategic minerals.

Analyze The United States must import more than 75% of the REEs that it uses. In what ways could reliance on other countries for rock and mineral resources be risky? How could the United States reduce those risks?

Rock and Mineral Extraction

The type of mining, or the method used to extract a particular rock or mineral resource, depends on the properties of the resource and the size, shape, concentration, and location of the deposit.

Surface Mining Methods

Deposits that are located on land and on or near the surface can be extracted using a surface mine. Some methods of surface mining include open-pit mining, quarrying, strip mining, hydraulic mining, and solar evaporation mining.

FIGURE 11: Methods for Extracting Rock and Mineral Resources

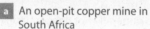

a An open-pit copper mine in South Africa

b A solar evaporation pond for mining salt in India

Open-Pit Mines As the name suggests, open-pit mines are giant holes in the ground. Explosives are used to break apart the rock, while giant trucks are used to haul it out of the mine. Some open-pit mining involves removing layers of rock or sediment above to expose the deposit. In some areas, so much rock is removed that the process is referred to as mountaintop removal. Copper and iron are commonly extracted from open-pit mines. Open-pit mines for sand, gravel, and building stones, such as granite and marble, are often referred to as quarries.

Strip Mining Sedimentary resources such as phosphates, salt, and aluminum commonly exist as flat layers beneath the surface. These can be extracted using strip mining, in which successive horizontal strips of overlying rock and resources are removed. As overlying rock is removed, it is piled on top of the previous strip.

Hydraulic Mining Placer deposits are loose ancient or modern river and stream sediments that contain dense and valuable minerals such as gold and platinum, and gemstones such as diamond, ruby, and sapphire. Many placers are mined using hydraulic mining, which involves loosening the sediments with high-pressure jets of water. The sediments then move though a system of sluice boxes designed to remove the valuable minerals.

Solar Evaporation Ponds Minerals that are soluble in water can be extracted from ground and surface water using evaporation. Salt water is pumped from underground or channeled from the surface into shallow ponds in hot, dry climates. Minerals crystallize as the water evaporates. Once the pond is dry, the minerals are harvested.

Explain Why can't all minerals be mined using solar evaporation ponds? Why can't all be extracted using hydraulic mining?

Subsurface Mining Methods

Subsurface mines are much more expensive to operate than surface mines and thus are reserved for more valuable deposits. There are several methods of subsurface mining. The method chosen depends on natural factors such as the properties of the resource being mined; the size, shape, and depth of the ore body; the strength of the surrounding rock; and the amount of groundwater present. It also depends on human factors such as labor costs, environmental laws, safety regulations, and the market price of the resource. Metal and other valuable minerals are extracted from ore, a natural material made of one or more minerals.

Explore Online

Hands-On Lab

Copper Recovery Extract solid copper from an iron nail.

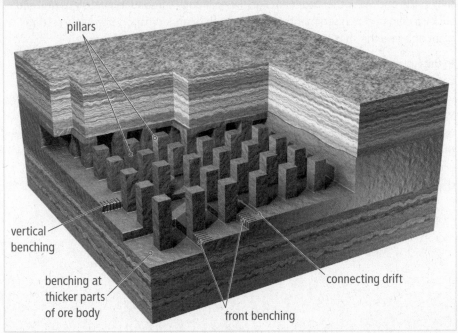

FIGURE 12: In a room-and-pillar mine, columns of ore are left over to support the ceiling and keep the mine from caving in.

pillars

vertical benching

benching at thicker parts of ore body

front benching

connecting drift

Explain Planning a subsurface mining operation often requires the expertise of both geologists and civil engineers. How are these roles important? What could happen if an operation were not planned properly?

Minerals that dissolve easily can be extracted using solution mining. Solution mining involves pumping hot water or acidic solvents down into the ground where they dissolve minerals like salt, sulfur, gold, and copper. The mineral-rich brine is then pumped up to the surface, where it can be processed.

If the rock surrounding an ore body is very hard, ore can be removed using block caving or stoping. In these methods, workers drill and blast from below, creating a pile of broken ore on the floor of the mine. The broken rock is then transported to the surface with machinery. In some mines, stoping creates giant underground rooms. In others, waste rock is poured or pumped back down into the mine to fill the empty space. This cut-and-fill method helps get rid of the waste and also support the mine.

The room-and-pillar method is often used for flat sedimentary ore bodies with a relatively weak or fractured sedimentary layer above. Rather than removing all of the ore, which would likely result in a mine collapse, rooms of ore are removed while pillars of ore are left standing to support the rock above.

Marine Mining

Some resources are concentrated in sediments on the seafloor. Spherical nodules on the deep seafloor are rich in metals like manganese, cobalt, and nickel. Rich deposits of copper, lead, zinc, cobalt, gold, and rare earth elements can form around submarine hot springs on the seafloor. Most of these resources lie in water that is 500 m or more below sea level. Therefore, the challenge of marine mining is the technological difficulty associated with extracting mineral deposits from deep water.

As of yet, however, the only resource worth the great expense of marine mining is diamond. Offshore diamond mining takes place primarily off the coast of southern Africa in waters that are less than 200 m deep. Diamond-rich sediments weather out of rock on the continent and are then transported by flowing water into the ocean, where they settle out with other sediments on the seafloor. Diamond mining ships drill and suck up diamond-rich sediments from the seafloor and transport them to a sorting plant onboard the ship. Waste is then dumped back out into the ocean.

In the future, marine mining may focus primarily on mining minerals containing copper, iron, and zinc from deep-sea hydrothermal vents. At present, hydrothermal vents in the western South Pacific Ocean are of particular interest to mining companies. Papua New Guinea is the only country to have allowed this form of mining in their waters. However, the potential environmental effects of this mining is raising concerns throughout the region. This is partly due to the fact that deep-sea vents have unique ecosystems. They provide habitats for little-known, deep-sea organisms that obtain their energy from chemicals rather than sunlight.

FIGURE 13: This offshore mining ship is exploring the seafloor sediment for diamonds off of Namibia in southwest Africa.

Analyze Different forms of mining have different economic, social, safety, and environmental risks and benefits. Compare the risks and benefits of one form of surface mining and one form of subsurface mining. Think about the costs and hazards, as well as the potential benefits in terms of the local or national economy or in terms of our ability to make new products.

Impacts of Mineral Use

Potential Effects of Mining

Mining (along with recycling of previously mined materials) is essential in order to meet many of the needs and wants of today's society. Recycling is the recovery of useful materials from waste. However, mining and processing of rock and mineral resources also has very serious environmental effects.

Explain What factors influence the effects of mining on the environment?

FIGURE 14: Both surface and subsurface mining can negatively impact the environment.

a Acid mine drainage from a copper mine in Romania has negatively affected this body of water.

b This hole opened up in the backyard of a home in Egremont, England when an old mine shaft collapsed.

Surface mining can destroy habitats and displace wildlife; send dust into the air, causing air pollution; and result in leaching, erosion, and subsequent pollution of streams, rivers, and other bodies of water. The vibrations and noise from drilling, explosions, and heavy trucks used in surface mining can also be very disruptive to people and other living things. Subsurface mining can pollute groundwater resources and can cause land subsidence such as that shown in Figure 14b. Mineral processing— the processes used to remove the valuable components from the ore rocks and minerals after they have been mined—can also cause land, water, and air pollution.

Mining can also have negative effects on individual mine workers. Mines that are not engineered, monitored, and maintained properly can collapse, flood, or overheat. Poor ventilation can result in the buildup of toxic and explosive gases and dust.

The specific effects of a mining operation depend on factors such as the mining methods that are used, the topography and climate of the area, the structure and chemistry of the ore body and the surrounding rocks, and the size of the operation. For example, a copper mine and smelting plant are likely to cause much more air and water pollution than a granite building-stone quarry.

Explore Online ▶

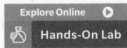 **Hands-On Lab**

Investigating Ore Deposits Model a geophysical survey to find metal ore deposits, and consider the costs and benefits of decisions.

Explain Mining operations can last for many years. How can the benefits of these operations be weighed against potential long-term environmental and social impacts?

The Social Effects of Mining

Mining can be an important part of a nation's economy. Mining projects provide jobs to local people in the community and wealth to the region in general. But in many cases, these short-term benefits are outweighed by other effects. In recent years, concerns over the environmental and social effects of mining have led people to protest mining operations. In some cases, protestors have been able to stall or stop mining projects completely before they've even begun.

For example, in 2013 an open-pit gold and silver mining project in the Andes Mountains of South America was stalled over concerns that mining would destroy glaciers and would affect indigenous people living in the area. In Romania, people protested plans to open an ancient gold and silver mine. They were concerned not only about cyanide used in the mining process, but also because the operation would destroy an archeological site: the oldest Roman gold mine galleries in the world. People in Greece protested a gold mine project because of concerns about groundwater and air pollution and also because they feared it would have negative effects on other aspects of the local economy, like tourism, fishing, farming, and beekeeping.

Regulation and Compliance

In order to reduce the effects of mining on the environment, countries have laws and regulations that govern how mines must be operated. The laws differ from country to country—laws are much stricter in some countries than in others. In the United States, mining companies must comply with laws such as the Clean Air Act, the Safe Drinking Water Act, the Solid Waste Disposal Act, the Endangered Species and Migratory Bird Treaty Acts, as well as the Surface Mining Control and Reclamation Act. Mining companies must also abide by strict health and safety regulations to protect people working in and around mines and processing facilities.

In order to operate a mine in the United States, a company must also have a reclamation plan. Reclamation is the process of returning the land to its former environmental condition. A reclamation plan describes exactly how the company plans to restore the landscape and ecosystems that the mine disrupted. Reclaimed surface mines have been turned into pasture, forestland, playing fields, and golf courses. Quarries are often flooded and turned into recreational lakes.

In order to ensure that a mining company abides by all standards and reclaims the site as planned, money is set aside in the form of a bond. If a company does not mine and reclaim a site according to the standards required by its permits, the company must give the bonds to the states, which use the funds to reclaim the site.

 Collaborate Choose one type of mine. How might this type of mine and mining operation affect the environment? How could the land be reclaimed after the mine ceases operating?

Hands-On Lab

Reclamation

PROCEDURE

1. Use a plastic spoon to remove the first layer of gelatin from a multilayered gelatin dessert cup and place it into a small bowl.
2. Remove the next layer of gelatin and discard it.
3. Restore the dessert cup by replacing the first layer of gelatin.

MATERIALS

- bowl, small
- gelatin desert cup, multilayered
- spoon, plastic

ANALYZE

1. What does the first layer of gelatin on the restored dessert cup represent?
2. Does the "reclaimed" dessert cup resemble the original, untouched dessert cup?
3. What factors would you address to make reclamation more successful?

Minimizing the Impact of Mineral Extraction

Decreasing the amount of a particular resource that must be mined to meet demands can reduce the negative effects of mining. For example, when engineers improve the ability to extract a particular metal from a rock, less rock needs to be mined. Materials that can be mined and processed with less damage to the environment can be substituted for those that cause more damage.

Everyone can help significantly reduce the need for mining simply by reducing our consumption, reusing products when possible, and recycling materials. Building smaller houses, recycling aluminum cans and glass jars, and buying a used car instead of a new one are all ways to reduce the effects of mining on the environment.

FIGURE 15: Recycling materials such as trash and scrap metal help to reduce the demand for resources that must be mined.

a This girl is helping to recycle items that have been carelessly disposed of in a neighborhood park.

b Scrap metal can be recycled for many elements, including iron, titanium, tungsten, vanadium, zinc, and zirconium.

 Predict How could improving recycling rates and recycling technology influence the effects of mining around the world?

Careers in Science

Recycling Technician

FIGURE 16: A technician is taking apart a television set in order to recycle parts at this technology center in Katō, Japan.

Mining rock and mineral resources is expensive in terms of both dollars and cost to the environment. While some resources are plentiful, others are in very limited supply. Recycling common materials like aluminum, glass, and steel, as well as less abundant materials such as rare earth elements, is important for both the environment and the economy.

Recycling technicians play a key role in this process. Recycling technicians may carry out a variety of jobs related to recycling. Some recycling technicians work for large businesses, universities, and government offices to create and manage recycling programs and motivate people to recycle. Others work for waste management companies to ensure that recycling is being collected properly and that people who want to recycle have what they need. Some recycling technicians work at recycling plants to make sure the materials are sorted properly.

Language Arts Connection Gather evidence to develop an argument for recycling in a specific community. Do the benefits of recycling outweigh the costs? Research the societal and environmental benefits as well as the financial costs and benefits of recycling in the community. Use reliable sources, such as government agencies, educational institutions, and personal interviews with authorities. When drawing evidence from these sources, ask yourself: Are the facts verifiable—that is, can they be proved to be true? Is the source an expert? Finally, develop your argument and present it to your peers. Be sure to cite specific evidence to support your claims.

| GPS FOR UNDERGROUND MINING | CONFLICT MINERALS | Go online to choose one of these other paths. |

Lesson Self-Check

CAN YOU EXPLAIN IT?

FIGURE 17: A smartphone is composed of many different elements.

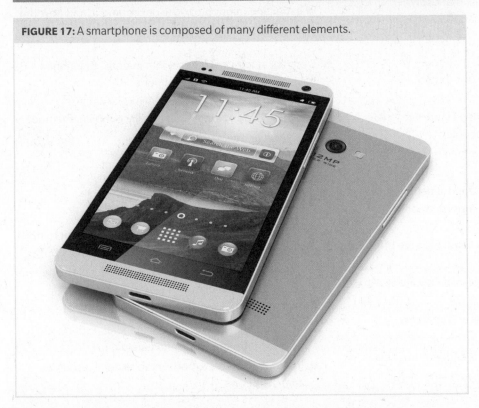

More than 70 different elements are found in the plastic and metal casing, touchscreen, battery, electronics, and circuitry that make up a smartphone. Each of these elements comes from either living things or non-living resources such as rocks and minerals. The silica that makes up the glass and the silicon in the computer chips come from quartz sand. The aluminum that makes the glass shatter resistant comes from an aluminum ore called bauxite.

Rare earth elements used to make the magnets in the speaker and microphone, the mechanism that causes the phone to vibrate, and the bright colors on the screen come from minerals like bastnäsite and monazite, which are found in some igneous rocks. Indium used to make the touchscreen is found in deposits along with copper that is used for wiring and lead used for solder. Tin in the touchscreen and that becomes the solder that binds the components together comes from the mineral cassiterite, which is found in igneous rocks and some sediments. Lithium used in the rechargeable batteries comes from lithium-rich brines and is mined using solar evaporation ponds. The smartphone case can be made of carbon from oil deposits or graphite deposits.

 Explain All elements that make up the products we use every day come from living things, like plants and animals, or non-living resources, such as rocks and minerals. Where do you think the elements that make up a smartphone come from? What rocks and minerals are they found in? What parts of the world do they come from?

Image Credits: (b) ©Scanrail/Getty Images

CHECKPOINTS

Check Your Understanding

1. Which of the following statements about rock and mineral resources is true? Choose all that apply.
   a. There are no valuable minerals in Antarctica.
   b. Rock and mineral resources are distributed evenly across the globe.
   c. Rock and mineral resources are distributed randomly across the globe.
   d. Most of the deposits shown on the Figure 4 resource map were used by prehistoric people.
   e. The cost of extracting valuable minerals is the same everywhere in the world.
   f. The value of a rock and mineral deposit depends on its size, shape, location, and concentration.

2. Which of the following statements about REEs are true? Choose all that apply.
   a. REEs can be mined profitably because they are easy to extract from rocks.
   b. REEs are considered to be critical and strategic minerals in the United State.
   c. The majority of REE production is currently in China.
   d. REEs are extracted from igneous rocks that occur commonly in Earth's crust.

3. The production of REEs has increased more than 1000% since 1965. Which is most likely driving the change in REE production?
   a. Increasing demand for organic foods
   b. Increasing demand for consumer electronics
   c. Increasing demand for better-insulated houses
   d. Increasing demand for drinks in unbreakable containers

4. The change in production of REEs has probably also resulted in which of the following? Choose all that apply.
   a. Increase in the abundance of REEs on Earth
   b. Decrease in water pollution near REE mines
   c. Increase in habitat destruction as a result of mining
   d. Increase in air pollution near mines and processing plants

5. Make a table of the rock and mineral resources that might be used in constructing a house. Include as columns in the table where you are likely to find these resources, how they might be mined or extracted, what the effect of extraction might be on the environment, and how the effects on the environment could be minimized.

6. Describe at least two effects that marine mining may have on the offshore environment.

7. Which of the following is not a surface-mining method?
   a. solar evaportion
   b. hydraulic mining
   c. room-and-pillar mining
   d. strip mining

8. Which of the following statements are true about mineral production in the United States? Choose all that apply.
   a. The United States produces the majority of the mineral resources that it uses.
   b. The United States is a major exporter of REEs.
   c. Among the major suppliers of mineral resources to the United States are China and Canada.
   d. The United States exports more mineral resources than it imports.

9. Which of the following mineral resources can be extracted using the solar evaporation method of mining?
   a. salt (halite)
   b. gold
   c. diamond
   d. copper

10. Which of the following statements are true about mine reclamation in the United State? Choose all that apply.
    a. Mining companies in the United State must set aside money for reclamation in the form of a bond.
    b. To operate a mine in the United State, a mining company must have a reclamation plan.
    c. Open-pit mines are often flooded and turned into recreational lakes.
    d. Mining companies in the United State must comply with a number of environmental laws.

11. Briefly describe how Native Americans used the mineral resources that they mined and quarried.

12. Titanium is light but strong. It has an important use in which of the following applications? Choose all that apply.
   a. joint replacement
   b. rechargeable batteries for hybrid cars
   c. magnets in electronic and medical equipment
   d. aircraft bodies

13. Solution mining is used in which of the following situations?
   a. when there is an ore body with a weak or fractured layer above it
   b. when very hard rock surrounds an ore body
   c. when there is sediment that needs to be loosened using high water pressure
   d. when there are minerals that dissolve easily

14. Which of the following are important reasons why we use REEs in electronics technology today? Choose all that apply.
   a. REEs are extremely light
   b. REEs resist impact and corrosion better than steel
   c. some REEs have luminescent properties
   d. some REEs can be used to make strong magnets

15. Which of the following were important mining localities in the ancient world? Choose all that apply.
   a. Timna, Israel
   b. Las Medulas, Spain
   c. Attica, Greece
   d. Skouriotissa, Cyprus

16. Which of the following are important mineral resources that can be obtained by hydraulic mining? Choose all that apply.
   a. gold
   b. ruby
   c. salt (halite)
   d. manganese

17. Describe some scenarios where people have opposed building a mine at a specific location.

18. List some of the factors that determine which type of mining would be used to extract a specific mineral resource. Use examples of both surface mining methods and subsurface mining methods.

19. Discuss some ways that people can reduce the impact of mineral resource extraction.

20. Explain what is meant by a critical and strategic mineral.

21. Explain how carbon fiber is produced and some of its applications in modern technology.

22. Describe a particular piece of modern technology that you want to build, the properties that you wish the piece to have, and the resources that you would build it from.

MAKE YOUR OWN STUDY GUIDE

 In your Evidence Notebook, design a study guide that supports the main ideas from this lesson:

Remember to include the following in your study guide:
- Support main ideas with details and examples.
- Record explanations for the phenomena you investigated.
- Describe how new technologies can have deep impacts on society and the environment, including some impacts that were not anticipated.
- Explain why science and technology may raise ethical issues for which science, by itself, does not provide answers and solutions.
- Explain why the analysis of costs and benefits is a critical aspect of decisions about technology.

Energy Resources

The Crescent Dunes Solar Energy Plant, located about 225 miles northwest of Las Vegas, can generate energy day and night. It can generate enough electricity to power 75,000 homes.

CAN YOU EXPLAIN IT?

FIGURE 1: Natural gas can be extracted from Earth by the hydraulic fracturing method.

Gather Evidence As you explore the lesson, gather evidence on the pros and cons of different energy resources.

Hydraulic fracturing, also called *fracking*, is the process by which materials are pumped underground to break up rock and release oil or natural gas. The materials include large amounts of water, sand and chemicals. Natural gas and other fossil fuels take millions of years to form and therefore exist in limited amounts. Once a fossil fuel is used, it cannot be quickly replaced.

At this time, most of the energy used in the United States is generated using fossil fuels, such as the natural gas extracted by hydraulic fracturing. The natural gas is used primarily to generate electricity. It also is used to heat about half the homes in the United States. Hydraulic fracturing, however, has troubling environmental consequences that will be discussed in more detail later in this lesson. Does the environmental impact of hydraulic fracturing outweigh the benefit of obtaining natural gas for energy?

Predict How might hydraulic fracturing be used to obtain energy from Earth's subsurface?

Image Credits: (t) ©Ethan Miller/Getty Images ; (b) ©Yaygin/Shutterstock

Petroleum and Natural Gas

Fossil fuels are compounds that contain hydrogen and carbon atoms and formed from the remains of living things. Because of their organic origin, coal, petroleum, and natural gas are known as fossil fuels. Fossil fuels are considered nonrenewable.

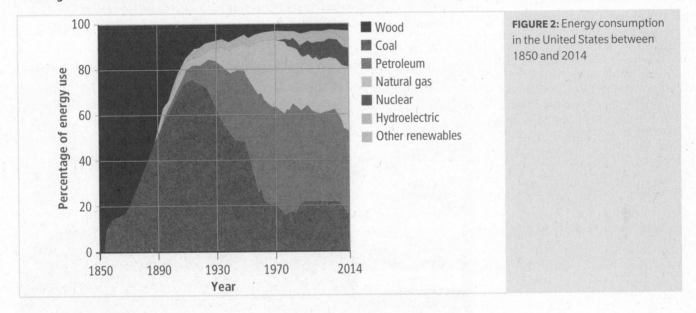

FIGURE 2: Energy consumption in the United States between 1850 and 2014

The Importance of Petroleum and Natural Gas

Petroleum is the largest source of energy used today and is a fundamental component of many consumer and commercial products. The majority of petroleum recovered from Earth is used to produce gasoline and diesel fuels for transportation.

Natural gas is the second largest source of energy used today and accounts for about 24% of energy in the United States. Most natural gas is used to generate electricity, but natural gas is also used for industrial, commercial, and residential applications, such as heating and cooking.

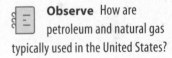 **Observe** How are petroleum and natural gas typically used in the United States?

FIGURE 3: Petroleum products and natural gas uses

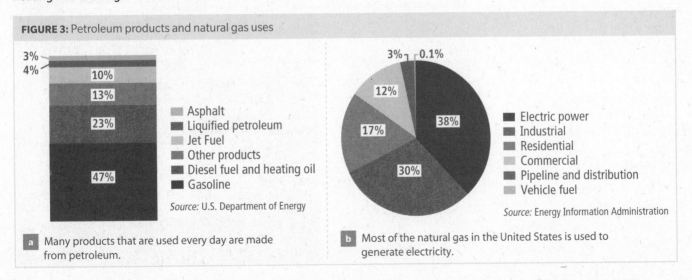

Source: U.S. Department of Energy

Source: Energy Information Administration

a Many products that are used every day are made from petroleum.

b Most of the natural gas in the United States is used to generate electricity.

Petroleum and Natural Gas Reservoirs

Explain What are the conditions necessary to produce a reservoir for petroleum or natural gas?

Petroleum and natural gas form in reservoirs, or pockets, in Earth's interior. Three components are required to produce these reservoirs. The first component is heat. The source rock, rich in organic material, must be located deep enough inside Earth to be subjected to temperatures sufficient to convert the organic carbon into petroleum. The second component is a permeable layer. A porous, permeable reservoir rock, such as sandstone or limestone, which contains pores large enough and with enough connections to serve as storage and migration sites for petroleum to accumulate is needed. The third component is an impermeable layer. A dense layer of rock must be located above the porous permeable layer to prevent petroleum from moving to the surface.

FIGURE 4: Petroleum and natural gas are found in pockets under layers of rock and sediment in Earth's interior.

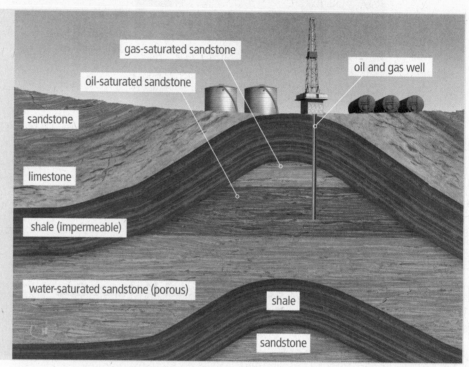

Extracting Petroleum and Natural Gas

FIGURE 5: This cross-section illustrates how carbon dioxide and water can be used to flush residual petroleum from the subsurface between wells during enhanced recovery.

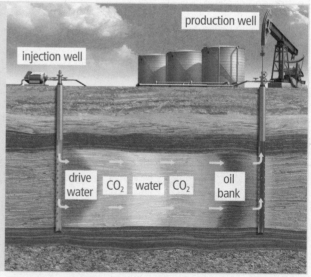

Three techniques are commonly used to extract petroleum and natural gas from Earth's interior. *Primary recovery* relies on underground pressure to drive petroleum to the surface. If the pressure falls, pumps are used to bring petroleum to the surface. During *secondary recovery*, water is injected into the rock to bring petroleum to the surface. In *enhanced recovery*, such as thermal recovery, gas injection and chemical flooding are used to bring the remaining petroleum to the surface.

Predict What are some methods used to extract petroleum and natural gas from the subsurface?

Petroleum and Natural Gas Extraction and the Environment

Extracting fossil fuels, such as petroleum or natural gas, from Earth's interior can affect air quality. Refining petroleum releases toxins into the atmosphere, and oil spills produce environmental hazards.

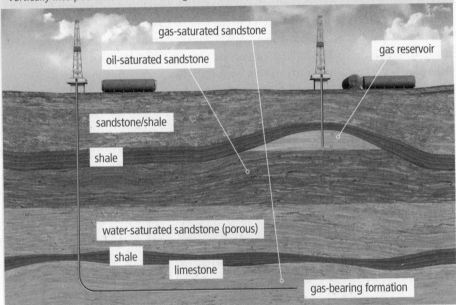
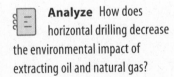

FIGURE 6: Fossil fuels can be extracted from Earth's interior by drilling horizontally as well as vertically into petroleum and natural gas reservoirs.

However, advanced drilling processes can minimize the environmental impact of extracting petroleum from Earth's interior. *Horizontal drilling* begins when a vertical hole is drilled into rock. Drilling is then turned horizontally to exploit a particular rock layer, which yields natural gas more readily and with fewer drill holes. During a process called *multilateral drilling*, the drill hole accesses multiple layers underground to more efficiently remove natural gas by using a single drill hole. *Extended reach drilling* is an advanced process that can cover great distances in the subsurface, which exceed traditional vertical drilling methods. *Complex path drilling* extracts petroleum and natural gas from a single drill well using several routes, which improves well efficiency.

In addition to these drilling processes, other technological innovations such as D and D seismic imaging are also utilized. Advanced imaging improves exploration efficiency by reducing the number of drill holes, minimizing environmental impact.

Analyze How does horizontal drilling decrease the environmental impact of extracting oil and natural gas?

Explain How have drilling technologies advanced to improve the efficiency of natural gas and petroleum extraction from the subsurface?

Coal, Tar Sands, and Oil Shale

The United States obtains 80% of its energy from fossil fuels. Although the extraction, processing, and use of fossil fuels contribute to the job market and the economy, there is a cost. The burning of fossil fuels causes long-term environmental damage by increasing greenhouse gases in the atmosphere, which elevates the average global temperature and reduces water quality. Pollution from fossil fuels can also be a health risk, and over-reliance on fossil fuels can potentially impact international relations and national security.

The Importance of Coal

 Predict How is coal used in various energy outlets?

For centuries, coal has been used to generate energy. Today, coal—the largest domestically produced source of energy in the United States—generates about 50% of the country's electricity. Approximately 900 million tons of coal were mined in 2015. The energy in coal is stored in the bonds of ancient plants that died millions of years ago. Coal is classified into three types: anthracite, bituminous, and lignite. These classifications are based on carbon content and rated from highest to lowest. Coal with the highest carbon content (anthracite) produces the most heat energy when burned.

World Coal Consumption, 2007

FIGURE 7: The circle graph shows the percentages of uses for coal.

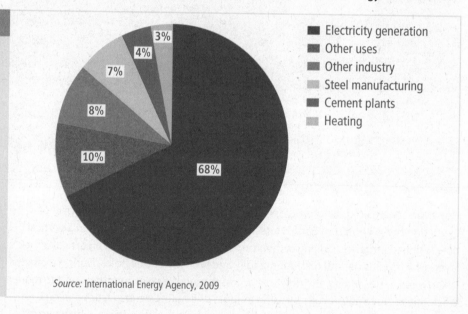

- Electricity generation
- Other uses
- Other industry
- Steel manufacturing
- Cement plants
- Heating

Source: International Energy Agency, 2009

Coal Extraction

 Predict What are the differences and similarities between strip mining and open-pit coal mining?

Surface mining processes to extract coal include strip mining, open-pit mining, and mountaintop removal mining. During these processes, the topsoil, vegetation, and rock are removed and placed to the side, which exposes the coal deposit at the surface. Strip mining is commonly conducted on fairly flat terrain in order to expose coal in long strips. Open-pit mines are large pits that are dug using heavy machinery to expose seams of coal. Mountaintop removal mining involves removing up to 1000 vertical feet of vegetation and rock from a mountain to expose the coal.

FIGURE 8: Coal is extracted from the surface using (a) mountaintop removal mining or from the subsurface using (b) longwall mining.

a Mountaintop removal coal mining

b Longwall mining

Coal can also be mined underground. Room-and-pillar mining uses machines to dig into Earth's surface. Large rooms are excavated along the coal seam. Some of the excess rock that is removed is used to support the room to prevent cave-ins. Coal is loaded onto shuttle cars, which transport the coal to the surface. Longwall mining uses mechanized shearers to cut pits into the earth. Long walls up to 600 feet wide are cut along the coal seam, allowing for up to 80% of coal removal. Temporary hydraulic roof supports are then used to hold up the roof during coal extraction.

Coal Mining and the Environment

All three types of coal contain sulfur, which is a major source of environmental pollution. Coal mining also results in land disturbance, soil erosion, noise pollution, water pollution (acid mine drainage), and mine subsidence. Acid mine drainage is caused by the outflow of acidic water from coal mines.

Only with careful planning and implementation of pollution-control measures, monitoring, and reclamation can the negative impact of coal mining on the environment be minimized.

 Analyze What are some of the environmental consequences of coal mining?

Problem Solving

Mountaintop Removal Coal Mining

Mountaintop removal coal mining is a process for mining coal in which all or a portion of a mountain is removed so that one or more seams of coal may be extracted. The removal of the rock that makes up the mountain is accomplished with explosives, and the rock that is broken up is placed in adjacent valleys. This type of mining has generated controversy because of its effects on water quality and on the terrestrial environment. Water-quality problems include the degradation of streams from toxic chemicals and the potentially lethal consequences to organisms, such as fish and birds. Terrestrial impacts include forest loss and fragmentation, soil loss, loss of biodiversity, and negative health effects on humans.

The Importance of Tar Sands and Oil Shale

Tar sands and oil shale offer new reserves of petroleum that have only recently become available through advances in drilling technologies. Tar sand contains bitumen, a thick, sticky substance that does not flow like petroleum. Tar sands can be mined and processed to extract the petroleum-rich bitumen, which is then refined into oil. Much of the world's petroleum is found in the subsurface as tar sands. Tar sands are found in the United States, specifically in eastern Utah along public lands.

Oil shale is a sedimentary rock that contains kerogen, a solid bituminous material. The kerogen formed millions of years ago when organic matter was deposited with fine-grained sediment on lake and ocean floors. The kerogen that is locked in the rock is released as hydrocarbons when the rock is heated. The largest deposits of oil shale in the world are found in portions of Colorado, Utah, and Wyoming. This oil reserve is not readily accessible; the recovery of oil from oil shale comes at a relatively high cost. In addition, numerous regulations prevent the leasing of land for oil shale production.

Extracting Tar Sands and Oil Shale

Because bitumen cannot be pumped from the ground like traditional petroleum reservoirs, it must be mined. Near-surface tar sands can be accessed by open-pit mining. Similar to mining for coal, open-pit mining for tar sands requires the removal of the topsoil, vegetation, and rock layers to expose the sticky tar sand layer. The tar sand is extracted and sent to an onsite facility. There the sticky sand is mixed with hot water and shaken to separate the bitumen from the sand. The bitumen floats to the surface. It is skimmed off and mixed with chemicals so it can be processed further.

Gather Evidence How do oil shale and tar sands differ from petroleum?

FIGURE 9: (a) Tar sands and (b) oil shale offer two reserves of fossil fuels that can be exploited as an energy resource.

a Hand sample of tar sands

b Oil shale outcrop

FIGURE 10: The process of recovering oil from tar sand requires steam injection (stage 1), followed by time for the steam to heat the viscous oil (stage 2). Once the oil has been heated, it, together with condensed steam, is pumped to the surface (stage 3).

stage 1 stage 2 stage 3

Subsurface mining techniques include steam injection, solvent injection, and firefloods. During steam injection, two wells are drilled deep into the subsurface to reach the tar sand reservoir. Steam is then injected into one well to heat the sand and release the bitumen. The second well is used to bring the bitumen to the surface. Steam injection is the method most commonly used to extract bitumen from subsurface reservoirs.

For solvent injection, two wells are drilled into the tar sand reservoir. A solvent is then mixed with the steam that is injected into one well, while the bitumen that is released is pumped to the surface through the second well. During firefloods, compressed air is injected into a well and partially burned to provide heat to reduce the viscosity of the bitumen, allowing it to flow in advance of the approaching fire toward the second well. The bitumen is then pumped to the surface.

Hydraulic fracturing is a common practice employed to remove natural gas from the subsurface of Earth. During hydraulic fracturing, a well is drilled into the subsurface into a rock unit that potentially contains natural gas. However, the subsurface rock is not permeable, which makes it impossible to pump the gas out using normal practices. So, a steel pipe, called a casing, is inserted into the well. The pipe contains holes, and millions of gallons of water, sand, and chemicals are released through the pipe and pumped into Earth's interior. These substances are injected into specific regions of the surrounding rock, causing it to break or fracture, releasing any gas that may be contained within the rock.

Explain What happens during the process of hydraulic fracturing?

FIGURE 11: In hydraulic fracturing, fluid is injected into a well to produce pressure that cracks or fractures the rock. The fractures enable the extraction of petroleum and natural gas. (a) Gun charges blast holes through the well casing and the surrounding rock. (b) Sand, water, and chemicals are pumped in at high pressure to fracture the rock further. (c) Sand particles prop the cracks open. Gas escapes through the cracks and flows up to the surface.

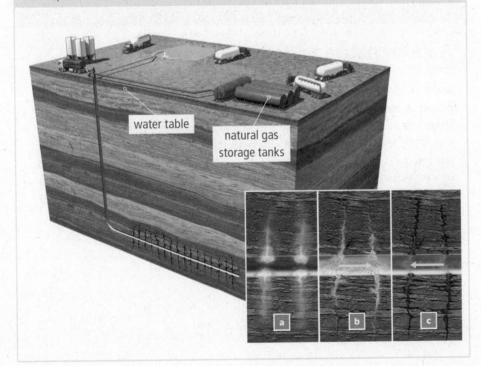

water table

natural gas storage tanks

a   b   c

Extracting Petroleum from Tar Sands and Oil Shale

Mining tar sands and oil shale can have serious environmental consequences. The mining processes used to extract tar sands from the subsurface disrupt the surrounding landscape and ecosystems. One gallon of gasoline refined from tar sands produces more carbon dioxide than one gallon of gasoline produced from conventional petroleum. The extraction and refining processes require three times more water than conventional petroleum extraction processes do. Every gallon of gasoline produced from tar sands requires about six gallons of fresh water. Most of this water contains toxic chemicals that are harmful to human health and the environment.

The environmental consequences of extracting oil shale from the subsurface parallel those for tar sands. The extraction process disturbs landscapes, negatively affecting the surrounding plants and animals. In addition, the extraction process requires large amounts of water. Refining oil shale is energy intensive and produces an estimated three times as many greenhouse gas emissions as refining petroleum does.

 Model How is petroleum extracted from oil shales?

Similar to oil shale and tar sand extraction, hydraulic fracturing also affects the landscape and water quality. Many of the chemicals used during the fracturing process are toxic to people and animals. These chemicals have been shown to affect respiratory, gastrointestinal, nervous, immune, cardiovascular, and endocrine systems. It takes only a small amount of fracturing chemicals to contaminate watersheds, groundwater, and soil. The hydraulic fracturing chemicals also affect air quality, which can result in headaches, dizziness, insomnia, nausea, blurred vision, and even blindness. In addition, the disposal of hydraulic fracturing fluids, which contain heavy metals, radionuclides, organics, and brines used during the extraction process, poses a serious health risk.

 Engineering

An Alternative to Hydraulic Fracturing

A new process is now under development that involves using electric heaters placed in deep vertical holes that have been drilled through a section of oil shale. The oil shale is heated until it reaches a temperature between 345 °C and 370 °C (650 °F and 700 °F), at which point oil is released from the shale. The released oil is gathered in collection wells within the heated zone. A freeze zone of refrigerated fluid is established around the perimeter of the area to be mined so that no groundwater enters the perimeter and no hydrocarbons are released from the perimeter.

 Explain What are the various techniques used to extract coal, bitumen (in tar sand), and kerogen (in oil shale) from the subsurface?

Solar and Wind Energy

Many types of energy resources are continually replenished and never run out. These resources are called renewable resources. Most renewable energy comes directly from natural resources such as the sun, the wind, the tides, moving water, and Earth's internal heat energy.

Active vs. Passive Solar Energy Systems

The sun is the primary source of energy on planet Earth. In fact, the amount of energy Earth absorbs from the sun in one hour is more energy than is actually used by everyone on the planet in one year. Solar power is a renewable energy source derived from the sun that can be used to provide heat and electricity.

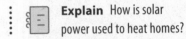

Explain How is solar power used to heat homes?

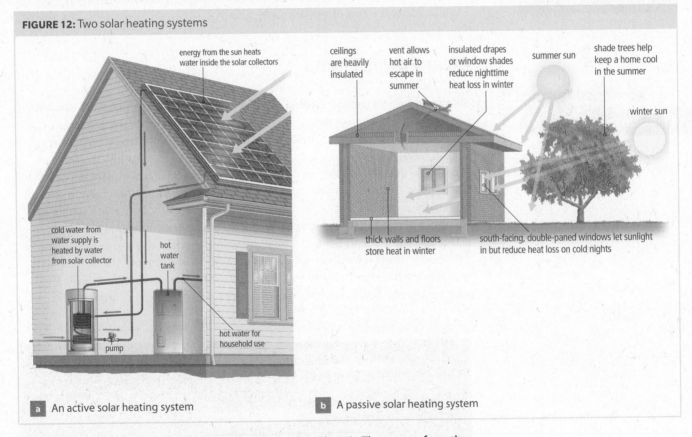

FIGURE 12: Two solar heating systems

energy from the sun heats water inside the solar collectors

cold water from water supply is heated by water from solar collector

hot water tank

hot water for household use

pump

ceilings are heavily insulated

vent allows hot air to escape in summer

insulated drapes or window shades reduce nighttime heat loss in winter

summer sun

shade trees help keep a home cool in the summer

winter sun

thick walls and floors store heat in winter

south-facing, double-paned windows let sunlight in but reduce heat loss on cold nights

a An active solar heating system

b A passive solar heating system

Active solar heating systems use solar energy to heat liquid or air. The energy from the sun is transferred to the fluid, which then carries it into a home or building. Passive solar heating takes advantage of a building's location, landscaping, and building materials to minimize energy use. A passive solar building reduces heating and cooling loads through energy-efficient strategies, such as window orientation, which can affect how much heat enters the building.

Analyze What are the pros and cons of solar energy?

FIGURE 13: Many residents install solar voltaic technology on their homes to harness the power of the sun.

Explore Online ▶

Hands-On Lab

Solar Cooker Design and build a solar cooker.

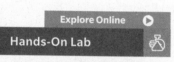

Analyze How do photovoltaic systems compare to solar power plants?

Photovoltaic Cells

Photovoltaic technology is used to convert visible light into electrical energy. Photovoltaics are composed of cells, which are connected to form chains that boost power output. The power is amplified further when chains are aligned in arrays. One or more arrays are connected to the electrical grid, which completes the photovoltaic system. This energy is then transferred to residents. Many states that receive consistent sunlight, such as California or Nevada, have greatly benefited from solar power.

Solar technologies offer clean energy that is available as long as the sun shines. This technology is easy to install. While the cost of solar technology is decreasing, it is not inexpensive. Some states offer tax credits to offset installation costs. In addition, excess energy that is generated from residential photovoltaic systems is returned to the electrical grid and offered as a credit to customers. The maintenance cost of photovoltaic systems is low compared to other systems.

One of the greatest limitations of solar energy is the intermittency and unpredictability of solar energy during different seasons. In order to maintain a continuous supply of energy based solely on solar power, batteries are required to store the energy—this can also add to the cost of a solar energy system.

Solar Power Plants

Solar power plants consist of a field of mirrors called *heliostats* that capture sunlight and heat a synthetic oil or salt, which is used to heat water. The water produces steam that turns a turbine to produce electricity that is transmitted by power lines to customers. While the installation of a solar power plant is expensive, it is far more economical than the installation of a new, cleaner, coal-fired power plant or nuclear power plant. In addition, solar power plants do not require additional fuels to operate, making them one of the cheapest power plants to run. Solar power costs as little as 1.14 cents per unit, compared to coal power that costs 4 cents per unit or nuclear power that costs 2 cents per unit. Like photovoltaic systems, the greatest drawback to solar power plants is when sunlight is limited. To sustain electricity, the power plants maintain a natural-gas boiler to ensure energy is available during cloudy days. Also, solar technology is still in its infancy, with maximum solar efficiency around 25%.

FIGURE 14: The Crescent Dunes Solar Energy Plant located in Nevada

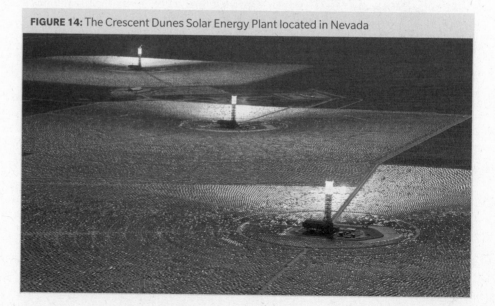

Power from the Wind

Earth's surface is not a uniform temperature. The differential heating around the planet produces pockets of high pressure and low pressure. Air moves along these pressure gradients from high to low, producing wind. Wind is a renewable energy resource that will continue to blow as long as the sun shines. Wind turbines harvest wind energy. Wind turns the blades of a wind turbine, which is attached to an internal shaft that turns a generator and produces electricity. This electricity is funneled through a centralized substation, then transmitted to homes, businesses, and schools.

 Explain How does a wind turbine generate electricity?

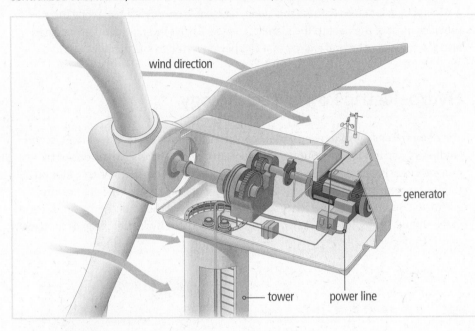

wind direction

generator

tower power line

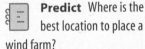

FIGURE 15: Wind turns the blades of the turbine, which spins a shaft connected to an electric generator.

Farming the Wind

Interest in harnessing the power of wind as an energy source originated in the 1970s around the same time the oil market fluctuated. Since then, the United States has made inroads into developing technologies to efficiently harvest wind power to generate electricity. The location of a wind farm is important because wind speed and duration must be fairly constant to be effective. Wind farms are often located on the top of smooth, rounded hills; on flat, open plains; along shorelines; or in mountain gaps where wind is funneled through a pass. Ideal conditions should produce a wind with a velocity of at least 23 km per hour (14 mph). Wind speeds that exceed this value can be dangerous for the windmills. When wind speed is too high, the windmill must be shut down to prevent damage. Most wind plants in the United States are privately owned. The wind-produced electricity is sold to the electric companies, where it is transmitted onto electrical grids and made available to the public.

The biggest drawback of wind-produced electricity is a limitation in the current electrical grid system in the United States. The transmission lines in the current grid system are too small to carry the heavy loads of energy produced by wind farms over a long distance.

Predict Where is the best location to place a wind farm?

FIGURE 16: A wind farm

Analyze What are the benefits of a wind farm?

Hydroelectric, Tidal, and Geothermal Energy

Solar and wind are the two most common forms of renewable energy. However, there are other types of renewable energy that also can be beneficial. Hydroelectric energy converts the energy in moving water into electricity. Tidal energy also harnesses the energy of moving water—tides are more predictable than wind, and new technologies are being developed to harness this clean, renewable energy source. While the sun provides most of the heat to the planet's surface, Earth's interior (geothermal heat) also produces geothermal energy that can be converted to electricity.

Hydroelectric Power Technology

The potential energy of moving water is powerful. Water can erode sediment, scour landforms, and is mighty enough to produce electricity. The energy produced by moving water is called hydroelectric power. Similar to windmills, moving water pushes turbines that power electrical generators. The generators convert the energy into electricity. Hydroelectric power accounts for about 7% of the total energy production in the United States. Idaho, Washington, and Oregon use hydroelectricity as their main power source.

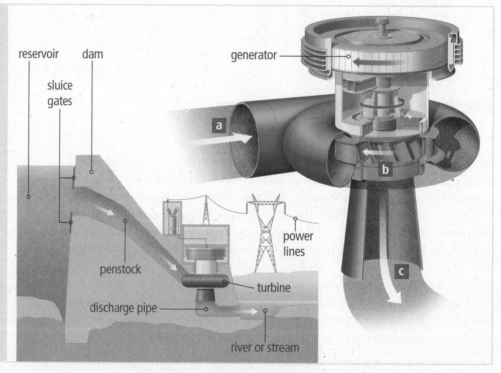

FIGURE 17: Hydroelectric power plants use moving water to run turbines. (a) The water supply flows down a channel (the penstock) from the reservoir. (b) Flowing water turns the turbine, which then turns the generator that generates electricity. (c) Water is discharged into a river or stream.

Explain How is the energy in moving water converted into electricity?

To produce hydroelectric power, a dam is built on a large river that has a significant drop in elevation. The dam stores water behind it in a reservoir. Near the bottom of the dam wall, water flows through a water intake. Gravity causes the water to fall through the penstock, a channel for conveying water to a waterwheel or turbine inside the dam. At the end of the penstock, moving water is forced through a turbine propeller. The shaft of the turbine is attached to the generator, which produces the electricity. Power lines are connected to the generator.

Pros and Cons of Hydroelectric Power

Hydroelectric power is beneficial because it is a clean, renewable energy resource that does not pollute the air, water, or land. Hydroelectric power is one of the cheapest and most efficient methods of producing electricity, and it can easily and rapidly meet peak demands for electricity in a region. In addition, hydroelectric power plants, once built, have fairly low operating costs.

Analyze How does construction of a dam affect the surrounding landscape and ecosystems?

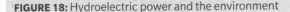

FIGURE 18: Hydroelectric power and the environment

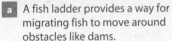

a A fish ladder provides a way for migrating fish to move around obstacles like dams.

b This lake in the Khao Sok National Park in Thailand was created after a dam was built.

However, building a dam to produce hydroelectric power has its drawbacks. The construction of a dam is very expensive. A dam can affect the surrounding environment by altering the landscape and preventing the normal flow of a river. A dam can also affect water quality and interfere with the migration of organisms upstream in a river. Additionally, dams can flood large areas of land.

Tidal Power Technology

Tidal stream power plants harness the energy produced in the tides. These systems work on the principle of kinetic energy produced by flowing water. As the tide rises, water enters a bay behind a dam. The gate then closes at high tide. The gate opens at low tide, and the water in the bay rushes through, turning a turbine that generates electricity. Tidal power is only limited by the number of available sites where tidal barriers can be placed.

Explain How is tidal barrier electricity similar to hydroelectric power?

FIGURE 19: Tidal barriers are constructed along a coastline with a large tidal range to take advantage of the power in moving water.

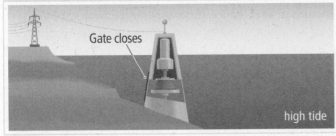

Gate closes

high tide

Gate opens

low tide

The Pros and Cons of Tidal Power

Predict What are the pros and cons of geothermal energy?

Tidal energy is a clean, renewable energy resource. It requires no fuel, so it is emission free. Tidal power is highly efficient and has a predictable output. In addition, tidal barriers can double as storm-surge barriers. Unfortunately, a tidal barrage plant is very costly to build and maintain. In fact, only a few plants are actually operating around the world. The placement of a tidal barrage plant requires a coastal area with an extreme range of high and low tides. The plants also have a profound, often negative, effect on the surrounding environment. Tidal power stations can decrease the salinity of tidal basins and can kill marine life.

FIGURE 20: The Sihwa Lake Tidal Power Station in South Korea was completed in 2011 at a cost of $355 million. The facility uses 10 submerged turbines.

Geothermal Power Technology

Explain What is geothermal energy?

Geothermal energy is energy derived from the heat of Earth. Geothermal energy can be tapped in areas of volcanic activity, as well as in geysers and hot springs, and can be recovered in several ways. The first is by direct use, where hot water from the subsurface is used to heat buildings. This process is used for buildings in Iceland. The second process used to tap geothermal energy is by the use of geothermal heat pumps. Air or antifreeze is pumped through pipes buried in the subsurface and the heated fluid is circulated through a building.

A geothermal power plant uses steam produced from superheated water in Earth's interior to rotate a turbine. The turbine activates a generator to produce electricity.

The United States is a global leader in installed geothermal capacity. Eighty percent of this capacity is located in California, where more than 40 geothermal plants provide nearly 7% of the state's electricity. In 2015, United States geothermal power plants accounted for 0.4% of the country's energy needs.

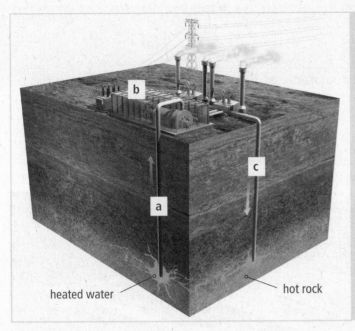

FIGURE 21: Geothermal power plants generate electricity according to the following process: (a) steam rises through a well; (b) steam drives turbines, which generate electricity; (c) leftover liquid water is pumped back into the hot rock.

heated water   hot rock

The Pros and Cons of Geothermal Power

Geothermal energy is a clean, renewable resource powered by the natural radioactive decay of elements in Earth's interior. Unlike wind and solar, it is virtually unlimited and can be used to heat and cool buildings. Geothermal energy requires no fuel and is almost emission free, and it produces a low carbon footprint. The drawbacks to geothermal energy are the limited locations where it can be accessed; a minimum temperature of 175 °C (350 °F) is required in the subsurface to generate electricity. Long-distance transmission tends to be inefficient and results in significant losses. Geothermal power also uses a large amount of water, and construction of power plants is costly.

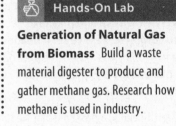

Explore Online ▶

🧪 **Hands-On Lab**

Generation of Natural Gas from Biomass Build a waste material digester to produce and gather methane gas. Research how methane is used in industry.

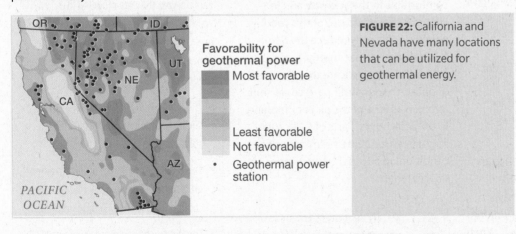

Favorability for geothermal power
- Most favorable

- Least favorable
- Not favorable
- • Geothermal power station

FIGURE 22: California and Nevada have many locations that can be utilized for geothermal energy.

Predict What are the pros and cons of geothermal energy?

Explain How does geothermal energy, hydroelectric energy, and tidal energy compare to solar or wind energy?

Guided Research

Harnessing the Power of the Sun

Is active solar power the only "real" solar power? Can passive solar technology also help to conserve Earth's fossil fuels and protect our environment? Researchers are investigating many ways to utilize the sun's energy.

Engineers are working to build bigger and better solar power plants. Someday, active solar power could replace coal or nuclear power. However, presently, the development of the complex systems needed to efficiently harness solar power and produce enough electricity to meet global demands is very expensive and may take decades to complete. Passive solar heating offers a low-tech, less expensive approach to solar energy and may be better suited for immediate use.

Traditionally, a passive solar heating system includes a thermal mass that stores heat, such as a thick concrete wall or barrels of water. These materials, however, are bulky, take up space, and may soon be obsolete. Researchers are testing thermal-mass materials that are up to 14 times more efficient at storing and transferring heat. These materials have been used to make a new product called a phase-change wallboard.

A phase change occurs when the state, or phase, of matter—solid, liquid, or gas—changes. Researchers have incorporated materials, such as paraffin wax, into normal gypsum drywall. When the outside temperature rises, the material in the wallboard slowly melts but remains at a constant temperature

FIGURE 23: This sunken house, built in the Chiltern Hills of England, has grass planted on the roof and the largest sliding glass doors in the world.

until it is entirely melted. It absorbs the sun's energy without getting hotter. At night, when the air outside cools, the material radiates heat while returning to its solid state. Phase-change wallboard can keep temperatures inside a building comfortable in the summer and in winter. Widespread use of this product would significantly reduce the demand for coal and nuclear energy. Simulations in Dallas, Texas, indicate that the use of phase-change wallboard could shift as much as 90% of the air conditioning to off-peak hours. Parts of California might even be able to eliminate air conditioning altogether by using this material.

 Analyze How can a simple change to a common building material help to reduce the demand for electricity?

Language Arts Connection Brainstorm a plan to simulate a model of phase-change solar-energy technology. Your simulation should include the following concepts, and you should explain how they are modeled in a written report. The simulation can be in the form of a computer model, a video, a mathematical model, a conceptual model, or a hands-on activity.

- The simulation should model a cost-saving technological approach to solar energy.

- The technology can be an improvement on traditional passive solar heating and cooling using phase-change materials.

- The phase-change material may be applied to walls, windows, ceilings, flooring, or attic insulation.

 FRANCE CUTS NUCLEAR POWER   **OIL WELL**   Go online to choose one of these other paths.

Lesson Self-Check

CAN YOU EXPLAIN IT?

FIGURE 24: A station that uses hydraulic fracturing to obtain natural gas

Both renewable and nonrenewable energy resources have both advantages and disadvantages in terms of their extraction and use. For instance, hydraulic fracturing is a method now used to extract natural gas from a specific rock unit in the subsurface. The rock that makes up the subsurface rock unit is impermeable, which means it is impossible to remove natural gas from the rock using conventional drilling methods. Instead, a steel pipe or casing is inserted into the well. This pipe contains a series of holes. A tremendous amount of water, sand, and chemicals is pumped through the pipe into the area of the subsurface where gas is contained in the rock. These substances are injected through the pipe into the rock, causing the rock to fracture and releasing petroleum and natural gas in the process. Therefore, the major benefit of hydraulic fracturing is that it allows access to natural gas in a way that is not available through traditional drilling. This will allow countries such as the United States to reduce their dependency on foreign petroleum sources. In addition, hydraulic fracturing is creating more new jobs.

Some disadvantages of hydraulic fracturing involve the chemicals used in the process. These chemicals can be toxic to both people and animals. They can also contaminate watersheds, groundwater, and soil. Because hydraulic fracturing uses so much water, it may also lead to a decrease in water supplies.

Analyze What environmental implications are associated with hydraulic fracturing to obtain petroleum and natural gas from the subsurface?

Explain Refer to the notes in your Evidence Notebook to explain the technology used in the hydraulic fracturing method of extracting petroleum and natural gas from oil shale.

Image Credits: ©Yarygin/Shutterstock

CHECKPOINTS

Check Your Understanding

1. What characteristic makes an energy resource renewable?
   a. It formed millions of years ago.
   b. It comes from nature.
   c. It is replenished every day.
   d. It does not pollute the environment.

2. Which technique is used to recover natural gas from the subsurface?
   a. Open-pit mines are dug.
   b. A vertical hole is drilled.
   c. Room-and-pillar mining is used.
   d. Longwall mining is used.

3. What additional step is required to recover bitumen from tar sands in the subsurface?
   a. Open-pit mines are dug.
   b. The resource is heated with steam or liberated with solvent.
   c. The bitumen is diluted before refining.
   d. Lateral drilling is performed.

4. How do new drilling methods for petroleum improve fossil fuel extraction efficiency and reduce the impact on the environment?

5. What technology is used to obtain energy from renewable resources? Choose all that apply.
   a. photovoltaic cells
   b. synthetic oil
   c. wind moving blades
   d. D models

6. Compare the pros and cons of using different renewable energy resources.

7. How might life be affected if all fossil fuels were no longer available?

8. Explain the process by which energy from tides is used to produce electricity.

9. What are the top three fossil fuels used for energy production in order from most used to least used?
   a. coal, petroleum, natural gas
   b. coal, wood, petroleum
   c. natural gas, wood, coal
   d. petroleum, coal, natural gas

10. Why might Las Vegas, Nevada, benefit from solar energy more than Portland, Oregon?

11. What factors might a community consider if it wanted to build a windmill farm in the area to offset energy needs with clean, renewable energy?

12. Which of the following substances is used to bring petroleum to the surface during secondary recovery?
    a. CO_2
    b. water
    c. steam
    d. solvent

13. Which of the following is a benefit of building a hydrothermal electric plant?
    a. Hydroelectric plants do not have to placed at specific locations.
    b. Hydroelectric plants are powered by the natural radioactive decay of elements.
    c. Hydroelectric plants can be used as storm-surge barriers.
    d. Hydrothermal electric plants have fairly low operating costs.

14. The world's largest source of oil shale is located in which of the following countries?
    a. Canada
    b. United States
    c. China
    d. Mexico

15. Which of the following is the biggest drawback to the use of wind energy in the United States?
    a. Transmission lines are too small to carry heavy loads.
    b. Very few locations have adequate wind velocity.
    c. Most wind farms are privately owned.
    d. Wind-produced energy is sold to electric companies.

16. Hydraulic fracturing is a method used to bring which of the following resources to Earth's surface? Choose all that apply.

   a. petroleum

   b. bitumen

   c. natural gas

   d. kerogen

17. Which of the following renewable energy resources are dependent on location for their success? Choose all that apply.

   a. hydroelectric energy

   b. solar energy

   c. wind energy

   d. geothermal energy

18. Which of the following components are necessary to produce petroleum and natural gas reservoirs? Choose all that apply.

   a. water

   b. heat

   c. a permeable layer

   d. an impermeable layer

19. Which of the following statements are true about a passive solar energy system? Choose all that apply.

   a. It uses solar energy to heat liquid or air.

   b. It takes advantage of a building's location, landscape, and building materials to minimize energy use.

   c. It reduces heating and cooling loads through energy-efficient strategies.

   d. It transfers energy from the sun to a fluid, where it is then carried into a home or building.

20. The most important use of petroleum is to produce

   a. diesel fuel and heating oil.

   b. jet fuel.

   c. asphalt.

   d. gasoline.

21. Which of the following is the most important use of coal?

   a. electricity generation

   b. steel manufacturing

   c. heating

   d. cement production

22. Which of the following nonrenewable energy resources are used primarily for the generation of electricity? Choose all that apply.

   a. coal

   b. petroleum

   c. nuclear energy

   d. natural gas

23. Explain how solar power plants produce electricity.

24. Describe the process by which petroleum is extracted from tar sands.

25. Describe some of the environmental problems that can potentially be caused by the use of hydraulic fracturing.

26. Explain where wind farms must be located to capture a sufficient wind velocity to help generate electricity.

27. Explain why states like California and Nevada are good locations to construct geothermal energy plants.

28. Describe the process of longwall coal mining.

29. Explain how mountaintop removal coal mining is different from open-pit coal mining.

MAKE YOUR OWN STUDY GUIDE

 In your Evidence Notebook, design a study guide that supports the main ideas in this lesson:

- The different extraction methods and uses of fossil fuels can pose environmental risks.
- There are environmental risks and practical limitations associated with renewable energy resources.
- Technological innovations can minimize the impacts of extracting resources.

Remember to include the following information in your study guide:

- Use examples that model main ideas.
- Record explanations for the phenomena you investigated.
- Use evidence to support your explanations. Your support can include drawings, data, graphs, laboratory conclusions, and other evidence recorded throughout the lesson.

A BOOK EXPLAINING
COMPLEX IDEAS USING
ONLY THE 1000 MOST
COMMON WORDS

STUFF IN THE EARTH WE CAN BURN

How we get things we need out of the ground

You've explored rock, mineral, and energy resources that are essential to life on Earth. What methods have humans devised to find and extract those valuable resources from deep inside Earth?

RANDALL MUNROE
XKCD.COM

THE STORY OF HOW LIVING THINGS GET POWER

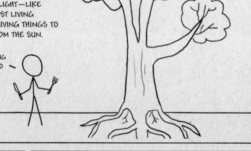

ALMOST ALL LIVING THINGS ARE POWERED BY THE SUN. SOME LIVING THINGS GET THEIR POWER STRAIGHT FROM THE SUN'S LIGHT—LIKE TREES, AND SOME THINGS THAT GROW IN THE SEA. MOST LIVING THINGS THAT DON'T EAT THE SUN'S LIGHT EAT OTHER LIVING THINGS TO GET *THEIR* POWER. IN THE END, THE POWER COMES FROM THE SUN.

LOOKS PRETTY DRY. I'M GOING TO NEED A LOT OF WATER TO EAT THE WHOLE THING!

WHEN THINGS DIE, SOME OF THAT POWER IS LEFT IN THEIR REMAINS, WHICH IS WHY YOU CAN GET POWER OUT OF DEAD TREES BY BURNING THEM. SOMETIMES, IF DEAD THINGS DON'T BURN OR GET EATEN, THEY GO INTO THE GROUND WITH THAT POWER STILL INSIDE THEM.

SO WHEN DO I GET THE POWER?

OVER A LONG TIME, UNDER THE WEIGHT AND HEAT OF THE EARTH, HUGE NUMBERS OF THESE REMAINS CAN CHANGE INTO DIFFERENT KINDS OF ROCKS, WATER, OR AIR . . . BUT EVEN AS THEY CHANGE, THEY HOLD ON TO THEIR POWER. WHEN WE FIND THESE REMAINS, WE CAN BURN THEM, AND GET ALL THAT POWER—GATHERED FROM THE SUN OVER HUGE STRETCHES OF TIME—AT ONCE.

— HOW DO I GET IT?

WHEN WE FIRST BUILT MACHINES POWERED BY FIRE, WE BURNED WOOD FROM THE FORESTS OF OUR TIME. WHEN THOSE WEREN'T ENOUGH, WE STARTED BURNING THE FORESTS OF THE PAST. ONE DAY, THOSE WILL RUN OUT, TOO, AND WE'LL HAVE TO GET POWER SOMEWHERE NEW— LIKE STRAIGHT FROM THE SUN, OR THE EARTH'S HEAT.

THAT CAN'T BE RIGHT . . .

BUT WE MAY HAVE TO CHANGE THE KIND OF POWER WE USE SOON, BEFORE WE FINISH BURNING ALL THE STUFF IN THE GROUND. IT TURNS OUT BURNING THAT STUFF IS CHANGING OUR AIR, IN A WAY THAT'S MAKING THE WORLD HOTTER. IF WE USE UP ALL THE BLACK ROCKS, FIRE WATER, AND FIRE AIR, THE PROBLEM IT MAKES MAY BE TOO BIG FOR US.

— IS THAT POWER?

HOW WE GET BLACK ROCKS OUT OF THE GROUND

If the rocks aren't very deep, we can make holes under the ground and carry them up with machines. This is how we used to get most of the rocks we burned.

As we built bigger earth-moving machines, we learned to just move all the trees and land out of the way to get the rocks.

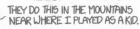

THEY DO THIS IN THE MOUNTAINS NEAR WHERE I PLAYED AS A KID.

Some rocks are inside mountains, so some companies have started blowing up the tops of the mountains so they can get the rocks out more easily.

HOW WE GET FIRE WATER AND FIRE AIR OUT OF THE GROUND

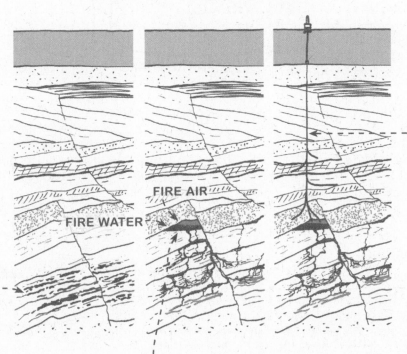

FIRE AIR

FIRE WATER

We make holes looking for places where lots of things died. When we find a pool, we push a stick down and pull up all the fire air and fire water.

Over time, some dead things slowly turn to fire water and fire air.

These are both lighter than rocks and rise up through tiny holes. When they reach a rock with no holes, they form pools, with the lighter air on top.

STUFF IN THE EARTH WE CAN BURN

This kind of work leaves pools full of heavy metals and strange kinds of water that was used to get the black rocks out. Sometimes you can notice the bright colors of these pools from the air. When companies are done making holes, they often leave the pools behind. People worry about whether the stuff in the pools could be bad for us. Sometimes birds land in the pools and die.

BLACK ROCKS

HOLES

One reason we make holes that bend is so we can reach under cities without bothering people.

Layers of rock from different times

HOW DEEP?

We can only get black rocks easily if they're not too deep in the ground. The biggest problem is that deeper in Earth, rocks are hotter. It's hard to get a lot of rock up out of the ground, and if the rocks are too hot, that makes everything so hard that it's not worth it.

There are other problems. You need to cut big rooms into the ground to get black rocks out, and it's hard to hold the roof up when there's so much rock piled up on it. Sometimes the roof falls, and people die.

STRANGE SHAPE

When a sea dries up, it leaves lots of this white stuff behind. Sometimes, the stuff gets covered in dirt and sand.

When the layers above the white stuff get heavier, it can make the white stuff start to rise up and push through the layers above. It looks like paint drops falling from a ceiling but going up.

ROCK BREAKING

Big, easy-to-reach pools of fire water are getting harder to find, so we've been trying new ideas for getting it from the ground. We've found that sometimes, rock has fire water or air you can burn stuck in it. To get it out, we push water into the ground so hard that it makes the rocks break. Then we push in small rocks or glass to hold the breaks open, and the fire water and fire air come out through the openings.

Making all these holes in the rock might mean that when we drink water, we'll also drink whatever stuff they use to get fire water out, since everything can run through the new holes in the rock.

Go online for more about *Thing Explainer*.

WHITE STUFF

This is white stuff, like what we put on food to make it better (although we mostly get the kind we eat from drying out sea-water). We make holes like this to get white stuff out, then we put it on our roads to get rid of snow and ice.

We sometimes use the spaces we leave behind to hold stuff, like fire water or fire air that we want to save to burn later.

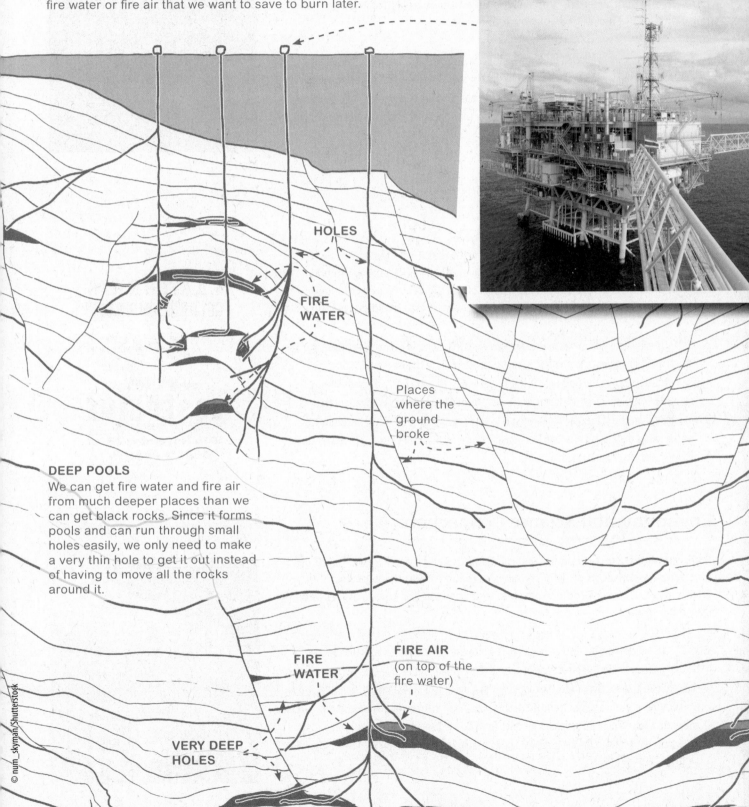

HOLES

FIRE WATER

Places where the ground broke

DEEP POOLS

We can get fire water and fire air from much deeper places than we can get black rocks. Since it forms pools and can run through small holes easily, we only need to make a very thin hole to get it out instead of having to move all the rocks around it.

FIRE WATER

FIRE AIR
(on top of the fire water)

VERY DEEP HOLES

© num_skyman/Shutterstock

Engineering Connection

Mining Asteroids As the human population increases and as new technologies like electronics are developed and improved, the demand for rare elements is increasing. Meanwhile, the supply of mineral resources is decreasing. There is only so much that can be mined from Earth's crust. One possible solution to this supply problem is to mine asteroids. Certain types of asteroids are rich in important and rare elements like nickel, gold, platinum, and rhodium.

> Use library and Internet resources to research plans for mining asteroids. What are some engineering challenges that need to be overcome to successfully mine asteroids? What are the safety and environmental risks? What are the potential benefits? Prepare a brief report describing the potential risks and benefits for someone who is thinking about investing in an asteroid mining project.

FIGURE 2: Scientists estimate that the asteroid 16 Psyche contains more than 1.7×10^{19} kg of nickel-iron. This is an illustration of a future NASA mission to explore 16 Psyche.

Social Studies Connection

Exploration, Colonialism, and Natural Resources Human civilization has been shaped by people's relationship with natural resources. The need and desire for mineral and energy resources such as gold, silver, tin, oil, and gas have fueled exploration and settlement of different parts of the globe as well as colonialism—the practice of invading and controlling another territory to exploit its resources.

> Use library or Internet resources to research the relationship between natural resources and exploration, expansion of a country, or colonialism. Choose a specific time and place in history such as the Gold Rush in the United States, the search for gold and silver in South and Central America, or more recent activity related to oil and gas exploration. Present your findings in one of the following forms: a) a map showing the locations of the resources and the routes that people traveled; b) a timeline of events; or c) a brief essay about the causes and effects of the exploration or invasion.

FIGURE 3: In the mid-1800s, the quest for gold drew tens of thousands of settlers to California from around the world.

Environmental Science Connection

Environmental Law Companies that mine for rock and mineral resources or drill for oil and gas must comply with certain laws that are designed to protect the environment. These laws differ from state to state within the United States, and they differ from country to country.

> Use library and Internet resources to research the environmental laws that affect mining, drilling, or processing of natural resources in your area or another area of your choice. How do these laws affect the companies that own the mines or drilling operations, the workers, the local environment, and the people who live in the region? Choose a specific law, and write a brief report that explains the law. Describe the benefits and the costs or drawbacks of the law to the environment and to people, such as company owners, workers, residents, and consumers.

FIGURE 4: The Clean Air Act was first passed in 1963 to control air pollution.

SYNTHESIZE THE UNIT

In your Evidence Notebook, create a concept map, graphic organizer, or outline using the Study Guides you created for each lesson in this unit. Be sure to use evidence to support your claims.

When synthesizing individual information, remember to follow these general steps:

- Find the central idea of each piece of information.
- Think about the relationships among the central ideas.
- Combine the ideas to come up with a new understanding.

Go online to access detailed lesson summaries for this unit.

DRIVING QUESTIONS

Look back to the Driving Questions from the opening section of this unit. In your Evidence Notebook, review and revise your previous answers to those questions. Use the evidence you gathered and other observations you made throughout the unit to support your claims.

PRACTICE AND REVIEW

Use the following scenario to answer Questions 1 through 4.

Black smoker chimneys are structures made of minerals that form around hot springs on the ocean floor, more than 2 km below the surface. Rare organisms live on and around the chimneys. A natural history museum wants to collect some black smoker chimneys for a new exhibit hall. They also want to better understand chimney ecosystems and how the chimneys form. Before setting off on the expedition, a team of biologists, chemists, geologists, and engineers gets together to plan how to cut the chimneys down and bring them up to the surface and back to the museum without damaging them and with minimal damage to the ecosystem. They ultimately decide to place a metal cage and ropes around each chimney, use an underwater chain saw to cut it down, and then use a long rope to pull it up to the surface.

1. Which question best conveys the engineering problem that needs to be solved?

  a. How do black smoker chimneys form?

  b. Can organisms that live around black smokers also live on the surface?

  c. How can we collect a black smoker chimney from the seafloor without damaging it?

  d. What is the temperature and pressure of the water that comes out of the black smoker chimneys?

2. The museum has 24 months and $2 million to plan and complete the project. They will have six full weeks of ship time to study the ecosystem and bring back the chimneys. These are all examples of

  a. Criteria

  b. Tradeoffs

  c. Problems

  d. Constraints

3. Indicate whether each activity below is an example of (a) modeling, (b) ranking criteria, (c) troubleshooting, or (d) evaluating tradeoffs.

  a. The team decides to spend the last day gathering more data about the seafloor instead of trying to bring up another chimney.

  b. The scientists discuss which is more important: collecting a chimney that is still growing or collecting a chimney that is no longer growing.

  c. The engineers calculate the weight of the chimney in water and then use that information to figure out how strong the rope used to pull the chimneys up must be.

  d. A piece of the first chimney breaks off on the way up to the surface. The engineers decide to secure the second chimney with more loops of rope.

4. Which is most likely to be true?

   a. The biologists, chemists, and geologists will agree on what part of the system is most important to study.

   b. Scientists and engineers on future expeditions to collect black smoker chimneys will use the design as a starting point.

   c. If the engineers are competent, the design for bringing up the chimneys will work well on the first try without any modification.

   d. If the scientists and engineers work hard enough, they will be able to meet all of the design criteria perfectly while working within all of their constraints.

5. A woman is trying to choose a new coat to buy. She can't decide between a sheepskin coat or a synthetic fleece coat. She wants to choose the coat that causes the least damage to the environment. How can she use life cycle analysis to help make this decision?

6. The availability and use of natural resources has affected the development of human society. Which of the following statements are true? Select all correct responses.

   a. Native elements like gold and copper were used before alloys like bronze.

   b. Humans could not use rock and mineral resources until fire was discovered.

   c. The first known use of rock and mineral resources was in sculpture and other artwork.

   d. Native Americans were not concerned with the physical properties of rocks and minerals.

   e. The need for rock, mineral, and energy resources has driven human exploration and settlement.

   f. The types of resources that early humans used depended on what was available nearby or through trade.

7. Why are minerals that are rich in rare earth elements considered to be "critical and strategic"?

8. What factors must a mining company take into account when deciding what method to use to mine for a particular resource? Identify at least three factors, and briefly explain how each affects the decision.

9. Evaluate the following statement:

   All forms of mining and drilling have costs and risks as well as benefits. The development of new technologies can change the balance of costs and risks to benefits.

   Do you agree or disagree with this statement? Use evidence and reasoning to support your answer.

10. A country passes a law to reduce its reliance on nonrenewable resources that are accessed through drilling and mining. Which of the following energy resources is it most likely to invest in? Choose all correct answers.

    a. Bitumen

    b. Coal

    c. Hydroelectric

    d. Natural gas

    e. Petroleum

    f. Solar

    g. Tidal

    h. Wind

11. Compare the costs and benefits of one type of fossil fuel with the costs and benefits of a renewable energy resource.

12. Describe the process that an engineering team might go through to design a way to reduce the environmental impact of extracting petroleum or natural gas.

UNIT PROJECT

Return to your unit project. Finalize your proposal so that it clearly explains how the current recycling system works, how well it serves your community, how it needs to be improved, and what the benefits of improving the system will be to the community and to the environment.

Remember these tips while you are finalizing your proposal:

· Is the way the system works now clearly described?

· Are the problems with the current system clearly identified?

· Is the evidence and reasoning for improving the system clear?

· Are the costs and benefits of your improved system clearly outlined?

· Did you include an action plan?

Carbon Fiber Solutions

If you compare modern sporting equipment to equipment that was made decades ago, you'll notice some differences. As new resources are discovered, new technologies and processes for mining and processing minerals are invented, and new materials are developed, engineers have replaced certain materials with others that are less expensive or have properties better suited for their function. One of the most popular new materials is carbon fiber.

FIGURE 5: Carbon fiber road bike

1. DEFINE THE PROBLEM

With your group, choose a type of sporting equipment that could be made using carbon fiber: for example, bicycles, rackets, bats, skis, snowboards, or skateboards.

Brainstorm the criteria that the particular piece of equipment needs to meet. Think about its purpose, how it is used by athletes, and what qualities make one design or brand better than another.

2. CONDUCT RESEARCH

On your own, conduct additional research into the properties of carbon fiber and the ways carbon fiber can be used in the sporting equipment you chose. Try to find out: What materials does carbon fiber replace? What are some important physical and chemical properties of carbon fiber? How much does carbon fiber cost relative to the materials it replaces? Where does carbon fiber come from? What are the possible environmental costs of using carbon fiber instead of more traditional materials? What are some other advantages and disadvantages of making this sporting equipment out of carbon fiber?

3. ANALYZE DATA

Get back together with your team to discuss your findings. Analyze the benefits and costs of using carbon fiber in the sporting equipment. Make a chart that compares equipment made using carbon fiber to equipment made without it. Include how well the equipment performs, the price of the equipment, and the environmental cost or risks of using carbon fiber versus using other materials.

4. EVALUATE THE SOLUTION

Do the benefits of using carbon fiber outweigh the costs? On your own, think about your personal priorities when it comes to buying sporting equipment. Which would you buy: the equipment made with carbon fiber or with some other set of materials? Be prepared to explain your reasoning to the group.

5. COMMUNICATE

Get back together with your group and share your thinking. Did everyone come to the same conclusion? Why or why not? Discuss what factors went into each person's thinking and how people weigh factors differently.

 CHECK YOUR WORK

Once you have completed this task, you should have the following:

- A description of a piece of sporting equipment and the criteria that it needs to meet
- A brief description of the important properties of carbon fiber and how it is used
- A matrix comparing the costs and benefits of a piece of sporting equipment made with carbon fiber to one made with other materials
- Your personal assessment of whether it is better to buy the equipment made with carbon fiber or with some other materials, supported by your reasoning

Earth in the Solar System

This view of Earth from the International
Space Station shows Asia at night.

Image Credits: ©NASA Johnson Space Center

FIGURE 1: The solar system consists of the sun, the eight planets, and all other objects that revolve around the sun.

not to scale

Eight planets travel around the sun, each in its own unique orbit. The gravitational attraction between the sun and each planet keeps the planets in their orbits.

 Predict What factors might scientists consider in distinguishing planets from smaller objects in the solar system such as dwarf planets?

DRIVING QUESTIONS

As you move through the unit, gather evidence to help you answer the following questions. In your Evidence Notebook, record what you already know about these topics and any questions you have about them.

1. How has gravity influenced the formation and motion of Earth over time?

2. How can we use our understanding of physical laws and the behavior of objects to understand Earth's formation and history in the solar system?

3. What factors affect climate on Earth?

4. How can you use evidence from Earth's surface to understand how climate has changed through time?

UNIT PROJECT

Go online to download the Unit Project Worksheet to help plan your project.

Model Another Solar System

How does knowledge of our solar system make it possible to model other solar systems? In this project, you will develop a model of another solar system—either a real system or one you make up. Your model should include one star that has a different mass than the sun, at least three planets, and one object in a highly eccentric orbit.

Solar System Formation

Comet Churyumov-Gerasimenko, as seen from the *Rosetta* spacecraft in 2014

CAN YOU EXPLAIN IT?

FIGURE 1: The ancient surface of Earth's moon is covered with impact craters that formed when other objects smashed into it and exploded.

 Gather Evidence
Record observations about the composition and structure of the solar system and the objects that make it up. As you explore the lesson, gather evidence that can be used to explain how the solar system formed.

On the lunar surface, nested impact craters ranging in size from microscopic to hundreds of kilometers in diameter cover the desolate moonscape. They bear witness to the violent history of the early solar system. On Earth's mostly watery surface, reminders of this period are harder to find. What is there to be learned from impact craters on the moon and on Earth?

Explain Why doesn't Earth's surface show the same violent history as the moon's surface?

The Solar System

If you compare a model of the solar system made today with models constructed in the past, you will find that they are different. The solar system itself has not changed significantly over the past 2000 years, but our understanding of it has.

Solar System Models

What comes to mind when you think about the solar system? You might remember seeing a recent full moon, the shimmering light of a distant star, or the brightness of a nearby planet. Like you, ancient people also noticed the objects in the night sky.

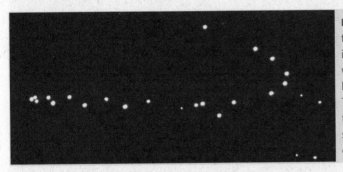

FIGURE 2: From night to night, some objects in the sky appear to wander relative to the background of stars. This figure shows the path of an object studied by ancient observers.

Explain What is a possible cause of the apparent motion of the object shown in Figure 2?

Early astronomers made careful observations to construct explanations and build models of the solar system. They were familiar with the daily motion of the sun and moon and discovered that throughout the year, different groups of stars appeared in the night sky. They also identified five starlike objects that wandered back and forth relative to more distant stars and called them planets. Based on their observations, these observers developed the geocentric model of the solar system. In this model, all the objects in the sky moved in circular paths around Earth. The paths of Mars, Jupiter, and Saturn had loops called epicycles that help explain and predict their apparent back-and-forth motion.

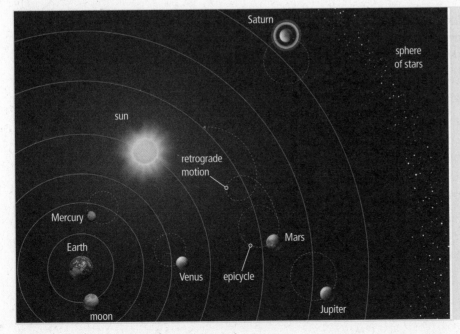

FIGURE 3: Geocentric models of the solar system explain careful observations such as the apparent motion of the sun, moon, planets, and stars across the sky.

Image Credits: (t) ©Larry W. Koehn/Science Source

The geocentric model explained observations well enough for hundreds of years. It also fit well with the thinking of the time—that Earth, being the most important object, lies at the center of the universe and that objects orbit in perfect circles.

However, as observers gathered more and more precise data, they needed to modify the model to make it more consistent with observations. It slowly became apparent that models with Earth at the center of the solar system and models with perfectly circular paths, or orbits, could not accurately predict astronomical events. By the 17th century, the geocentric model with circular orbits had been replaced by a heliocentric model with slightly elongated orbits.

FIGURE 4: This modern heliocentric model of the solar system is consistent with detailed observations and measurements made from Earth and from space, using modern technology.

FIGURE 5: Mercury, Venus, Mars, Jupiter, and Saturn can all be seen without a telescope and thus have been known to us for thousands of years.

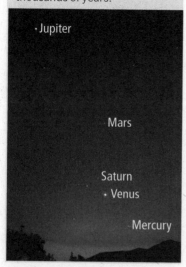

Solar System Components

Compare the modern model of the solar system with the geocentric model. You should notice the difference in its organizing structure, with the sun at the center, and the addition of more objects.

Since the heliocentric model was first introduced in the 1500s, it has been modified even further, primarily with the help of telescopes and space probes.

With Earth-based telescopes, scientists discovered the asteroid belt, Uranus, Neptune, and Pluto. With space-based telescopes, space probes, and landers, they have been able to discover more objects and also better understand the composition and motion of these objects.

Explain The geocentric model of the solar system was used by most observers to describe the solar system until the 17th century when they began to accept the heliocentric model. Why do you think the geocentric model was popular for so long? What do you think caused people to begin to favor the heliocentric model?

Image Credits: (b) ©John Sanford/Science Source

Telescopes also enabled astronomers to make much more precise measurements of the locations of stars at different times of year, which enabled them to calculate distances to stars. Once this was possible, astronomers realized that stars are much farther away than the planets and are not part of the solar system at all.

Our understanding has also changed as a result of unusual astronomical events. For example, before the late 1700s, scientists generally did not consider comets to be part of the solar system. But in 1758, a comet that had appeared 75 years earlier returned as predicted by Edmund Halley, proving that at least some comets do orbit the sun.

FIGURE 6: More precise observations lead to a better classification of solar system objects.

a Terrestrial planet Mars

b Gas giant planet Saturn

e Comet Churyumov-Gerasimenko

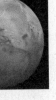
c Dwarf planet and Kuiper belt object Eris

d Asteroid Vesta

Explain Compare the components of the geocentric and the modern heliocentric model. Why does the modern model include so much more detail than models developed hundreds of years ago?

Collaborate With a partner, compare characteristics of different types of objects in the solar system. Research specific examples of each type of object to support your comparisons.

Models Change

A modern, heliocentric model of the solar system includes eight major planets, hundreds of moons, an asteroid belt, and objects in regions beyond the orbit of the major planets. It includes solid bodies (rock and solid ice), atmospheres, and different forms of energy. Objects interact through matter, gravity, light, and magnetic fields. The model is based on many different types of observations, which are ongoing.

The heliocentric model helps astronomers understand what they observe. It also helps them make accurate predictions. The winding path of Mars, as seen from Earth, makes sense if you model both of these objects' orbits around the sun. Earth orbits faster and sometimes passes Mars. As Earth passes, Mars seems to move backward.

Today, many people, including astronomers, still use a geocentric model to describe common events such as sunrise and sunset. The model is simple enough to be useful, though only within limits.

 Model How would Earth appear to move if you were viewing from Mars? Use people or objects to model how the position of a moving object changes relative to distant objects as you pass.

FIGURE 7: Apparent motion of Mars as viewed from Earth

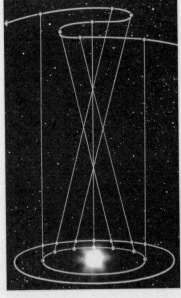

Solar System Formation

Gather Evidence
Assuming the solar system is a closed system (no material has entered or left the system since it began to form), what was the composition of the material that the solar system came from?

Our current model of the solar system illustrates our understanding of its structure and composition as it exists today. By studying its characteristics and gathering evidence, scientists developed a model to explain how the solar system and Earth formed.

Observations and Characteristics

How is matter distributed in the solar system? There are trillions of tons of material in the solar system, but it is not distributed evenly throughout. More than 99.8% of the mass of the solar system, or about 1.99×10^{30} kg, is found in the sun. Most of the rest is concentrated in the planets. The sun is composed almost entirely of hydrogen and helium. All other elements make up only about 2% of the composition of the sun.

Analyze Compare the densities of the inner and outer planets. What can explain these differences?

Density Distribution

FIGURE 8: Comparing the masses and densities of the planets and sun confirms the fact that material is not mixed evenly throughout the solar system.

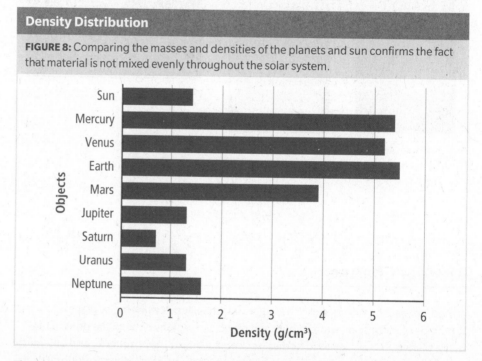

The sun may have most of the mass in the solar system, but Mercury, the smallest planet, has more than three times its average density. How is that possible? Recall that density is the ratio between the mass and volume of a substance. The sun is the largest object in the solar system, larger than Jupiter, the largest planet.

What else do you notice about the relative average densities of the inner and outer planets? What about their relative sizes? The inner planets have relatively high average densities, while the outer planets have very low average densities. However, although they are less dense, the outer planets are much more massive. In fact, together, the outer planets contain more than 99% of the total mass of the planets.

 Explain What is the relationship between the size, mass, average density, composition, and location of the planets?

FIGURE 9: The density of a planet reflects its composition and structure.

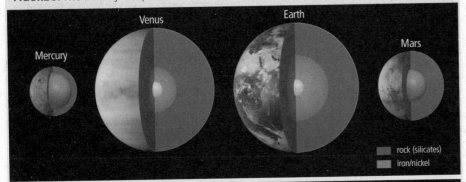

rock (silicates)
iron/nickel

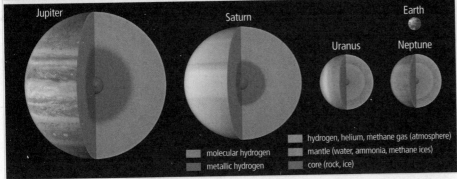

molecular hydrogen
metallic hydrogen

hydrogen, helium, methane gas (atmosphere)
mantle (water, ammonia, methane ices)
core (rock, ice)

Explain How do you think the compositions of the planets reflect the distribution of different types of material early in the evolution of the solar system?

Examine the chart below. How do distance from the sun and composition of the class of object seem to be related? The objects seem to be sorted based on composition and distance from the sun. The inner planets and the asteroid belt are rich in materials such as iron and silicates. These materials can condense at temperatures such as those that exist near the sun. The outer planets and the objects of the Kuiper Belt and the Oort cloud are rich in materials that condense mostly at low temperatures, such as those that exist farther away from the sun. These materials, known as volatiles, evaporate quickly at typical Earth temperatures and pressures.

Explain Spectroscopic measurements, or measurements of wavelengths of reflected sunlight, revealed that the tail of Comet Hale-Bopp is made of dust and gases such as water, carbon dioxide, methane, and ammonia. What does this suggest about the composition of a comet and the region in which comets formed?

Objects in the Solar System			
Class of object	Solar system region	Distance from sun (AU*)	Composition
terrestrial planets	inner solar system	0–2	rock and metal
asteroids	asteroid belt	2–5	rock and metal
moons	inner and outer solar system	1–30	rock and metal
gas giants	outer solar system	5–30	gas, ice, and metal
dwarf planets and **short-period comets	Kuiper Belt	30–50	rock and ice
**long-period comets	Oort cloud	5000–100 000	rock and ice

*AU: astronomical units; 1 AU = the average distance between Earth and the sun

** Refer to the length of a comet's orbit

As comets approach the sun, in elongated orbits that can take hundreds or thousands of years, they provide evidence to explain the difference in composition between groups of objects in the solar system. Comets are made of dust particles trapped in a mixture of frozen water, carbon dioxide, methane, and ammonia.

FIGURE 10: Comet Hale-Bopp forms a tail as it approaches the sun.

As a comet moves close to the sun, it becomes active. Solar radiation heats up the comet's icy surface and produces a coma, a cloud of particles and gas around the comet's solid nucleus. A tail may also form. The tail points away from the sun, regardless of the comet's motion. The coma and tail grow as the comet nears the sun, then fade and shrink as the comet gains distance from the sun. When the comet is far from the sun, it again becomes inactive.

Explain How does the composition of the objects in the solar system appear to be related to distance from the sun? Use evidence and reasoning to support your claim.

FIGURE 11: The tail of a comet forms when the comet enters a region of the solar system where the temperature is high enough to vaporize ices.

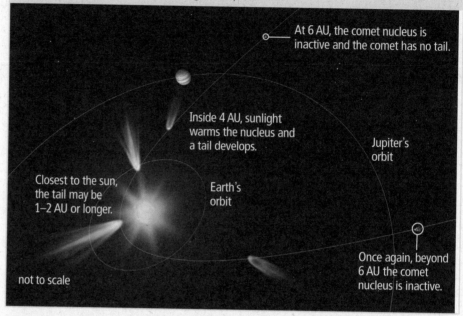

At 6 AU, the comet nucleus is inactive and the comet has no tail.

Inside 4 AU, sunlight warms the nucleus and a tail develops.

Jupiter's orbit

Closest to the sun, the tail may be 1–2 AU or longer.

Earth's orbit

Once again, beyond 6 AU the comet nucleus is inactive.

not to scale

Finally, studying the shape of the solar system and the motion of objects within it can help develop a model of its formation. Most of the objects in the solar system orbit the sun on roughly the same plane. Thus, the solar system is essentially disk-shaped, with a bulge in the center. All of the objects revolve around the sun in the same direction that the sun spins: counterclockwise as viewed from above the sun's north pole.

Beginning and Formation

Scientists infer that the solar system began as a cloud of dust, ice, and gas, called a nebula, roughly 4.6 billion years ago. With powerful telescopes, we have observed distant nebula in space. According to the nebular theory, the cloud collapsed to form the sun, planets, and all of the other solar system objects that exist today.

About 4.6 billion years ago, some force disturbed the nebula, causing it to collapse under its own gravity. This could have been a result of gravity from a star passing by or the shockwave from an exploding star. Whatever the cause, as the nebula collapsed and became smaller, its density and temperature increased. Material began to coalesce and accumulate in the center. As more and more material accumulated, the gravitational pull toward the center increased.

FIGURE 12: The solar system began in a nebula like this, as a swirling cloud of hydrogen and helium gas, dust (including minerals), and ices of water, methane, and carbon dioxide.

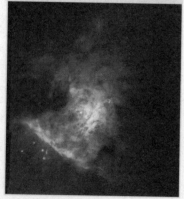

Explain What is the evidence and reasoning supporting the claim that the solar nebula was composed primarily of hydrogen and helium, with smaller amounts of other elements such as iron, silicon, and oxygen?

FIGURE 13: Cloud collapse and flattening

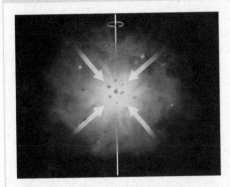

a **Collapse** The nebula collapsed. Gravity pulled most mass toward the center.

b **Flattening** The cloud flattened into a disk as it collapsed.

As a region of the solar nebula collapsed, gravity pulled most of the mass toward the center of the nebula. As the nebula contracted, it began to rotate. As the rotation grew faster, the nebula flattened out into a disk. This disk, which is called a protoplanetary disk, is where the central star, the sun, formed.

FIGURE 14: Protosun and planet formation

a **Fusion** As fusion began, energy was released, heating up the surrounding disk and pushing volatile materials outward.

b **Accretion** Near the protosun, iron, nickel, and silicates came together to form the inner planets. Ice accreted in the cooler outer part of the solar system, while hydrogen and helium accumulated around larger planets.

As the protostellar disk continued to contract, most of the matter ended up in the center of the disk. Friction from matter that fell into the disk heated up its center to millions of degrees, eventually reaching its current temperature of 15 000 000 °C. This intense heat in a densely packed space caused the fusion of hydrogen atoms into helium atoms. The process of fusion released large amounts of energy. This release of energy caused outward pressure that again balanced the inward pull of gravity. As the gas and dust stopped collapsing, the sun was born.

The energy emitted by the sun caused the surrounding disk to heat up even more. The high temperatures near the young sun kept volatile materials such as water, carbon dioxide, ammonia, and methane in that region in gas form. At the same time, a stream of charge particles emitted by the sun called the solar wind pushed these materials, along with leftover hydrogen, helium, and other light gases, toward the outer part of the disk, leaving behind only those materials that could remain solid at high temperatures.

Gather Evidence
According to the nebular theory, as the nebula collapsed, it began to rotate. All of the material began to move in one direction around the center. What observations about the solar system today support this claim?

Gather Evidence
What is the evidence that volatile materials were pushed away from the center of the solar system and out toward the outer part of the disk?

Image Credits: (t) (bl) (br) ©NASA/JPL–Caltech

As the sun was forming, dust grains collided and stuck together. The resulting dust granules grew in size and increased in number. Over time, dust granules increased in size until they had become meter-sized bodies. Collisions between these bodies formed larger bodies that were kilometers across. These larger bodies, from which planets formed, are called planetesimals. The protostellar disk had become the protoplanetary disk in which the planets would form.

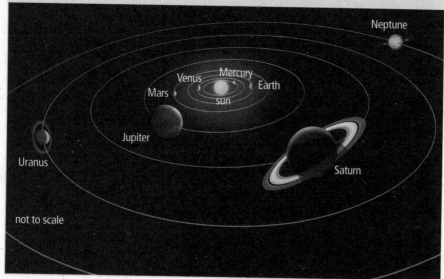

FIGURE 15: Clearing While the solar wind blew the remaining gas and tiny dust particles out of the system, the newly formed planets swept up larger pieces of loose debris, clearing their orbits of materials.

The inner part of the protoplanetary disk was so hot that only rocks and metals were in solid form. Therefore, rocky, metallic planets formed in the inner disk. These planets formed from the collisions and mergers of rocky planetesimals. These inner planets are called the terrestrial planets.

In the cold, outer disk, ices, gases, metals, and rocks were all found. At first, massive planets of made icy and rocky planetesimals may have formed. The gravity of these planets was so strong that they captured gas and other matter as they grew. Therefore, planets that formed in the outer disk have rocky or metallic cores and deep atmospheres of gas and ice. These outer planets are the gas giant planets.

By the time the surfaces of the inner planets had cooled enough to form crusts, most of the material in the disk had been incorporated into the planets—but not all. Enough was left over that the surfaces continued to be pelted by rocks for millions of years, leaving impact craters as evidence. Material between Jupiter and Mars never accumulated to form a single planet and instead remains as the asteroid belt, while material beyond Neptune seems to be distributed in a wide band called the Kuiper Belt.

Extrasolar System Observations

Did the solar system really form from a collapsing cloud of dust and gas? Are there other solar systems out there, and if so, did they form in the same way? The nebular theory was originally developed based only on observations of our solar system. For many years, it was impossible to confirm the model because we had only one example of a solar system, and of course, we are not able to travel back in time.

FIGURE 16: HL Tauri, a young sun-like star located 450 light years from Earth

Recent surface-based observations have revealed that in fact there are uncountable solar systems in the universe. We now not only have images of some of these systems and planets, but we also have images of young stars surrounded by disks of gas and dust—protoplanetary disks. These observations of other systems confirm many of our ideas, but they cause us to question others. For example, in some systems, Jupiter-sized planets made of very low density material orbit extremely close to their stars. It is possible that these planets formed farther from their stars and their orbits decayed.

 Evaluate Why are observations of objects outside our solar system important for evaluating the nebular theory of solar system formation?

Evidence of Earth's Early History

The solar system and Earth formed roughly 4.6 billion years ago through the collapse of a cloud of gas and dust. What evidence can we use to attempt a reconstruction of the early history of Earth and its neighbor?

FIGURE 17: Manicouagan impact crater, Canada

Explain The surface of Mercury shows abundant evidence for accretion in the form of impact craters covering the surface. If Earth formed at the same time as Mercury and through the same process of accretion, why does Earth have so few craters?

From Physical Characteristics

Each of the terrestrial planets has a hard, rocky crust. All but Mercury are surrounded by thin atmospheres of gas. Only Earth has liquid water on the surface. Mercury and the moon are covered in impact craters, but Earth and Venus have very few. What can the number and condition of craters on a planet reveal about its geologic history?

FIGURE 18: Earth is the largest and densest of the four terrestrial planets.

Mercury   Venus   Earth   Mars

Explain Earth and the other terrestrial planets are much smaller, denser, and less massive than the outer planets, and they are composed of silicate rock and metal rather than gases and ices. What does this tell you about Earth's early history?

We know through direct observations and through inferences that internal and surface processes have changed Earth's surface significantly since it formed. This is also true for Mars and Venus and to a lesser extent for the moon and Mercury. As a result, much of the evidence for Earth's early history has been erased. However, we can infer something about its history by its structure.

Earth and the other planets are differentiated: they have layers of increasing density toward the center. This tells us that the bodies were once molten, allowing dense material to sink, pushing lighter materials to the surface. The energy that caused early Earth to melt is thought to have come in part from the energy of collisions with small, rocky bodies, which transformed the energy of motion into thermal energy that melted the planet.

Impact craters are evidence that planets formed and grew through accretion—the coming together of smaller objects in space. There are very few impact craters remaining on Earth's surface—most have been weathered and eroded. However, the moon shows a better record of impacts, providing evidence that accretion continued well after planets had formed. Many meteorites appear to be unchanged since the solar system formed. Because the minerals that make up these rocks formed when the planets formed, they have been used to estimate the composition of the early solar system and the age of Earth.

 Engineering

FIGURE 19: The Barringer Crater (Meteor Crater) in Arizona is 1200 m across and 170 m deep.

Design an Impact Crater Investigation

Until the 1950s, most scientists didn't agree on the origins of craters. Some scientists designed lab experiments to model impact crater formation. Others conducted field studies. Ultimately, scientists were able to use what they learned to figure out how craters on Earth and in the solar system formed. We now know that Meteor Crater formed 50 000 years ago when an asteroid 50 m across struck Earth at 65 000 km/h.

Investigate Plan and design an investigation to learn more about impact craters. What materials would you use to represent Earth's surface and meteorites? What independent variables could you test? What dependent variables could you measure? What variables would you need to control during the investigation? What questions would this investigation help answer?

Absolute Age

 Explain Briefly explain what Earth's composition, its size and mass relative to other planets, and the presence of impact craters on it and other objects in the solar system indicate about the formation of the solar system and Earth's history.

Problem Solving

Use graphs to model how systems change over time. This graph in Figure 20 shows how the percentage of the parent material changes as it decays. If you know the ratio of parent to daughter atoms in the sample, you can use a graph like this to figure out how old the sample is.

Evidence from the composition and structure of solar system objects provide clues about how it formed, but how do we know when it formed and how old the objects in it are? The most important evidence comes from radioactive decay.

Radioactive Decay

FIGURE 20: Over the course of one half-life, half the parent atoms in a sample decay to form daughter atoms.

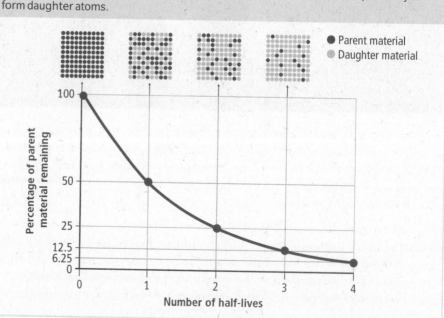

Some rocks and minerals contain trace amounts of elements that change, or decay, from one form to another. These radioactive elements decay at a constant rate that is not affected by the environment or by the passage of time. The graph in Figure 20 shows how a radioactive sample decays at a constant rate from parent material to daughter material. The time when exactly half of the starting parent material remains in the sample is called a half-life.

FIGURE 21: **Oldest-known minerals** Radiometric dating of zircon crystals such as this one from the Jack Hills in Australia reveals that they may have formed as long as 4.375 billion years ago.

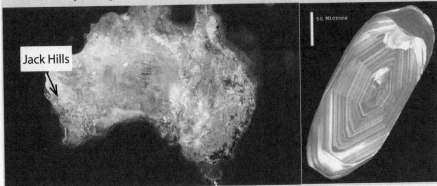

Jack Hills

Because of plate tectonics, there are very few rocks on the surface that can provide evidence for conditions early in Earth's history. However, geologists make inferences from the samples available. Earth's age can be estimated by measuring the absolute age of ancient materials such as meteorites, rocks from the moon, and minerals in ancient rocks on Earth that contain radioactive elements.

Some of the oldest rock on the planet's surface is found in Canada, Greenland, Africa, and Australia. The oldest mineral crystals analyzed so far, which appear to have formed when Earth around 4.4 billion years old, provide evidence that Earth had a continental crust and likely even surface waters. However, because there are so few samples of rocks and minerals this old, it is difficult to confirm the result. There are still many outstanding questions, such as when did the crust, oceans, and atmosphere form? When did plate tectonics start? When was Earth hospitable for life?

Earth's Beginnings

When exactly did Earth accrete most of its mass? When did large objects stop crashing into Earth on a regular basis? It is hard to say. Most of Earth's mass probably accumulated during the first few tens of millions of years of its formation. Scientists think that about 4.5 billion years ago a smaller planet smashed into Earth, forming the moon. Recent models suggest that between 4.5 and 3.8 billion years ago Earth may have been hit by numerous giant asteroids. These impacts would have mixed, melted, and buried rocks on the surface and boiled off the early oceans.

 Explain The moon provides some of the most direct evidence supporting the claim that Earth was bombarded during its early history. What is the form of this evidence, and what is the reasoning that connects this evidence to the claim?

Explore Online

Hands-On Lab

Simulation of Nuclear Decay
Use pennies and paper to simulate nuclear decay and generate data for analysis.

Explain Why do you think it is difficult to determine the age of Earth with radiometric dating of minerals that formed on Earth?

Collaborate
What can be inferred about Earth from the discovery of a crystal that has a radiometric age of 4.375 billion years? What cannot be inferred?

Guided Research

Taurus Molecular Cloud

FIGURE 23: The HL Tauri system, as viewed by a radio telescope on Earth

HL Tauri is a young, sunlike star in the Taurus molecular cloud, 450 light-years from Earth. In 2014, radio telescope images from the Atacama Large Millimeter/submillimeter Array (ALMA) revealed what appears to be a protoplanetary disk: a set of bright rings of material surrounding the star.

The star is very young—only about one million years old—and scientists were surprised to discover a disk surrounding such a young star.

Collaborate Conduct research to find out more about the HL Tauri system. How is it similar to and different from our solar system? Assuming it is forming according to the nebular theory, at what stage of formation is it currently? What technology has been used to image HL Tauri, and what types of data do these forms of technology help us collect or analyze?

| MODELING IMPACT CRATERS | THE OORT CLOUD | Go online to choose one of these other paths. |

Image Credits: ©Science Source

Lesson Self-Check

FIGURE 24: Impact craters on the moon's surface record part of the solar system history.

FIGURE 25: Manicouagan crater in Québec, Canada

Take another look at this picture of the moon. On Earth, evidence of this early, violent period in the history of the solar system has been erased by the processes that tear down and build up the land. The Manicouagan impact crater in Canada, believed to be the oldest crater on Earth, is only about 214 million years old.

Radiometric evidence from lunar rock samples brought back to Earth suggests that most of the lunar craters formed within a narrow period of time around 4 billion years ago. Scientists can draw conclusions about the early history of the moon based on this evidence. They can also make inferences about conditions on Earth, other planets and moons, and the solar system at the time the craters were formed.

The radiometric evidence from lunar rock samples confirms that the moon already had a solid surface 4 billion years ago. It also suggests that there was a sudden increase in the number of impactors—asteroids, comets, and other solar system debris—at the time. Evidence suggests that this increase lasted approximately 200–300 million years.

Today, large asteroid and comet impacts on planets and moons are very rare. However, every year for a few days during mid–July to mid–August, Earth passes through the Perseid Cloud. Small debris, left over by a comet that crosses Earth's orbit every 133 years, strikes Earth and burn up in its atmosphere.

 Explain What can the existence of craters on the moon and on other planets tell us about the early history of solar system?

CHECKPOINTS

Check Your Understanding

1. Although the geocentric model of the solar system was incorrect, there were aspects of it that were relatively accurate. Identify which components of the geocentric model (prior to the 1700s) are accurate and which are inaccurate.
   a. The sun orbits Earth.
   b. The moon orbits Earth.
   c. Planets are closer than stars.
   d. Orbits and epicycles are perfectly circular.
   e. Saturn is farther away from Earth than Jupiter.
   f. Stars are farther away than planets but not much farther away.

2. Over the centuries, scientists have constructed models and explanations of the solar system based on evidence and reasoning. Compare the evidence and reasoning used to support the geocentric model with the evidence and reasoning used to support the modern model of the solar system.

3. A model for how the solar system formed must explain observations and reasoning. Identify each statement as an example of an observation or reasoning. If a statement is false or invalid, identify it as such.
   a. Most of the mass of the solar system is in the sun.
   b. The sun is composed primarily of hydrogen and helium.
   c. The sun formed more than 13.8 billion years ago when the universe formed.
   d. Most objects in the solar system orbit the sun in the same direction.
   e. If most of the mass of the solar system is in the sun and the sun is mostly hydrogen and helium, then the solar system must primarily be hydrogen and helium.

4. Modern telescopes have allowed us to see far beyond the solar system. We have been able to capture images of nebulae, regions where stars are forming, stars of different ages, and planets that orbit other stars. Write two scientific questions about solar system formation that observations of other nebulae, stars, and solar systems can help us answer.

5. Complete items a–c to demonstrate how a systems approach can be used to describe the solar system and its formation.
   a. What are the primary components of matter in the solar system?
   b. What are the energy components of the solar system?
   c. Identify some processes that are at work (or have been at work) in the system.

6. Use the following words and phrases to complete the paragraph below describing events in the formation of the solar system.

increased	*planetesimals*
dust particles	*gravity*
fusion	*accretion*
flattened	*collapse*
solid core	*star*
cloud of dust and gas	*massive bulge*

   The solar system began as a swirling ____. Some disturbance caused the cloud to ____. As this happened, the density, temperature, and pressure within the cloud ____. As material swirled toward the center, the cloud ____ into a disk. A ____ developed at the center of the disk as mass accumulated there under the force of ____. At some point, ____ began and the bulge became a ____. At the same time, in the surrounding disk, ____ came together to form rocks. These rocks came together to form ____ which grew larger through ____ to form the inner planets and the ____ of the outer planets.

7. Zircon crystals, which form in igneous and metamorphic rocks, contain trace amounts of uranium-238, a radioactive element which decays to lead-206 over time. Scientists measure the ratios of U-238 and Pb-206 to estimate when the crystal formed. The half-life of U-238 is about 4.5 billion years.

   a. If the ratio of U-238 to Pb-206 atoms is 1:1, how old is the zircon crystal?

   b. A scientist measures the U-238:Pb-206 ratio of a single sample from a rock from the continental crust. The ratio is 1:3. What can the scientist conclude from this sample alone?

8. Which of the following observations support or are explained by the nebular theory (as outlined in this lesson)?

   a. Planets orbit in one direction around the sun.

   b. Venus has a thick atmosphere of carbon dioxide.

   c. The inner planets are denser, smaller, and less massive than the outer planets.

   d. Helium and hydrogen gas are evenly distributed in the solar system.

   e. In other solar systems, there are giant, low-density planets orbiting very close to their stars.

MAKE YOUR OWN STUDY GUIDE

 In your Evidence Notebook, design a study guide that supports the main ideas from this lesson:

1. The solar system consists of a star orbited by smaller objects made of rock, ice, and gas.

2. Models of the solar system have changed over time based on improved observations, improvements in technology, and changes in scientific thinking.

3. The solar system is thought to have formed about 4.6 billion years ago from a giant cloud of gas, dust, and ice that collapsed to form the sun and planetary bodies.

4. The nebular theory explains observations of the solar system and is supported by observations of other solar systems.

Remember to include the following in your study guide:

- Support main ideas about the composition, structure, and formation of the solar system with details and examples.
- Record explanations for the structure and composition of the solar system.
- Describe how the solar system has changed over time and how it has remained the same.

4.2

Gravity and Orbits

An orrery is a physical model of the relative motions of the planets.

CAN YOU EXPLAIN IT?

FIGURE 1: Mercury's transit of the sun in 2016

Explore Online

 Gather Evidence As you explore the lesson, gather evidence about how solar system bodies behave.

Mercury and Venus are closer to the sun than Earth is, and sometimes we can see them move in front of the sun. This is a rare astronomical event called a *transit*. In the above images, you are seeing Mercury cross between the sun and Earth. Mercury appears as a tiny black dot on the surface of the sun.

The movements of planetary bodies appear to go from left to right, or right to left depending on how the planet is moving relative to Earth and where the observer is standing on Earth.

Analyze How does Mercury appear to be moving relative to Earth? Why do you think the motion is so different from Earth's motion?

Planetary Movement

Planets are always moving. Even the name *planet* comes from the Greek word for "wander." Ancient astronomers noticed that planets appeared to drift across the night sky, unlike the apparently fixed stars behind them. Modern astronomers have more sophisticated ways of observing planetary motion and have been able to study the particular paths that follow around the sun.

Predict Why do you think the planets are in motion? What would happen if a planet were suddenly stopped?

Planetary Motion

One feature that is consistent for all planets in our solar system is the curved paths that they take through space. No planet travels in a straight line; rather, they all move in closed loops around the sun. Though astronomers have long known this to be the case, it is only in the last few hundred years that we have been able to explain why this occurs.

Collaborate With a partner, consider a hypothetical planet that is not moving relative to the sun. What would immediately follow the scenario presented in Figure 2a?

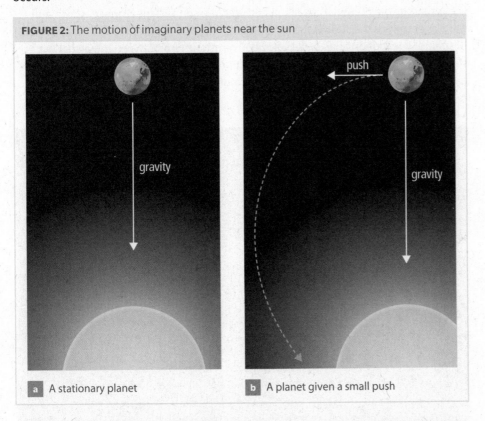

FIGURE 2: The motion of imaginary planets near the sun

push

gravity

gravity

a A stationary planet

b A planet given a small push

Predict The planet is given a small push, as shown in Figure 2b. What would happen to the planet immediately after the push?

If a planet were to somehow stop moving relative to the sun, we would witness the planet fall into the sun in the same way that a dropped baseball would fall toward Earth. Suppose that we could give the planet a small "push," as in Figure 2b. In that case, the planet would follow a trajectory similar to a thrown baseball on Earth before ultimately crashing into the sun.

FIGURE 3: The interaction that produces a closed-loop orbit

straight-line motion

gravity

Collaborate The planet is given a large push, as shown in Figure 3. With a partner, discuss what would immediately follow in the scenario.

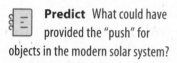

Predict What could have provided the "push" for objects in the modern solar system?

If there were no sun, planets would tend to move in a straight line at a steady velocity until they interacted with something else. The reason planets do not move in a straight line is that the gravitational attraction between the sun and the planet tends to pull the planet toward the sun. As this pull is happening, the planet still has a component of straight line motion at its initial velocity. The interaction between the planet's straight line motion and gravitational attraction produces a closed-loop path called an orbit. All solar system bodies are in an orbit around the sun or one another.

FIGURE 4: The formation of the solar system

Planets in our solar system were never "pushed" into their orbits; they all gained their orbital velocity in the early days of the solar system. When the proto-planetary dust cloud collapsed, its overall motion became part of the overall motion of the early planets

Orbit Shape and Mechanics

Explore Online ▶

🧪 **Hands-On Lab**

Modeling Orbits Use a model to study the elliptical orbits of planets.

FIGURE 5: The modern solar system

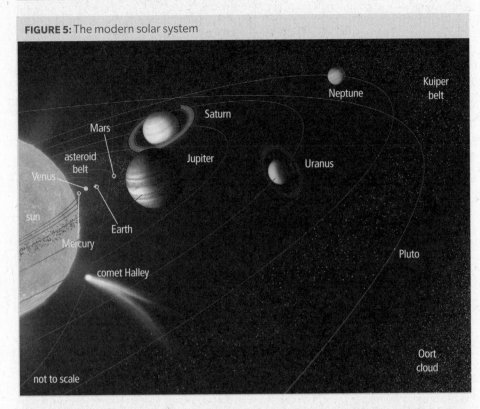

The orbit developed in the example of Figure 3 is fairly similar to the orbits of most modern-day planets. Each orbit is not a perfect circle but is actually an oval, or an ellipse. The sun is not quite at the center of each orbit. A 17th century German astronomer and scientist named Johannes Kepler developed three laws to describe the nature of planetary motion. Kepler's first law states that the orbit of a planet is an ellipse with the sun at a focus, one of the two defining points of the ellipse. For a circle, both foci are at the center of the circle. An ellipse has symmetry along two lines, each called an axis. There is a long axis and a short axis. The foci of an ellipse lie on the long axis and are equally spaced from the center.

FIGURE 6: Kepler's first law

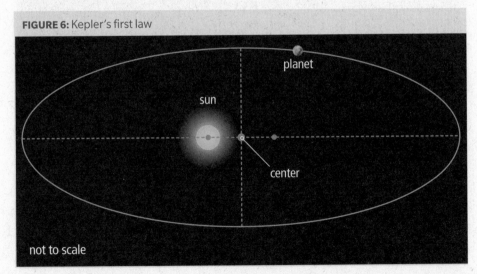

Gather Evidence
Describe the ellipses in the image shown. Which orbits appear to be nearly circular? Which orbits appear stretched?

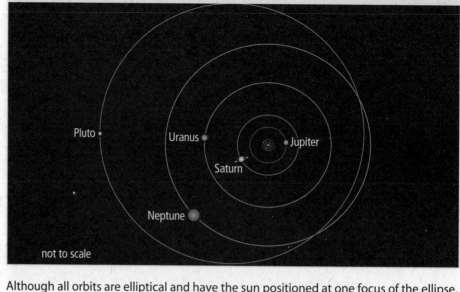

FIGURE 7: The shapes of modern-day planetary orbits

Pluto

Uranus

Saturn

Jupiter

Neptune

not to scale

Although all orbits are elliptical and have the sun positioned at one focus of the ellipse, not all orbits are alike. Ellipses range from almost circular to stretched ovals. The degree of elongation of an elliptical orbit is called eccentricity (ranging from 0 to 1). A circle has an eccentricity of zero. The more stretched an orbit appears, the greater its eccentricity and the closer its value approaches 1.

Explain Look at the comet in Figure 8. Describe the comet's orbit in terms of eccentricity.

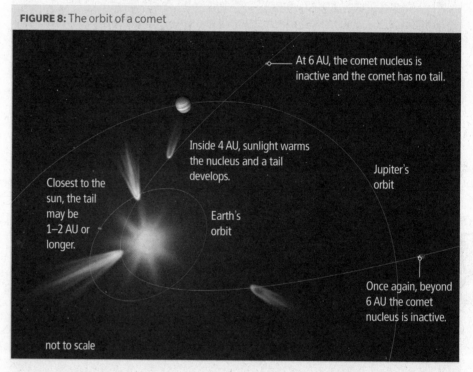

FIGURE 8: The orbit of a comet

At 6 AU, the comet nucleus is inactive and the comet has no tail.

Inside 4 AU, sunlight warms the nucleus and a tail develops.

Jupiter's orbit

Closest to the sun, the tail may be 1–2 AU or longer.

Earth's orbit

Once again, beyond 6 AU the comet nucleus is inactive.

not to scale

As can be seen in Figure 8, the eccentricity of the orbits of solar system bodies varies considerably. In fact, eccentricity is one of the factors that is considered in defining the different types of solar system bodies. Pluto, a dwarf planet, has a highly eccentric orbit, while comets can have even more eccentric orbits.

Explain What path do the planets of our solar system take around the sun? Why?

Planetary Motion

Measurements of interplanetary distances and motion can be made using a geometric method known as parallax. Parallax is the apparent shift of an object with respect to the background. As Earth revolves around the sun, astronomers measure an object's apparent shift against the background of more distant bodies from two different locations on Earth or at two different times.

Analyze Do objects closer to or farther from Earth have a greater change in apparent position as Earth moves?

In 1672, Italian astronomer Giovanni Cassini was able to use the parallax method to compute the approximate distance of Mars from Earth. Cassini made observations of Mars from Paris, while a colleague made observations at the same time from French Guiana in northern South America. In 1761, by observing the planet Venus against the background of the solar disk from different locations on Earth, astronomers were able to determine the approximate distance of Earth from the sun.

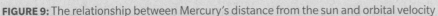
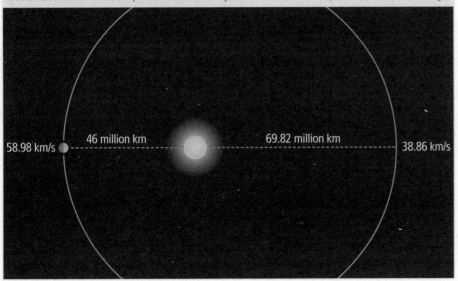

FIGURE 9: The relationship between Mercury's distance from the sun and orbital velocity

58.98 km/s — 46 million km — 69.82 million km — 38.86 km/s

Changes in Velocity Within an Orbit

Kepler's second law of planetary motion describes orbital velocity. Kepler discovered a unique relationship when he drew a line from a planet to the sun, which lies at one focus of its elliptical orbit. He found that a planet moves more rapidly when it is closer to the sun and less rapidly when it is farther from the sun. This change in velocity happens because as a planet moves around its orbit, it sweeps out equal areas in equal times. Near the sun, when the planet is moving faster, it sweeps out an area that is short but wide. Far from the sun, a planet sweeps out an area that is long but narrow in an equal amount of time.

Collaborate What do you think happens to the speed at the different regions? Recall that generally velocity is the ratio of distance over time.

Mercury has an orbit that is highly eccentric. Mercury's orbit passes about 46 million km from the sun at it closest, but at it farthest the orbit is 70 million km from the sun. When nearest the sun, Mercury reaches its maximum orbital velocity of 58.98 km/s, and when farthest from the sun Mercury reaches its minimum orbital velocity of 38.86 km/s.

Moons of Jupiter Perform calculations to model and explain the orbits of Jupiter's moons.

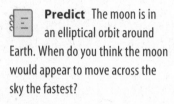

Predict The moon is in an elliptical orbit around Earth. When do you think the moon would appear to move across the sky the fastest?

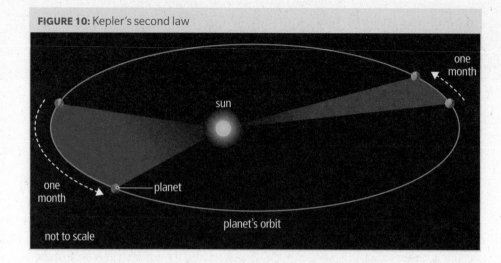

FIGURE 10: Kepler's second law

one month

sun

planet

one month

planet's orbit

not to scale

FIGURE 11: The moon follows an elliptical path around Earth. The elliptical shape is exaggerated in this diagram. The moon's actual orbit is much closer to a circle.

perigee

apogee

Relating Planetary Orbits and Time

When Kepler looked at how long it took for the planets to orbit the sun and at the sizes of their orbits, he found a further relationship. He discovered that the square of the orbital period—the time it takes a planet to complete one full orbit around the sun—was proportional to the cube of the planet's average distance from the sun. This is Kepler's third law of planetary motion. When the units are years for the orbital period and astronomical units (AU) for the distance, the law can be written: (orbital period in years)^2 = (average distance from the sun in AU)^3 or $P^2 = a^3$. This law is true for every planet in the solar system.

Using Kepler's second law together with his third law tells us that the more distant planets in the solar system move at slower speeds in their orbits around the sun than planets located closer to the sun. For example, Neptune, the most distant planet in the solar system, has the lowest mean orbital velocity of any of the planets at 5.43 km/s. Mercury, located closest to the sun, has the greatest mean orbital velocity of the planets at 47.87 km/s.

Problem Solving

Orbital Velocity Consider doubling the average orbital radius of Mercury. The planet would have double the distance to travel. What effect would you predict this change would have on the planet's average velocity?

Explain How are distance from the sun and orbital velocity related?

Gravity and the Motion of Planets

Kepler's laws help scientists describe *how* planets move around the sun, but they do not explain why planets move around the sun in varying orbits. To do that, we will need to include the contributions of 17th-century physicist and mathematician, Isaac Newton.

Gravity

As you've already discovered, gravity is responsible for the shape of orbits. Gravity is the natural attraction between physical bodies due to their masses. Their masses produce a force, which is a push or a pull in a particular direction. However, gravity only pulls—it doesn't push. Two objects pull on each other with equal force.

FIGURE 12: Trajectory of an imaginary planet without the influence of the sun

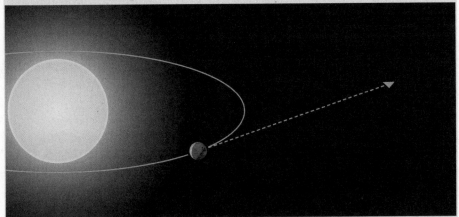

An object in space keeps moving because there is no friction to slow it down. The force of gravity from a massive object, such as the sun, can pull an object and change its path into a closed orbit. A continuous force is needed to maintain the orbit. As you will see, the force depends on mass and distance, so it varies over an elliptical orbit.

FIGURE 13: A change in mass directly affects the gravitational force experienced by both bodies.

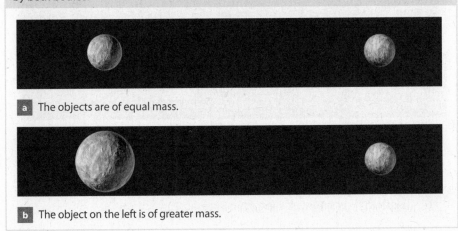

a The objects are of equal mass.

b The object on the left is of greater mass.

Predict Without the sun, planets would move through space in a straight line. What do you think pushes them from this straight path?

Collaborate In Figure 13, which pair of objects do you think would experience the larger gravitational force? Why?

Sir Isaac Newton studied the relationship between the motion of the planets and the force of gravity. In his investigation, he found that more massive objects experience a greater gravitational pull.

The relationship between mass and gravity is linear, which means that any change in mass is reflected in the pull of gravity. For example, doubling the mass of one object in a system would double the pull of gravity on the objects in the system.

FIGURE 14: Mass affects the gravitational force experienced by both bodies.

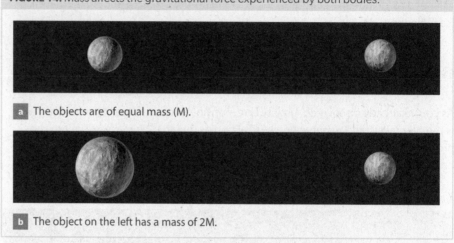

a The objects are of equal mass (M).

b The object on the left has a mass of 2M.

Expain Assuming that the planets in both Figures 14a and 14b are the same distance apart, how does the strength of the gravitational force between the planets in 14a differ from that between the planets in 14b?

Sir Isaac Newton also discovered a relationsip between the distance separating objects and the gravitational pull they experience. Objects far away from one another experience a smaller gravitational force than they would if they were closer together. This relationship is not linear, however. The gravitational pull experienced by two objects decreases proportionally to the distance between them *squared*. For example, doubling the distance separating two objects would actually result in them experiencing one-fourth the gravitational pull.

FIGURE 15: Distance affects the gravitational force experienced by both bodies.

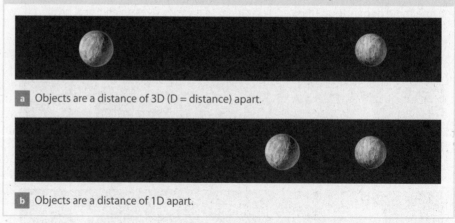

a Objects are a distance of 3D (D = distance) apart.

b Objects are a distance of 1D apart.

Explain In Figure 15, how would the strength of the gravitational force between the planets in 15b differ from that between the planets in 15a?

Real Orbits

Orbits are elliptical. The distance is constantly changing, so the force is constantly changing. The force due to gravity also changes the speed of the object in an elliptical orbit. The object speeds up and slows down. Mercury and Mars both have enough change in speed and distance as they move in their orbits that early astronomers noticed the changes.

FIGURE 16: The International Space Station in orbit around Earth

An orbit can change over time. The gravitational force from one planet can change the orbit of another planet. The International Space Station uses engines to routinely change the altitude of its orbit around Earth. This allows the station to avoid potentially damaging debris and counteract the drag caused by the very thin high atmosphere.

 Collaborate What do you think would happen to the orbit of a body if its velocity was increased? What would happen if it was decreased?

If a force causes an object to speed up while moving along its orbit, the distance—the axis of the orbit—will increase. If a force slows the object, the orbit will become smaller. The International Space Station sometimes gets a "push" from other vehicles to raise its speed and orbit. Orbital vehicles are often slowed down at the end of their lifetimes to cause their orbit to degenerate into the atmosphere where they disintegrate.

 Explain Describe the relationship between gravity and planetary motion. What aspects will have the greatest influence on the orbits of objects?

Guided Research

Space Junk

NASA tracks approximately 500 thousand pieces of orbital debris (also known as 'space junk'), which can circle Earth at speeds up to 8 km/s. This is so fast that a small piece of 'junk' can damage a large spacecraft.

The size of the debris is important. About 4% of the junk in space is bigger than a softball. Similar-sized hail on Earth can destroy roofs of cars and houses. At much higher speeds,

consider the damage softball-sized junk could cause.

While most natural debris orbits the sun, manufactured junk orbits Earth. Types of manufactured debris include abandoned spacecraft, satellites, and other mission-related debris.

Several methods have been developed to deal with these potentially destructive pieces. For example, NASA changes the planned orbits of

its spacecraft to avoid damage from space debris. Once in space, NASA uses thrusters that go with or against the orbital motion to change the spacecraft's velocity, keeping any junk a safe distance away from the spacecraft.

Degenerating orbits are another method for dealing with space junk. The degenerating orbit sends a satellite into a spin that causes it to burn up in the atmosphere.

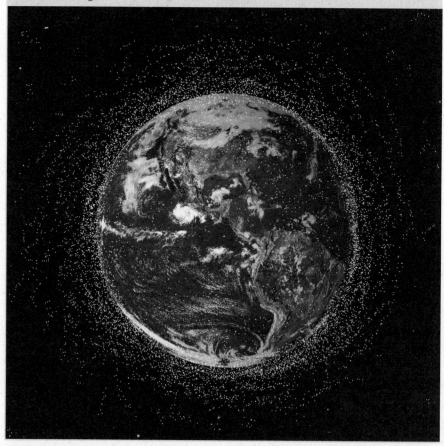

FIGURE 17: Rings of orbital debris encircle Earth.

Explain Explain how you would solve the problem of space debris. First, construct a hypothesis based on valid and reliable evidence. Consider theories and laws that describe motion in space. Then, apply scientific reasoning to link evidence to your claims. Assess the extent to which your data and reasoning support any conclusion.

Language Arts Connection What are the dangers and effects of the accumulation of space debris both now and in the future? Which of the proposed solutions do you think would work best?

NASA SCIENTIST   THE INTERNATIONAL SPACE STATION   Go online to choose one of these other paths.

Lesson Self-Check

CAN YOU EXPLAIN IT?

FIGURE 18: Mercury's transit of the sun in 2016

Explore Online ▶

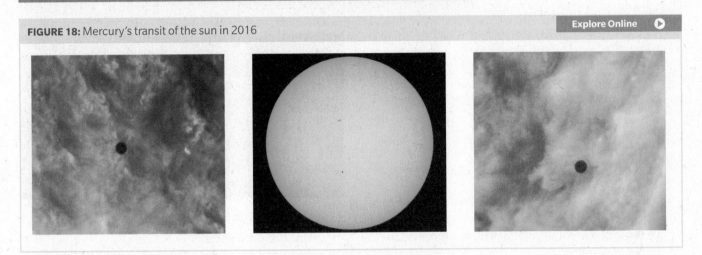

Mercury has a very strange orbit that scientists have only recently been able to explain. It has a very high eccentricity compared to Earth, and sometimes it looks as though it's moving backward. Because it is so close to the sun, it is heavily influenced by the sun's gravity. Sometimes, Mercury is very close to the sun and only 46 million km away. At its farthest point from the sun, it is 70 million km away.

For a long time scientists could not determine the orbit of Mercury. Some scientists thought there was a smaller planet or an asteroid belt near Mercury affecting its orbit, but they could not locate any objects nearby. Mercury's orbit is constantly changing. If a pin were stuck in the center of the orbit, the ellipse of Mercury's orbit would rotate around the pin. This is called *precession*. Scientists had a hard time explaining the precession of Mercury's orbit until Einstein developed his theory of general relativity in 1915. The theory describes the relationship between gravity, space, and mass. Any object orbiting as close to the sun as Mercury will experience this orbit precession effect because space is slightly warped by the sun's enormous gravity at these distances. Some scientists think that an impact from an asteroid may have set Mercury into its strange orbit.

 Explain How does Mercury appear to be moving relative to Earth? Why do you think its motion is so different from Earth's?

CHECKPOINTS

Check Your Understanding

1. Which object has the greatest eccentricity in its orbit?

  a. Pluto

  b. Saturn

  c. Jupiter

  d. Neptune

2. What gave planets their initial velocity

  a. gravity

  b. sun

  c. the formation of the solar system

  d. Kepler's third law

3. Using Newton's Law of Gravitation, if there are two objects exerting the force of gravity on each other and the mass of one of the objects is quadrupled, then the force between them is

  a. doubled.

  b. quartered.

  c. tripled.

  d. quadrupled.

4. Match the phrase from Kepler's laws to the quick descriptor:

  a. Kepler's 3rd law

  b. Kepler's 1st law

  c. Kepler's 2nd law

  1. The ellipitical path of the planets around the sun includes the center of the sun at one focus.

  2. The ratio of squares of the periods of two planets is equal to the ratio of cubes of the average distance from the sun.

  3. This law describes an imaginary line from the center of the sun to the center of the planet that sweeps through equal areas in equal time intervals.

5. For Figure 19, which statement accurately describes the difference between the gravitational force experienced by the top and bottom objects?

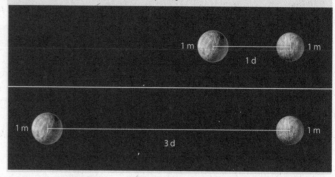

FIGURE 19: The bottom objects are separated by three times the distance between the top objects.

  a. The force between the top objects is one third that of the bottom objects.

  b. The force between the top objects is three times that of the bottom objects.

  c. The force between the top objects is one ninth that of the bottom objects.

  d. The force between the top objects is one half that of the bottom objects.

6. Using Newton's law of gravitation, if there are two objects exerting the force of gravity on each other and the mass of both of the objects is halved, then the force between them is

  a. doubled.

  b. quartered.

  c. tripled.

  d. quadrupled.

7. How does the ISS help manage space junk?

  a. It alters its own orbit to avoid known space junk.

  b. It slows down the orbit of the decommissioned satellite.

  c. It speeds up the orbit of the decommissioned satellite.

  d. It places a decommissioned satellite in a graveyard orbit.

8. Consider the orbital period and average distances from the sun for the planets listed below:

	Planet	Period (y)	Average distance (Au)
a.	Mercury	0.2	0.4
b.	Earth	1	1
c.	Saturn	29.5	9.5
d.	Neptune	165	30

Using the $\frac{p^2}{a^3}$ = constant ratio described in this unit, what is the approximate constant for each planet?

9. What are the foci of an ellipse?

a. the farthest points from the center

b. points near the center (lying along the long axis)

c. the closest points to the center

d. points near the center (lying along the short axis)

10. At which point in its orbit is a planet traveling the fastest?

a. when it is farthest from the sun

b. when it is traveling towards the sun

c. when it is traveling away from the sun

d. when it is closest to the sun

11. Which of these statements accurately describes how a satellite stays in orbit?

a. It is outside of Earth's gravity.

b. It is continuously falling and missing the Earth.

c. Its thrust is stronger than Earth's gravitational pull.

d. It is moving so fast that gravity doesn't affect it

Earth and the Sun

Earth and the sun interact through energy.

CAN YOU EXPLAIN IT?

FIGURE 1: Between 850 and 630 million years ago, Earth may have been almost completely covered in ice.

About 10% of Earth's surface today is covered in ice. Massive ice sheets cover most of Antarctica and Greenland, while sea ice covers the Arctic Ocean. Glaciers are also found in temperate and even tropical latitudes, but only at very high elevations where the air is significantly cooler than it is at sea level. Hundreds of millions of years ago, however, conditions may have been very different.

Evidence for glaciers at sea level near the equator suggests that Earth was much colder than it is today. Why would Earth have been significantly colder in the past?

Gather Evidence
As you explore the lesson, gather evidence to help explain how the amount of solar energy reaching Earth changes over time and how these changes can affect Earth's global climate.

Infer Where do you find ice sheets on Earth today? What are conditions like in these places? Use evidence to make an inference about Earth's conditions 700 million years ago, when ice sheets and glaciers where found near the equator.

Image Credits: (t) ©Louise Murray/Alamy; (b) ©Chris Butler/Science Source

The Earth-Sun System

Think about the last time you went outside. How does the interaction between Earth and the sun affect your life? Most of what we see outside during the daytime is visible because of sunlight. The warm air, wind, and rain that we feel exist because of the sun's energy.

In addition to light, the sun also emits streams of charged particles called the solar wind. Earth's magnetic field—which originates in Earth's core—exerts a force on those particles, causing them to deflect toward the poles. There they interact with the gases in Earth's atmosphere, causing the greenish-purplish glow of the aurora. The aurora is an example of the many interactions in the Earth-sun system.

FIGURE 2: An aurora, as seen from the International Space Station in 2012, is the result of the interaction between the solar wind and Earth's magnetic field and atmosphere.

Analyze Think about your everyday experiences. How are they affected by your interactions with the sun or by Earth's interactions with the sun?

Earth-Sun System Components

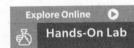

Explore Online ▶

Hands-On Lab

Earth-Sun Motion Design an experiment to measure the movement of Earth.

Suppose you travel back in time to Earth's past and find yourself on a planet that is covered in ice—snowball Earth! How would you go about understanding this frozen version of Earth? You learned that in science it is useful to think of events or phenomena as occurring within a system. Large-scale changes to Earth may involve many of its systems. A change that affects Earth's temperature may also involve Earth-sun system interactions.

Matter and energy are components of the Earth-sun system. Most of the matter and the energy in the system is concentrated in the sun. Composed mostly of hydrogen and helium atoms, the sun is 330 000 times as massive as Earth and has a volume at least 1 300 000 times as great as Earth's. Though matter is concentrated in the sun, Earth has a greater average density. Earth has an average density more than five times as great as the average density of the sun. It has a thin atmosphere made up mostly of nitrogen and oxygen, a solid surface that is largely covered in water, rock, ice, and living things, and a dense metallic core made of nickel and iron. Earth is orbited by the moon, a small rocky body without a significant atmosphere.

Image Credits: ©Science Source

Predict Choose a force, a form of energy, or a motion that is important to the interactions between Earth and the sun. How would your experience on Earth be different if that force, energy, or motion changed or did not exist?

The Earth-sun system includes not only Earth and the sun and the materials they are made of, but also the solar energy emitted from the sun, the gravitational forces keeping the objects close together and moving in their orbits, and the processes that are affected by sunlight and gravity.

Every 365 days, Earth completes one orbit around the sun. Earth's orbital motion is important, because it ensures that Earth stays at approximately the same distance from the sun throughout the year and receives a steady supply of energy from it. Although the total amount of energy that Earth receives does not change significantly throughout the year, the way that energy is distributed on the surface does vary.

Approximately once every 24 hours, Earth completes one rotation on its axis. This rotation results in the cycle of day and night. Earth's axis is not perpendicular to its path around the sun. Instead, it is constantly pointed toward Polaris—the North Star. As Earth orbits the sun, the orientation of its axis stays the same relative to Polaris, but it changes relative to the sun. In January, for example, the North Pole is pointed away from the sun, while in July it is pointed toward the sun.

Earth-Sun-Moon System Interactions

Interactions between Earth and the sun occur mainly through gravity and energy. The gravitational effects of the sun on Earth's surface are very difficult to notice. These effects are easier to observe when the moon is included as part of this system.

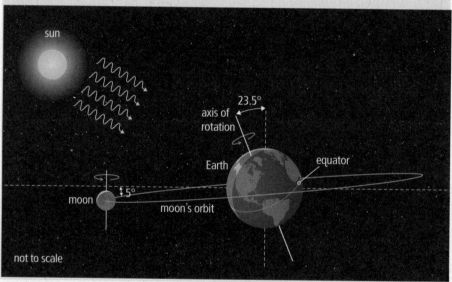

FIGURE 3: The force of gravity and inertia keeps the moon in orbit around Earth and the Earth-moon system in orbit around the sun.

Gravity

Model Make a drawing to compare the location of the moon relative to the sun and Earth during the new moon with the location of the moon during the first quarter. How does this model help explain the difference between spring tides and neap tides?

Tides are an example of how Earth, the sun, and the moon interact through gravity. Figure 4 shows the position of the moon relative to Earth and the sun at four different times in the moon's orbit. The difference between high and low tide is greatest at the new and full moon, and least during the first- and third-quarter moons. The changing gravitational interactions between the moon, sun, and Earth as the moon orbits Earth cause the difference between these tides, known as spring and neap tides.

FIGURE 4: Although the moon's gravity is the main reason for tides on Earth, the sun's gravity also has an effect.

spring tides

sun moon (new) Earth moon (full)

not to scale

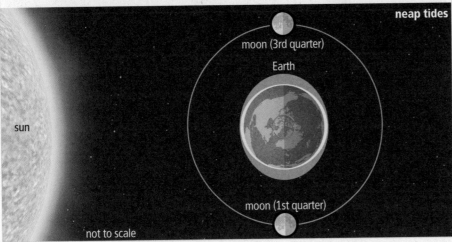

neap tides

moon (3rd quarter)

sun Earth

moon (1st quarter)

not to scale

FIGURE 5: Extreme low and high tides occur when the effects of the gravitational pull of the sun and the moon are added together.

The gravitational force between Earth and the sun is, in part, responsible for Earth's motion in space. At any given time, a planet is moving through space in two directions: straight forward and straight toward the center of the sun. Where do these two motions come from? A planet's forward motion is a result of its inertia, the tendency to keep moving as it has been moving since it formed. The motion toward the sun is a result of the gravitational force between the sun and the planet. The planet continuously accelerates toward the sun. It doesn't fall into the sun because of its inertia.

Earth's orbit is not perfectly circular. As a result, the distance between Earth and the sun varies slightly throughout the year. In January, Earth is about 5 million km closer to the sun than it is in July. Because the gravitational pull between two objects increases with decreasing distance, objects orbit faster when they are closer. In January, Earth moves through space slightly faster than it does in July.

Explain How does gravity affect the motion of Mercury relative to the sun? How is this effect similar to and different from the effect of gravity on the motion of the Earth-moon system around the sun?

Energy

Solar energy travels through space in the form of electromagnetic radiation. Of the light emitted by the sun, 41% is visible light, another 9% is ultraviolet light, and 50% is infrared radiation.

FIGURE 6: Light is emitted by the sun and then absorbed, reflected, refracted, and radiated by materials on Earth's surface and in the atmosphere.

Image Credits: ©Irisphoto1/Fotolia; ©Louise Murray/Alamy

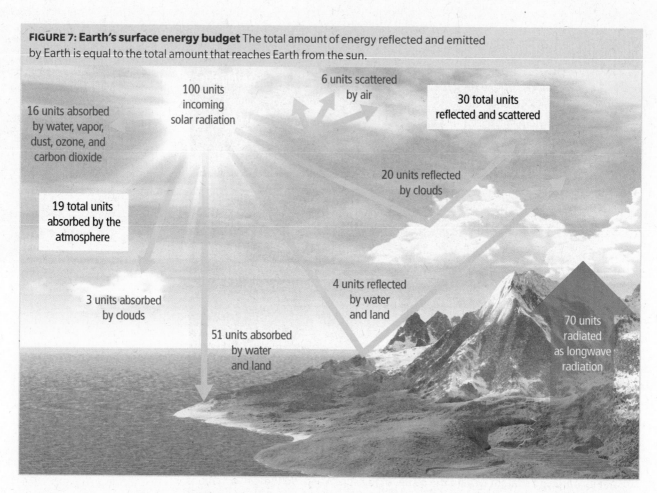

FIGURE 7: Earth's surface energy budget The total amount of energy reflected and emitted by Earth is equal to the total amount that reaches Earth from the sun.

100 units incoming solar radiation

6 units scattered by air

30 total units reflected and scattered

16 units absorbed by water, vapor, dust, ozone, and carbon dioxide

20 units reflected by clouds

19 total units absorbed by the atmosphere

3 units absorbed by clouds

4 units reflected by water and land

70 units radiated as longwave radiation

51 units absorbed by water and land

When solar energy reaches Earth, it interacts with the atmosphere and surface. Some is reflected off clouds, land, water, and ice. Earth is visible from space because of the sunlight that reflects off it. Light that is not reflected is absorbed by rock and water on the surface and by gases in the atmosphere. Once light is absorbed, it causes the material to heat up. The ground is hotter during the day than at night, because it absorbs sunlight. As a material heats up, it emits energy in the form of invisible infrared radiation. Earth's surface radiates infrared energy out toward space, but some is absorbed by Earth's atmosphere.

Overall, the amount of solar energy that reaches Earth from space is balanced by the amount that is reflected and radiated back to space. However, gases in the atmosphere, known as greenhouse gases, absorb and give off infrared radiation. As a result, Earth's atmosphere absorbs some of the outgoing radiation and keeps it in the Earth system for a while, which raises Earth's surface temperature. This process is called the *greenhouse effect*.

Without the greenhouse effect, much of Earth's heat energy would be lost almost immediately to outer space. Earth's average surface temperature would be about 33°C cooler than it is now. The greenhouse effect has helped Earth thrive as a planet. Recently, however, there has been such a significant increase in the levels of carbon dioxide in the atmosphere that Earth's energy budget may be out of balance. Many scientist warn of the possibilities of global climate change.

Math connection

Calculate The albedo of a surface is a measure of how reflective it is. To calculate the albedo, divide the amount of solar energy reflected by the surface by the total amount of solar energy that reaches Earth. What is Earth's albedo?

Predict Think about how light moves through different materials. What are some factors that could change the amount of sunlight absorbed by Earth's surface and atmosphere?

Solar Energy in Earth's Systems

Energy is continuously moving outward from the sun in all directions. The amount of energy that reaches Earth does not change significantly from hour to hour, day to day, or even month to month. In spite of this, however, we can feel differences from place to place and from season to season.

Energy in Systems

A diagram of Earth's energy budget is a model showing the ways that energy moves to and from Earth. What this model does not show is how solar energy flows within Earth's systems. It does not show all the ways that the flow of solar energy influences Earth's surface—how it affects the atmosphere, the hydrosphere, lithosphere, or the biosphere. When we study the importance of solar energy to Earth systems, it is useful to examine what happens when the amount of solar energy in a location changes.

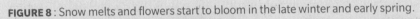
FIGURE 8 : Snow melts and flowers start to bloom in the late winter and early spring.

Explain Do you agree or disagree with the following statement? Without the sun, there would be no changes in the weather on Earth. Use reasoning to support your argument.

You learned that when solar energy reaches Earth, it interacts with matter on the surface and in the atmosphere. While the amount of energy emitted by the sun is nearly constant, its distribution over Earth's surface changes. During the spring, the amount of energy reaching a particular part of Earth increases. With more direct sunlight and more hours of daylight, the amount of energy absorbed by the ground increases. The ground heats up more and emits more energy, warming the air above. The warmer air, along with the increase in intensity of light and the switch from snowfall to rain, causes the snow to melt. The meltwater seeps into the ground. With less snow reflecting the sunlight, more light is absorbed by the ground. The warmth and water trigger the growth of spring flowers. Once the plants are above ground, their leaves use the sunlight and water during the process of photosynthesis, converting sunlight into chemical energy within the plant. Animals such as deer and squirrels eat the flowers, using the stored sunlight in them to live and grow.

FIGURE 9: Solar energy drives the water cycle and the global wind systems.

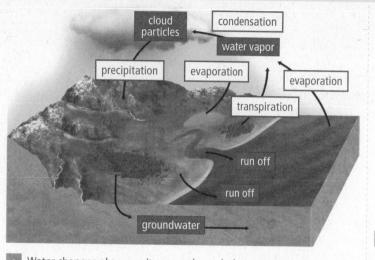

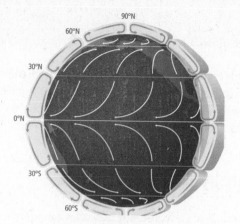

a Water changes phases as it moves through the water cycle. These changes are driven by energy from the sun.

b Uneven heating of Earth's surface results in global winds. Rising warm air and sinking cool air currents (red and blue arrows) form patterns that produce surface winds (white arrows).

Collaborate With a partner, explain how each part of the water cycle would be affected if the amount of solar energy reaching the surface in a given place changed. Use reasoning to support your explanations.

Sunlight has a profound effect on individual Earth's systems. It is a major factor in Earth's global cycles and processes. Sunlight provides the energy that causes water to change form as it moves through the water cycle. Solar energy drives local and global wind patterns, which develop as the sun heats up parts of Earth more, or more quickly, than other parts of the planet. Differences in weather from place to place, and changes in weather from day to day, are also a result of differences in the way sunlight interacts with Earth's different surfaces over distance and time. Because the sun is the main source of energy for living things on Earth, sunlight is also key in the cycling of carbon and oxygen between the atmosphere and living things. Plants, for example, use more oxygen in spring and summer when the length of day and sunlight intensity increases.

Distribution of Solar Energy on Earth's Surface

If you live in a region with distinct seasons, you are familiar with the cyclic pattern of temperature, precipitation, and daylight change that occurs during the year. These changes are a result of Earth's shape, the tilt of its axis, and its orbit around the sun.

FIGURE 10: Earth's shape and axial tilt affect the amount of energy received by different regions of the planet.

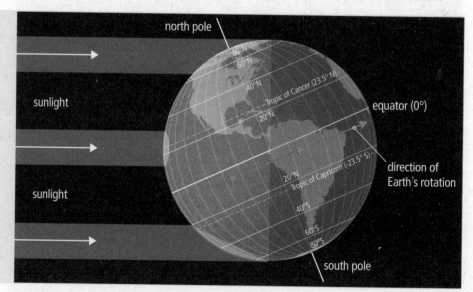

Therefore, the total amount of solar energy that tropical regions receive is significantly greater than that of polar regions. This difference in energy distribution affects climate and drives the movement of winds and ocean currents.

Because Earth's tilt relative to the sun changes as it orbits the sun, the concentration of sunlight in any given area changes throughout the year. This results in seasons. During the June solstice, when the North Pole is tilted toward the sun, the sunlight is most intense at 23.5°N of the equator. The Northern Hemisphere experiences the warmer temperatures and longer days of summer, while the Southern Hemisphere experiences winter. During the December solstice, when the North Pole is tilted away from the sun, sunlight falls most directly at 23.5°S of the equator. The Northern Hemisphere experiences lower temperatures and shorter days of winter, while the Southern Hemisphere experiences summer. During the spring and fall equinoxes, in March and September, respectively, Earth's axis is not tilted away or toward the sun, and sunlight is most intense at the equator. All areas of Earth receive 12 hours of daylight, and there is no difference in the amount of energy received by either hemisphere.

 Explain In January, the days are longer and the weather is warmer in South America than in North America. Explain this difference in terms of interactions between Earth and the sun.

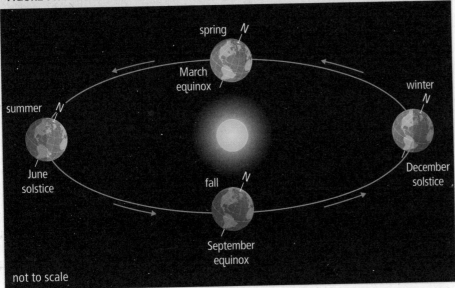

FIGURE 11: Seasons in the northern hemisphere

spring

March equinox

summer

June solstice

winter

December solstice

fall

September equinox

not to scale

The effect of seasonal changes on temperature and daylight are most dramatic near the poles and least dramatic near the equator. In March and September, both poles experience 12 hours of daylight. But in December, the North Pole is pointing away from the sun at such an angle that the region does not experience any hours of daylight whatsoever. At the same time, the South Pole is pointing toward the sun at such an angle that it experiences a full 24 hours of daylight. This situation is reversed in June. At the equator, however, the difference in intensity of light and number of daylight hours changes much less throughout the year than it does at the poles.

Explore Online ▶

Hands-On Lab

Positions of Sunrise and Sunset Collect and analyze data describing the positions of sunrise and sunset, and then make predictions for future months.

Model Make a sketch that shows why the intensity of sunlight differs from place to place because Earth is spherical. Use the sketch to show why areas that are tilted directly toward the sun receive more solar energy than those that are not.

Earth-Sun System and Climate Change

Studying the current conditions of the Earth-sun system helps us understand Earth's daily and seasonal changes in weather, differences in climate from place to place, and Earth's global climate conditions in general. However, evidence in the rock and fossil record suggests that Earth's global climate has changed significantly in the past. Earth has experienced much cooler and much warmer periods. The current variations of the Earth-sun system cannot explain these changes. Could solar radiation, Earth's tilt, and its orbit have changed over time, and if so, could these factors explain changes in Earth's climate?

Solar Variability

Since 1978, scientists have used satellites to measure the amount of sunlight that reaches the top of the atmosphere. Measuring sunlight away from Earth's surface allows us to see patterns that are related to the amount of energy given off by the sun, rather than daily and seasonal patterns related to Earth's rotation and orbit.

For centuries, scientists have known that the amount of energy emitted by the sun changes over time. It fluctuates on a cycle of about 11 years. For example, in 1999 the sun emitted about 0.1% more energy than in 1996, but about the same as it did in 1988. It turns out that the amount of energy that the sun emits is related to sunspot activity. Sunspots are darker spots within the sun's bright surface. The number of sunspots visible each month varies between almost 0 to nearly 200. In general, the more sunspots there are, the more energy is being emitted by the sun.

This relationship between sunspots and solar energy is very useful. We have only a few decades of actual measurements of solar energy, but we have more than 400 years of scientific observations of sunspots, beginning with Galileo in 1610. We can therefore use historical records of sunspots to infer changes in solar energy.

Analyze Describe the relationship between sunspot activity and average change in air temperature between 1860 and 1960. What explains this relationship?

Sunspot Activity and Change in Air Temperature, 1860–2000

FIGURE 12: Plots showing sunspot activity and solar energy reaching Earth's upper atmosphere

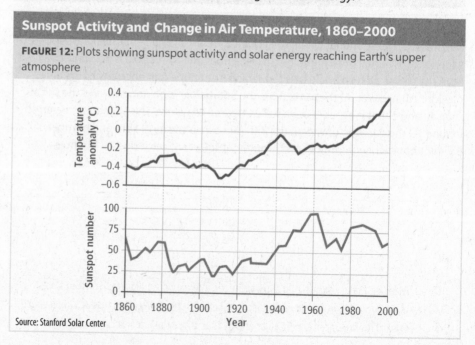

Source: Stanford Solar Center

How do changes due to sunspot activity affect Earth's climate? By comparing graphs of sunspot cycles and average global temperature change over time, it becomes apparent that even a small change in energy emitted by the sun does affect Earth's climate. Perhaps the most dramatic example is known as the Maunder Minimum. Between 1645 and 1700, there were very few sunspots. This corresponded to a particularly cold period in Europe, part of a period known as the Little Ice Age.

In addition to the 11-year sunspot cycle, the sun appears to go through other longer period cycles as well. As the sun ages, it is becoming hotter and brighter. However, this change is very slow.

Predict Suppose the sun went through several decades of very low sunspot activity. How could this affect Earth's surface? Support your prediction with evidence and reasoning.

Changes in Earth's Motion

The amount of energy that reaches Earth depends not only on the amount of energy emitted by the sun, but also on changes in Earth's motion in space.

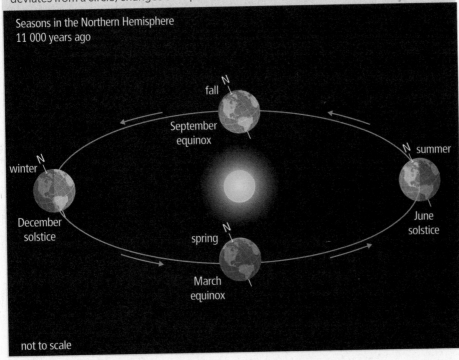

FIGURE 13: Earth's orbit can be more or less circular. Its eccentricity, or how much it deviates from a circle, changes over periods of about 100 000 years and 413 000 years.

Seasons in the Northern Hemisphere
11 000 years ago

not to scale

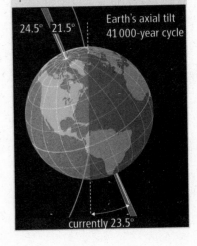

FIGURE 14: Earth's tilt varies between 21.5° and 24.5° over a period of about 41 000 years.

Earth's axial tilt
41 000-year cycle

24.5° 21.5°

currently 23.5°

At its closest point, Earth is 147.1 million km from the sun. At its farthest point, it is 152.1 million km from the sun. As a result, about 7% more solar energy reaches Earth in January than in July. Over time, however, Earth's orbit becomes more elliptical and less elliptical, or eccentric. As a result, the difference between its closest and farthest approach to the sun changes. When Earth's orbit is more circular, Earth spends more time closer to the sun. When Earth's orbit is more eccentric, Earth spends more time farther from the sun.

Changes in the eccentricity of Earth's orbit can affect the differences between seasons. For example, if Earth is closer to the sun during the summer, summer will be slightly warmer. Eccentricity can also affect the total amount of energy received from the sun. When Earth's orbit is more circular, it receives slightly more solar energy during the year than when it is more elliptical. This results in slight fluctuations in temperature over tens of thousands of years.

Analyze How might changes in eccentricity affect the amount of solar energy reaching Earth?

FIGURE 15: The direction that Earth's axis points in space changes slowly over time.

Model Make a sketch to show what Earth would look like at different points in its orbit if its axis were pointing to a different star in space. How might this change affect seasons on Earth? Use reasoning to support your claim.

Analyze Describe the relationship between solar energy reaching the Northern Hemisphere in July to average air temperature in Antarctica. What could explain the relationship?

Earth is currently tilted about 23.5° relative to its orbital plane. However, about 10 000 years ago Earth's tilt was about 24.5°, and 30 000 years ago its tilt was about 22.2°. The more Earth's axis is tilted, the greater the differences between seasons—winters are colder and summers are warmer. The smaller the tilt, the less the weather changes from season to season. Scientists think that axial tilt affects global climate—not just seasonal changes. When the tilt is smaller, less winter snow melts during the cooler summers. This can result in the expansion of glaciers and ice sheets.

Presently, Earth's axis points toward Polaris, the North Star. Over a period of about 26 000 years, however, the axis itself rotates. This motion is called precession, and it is similar to the wobble of a spinning top. Because of precession, the direction that Earth's axis points in space changes, which affects the timing of the seasons. Today, for example, summer in the Southern Hemisphere occurs when Earth is closest to the sun. However, 11 000 years ago, Earth's axis pointed in the opposite direction, just as it does today, and summer occurred in the Northern Hemisphere when Earth was closest to the sun.

Independently, the effect on seasons or global climate of each of these changes in Earth's motion in space—its eccentricity, tilt, and precession—is clear. But because all of these changes occur at the same time, understanding the combined effect is complicated. Scientists use mathematical and computer models to understand the combined effects of Earth's motion in space.

Explain Earth has gone through many cycles of ice ages followed by periods of warmer climate. How might these cycles be related to patterns of solar output and patterns of change in Earth's motion in space?

Evidence of Past Climate

Evidence shows that over thousands of years, Earth has gone through many glacial periods. These periods are separated from each other by interglacial periods—periods of warmer weather, melting of ice sheets, and rises in sea level. But how can we determine the timing of glacial and interglacial periods?

Milankovitch Cycles and Temperature from the Vostok Ice Core

FIGURE 16: Geologists compared temperature data to Milankovitch models to test the hypothesis that ice ages are a result of changes in Earth's motion in space.

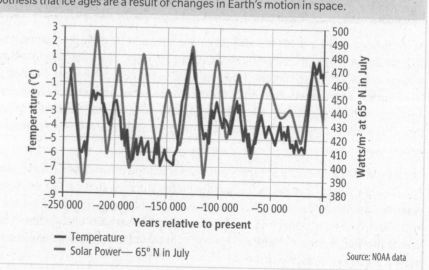

— Temperature
— Solar Power— 65° N in July

Source: NOAA data

Image Credits: ©Robert Simmon/NASA Goddard Space Flight Center

In the early 20th century, Serbian scientist and engineer Milutin Milankovitch developed a model to show how a combination of changes in Earth's motion would affect solar radiation reaching the Northern Hemisphere and, therefore, Earth's glaciation patterns. When Milkankovitch developed his model, it was difficult to put precise dates on when each glacial and interglacial period occurred.

In the 1970s, scientists developed new methods for estimating global temperatures using natural recorders of climate variability, such as tree rings, fossils, and glacial ice cores. Scientists study the texture and composition of layers in ice cores to infer the timing and duration of glacial and interglacial periods. The graph in Figure 16 combines data from Antarctic ice cores with calculations of solar radiation to show global changes in Earth's temperature over time. In order to accurately time interglacial and glacial periods, scientists study the ratio of different types of oxygen in ice cores and in the shells of marine fossils. They also measure the thickness of annual growth rings in old and fossilized trees to determine past climate conditions.

Patterns

FIGURE 17: Patterns in tree rings, ice cores, layers of sedimentary rock, and locations of rocks transported by glaciers all reveal that Earth has gone through cycles of cooler and warmer climates.

a Tree rings reveal information about climate when the tree was growing.

b Rock layers contain fossils that can be used to figure out ocean temperatures.

c Ice cores can be used to infer snowfall rates and air temperature.

d Glacial erratics are evidence that ice once covered an area.

Pattern Evidence

In order for an idea to be accepted as scientific theory, it must not only make sense theoretically and mathematically, it must also be supported by an abundance of evidence. Milankovitch's idea that patterns of changes in Earth's motion cause patterns of change in Earth's climate is supported by many observations and measurements from many different places on Earth.

Evaluate Which of the types of evidence shown in the images are most useful for constructing a record of climate change over thousands or millions of years? Use reasoning to support your response.

Predict How could you use an understanding of Earth's motion in space to predict changes in global climate over the next few hundred thousand years? How could it be possible to predict future climate with complete accuracy?

Data Analysis

Cycles of Glaciation

In the early 20th century, Milutin Milankovitch developed a model to test his hypothesis that cycles of glacial-interglacial periods in Earth history could have been caused by changes in Earth's motion in space. The result was a graph similar to the graph at the bottom of Figure 18, which shows a clear pattern of increasing and decreasing amounts of incoming solar radiation—insolation—reaching the Northern Hemisphere in July. These periodic changes in Earth's orbit are now known as *Milankovitch cycles,* and they correlate strongly to patterns of glacial and interglacial periods on Earth.

Use the graphs, along with what you have already learned in this lesson, to answer the following questions.

1. Over the past 600 000 years, when was Earth's orbit most elliptical? When was it least elliptical?

2. How does ellipticity affect the total amount of solar energy that reaches Earth?

3. Over the past 600 000 years, when was Earth's axis tilted most? When was it tilted least?

4. Assuming Earth's orbit is the same as it is today, how does tilt affect the amount of energy reaching the Northern Hemisphere in July?

5. The day of perihelion is the day when Earth is closest to the sun. Describe how the day of perihelion changes over time.

6. How does the day of perihelion affect climate?

7. How would you describe the way that eccentricity, tilt, and the time of perihelion together seem to affect the amount of energy reaching the Northern Hemisphere in July?

 Explain Why is the graph of northern summer insolation not a perfectly regular pattern?

Milankovitch Cycles

FIGURE 18 Combined changes in eccentricity, axial tilt, and precession affect seasonality and the difference between seasons.

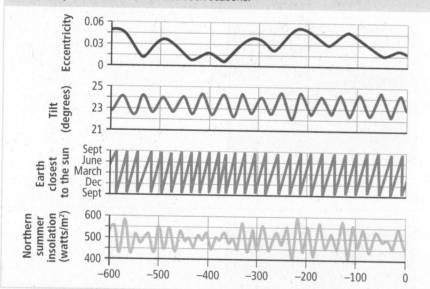

 **Language Arts Connection** Research how variations in Earth's orbit determine the intensity of sunlight that falls in the far North during the summer months and how weak summer sunlight over a period of years can cause snow accumulation that can lead to ice ages. Present your findings in the form of an infographic, a poster presentation, or a slide-show presentation.

MILANKOVITCH CYCLES ON MARS   **CLIMATE FEEDBACK**   Go online to choose one of these other paths.

Lesson Self-Check

CAN YOU EXPLAIN IT ?

FIGURE 19: Between 850 and 630 million years ago, Earth may have been almost completely covered in ice.

Ice sheets currently cover most of Antarctica and Greenland. The North Pole itself is an ocean, which is almost permanently covered in sea ice. Glaciers are also found in temperate and even tropical latitudes. Glaciers like these, including the Furtwängler Glacier located almost on the equator at the summit of Mt. Kilimanjaro, are found at very high elevations, where the air is significantly cooler than it is at sea level.

It is not surprising that the geologic record holds evidence for the existence of glaciers and ice sheets in the past. Twenty thousand years ago, for example, a vast ice sheet extended as far south as New York and Pennsylvania. The evidence for these ice sheets, along with vast quantities of other evidence, indicates that at the time Earth was about 5 °C cooler than it is today. Evidence from sedimentary rocks and fossils also shows that Earth has gone through major changes in climate over the past 600 million years.

What is surprising, however, is the evidence that earlier in Earth history—around 700 million years ago—the entire Earth could have been covered in ice. Geologists refer to this possible period as the Snowball Earth. What could cause Earth to become covered in ice? What caused other major changes in climate shown in the rock and fossil record? Geologists think that changes in climate are a result of a combination of factors, including changes in energy radiated by the sun, changes in Earth's orbit and tilt, changes in the composition of the atmosphere, episodes of volcanism and mountain building, and changes in the locations of continents and oceans.

Explain What conditions affect how warm Earth's surface is? What could have been different 700 million years ago that resulted in more of Earth's surface being covered in ice?

CHECKPOINTS

Check Your Understanding

1. A system can be described by its components and the processes that occur within it.

   Identify the components of matter, energy, and force in the Earth-sun system.
   a. matter:_____
   b. energy:_____
   c. force:_____

2. Give examples of processes that occur within the Earth-sun system:
   a. process that involves energy only: _____
   b. process that involves interaction between force and matter: _____
   c. process that involves interaction between energy and matter: _____

3. Which of the following statements accurately describe interactions in the Earth-sun system? Choose all that apply.
   a. Without gravity, Earth would not move at all through space.
   b. Different regions of Earth receive different amounts of solar energy.
   c. As Earth warms up, the amount of energy emitted by the sun increases, decreasing volcanic activity on Earth's surface.
   d. If Earth were not tilted, it would be heated evenly over the entire surface.
   e. Energy absorbed by Earth's surface flows into Earth's interior to keep it warm.
   f. The total amount of energy that reaches Earth depends on its distance from the sun.

4. A student wants to explain why polar climates are cooler than tropical climates. Describe a 3D model that the student could make out of simple materials in order to explain this. Explain what each part of the model represents and how the student would use the model to explain differences in climate.

5. Organize the following statements into four cause-and-effect pairs.
   • Earth's tilt increases.
   • Sunspot activity increases.
   • The timing of the seasons changes.
   • More radiation is emitted by the sun.
   • Earth's axis and orbit precess (wobble).
   • Earth receives slightly less solar radiation.
   • Seasonal differences in weather are greater.
   • Earth's orbit becomes more eccentric (more elliptical).

6. For each change, identify the timescale over which the change occurs: hours, months, years, thousands of years, or billions of years.
   a. Earth rotates on its axis.
   b. The tilt of Earth's axis changes.
   c. The sun gets hotter as it evolves.
   d. The shape of Earth's orbit changes.
   e. The orientation of Earth's axis changes as it orbits the sun.
   f. The number of sunspots observed increases and decreases.

7. Scientists think that between 1645 and 1715, the sun went through a period of emitting less solar energy. The image below shows Earth's energy budget today.

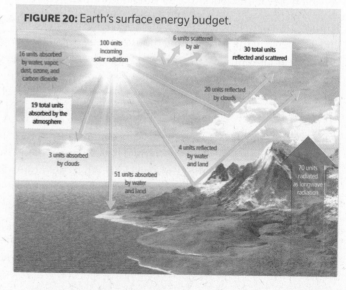

FIGURE 20: Earth's surface energy budget.

100 units incoming solar radiation

6 units scattered by air

30 total units reflected and scattered

16 units absorbed by water, vapor, dust, ozone, and carbon dioxide

20 units reflected by clouds

19 total units absorbed by the atmosphere

3 units absorbed by clouds

4 units reflected by water and land

51 units absorbed by water and land

70 units radiated as longwave radiation

Describe three ways that the energy budget diagram for 1645–1715 would be different.

8. How and why could a change in solar output affect Earth's water cycle?

9. Which of the following are most likely causes of glacial periods over the past 2 million years? Choose all that apply.
   a. decrease in tilt of Earth's axis
   b. increasing eccentricity of Earth's orbit
   c. decreasing rate of fusion in the sun over time
   d. decreasing volcanic activity on Earth's surface
   e. increasing difference between high and low tides
   f. decreasing force of gravity between Earth and the sun
   g. increasing frequency of comets entering the inner solar system

10. Which of the following are Milankovitch cycles? Choose all that apply.
   a. eccentricity
   b. sunspot cycle
   c. precession
   d. axial tilt

11. Explain how changes in the tilt of Earth's axis can affect the differences between seasons.

12. At what time of year is the North Pole in complete darkness?
   a. during the June solstice
   b. during the spring equinox
   c. during the fall equinox
   d. during the December solstice

13. When it is summer is Australia, it is
   a. fall in the United States
   b. winter in the United States
   c. spring in the United States
   d. summer in the United States

14. Which of the following methods would scientists use to determine global changes in Earth's climate over time?
   a. by examining ice cores
   b. by examining tree rings
   c. by examining sedimentary strata
   d. by examining glacial eccentrics

15. What aspect of Earth's orbit changes in cycles of 23 000 years? Of 41 000 years? of 100 000 years?

16. What is the variation in the periodicity of long-term changes in eccentricity?
   a. 25 700 years
   b. 100 000 and 413 000 years
   c. 41 000 years
   d. 23 000 years

17. What would be consequence for incoming solar radiation and the seasons if Earth had no tilt? a 90° tilt?

18. In approximately 13 000 years, Earth's axis will point toward the star Vega. Twenty-six thousand years from now, where will Earth's axis be pointing?

MAKE YOUR OWN STUDY GUIDE

 In your Evidence Notebook, design a study guide that supports the main ideas in this lesson:
- The sun and Earth are part of a system of interacting components of matter and energy.
- Almost all of Earth's surface energy originate as sunlight.
- Sunlight affects different parts of Earth in different ways depending on latitude, time of year, and surface characteristics.
- Gravity holds Earth in orbit around the sun, ensuring that a steady supply of energy reaches Earth.
- Changes in the amount of energy emitted by the sun and the amount reaching Earth in total and at different times of year can affect Earth's global climate.

Remember to include the following information in your study guide:
- Support main ideas about Earth-sun interactions with specific examples.
- Record explanations for patterns in the interactions between Earth and the sun.
- Evaluate evidence for the effects of changes in the Earth-sun system over time.

A BOOK EXPLAINING
COMPLEX IDEAS USING
ONLY THE 1000 MOST
COMMON WORDS →

RANDALL MUNROE
XKCD.COM

WORLDS AROUND THE SUN

The system made up of the sun and the bodies that travel around it

Understanding the formation and characteristics of our solar system and its planets can help scientists plan investigations to study planets and solar systems around other stars in the universe. Here's a look at our solar system.

THE STORY OF OUR WORLD AND BEYOND

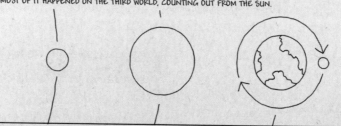

THE SUN IS THE BIGGEST THING NEAR US. OUR WORLD AND EVERYTHING NEAR IT GOES AROUND THE SUN. SOME OF THE WORLDS THAT GO AROUND THE SUN ARE BIG ENOUGH THAT THEY HAVE THEIR OWN MOONS—LITTLE WORLDS THAT GO AROUND THEM AS THEY ALL GO AROUND THE SUN. ALL OF OUR HISTORY HAPPENED IN THIS PICTURE. MOST OF IT HAPPENED ON THE THIRD WORLD, COUNTING OUT FROM THE SUN.

THE LITTLE RED WORLD

This world had seas on it when it was very young, but now it's cold and the seas are gone. It's called the red world because there's metal in the sand, and it turned red over time for the same reason that old keys or trucks turn red on Earth if you leave them outside for a long time.

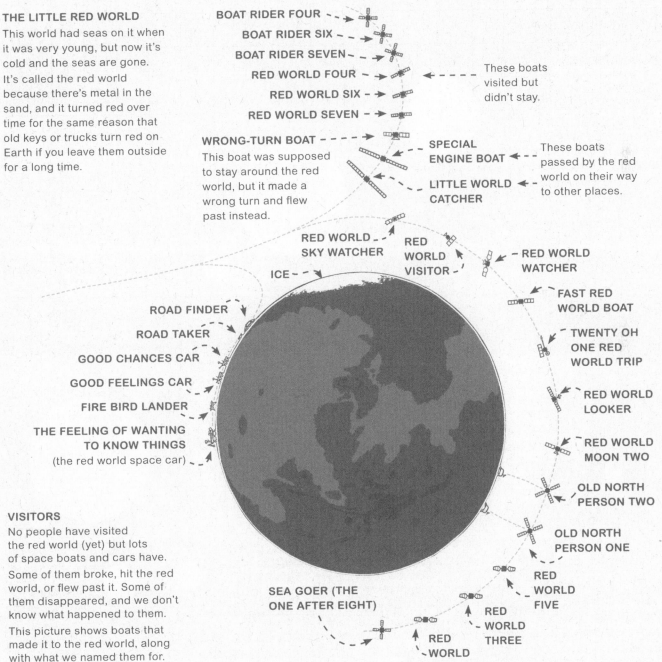

BOAT RIDER FOUR

BOAT RIDER SIX

BOAT RIDER SEVEN

RED WORLD FOUR

RED WORLD SIX

RED WORLD SEVEN

These boats visited but didn't stay.

WRONG-TURN BOAT
This boat was supposed to stay around the red world, but it made a wrong turn and flew past instead.

SPECIAL ENGINE BOAT

LITTLE WORLD CATCHER

These boats passed by the red world on their way to other places.

RED WORLD SKY WATCHER

RED WORLD VISITOR

ICE

RED WORLD WATCHER

ROAD FINDER

ROAD TAKER

GOOD CHANCES CAR

GOOD FEELINGS CAR

FIRE BIRD LANDER

THE FEELING OF WANTING TO KNOW THINGS
(the red world space car)

FAST RED WORLD BOAT

TWENTY OH ONE RED WORLD TRIP

RED WORLD LOOKER

RED WORLD MOON TWO

OLD NORTH PERSON TWO

OLD NORTH PERSON ONE

RED WORLD FIVE

RED WORLD THREE

RED WORLD ONE

SEA GOER (THE ONE AFTER EIGHT)

VISITORS

No people have visited the red world (yet) but lots of space boats and cars have.

Some of them broke, hit the red world, or flew past it. Some of them disappeared, and we don't know what happened to them.

This picture shows boats that made it to the red world, along with what we named them for.

WORLDS AROUND THE SUN

LOST WORLD
This world is strange because it used to go around the Sun alone, but one day it came too close to the cold wind world and now it lives there.

BIG TRIP TAKER TWO
Big Trip Taker Two is the only boat to visit the two outer worlds.

These two air worlds are smaller than the ring world and the huge air world. They have more kinds of water in their air, which makes them more blue.

RING WORLD BOAT
This boat visited the ring world to learn more about it—and to get a closer look at the cloud moon.

This world is far from the Sun. It has the coldest air and the fastest winds.

BIG TRIP TAKER ONE
We were so surprised when an earlier boat saw clouds around the cloud moon, we told Big Trip Taker One to change plans and fly past the cloud moon for a closer look. This took it off the road to the other worlds, and it headed out into space. It's now traveled farther from home than anything humans have built.

CLOUD MOON
This world is very strange—it's the only moon covered in thick clouds. The air there is even thicker than Earth's. It would be nice if it were the kind of air we can breathe, but it's not.

RING WORLD
All the big air worlds have thin rings, but this world's are huge and bright.

These two worlds are huge balls of air and water with some rocks in the middle.

BIG WORLD BOAT
This boat visited the big world and its moons. Once it was done with its job, we told it to fly into the huge air world so it would burn up in the air, just like old space boats sometimes do on Earth.

We did that because we were worried that if we didn't, it would hit one of the other worlds and spread Earth's tiny animals there. We don't know if there are any other animals on those worlds, but if there are, we don't want our animals to eat them before we can look at them.

BIG WORLD
This is the biggest world around the Sun. It's mostly made of air. Some of its moons are almost as big as our world.

OLD CIRCLE-COVERED MOON
This moon got hit by lots of rocks once, which left it covered in circle-shaped holes, just like our Moon.

DARK WORLDS
Out past the cold wind world, there are lots of little ice worlds moving very slowly around the far-away Sun.

ICE WATER MOON
This world has ice on the outside, but it's warmer on the inside, and there's water under the ice.
Since there's warm water, lots of people want to go there to look for animals. We don't know if there are animals there, but if there are, we want to know about them.

BIG MOON
This is the biggest and heaviest moon near the Sun.

Go online for more about *Thing Explainer*.

SPECIAL ENGINE BOAT
This boat visited two of the little worlds between the red world and the huge world. It's pushed by a special engine that's powered by the Sun.

It was the first boat to visit two different worlds and stay for a while at each of them.

LITTLE RED WORLD

RED WORLD SPACE CAR

HOT SKY WORLD
This world is about as big as our world, but it's much hotter. One reason it's hot is that it's closer to the Sun. The other reason is that it has more air than our world, which keeps it warm, sort of like a thick coat around the whole world.

People used to think this world would be nice to live on. But if you visit this world, you will have lots of problems.

The air is really hot. If you land there, you will be on fire, and you will not come home. The air is really heavy. If you land there, it will be like you're deep under the sea. The sky will press down on you and make you get smaller, and you will not come home. The air isn't the kind of air humans breathe. If you try to breathe it, you will not come home. The air is also full of a kind of water that's bad for your skin. If it touches you, you might come home, but without your skin.

THE SUN
The Sun is a star. It looks bigger and brighter than other stars because it's much closer to us. But it turns out it really *is* bigger and brighter than other stars.

For a while, we thought it was smaller than other stars, because most of the stars we looked at turned out to be bigger than it. But it turns out there are lots of stars that are less bright; they're just harder to see.

SMALL ROCK WORLD
This world is hard to see because it's right next to the bright Sun. It turns very slowly, so the day side gets very hot and the night side gets very cold.

OUR WORLD
There are animals and trees and a blue sky here. You probably live here, too; it's very hard to leave.

THE MOON
Other moons have names, but our moon is just called the Moon. Some people visited it once.

We're not sure where it came from. We think another world probably hit our world when it was very young and lots of pieces flew off, and then the pieces fell together and made the new baby world. But we don't know for sure yet.

SMELLY YELLOW MOON
This world has lots of color, but the color doesn't look very nice. It looks kind of like fire, but even more like food that came out of someone's mouth. It's covered in stuff that smells like old food.

Physics Connection

Exploring Rotational Motion An object that spins about its center of mass is said to be in rotational motion. The sun, planets, and moons of the solar system all exhibit rotational motion. Everyday examples of rotational motion include the spinning of a football as it flies through the air or a figure skater as she executes a spin. As a skater draws her hands closer to her body, more of her mass is near the axis of rotation. As a result, the speed of rotation increases.

> Use library or Internet resources to learn more about rotational motion. Then investigate the rotational motion of one of the planets in the solar system. How does its speed of rotation compare with those of other planets? What factors might cause the speed of rotation to change?

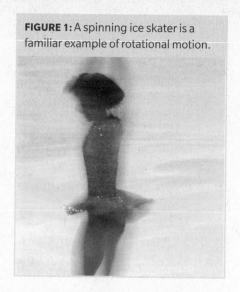

FIGURE 1: A spinning ice skater is a familiar example of rotational motion.

Social Studies Connection

Traditional Calendars Many cultures developed calendars to keep track of time. The calendars are based on patterns of changes in the Earth-sun-moon system. Many of the calendars developed hundreds to thousands of years ago are almost as accurate as the calendars we use today. In equatorial regions, purely lunar calendars are more common. Cultures in higher latitudes tended to have solar calendars with lunar subdivisions.

> Using library and Internet resources, research the calendar system developed by a specific culture, such as the Mayan calendar, the Chinese calendar (four seasons and eight nodes), the Egyptian (Ptolemaic) calendar, or one from another culture. Why might some cultures use a lunar-based calendar, while other cultures use solar-based calendars? Write a blog entry explaining how the calendar was developed. How was the calendar used by that culture?

FIGURE 2: An Aztec calendar

Art Connection

Sun in Art The sun is an integral part of our lives. Artists have rendered the sun since the earliest forms of art. But art changes through time. How has the sun been represented in art through time?

> Use library and Internet resources to find three examples of how the sun has been rendered by artists through time. Prepare a presentation that includes an image of a piece showing the sun with the artist's name or, if the artist is unknown, the period when the art was created. Write a short paragraph identifying similarities or differences in how the sun was represented and how these representations differ from our scientific understanding of the sun.

FIGURE 3: Vincent van Gogh's painting *The Sower*

SYNTHESIZE THE UNIT

In your Evidence Notebook, create a concept map, graphic organizer, or outline using the Study Guides you created for each lesson in this unit. Be sure to use evidence to support your claims.

When synthesizing individual information, remember to follow these general steps:

· Find the central idea of each piece of information.
· Think about the relationships among the central ideas.
· Combine the ideas to come up with a new understanding.

Go online to access detailed lesson summaries for this unit.

DRIVING QUESTIONS

Look back to the Driving Questions from the opening section of this unit. In your Evidence Notebook, review and revise your previous answers to those questions. Use the evidence you gathered and other observations you made throughout the unit to support your claims.

PRACTICE AND REVIEW

1. Earth's orbit changes through time. The shape of the orbit changes. The tilt changes, and the position of the planet changes in its orbit. How do changes in Earth's orbit affect planetary climate?

FIGURE 4: The Earth during the Last Glacial Maximum 20 000 years ago.

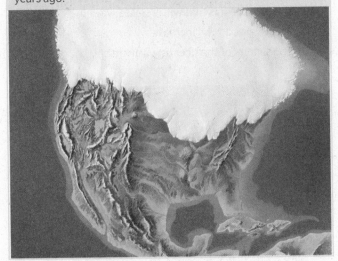

2. During the last ice age, water was trapped as ice on land. What effect did this have on the planet? Select all correct statements.

  a. Sea level decreased.
  b. Ice depressed land.
  c. Ice decreased planetary albedo
  d. With ice on land, the ocean was warmer.

3. Which statements are true about the heliocentric model? Select all correct responses.

  a. The model includes elliptical orbits.
  b. It is based on the assumption that the stars are much closer to Earth than they actually are.
  c. The sun is the center of the solar system.
  d. It was developed by mathematician and astronomer Nicolaus Copernicus.

4. How might the energy budget of Venus differ from Earth's energy budget?

5. Which of the following accurately compare the inner planets and outer planets of the solar system? Select all correct responses.

  a. The inner planets have a much greater density than the outer planets.
  b. The total mass of the inner planets is much greater than the total mass of the outer planets.
  c. The inner planets are composed mostly of solid rock, and the outer planets are composed mostly of gases.
  d. The outer planets have a much greater density than the inner planets.

6. A common misconception is that seasons are related to Earth's distance from the sun. What is one piece of evidence that demonstrates that this idea is mistaken?

7. Eccentricity is a measure of how stretched an elliptical orbit is. Which objects in the solar system have orbits with the greatest eccentricity?

   a. asteroids

   b. comets

   c. the inner planets

   d. the outer planets

8. Create a model in your Evidence Notebook to show the orbital shape, planetary tilt, and position of Earth in its orbit today.

9. Which statements accurately describe Earth's orbit around the sun? Select all correct responses.

   a. The gravitational attraction between Earth and the sun causes Earth to orbit the sun rather than flying off into space.

   b. Earth orbits the sun faster than Mercury.

   c. Earth orbits the sun faster than Jupiter.

   d. Earth's orbit is circular.

10. How does high albedo affect the planetary climate?

    a. High planetary albedo means more sunlight is reflected, and the planet warms.

    b. High planetary albedo means less sunlight is reflected, and the planet warms.

    c. High planetary albedo means more sunlight is reflected, and the planet cools.

    d. High planetary albedo means less sunlight is reflected, and the planet cools.

11. How would increasing the tilt of Earth's axis affect the amount of daylight throughout the year?

12. How do sunspots affect the solar radiation emitted by the sun?

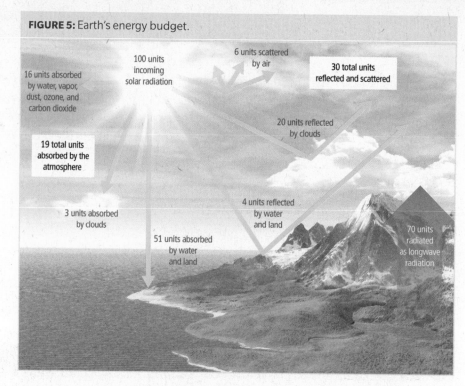

FIGURE 5: Earth's energy budget.

100 units incoming solar radiation

16 units absorbed by water, vapor, dust, ozone, and carbon dioxide

6 units scattered by air

30 total units reflected and scattered

20 units reflected by clouds

19 total units absorbed by the atmosphere

3 units absorbed by clouds

4 units reflected by water and land

51 units absorbed by water and land

70 units radiated as longwave radiation

13. Use Figure 6 to explain how a volcanic eruption can affect climate.

14. As the planet warms, which outcomes are likely? Select all correct responses.

    a. Ice will melt and planetary albedo will decrease.

    b. The atmosphere will hold more water vapor, a greenhouse gas that will increase warming.

    c. Earth's albedo will increase.

    d. The salinity of the oceans will increase.

UNIT PROJECT

Return to your unit project. Prepare your research and materials into a presentation to share with the class. In your final presentation, evaluate the strengths and limitations of your model.

Remember these tips while evaluating:

- Look at the empirical evidence—evidence based on observations and data. Does the evidence support your model?

- Consider the accuracy of your model. Is it consistent with all the evidence that you gathered?

- Consider predictions you could make based on your model.

Seasonal Changes on Mars

Like Earth, Mars also has polar icecaps. However, on Mars the polar ice is made of frozen carbon dioxide rather than water. One cap vanishes for part of the Martian year. The other icecap also grows and shrinks but is present year-round.

Use what you have learned about solar energy and planetary orbits to construct an explanation for the patterns of annual changes in icecap patterns on Mars. How are these patterns similar to and different from those of Earth's polar icecaps?

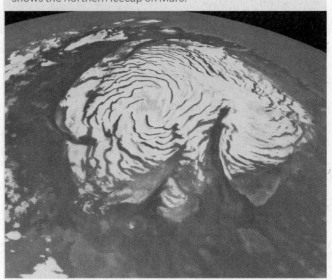

FIGURE 7: This image from NASA's Mars Global Surveyor shows the northern icecap on Mars.

1. ASK A QUESTION

With your team, define the specific question to be answered. Identify all of the factors you will explore to answer the question and the characteristics a complete answer should have.

2. PLAN AND CONDUCT RESEARCH

With your team, review what you know about seasonal changes on Earth. How do those changes relate to Earth's orbit and the tilt of Earth's axis? Then make a plan for what information about Mars you need to gather to explain seasonal changes on that planet.

3. ANALYZE DATA

Analyze the results of your research, including any data you gathered about the orbit of Mars and the tilt of the planet's axis. Also identify any additional information you may need.

4. CONSTRUCT AN EXPLANATION

Based on the results of your research, state a claim that answers your original question about seasonal patterns on Mars. Use scientific reasoning to support your claim with the evidence you have collected. Your explanation should also include a comparison of the polar ice patterns on Mars with those on Earth and identify the key reasons for any differences.

5.COMMUNICATE

Work with your team to develop a presentation of your explanation. Your presentation should include images and data to help support your claim.

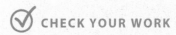 CHECK YOUR WORK

The presentation should include the following information:

- an accurate description of how polar ice changes over the course of a Martian year and how those patterns compare with patterns on Earth
- a clearly stated claim that connects the patterns to the main causes of the patterns
- images and data to support the claim
- a well-stated argument that uses reasoning to connect evidence to the claim

UNIT 5

Space

A pair of galaxies collides approximately
134 million light-years away in the
constellation Ursa Major.

Image Credit: ©Science Source

In 1966, astronomer Halton Arp published his *Atlas of Peculiar Galaxies*, a collection of images of 338 nearby galaxies that did not fit into any of the established categories of galaxy shapes. His goal was to give astronomers data they could use to study the evolution of galaxies. Today, we know that most of the objects from the catalog are actually interacting or colliding galaxies. They continue to be referred to mainly by their Arp number.

The colliding galaxies you see here are called Arp 299. Astronomers have discovered that a massive black hole in the center of the galaxy on the right is consuming the galaxy on the left. Keep in mind that these galaxies are 134 million light-years away. That means they are so distant that it takes 134 million years for light from these galaxies to reach Earth.

 Predict What tools and techniques do you think scientists use to study galaxies and other objects across the vast distances of space?

DRIVING QUESTIONS

As you move through the unit, gather evidence to help you answer the following questions. In your Evidence Notebook, record what you already know about these topics and any questions you have about them.

1. How do scientists study objects in space that are at vast distances from Earth?

2. What types of evidence enable scientists to make inferences about the sizes, temperatures, and distances of stars?

3. How are scientific inquiry and engineering design interrelated in the field of astronomy? How might new instruments and tools help astronomers expand their knowledge of the universe?

4. How do astronomers interpret lines of evidence to support a theory that explains the formation and history of the universe?

UNIT PROJECT

Citizen Science

Go online to download the Unit Project Worksheet to help plan your project.

Astronomy is a field that offers many opportunities for amateurs to collaborate with professional scientists. Anyone who is interested can choose from a wide range of citizen science projects to help gather, analyze, and interpret data for astronomers. In this unit project, you will choose a citizen science project to participate in and then prepare a presentation about the project and what you learned through your participation.

Observing Matter in Space

Complex surface features within Jezero Crater, Mars

CAN YOU EXPLAIN IT?

When you imagine outer space, you may picture objects such as stars, asteroids, and comets. Because most objects in space are too far to visit, scientists must gather information from observations made at great distances from the objects.

FIGURE 1: Horsehead Nebula

Gather Evidence
Record information about the Horsehead Nebula. As you explore the lesson, gather evidence about these particular colors as well as other information to help you interpret this image.

The Horsehead Nebula is a cloud of gas and dust located about 1500 light-years from Earth. Light moves very fast and very far in a year. But even if humans could travel at the speed of light, it would take 1500 years—approximately 20 times the average human lifespan—to reach the Horsehead Nebula. Scientists must study such objects from a distance by using various instruments and techniques. Most of the information comes from the light from these objects that reaches Earth.

Observe the colors and other details in the photo of the Horsehead Nebula. In this image, you might notice a dark "horsehead" shape and lighter areas of different colors.

 Predict What explanation can you suggest for what might be causing the horsehead shape in this nebula?

Types of Observations

Every object in the universe that has mass and takes up space is composed of matter. By studying meteorites that crash to Earth and analyzing samples obtained from past visits to the moon's surface, scientists gather direct evidence of the nature of some of this matter. However, most matter in the universe is too far away to be accessible to humans.

You have made observations of objects far beyond our solar system by gazing at stars. Scientists usually observe distant objects with the help of instruments on Earth, in Earth's orbit, and on spacecraft.

Collaborate With a partner, list what you already know about different ways of studying objects in space.

Observing Nearby Objects

FIGURE 2: Instruments for observing and exploring space

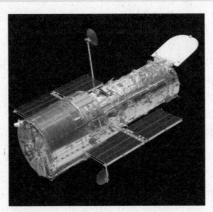

a Ground-Based Telescope: gathers and concentrates light or other radiation, enabling observations of faint objects at great distances in space

b Satellite Observatory: gathers and concentrates light or other radiation without the interference of Earth's atmosphere

c Spacecraft: obtains images and direct measurements of materials, fields, and properties of nearby objects

Earth's surface is an easily accessible place to set up a telescope to observe objects and other matter in the universe. However, some properties of the atmosphere can interfere with astronomical observations. Many telescopes are placed on high mountains to avoid clouds and distortions from Earth's atmosphere. Telescopes may travel on planes or balloons to escape more of the atmosphere, though briefly.

Earth-orbiting satellites are not much closer to most of the objects being studied. However, energy reaches a satellite without first being affected by the atmosphere.

A spacecraft sent to one of Earth's neighbors can get a close-up view. It also has the advantage of being able to interact with the object. A spacecraft might make direct measurements of a planet's magnetic field or look at an asteroid in directions that can't be seen from Earth. It might drop a lander or probe to measure wind speeds and temperatures, determine atmospheric humidity and the amount of radiation received at the surface, or determine the composition beneath the visible surface.

Analyze When scientists evaluate tradeoffs between a telescope on the ground and a telescope in Earth orbit, how much do you think they count the difference in distance the telescopes will be in comparison to the objects being observed? Support your opinion.

Observing Distant Objects

For objects that are very distant, such as stars and galaxies, observations cannot be made by spacecraft. As a result, we use Earth and near-Earth-based telescopes to help us gather information by collecting the light from distant objects.

Gather Evidence

Look at the example beam of starlight. Compare the width of the beam as it enters the telescope with the width of the beam as it leaves through the telescope's eyepiece. How does the telescope affect the light?

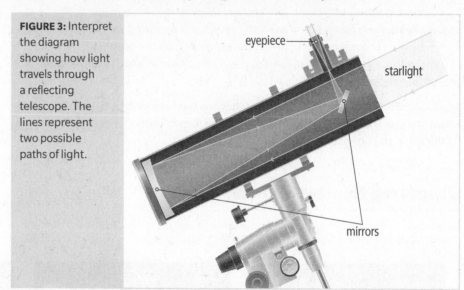

FIGURE 3: Interpret the diagram showing how light travels through a reflecting telescope. The lines represent two possible paths of light.

eyepiece

starlight

mirrors

Although telescopes make objects seem bigger, their main job is to make objects appear brighter. As light bounces off mirrors within the telescope housing, it becomes more concentrated. Larger telescopes have larger mirrors. For this reason, they can capture more light and are used to observe fainter objects. The larger the mirror, the greater the distance at which an object can be observed.

Instruments are used in place of the telescope's eyepiece to measure, record, and analyze light. For example, cameras take images of distant objects. Spectrographs break the object's light into its component parts to produce a spectrum. Spectra provide valuable data about the nature of matter in our universe.

Explain Why is a larger telescope needed to observe objects that emit or reflect less light?

The Electromagnetic Spectrum

Visible light is only a portion of the electromagnetic, or EM, energy that radiates through space. Telescopes and other instruments can be made to measure, record, and analyze this radiation. Because this radiation is the only source of information about many objects in space, scientists try to analyze it in as many ways as possible.

The electromagnetic spectrum ranges from gamma rays through radio waves. Despite the different characteristics, radio waves, microwaves, infrared radiation, visible light, ultraviolet radiation, x-rays, and gamma rays are names for frequency ranges of the same thing—electromagnetic waves. Each electromagnetic wave can be measured by its frequency, energy, or wavelength. Wavelength refers to the distance between successive wave peaks. Frequency refers to the number of peaks passing a stationary point during a given time, which can also be thought of as the number of cycles in a given time. Closer peaks give higher frequencies. Higher frequencies deliver more energy in a given time, too.

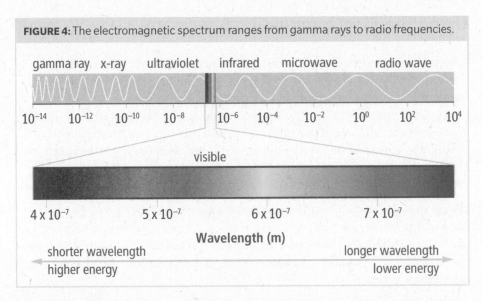

FIGURE 4: The electromagnetic spectrum ranges from gamma rays to radio frequencies.

gamma ray   x-ray   ultraviolet   infrared   microwave   radio wave

10^{-14} 10^{-12} 10^{-10} 10^{-8} 10^{-6} 10^{-4} 10^{-2} 10^{0} 10^{2} 10^{4}

visible

4×10^{-7} 5×10^{-7} 6×10^{-7} 7×10^{-7}

Wavelength (m)

shorter wavelength   longer wavelength
higher energy   lower energy

Explain What part of the electromagnetic spectrum was used to obtain the image of the Horsehead Nebula? Why do you think so?

The ranges of EM radiation have different names because each interacts with matter somewhat differently. Radio waves will not burn your skin, whereas ultraviolet waves might. From this contrast, you might infer—correctly—that radio waves have lower frequencies and energies than ultraviolet. X-rays pass through your skin but can give information about your bones. You might use microwaves to cook your food or an infrared "heat" lamp to keep it warm.

In space, the pattern is similar. An image taken in the infrared range will give information that's different from an image in visible light. An infrared image of a kitchen would show hot food or surfaces as bright and cooler areas as dark. In an infrared image of the Messier 101 galaxy, red shows areas where dust is illuminated by young stars. The same dust might reflect visible light and appear bright or might block visible light and appear dark. The x-ray image provides information about hot, turbulent regions of the galaxy.

FIGURE 5: Images of the Messier 101 galaxy taken in different spectral ranges. Colors have been chosen to represent the radiation that isn't visible. Because they interact with matter differently, the infrared radiation, visible light, and x-rays show different aspects of the galaxy.

a infared   **b** visible   **c** x-ray

Using the Electromagnetic Spectrum

Analyze Compare the protective effects of Earth's atmosphere with the ease or difficulty in observing ultraviolet radiation.

Earth's atmosphere helps maintain the habitability of the planet by the way it interacts with EM radiation. Visible light and radio waves from the sun pass through the atmosphere and are absorbed by Earth's surface. The surface then emits infrared waves, which may interact with the atmosphere before the energy escapes to space. Visible light and radio waves from other objects in space also pass through Earth's atmosphere and can be observed using ground-based telescopes. Infrared light from space can be observed at ground level but is contaminated by infrared radiation from the atmosphere. High altitude and space are better locations for an infrared telescope.

Life can exist on Earth's surface because the atmosphere absorbs harmful gamma rays and x-rays before they reach Earth's surface. As a result, instruments built to detect gamma or x-ray radiation from space are ineffective at Earth's surface—they must be placed above the atmosphere. A location in orbit or beyond is essential for detecting high-energy waves.

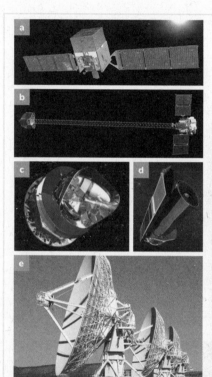

FIGURE 6: The diagram shows the absorption of electromagnetic radiation by Earth's atmosphere. For each EM range, notice the lowest altitude from which observations can be made. Also match the ranges with the telescopes at the left: (a) Fermi Gamma-ray Space Telescope, (b) NuSTAR (x-ray), (c) Planck Telescope (microwave), (d) Spitzer Space Telescope (infrared), and (e) Very Large Array (radio).

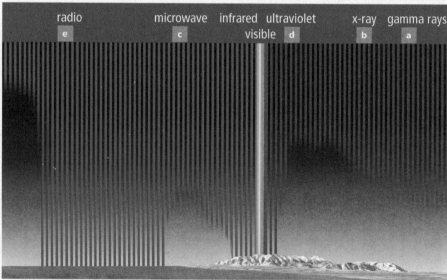

The figure shows how far different frequencies travel into Earth's atmosphere. Some radiation reaches only to high altitudes. Notice the variation, even within ranges. Some very narrow frequency ranges are exceptions to the general trends.

There are tradeoffs in the placement of telescopes. An infrared or visible-light telescope may reasonably be built and operated on a mountaintop. Locating such telescopes at high elevations generally makes a significant improvement in observations. However, it would be expensive and difficult to build a line of radio telescopes on such uneven ground. Telescopes for all ranges may be more effective in space, but the costs and benefits vary greatly. Yet even the difficulty of placing a large radio dish in space may be justified for some observations.

 Explain Summarize the ways of observing objects and other matter in space. What would be needed to obtain the image of the Horsehead Nebula?

The Doppler Effect

Electromagnetic waves are produced by and interact with matter. For this reason, their frequencies can contain information about the matter. A change in frequency can be a sign of matter in motion. The frequencies of other types of waves, such as sound waves, are affected in the same way by the motion of an object. This observed change in frequency when there is relative motion between an object and the observer is called the Doppler effect.

Observing the Doppler Effect

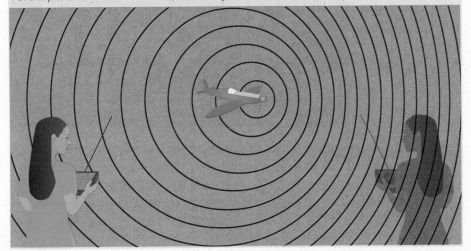

FIGURE 7: Notice how the lines depicting the sound waves are more compressed in front of the plane. Contrast the sounds heard by an observer at the two positions shown.

Collaborate Work with a partner to list examples of when you have known about the motion of an object from a change in how it sounds.

You have probably noticed the pitch of an approaching car, train, or other vehicle rise as it approaches and then become lower as it passes. Compare this experience with the circles in the figure that represent sound waves. Each circle expands outward from the point where it started. But the plane moves as it gives off sound waves. The sound waves in front of the plane, as they would be experienced by a person on the ground, appear compressed. The peaks are closer together, and so the waves have a higher frequency than they would for a plane that is not moving relative to the observer. The sound has a higher pitch. Behind the plane, the waves appear spread out to a lower frequency and lower pitch.

The higher energy of the compressed, higher-frequency approaching sound is balanced by opposite characteristics of the receding sound. The total energy carried by this plane's sound waves is constant, regardless of whether you observe them from the plane or from the ground.

 Predict How does the sound of an airplane change as it passes and flies away from an observer? What happens to the frequency of the sound waves?

The Doppler Effect for Light

Order and Consistency

Universal Laws As you learn about how light can show motion, think about how scientists make use of basic laws that apply throughout the universe.

Electromagnetic waves are also subject to the Doppler effect. Many technologies rely on frequency shifts to measure the motion of objects. For example, police radar guns bounce microwaves or radio waves off of approaching cars. The device detects and uses the change in frequency of the returning waves to calculate the speed of a car. In meteorology, Doppler radar is used to track storm systems and determine wind direction. It can determine the velocity of raindrops, from which precipitation amounts can be estimated. The same pattern is observed in the light from objects in space—frequency shifts can be used to measure motion.

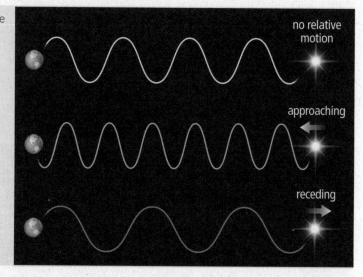

FIGURE 8: Compare the waves. As the middle star moves toward the observer, the waves it gives off are compressed, resulting in a higher frequency.

no relative motion

approaching

receding

Doppler shifts can be measured to identify whether stars and galaxies are moving toward or away from Earth. To measure a shift, scientists compare bright or dark lines in an object's spectrum with unshifted bright lines in a laboratory spectrum. A set of lines will all be shifted in the same way, relative to the laboratory spectrum, if they were produced by a moving object. If the object is moving toward the observer, the waves are compressed, and the frequency of each line increases.

Explain Use Figures 8 and 9 together to describe what happens when an object is receding from an observer. What happens to the frequency and energy of light from the lower star in Figure 8?

FIGURE 9: The normal lines associated with hydrogen (H) are shown in the top band. The shift toward the blue end in the middle band indicates a star moving toward Earth. The shift to the red end in the bottom band means the star is moving away.

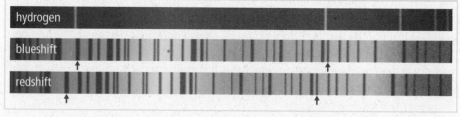

hydrogen

blueshift

redshift

An increase of frequency shifts all of the lines toward the blue end of the visible light spectrum. This effect—from an approaching object—is called a *blueshift*. In contrast, the lines from receding objects are shifted toward the red end of the spectrum. This effect is called a *redshift*. Scientists use red and blue rather than left or right, even for other EM ranges, because a spectrum can be turned or flipped.

 Gather Evidence What evidence do you have to demonstrate that spectra can be used reliably to measure motion?

Applying the Doppler Effect

The Doppler effect is limited to measuring motion that is toward or away from an observer. If an object maintains the same distance from you as it moves across your field of view, you would not be able to measure a spectral shift.

FIGURE 10: The spiral galaxy, designated NGC 4414, is rotating counterclockwise.

Predict What Doppler shift do you expect for the part of the galaxy labeled C, relative to B? Explain why you think so.

The outer part of the pictured galaxy is a flat, turning disk. If a spectrum from location A were compared with a spectrum from location B, the lines would show a Doppler shift. Stars and other matter at location A appear to be moving toward Earth relative to stars and other matter at B—the lines are blueshifted. This type of relative shift can show how an object is turning or how different parts are moving. Overall, the galaxy is redshifted relative to a laboratory spectrum, which shows that the galaxy is receding.

Data Analysis

Doppler Shifts in the Universe

Laboratory measurements give the wavelengths at which different elements emit and absorb light. By comparing these wavelengths with the spectra of objects in space, Doppler shifts can be measured, and velocities can be calculated. The Doppler shifts of galaxies fall into a pattern that has been used to help understand the history of the universe.

Explore Online ▶

Analyzing and Interpreting Data
Measure Doppler shifts of galaxies to find a pattern of motion in the universe as you explore Shifting Galaxies online.

Explain Record information about how light from objects in space can provide information about motion. How much do you expect Doppler shifts to affect the colors that you see in an image?

Spectra

A spectrum is a representation of an object's light spread into component frequencies. Spectra are important analytical tools that help astronomers get information from the light of distant objects.

Studying a Spectrum

Predict What would happen if you aimed light from the magenta part of the Horsehead Nebula through a spectrograph?

Explore Online ▶

Hands-On Lab 🧪

Make and Use a Spectroscope Build your own spectroscope and use it to examine different sources of light.

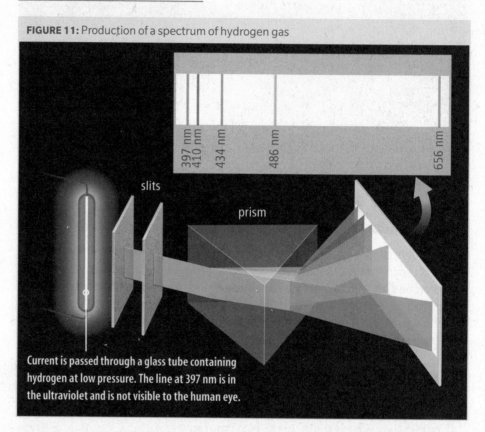

FIGURE 11: Production of a spectrum of hydrogen gas

397 nm
410 nm
434 nm
486 nm
656 nm

slits

prism

Current is passed through a glass tube containing hydrogen at low pressure. The line at 397 nm is in the ultraviolet and is not visible to the human eye.

Spectrographs are routinely used with telescopes to analyze the light of distant objects. A spectrograph breaks light into its component colors by using a prism or diffraction grating. For example, hydrogen gas glows a bright pink or purple-red called magenta, as shown in Figure 11. However, the spectrum of hydrogen shows that the magenta is made up of different specific frequencies—different wavelengths and colors. Each frequency shows as a thin, bright line in hydrogen's spectrum.

There are three main types of spectra: bright lines, dark lines, and smooth color without lines. A glowing gas typically produces, or emits, light of specific frequencies. The resulting spectrum has bright lines and is called an emission spectrum. A gas can also absorb light and produce dark lines. The result is called an absorption spectrum. Absorption and emission spectra can be used to determine the composition of a gas. Other materials give off light of a wide range of frequencies. The resulting spectrum looks like a rainbow—a continuous change from one color to the next, without lines. It is called a continuum or continuous spectrum and can provide information about temperature.

FIGURE 12: Compare the features of the three spectra.

a emission spectrum

b absorption spectrum

c continuous spectrum

Spectral Analysis

A spectrum provides information about the nature of matter in space. A continuous spectrum is produced by hot, dense matter that radiates light in a wide range of frequencies. For example, the plasma at the visible surface of a star and the wire of an incandescent light bulb both produce continuous spectra.

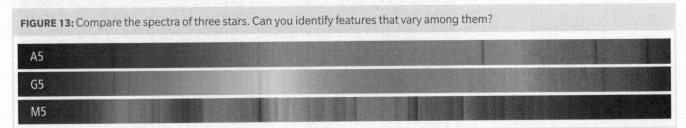

FIGURE 13: Compare the spectra of three stars. Can you identify features that vary among them?

A5

G5

M5

The three features—emission lines, absorption lines, and continuum—can appear together in a single spectrum. Scientists analyze the features separately because the features give different types of information. Figure 13 shows the spectra of stars, labeled A5, G5, and M5. Each spectrum shows a broad, bright band, or continuous feature. The brightest part of the continuum varies among stars and can provide information about temperature.

You can see absorption lines in all three spectra. However, the absorption lines vary in number, spacing, and strength. Absorption lines from different gases are superimposed. Some of the strong, dark lines in spectrum A5 are from hydrogen and can also be seen in spectrum G5. The spectrum labeled M5 shows many more absorption lines. Some emission lines can be detected through a more detailed analysis. Scientists may compare absorption and emission lines to learn about the structure of an object.

Explain Describe how you can compare the materials that are present in the stars whose spectra are shown. Include the types of features as you cite your evidence.

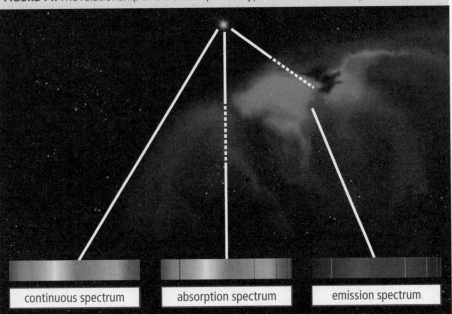

FIGURE 14: The relationship of the three spectral types obtained from objects in space

continuous spectrum   absorption spectrum   emission spectrum

Gather Evidence How might you interpret the spectrum of a star in order to understand its outer layers?

If a continuous light source is behind a gas, the gas can produce absorption lines. The same light source can add energy to the gas, causing it to glow with emission lines. The light of emission lines can be most easily detected against a dark background.

Matching Spectra

FIGURE 15: The absorption spectrum of an unknown element is shown. Can you identify the element by comparing its spectrum to the emission spectra?

| unknown |
| helium |
| carbon |
| hydrogen |

Absorption and emission spectra result when the electrons of the atoms gain or lose energy. The atom gains energy by absorbing a photon—a particle of light. It loses energy by giving off, or emitting, a photon. The energy lost or gained by the atom exactly matches the energy—or frequency—of the photon.

In an atom of hydrogen, the electron can stay only at very specific energy levels, as depicted in Figure 16. The electron can gain or lose only the exact amount of energy needed to move between two energy levels. As a result, it can absorb or emit only photons of those exact amounts of energy. The atom does not absorb light of other frequencies.

As you have learned, continuous light consists of a range of frequencies. When continuous light shines on hydrogen gas, most of the light passes through the gas. The hydrogen atoms absorb only light at specific frequencies, leaving dark lines or gaps. The continuous spectrum now has hydrogen absorption lines superimposed on it.

When a hydrogen atom absorbs a photon, it becomes energized. When the atom loses this same amount of energy, it produces a photon of the same frequency. This emitted photon contributes to the bright line of an emission spectrum. The bright and dark lines of hydrogen's two types of spectra match because hydrogen's electron is restricted to moving between the same energy levels, whether the atom is gaining or losing energy. Different elements have different energy levels. The transitions between these energies gives each element a characteristic spectrum.

Explain Suppose an element had more energy levels than hydrogen. How would you expect its spectrum to differ from hydrogen's spectrum?

FIGURE 16: As hydrogen's electron changes energy levels, it contributes to the lines of absorption and emission spectra.

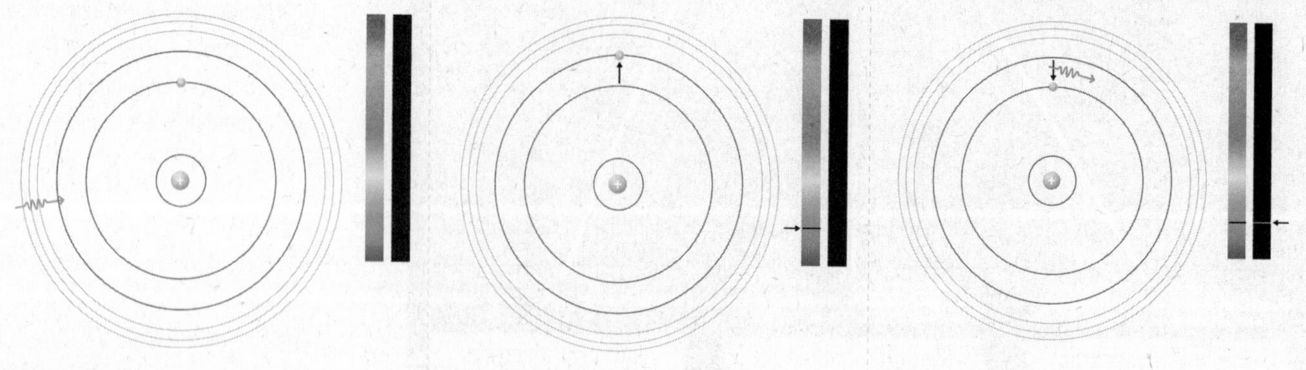

a A photon approaches an atom of hydrogen.

b If the energy is exactly right, the electron gains energy and contributes to an absorption line.

c As the electron returns to a lower energy level, it produces a photon that contributes to an emission line.

Spectra of elements can be produced in laboratories. Emission spectra are easier to produce and more common than absorption spectra. The results can be used to identify lines in emission or absorption spectra from space or from materials on Earth.

 Predict If hydrogen gas were illuminated by emission from another gas, rather than by a continuous source, how would the spectrum appear?

Explaining Observations

FIGURE 17: Spectra connect phenomena at the very large scale of objects in space to phenomena at the very small scale of atoms.

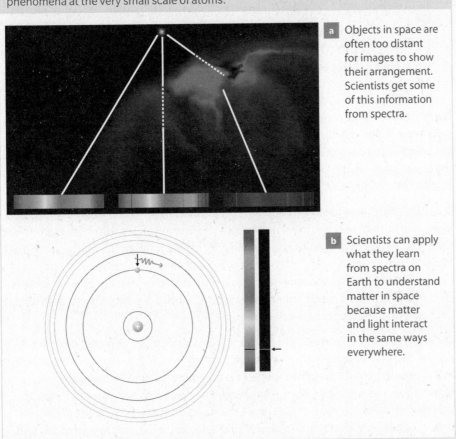

a Objects in space are often too distant for images to show their arrangement. Scientists get some of this information from spectra.

b Scientists can apply what they learn from spectra on Earth to understand matter in space because matter and light interact in the same ways everywhere.

Predict Do you expect bright emission lines from the red gas (third spectrum in Figure 17a) to be present in either of the other two spectra?

When you see an absorption spectrum, you are seeing two objects or two components of an object. The absorbing gas is in between the continuous source and the spectrograph. The continuous source could be very far behind the gas or very close to it. In contrast, a continuous spectrum with no lines indicates that the path of light is free from absorbing gases. In contrast, an emission spectrum shows just one object but with a source of energy. Scientists can often infer the location of the star or other energy source relative to a gas in space.

 Explain Record the main ideas from this Exploration. How might knowledge of spectra help you interpret the colors and dark areas of the Horsehead Nebula?

Studying Objects

Data can be gathered from spectra, images, observations of particles, other observations, and the way these data change over time. Scientists then derive information about properties such as motion, temperature, and composition of objects in space.

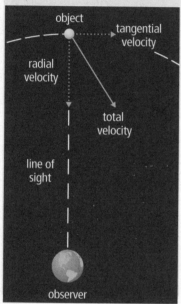

FIGURE 18: Directions of motion

Motion

Collaborate Work with a partner to analyze how you determine the motion of a distant object. Include objects in the sky, such as birds, planes, and clouds, as well as objects on the ground or in water. Think about the types of information you observe directly and the types you approximate or infer.

Astronomers use several methods for determining the motion of objects in space. The Doppler effect can be used to measure motion toward or away from an observer, called radial motion. This is motion along the line of sight, shown in Figure 18. Motion across the sky, called tangential motion, can be observed for many nearby objects. If the distance to the object is known, a velocity can be calculated. Any velocity can be broken into a radial part and a tangential part, which may be known through different observations.

There are other ways to study motion in space. When astronomers observe one object passing in front of another, the data can give information about their sizes, speeds, and distances. Periodic changes can be used to infer orbital motion. The masses, distance, and period are related, so if some are known, others may be calculated. Distance is needed for many of these calculations and is determined in a variety of ways, such as by comparing various measurements of star brightness. For some objects, distance can even be estimated from radial velocity.

Objects also seem to move due to Earth's motion rather than the object's motion. A nearby object will appear to have different positions, relative to more distant objects, as it is viewed from different directions. This phenomenon is called parallax. For an object as near as the moon, careful measurements from opposite sides of Earth can show parallax. For the nearest stars, even the views from opposite points of Earth's orbit produce only a fraction of a degree of change in the object's apparent position. Most objects in space are much too distant to measure by parallax.

Math Connection

Connect the ideas of radial and tangential to your knowledge of geometry. Imagine the observer at the center of a circle. Compare a radius and a tangent of the circle to the velocities shown in the figure.

FIGURE 19: Imagine looking along the arrows to see the views shown. What would change if the object were more distant?

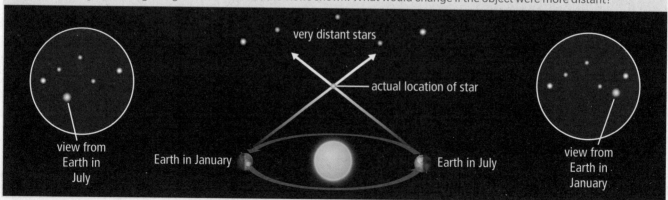

Modeling Parallax

PROCEDURE

1. Hold your thumb at arm's length. Close your left eye, and note the position of your thumb relative to a distant object, such as a tree or a picture on the wall.

2. Without moving your head, open your left eye and close your right eye. Again note the position of your thumb relative to the distant object. How does the amount of observed parallax change if your thumb is closer to your eyes?

📋 **Analyze** Describe the parallax you observed. How might parallax help you tell the difference between a distant airplane and a nearby model airplane?

Temperature

You may have noticed a hot object, such as the coil of an electric range, change color as it grows hotter. It first glows dull red, then brighter red, orange, yellow, and possibly white. If the material gets even hotter, it may take on a slight blue tint. This type of color is determined mostly by the temperature rather than by the material. Hot or molten metal, pottery in a kiln, and the surface materials of a star all show the same colors at the same temperatures. Color can provide data about temperature.

Notice that the progression from red to yellow represents light of increasing frequencies and energies. Recall how a continuous spectrum shows a wide range of frequencies. Hot objects emit mostly at the red end of the spectrum, but very hot objects emit across the entire visible spectrum. The result appears white or bluish-white to the human eye.

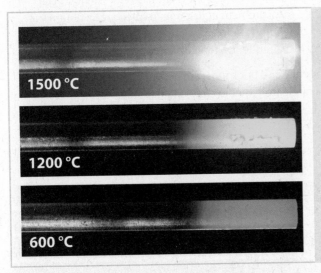

FIGURE 20: Notice the changes in color and brightness as a steel bar is heated (bottom to top). The amount of change is distorted by the photography and printing.

1500 °C

1200 °C

600 °C

📋 **Predict** Star types include red giants and white dwarfs. Which would you expect to be hotter?

Explore Online ▶

🧪 **Hands-On Lab**

Blackbody Radiation View the colors and brightnesses produced by incandescent light bulb filaments as you vary the temperature.

The brightness of a material also changes with temperature. The first dull-red glow might be too faint to notice, but the hotter, yellow glow is much brighter. Both color and brightness patterns convey temperature information. These patterns extend into other ranges of EM radiation. Materials at temperatures comfortable to touch tend to glow with infrared radiation. Because of this relationship, continuous spectra, especially infrared spectra, are sometimes called thermal spectra.

FIGURE 21: The lines represent spectra of materials at different temperatures.

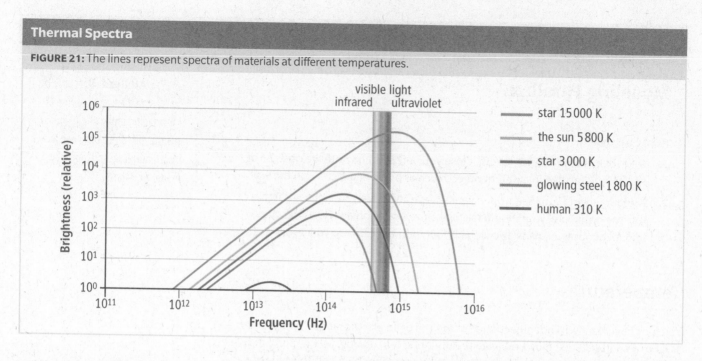

Explain Why do humans often associate the color blue with cold? Remember that most everyday objects are seen by reflected light.

Each line on the graph represents the continuous spectrum for a particular temperature. The lines show how color and brightness at different temperatures are related to a material's spectrum through several ranges of EM radiation. The brightest part of the curve, the peak, is roughly related to the color in visible light. But more generally, the peak frequency of emitted energy is higher at greater temperatures. A hot, blue star has a higher peak frequency than a cooler, red star.

In visible light, or in any other range or specific frequency, a material is brighter when it is hotter. A hot, blue star gives off more visible light, more infrared radiation, and more ultraviolet radiation than a cooler, red star of the same size. If scientists can account for size and distance, a measurement at just one frequency can determine an object's temperature. In a different situation, if scientists can measure enough frequencies to determine the peak frequency, then distance might be calculated.

These same patterns of frequency and brightness are used on Earth, mostly in the infrared range. Applications range from medicine to engineering and law enforcement.

Composition

FIGURE 22: Use the emission line spectra to identify some of the gases in the stars. You may find that some elements are difficult to identify with certainty. Do Doppler shifts affect your identifications of elements?

Recall that spectral lines can be used to identify elements. The idea is simple, but identifying absorption lines in stars can be complicated. Some lines may overlap or may be poorly developed. In many stars, simple molecules produce additional dark lines in the spectrum. The amount of each material, the temperature, and other conditions can affect the strengths of the lines.

The frequencies of absorption lines in stars may not perfectly match the lab spectra. The lines may have Doppler shifts due to a star's overall motion. Other types of motion can broaden the lines, such as when the turning of an object shifts the lines in both directions at once. Material that is expanding, convecting, or in other complex motions may have very complicated—and data-rich—Doppler shifts.

Gather Evidence
Continue taking notes of the ways spectra can provide information about objects in space.

Combining Observations

FIGURE 23: When an image from radio waves (red) is added to visible light, the spiral galaxy shows new characteristics: large lobes or jets of material that seem to be coming from the center of the galaxy.

visible light

radio waves

Analyze Compare the radio image of the galaxy with that of visible light. How do they differ? What can you infer from the differences you observe?

You have seen how one type of observation can give information about several properties. Different types of observations can be used to untangle these properties, and they can be combined with models to determine additional properties, such as mass. In Figure 23, radio waves show a different shape and size than the visible galaxy. Additional x-ray spectra (not shown) indicate that something energetic is happening at this galaxy's center. Further observation and modeling lead to the inference that black holes may be located at the centers of this and other galaxies.

Explain Review and summarize the ways different types of observations provide a range of information about matter in space.

Data Analysis

Spectral Analysis

FIGURE 24: Study the glowing gas and its spectrum. Try to identify the mystery substance by comparing its spectrum with known spectra. Can you rule out any elements? Use any information available to you.

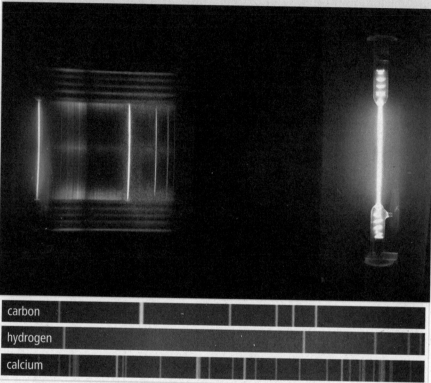

Language Arts Connection

To evaluate information presented in different formats, examine the information carefully to judge its value or worth. In science, you may encounter information in these formats, among others:

- prose (text)
- visuals (photographs, video clips, animation)
- quantitative data (tables, graphs)

For guidance on evaluating information presented in different formats, see the Learning Resources for this lesson.

As you look at the figure above, compare the reference spectra with the spectrum of the mystery substance. Use the knowledge you have gained from this lesson as you try to identify the substance. Judge whether you have enough information to identify the element(s) present in the substance pictured. Even if you can't identify the substance, you should be able to rule out one or more of the elements.

Although none of the known spectra may match the mystery spectrum exactly, the color and spectrum are similar to a known element and can give you clues. The mystery substance is not a single element but a familiar compound that includes one of the elements shown.

Explain In your evidence notebook, record your reasoning about the mystery substance. Consider how spectra are used for studying objects and materials on Earth, and then evaluate how reliable spectra are for studying objects in space.

SPECTROSCOPIST

MAKE AND USE A SPECTROSCOPE

THE ELECTROMAGNETIC SPECTRUM

Go online to choose one of these other three paths.

Lesson Self-Check

CAN YOU EXPLAIN IT?

FIGURE 25: Close-up of the Horsehead Nebula in visible light

Take a fresh look at the image of the Horsehead Nebula in visible light. Think about the different types of information that visible light can provide. Consider how matter gives off light and how color can give information about the properties of matter. Observe the dark shape that resembles a horse's head. Is it a gap in the reddish area, or is it something else?

Scientists can use different parts of the electromagnetic spectrum to gain more information. Figure 26 shows the Horsehead Nebula in a combination of visible light and infrared radiation.

As you consider both images, use the following questions to help you think more about the Horsehead Nebula.

- What colors do you observe, and what can you infer from them? Does their shape or relative position influence your interpretation?
- Why are there darker and lighter areas?
- What is the nature of the "horsehead" region?
- Did the image from infrared light affect your interpretation of this dark area? Does it affect how you think about the nearby dark areas?

Explain What do you think is producing the dark, horsehead-shaped area in this nebula? Include evidence to support your claim.

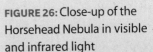

Analyze Review the notes you made in your Evidence Notebook to help you construct an explanation of the Horsehead Nebula.

FIGURE 26: Close-up of the Horsehead Nebula in visible and infrared light

CHECKPOINTS

Check Your Understanding

1. Select and record the correct responses to complete the following statements.

   You have learned that the frequency of sound waves reaching a stationary observer will change depending on whether the source of the sound is approaching or receding. Suppose an ambulance is approaching and then passes you and drives away without changing speed. As an ambulance approaches, the sound waves (expand, compress), resulting in a (higher, lower)-frequency wave. As the ambulance passes, the pitch (increases to a higher frequency, drops to a lower frequency).

2. Which of these statements describes a way scientists can study an object in space regardless of its distance from Earth?

   a. A spacecraft is sent to visit and analyze matter from the object.

   b. Scientists collect and analyze matter from the object that reaches Earth.

   c. A telescope in orbit concentrates electromagnetic radiation from the object, and a spectrograph or other instrument is used to analyze the EM radiation.

   d. A telescope on the ground concentrates electromagnetic radiation from an object that gives off only x-rays.

3. Suppose you observe absorption spectra from three galaxies. All contain the same number of absorption lines. The lines have the same spacing in all three spectra. Lines in the first spectrum show blue shift, lines in the second match laboratory emission lines, and lines in the third show red shift. Which of the following statements is correct?

   a. The differences in the line positions are due to differences between absorption spectra and emission spectra.

   b. The differences in the line positions show that the galaxies are composed of different elements.

   c. The blueshifted lines of the first galaxy show that it is moving away from Earth.

   d. The redshifted lines of the third galaxy show that it is moving away from Earth.

4. Compare the spectrum of a star with the spectra of elements provided in Figure 27. For each element, record whether it is clearly present, possibly present, or clearly not present in the star.

FIGURE 27

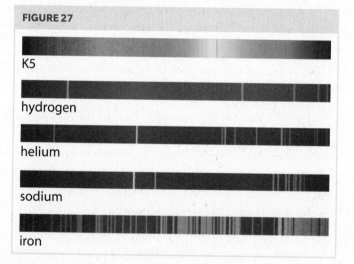

K5

hydrogen

helium

sodium

iron

5. Look at the spectrum of the star in Figure 27. What type of spectrum is it? What features does it show?

6. In addition to the elements present in a star, what other information might scientists obtain by studying the star's spectrum?

7. What can parallax be used to determine?

   a. the composition of stars based on the spectra of their starlight

   b. the distance to a star that is within 1,000 light years of Earth

   c. the temperature of the surface of a star that is within 1,000 light years of Earth

   d. the distance to extremely distant stars

8. Several of the world's most powerful reflecting telescopes are located at the summit of Mauna Kea in Hawaii, nearly 14,000 feet above sea level. What ranges of the EM spectrum are better observed at such a location than at sea level? What ranges are not observable even at that height?

9. Blue giants and red giants are two major categories of stars. Based on what you have learned about the relationship between temperature and color, which of these types of stars would you expect to be hotter? Explain your reasoning.

 In your Evidence Notebook, design a study guide that helps you explain how scientists use remote observations of temperature, composition, and motion to study objects in space.

Remember to include the following in your study guide:
- Support main ideas with details and examples.
- Record explanations for the phenomena you observed.
- Reflect on how scientists make use of basic laws that apply throughout the universe.

Use the crosscutting concept that energy is neither created nor destroyed to help interpret observations, such as the relationships among the three main types of spectra.

Stars

Solar flares increase the sun's energy output.

CAN YOU EXPLAIN IT?

FIGURE 1: The Orion constellation

Gather Evidence
Record observations about the differences you see among the stars that form Orion. Gather evidence to help explain these observations.

The constellation Orion is visible in the Northern Hemisphere in the winter sky. In Greek mythology, Orion is the Hunter. Three bright stars across the center mark Orion's belt and are often easy to spot. The middle of the 3 bright objects oriented downward below Orion's belt is the Orion nebula, a cloud of gas and dust, rather than a star.

Observe Notice that the stars in the constellation Orion are of different colors. What do you think might be causing these differences in color?

Energy and the Sun

The sun is Earth's nearest and best studied star. Not all stars share the sun's characteristics of mass and temperature, but scientists can still apply what they learn about the sun to stars in general.

Solar Fusion

Stars go through various stages during their life cycle, which you will learn more about later in this lesson. A star's life begins when high temperatures and pressures within its core make possible the start of nuclear fusion. In the process of nuclear fusion, two or more nuclei combine to form a larger nucleus. Fusion in the sun and other stars begins when two hydrogen nuclei collide and combine. This process releases energy and changes one of the hydrogen nuclei into a neutron. The combined hydrogen nuclei become deuterium, which is a form of hydrogen that contains one proton and one neutron in its nucleus. Deuterium nuclei then may collide and combine with other hydrogen nuclei to produce helium, subatomic particles, and additional energy.

Solar Nuclear Fusion

FIGURE 2: Energy is generated in the sun by the process of solar nuclear fusion. Each step produces different amounts of energy, labeled in energy units of megaelectron volts (MeV).

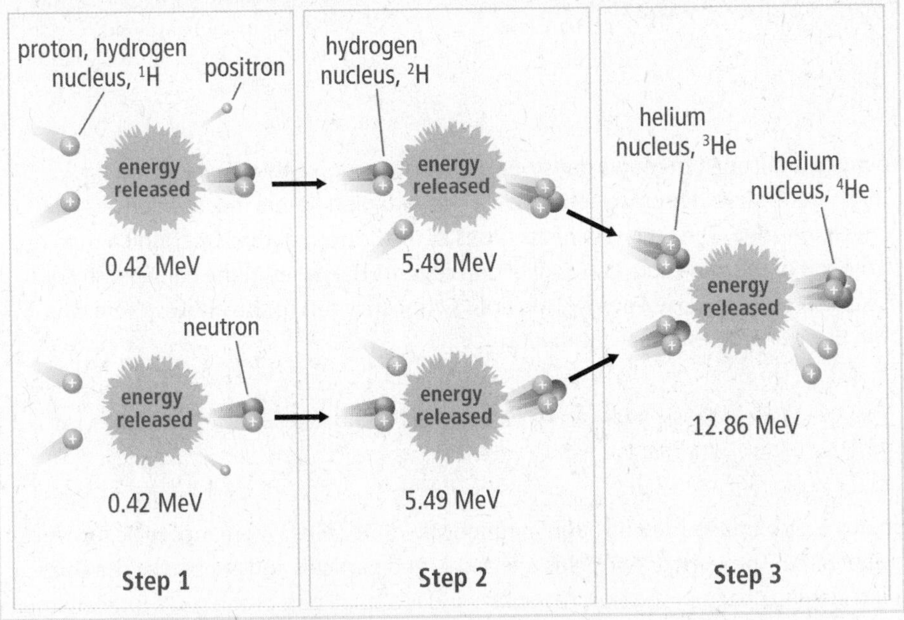

proton, hydrogen nucleus, ^{1}H   positron   hydrogen nucleus, ^{2}H

helium nucleus, ^{3}He   helium nucleus, ^{4}He

energy released   0.42 MeV

energy released   5.49 MeV

neutron

energy released   0.42 MeV

energy released   5.49 MeV

energy released   12.86 MeV

Step 1   Step 2   Step 3

Analyze
Examine the fusion process in Figure 2. Which step releases the most particles? Which releases the most massive particles? Which releases the fewest particles? Rank the steps by how much energy they release, from least to greatest.

Explore Online ▸

Hands-On Lab

Modeling Fusion
Use coins to create a simple model of a nuclear fusion reaction.

When a star's supply of hydrogen runs low, the star begins to fuse helium into heavier elements. This marks the start of a new stage in the life cycle of the star. Later in the lesson, we will explore the life cycle of stars in greater detail. Over its lifetime, a star may generate elements with increasingly higher numbers of neutrons and protons in their nucleus, up to iron. The fusion of iron consumes energy, so it and heavier elements form through other processes.

FIGURE 3: Nuclear fusion in the sun's core produces tremendous amounts of energy that move through the sun's layers.

The core Nuclear fusion of hydrogen forms helium in the sun's core, which releases energy from this extremely dense and hot layer.

Radiative zone Energy produced by fusion in the core radiates through this dense layer. It can take 100 000 years for the energy to reach the next layer.

Convection zone Energy from the radiative zone heats matter at the bottom of this zone, causing it to expand and rise. Matter rises, cools, and sinks, forming convection cells. Energy from the interior continues to warm cooled sinking matter, while energy is given off at the top of the convection cell.

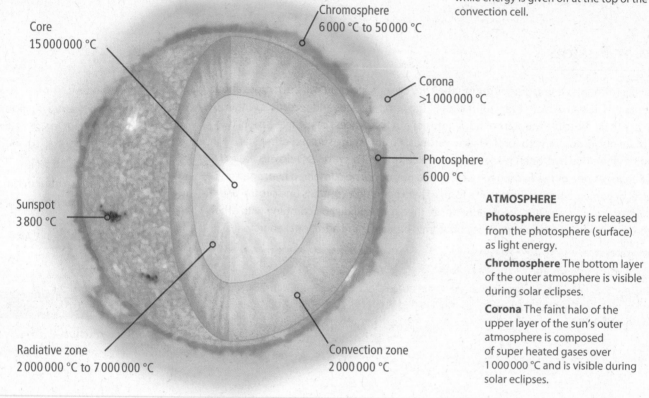

Core
15 000 000 °C

Chromosphere
6 000 °C to 50 000 °C

Corona
>1 000 000 °C

Photosphere
6 000 °C

Sunspot
3 800 °C

Radiative zone
2 000 000 °C to 7 000 000 °C

Convection zone
2 000 000 °C

ATMOSPHERE

Photosphere Energy is released from the photosphere (surface) as light energy.

Chromosphere The bottom layer of the outer atmosphere is visible during solar eclipses.

Corona The faint halo of the upper layer of the sun's outer atmosphere is composed of super heated gases over 1 000 000 °C and is visible during solar eclipses.

Analyze Study how energy is transferred between the sun's radiative and convection zones. Develop a diagram to model the process.

Energy produced in the sun's dense core travels through a thick layer called the radiative zone as electromagnetic waves. This radiation enters the less-dense convection zone. The radiation heats gases at the bottom of the zone, which then rise to the top of the zone, forming convection cells. As the gases in the convection cells rise to the top, they lose energy. That energy transfers out to the photosphere, and from there energy escapes as radiation.

Model Using a diagram, explain and label the four steps of energy generation and transfer in the sun.

Energy is also transmitted through magnetic fields, regions where magnetic forces can be detected. These magnetic fields affect charged particles and are part of the solar wind flowing out from the sun. The solar wind is a small part of the sun's total energy.

The sun radiates energy in all directions from its surface, but only a small portion reaches Earth. The frequencies of radiation emitted by the sun include about 50% infrared, 40% visible light, 9% ultraviolet, and 1% other wavelengths. Because of absorption by the atmosphere, the energy that reaches Earth's surface is mostly visible light—with only some infrared and an even smaller amount of ultraviolet radiation.

Solar Variation

Scientists use the term *solar activity* to refer to variations in the energy output of the sun. Solar activity includes such phenomena as solar flares and coronal mass ejections. Patterns of solar activity take place across a wide range of time scales. One such pattern is a predictable cycle of sunspot activity. A sunspot is a darker area of the photosphere with lower temperatures due to slower convection caused by magnetic fields. Sunspots reappear with regularity on a cycle of approximately 11 years.

 Math Connection

Sunspots Recorded

FIGURE 4: Explore the variation in sunspot frequency to understand the time scale of this solar activity.

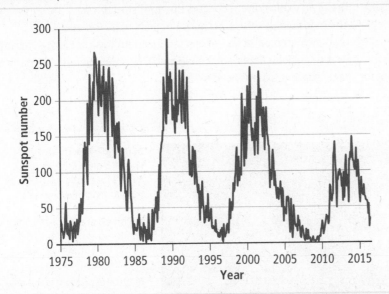

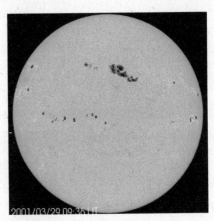

Sunspots are cooler areas in the photosphere. They are related to changes in the sun's magnetic fields.

Explain   Look at the graph. Which years had the fewest sunspots, and which the most? When would you predict the next cycle will begin and peak?

Sunspot cycles begin when the number of sunspots is very small but slowly increases. Initially, sunspots appear in groups about midway between the sun's equator and the poles. The number of sunspots increases over the next few years and can reach a peak of 100 or more. The sunspots at higher latitudes, closest to the sun's poles, slowly disappear, and new ones appear near the sun's equator. After the peak, the number of sunspots decreases until a minimum is reached. Another 11-year cycle starts when the number of sunspots begins to increase again.

Hypothesize   What effect does solar activity have on the sun's energy output?

The Solar Wind

The sun's corona is a huge region of gas with a temperature above 1 000 000 degrees Celsius. The solar wind originates because of the dynamic nature of the sun and consists mostly of protons and electrons that shoot out from the sun's surface. The massive amount of electrically charged particles influences conditions in space near Earth and in Earth's upper atmosphere. This phenomenon, known as *space weather*, can affect radio communication, spacecraft, and even GPS navigation systems.

Disturbances in the magnetic fields of the sun's surface cause such things as solar flares, coronal mass ejections, and the solar wind. Solar flares occur when magnetic fields realign and release vast amounts of light energy in the process. Observed as a flash of light, solar flares can be seen on Earth 8 minutes after they occur, because it takes light that long to travel the distance between the sun and Earth. They often occur at the same time as coronal mass ejections, or CMEs, but they are not the same thing. CMEs are more of an explosion that occurs due to disturbances in the sun's magnetic field. As the fields realign, the sun sheds or ejects mass from its corona. In this type of event, the ejected particles—if ejected in a path toward Earth—do not reach Earth for several days. Solar flares, solar wind, and CMEs direct energetic particles that account for space weather experienced on Earth.

FIGURE 5: Solar processes eject high-energy particles that reach Earth and interact with its magnetic field.

Solar Wind Charged particles, mostly protons and electrons, flow outward from the sun at speeds up to 900 km/s (2 000 000 mi/hr). The particles are deflected around Earth. They may cause disturbances when they come into contact with Earth's magnetic field.

Magnetic Field Lines Without the sun's influence, Earth's magnetic field would be symmetrical. However, forces from the solar wind distort Earth's magnetic field, compressing it on the side facing the sun and extending it on the opposite side.

Magnetosphere It is the area around Earth where solar wind is deflected because of Earth's magnetic field. Particles that reach Earth's atmosphere near the poles produce auroras (northern and southern lights near the poles).

Explain List the observations, evidence, and claims that allow you to understand the production and release of energy from the sun. Explain whether these facts are unique to the sun or would apply to all stars.

Image Credits: ©SOHO (ESA & NASA)

Properties of Stars

A good understanding of properties of stars such as stellar brightness, temperature, luminosity, mass, and size is necessary to identify and study individual stars. Although stars appear as individual points of light, scientists have learned that nearly one-third of the stars in the Milky Way are actually binary (paired) or triplet stars.

Stellar Brightness

A bright object, such as a spotlight, appears dimmer from a great distance than when it is close to you. Similarly, stars that are brighter than our sun but located farther away appear dimmer to us. Two scales have been developed to describe stars' brightness—the apparent magnitude scale and the absolute magnitude scale.

Predict How do the apparent and absolute magnitudes of a small, bright star compare to those of a large, dim star?

Common Name	Distance (Light-Years)	Apparent Magnitude	Absolute Magnitude
Sun	0.000016	−26.72	4.8
Sirius	8.6	−1.46	1.4
Capella	42	0.08	−0.48
Rigel	770	0.12	−8.1
Betelgeuse	640	0.50	−7.2
Spica	260	0.98	−3.2
Pollux	34	1.14	0.7
Deneb	1500	1.25	−7.2
Regulus	70	1.35	−0.3

Apparent magnitude measures brightness as perceived by an observer on Earth. Hipparchus, an ancient Greek astronomer, first cataloged star brightness. He assigned the brightest stars he could see a magnitude of 0. Dimmer stars were assigned magnitudes of 1, 2, and so on. Using telescopes, modern astronomers observed stars brighter than Hipparchus's zero, so they began to use negative numbers for the apparent magnitude of these brighter stars.

Absolute magnitude is a measure of how bright stars would appear if they were all at the same standard distance from Earth. From Earth, the sun is the brightest star we see. As such, its apparent magnitude is the highest—represented by the large negative number. However, if we were able to put the sun next to Betelgeuse, a star in the constellation Orion, at the same distance from Earth, Betelgeuse's absolute magnitude would be greater. Rigel is the brightest star listed; the sun is the dimmest.

Distance affects the perceived brightness of a star. If you observed Capella in the night sky, you might never think it could be brighter than the sun. However, if you placed Capella next to the sun and equidistant from Earth to observe their absolute magnitudes, Capella would appear 12 times brighter.

Analyze For which star in the chart are apparent and asbolute magnitude most nearly equal? Based on that fact, what can you infer about the standard distance astronomers use to calculate absolute magnitude?

Temperature and Color

Color and temperature are not always related, but color is generally a good indicator of a star's surface temperature. From spectral analysis, remember that lower frequencies are associated with lower energy. In the visible light spectrum, the color red is the lowest frequency and is associated with the lowest energy. A red star is cooler, emitting less energy than a blue star of the same size.

FIGURE 6: The color of a star can provide information about its temperature.

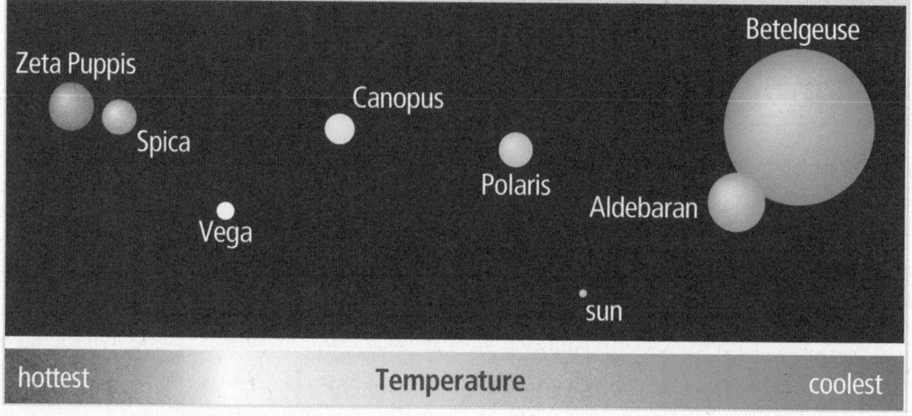

Zeta Puppis
Spica
Vega
Canopus
Polaris
Betelgeuse
Aldebaran
sun
hottest
Temperature
coolest

Evidence In your notebook, list the stars in Figure 6 in order from hottest to coolest.

Size and Mass of Stars

An object's mass is a measure of how many atoms it contains. In general, larger stars contain more atoms than smaller stars and are more massive. The conditions under which a star forms determine its initial mass. The greater the initial mass of the star, the brighter and hotter it is and the more quickly it goes through its life cycle.

Scientists can generally estimate the size of a star by considering the color, the amount of energy it emits, and its temperature. Stellar size and distance influence the apparent magnitude of a star. A cooler, bigger star could exhibit the same apparent magnitude as a smaller, hotter star because it has a greater light-emitting surface area.

Math Connection

Density Stars vary greatly with respect to mass, size, and volume. For example, a red giant is approximately 14 times more massive than a red dwarf, but its radius can be up to 10 000 times that of a red dwarf. Volume is a factor of size, and density is determined by mass and volume. A red giant has 14 times the mass in a much larger volume than a red dwarf's, so its density is much lower than the red dwarf's.

FIGURE 7: The illustration shows how the sun compares in size with both giant and dwarf stars. The supergiant star Betelgeuse has a radius more than a thousand times that of the sun. Thus only a small portion of Betelgeuse is represented in this diagram.

Zeta Puppis
sun
Betelgeuse
Sirius B
Proxima Centauri
sun
Zeta Puppis

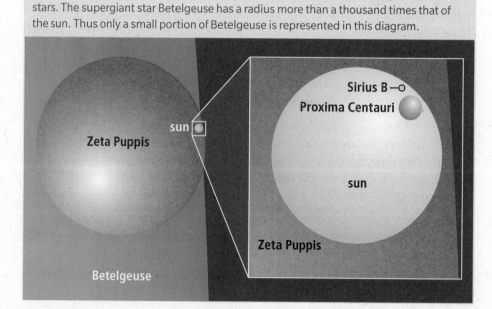

Eighty-five to 90 percent of stars show identifiable patterns with respect to temperature, brightness, mass, size, and density. Stars with larger diameters are generally more massive, hotter, and brighter than stars with smaller diameters. Smaller stars are less massive, cooler, and dimmer than their larger counterparts. Our sun is a star of average mass, size, brightness, and temperature.

Some stars are very large but not very hot or massive. These stars, known as giants and supergiants, are quite bright but not very dense. They are dying stars and have begun fusing helium as their supply of hydrogen has run low. Other outlier stars include white dwarf stars, which are small, very hot, and dense. White dwarfs have masses close to our sun's but volumes only slightly larger than Earth's. A white dwarf star is in a later stage of its life and mostly emits thermal energy.

Diagram of Star Properties and Types

A graph called the Hertzsprung-Russell diagram, or HR diagram, plots star brightness on one axis and star temperature on another. Around 85% to 90% of all stars plot within a band across the middle of the diagram. These are called main-sequence stars because these stars are fusing hydrogen in their cores.

The HR diagram serves as a model for predicting the characteristics of stars at different life-cycle stages. For example, stars not on the main sequence are not fusing hydrogen. They are either very young or old stars nearing the next stage of stellar evolution. If a non-main-sequence star plots on the lower left of the diagram, the star can be described as small, dim, dense, and very hot. These are the late-stage characteristics of stars like our sun.

Evaluate Rigel is the bright blue star at the bottom right of Orion. Where would Rigel appear on the HR diagram? Explain your reasoning.

FIGURE 8: The Hertzsprung-Russell diagram of star type and absolute magnitude.

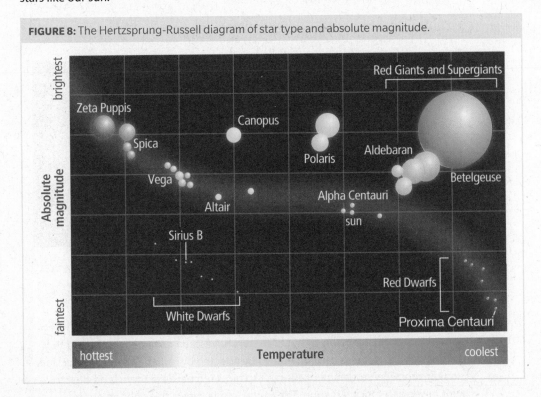

 Collaborate With a partner, choose a star to compare with the sun. Compare density, size, mass, temperature, and brightness as shown on the HR diagram.

Star-Forming Regions

Interstellar space begins where the influence of a star's solar wind on its surroundings stops. The space between stars is characterized by lower-energy gas and dust particles. Stars can form in the regions of space where interstellar materials are more densely concentrated.

The Interstellar Medium

The term interstellar medium refers to the matter found in the space between stars in a galaxy. This space is mostly empty, but the particles in the interstellar medium account for at least 10% of all observable matter in the Milky Way. The matter is unevenly distributed, dispersed in some places and clumped in others. Some denser regions consist of hydrogen and helium left over from the formation of the universe. Other regions contain dust, ice, and heavier elements blasted into the medium during the explosive end stages of earlier generations of stars.

In some regions of interstellar space, gravitational forces cause the interstellar medium to form denser cloud-like formations of gas and dust called *nebulas*. Not all nebulas are alike. Some reflect the light of nearby stars, while others look dark because dust blocks out the light from stars behind them. Still others have large amounts of glowing, ionized gases and appear bright.

FIGURE 9: Origins of elements in the interstellar medium

Universe Formation	Hydrogen
	Helium
	Lithium [trace amounts]
Matter from Stars	Hydrogen
	Helium
	Carbon
	Neon
	Oxygen
	Sulfur
	Silicon
	Iron

Infer How could a scientist use the composition of the interstellar medium in a region of space to understand that region's past?

FIGURE 10: The Pleiades star cluster and the Eagle nebula

a The Pleiades star cluster

b The Eagle nebula

In some nebulas, dust can scatter high-frequency radiation more than lower-frequency, causing them to appear blue in true-color images of space. The Pleiades is a star cluster in which hot blue stars have been observed, indicating that it is also a nebula. Nebulas can sometimes be affected by radiation from nearby stars, which can ionize hydrogen gas, causing it to glow red because there is no dust to scatter lower-frequency radiation. The Eagle nebula shows this phenomenon.

Evaluate How is the effect of nebulas on star light similar to the effect Earth's atmosphere has on sunlight?

From Nebula to Star

Star formation may begin when matter in a nebula collides and parts of the nebula collapse, forming dense regions of gas and dust. Increasing gravitational forces draw in additional materials toward these dense regions, and protostars begin to form. The amount of matter available and how much of it comes together determine the size of any stars that would eventually form.

Once enough material has collapsed to form protostars, they begin to glow due to their increasing temperature. Depending on mass, fusion may begin at the core of a protostar in a few million years or in tens of millions of years. Once fusion begins, a protostar becomes a star. Stellar winds clear away remaining gas and dust that has not clumped together, blasting this matter into regions where it could trigger other stars to form.

Evidence List and explain similarities between the composition of the interstellar medium and nebulas. What are some significant differences between the two features?

FIGURE 11: First stages of star formation.

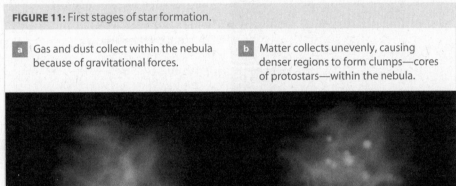

a Gas and dust collect within the nebula because of gravitational forces.

b Matter collects unevenly, causing denser regions to form clumps—cores of protostars—within the nebula.

Analyze: Describe the energy and matter interactions at each of the star-forming events shown at the left.

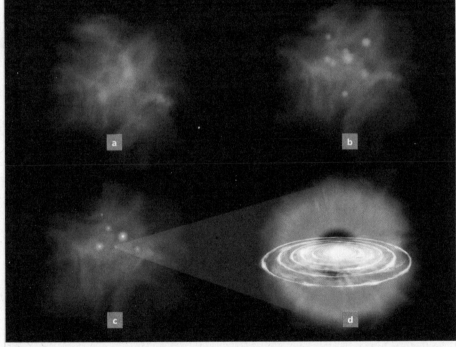

c Protostar cores' density and temperature increase as more gas and dust accumulate; cores begin to glow.

d Fusion begins, and a star is born. infalling matter forms a disk around the star's equator while solar wind clears away matter in other directions.

Using Patterns to Analyze a Space Image

As you have seen, elements display the same properties, whether they are being observed in the laboratory or at vast distances away in space. Scientists can use properties of elements to identify patterns and make inferences about galaxies and other objects located at great distances. Take a look at some of the patterns we can observe in this distant galaxy called Messier 74.

FIGURE 12: The galaxy Messier 74 observed in visible light

Foreground star Many of the compact, bright spots are not part of galaxy Messier 74 but are much closer. They are stars within our own galaxy.

Spiral arms The spiral pattern consists of density waves, like sound waves, spiraling outward as the galaxy rotates. The increased density helps to trigger star formation.

Central bulge The bright center of a spiral galaxy is commonly yellow because it is made up mostly of older, longer-lived stars.

Dust nebula Blue generally indicates a nebula of dust, often lit from within by new hot blue stars. These stars tend to be of high mass and have short lifespans. Thus blue is often a sign of ongoing star formation.

Gas nebula Hazy patches of red and pink indicate glowing hydrogen gas.

Dust lanes The dark patches are not empty areas but dust that blocks light from objects behind it.

Messier 74 is about 32 million light-years from Earth, but we can use patterns observed in the laboratory to make inferences about the galaxy based on the visible light it gives off. Observations made in other ranges of EM radiation can reveal other patterns. For example, infrared images made by the Spitzer Space Telescope have indicated the presence of organic (carbon-based) molecules in Messier 74.

 Analyze How might you use patterns of color to identify regions of older and younger stars within a galaxy?

 Gather Evidence Make notes about patterns you've observed in this Exploration that could help you interpret images of nebulas, such as the Horsehead nebula shown in lesson 1.

Matter Transformations in Stars

Stars go through different stages as they age. The life story of a particular star depends on its initial mass. With the exception of the final steps of stellar evolution, the life cycle of stars can be tracked on the HR diagram.

Fusing Hydrogen into Helium

Once a protostar gathers enough material to reach a critical mass and temperature, fusion of hydrogen to helium begins in its core, and the protostar becomes a star. Fusion creates a high-pressure region that exerts an outward force, while gravitational forces try to collapse and condense the star. The star will expand until the force due to fusion and the force of gravity are equal. Forces due to fusion and gravity increase or decrease in tandem, counterbalancing each other by constant adjustments until a new equilibrium is reached. Stars that have achieved and maintain this delicate balance exist within the HR diagram main-sequence band.

Higher-mass protostars begin fusion sooner than less massive ones. A protostar with a mass near that of the sun would take tens of millions of years before fusion begins. In contrast, a protostar five times as massive could begin fusing in a mere million years.

Stars with higher masses also burn through their available fuel faster. For this reason, more massive stars spend less time on the main sequence than less massive stars, and their life cycles are shorter—some last only a million years or so. The least massive main-sequence stars, red dwarf stars, can live trillions of years!

A star remains on the main sequence as long as it is burning hydrogen and the balance between gravitational forces and fusion/radiation forces is maintained.

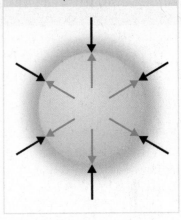

FIGURE 13: When the inward force of gravity balances outward pressure from fusion and radiation, the star has reached equilibrium.

Collaborate With a partner, model the opposing forces of gravity and pressure due to fusion within a star by gently pressing your hands together. What happens if one person presses slightly harder? Can you keep your hands in the same place while varying amounts of pressure?

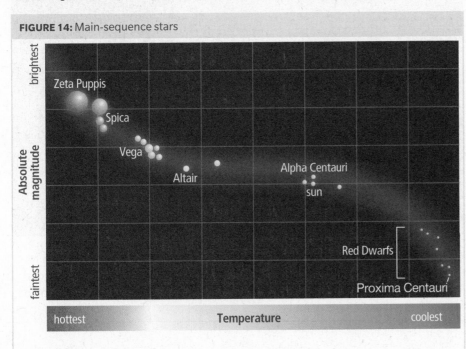

FIGURE 14: Main-sequence stars

brightest

Zeta Puppis

Spica

Vega

Altair

Alpha Centauri

sun

Absolute magnitude

faintest

Red Dwarfs

Proxima Centauri

hottest   **Temperature**   coolest

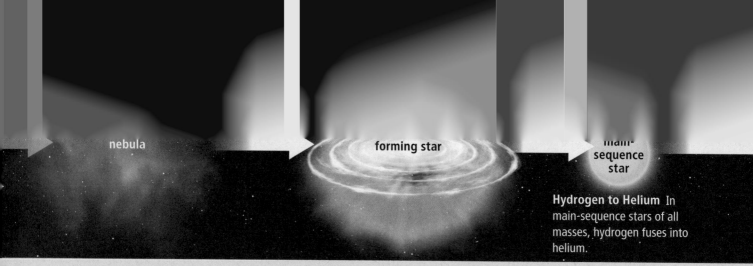

nebula

forming star

main-sequence star

Hydrogen to Helium In main-sequence stars of all masses, hydrogen fuses into helium.

FIGURE 15: The life cycle of a star begins as a nebula and ends as a nebula.

Fusing Elements Beyond Helium

Explain What makes it possible for high-mass stars to continue fusing elements beyond carbon?

As a star uses up its hydrogen, it begins to form heavier elements—elements with higher atomic numbers on the periodic table. Again, the mass of the star determines which elements it will form. All stars begin by fusing helium to form carbon after hydrogen runs low. For stars with a mass about the same as our sun's, the process stops with carbon fusing into oxygen. Hotter, more massive stars can fuse other elements, including nitrogen and neon. In the most massive stars, this process continues up to the formation of iron.

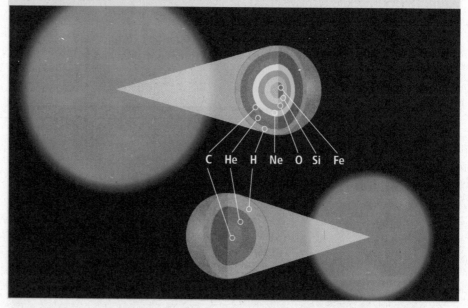

FIGURE 16: Compare the shells of elements formed by fusion in low-mass and high-mass stars.

C   He   H   Ne   O   Si   Fe

When a star has used up the hydrogen in its core, fusion stops, and gravity begins to take over. The core shrinks, and its contraction produces additional heat. This triggers fusion in a shell outside the core where hydrogen still exists. The entire star begins to expand and becomes a red giant.

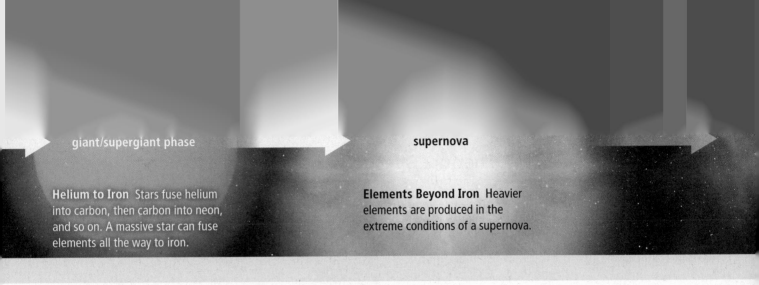

giant/supergiant phase

Helium to Iron Stars fuse helium into carbon, then carbon into neon, and so on. A massive star can fuse elements all the way to iron.

supernova

Elements Beyond Iron Heavier elements are produced in the extreme conditions of a supernova.

The core temperature rises to the point at which helium can fuse into carbon and oxygen. In a star with a mass similar to the sun's, the temperature never rises enough for these heavier elements to fuse. A carbon-oxygen core forms, and hydrogen and helium fusion reactions continue in the layers surrounding the core. Eventually the outer shells of gas will be shed by the star, leaving behind the intensely hot carbon-oxygen core—a white dwarf.

The expelled layers of the star absorb ultraviolet radiation from the white dwarf and give off visible light. The resulting glowing halo of gases is called a planetary nebula because 18th-century astronomers thought such halos looked like the discs of planets. The nebula fades as it sheds into space its dust and gas, enriched in heavier elements from which new stars can form. Only the white dwarf remains.

Fusing Heavy Elements

The late stages of massive stars follow a different pattern. These massive stars become red supergiants as they fuse progressively heavier elements up to iron. The fusion of iron nuclei does not release energy but rather absorbs energy. For this reason, the attempt to fuse iron causes the core to collapse suddenly and produce a shock wave that blasts the star's outer layers into space. This brilliant explosion, called a supernova, produces conditions that allow the fusion of heavier elements up to uranium. Thus, supernovas are the source of all naturally occurring elements heavier than iron.

The collapsed core of the massive star becomes a neutron star. As its name suggests, a neutron star is composed almost entirely of neutrons and has a superdense core comparable to that of an atomic nucleus. It can have a radius as small as 11 km but have a mass nearly twice that of the sun.

Neutron stars rotate rapidly, and some highly magnetized ones give off electromagnetic radiation that appears in pulses. These neutron stars are called pulsars. The appearance of pulses is due to the rotation of the neutron star; the pulse is only observed when the beam of radiation is oriented toward Earth. The discovery of the first pulsar by astronomer Jocelyn Bell in 1967 provided the first direct evidence for the existence of neutron stars.

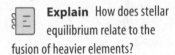

Explain How does stellar equilibrium relate to the fusion of heavier elements?

Explain How does the mass of a star affect that star's end-stage evolution?

Hands-On Lab

Thermal Spectra

Predict How do you think the strength of a battery might affect the color of light produced by the bulb?

Using a few items that you can find around the house, investigate the relationships among energy, color, and temperature.

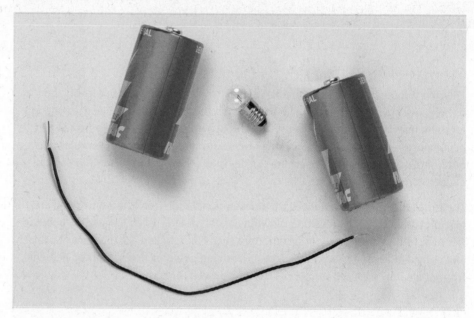

MATERIALS

- light bulb
- weak D battery
- strong D battery
- insulated wire that is stripped at each end

PROCEDURE

1. Using the wire, the light bulb, and the weak D battery, complete a circuit so that the bulb illuminates (HINT: Place one end of the wire on the bottom of the battery, and place the other end on the side of the light bulb. Now place the tip of the light bulb to the tip of the battery).

2. Note the color of the filament's glow and the temperature of the bulb.

3. Repeat with the strong D battery.

4. Compare the filament colors and the bulb temperatures when using the different-strength batteries.

ANALYZE

How do your observations from this lab relate to what you have learned about energy, color, and temperature in stars?

Explain Describe how your observations support the claim that color can be reliably used to determine the temperature of distant objects.

| STAR EVOLUTION | COMPARING STARS | STAR CLASSIFICATION | Go online to choose one of these other paths. |

Lesson Self-Check

CAN YOU EXPLAIN IT?

FIGURE 18: The Orion constellation

FIGURE 19: Our sun is a yellow, main-sequence star.

Take another look at the stars in the Orion constellation. As you develop your explanation, apply the evidence you have gathered in this unit:

- Consider the reasons objects in space are different colors.
- Look through the interpretation of other space images. Do any of those ideas apply to the stars in Orion?
- Think about what you have learned about stars. How do different factors affect star color?
- Do any other observations, such as brightness, help you make inferences?
- In your explanation, list the inferences that you can make from the colors. Also, list any additional inferences that an astronomer might be able to make from the colors.

 Analyze Refer to the notes in your Evidence Notebook to review what you've learned about the properties of stars and their life cycles.

Explain What causes the stars in the Orion Constellation to appear different colors? What else can you learn from the colors?

CHECKPOINTS

Check Your Understanding

1. Where in our sun is energy produced, and how does the process occur?

    a. Nuclear fusion produces energy in the core of stars, including our sun.

    b. Energy is produced in a star's corona by nuclear fission.

    c. A star's radiative zone produces energy by nuclear fusion.

    d. All stars generate energy by nuclear fusion at the top of convection cells.

2. Which statements correctly describe characteristics of nebula gas and dust? Select all correct answers.

    a. The dust and gas of planetary nebulae form planets.

    b. Denser regions of gas and dust are where star formation can begin.

    c. In visible light, dust may appear either blue or dark, and ionized hydrogen appears magenta or red.

    d. Very dense clusters of dust create barriers to scientists, who cannot observe the region of space behind them.

3. Construct the chart in your Evidence Notebook. Complete the chart by correctly sorting the phases of stellar evolution listed below. There may be more than one answer for each description.

Description	Phase
Collapse due to gravitational forces forms a dense accumulation of gas and dust.	
Gravitational forces are stronger than the outward force of fusion.	
Hydrogen is fusing to form helium in the star's core.	

Late in stellar evolution   A star on the main sequence

A protostar   Early in stellar evolution

A dying star

4. Through your telescope, you observe a star in the constellation Orion. It appears reddish in color and is quite bright compared to other stars in the sky. Where in its life cycle do you think this star is currently? Refer to the HR diagram in Exploration 2 to help you.

5. Construct the chart below in your Evidence Notebook. Determine the components that are present or needed to form each space feature. There may be more than one answer for each feature.

Space feature	Contents
Interstellar space	
Stars	
Nebulas	

hydrogen   helium   dust

6. Through laboratory studies, the spectra of many gases are known. This allows scientists to do what?

    a. Scientists can better understand the composition of the gases in our atmosphere and how they absorb electromagnetic radiation.

    b. By comparing the spectra of known gases to those of objects at great distances, scientists can identify the composition of large-scale features such as nebulae, stars, and galaxies.

    c. Spectral analysis allows scientists to understand the motion of objects in space relative to Earth if they have radial motion.

    d. Scientists can determine the temperature of a star.

Use Figure 20 to answer questions 7 and 8.

FIGURE 20

7. Figure 20 shows something important about how the sun affects Earth. Which of the following statements describes the process that is illustrated?

   a. The sun causes Earth's magnetic field to be strongest in the direction of Earth's poles and weaker with distance from Earth.

   b. Sunspots change solar energy output and occur in predictable patterns.

   c. High-energy solar particles are released during solar events, but most are deflected by Earth's magnetic field.

   d. Solar flares release vast amounts of light energy and are related to changes in the sun's magnetic field.

8. Which of the following best explains the effect solar wind has on Earth's magnetic field?

   a. It reduces the field generated by Earth's core.

   b. It causes Earth's field to be stronger everywhere.

   c. It shifts the field in a direction away from the sun.

   d. It causes the shape of the field to be more uniform.

MAKE YOUR OWN STUDY GUIDE

In your Evidence Notebook, design a study guide that helps you explain how scientists use remote observations of temperature, composition, and motion to study objects in space.

Remember to include the following in your study guide:

• Support main ideas with details and examples.

• Record explanations for the phenomena you observed.

• Reflect on how scientists make use of basic laws that apply throughout the universe.

Use the crosscutting concept that energy is neither created nor destroyed to help interpret observations, such as the production of energy in the sun.

The Universe

The central region of our galaxy, the Milky Way

Image Credits: (t) NASA/JPL-Caltech/ESA/CXC/STScI; (b) ©Johns Hopkins University Applied Physics/Southwest Research Institute/ NASA Jet Propulsion Laboratory

CAN YOU EXPLAIN IT?

FIGURE 1: The dwarf planet Pluto pictured from a distance of 768 000 km (477 000 mi) by the *New Horizons* spacecraft in 2015

Gather Evidence
As you explore the lesson, gather and record evidence about the extent of the solar system. Use this evidence to help explain what you see.

From subatomic particles to planets, galaxies, and multigalaxy structures, the scales of objects in our universe vary tremendously. Although we used to think of the dwarf planet Pluto as the most distant part of our solar system, new theories and data have led us to reevaluate the limits of our solar neighborhood.

In recent years, studies into the existence of distant sun-bound objects as well as the influence of the sun's magnetic field and solar wind have caused scientists to review and revise old notions about the extent of the solar system.

 Predict How do you think that we should define the edge of our solar system? What are some factors that might need to be considered?

The Scale of the Universe

Whether an object is considered large or small, near or far, depends upon the perspective of the observer. Within our solar system, Venus is our nearest planetary neighbor, a mere 40 million km (25 million mi) away when the two planets are closest together in their orbits. The diameter of our solar system is thousands of times that distance, but our whole solar system is quite small when compared with the Milky Way galaxy. Objects in the universe range in size over several orders of magnitude, as do the distances between them.

The Solar System

How far is the moon, our closest celestial neighbor, from Earth? Do you think of it as being close or far away? How big is it? Do you think of it as being big or small? One way to consider the distance is in terms of the number of Earths that could fit in the space between. To think about the distance, we can compare it with the size of Earth. Look at the image to the right, which is drawn to scale.

 Analyze Approximately how many Earths could fit in the space between Earth and the moon? How many of Earth's moon?

Approximately 30 Earths—each with a diameter of about 12 740 km (7 917 mi)—could fit in the space between Earth and the moon. It takes just 1 second for the moon's reflected light, traveling at almost 300 000 km/sec (about 186 000 mi/sec), to reach Earth. The moon's diameter is just over a quarter of Earth's diameter. If you imagine Earth as a basketball and the moon as a tennis ball, a scale model of the Earth-moon system would place the tennis ball about 24 feet away from the basketball.

The solar system consists of a central star (the sun), eight planets, and at least six known dwarf planets, all of which orbit the sun. Moons orbit around six of the planets and around three of the known dwarf planets.

Smaller objects are found in different parts of the solar system. The main asteroid belt, between Mars and Jupiter, holds hundreds of thousands of bodies that range in size from small specks of dust to the dwarf planet Ceres, which is 946 km in diameter. Farther out, beyond the orbit of the most distant planet, Neptune, is the Kuiper belt. This is a ring of rocky and icy bodies that is many times larger than the asteroid belt between Mars and Jupiter. The Kuiper belt includes Pluto and several other icy dwarf planets. Far beyond the Kuiper belt lies the Oort cloud, a collection of trillions of icy bodies that were cast into highly eccentric orbits during the formation of the solar system and are weakly held at the limits of the sun's gravitational influence.

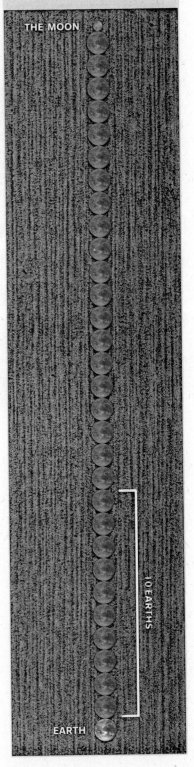

FIGURE 2: The average distance between Earth and the moon is 384 400 km (238 900 mi).

THE MOON

10 EARTHS

EARTH

FIGURE 3: Objects in our solar system vary greatly in size.

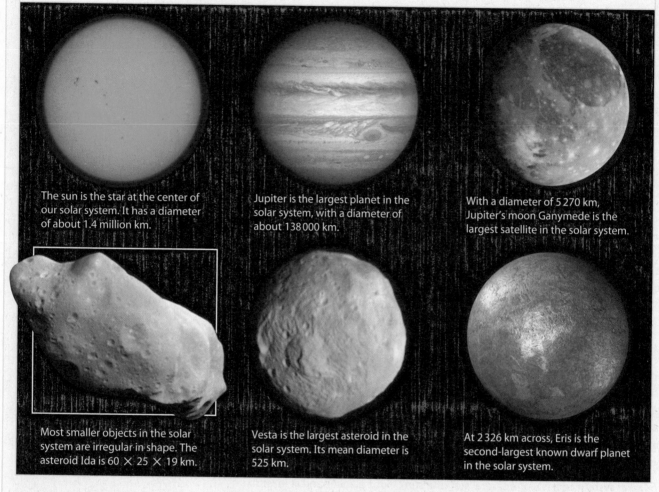

The sun is the star at the center of our solar system. It has a diameter of about 1.4 million km.

Jupiter is the largest planet in the solar system, with a diameter of about 138 000 km.

With a diameter of 5 270 km, Jupiter's moon Ganymede is the largest satellite in the solar system.

Most smaller objects in the solar system are irregular in shape. The asteroid Ida is 60 × 25 × 19 km.

Vesta is the largest asteroid in the solar system. Its mean diameter is 525 km.

At 2 326 km across, Eris is the second-largest known dwarf planet in the solar system.

Analyze: The objects shown above appear to be about the same size, but they are not. What is the order of the objects from largest to smallest?

Explain How does the distance to an object in space affect its apparent size?

Objects in our solar system range in size from dust particles of less than a micron (one-millionth of a meter) to our solar system itself with a diameter in the billions of kilometers. Distances between objects in our solar system seem immense, but when we compare those distances with the distances between objects outside of our solar system, it becomes clear that we are quite close by cosmic standards.

Consider the following: You can look toward the sky and observe the moon and planet Mercury. Which object is smaller? From your location on Earth, Mercury looks significantly smaller than the moon. However, Mercury only appears to be smaller because it is so much farther away. Now think about the sun's brightness. It is the brightest object in our sky not only because it emits a significant amount of light, but also because it is so close to Earth. When studying celestial objects, those that are farther away appear less bright because the light they emit is spread over a greater area.

Comparing Size and Distance

To get a good feel for the huge sizes of objects within our solar system and beyond, it is useful to compare objects with one another. It may be difficult to picture the size of the star Betelgeuse because its diameter is 1.6 billion km. However, knowing that it is more than 1000 times the diameter of the sun gives us a better sense of its immense size.

 Scale, proportion, and quantity

What units are used to describe the sizes of objects in the universe?

FIGURE 4: Objects in the universe vary greatly in size.

a Sun: star at the center of our solar system. Radius: 695 700 km

b Betelgeuse (model): distant red giant star Radius: about 1000 R_{sun}

c Jupiter: gas giant planet. Radius: 71 500 km

d Wasp 17b (model): exoplanet of a distant star Radius: 1.991 R_J

The radius and mass of a star are commonly given in terms of the radius and mass of the sun: a star that is 2 R_{sun} and 1.5 M_{sun} has a radius twice that of the sun and a mass 1.5 times greater. Large planets or objects are compared to Jupiter—R_J means "times the radius of Jupiter."

To convert a "solar radius" into a radius in kilometers, multiply by the radius of the sun. For objects that are described in terms of R_J, multiply by the radius of Jupiter.

Jupiter, our solar system's largest planet, has a radius nearly half that of the largest discovered planet outside our solar system, and the sun has a radius approximately 700 times smaller than the largest star in our galaxy. Comparisons such as these are useful for understanding and visualizing the magnitude of sizes of objects in the solar system and the universe.

Distances within our solar system are quite large compared with everyday distances on Earth. Therefore, scientists choose to discuss distances in comparison with the average distance between Earth and the sun. This distance of 150 million km (93 million mi) is designated as one astronomical unit (AU). Jupiter is 5.2 AU from the sun, or approximately 5 times farther than Earth; Pluto is 39.5 AU from the sun—almost 40 times farther than Earth.

When comparing measurements of objects, it is important to know what you are comparing. The size of an object can be described in terms of its radius, diameter, or volume. Objects are also often described in terms of mass, which depends on density and volume.

Explore Online ▶

 Hands-On Lab

It's a Long Way to Neptune!
Interpret and apply data to create an accurate scale model of the solar system using adding machine tape.

Image Credits: (l) ©Digital Vision/Getty Images; (cr) ©ESA/A. Simon/NASA Goddard Space Flight Center; (r) ©ESA/NASA Jet Propulsion Laboratory

Light-Years

Explain Why do you think distances within our solar system are not expressed in terms of light-years?

Large distances within our solar system are more easily managed by using the comparative astronomical unit (AU) as the standard. As greater distances are considered, such as those beyond our solar system, another standard of measurement is necessary because even the magnitude of AU numbers can become extremely large. Astronomers use the light-year (ly) as a standard of measuring vast distances in space.

One light-year is defined as the distance light travels in 1 year, approximately 9.5×10^{12} km, or nearly 6 trillion miles. Consider that sunlight takes 8 minutes to travel from the sun to Earth. This distance is less than 0.00002 of a light-year! It takes light just over 7 hours to reach the farthest extent of the Kuiper belt, a distance of approximately 55 AU, or just under 0.0009 light-years.

Some objects are so far away from Earth, it has taken millions of years for their light to reach us.

Explain Why is the light-year a necessary standard for communicating the distances of many objects beyond our solar system?

Math Connection

Orders of Magnitude What do we mean when we say that a distance of one light-year is nearly 5 orders of magnitude greater than one AU? "Order of magnitude" refers to powers of ten. One order of magnitude greater = 10 times greater. Two orders of magnitude greater = 10^2, or 100, times greater, and so on.

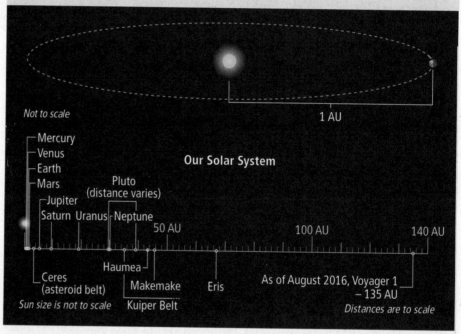

FIGURE 5: One AU is the average distance between Earth and the sun. Most distances within the solar system are described in km or in AU.

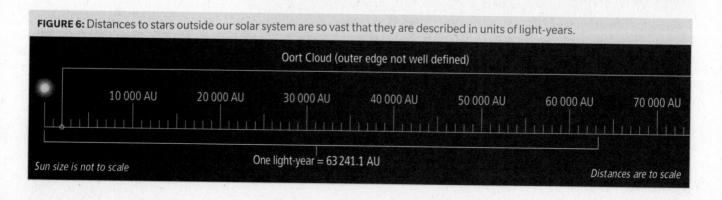

FIGURE 6: Distances to stars outside our solar system are so vast that they are described in units of light-years.

Nebulae and Star Clusters

A nebula is a large region of dust, gas, and stars within a galaxy. Nebulae, like the Tarantula nebula shown below, contain star clusters, groups of stars of approximately the same age that are gravitationally bound to one another and are relatively close together. Nebulae are often referred to as the birthplaces of stars.

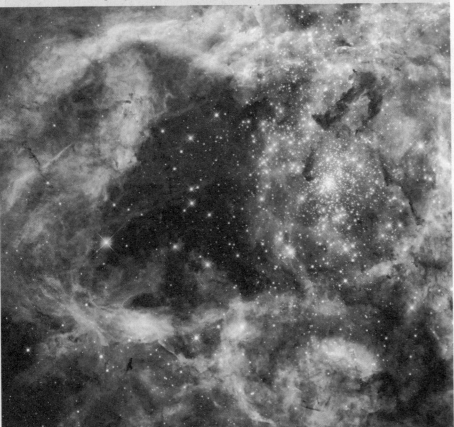

FIGURE 7: Star clusters in the Tarantula nebula of the Large Magellanic Cloud. The nebula is more than 1 000 light-years across and is about 180 000 light-years from Earth.

How do nebulae and star clusters differ in size from our solar system? Nebulae and star clusters are much larger than solar systems, which consist of a single star (or double star) and the planets and other objects that orbit the star. The stars within a cluster may appear close together—about 1 light-year apart. If our solar system were part of a star cluster, we would expect to observe more than one star like the sun relatively near us. In fact, our sun's closest stellar neighbor, a group of stars known as Alpha Centauri, is about 4 light-years away and may be nearly 2 billion years older than the sun.

The Milky Way Galaxy

Our galaxy, the Milky Way, is a barred spiral galaxy, which is a spiral galaxy that has a bar-shaped structure of stars at its center. The Milky Way has at least four major spiral arms and several shorter spiral arm segments extending from the center bar. Our solar system is located on the Orion Spur—an outer arm of the Milky Way galaxy. As the entire galaxy rotates, our solar system completes a 360-degree journey about every 240 million years.

Analyze How does the size of our solar system compare to the size of the Tarantula nebula? How do both compare to the size of the Milky Way galaxy? (Our solar system has a radius of approximately 100 AU. The Milky Way is about 100 000 light-years across.)

FIGURE 8: The Milky Way galaxy

a Seen from Earth

b As it would appear if we could view it from a great distance

Analyze Use what you know about the size and structure of the Milky Way to explain how the mass of a galaxy compares to the masses of a nebula, a star, and a solar system.

Analyze The largest object in our solar system is the sun, which has a diameter of 1.4 million km. In comparison, the Virgo Supercluster has a diameter of 110 million light-years. How do the sizes of these objects support or refute your perception of the sizes of objects in the universe?

The Big Picture

The Milky Way and more than 50 other galaxies are bound together by gravitational forces in a cluster called the *Local Group*. The Local Group is about 10 million light-years across and is part of the Virgo Supercluster, a tightly packed group of galaxies approximately 110 million light-years in diameter. It is huge, and yet there are even larger structures. The Great Sloan Wall, for example, is a "filament" of galaxies that is 1.38 billion light-years long. The largest known structure, the Hercules-Corona Borealis Great Wall, is 10 billion light-years across.

FIGURE 9: The largest scales of the universe

a The Virgo Supercluster, a large group of galaxy clusters, is 110 million light-years across.

b A map of a slice of the universe

Universe Orders of Magnitude

Analyze Sort the four objects in the following fictional story by order of magnitude: "A planet with a radius 10 times that of Saturn was discovered late last week by amateur astronomers. The planet is orbiting a red supergiant star in the Horologium nebula."

Astronomers estimate that the distance to the edge of the universe extends at least 46 billion light-years. That might seem surprising given that evidence indicates that the universe is about 13.8 billion years old. Some of the light and other electromagnetic radiation that we observe today was emitted by objects that used to be much closer but now are more than 13.8 billion light-years away because of the expansion of the universe. Even so, some objects are too far away for light from them to have reached Earth. For this reason, astronomers sometimes use the term *observable universe* to distinguish the part of the universe we can observe from the total extent of the universe.

Analyze Recall that an order of magnitude is equal to one power of 10. Compare the sizes of the objects described above in terms of orders of magnitude.

Image Credits: (l) ©NASA, ESA, the Hubble Heritage Team (STScI/AURA), J. Blakeslee (NRC Herzberg Astrophysics Program, Dominion Astrophysical Observatory), and H. Ford (JHU); (r) ©Markus Guthackl Entities of the...

Patterns in the Universe

Patterns of various types and at various scales are found throughout the universe. Stars of similar ages are found within certain types of star clusters. Galaxies typically fall into one of three types based on shape. And various sizes of rotating disks are found not only around stars and large planets, but also within galaxy centers and around black holes.

Young Stars and Old Stars

Our universe contains an estimated 100 octillion (a 1 followed by 29 zeros) stars, both old and young. To determine the age of a star, astronomers can study the star's spectrum. When our universe first formed, particles collided to form hydrogen. Stars that contain mostly hydrogen are, therefore, older stars. Stars whose spectra reveal compositions that have heavier elements must have formed after those elements were introduced into interstellar space by supernovae. They are younger stars.

Spectra reveal a pattern in the distribution of young and old stars, based on the type of cluster containing the star. Open clusters tend to be made up of young stars, whereas globular clusters are dominated by older stars.

FIGURE 10: Globular cluster M80 contains hundreds of thousands of stars. M80 is 30 000 light-years away.

Gather Evidence
What elements would you expect to find in the stars in the globular cluster M80?

Summarize Summarize the evidence supporting the observed pattern of star ages with respect to the type of star cluster in which they are predominantly observed.

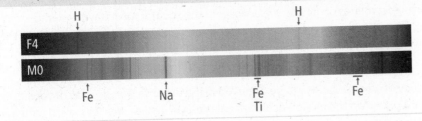

FIGURE 11: Spectrum of an old metal-poor star with weak metal absorption lines (top) vs. the spectrum of a young star (bottom) that is metal-rich and has strong lines

Types of Galaxies

There are three main types of galaxies in the universe, and each has different characteristics. Classification of galaxies is based upon their shape. Galaxies are categorized as spiral, elliptical, or irregular.

FIGURE 12: Galaxies are classified based on their shape.

a Spiral galaxy

b Elliptical galaxy

c Irregular galaxy

Image Credits: (c) ©NOAO/AURA/NSF/Science Source; (tr) ©Hubble Heritage Team/STScI/Aura/NASA; (bl) ©NASA/Gemini Observatory, GMOS Team; (bc) ©NASA, ESA, R.M. Crockett (University of Oxford, U.K.), S. Kaviraj (Imperial College London and University of Oxford, U.K.), J. Silk (University of Oxford, U.K.), R. O'Connell (University of V; © (br) ESA/Hubble, NASA, D. Calzetti (UMass) and the LEGUS Team

Patterns in Motion

You know that the moon orbits Earth and the Earth-moon system orbits the sun. As this occurs, Earth spins on its axis every 24 hours, with one rotation defining the length of an Earth day. Objects rotating and orbiting around other objects are found throughout the universe. The observed motion results from the gravitational attraction that formed these objects.

FIGURE 13: The same motion is observed when the moon orbits Earth, when ring particles orbit the planet Saturn, and when stars and nebulae orbit the center of a galaxy.

a **Saturn's rings** Orbiting icy and rocky material form Saturn's rings.

b **Galaxy** Objects form a spiral pattern as they orbit within a galaxy.

c **Jets of matter** Many objects have matter shooting out along the poles.

Explain Describe the patterns of motion you have learned, and evaluate how they tell us about the processes shaping the evolution of the universe.

As an object rotates on its axis, areas closer to the equator must travel faster to complete a 360-degree rotation than areas located near the poles. Consequently, the object flattens in the polar regions over time. Perfectly spherical objects are rarely observed in the universe because some degree of rotation is common.

A variety of other patterns can be observed in the universe. For example, Doppler shifts reveal a pattern in the motion of distant galaxies. On a much smaller scale, a pattern of motion results when small charged particles shed from stars in solar wind intercept the magnetic field of another object.

This pattern can be observed when the gravitational fields of planets redirect the solar wind generated by our sun, protecting their surfaces from high-energy particles. On a larger scale, the solar wind and the sun's magnetic field redirect particles from the interstellar medium, creating a bubble around our solar system called the *heliosphere*. The boundary of the heliosphere lies well beyond the planets in the vicinity of the Kuiper belt. The Oort cloud lies far beyond the edge of the heliosphere and is thought to be the farthest point at which the sun's gravity can tie objects to the solar system.

FIGURE 14: Small charged particles are deflected by a magnetic field much as the orientation of iron filings is affected by a bar magnet.

Extrasolar Planetary Systems

People have long speculated about the possible existence of planets around other stars, but the first confirmed discoveries of exoplanets came in the 1990s. In 2008, astronomers directly observed three planets around the nearby star HR 8799, and in 2009, the Kepler spacecraft was launched with the mission of identifying exoplanets. By 2016, more than 3500 exoplanets had been discovered.

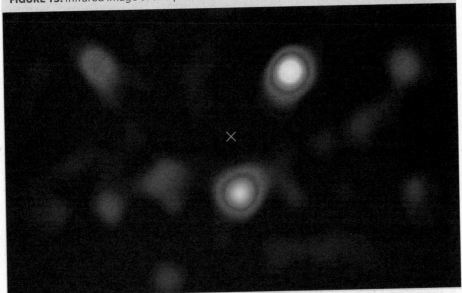

FIGURE 15: Infrared image of two planets in the HR 8799 planetary system

Systems and Methods for Detecting Exoplanets

Unlike HR 8799, most stars are too far away for us to directly observe planets in orbit around them. Instead, scientists rely on evidence based on known behavior patterns of motion and light. For example, the transit method is based upon a measurable dimming of a star's light as a planet travels in front of the star during its orbit. The dimming is cyclical; it occurs every time the planet is in front of the star. This method will not "see" a planet if the planet's path is not aligned with both the star and the spacecraft or Earth-based observer.

A second method, the radial velocity method, depends on the Doppler effect. A star moves slightly in response to an orbiting planet. If the planet is massive or close to its star, the star will be pulled by the gravitational attraction between the two objects. Doppler shifts as small as 1 meter/second are measurable and indicate the presence of a large exoplanet orbiting the star.

FIGURE 16: The transit of Mercury across the sun

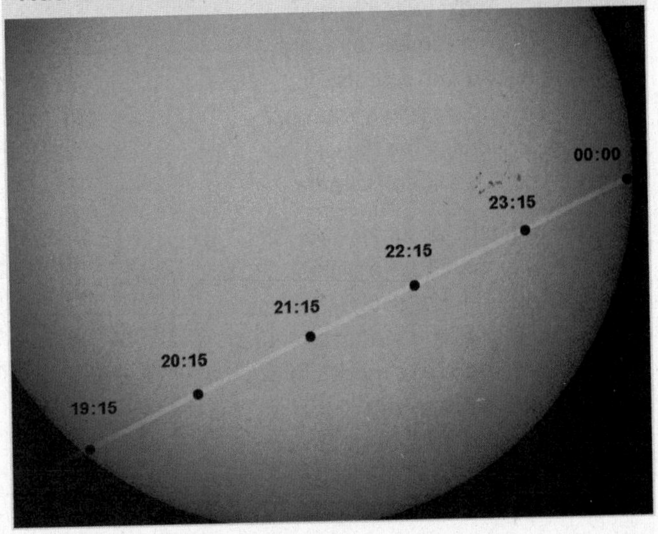

00:00
23:15
22:15
21:15
20:15
19:15

Explain What are some of the limitations of the transit and radial velocity methods in locating a planet of Earth's size in orbit around another star?

Image Credits: (t) ©JPL-Caltech/Palomar Observatory/NASA Jet Propulsion Laboratory; (b) ©ESA/NASA/Solar and Heliospheric Observatory (SOHO)

Guided Research

Mapping the Milky Way

For hundreds of years, scientists have sought to create accurate depictions of our cosmic surroundings. Early models of the solar system were drafted and revised to keep up with new observations and data. These models could all be two-dimensional since most solar system bodies orbit in a similar plane. However, as our advanced technology extended our powers of observation beyond the edges of our solar system to the Milky Way as a whole, it became apparent that a two-dimensional model wouldn't be able to accurately capture the arrangement of stars and objects in our galactic neighborhood.

In the early 2000s, the European Space Agency (ESA) set out to create the most detailed map of our galaxy to date. To accomplish this task, they constructed a high-power telescope called *Gaia* and set it in a special orbit around the sun that would keep it close to Earth at all times. To record the positions and movements of stars around us, Gaia slowly rotates, capturing portions of the sky with an extremely high-resolution camera.

After capturing the positions and movements of more than a billion objects, Gaia sends the data to stations on Earth for processing so that scientists can begin constructing a model. Unlike earlier models of space, this model is three-dimensional, with height, width, depth, and motion, and comes closer to capturing the actual structure of the galaxy than any before it.

FIGURE 17: The telescope Gaia collected data to make this 3D map of the Milky Way in 2016, showing the position and brightness of more than 1 billion stars.

Engineering Often, constructing and launching a spacecraft is only the beginning of the work for spacecraft engineers. Once the spacecraft is operational, the data it captures needs to be analyzed and changed into a format that is easy for scientists to use. Because of the incredible amount of information captured by Gaia as it mapped over a billion objects, engineers had to design new data-processing software in order to efficiently translate the data into a working 3-D model.

Language Arts Connection Scientists are currently using the data from Gaia to learn about the structure of the galaxy as well as how stars change and evolve. Write a proposal for other ways that the 3D map of the galaxy created by Gaia could be used either now or in years to come.

| EXPLORING THE UNIVERSE | DESIGN YOUR OWN SCALE MODEL | ON THE UNIVERSE SCALE | Go online to choose one of these other three paths. |

Lesson Self-Check

CAN YOU EXPLAIN IT?

Explain Refer to the notes in your Evidence Notebook to explain what you've learned about the extent of the solar system.

Where the outer edge of our solar system lies is the subject of debate among scientists. In developing your answer, consider several different interpretations of the solar system's boundary. If you consider the extent of the sun's solar wind (sometimes thought of as the equivalent of the sun's atmosphere), the boundary might lie at the edge of the heliosphere. However, if you consider the distance at which the sun's gravitation overcomes that of neighboring stars, the boundary may be as far out as the edge of the Oort cloud. There are even other factors to consider, such as the effects of the sun's light and how the sun's gravity interacts with neighboring stars.

The Voyager 1 spacecraft, which was launched in 1977 with the intention of exploring Jupiter and Saturn, is currently the farthest spacecraft from Earth. In August 2012, Voyager 1 passed the edge of the heliosphere and entered what some scientists refer to as interstellar space, making it the first and only spacecraft to do so. After a multi-decade mission and over 20 billion km, Voyager 1 is still sending us data on the space beyond the sun's magnetic influence.

Analyze How do you think we should define the edge of our solar system? What are some factors that might need to be considered?

CHECKPOINTS

Check Your Understanding

1. The sun's diameter is approximately 1.4×10^6 km, and the Earth's is just under 1.3×10^4 km. The Milky Way is about 9.5×10^{17} km across. Which statement is true?

   a. The sun is 2 times wider than Earth; the Milky Way is 11 times wider than the sun.

   b. The sun is 100 orders of magnitude wider than Earth; the Milky Way is 100 billion orders of magnitude wider than the sun.

   c. The sun is 2 AU wider than Earth; the Milky Way is 11 light-years wider than the sun.

   d. The sun is 2 orders of magnitude wider than Earth; the Milky Way is 12 orders of magnitude wider than the sun.

2. What is the correct order of the following objects and measurements, from smallest to largest? (Hint: Look carefully at the units.)

Hydrogen atom	2.4×10^{-15} m
Distance to nearest white dwarf star	8.58 ly
Diameter of nearest white dwarf star	2 million km
Distance to Orion nebula	1 344 ly
Diameter of Earth	13 000 km
Distance to Alpha Centauri	4.4 ly

3. In your Evidence Notebook, make a Venn diagram to compare and contrast two types of star clusters: open clusters and globular clusters. Include the following characteristics in your diagram.

   Older stars

   Younger stars

   Metal-poor stars (H, He only)

   Metal-rich stars (heavier elements present)

   Held together by gravitational forces

4. Which of the following accurately describe the reason for or result of patterns of motion in our universe? Choose all correct answers.

   a. Reason: Gravitational attraction caused materials to accrete in a central mass; motion typically began around a central axis.

   b. Result: Supernovae occur due to the immense centrifugal force generated by the spinning of a star.

   c. Result: Planets spin, rings move around planets, planets journey around the sun, stars spin, galaxies spin.

   d. Reason: Motion observed is residual motion resulting from the physical forces of the big bang.

5. Look at the image of the galaxy in Figure 19. What type of galaxy is this? Based on your observations, do you think the galaxy is rotating in a clockwise or counterclockwise direction? Explain your reasoning.

FIGURE 19

Image Credits: ©NASA/Gemini Observatory, GMOS Team

6. Which group of characteristics could you infer was observed by studying a star cluster?

 a. Observations indicate a well-shaped structure with many closely spaced stars. Spectra indicate dominantly cooler, younger stars.

 b. Observations indicate an irregularly shaped structure with many closely spaced stars. Spectra indicate dominantly hotter, younger stars.

 c Observations indicate a well-shaped structure with many closely spaced stars. Spectra indicate dominantly older, hotter stars.

 d. Observations indicate an irregularly shaped structure with many closely spaced stars. Spectra indicate dominantly older and cooler stars.

7. Match each distance to the unit that is best used to describe it.

 a. Distance to Madrid, Spain

 b. Distance to edge of observable universe

 c. Distance to Andromeda galaxy

 d. Distance to Pluto

 1. Light-year

 2. Gigalight-year (one billion light-years)

 3. Astronomical unit

 4. Kilometer

BUILD YOUR OWN STUDY GUIDE

 In your Evidence Notebook, design a study guide that helps you explain the scale of the universe and patterns in the universe.

Remember to include the following in your study guide:
- Support main ideas with details and examples.
- Record explanations for the phenomena you investigated.
- Reflect on how scientists use basic laws that apply throughout the universe.

Use the crosscutting concept that patterns occur on different scales to help interpret observations, such as the relationship between a star's age and its composition.

Evidence for the Big Bang

Full-sky image of
cosmic microwave
background radiation from
the COBE spacecraft

CAN YOU EXPLAIN IT?

FIGURE 1: Some of the oldest galaxies observed are seen here in part of an image known as the Hubble Deep Field South.

 Gather Evidence As
you explore the lesson,
record evidence to help explain how
matter has formed over the history
of the universe.

The Hubble Space Telescope, launched in 1990, has captured amazing images and greatly expanded our knowledge of the universe. This photo shows some of the oldest and most distant galaxies visible from Earth's Southern Hemisphere. Some of these galaxies are estimated to be as much as 13 billion years old.

Predict How is it possible for us to know about events that happened in the universe billions of years ago? What kinds of evidence do you think might support a theory of how the universe developed?

What Is the Big Bang Theory?

The Hubble Space Telescope is named in honor of the astronomer Edwin Hubble, who made a discovery in the 1920s that had a profound effect on our understanding of the universe. From his study of the motion of galaxies, Hubble concluded that the universe is expanding. Today, the commonly accepted theory that explains the formation and expansion of the universe is called the big bang theory. The theory states that about 13.8 billion years ago, the universe expanded suddenly from a very hot, condensed state. Despite the name "big bang," the event was not an explosion but an expansion of space itself.

The Big Bang Timeline

Take a look at the timeline of the universe based on the big bang theory. Notice that protons, neutrons, and electrons formed almost immediately and by 3 minutes, protons and neutrons had combined to form nuclei. However, it took more than 300 000 years before electrons could combine with nuclei to form stable atoms. And a few hundred million more years would pass before the first galaxies began to form.

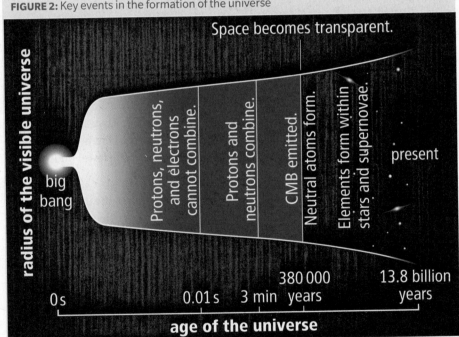

FIGURE 2: Key events in the formation of the universe

Interpreting Evidence

Humans have observed the universe for only a tiny sliver of the time it has existed, and we see only the current stage of its evolution. So how is it possible for scientists to construct an account of events that took place in the universe billions of years ago?

FIGURE 3: What clues can help you figure out what time of year this tree fell?

To understand how astronomers can describe the formation and history of the universe, it may help to first consider a more familiar real-world experience, such as the fallen tree in the photo. You were not there to observe the tree falling, but you can use evidence from the photo to come up with a possible explanation of when and how it probably fell..

 Collaborate Discuss the photo with a partner. During which season of the year do you think the tree fell? You may want to consider such clues as the presence, color, and size of leaves.

You and your partner probably came up with a pretty good answer to when the tree fell. A botanist with detailed knowledge of trees could give an even more specific answer. Each spring, deciduous trees form buds that grow into leaves over time. Suppose that early in the spring, a storm blows down a tree. Given the degree of leaf development, a botanist could easily determine when the tree fell by calculating the time that elapsed between the formation of the initial bud and when the tree fell. By the same reasoning, if the tree fell later in the spring, it would have fewer buds and more advanced leaf development.

Like the growth of the buds and leaves, events in the formation of the universe took place over a finite period of time. Because the same basic laws of physics have applied throughout all of space and time, scientists can use modern knowledge to learn about early stages of the development of the universe. For example, today we know that nuclear fusion in stars results from particle collisions, and so we can infer that the first nuclei and atoms also formed through particle collisions. Similarly, the Doppler effect that we are familiar with from everyday life also has an influence on how we measure the universe's first visible light. In upcoming Explorations, you will take a closer look at how scientists interpret evidence to explain the history of the universe.

 Explain Scientific knowledge is based on the assumption that the same natural laws operated in the past as they do today. How is this assumption important for the interpretation of evidence that supports the big bang theory?

Evidence of the Expanding Universe

Recall what you learned about the Doppler effect and redshift earlier in this unit. Light from stars and galaxies that are moving away from Earth is shifted toward the red end of the spectrum, while light from approaching objects is shifted toward the blue end of the spectrum. A discovery about the motion of galaxies became one of the major breakthroughs in modern astronomy.

Hubble's Discovery

During the 1920s, Edwin Hubble collected and studied the spectra of 46 galaxies. He determined that, except for a few nearby galaxies, all of the galaxies had spectra that showed redshift. By measuring the amount of redshift, he determined the speeds at which the galaxies were moving away from Earth. Then after comparing each galaxy's speed with its distance, Hubble announced in 1929 that the farther away a galaxy is, the faster it is moving away from Earth. His findings became the first persuasive evidence for the argument that the universe is expanding.

The idea that galaxies are moving away at a velocity that is proportional to their distance is known as Hubble's law. Many more galaxies have been observed since Hubble's time, and they all follow the same pattern. In 2016, researchers used a camera on the Hubble Space Telescope to obtain the spectrum of the oldest and most distant galaxy yet discovered. The galaxy, called GN-z11, formed just 400 million years after the big bang.

It is tempting to assume that because the galaxies are moving away from us, the Milky Way must be at the center of the expanding universe. But the relationship between distance and velocity would be the same from any point of observation in the universe. Although we may imagine that the galaxies are moving away from each other through space, it is space itself that is expanding and carrying matter with it.

 Problem Solving

Rate, Time, and Distance
Remember: distance = rate × time. For all four galaxies, the duration of the time that you are observing the motion is the same: the time between T1 and T2.

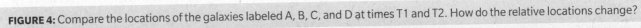

FIGURE 4: Compare the locations of the galaxies labeled A, B, C, and D at times T1 and T2. How do the relative locations change?

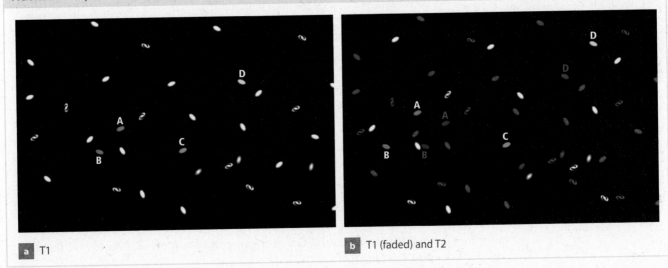

a T1

b T1 (faded) and T2

Modeling the Expanding Universe

MATERIALS

- balloon
- binder clip
- marker
- pen, ballpoint
- rubber band, thick
- ruler, metric
- scissors
- string

You can use simple hands-on models to develop a better a sense of how rates of expansion affect objects in the universe. Try these two models using a rubber band and a balloon.

PROCEDURE

Part A

1. Use **scissors** to cut open a **thick rubber band.** Spread the rubber band against a **ruler** without stretching the band.

2. Use a **ballpoint pen** to mark the zero point at one end of the the rubber band and then mark each centimeter from 1 cm to 5 cm as shown in Figure 5.

3. Hold the first mark (0 cm) in place next to the ruler while stretching the rubber band until the last mark (5 cm) aligns with the 10 cm mark on the ruler.

4. Observe and measure how many centimeters each mark has moved from its original location. Record your observations.

FIGURE 5: Part A

Part B

5. Use a **marker** to make 3 dots in a row on an uninflated **balloon.** Label them "A," "B," and "C." Dot B should be closer to A than dot C is to B.

6. Blow the balloon up just until it is taut. Use the **binder clip** to seal the balloon temporarily, but do not tie the neck.

7. Use **string** and a **ruler** to measure the distances between A and B, B and C, and A and C as shown in Figure 6.

8. With the balloon still inflated, blow into the balloon until its diameter is twice as large.

9. Measure the distances between A and B, B and C, and A and C. For each set of dots, subtract the original distances measured in step 7 from the new distances. Then, divide by 2, because the balloon is twice as large. This calculation will give you the rate of change for each pair of dots.

10. Repeat steps 8 and 9.

FIGURE 6: Part B

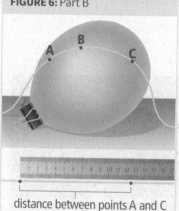

distance between points A and C

ANALYSIS

1. By how many centimeters did each mark move when the rubber band was stretched? What does this tell you about the rate of movement relative to the distance from the stretching point?

2. How is the rubber-band model similar to the expanding universe? How is it different?

3. With the balloon model, for which pair of points did the distance show the greatest rate of change: A and B, B and C, or A and C?

4. Suppose dot A represents Earth and that dots B and C represent galaxies. How does the rate at which galaxies are moving away from us relate to how far they are from Earth?

The Raisin-Bread Model

Another model can help with picturing the expansion of the universe. Imagine a loaf of raisin bread rising. Raisins that are farther apart in the dough when it begins rising move farther apart faster because there is more dough expanding between them. The entire loaf is expanding and carrying the raisins along with it. In the same way, the distances between galaxies are increasing as the universe itself expands.

FIGURE 7: In the raisin-bread model, you can see that the raisins move farther and farther apart as the bread rises and expands.

 Systems and System Models

Comparing Models

As you have seen, a variety of models can be helpful in understanding the biggest system of all—the universe. The rubber-band model and the balloon model are simple physical models. The raisin-bread model is a conceptual model that uses a real-life example to help us better visualize the expansion of space.

Scientists use several types of mathematical models, together, to develop an understanding of the formation and history of the universe. They use equations from physics experiments and theories to model the extreme conditions of the early universe. Models are also used to extrapolate those conditions to what should be observed, such as slight temperature variations in the early universe.

 Explain How does the analysis of spectra from galaxies provide evidence to support the big bang theory?

Evidence from the Early Universe

Powerful ground-based and space telescopes today make available vast amounts of data about the current universe. Some of these data provide evidence for conditions in the early universe that helps support the big bang theory.

The Early Universe

We know from galaxies that the universe is expanding today. But if we could reverse that expansion and go back in time to just after the big bang, we would find that all matter in the universe was in a superhot, superdense state. Within a fraction of a second, the universe had expanded and cooled enough that basic particles such as protons, neutrons, and electrons could form.

Figure 11 shows that protons, neutrons, and electrons were densely packed in the early universe. This state of matter that consists of charged particles rather than neutral atoms is called a plasma. The particles continually collided with one another, perhaps combining but only very briefly. There were also photons, or massless particles of electromagnetic radiation, shown by the squiggly arrows in the illustration. Because of the extreme density, photons traveled only a short distance before colliding with other particles. Light could not pass through the matter, and so this earliest phase is called the opaque universe.

Analyze
How does the illustration help you visualize why light could not pass through matter in the early universe?

FIGURE 11: Collisions of elementary particles—protons, neutrons, and electrons—within the plasma of the early universe. The matter is so dense that photons cannot travel very far before colliding with other particles.

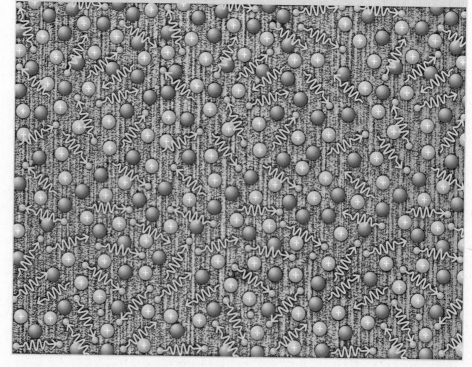

The universe continued expanding. Particles collided less often, and so the temperature dropped. After about three minutes, protons and neutrons could combine without being broken apart immediately by collisions. Most neutrons ended up in helium nuclei.

As the universe continued expanding and cooling, protons could capture electrons without losing them again in collisions—neutral hydrogen atoms formed. Similarly, neutral helium atoms formed. The universe was no longer a plasma. Photons don't interact with neutral atoms nearly as much as they do with electrons in a plasma, so the universe became transparent. Photons could travel for long distances without being further affected by matter. Many of those photons are still traveling today.

FIGURE 12: As the early universe expanded, it changed from a hot plasma with individual particles (left) to a hot plasma with nuclei as well as particles (center) to a much cooler, transparent state of neutral atoms and separate photons (right).

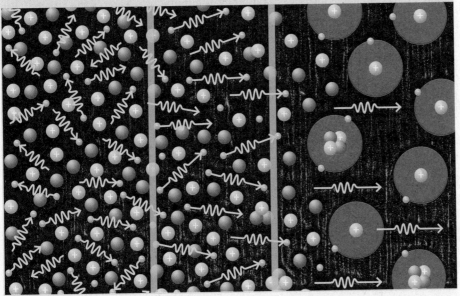

 Explain How did the formation of hydrogen and helium atoms make it possible for the universe to become transparent?

The Oldest Light in the Universe

It's hard to depict—and perhaps hard to imagine—but expanding space filled with particles and photons. Some of those particles of matter eventually ended up as you. Your current location was once within the opaque plasma that cooled and became transparent.

The photons that were near Earth's current location are long gone, but some of the photons from very distant locations are just reaching Earth now. They have been traveling from all of the locations that are now almost 14 billion light years away, in every direction. Some of the photons from Earth's location are now reaching those same distant places. Light didn't come just from a surface but from throughout the volume of space. When the universe became transparent, light started traveling from every point in all directions.

The Cosmic Microwave Background

Scientists accidentally detected the universe's earliest light in 1964, a discovery that became perhaps the most persuasive evidence in support of the big bang theory. Radio astronomers Arno Penzias and Robert Wilson were working to eliminate interference from an antenna they were attempting to use to detect radio signals from satellites. After removing interference from sources on Earth, they found a mysterious microwave signal coming from all directions in the sky. In consultation with other physicists, they determined that this cosmic microwave background (CMB) radiation is the remnant of the first light emitted 380 000 years after the big bang.

Space continued to expand after the radiation left the early plasma. Over time, the waves have stretched to longer wavelengths (lower frequencies) due to the expansion of the universe. Although the reason for the shift is different than a Doppler shift, it is related to motion and is also called a redshift. The shift is so great that the radiation is now in the microwave range.

The Cosmic Background Explorer (COBE) space mission was launched in 1989 to study the cosmic microwave background. Recall that the frequency of radiation can give information about temperature. COBE found the temperature of the CMB to be −270.4 °C, or just about 3 degrees above absolute zero. The temperature varies by tiny amounts in different directions. These tiny variations are also consistent with the details of the big bang theory.

 Gather Evidence
In your Evidence Notebook, make notes about how the CMB provides evidence that supports the big bang theory.

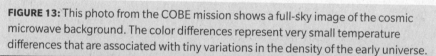 **Collaborate** Add a wave shape to your elastic band and balloon models of the expanding universe. What happens to the wavelength as you double the size of each model?

FIGURE 13: This photo from the COBE mission shows a full-sky image of the cosmic microwave background. The color differences represent very small temperature differences that are associated with tiny variations in the density of the early universe.

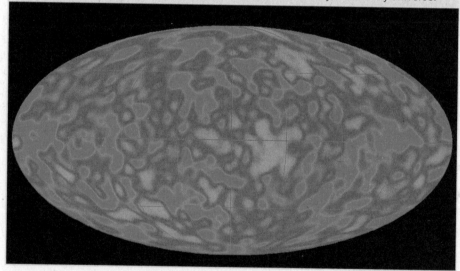

The tiny density variations in the CMB were mapped even more precisely by the Planck space telescope. The data gathered by Planck between 2009 and 2013 also enabled astronomers to calculate the age of the universe more precisely than ever before.

Consistency in Natural Systems

You may wonder how it is possible for scientists to know what would have happened just after the big bang. First of all, it's important to remember that scientific knowledge is based on the assumption that natural laws operate today as they did in the past. The mathematical models that physicists use to describe the present-day universe can also be used to predict what would have happened under the conditions of extreme temperature and pressure in the early universe.

Today, physicists can also use particle accelerators to observe the behavior or particles at extreme temperatures and pressures. In 2015, for example, researchers working at the Large Hadron Collider in Switzerland and France began experiments intended to simulate the conditions of the early universe.

Relative Abundances of Elements

The relative abundances of light elements (hydrogen and helium) in the universe are another important piece of evidence for the big bang theory. Recall that the big bang model indicates that protons and neutrons combined and formed nuclei within 3 minutes after the big bang. According to the theory, the conditions at that point in time should have resulted in hydrogen and helium being formed in a 3:1 ratio by mass. In other words, the total mass should have been about 75% hydrogen and 25% helium.

Collaborate Work with a partner to model the ratio of hydrogen to helium. Start with 2 dimes to represent neutrons and 14 pennies to represent protons. Arrange your "particles" to make as much helium as possible. Then calculate the mass ratio of hydrogen to helium. (Both protons and neutrons have a mass of approximately 1 atomic mass unit.)

Astronomers can estimate the primordial abundance of elements in the universe by analyzing "uncontaminated" regions of space. These regions must not only be far from us—and thus represent space in the distant past—but must also be far away from stars and nebulas that formed more recently and contain other elements that could interfere with observations.

Observations of these regions that are uncontaminated by processes of nearby stars or nebulas indicate an abundance of hydrogen and helium: 75% hydrogen by mass and at least 23% helium. Other light elements, such as lithium and beryllium, are present in trace amounts. Again, these observational data are strongly consistent with the predictions of the big bang theory.

Explain Record the significant information and observations you have made that will help you explain how evidence supports the big bang theory.

Guided Research

Contributors to the Big Bang Theory

As you have seen, astronomers have been developing and testing the big bang theory for nearly 100 years now. Like any scientific theory, the big bang theory builds on the work of many scientists and is supported by multiple lines of evidence. Today, space telescopes and other sophisticated instruments enable astronomers to test the predictions of the big bang theory in ever more precise and detailed ways.

Select one of the following options to learn more about the people who have contributed to the development and testing of the big bang theory.

Option 1: Edwin Hubble: Research to learn more about how Hubble determined that a galaxy's velocity is proportional to its distance.

Option 2: Georges Henri Joseph Édouard Lemaître: Lemaître was a Belgian astronomer who first proposed the theory that eventually became known as the big bang theory. Research how he came to propose his ideas about the expansion of the universe.

Option 3: Robert Wilson and Arno Penzias: Investigate to learn more about how these two radio astronomers discovered the existence of the cosmic microwave background. Who were the other physicists they consulted, and why was that collaboration so important?

Option 4: Fred Hoyle: The British astronomer Fred Hoyle coined the term *big bang*, but he was actually a major opponent of the big bang theory. He supported a competing theory called the steady state theory. Research to learn more about the steady state theory and why astronomers eventually rejected it in favor of the big bang theory.

FIGURE 14: Launched in 2009, the Planck space telescope gathered data about the cosmic microwave background, which provided powerful confirmation for the big bang theory.

Language Arts Connection Prepare an informative written report or oral presentation to share the results of your research with your classmates.

Informative/explanatory writing is a well-organized analysis of a topic. This type of writing tells how or why. Be sure to:

- provide an introduction that clearly states the topic and engages readers
- organize your ideas to make important connections and distinctions
- include details that support your ideas
- provide a conclusion that supports your explanation.

You can find guidance on writing an informative/explanatory essay in the Learning Resources for this lesson.

| SUMMARIZING EVIDENCE | SCIENCE WRITER | Go online to choose one of these other paths. |

Lesson Self-Check

CAN YOU EXPLAIN IT?

FIGURE 20: This image, part of a composite of images known as the Hubble Deep Field South, includes some of the oldest galaxies ever observed.

To gather the light from deep space that makes up the image above, the Hubble Space Telescope focused on one area of space for ten days. Most observations are made over hours, not days, and are not able to gather enough light to see so far away and so far back in time. The images revealed an immense region of more than 3,000 galaxies, including some of the oldest ever observed. The light from these very distant galaxies has taken billions of years to arrive at Earth. The observed colors of the galaxies have been affected by their motion.

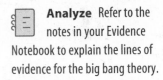 **Analyze** Refer to the notes in your Evidence Notebook to explain the lines of evidence for the big bang theory.

 Explain How does studying these extremely distant galaxies help astronomers learn about the early universe and its development?

CHECKPOINTS

Check Your Understanding

1. The sketch below presents a different model of universe expansion, one in which expansion is in one direction from a single point. If X were Earth, how would a spectrum from galaxy A most likely differ from that of galaxy B?

■- - - - - A - - - - - - X - - - - - - B - - - - -→

   a. Spectra A and B would not differ.

   b. Spectrum A would show a redshift and spectrum B a blueshift.

   c. Spectrum A would show a redshift, and spectrum B would not be shifted.

   d. Spectrum A would show a blueshift and spectrum B a redshift.

2. Put the following terms associated with the evolution of the universe in order from earliest to most recent.

   Transparent

   Stable nuclei

   Photons not destroyed

   Plasma

   Complex molecules

   Hydrogen atom

3. For each statement (a) through (d) below, identify whether it describes a process or characteristic associated with hydrogen, helium, or both hydrogen and helium.

   a. This formed when cooling temperatures allowed collisions to form stable nuclei.

   b. This accounts for approximately 25% of the universe's mass.

   c. The amount of this would be different had our universe's rate of expansion been different

   d. Isotopes of this include deuterium and tritium

4. Which of the following are true regarding the cosmic microwave background? Choose all correct answers.

   a. Radiation released when the universe became transparent is an indication of the temperature at the time.

   b. The expansion of the universe caused changes in visible-light frequencies.

   c. Detection of CMB from every direction in space indicates the universe is expanding in all directions.

   d. If the universe were not expanding, we would observe the universe's earliest generated light as visible light.

5. Match the lines of evidence on the left to one or more aspects of the big bang theory that it supports on the right.

   a. Motion of galaxies

   b. Cosmic microwave background

   c. Ratio of H to He

   1. Universe is expanding in all directions

   2. Distant galaxies moving away from us faster

   3. Expansion rate estimated with confidence

   4. Know timing of initial element formation

6. The first hydrogen and helium formed through the fusion of subatomic particles in the early universe. How do the relative abundances of hydrogen and helium in the present-day universe provide evidence for the big bang theory?

7. Observations of galaxy motion indicate that the universe is expanding in all directions. Do scientists infer, therefore, that the Milky Way's position in space is static? Choose the best answer.

  a. No. The ratio of H:He indicates the rate of current expansion includes all objects in the universe.

  b. Yes. The fact that CMB is coming from all directions as well further supports this conclusion.

  c. No. If we were in another galaxy, the Milky Way would be travelling away from us.

  d. Yes. If the Milky Way were moving too, we would see a different pattern of galaxy motion around us.

8. Observations of spectra from the Andromeda galaxy show that it is moving toward the Milky Way galaxy. Scientists estimate that the galaxies will merge in about 4 billion years. Is this evidence against the big bang theory? Explain your answer.

9. Telescopes such as the Hubble Space Telescope allow us to see back in time. Use an example to explain what this means and how it is possible.

10. Based on what you have learned so far, do you think it would be possible to detect light and create images of what the universe looked like in the seconds or minutes after the big bang? Explain your reasoning.

BUILD YOUR OWN STUDY GUIDE

In your Evidence Notebook, design a study guide that helps you explain the three main lines of evidence scientists use to support the big bang theory.

Remember to include the following in your study guide:
- Support main ideas with details and examples.
- Record explanations for the phenomena you investigated.
- Use evidence to show how scientists use basic physical laws that apply throughout time and space.

Use the crosscutting concept that energy is neither created nor destroyed to help interpret observations, such as the relationships among the three main types of spectra.

A BOOK EXPLAINING
COMPLEX IDEAS USING
ONLY THE 1,000 MOST
COMMON WORDS

RANDALL MUNROE
XKCD.COM

OUR STAR
How the sun turns matter into heat and light we can use

You know that Earth is a large and complex system. The sun and radioactive decay are the two main sources of energy in the Earth system. What is the source of the sun's energy?

THE STORY OF STAR POWER

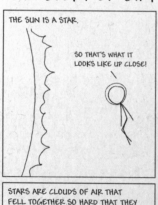

THE SUN IS A STAR.

SO THAT'S WHAT IT LOOKS LIKE UP CLOSE!

IT'S LIKE OTHER STARS, BUT LOOKS BRIGHTER BECAUSE IT'S CLOSER.

TOO CLOSE! TOO CLOSE!

THE SUN IS SO BRIGHT THAT WE CAN ONLY SEE OTHER STARS WHEN ITS LIGHT IS BLOCKED BY THE EARTH.

HEY, LOOK! THERE'S ANOTHER ONE!

STARS ARE CLOUDS OF AIR THAT FELL TOGETHER SO HARD THAT THEY STARTED BURNING.

SIGH . . .

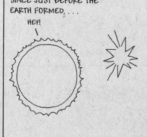

THE SUN'S AIR HAS BEEN BURNING SINCE JUST BEFORE THE EARTH FORMED, . . .

HEY!

. . . AND WILL KEEP BURNING FOR ABOUT THAT LONG INTO THE FUTURE.

HELLO!

AFTER THE SUN RUNS OUT OF AIR TO BURN, IT WILL GET VERY BIG FOR A SHORT TIME, BLOW OUT LOTS OF HEAT, . . .

OW! OW! OW!

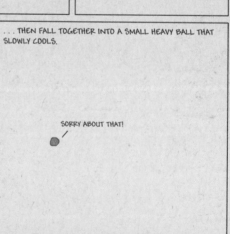

. . . THEN FALL TOGETHER INTO A SMALL HEAVY BALL THAT SLOWLY COOLS.

SORRY ABOUT THAT!

WHY STARS HAPPEN

To imagine how weights pull each other together, a lot of people say to imagine them sitting on a sheet. This doesn't always give you the right idea, but it works pretty well here.

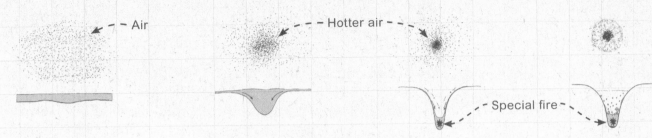

- Air
- Hotter air
- Special fire

1. AIR CLOUD

A star begins as a cloud of air in space. This cloud is always moving, pushing, and feeling waves go through it, like the surface of the sea.

After a while, a pocket of air happens to get close enough together that the pull of its weight becomes stronger than the force keeping it spread out.

As the air falls together, it gets heavier. This makes it pull harder, which pulls in more air.

As air falls together, it also gets hotter. This heat is how the air pushes back against whatever is pushing it together.

But in this cloud, that heat isn't as strong as the pull of the air's own weight, so it keeps getting smaller and hotter.

2. SPECIAL FIRE

The air seems like it might keep getting smaller and hotter like this forever. But when it gets hot enough, a new kind of heat is made.

When air is pushed together hard enough, the pieces it's made of can stick together. When they do, they let out a lot of light and heat. This is the heat that powers our largest city-burning war machines.

When a cloud of air gets hot enough, this kind of fire starts, and a great heat blows out from where it burns.

This hot wind is strong enough to fight the force pulling the air together. The air gets hotter, but stops getting smaller. A star is born.

The force pushing away and the force pushing in stop each other. If the star falls a little closer together, it makes the fire burn much hotter, pushing it back out.

A star like the Sun has enough air to burn for a very long time—long enough for worlds and life to form. But it can't burn forever.

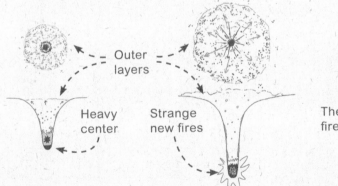

- Outer layers
- Heavy center
- Strange new fires

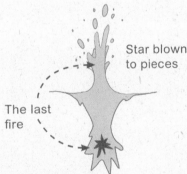

- Star blown to pieces
- The last fire

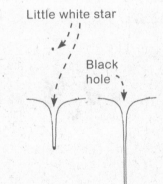

- Little white star
- Black hole

3. NEW AIR

When the star burns air by pushing it together, it makes a new kind of heavier air. This kind of air doesn't burn as well, so it gathers, not burned, in the center of the star.

The new air's weight pulls the star together, making the fire burn hotter. The wind from this hotter fire blows the outer parts of the star out farther. Over time, the star grows.

When it starts running out of air to burn, the center falls even closer together, lighting new kinds of fire that blow the outer layers farther away from the star. The star gets very, very big . . . and as the fires begin to die, the force holding back the star's weight disappears, and it starts to fall in on itself.

4. THE LAST FIRE

As the dying star falls together, it becomes even hotter than ever before. In this heat, even things that couldn't burn before start to burn, creating new and strange kinds of air. (Much of the stuff we're made of here on Earth comes from a fire like this.)

A lot of heat and light pour out from this last fire, and for a moment, the star can become the brightest thing in all of space.

5. WHAT'S LEFT

The heat blows much of the star away into space. Sometimes, what's left of the star will fall together until it becomes a bright white ball of hard air that slowly cools. Someday, this will happen to the Sun.

If the star is bigger than the Sun, it may have too much weight to stop even there. The weight of the hard ball will make it keep falling in on itself, until it becomes so strong it pulls in even light, leaving behind a black hole in space.

OUR STAR

AIR AROUND THE SUN

The Sun has air around it, like the Earth, but it doesn't have a hard surface under that air. It just keeps getting thicker, all the way to the center.

The air around the Sun is even hotter than some of the inside parts, which is very strange. We're not sure why it's like that.

CENTER

The middle of the Sun is where most of the weight is gathered and where the special fire happens. This special fire only starts if you push air together very, very hard. (This is the fire that powers our biggest city-burning machines.)

FIRE LIGHT

Around the center of the Sun, hot air doesn't rise. Hot air only rises when there's cooler air above it, and near the center of the Sun, *all* the air is hot. Instead, the heat is carried through the Sun by light, just like how light carries the Sun's heat to your face.

The light takes a winding path through the Sun's air. The path is so long that it can take a very long time to reach the surface—as long as hundreds of human lives.

DARK SPOTS

Sometimes dark, cooler spots appear on the Sun, caused by power running through the Sun's surface. Big fire storms often come from places with dark spots.

HOW MUCH HEAT?

Although it's very hot, the fire doesn't actually make new heat very fast. An area of air at the Sun's center makes about as much heat as the body of a cold-blooded animal of the same size.

Even though that doesn't seem like a lot, the Sun is so big—and it has such a thick coat of air around it—that the heat adds up, making it much hotter than any animal.

HOT AIR

The air on fire at the center of the Sun blows light and heat out in all directions. The air in the Sun is trying to fall toward the center, but the light and heat keep blowing it away.

Near the surface of the Sun, the air shakes and rises and turns over, much like a cup of water when you heat it up.

The fire from the center of the Sun heats the air. The air rises and turns over, carrying heat to the surface, where the heat is sent out to space (most of it as light). Some of the air is blown away too, but most of it—cooler, thanks to its trip to space—falls back down to heat up again.

FIRE STORMS

The air in the Sun makes power as it moves (for the same reason that a turning wheel can make power run through metal lines). Sometimes, the power runs through the Sun's surface and blows some of the Sun's fire out into space. These fire storms carry power with them, and if they hit Earth, they can break our computers and power lines.

THE END OF THE EARTH

When the Sun gets very big, its edge will reach the Earth, and Earth will fall in and burn up. You don't need to worry about that now, though. If we want to stay alive past the Sun's death, there are lots of other problems we'll have to face first. Worrying about that one now would be like worrying that one day a tree will grow where you're standing.

Engineering Connection

Designing Space Telescopes Engineers have long played a vital role in designing and building telescopes and other instruments for studying space. Since the 1970s, engineers have also been involved in designing telescopes to be launched into space. These space telescopes present their own unique set of engineering design challenges. The James Webb Space Telescope, a major space observatory scheduled to launch in 2018, will greatly extend astronomers' ability to observe in the visible and infrared regions of the spectrum.

> Use library and Internet resources to learn more about the James Webb Space Telescope. Then work with a partner to develop a list of criteria and constraints for the design of one of the key components, such as the mirror or sunshield protection.

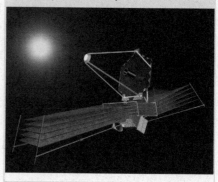

FIGURE 1: Artist's drawing of the James Webb Space Telescope

Social Studies Connection

Light Pollution Less than 100 years ago, people could see a starry sky wherever they lived. A research study published in 2016 found that more than 99% of the United States population now lives under light-polluted skies. Light pollution, or the excessive use of artificial lighting, not only limits our ability to see stars, but also has serious consequences for the environment, wildlife, and climate.

> The International Dark-Sky Association works to protect the night sky for present and future generations. Use Internet resources to learn about the work of the International Dark-Sky Association or other groups working to address light pollution. Then create a flyer, blog post, or other communication to educate others about what they can do to help reduce light pollution.

FIGURE 2: Light pollution over Los Angeles

Technology Connection

Space Weather Space weather involves conditions in space that affect Earth and its technological systems. Space weather results from the activity of the sun and its effects on Earth's magnetic field and atmosphere. Storms that originate from solar activity can disrupt a wide range of technologies, including satellites, communication systems, and the electric power grid. The National Oceanic and Atmospheric Administration operates a Space Weather Prediction Center that provides forecasts to help users deal with disruptions caused by severe space weather.

> Use the Space Weather Prediction Center's webpage and other Internet resources to learn more about space weather. Then work with a partner or small group to prepare a space weather forecast. Assume that a major geomagnetic storm is expected. Identify users to alert, and detail the disruptions that they should expect. Your forecast can take the form of a script, video, or other medium of your choice.

FIGURE 3: Solar prominence image captured by the Solar Dynamics Observatory

SYNTHESIZE THE UNIT

In your Evidence Notebook, create a concept map, graphic organizer, or outline using the Study Guides you created for each lesson in this unit. Be sure to use evidence to support your claims.

When synthesizing individual information, remember to follow these general steps:

- Find the central idea of each piece of information.
- Think about the relationships between the central ideas.
- Combine the ideas to come up with a new understanding.

DRIVING QUESTIONS

Look back to the Driving Questions from the opening section of this unit. In your Evidence Notebook, review and revise your previous answers to those questions. Use the evidence you gathered and other observations you made throughout the unit to support your claims.

PRACTICE AND REVIEW

1. Which of the following statements about an emission spectrum are true? Select all correct answers.
   a. It is a series of bright lines against a dark background.
   b. It is a continuous spectrum crossed by a number of dark lines.
   c. The lines show which wavelengths of light a star is producing.
   d. Each element has a unique emission spectrum.

2. If the spectral lines from a star are shifted toward the red end of the spectrum, which of the following must be true?
   a. The star is moving toward Earth.
   b. The star is getting hotter.
   c. The star is moving away from Earth.
   d. The star is getting cooler.

3. What causes strong magnetic fields on regions of the sun to lead to sunspots?
   a. Convection slows and energy decreases.
   b. Convection increases and energy increases.
   c. Radiation slows and energy decreases.
   d. Radiation increases and energy increases.

4. During a star's main-sequence stage, how is energy generated in the star's core?
   a. Hydrogen fuses into helium.
   b. Helium fuses into carbon.
   c. Carbon and helium fuse into oxygen.
   d. Helium decays into hydrogen.

5. What is the apparent magnitude of a star a measure of?
   a. the apparent shift in position of a star when viewed from different locations
   b. the brightness of the star as seen from Earth
   c. the brightness of the star if it were at a distance of 32.6 light-years from Earth
   d. the apparent shift in the wavelength of the star's light

6. In your Evidence Notebook, draw a model to represent how the energy produced in the core of the sun travels to the surface of planets in the solar system.

7. Why does the amount of energy Earth receives from the sun vary over time? Describe one of the patterns of variation.

8. Based on what we know about the chemical elements present on Earth, what inference can you make about the relative age of the sun? In other words, did the sun form relatively early or relatively late in the history of the universe? Explain your answer.

A theory is a proposed explanation for a wide range of observations and experimental data that is supported by multiple lines of evidence. Answer questions 9–11 about the big bang theory.

9. What does the big bang theory tell us about the early universe?

10. Scientific knowledge assumes that natural laws operate today as they did in the past and will continue to do so in the future. Explain the importance of this assumption for the big bang theory.

11. What are three lines of evidence that support the big bang theory? Choose one of these lines of evidence, and explain its significance for the theory.

Use the photos of the spiral and elliptical galaxies in Figure 4 to answer questions 12–14.

FIGURE 4: Galaxy types

| **a** Spiral | **b** Elliptical |

12. What inference can you make about the relative ages of these two galaxies?

13. In which type of galaxy is our solar system located? How would you describe the general location of our solar system within the galaxy?

14. In what parts of a spiral galaxy would you most likely find collections of very bright stars? Why?

Use the HR diagram to answer questions 15–17.

FIGURE 5: HR diagram

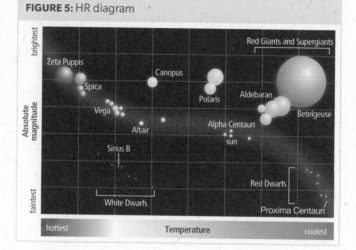

15. How will the sun's HR-diagram position change as the sun gets older?

16. In the diagram, both Betelgeuse and Proxima Centauri are shown in red. What does that indicate about the surface temperatures of these two stars? Why is Proxima Centauri so much less luminous than Betelgeuse?

17. Of the stars labeled on this diagram, which will likely have the longest lifespan? Which will have the shortest lifespan? Explain your answers.

UNIT PROJECT

Return to your unit project. Prepare your research and materials into a presentation to share with the class.

When preparing an oral presentation, remember these tips:

- Include a clear, logical, and well-defended claim.
- Provide evidence to support your claim.
- Present an introduction, a logically structured body, and a conclusion.
- Use clear and appropriate language.
- Use emphasis, volume, and gestures to engage listeners.
- Make eye contact with your audience, and speak at a volume that all can hear.

Image Credits: (cr) © NASA, ESA, R.M. Crockett (University of Oxford, U.K.), S. Kaviraj (Imperial College London and University of Oxford, U.K.), J. Silk (University of Oxford, U.K.), M. Mutchler (Space Telescope Science Institute, Baltimore, USA), R. O'Connell (University of Virginia, Charlottesville, USA), and the WFC3 Scientific Oversight Committee; (d) NASA/Gemini Observatory, GMOS Team;

Explaining the Abundance of Elements

The table presents data about the most abundant elements in the Milky Way galaxy. Based on what you have learned about the way stars produce elements over their life cycle, develop a claim supported by evidence to explain why these elements are the most abundant.

1. STATE A CLAIM

Based on what you know now, draft a preliminary claim that explains the relationship between stars and the most common elements. Record any questions you have, and list any information you will need to refine and support your claim.

2. GATHER EVIDENCE

Use Internet or library resources to investigate the details of the formation of elements through a star's life cycle. Consider the following questions to guide your research:

- What are the most common fusion processes that take place in stars with masses similar to that of the sun?
- What other fusion processes take place in more massive stars?
- Why are there no elements with atomic numbers greater than 26 on the list?

3. ANALYZE DATA

Use the evidence that you have gathered to revise and refine your original claim as necessary. Then construct your argument, using reasoning to explain how your evidence connects to or supports your claim.

4. COMMUNICATE

Prepare a written presentation of your argument in one or more well-developed paragraphs. You may choose to incorporate diagrams or other visuals in support of your argument, but be sure that your text clearly references them and points out their significance.

FIGURE 6: Ten Most Abundant Elements in the Milky Way Galaxy

Element	Atomic number	Mass fraction (parts per million)
Hydrogen	1	739 000
Helium	2	240 000
Oxygen	8	10 400
Carbon	6	4 600
Neon	10	1 340
Iron	26	1 090
Nitrogen	7	960
Silicon	14	650
Magnesium	12	580
Sulfur	16	440

Source: Ken Croswell, *Alchemy of the Heavens*

 CHECK YOUR WORK

A well-crafted argument should meet the following criteria:

- The claim is clearly stated and can be supported by evidence.
- The evidence is empirical, relevant to the claim, and sufficient to support it.
- The reasoning is logical, uses scientific principles to connect the evidence to the claim, and contains no logical flaws or fallacies.

UNIT 6

Plate Tectonics

Bardarbunga volcano erupting on Iceland in September 2014

Image Credit: © Jeff Vanuga/Corbis/Getty Images

FIGURE 1: Fissure eruption on Iceland

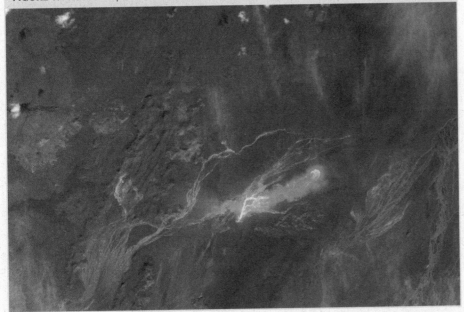

The island of Iceland has more than 30 active volcanoes and is made almost entirely of basaltic lava. The island lies on the boundary between the North American and Eurasian tectonic plates, and it is growing as the plates move apart.

 Predict How might Iceland provide evidence to help understand Earth's structure and composition and the processes that affect Earth's surface?

DRIVING QUESTIONS

As you move through the unit, gather evidence to help you answer the following questions. In your Evidence Notebook, record what you already know about these topics and any questions you have about them.

1. How do we know the structure of Earth's interior?

2. What evidence supports the claim that Earth's surface is made up of slabs of rock that are moving relative to each other?

3. How does the flow of energy from Earth's interior affect its surface?

4. How do plate motions affect people?

UNIT PROJECT

 Go online to download the Unit Project Worksheet to help plan your project.

Modeling Subduction

New oceanic crust is continuously forming, while old crust is being destroyed. How does this happen? Develop a model that shows how ocean crust is being destroyed in a specific area of the ocean floor. How do we know the crust is being destroyed there? What else happens in these areas?

Earth's Dynamic Interior

Earth's magnetism, which causes the auroras, is evidence of Earth's dynamic interior.

FIGURE 1: Edmond Halley

CAN YOU EXPLAIN IT?

In the late 1600s, English astronomer Edmond Halley presented a model of Earth's structure. Halley originally claimed that Earth was composed of an outer rocky shell and an inner rocky sphere, separated by a wide gap filled with glowing air. He thought that Earth had two sets of magnetic poles: one permanent set that originated on the surface, and another set that originated in the inner sphere. Halley believed that the inner set of magnet poles moved over time because the inner sphere rotated slightly slower than the outer shell. He also thought that the inner sphere was just as habitable as the surface.

Halley knew that his model was hypothetical and might not be completely correct, but he thought that it could explain some important observations, calculations, and inferences about Earth's properties. His model was based on information and evidence available at the time, but it was also based on some nonscientific beliefs that many people at the time accepted. The idea that Earth is hollow was not new—many people thought that there were vast caverns that extended deep into Earth's interior.

Gather Evidence

Record evidence about the composition and structure of Earth's interior. As you explore the lesson, gather evidence to help explain how and why our understanding of Earth's interior changes over time.

 Model Suppose that you know very little about Earth's interior and wanted to find out how accurate Halley's model was. How would you go about evaluating the validity of the model? What sort of evidence would you need to collect and how could you collect it?

Image Credits: (t) ©SurangaSL/Shutterstock, (b) ©Erich Lessing/Art Resource, NY

Evidence of Structure and Composition

The structure and composition of Earth's surface are relatively easy to determine through direct observations and sampling. On land and at sea, we can conduct field investigations and collect rocks and sediment.

FIGURE 2: Earth's interior is divided into three distinct layers based on composition.

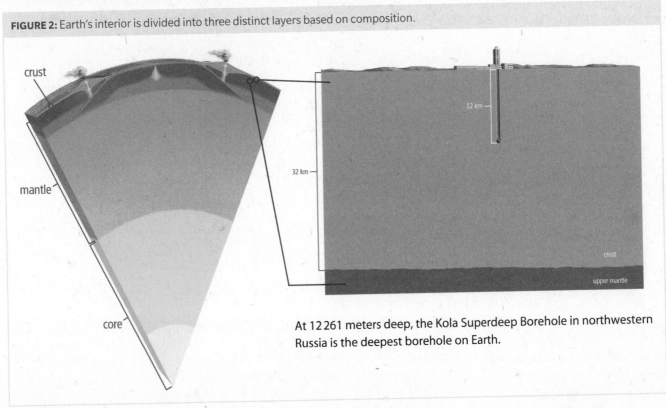

At 12 261 meters deep, the Kola Superdeep Borehole in northwestern Russia is the deepest borehole on Earth.

On land, we can investigate quarries, mines, and road cuts. The investigation of the ocean floor is more difficult, but it can be done with ships and sampling equipment such as drills and dredges. Investigating Earth's deep interior, however, is more difficult. One way scientists have tried to get a better understanding of Earth's interior is through drilling. The deepest hole ever drilled, the Kola Superdeep Borehole, is 12 261 meters deep. Twelve kilometers below Earth's surface seems deep, but it is only one-third of the way through the continental crust and only 1/500th of the total distance to Earth's center.

Drilling through the deep crust and into the upper mantle would be expensive and difficult. However, scientists from the International Ocean Discovery Program continue their attempt to drill to the mantle. If successful, it will provide important information about the composition, temperature, pressure, and other properties of the crust and uppermost mantle. But scientists still won't be able to sample the lower mantle or the core. To understand the composition and structure of Earth's interior as a whole, and to understand how it changes over time, scientists gather and analyze direct evidence, such as drilling samples, along with indirect evidence from energy released during earthquakes, gravity measurements, laboratory experiments, and chemical analysis of small fragments of mantle rock found within other rock.

Explain Why haven't scientists collected samples from Earth's core?

Models of Earth's Layers

Explain The Earth's layers models in Figure 3 show the characteristics of Earth's interior. What are some of the limitations of the compositional and structural models shown?

FIGURE 3: Models of the Solid Earth Earth's interior can be divided into distinct layers based on chemical and physical properties.

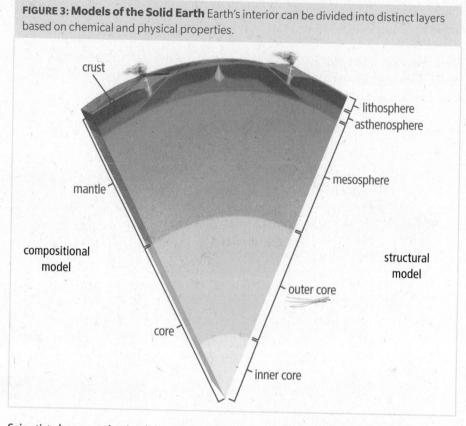

crust

lithosphere

asthenosphere

mesosphere

mantle

compositional model

structural model

outer core

core

inner core

Explain The terms "crust" and "lithosphere" are often used interchangeably, but they are not the same thing. How are the crust and lithosphere similar? How are they different? Why do you think people confuse the terms?

Scientists have synthesized the results of investigations to develop models that summarize our understanding of Earth's interior. The two most basic models are the compositional model and the structural model. Earth's compositional layers—crust, mantle, and core—are distinguished by their chemical composition, the minerals and rock they are made of. Its structural layers—lithosphere, asthenosphere, mesosphere, outer core, and inner core—are distinguished by physical properties such as temperature, physical state, and whether the layers flow or behave rigidly.

The models shown in Figure 3 are simple and appear to show that each layer is homogenous, the same throughout, and that the boundaries between the layers are sharp and even. In reality, Earth's interior is much more complicated. The exact composition and the physical properties of the rock vary from place to place. While some boundaries are relatively distinct and smooth, others are more blurry or uneven. Geologists who study Earth's interior have developed more detailed models that show additional layers and sublayers.

Like many scientific models, the models of Earth's interior are based on evidence and reasoning: direct observations, specific measurements, and the application of scientific laws and principles to make inferences about areas that cannot be observed or measured directly. Over time, these models have been modified and refined as new evidence has been gathered. Whenever you are presented with a model or a claim, it is important to ask: How do we know? Where did this information come from? What is still unknown?

Outer Layers

The outermost compositional layer of Earth is the crust. The crust along with part of the mantle below make up Earth's outermost structural layer, the lithosphere.

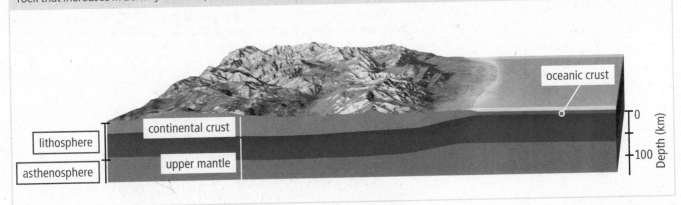

FIGURE 4: Earth's lithosphere, which includes the crust and uppermost mantle, is made of rigid silicate rock that increases in density and temperature with depth.

Our understanding of the lithosphere is based on evidence from rocks and rock formations, remote sensing of subsurface features, and laboratory experiments. We can, for example, study granites, gabbros, and other rocks exposed by erosion to infer the composition, temperature, pressure, and structure of the deep crust. Scientists can examine the rocks, mineral crystals, and gases that result from volcanic eruptions to gather evidence of the chemical composition and physical properties of the crust and mantle below. Finally, we can use data from earthquakes to infer physical properties and boundaries within the lithosphere. Seismic waves—waves caused by earthquakes—reflect off boundaries and refract—change speed and direction—when they move from one material into another. One good example of this occurs in a zone relatively near Earth's surface where seismic waves refract, which indicates a transition between two layers. This zone marks the boundary between the crust and mantle and is called the Mohorovičić discontinuity, or the Moho for short.

Explain What types of investigations are required to develop a complete and accurate model of the crust and lithosphere? Why is it important to draw conclusions based on many different observations and measurements, and types of investigations?

Collaborate Look at the diagram of the lithosphere. Which of the major features shown can be studied directly? Which can be understood only through indirect observations or interpretations of other forms of data?

Structure and Function

Volume of a sphere $= \frac{4}{3}\pi r^3$, where $r = $ radius

$$density = \frac{mass}{volume}$$

To figure out Earth's compositional structure, it is helpful to know its average density. Earth's density is related to the density of elements and minerals it is made of. Surface rock has an average density of 2.7–2.9 g/cm³. To calculate Earth's density, we need to know its mass and volume. Earth's mass can be calculated based on gravity measurements.

Analyze Earth's mass is 5.98×10^{24} kg and its radius is 6371 km. Calculate Earth's average density. How does it compare to the average density of rocks on Earth's surface?

Middle Layers

Earth's average density is about 5.5 g/cm^3. Since the crust has an average density of less than 3.0 g/cm^3, there must be materials deeper within Earth that are much denser than those on the surface. Most of those materials—about 83% of Earth's volume—are in the middle compositional layer of Earth known as the mantle. The mantle is denser than the crust because it is made of a higher proportion of heavier elements and because it is compressed by the weight of the crust above. The mantle can be divided into three structural layers based on their physical properties. The part of the mantle just above the core is called the mesosphere.

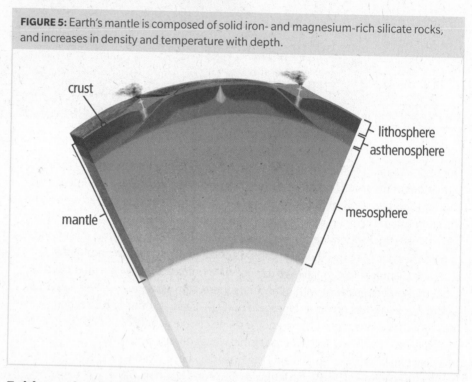

FIGURE 5: Earth's mantle is composed of solid iron- and magnesium-rich silicate rocks, and increases in density and temperature with depth.

Analyze If you were planning an investigation to drill into Earth's mantle, where do you think would be the best place to drill? Why?

Evidence from Rocks

Because Earth's mantle is so far underground, it is almost impossible to sample directly. Most of our understanding of the mantle comes from inferences based on the rocks we can examine on the surface, geophysical measurements, and laboratory experiments.

For example, the basaltic lava that erupts on the ocean floor is thought to be composed of mantle rock. Geologists use the chemical and physical properties of basalt to infer what the composition of the mantle must be. This approach to determine the characteristics of the mantle is consistent with estimates of the density of the mantle based on measurements of Earth's gravity and the way Earth moves in space.

In a few places on Earth, large sections of the oceanic lithosphere have been pushed up on land. At the base of these structures are rocks called peridotite, which are similar to basalt but have more iron and magnesium and less silica. Geologists think these are actual samples of Earth's mantle.

Evidence from Earthquakes

Most of our understanding of the details of Earth's structure—whether layers are solid or liquid, how hot they are, and where the boundaries between layers are—comes from analyzing data from earthquakes.

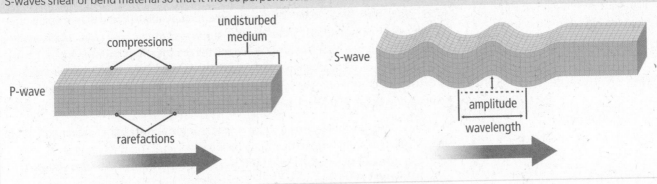

FIGURE 6: Seismic Waves P-waves expand and contract material so that it moves along the same direction as the wave is moving. S-waves shear or bend material so that it moves perpendicular to the direction of the wave.

When an earthquake occurs, masses of rock bend and then break and snap back suddenly. This causes waves of energy called seismic waves to move out in all directions. Two main types of seismic waves move through Earth's interior: P-waves and S-waves. The behavior of seismic waves depends on the properties of the material that the waves move through. Both P-waves and S-waves refract as they move from one material to another. In general, they move faster through denser, more rigid material, and slower through less dense or less rigid material. They also reflect off of different layers.

Scientists analyze the behavior of seismic waves—how they change speed and direction—to infer the density and composition of rocks, the thickness of rock layers, and the physical state of the layers. For example, the fact that the velocity of seismic waves increases with depth in the lithosphere provides evidence that density increases with depth. We know where the Moho is because there is a strong refraction of seismic waves in this zone. Because the velocity of the waves decreases suddenly, scientists infer that the lithosphere ends and the next-lower layer, the asthenosphere, begins. From this evidence, scientists infer that rocks in the asthenosphere are not rigid, but are plastic, or very bendable, like putty or clay, and close to their melting point.

Analyze Think about the density and physical state of Earth's different layers. How would you expect the velocities of P-waves and S-waves to change as they move from the solid crust to the solid mantle to the liquid outer core?

Explore Online ▶

Hands-On Lab

Modeling Earthquake Waves Use a spring toy to model P-waves and S-waves.

Data Analysis

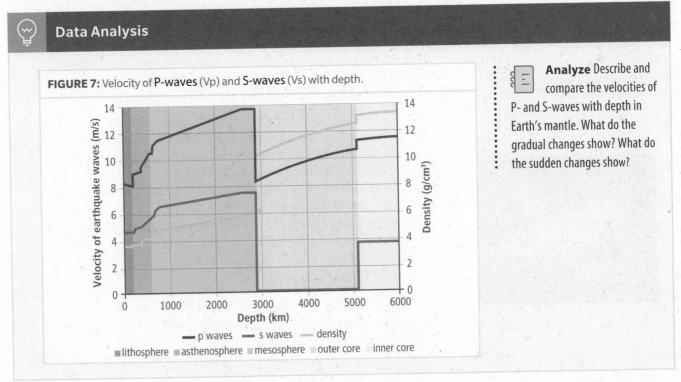

FIGURE 7: Velocity of **P-waves** (Vp) and **S-waves** (Vs) with depth.

— p waves — s waves — density

■ lithosphere ■ asthenosphere ■ mesosphere ■ outer core ■ inner core

Analyze Describe and compare the velocities of P- and S-waves with depth in Earth's mantle. What do the gradual changes show? What do the sudden changes show?

Image Credits: (d) ©Tom McHugh/Science Source; (cr) ©Mark Williamson/Science Source; (bl) ©NASA/JPL–Caltech

Explain Is it possible to estimate Earth's average composition by analyzing rocks on Earth's surface? Explain why or why not.

Evidence from Outer Space

To estimate the composition of the mantle and other interior layers, we need to have a good idea of the proportion of different elements that make up the planet as a whole. If Earth were homogeneous, or the same all the way through, we could do this easily by analyzing surface rock. But other evidence tells us that it isn't homogenous. Earth is separated into layers of different composition. Fortunately, there are a few rocks on Earth's surface that provide good evidence for Earth's composition and for the composition of the mantle and core: meteorites.

Meteorites are rock that fall to Earth from space. Some appear to be unchanged since the solar system formed nearly 4.6 billion years ago, and thus provide information about the materials that formed Earth at the time of the solar system's beginning. Geologists think that Earth's average composition is about the same as the composition of these meteorites. Other meteorites appear to be broken pieces of crust, mantle, and core of other bodies in space— such as the moon, Mars, and large asteroids—and provide additional evidence for the layering of Earth's interior.

FIGURE 8: Meteorites provide evidence of Earth's composition.

a Many stony meteorites are similar to rock on Earth's crust but appear to be unchanged since they formed 4.56 billion years ago.

b Geologists think that iron meteorites are broken pieces of the cores of small bodies

Stability and Change

FIGURE 9: Most of the mass in this rotating cloud of dust and gas came together to form the Sun, while the rest formed the planets, moons, asteroids, and comets.

Like the other planets, dwarf planets, and large moons in the solar system, Earth is differentiated. That is, its components are separated into layers based on density. How did this happen?

Earth formed more than 4.56 billion years ago through a process called accretion. During accretion, solid pieces came together to form larger pieces, which collided with other large pieces to form larger planetary bodies. The growing planetary bodies heated up as kinetic energy was transformed into thermal energy during these collisions. Bodies that were massive enough gained enough energy to melt completely. Over time, dense elements sank toward the center under the force of gravity, pushing lighter elements up to the surface. We don't know exactly when this differentiation took place, but it was within 100 million years of Earth's formation.

Analyze Some types of stony meteorites are undifferentiated. Scientists think that they come from small objects that never went through differentiation. Why were they not differentiated?

Laboratory Evidence

Another way that scientists can infer what the deep Earth is made of and how its properties differ from place to place is by making measurements and conducting experiments in the lab. We can measure the density of different types of rock and then use that information to infer what types of rock could be present in different places.

Laboratory experiments also help us understand how rocks and minerals are affected by changes in pressure, temperature, water content, and other variables. For example, we know that both pressure and temperature increase with depth. Geologists can heat and squeeze upper mantle rocks in the lab to find out how these changes affect them. When the temperature and pressure on mantle rock are increased to match the conditions that exist at a depth of about 400 km, one mineral transforms into a denser mineral of the same composition. This evidence supports the claim that there is a change in density of the mantle at about 400 km even though the composition remains the same. Experiments show that there are a number of depths in the mantle where changes like these take place.

We also know from experiments that mantle rock melts at lower temperatures when water is added to them and when the pressure decreases. This helps us understand why seismic waves travel more slowly through some parts of the mantle: They seem to be softer even though they are the same temperature as solid rock around them.

Analyze Laboratory experiments show that the density of the mantle changes at a depth of about 400 km even if the composition doesn't. If this is true, what should we expect the seismic evidence to show?

FIGURE 10: To better understand the composition of Earth's deep interior, scientists conduct experiments at extremely high temperatures and pressures. In the diamond anvil cell shown, a tiny sample is squeezed between two diamonds to generate pressure and then heated with a laser to reach high temperatures.

Evidence from laboratory experiments is just one part of the puzzle. Scientists combine experimental evidence with evidence from surface rock samples, drill core samples, measurements of Earth's gravitational and magnetic fields, and seismic data to get a more complete picture of Earth's interior.

Inner Layers

There is no direct evidence for the composition and physical properties of the core, which includes Earth's innermost layers. There are no pieces of the core on the surface, and it is physically impossible to drill 2900 km below Earth's surface to collect a sample. However, scientists can use similar techniques for inferring the characteristics of the innermost layers as they do for the mantle.

Analyze How are Earth's inner layers different from its middle and outer layers?

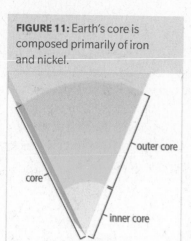

FIGURE 11: Earth's core is composed primarily of iron and nickel.

core

outer core

inner core

Seismic data show that there are two internal layers: an outer core that is liquid and an inner core that is solid. Earth's mass is greater than it would be if Earth were composed entirely from materials found at Earth's surface. We know this because of Earth's gravitational interaction with the sun. Scientists infer from this that Earth must have a core made of a very dense material, such as an iron-nickel alloy. The composition of meteorites supports the idea that there is a large amount of iron in Earth and that it is concentrated in the core. Experiments to figure out at what temperature and pressure different iron alloys crystallize help us infer what the exact composition of the core is and how its composition changes with depth.

 Analyze Look back at the graph showing how seismic wave velocity changes with depth. What is the evidence that Earth's outer core is liquid?

FIGURE 12: The existence of the aurora and and the behavior of a compass needle both provide information about Earth's deep interior.

a Aurora

b Compass needle

 Analyze Look carefully at the two images. Do research to find out what these two phenomena have in common. What do they both tell us about Earth?

Earth's magnetic field is additional evidence supporting the claim that Earth has an iron-rich core. Earth's magnetic field is similar to that of a bar magnet: One pole is located near the North Pole and the other near the South Pole. We know this because of measurements made using compasses and other instruments, such as magnetometers. We can infer from mapping thousands of measurements around the globe that the magnetic field originates from deep within Earth, not somewhere on the surface. We can conclude that Earth has had a magnetic field for a long time because evidence is recorded in ancient rocks more than 4 billion years old.

It makes sense that the core is made of a material such as iron that is a good electrical conductor. You can think of the outer core as working something like an electromagnet. The flow of liquid iron in the outer core generates an electric current that in turn produces a magnetic field. As we will see in the next section, observations that the magnetic field changes over time are further evidence that the outer core is liquid.

 Explain Scientists conduct a variety of investigations to understand Earth's composition and structure. Summarize the different types of investigations described in this lesson and provide at least one example of how each is used to understand Earth's interior.

Earth's Dynamic Interior

The Earth's interior models we have explored so far are static models. They are based on concentric compositional and structural layers of Earth at a single point in time. They are also very general, showing the broad structure, not details. But Earth's interior is dynamic with matter and energy in constant motion.

Core Dynamics

As with the composition and structure, the motion of Earth's interior layers is determined by making inferences. We know from direct observations that Earth has a magnetic field. Measurements show that the strength of the field and the location of the poles change slightly from year to year. We also know, by analyzing rock, that the orientation of Earth's magnetic field reverses every few hundred thousand years—the poles switch.

Gather Evidence What is the evidence and reasoning that supports the claim that Earth's magnetic field is generated by motion of liquid metal, and not a permanent, solid magnet deep inside Earth?

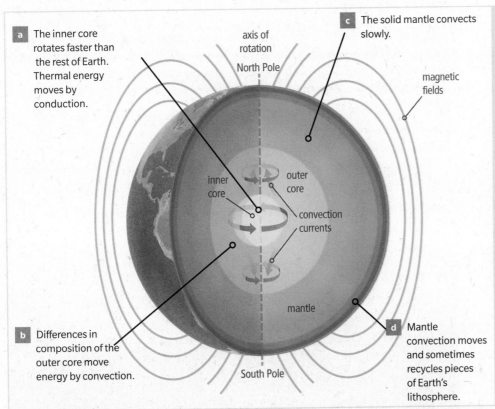

a The inner core rotates faster than the rest of Earth. Thermal energy moves by conduction.

b Differences in composition of the outer core move energy by convection.

c The solid mantle convects slowly.

d Mantle convection moves and sometimes recycles pieces of Earth's lithosphere.

axis of rotation
North Pole
magnetic fields
inner core
outer core
convection currents
mantle
South Pole

FIGURE 13: Earth's magnetic field and evidence of its frequent reversals over time point to an interior that is dynamic. The motion of magnetized materials in the core generates an electric current, which further strengthens the magnetic field.

Because minerals lose their magnetism at high temperatures, it is not possible that a permanent magnet exists deep within Earth. However, temporary magnetic fields can be generated by electric currents, and the field of a temporary magnet can change in strength and orientation over time, depending on changes in the current. Geologists have inferred from this evidence that Earth's changing magnetic field is caused by the motion of liquid iron in the outer core. As long as the iron keeps moving, the electric current keeps flowing, and there is a magnetic field. Geologists think that the magnetic field changes as the circulation of liquid iron in the outer core changes.

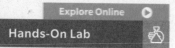
Liquid and Solid Cores
Use simple objects to quickly model Earth's core.

Mantle Convection

FIGURE 14: Convection cells are much more complicated than shown in this simple two-dimensional model. Geologists are not sure whether they extend to the core-mantle boundary, if they occur only in the upper mantle, or if there are two separate systems.

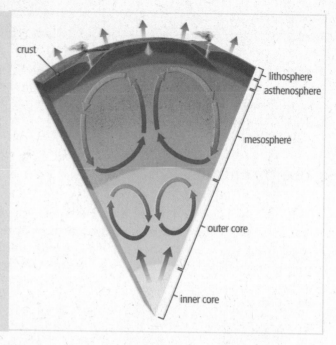

Explain What causes convection in the outer core? Why doesn't the inner core convect as well?

The flow of the solid rock of the mantle is driven by differences in density, which are caused by differences in temperature. Cool, dense material sinks and allows less dense material to rise. The motion continues as the sinking material eventually heats up enough to rise again, while the rising material, now near the top of the mantle, cools off enough to sink again.

Evidence from features on Earth's surface, from seismic waves, and from computer modeling indicates that this motion occurs in large convection cells: There are areas in the mantle where most of the material is colder and denser and is therefore sinking, and other areas where most of the material is warmer and lighter and is rising.

Convection occurs in the mantle at a rate of a few centimeters per year.

Analyze How does convection move both matter and energy in Earth's mantle?

FIGURE 15: Convection brings hot material up from the mantle toward Earth's surface, where it may melt and erupt, forming volcanoes. As the lava cools, the magnetic fields of the iron-rich mineral crystals within it align to Earth's magnetic field.

The Lithosphere

Earth's lithosphere is cold and rigid and does not experience convection in the same way as the mantle below. However, it does move and change slowly over time, in part because of mantle convection. Many of the features we see on Earth's surface and the processes that we can observe are evidence of this motion. Earth's surface is shaped not only by processes such as weathering and erosion that are driven by solar energy but also by processes that are driven by its internal energy.

Explain How is each feature shown in Figure 16 related to the motion of matter and energy in the mantle and core below?

FIGURE 16: Mountain chains and rift valleys are surface features formed by processes driven by Earth's internal energy.

a Mountain chains form as great masses of lithosphere crash into each other, crumpling and thickening the crust. These lithospheric masses are driven by the horizontal motion of convecting rock in the asthenosphere below.

b One of the ways in which rift valleys form is as hot, rising convective material in the upper mantle causes thinning and spreading in the crust.

Connecting Evidence

Although Earth's core is more than 2,800 km under ground, its influence can be felt high in the atmosphere. The shimmering lights of the aurora are caused by interactions between charged particles from the sun and gases in the atmosphere. The aurora occurs near the poles because Earth's magnetic field traps and channels the particles toward the poles.

 Explain Explain the connections, if any, between the aurora and the composition, structure, and motion of matter and energy in Earth's core, mantle, and lithosphere.

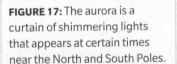

FIGURE 17: The aurora is a curtain of shimmering lights that appears at certain times near the North and South Poles.

Guided Research

Seismic Tomography

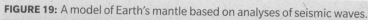

FIGURE 19: A model of Earth's mantle based on analyses of seismic waves.

Collaborate Models of Earth can be used to answer questions, and investigations can be used to improve models. For each type of model (compositional, structural, and dynamic), work with a teammate to come up with a specific question that could be answered using the model. Describe the steps you would follow to answer the question.

To develop a more accurate and detailed model of Earth, scientists collect and analyze seismic data from thousands of earthquakes at many seismic stations around the world. Scientists use the basic structural model of Earth to calculate how long it should take each wave to travel from the earthquake focus to the seismic station. They then compare this calculation with the actual travel time. Where there are differences between the actual data and the model calculations, they know that the model needs to be adjusted.

This diagram shows how the actual seismic wave velocity differs from the expected velocity. Areas in red are regions where the seismic waves are slower than expected. Continue your research about seismic tomography by asking more questions about this technique and the models it helps generate.

- How are the seismic wave data displayed?
- What do the red and blue colors mean and what do they tell us about those areas?
- What are some other applications that use similar techniques?
- How does the model generated with seismic wave data compare with other models of Earth's mantle?

| INTERIOR OF OTHER WORLDS | MODELING EARTHQUAKE WAVES | OBSERVATIONS OF EARTH | Go online to choose one of these other three paths. |

Lesson Self-Check

FIGURE 19: Halley's original model of Earth's interior included a layer of atmosphere between a rocky outer shell and a rocky core. Over time, Halley refined his hollow Earth model. In this model from 1692, Earth has seven alternating layers of rock and air.

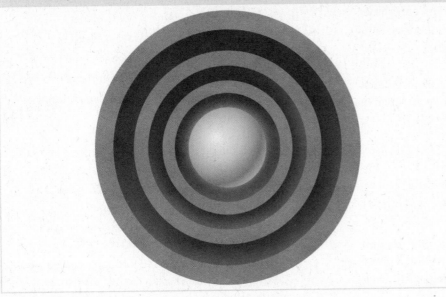

Analyze Examine Halley's model and compare it to a modern model of Earth. How would you now evaluate the validity of Halley's model? What evidence would you collect and how would you collect it?

Three hundred years ago, many people, including prominent scientists, thought that there were vast caverns in Earth's interior. Astronomer Edmond Halley thought that beneath Earth's outer shell of rock there was a wide gap filled with luminous air. He thought that within that gap, there was another rocky sphere, possibly inhabited with life. Halley later modified his model, adding several more layers of air and rock. Halley's model was based on observations, measurements, and ways of thinking at the time. When Halley saw the aurora, for example, he thought it was light coming through a hole near the North Pole. He thought the aurora was evidence that there was a glowing inner layer of air beneath Earth's surface.

We now know that Halley's models and other similar hollow Earth models are not correct. That is, they are not consistent with scientific evidence that we have today. Seismic data show that Earth is layered, but that the density of those layers increases with depth. Measurements of Earth's gravity, investigations of its magnetic field, and analyses of rocks on the surface also support this interpretation that Earth's interior is composed of solid and liquid layers, but not gas. If Earth's interior did consist of alternating layers of air and rock, our observations and measurements would be very different. Modern models of Earth's interior are different because they are based on information that Halley and other scientists did not have 300 years ago.

FIGURE 20: Modern scientific model of Earth.

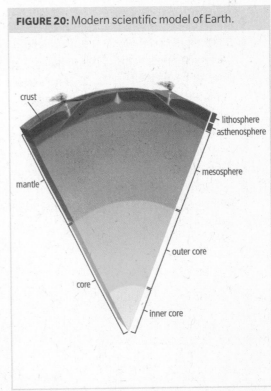

crust
mantle
core
lithosphere
asthenosphere
mesosphere
outer core
inner core

CHECKPOINTS

Check Your Understanding

1. Suppose you need to make a model of Earth's composition and structure using cereal and melted marshmallows to hold the cereal together in a ball. Which model would be most accurate? Explain what makes it more accurate than the other models.

   a. a ball of crushed cornflakes

   b. a ball of muesli (a mixture of oats, nuts, and fruit)

   c. a ball with raisins in the center, a middle layer of oats, and an outer layer of crushed cornflakes

2. A museum is designing an exhibit that allows visitors to examine "pieces" of each of Earth's layers. Match the sample to the layer that it best represents.

   a. Basalt   **1.** Core

   b. Granite   **2.** Mantle

   c. Peridotite   **3.** Oceanic crust

   d. Iron meteorite   **4.** Continental crust

3. Our understanding of the composition, structure, and dynamics of Earth's interior is based on direct and indirect evidence. Match each interpretation about Earth's core with evidence that supports it.

   Evidence

   a. Some types of seismic waves disappear at the base of the mantle.

   b. Some rocks show evidence that Earth's magnetic poles have reversed over time.

   c. Earth's bulk density is 5.5 g/cm^3, but the rocks of the crust have a density of only 2.7–3.0 g/cm^3.

   Interpretation

   1. Earth's outer core is liquid.

   2. Earth's core is composed of iron and nickel.

   3. The convection currents in the outer core change direction every few hundred thousand years.

4. A geologist is studying another planet. She wants to make a compositional model and a structural model of the planet's interior. To do this, she needs to design investigations to answer a number of scientific questions. For each question, state whether the answer will help develop a compositional model, a structural model, or both.

   a. Is there a magnetic field?

   b. What is the average density of the planet?

   c. At what depths do seismic waves reflect?

   d. Does the magnetic field change over time?

   e. What rock types are found on the surface?

   f. At what speed do seismic waves travel through different layers?

5. A student is building a model to demonstrate and explain mantle convection. Which model is most accurate?

   a. Toy bulldozers are placed on opposite sides of a carpet, causing the carpet to crumple.

   b. A bar magnet is placed inside a ball, causing iron filings to form a pattern around the ball.

   c. An electric current is passed through a copper wire surrounding a nail, causing the nail to become magnetized.

   d. A lamp heats a waxy substance in the bottom of a container, causing it to rise up to the top of the container, where it cools and then sinks again.

6. Describe how convection results in the motion of both matter and energy in Earth's mantle.

7. Rocks on Earth's surface can provide evidence for the composition of Earth's interior.

Which of the following statements are true?

a. Measuring the magnetic field around a volcanic rock can help us understand processes in Earth's core.

b. Analyzing the composition of a oceanic basaltic rock can help us understand the composition of Earth's mantle.

c. Measuring the temperature of a volcanic rock can help us understand the temperature in Earth's core.

d. Calculating the density of a volcanic rock can help us estimate the density of the crust.

8. Think about Halley's original hollow Earth model, in which there are two thick, rocky layers with a wide layer of glowing air in between. In what ways is Halley's model of Earth's interior similar to and different from the modern models? Consider composition, structure, and properties of the various layers.

9. What if Halley's model were correct? How do you think seismic waves would behave as they traveled through Earth? How would seismic evidence of Earth's interior be different?

MAKE YOUR OWN STUDY GUIDE

 In your Evidence Notebook, design a study guide that helps you describe and compare the different layers of Earth's interior and describe the scientific evidence that supports our interpretation of Earth's interior.

Remember to include the following in your study guide:

• two dimensional models (diagrams) to describe Earth's interior

• specific examples of observations, measurements, and experimental results that support the models of Earth's interior

• descriptions of how matter is arranged within Earth and how matter and energy move within Earth

Tectonic Plates

The Himalayas separate the Indian subcontinent from the Tibetan Plateau.

The Big One!

FIGURE 2: This is part of the San Andreas fault zone. What evidence of motion do you see?

FIGURE 1: The San Andreas is a complex fault system where major earthquakes have occurred. The lithosphere on the western side of the fault is moving northwest relative to the lithosphere on the eastern side.

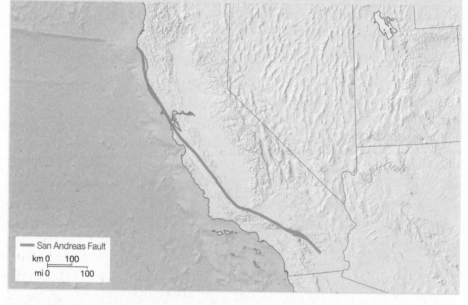

San Andreas Fault
km 0   100
mi 0   100

 Gather Evidence
Record observations for the existence of tectonic plates. As you explore the lesson, gather evidence to help you describe what tectonic plates are and how they move relative to each other.

In the 1978 movie classic *Superman*, supervillain Lex Luthor reveals his evil plan to set off a 500-megaton bomb along the San Andreas fault, causing a big earthquake that results in the west coast of California to fall into the Pacific Ocean. Once this happens, all of the land east of the fault—land that Lex Luthor owns—will become extremely valuable oceanfront property.

Explain Think about Lex Luthor's plan. Assuming Superman does not stop Lex Luthor, could Luthor's plan work? Why or why not?

Motion of Earth's Surface

Think about Earth's nonliving surface: the sediment, rock, and human-made materials and structures that cover it. Although they do not move on their own, we've all seen that they can move. Water and gravity move sediment down steep slopes. The impact of a boulder with another splits both rocks in two. Tree roots break apart sidewalks. High winds tear roofs off houses.

But what about the rock of Earth's lithosphere? Can rock 100 km thick and covering 500 million square kilometers of Earth's surface move? Can it break? If so, are there any patterns to the motion and fractures?

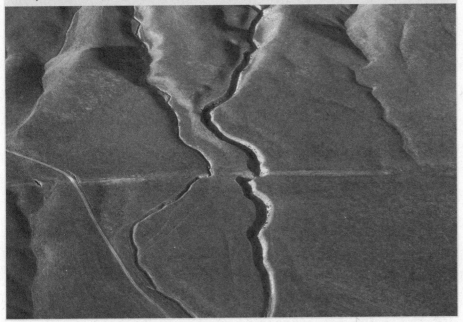

FIGURE 3: This portion of the San Andreas fault zone in California cuts through a stream valley and a road.

Analyze Describe the relative motion along the fault. Where is the fault? Which way are the rocks on the far side of the fault moving relative to the rocks on the near side?

The San Andreas fault, like other faults, is a break in rock along which the rock can slide. In Figure 3, you can see the line of the fault and how the stream seems to be offset at that line. This offset is evidence that the land has shifted over time. The ground in the top half of the picture, above the fault line, appears to have moved to the right, relative to the ground on the bottom half. The road on the left is not broken and must have been built or rebuilt since the ground moved.

Observations and measurements show that motion occurs all along the 1300-km-long San Andreas fault system. This motion is causing features along the ground to move past each other at an average rate of about 5 centimeters per year. The San Andreas fault is not unique; in many other locations around the world, there is evidence that segments of Earth's surface shift over time.

Faults show that parts of Earth's surface move relative to other parts. But just how much of Earth's surface is moving, and how?

Explain How could a geologist estimate the rate of motion along a fault?

Patterns of Motion and Surface Features

To investigate motion of the lithosphere on a global scale, geologists make measurements using the global positioning system, or GPS.

Interpret Examine the map. Describe at least two ways the motion of the lithosphere varies over distance. Use examples to support your claims.

Collaborate With a partner, identify a region where GPS receivers show a sharp change in the direction of motion. Then apply the claim-evidence-reasoning strategy to construct an explanation.

FIGURE 4: These arrows show the motion of the lithosphere based on GPS measurements.

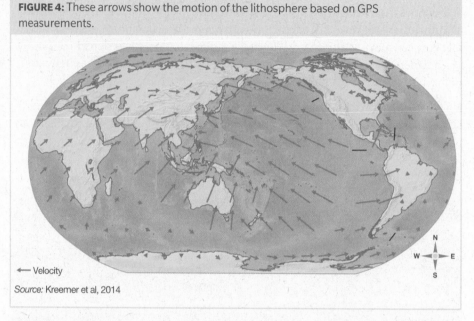

← Velocity

Source: Kreemer et al, 2014

The map in Figure 4 shows the motion of the lithosphere as velocity vectors—arrows that show speed and direction. The longer the arrow, the faster the lithosphere is moving. For example, locations in Hawaii are moving about 70 mm toward the northwest each year, while those in Puerto Rico are moving at a velocity of about 15 mm per year toward the northeast. In some places, such as the Central Pacific, motion is consistent over a large area.

FIGURE 5: The Andes Mountains straddle the western coast of South America. Arrows based on GPS measuremens show the direction of surface motion in this region.

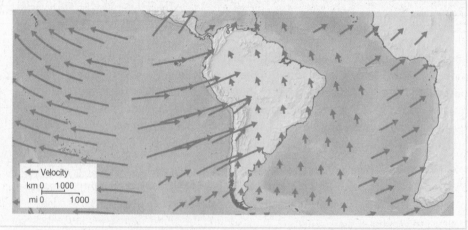

← Velocity

km 0   1000

mi 0   1000

Draw Conclusions Examine the maps on this page. Make a claim, supported by evidence and reasoning, about the location of topographic features and lithospheric motion.

Along its western coast, South America is moving toward the north. The Pacific Ocean floor is moving faster and toward the east. The two regions are moving toward each other. Along these regions' boundaries are a deep submarine valley, or trench, and a high mountain range, the Andes Mountains. In other places where regions interact, distinct topographic features can be observed. For example, the Cascade Range is located along western North America and the eastern Pacific Ocean floor.

Image Credits: (bl) ©ykumsri/Fotolia

Patterns in Earthquakes and Volcanoes

Are there distinct patterns to large-scale motion of Earth's surface? How does ground motion relate to other geological phenomena? One way to answer these questions is to analyze the distribution of earthquakes and volcanoes on Earth's surface.

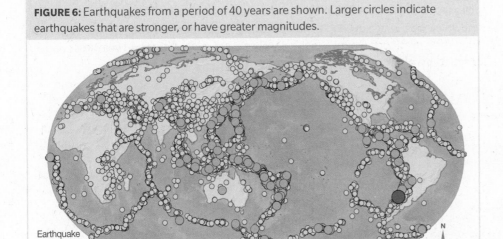

FIGURE 6: Earthquakes from a period of 40 years are shown. Larger circles indicate earthquakes that are stronger, or have greater magnitudes.

Earthquake Magnitude
- 8.0–8.9
- 6.0–7.9
- 4.0–5.9

Analyze Look at the maps on this page. How would you compare the distribution of earthquakes and volcanoes?

Explore Online ▶

🧪 **Hands-On Lab**

Where do Earthquakes Happen? Collect data and identify patterns in the occurrence of earthquakes.

An earthquake occurs when energy is released as masses of rock break or move. Scientists measure the shaking to determine the precise location of an earthquake's epicenter, the point on Earth's surface above the earthquake's starting point, or focus. A map of epicenters reveals that they are not distributed evenly or randomly over Earth's surface.

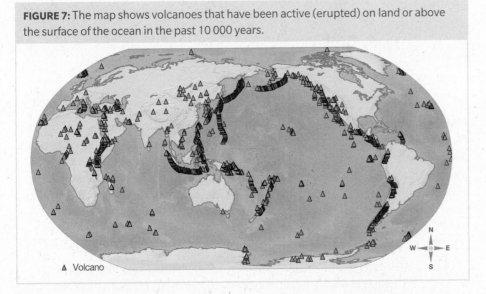

FIGURE 7: The map shows volcanoes that have been active (erupted) on land or above the surface of the ocean in the past 10 000 years.

△ Volcano

Volcanic eruptions occur when magma, a mixture of liquid rock, solid crystals, and gas, moves up from the mantle and crust and out onto the surface. Volcanic activity can be observed by those close to the eruption and can be monitored from afar with cameras and instruments that measure effects like temperature changes, ground motion, and gas emissions. A map of volcanic centers shows that, like earthquakes, eruptions do not occur evenly or randomly over Earth's surface.

In most places where earthquakes are common, there are volcanoes nearby and vice versa. Volcanoes and earthquakes are sometimes linked but are often independent events. When a volcano erupts, often the rising magma triggers earthquake activity. At volcanic centers around the world, earthquakes may trigger volcanic eruptions. Cracks can form that may act as pipelines for magma to rise as the crust moves during a major earthquake.

The maps in Figures 6 and 7 show that there is a distinct pattern to both earthquakes and volcanoes, which overlap almost perfectly. In addition, the map in Figure 8 suggests a relationship between the distribution of earthquakes and volcanoes and the patterns of ground motion measured by GPS.

FIGURE 8: Surface motion, earthquakes, and volcanoes reveal a pattern about boundaries and relative motion of large chunks of Earth's surface.

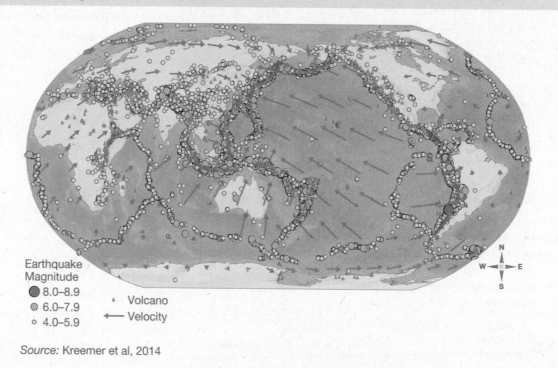

Earthquake Magnitude

- 8.0–8.9
- 6.0–7.9
- 4.0–5.9

▲ Volcano

⟵ Velocity

Source: Kreemer et al, 2014

What conclusions can we draw by studying GPS measurements of ground motion and the patterns in the distribution of earthquakes and volcanoes? The GPS measurements show that large areas of Earth's solid surface are moving. Earthquakes and volcanoes are common at locations where pieces of Earth's solid surface move toward or away from each other—that is, earthquakes and volcanic eruptions generally occur in areas along the edges of two rigid regions that are moving at different speeds or directions.

Analyze Compare the patterns of ground motion, earthquakes, and volcanic eruptions, shown on the maps in Figures 6, 7, and 8. Describe the patterns and how they seem to be related to each other. Use specific examples to support your claim

A Model of Earth's Surface

We saw from the GPS map that South America and the eastern Pacific Ocean floor are moving as separate pieces toward each other. Figure 5 shows that there is a long mountain chain and a deep ocean valley between these two lithospheric pieces. These features are not unique to South America and the eastern Pacific Ocean floor; other locations also show this pattern of mountains and trenches. In each of these other locations, pieces of Earth's surface are in motion relative to each other. The maps you have explored present just some of the measurements and observations scientists have made about the processes acting on Earth's solid surface and the motion of the solid surface over time. These data, along with numerous additional observations, measurements, experiments, and calculations, have been put together to form the tectonic plate model of Earth's surface. In this model, Earth's outer layer, its lithosphere, is divided into distinct pieces known as tectonic plates. Each plate moves as a rigid mass over the asthenosphere below. In general, all points on a particular plate move together. The plate boundaries can be recognized by certain types of features as well as by events such as earthquakes and volcanoes. The velocity of Earth's surface changes at a plate boundary.

Explore Online ▶

🧪 **Hands-On Lab**

Eggshell Tectonics Model Earth's tectonic plates using a hard-boiled egg. Investigate plate movements using the model.

FIGURE 9: Earth's lithosphere can be divided into about a dozen major tectonic plates, several minor plates, and some "micro" plates not shown on this map.

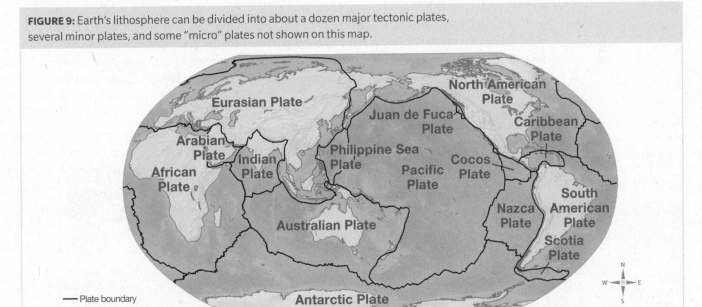

A map of Earth's tectonic plates, like any other map, is a model—it is a simplification of the real thing. The map shows our current understanding of the motion of the solid surface on a large scale. It does not show details of motion at any particular point on the surface, nor does it show exactly how sharp the boundaries are or what is happening at those boundaries. If you compare this map to more detailed tectonic maps or to more recent versions, you are likely to find differences. Like all models, this map will be revised as new evidence is collected.

Predict How do you think maps of tectonic plates have changed over time? Why have they changed? In what ways might a plate map published 100 years from now be different from the map shown here?

Explain How is your understanding of Earth's surface different after exploring this lesson? Look back at the maps and figures in this lesson, and make a list of patterns you can observe regarding the motion of lithospheric plates.

Earth's Lithospheric Plates

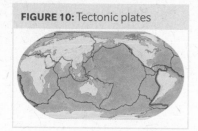

FIGURE 10: Tectonic plates

There are about a dozen major tectonic plates on Earth. Although they all vary in terms of size, shape, motion, and location, they have a number of characteristics in common.

The South American plate is in many ways representative of tectonic plates in general. It includes a variety of features such as mountains, valleys, and plains both on land and undersea. Like many but not all plates, it is made up of both continental and oceanic crust.

 Gather Evidence Make at least five specific observations about the South American plate. Think about the plate's characteristics both on land and under the sea—its boundaries, shape, motion, and relationship to other plates.

Composition of Earth's Plates

One aspect of the plates that is not apparent from the tectonic plate map is their composition. Rocks and sediment on the surface of Earth's continents can be examined and described. But is the surface of continents representative of an entire plate? Are the materials on and under the ocean floor the same as those of the continents?

FIGURE 11: The South American plate includes both continental and oceanic crust.

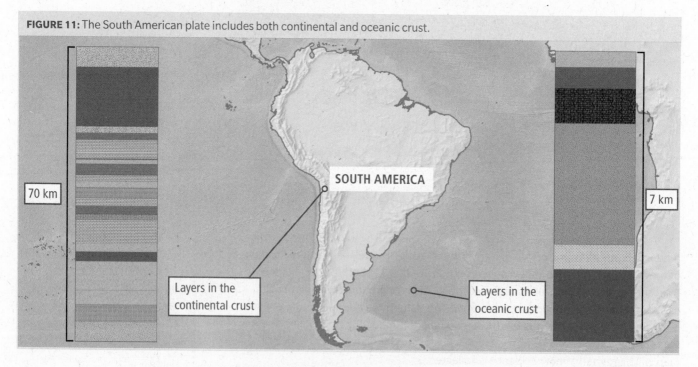

70 km

SOUTH AMERICA

7 km

Layers in the continental crust

Layers in the oceanic crust

One way to answer these questions is by examining the layers of rock in different plate locations. Geologists study the sequences of rock that are exposed on Earth's surface, rock found underground in mines, and land and seafloor rock core samples to gather evidence about the composition and structure of plates. Gravitational, seismic, and magnetic data also contribute to the picture.

If you look carefully at the map of Earth's tectonic plates, you will notice that some plates include both continents and ocean floor, while others consist only of ocean floor. Figure 11 shows typical continental and oceanic crust rock layers. It shows that continental crust is thicker and made of a much wider variety of rock types than the oceanic crust.

 Analyze Compare the rock layers from the different parts of the South American plate. How are they similar? How are they different? What do the sections tell you about what the crust is made of and how it formed?

Patterns

The composition and structure of the crust reflect the processes that shape plates. The South American plate is typical of many plates, composed of both continental and oceanic crust. Igneous, sedimentary, and metamorphic rock are all found in continental crust, though light-colored granitic igneous rocks are predominant. Oceanic crust is largely composed of dark-colored basaltic rock.

Characteristics	Continental Crust	Oceanic Crust
Composition	Granite (felsic)	Basaltic (mafic)
Thickness	30 km	7 km
Density	2.7 g/cm^3	2.9 g/cm^3
Mantle composition	Peridotite (ultramafic)	Peridotite (ultramafic)
Location	Most found on continents or their shallow edges (continental shelves)	Most found under the ocean or on oceanic islands; rare on continents

FIGURE 12: Rock of Earth's crust

a Basalt

b Granite

 Analyze Examine Figure 12 and the information in this feature. What specific characteristics of the South American plate exemplify the general characteristics of plates described above? If there are any, can you explain discrepancies between the two?

Although most landmasses are part of the continental crust and most of the sea floor is part of the oceanic crust, crust is not classified by whether or not it is underwater—parts of the continental crust are submerged. Some parts of the oceanic crust rise above the ocean surface to form islands. It is also important to understand that all of these descriptions are generalizations. In any particular place in the continental or oceanic crust, the composition could be more or less typical. There is also a type of crust called *transitional crust*, which is found between oceanic and continental crust and has characteristics of both.

Characteristics of Earth's Plates

Each of the two rock layer columns in Figure 11 is a model of the crust in a very small area of the South American plate. Geologists combine observations and measurements from thousands of investigations of lithospheric rocks from across the globe to understand the characteristics of the lithospheric plates such as structure, density, and age.

FIGURE 13: Model showing the characteristics of a tectonic plate

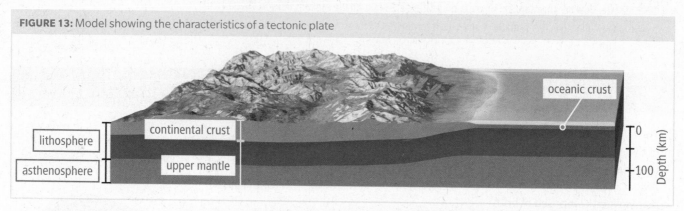

Gather Evidence
Look carefully at the diagrams showing the general structure of Earth's plates. Make at least five observations about the oceanic crust, the continental crust, or the differences between them.

Analyze In your notebook, make a table with two columns. In the first column, make a list of surface features and locations on plates (e.g., mountains, plains, continental shelf, abyssal plain). In the second column, describe each feature using one or more of the following terms: *thin, thick, granitic, basaltic, buoyant, dense.*

The cross-section model of a tectonic plate in Figure 13 provides an overview of the composition and structure of the lithosphere. It illustrates that oceanic crust is much thinner than continental crust. Both the oceanic and continental crust along with the lithosphere below them float on the aesthenosphere. Because oceanic crust is denser, oceanic lithosphere sinks deeper than continental lithosphere. Oceans are found above oceanic crust because oceanic crust has a lower elevation than most continental crust and gravity pulls water into low areas. The continental crust is thick and floats high on the mantle the same way an iceberg or a log floats on water.

FIGURE 14: The transition zone between continental and oceanic crust holds clues about the evolution of plates.

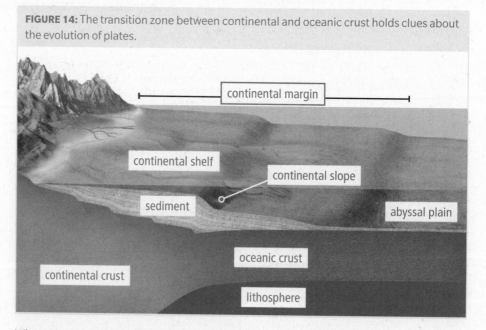

Where does continental crust stop and oceanic crust begin? The transition is within the continental margin, which includes the continental shelf and nearby sediment. Beyond is oceanic crust. On the scale shown in Figure 13, the transition is fairly sharp. On a finer scale, however, there is a narrow transition region between the two. A deep oceanic trench off the western coast of South America sharply divides the two types of crust.

In places such as the eastern coast of that continent, the transition isn't as obvious, but it is still there. This kind of transition, called the *continent-ocean boundary*, is of great importance to the study of the evolution of plates—how they formed and are shaped by internal processes that can bring them together and pull them apart.

The ages of continental and oceanic lithosphere differ greatly. Geologists determine the ages of rocks in a variety of ways. They might observe the relative position of rock layers or the fossil content of rocks to infer their ages. Geologists might also use more accurate methods to determine the absolute age of rocks, such as looking at the magnetic signatures of rocks or the patterns of radioactive elements in rocks.

The age of oceanic crust shows a clear and consistent pattern. Ocean floor rock is oldest near continental margins and youngest away from it. The pattern of ages on the continents is not as clear. In some places, the ages progress steadily from young to old toward the center of continents, but in other places, young and old continental crusts are mixed together.

Analyze: The map shows the ages of oceanic crust of the South American plate. Use the map to estimate the ages of the crust in the following regions: (a) the oceanic crust just off the western coast of South America, (b) the Central Pacific, and (c) the area just off the eastern coast of South America.

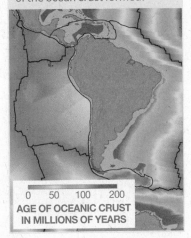

FIGURE 15: Age of the oceanic crust in the South Atlantic and South Pacific: This map shows when the basalts and gabbros of the ocean crust formed.

0   50   100   200
AGE OF OCEANIC CRUST IN MILLIONS OF YEARS

Analyze a Plate

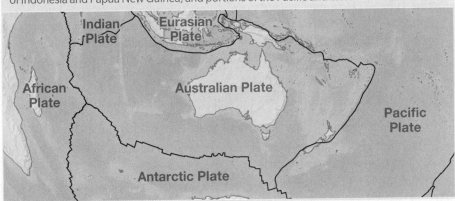

FIGURE 16: The Australian plate includes the continent of Australia, part of New Zealand, part of Indonesia and Papua New Guinea, and portions of the Pacific and Indian Ocean floors.

The Australian plate consists of both oceanic and continental lithosphere moving about 90 mm per year toward the northeast relative to the Pacific plate. The continental part of the plate includes the continent of Australia, the continental shelf surrounding Australia, and many islands to the north of Australia. The oceanic portion of the plate includes the deep seafloor to the east, west, and south of the continent.

Model Draw a simple cross-section of the Australian plate from the middle of Australia, south into the Indian Ocean. Identify the parts of the plate, and describe each part using words like *granitic*, *basaltic*, *old*, *young*, *dense*, and *buoyant*.

Data Analysis

Relative and Absolute Plate Motion

FIGURE 17: Absolute plate motion

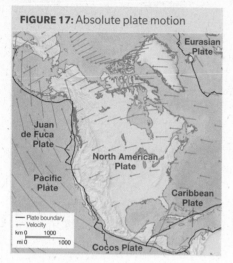

FIGURE 18: Relative motion of Earth's tectonic plates.

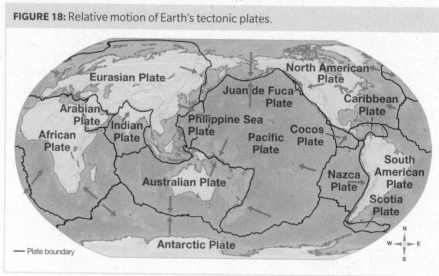

Collaborate Look at Figure 18. Choose a location along the edge of the North American plate. Analyze the motion of the plate in this location and the motion of the plate next to it. How are the plates moving relative to each other? How do the separate motions shown in Figure 17 combine to produce this relative motion? Make a sketch to show what is happening and how the plate will change.

Models can be used to generate and analyze data. Figure 18 is a simple model of the Earth's lithospheric plates. It shows the motion of each plate relative to each other. Figure 17 is a more complex model, showing the absolute motion of the North American plate. Absolute motion is the motion relative to a fixed point deep within Earth or out in space. On both models, the direction of plate motion is indicated by the arrows. Scientists choose a model based on the question they are trying to answer.

Examine the lithospheric plate models. Then answer the following questions:

a. What do you think are the advantages of each model?

b. When would using the absolute motion model be preferable to using the relative motion model?

c. Describe how the motion of the North American plate is depicted in each map.

In the relative motion map, look at the North American plate.

a. How do the plate's western and eastern boundaries differ?

b. Use a topographic or relief map to explain how continental features on the eastern and western coasts of North America reflect the location of the plate's boundaries.

| SAMPLING OCEANIC CRUST | TRANSITION CRUST | PLATE MOTION, STRESSES, AND EARTHQUAKES | Go online to choose one of these other three paths. |

Lesson Self-Check

CAN YOU EXPLAIN IT?

FIGURE 19: The San Andreas fault lies along the boundary between the Pacific and North American tectonic plates. The Pacific plate is moving roughly 50 mm per year to the northwest relative to the North American plate. Along the fault, the rocks of the crust are sheared and broken.

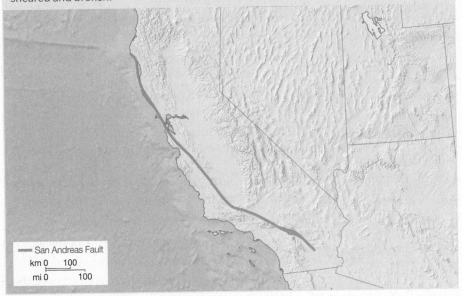

San Andreas Fault
km 0   100
mi 0   100

FIGURE 20: San Andreas fault aerial view

Recall that Lex Luthor was planning to plant explosives along the San Andreas fault in order to tip the west coast of California into the ocean. Would this work? To answer this question, look carefully at the map. Think about what you have learned about what plates are made of and how plates move relative to each other.

Ask yourself the following questions:

· Which plate is the coast of California on?

· What type of crust makes up the coast of California?

· What is this crust made of? Is it dense or buoyant?

· What would actually happen if the western side of the San Andreas were completely detached from the eastern side? Would the land fall into the ocean?

Analyze Refer to the notes in your Evidence Notebook to explain how faults and evidence of motion along faults are related to tectonic plates.

Explain Assuming Superman does not stop Lex Luthor, could Luthor's plan work? Are any parts of his plan supported by evidence? Use what you have learned about lithospheric plate motion and the composition and structure of plates to explain your answer.

CHECKPOINTS

Check Your Understanding

1. Identify which statements accurately describe the relationship between lithospheric plates and ground motion. Record and correct those that are not true.

   a. Plates are defined in part by the fact that they move as a single coherent mass.

   b. In general, every point on a single plate is moving at the same velocity.

   c. Plates move either directly toward, directly away, or parallel to each other.

   d. Plate motion is fast enough to be measured.

2. Which of these maps would be most useful in determining the location of lithospheric plates?

   a. A map of granitic rocks and basaltic rocks

   b. A map of earthquake epicenters and active volcanoes

   c. A map of the boundaries between dry land and ocean water

   d. A map of the boundaries between continental crust and oceanic crust

3. Write true statements that explain how we learn about plates by matching each piece of evidence on the left to all tools or methods used to collect the evidence on the right.

   a. The lithosphere is about 100 km thick.

   b. The oceanic crust is composed of mafic rocks.

   c. The oceanic lithosphere is between 0 and 180 million years old.

   d. Puerto Rico is moving at a velocity of about 15 mm/year toward the northeast.

   1. Seismic surveys

   2. Global positioning system

   3. Measuring sediment thickness

   4. Measuring ratios of radioactive isotopes

   5. Collecting and analyzing samples of rock and sediment

4. A student is using a physical model of the South American plate to better understand lithospheric plates in general. The model is small enough to manipulate and fit on a desk. Which questions would the student most likely be able to answer using the model?

   a. Are there any plates made only of oceanic lithosphere?

   b. Is the east coast of South America a plate boundary or is it in the middle of the plate?

   c. How is the South American plate moving relative to the African and North American plates?

   d. How thick is the crust beneath the Andes relative to the crust beneath the Atlantic Ocean?

   e. Exactly what rock types are found at a depth of 10.5 km on this plate?

   f. Where on the South American plate would it be easiest to drill through the crust and into the mantle?

5. Which statements accurately describe the pattern of ages observed on the continental and oceanic lithosphere?

   a. The continental lithosphere shows a pattern of increasing age away from the center of a continent.

   b. The oceanic lithosphere shows a pattern of increasing age away from a plate boundary that is in the middle of the ocean.

   c. The oceanic lithosphere shows a pattern of decreasing age away from a plate boundary that is along the edge of a continent.

   d. The continental lithosphere shows a pattern of increasing age away from a plate boundary that is in the middle of a continent.

6. Look at the African plate in Figure 21.

FIGURE 21: Age of oceanic crust

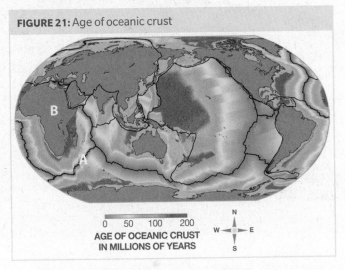

AGE OF OCEANIC CRUST
IN MILLIONS OF YEARS
0   50   100   200

Select from the following descriptions those that would apply to Locations A or B on the map. Some may apply to both and some may apply to neither. Give an explanation for your selections.

Mafic	Buoyant crust
Felsic	Part of a lithospheric plate
Thin crust	Not part of a lithospheric plate
Thick crust	Zero to billions of years old
Dense crust	Less than 200 million years old

FIGURE 22: Absolute plate motion

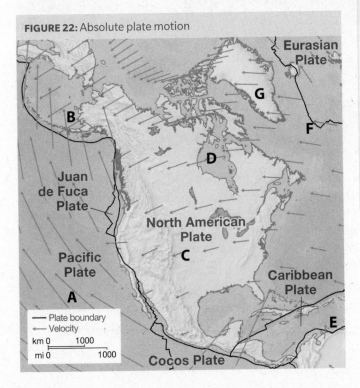

Eurasian Plate
G
B
F
D
Juan de Fuca Plate
North American Plate
C
Pacific Plate
A
Caribbean Plate
E

— Plate boundary
← Velocity
km 0   1000
mi 0   1000
Cocos Plate

7. A geologist wants to study current lithospheric plate boundaries. Look at Figure 22. Where would be the best places for the geologist to conduct field work to learn more about the rocks along plate boundaries? List all that apply.

8. Some geologists are planning where to do their summer fieldwork. Each geologist has a different question that he or she is trying to answer. Make a list matching each question to the best location for the fieldwork shown in Figure 22.

a. How old is the oldest oceanic crust?

b. How thick can the lithosphere be?

c. What is the composition of lava that erupts along a plate boundary where two plates are moving apart?

d. Why do so many powerful earthquakes occur deep underground along plate boundaries between the oceanic and continental lithosphere?

MAKE YOUR OWN STUDY GUIDE

In your Evidence Notebook, design a study guide that helps you explain how scientists study the composition, structure, and motion of Earth's tectonic plates.

Remember to include the following in your study guide:

- Support main ideas with details and examples.
- Record explanations for the phenomena you observed.
- Reflect on how scientists make use of basic laws that apply throughout the universe.

Use the crosscutting concept that empirical evidence is needed to identify patterns, such as the pattern present in the structure, composition, and age of lithospheric plates.

Plate Interactions

The Himalayan mountain range includes many of the highest peaks on Earth.

CAN YOU EXPLAIN IT?

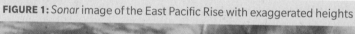

FIGURE 1: *Sonar* image of the East Pacific Rise with exaggerated heights

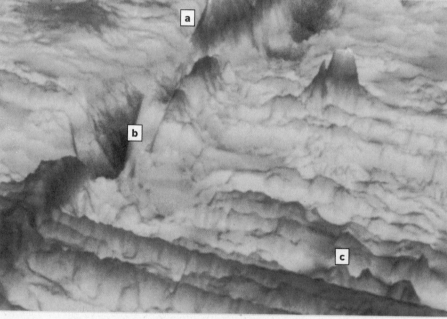

Gather Evidence
Record evidence for interactions between tectonic plates. As you explore the lesson, gather evidence to help explain landforms and geological processes that occur along plate boundaries and the processes that drive plate motion.

This *sonar* image shows part of the East Pacific Rise, a long underwater volcanic ridge that lies on the Pacific Ocean floor. White areas are high (shallower) and blue areas are low (deeper). The segment of the East Pacific Rise labeled *a* is separated from segment *c* by 85 km. At right angles to the segments is a long, straight zone of ridges and a valley (*b*). It connects the ends of the segments and continues beyond them in both directions. It is not volcanic.

Predict The area shown in Figure 1 includes two tectonic plates. Which areas do you think belong to each plate? Draw a diagram to show the two plates and their relative motions.

Image Credits: (t) ©Mark Williamson/Oxford Scientific/Getty Images; (c) ©Dr. Ken MacDonald/Science Source

Divergent Boundaries

Earth's surface is divided into about a dozen large slabs of rock known as lithospheric plates. The plates are from 80 km to 200 km thick. Each plate is composed of rigid crust and mantle rock. While some plates have only oceanic crust, others include both oceanic and continental crust. Each plate moves slowly (several centimeters per year) over the asthenosphere below.

As each plate moves with its own speed and direction, it interacts with others. What happens to Earth's crust where two plates are moving apart? What geologic events occur as two plates grind past each other? What landforms result where two plates crash into each other? What evidence do these structures and processes provide about plates and plate motion?

FIGURE 2: The South American Plate covers an area of 43 600 000 km² and comprises both the continent of South America and the seafloor westward of the Mid-Atlantic Ridge in the South Atlantic Ocean.

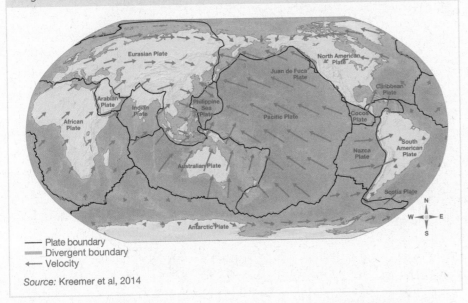

Plate boundary
Divergent boundary
Velocity

Source: Kreemer et al, 2014

Analyze
Look carefully at the boundaries between the South American Plate and the surrounding plates. Describe and compare the three types of relative motion illustrated and the three types of boundaries that you observe.

Recall that plate motion can be described relative to a fixed point (absolute motion) or relative to another plate (relative motion). The relative motion of a plate depends on its motion and the motion of surrounding plates.

Plates can be compared to other plates based on velocity—the speed and direction of motion. Because each plate has a different velocity compared to surrounding plates, and because plates are in contact with each other (along plate boundaries), they interact along these boundaries. Whether two plates are colliding, moving apart, or grinding past each other depends on the relative velocities at the plate boundaries. The results of these interactions depend on how plates are moving with respect to one another and also on the types of crust and lithosphere found along the boundaries.

Relative motion between plates can be broadly classified as divergent, convergent, and transform. At divergent plate boundaries, plates move away from each other, forming great valleys called rifts. Volcanic activity and shallow earthquakes occur at divergent boundaries. At convergent boundaries, plates move toward each other,

Analyze
What determines whether the relative motion between two plates at a boundary is toward, away from, or past each other?

causing the lithosphere to bend or crumple. The folding of rock, volcanism (volcanic activity), mountain building (orogeny), and deep earthquakes occur at convergent plate boundaries. At transform boundaries, plates move past one another. Strike-slip faulting and shallow earthquakes occur along transform boundaries, but no volcanism occurs there.

Divergent Plate Boundaries

Gather Evidence

Where are most divergent boundaries located on Earth?

Divergent boundaries can occur in places like the middle of the North Atlantic Ocean, where the motion of the two plates is in opposite directions. They can also occur where two plates are moving in the same direction, but at different speeds—the plate "ahead" is moving faster than the other. This type of motion is occurring between the Australian and African Plates.

FIGURE 3: Earth's major tectonic plates: the arrows on this map show velocity. Each arrow shows the direction and speed of plate motion. Longer arrows mean greater speed.

Eurasian Plate

Juan de Fuca Plate

North American Plate

Arabian Plate

Indian Plate

Philippine Sea Plate

Caribbean Plate

African Plate

Pacific Plate

Cocos Plate

Australian Plate

Nazca Plate

South American Plate

Antarctic Plate

Scotia Plate

— Plate boundary
══ Divergent boundary
← Velocity

Source: Kreemer et al, 2014

Collaborate Use the map to determine relative motion between plates. Which boundaries are divergent? How can you tell?

The majority of divergent boundary segments occur on the ocean floors between plates of oceanic lithosphere—generally close to the center of the ocean. In a few places, however, divergent boundaries exist on land where two plates of continental lithosphere are moving apart. There are no divergent boundaries at the edge of continental and oceanic lithosphere.

Features Found at Divergent Boundaries

The East African Rift is a system of valleys, mountains, and faults in northeastern Africa. The rift system, which is more than 3,000 km long and 30-100 km wide, lies along one of the few divergent boundaries found on continental lithosphere. It is forming as the African continental lithosphere is being ripped apart into two separate plates.

FIGURE 4: The East African Rift lies in the northeastern part of the African continent. It extends from the Red Sea and Gulf of Aden south to Malawi. The rift is caused by motion at the divergent boundary between the African plate to the west and the Somalian plate to the east.

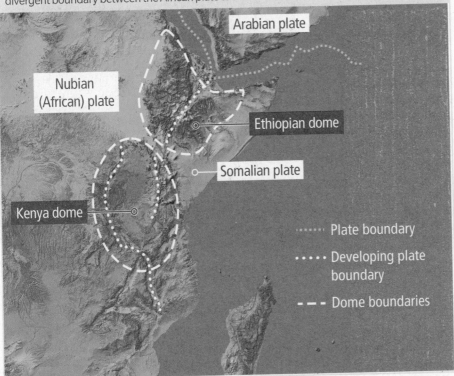

Features of the East African Rift system include things that are common to many rift systems: normal faults, valleys that form when blocks of crust drop down along normal faults, long narrow lakes filling the valleys, volcanoes, and broad uplifted regions called domes (a feature found often at continental rifts). Weak, shallow earthquakes are also common along rifts.

Because rifting occurs over millions of years, and because there are few continental rifts to study, how continental rifting begins is not well understood. However, geologists can use evidence from present day and ancient continental rifts, along with information about Earth's interior, to develop a basic model of how continents break apart. This is shown in Figure 5.

Different regions of the East African Rift are at slightly different stages of rifting. In general, the rift is between stages (a) and (b) in Figure 5: The continental lithosphere is in the process of stretching and thinning, and the rift currently consists of continental blocks that have dropped down along normal faults. The volcanism along the rift is a result of melting rocks from both the mantle and continental crust. If rifting continues, the crust will continue to thin and, eventually, dense basaltic lava will form new oceanic crust.

Predict What kinds of features would you expect to see along a divergent boundary?

Predict If rifting continues along the East African Rift, how will the continent of Africa change in that region?

Ocean water will flood in from the Red Sea and the Gulf of Aden, and a new ocean will begin to form. Geologists think that the rift will not pull apart at the same time along the entire valley, but will instead start in the north and continue southward from the Gulf of Aden and Red Sea, like a piece of paper tearing in two.

FIGURE 5: Continental rifting and seafloor spreading

a Rifting begins as hot mantle rock flows below the lithosphere. This exerts an upward force on the upper lithosphere, causing it to thin, weaken, and dome upward. Faults and fractures form in the crust as it bends upward. Magma generated by melting of the continental crust begins to erupt on the surface.

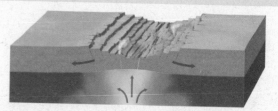

b Blocks of crust move downward along faults and form valleys. The rift valley—a new divergent plate boundary—begins to form. Eventually, the lithosphere becomes so thin that partial melting of the mantle results in the eruption of basaltic lavas. Denser oceanic crust begins to form.

c As the two plates move apart, the mantle rock along the rift continues to melt. Magma rises and fills the gap between the plates, forming more oceanic crust. Ocean water floods the low valley. The rift is now an oceanic rift.

d As the plates continue to move apart, the continents move farther apart and the ocean floor and oceanic lithosphere continue to grow.

Seafloor Spreading

There are two types of divergent plate boundaries: continent-continent plate boundaries and ocean-ocean plate boundaries. As you can see from the model of continental rifting, continent-continent divergent boundaries become ocean-ocean divergent boundaries over time. Continental rifting eventually leads to the formation of new ocean crust.

Divergent boundaries are also called *constructive plate boundaries* because new crust forms at these boundaries. On the ocean floor, divergent boundaries are marked by long volcanic ridges known as mid-ocean ridges. As the plates move away from each other, magma fills the gap and cools to become part of each plate. The new ocean crust that forms at the ridge moves off to either side of the ridge as part of each plate.

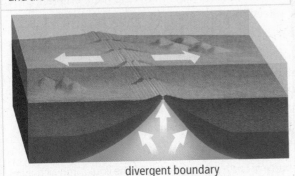

FIGURE 6: Most divergent plate boundaries are boundaries between plates of oceanic lithosphere and are found on the seafloor.

divergent boundary

Magnetic Reversal Timescale

As magma cools and solidifies to form rock, small crystals of iron minerals align with Earth's magnetic field. So, rocks on the seafloor contain a record of magnetic field direction. Positive seafloor anomalies show periods of time during which Earth's magnetic field was strong and had normal polarity—a magnetic field that pointed north. Negative seafloor anomalies show periods of time during which Earth's magnetic field was weak and had reverse polarity—a magnetic field that pointed south. They form a pattern in the seafloor that scientists have used to put together a timescale of reversals in Earth's magnetic field that extends back in time 155 million years.

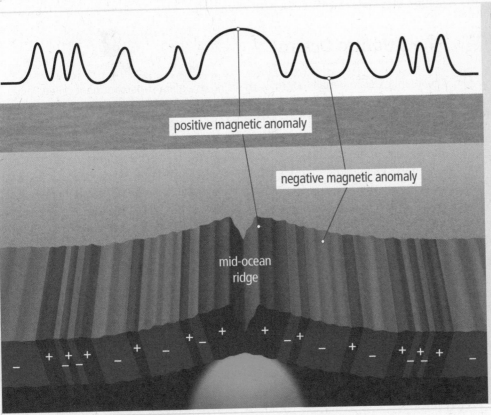

positive magnetic anomaly

negative magnetic anomaly

mid-ocean ridge

FIGURE 7: The positive and negative symbols indicate periods of normal and reverse polarity in Earth's magnetic field.

 Collaborate The pattern of magnetic anomalies is generally symmetrical about the mid-ocean ridge. Why do you think this is? How can the magnetic anomalies be used as evidence to support the claim that a mid-ocean ridge is a boundary between plates that are moving apart?

Basaltic magmas contain small crystals of the iron-rich mineral magnetite, which are easily magnetized. Magnetite becomes permanently magnetized parallel to Earth's existing magnetic field when basaltic magma cools and solidifies at a mid-ocean ridge. These magnetized rocks are pushed in both directions away from the ridge toward the continents in a process called *seafloor spreading*. As the polarity of Earth's magnetic field changes over time, a pattern of alternating normal and reversed polarity develops in the seafloor. Scientists can use this pattern of bands to help them estimate the age of the seafloor and its rate of spreading.

Seafloor anomalies indicate that Earth's magnetic field has not always pointed north, as it does now. Earth's North Magnetic Pole and South Magnetic Pole have reversed perhaps hundreds of times throughout the planet's history. This means that Earth's North Magnetic Pole has become the South Magnetic Pole, and, at the same time, Earth's South Magnetic Pole has become the North Magnetic Pole. During the past 20 million years, Earth's Magnetic North and South Poles have reversed approximately every 200 000 to 300 000 years. The last major reversal was 780 000 years ago.

As discussed in Lesson 1, the source of Earth's magnetic field is the liquid, iron-rich outer core of Earth. This liquid moves within the core as a result of heat convection deep within the core and the rotation of the planet. Because Earth's core is located too deep within Earth for scientists to measure directly, they must make observations about changes in the magnetic field. Scientists have observed that the Magnetic North Pole is currently migrating northward at a rate of almost 65 km per year.

The Atlantic Ocean

The Atlantic Ocean began to form with rifting of a giant supercontinent called Pangaea about 215 million years ago. As the continental plate began to split, the continental crust thinned and faulted. Eventually, the crust was so thin that basalt began to erupt along the new plate boundary and new oceanic crust began to form. As the plates moved apart, more basaltic lava erupted along the new plate boundary and the ocean basin grew. Water flooded this new low area and the Atlantic Ocean itself began to form. The basaltic lava that erupted along the new mid-ocean ridge was magnetized as it cooled. With time, the new oceanic crust was carried away from either side of the ridge. As it aged, the crust grew cooler and denser, sank deeper into the ocean, and accumulated more and more sediment.

If you were to make numerous observations and measurements from different parts of the Atlantic, you would find that the age of the ocean crust in the Atlantic Ocean varies from place to place and that the rate of spreading also varies. No single estimate is representative of the ocean as a whole. The age increases with distance from the Mid-Atlantic ridge. In addition, it varies from north to south. Pangaea began rifting in the Northern Hemisphere and continued southward. As a result, the oldest ocean crust in the northern Atlantic is older than the oldest ocean crust in the southern Atlantic.

Explain The Mid-Atlantic Ridge is the mid-ocean ridge that runs down the center of the Atlantic Ocean. The Atlantic Ocean is between 3000 and 7000 km across and continues to grow. What is a way that you could estimate when rifting began to form the Atlantic Ocean basin?

Explain Explain how the landforms and geological processes that are observed along divergent plate boundaries are related to plate movement.

Convergent Boundaries

Plate Collisions

Although new crust forms at divergent boundaries, and the ocean surface area increases as a result of seafloor spreading, Earth's overall surface area does not increase. This means that there must be places where plates are coming together and decreasing in size. This type of boundary is known as a convergent boundary.

Analyze How could you use plate velocities to identify convergent boundaries?

FIGURE 8: Plates collide at convergent boundaries.

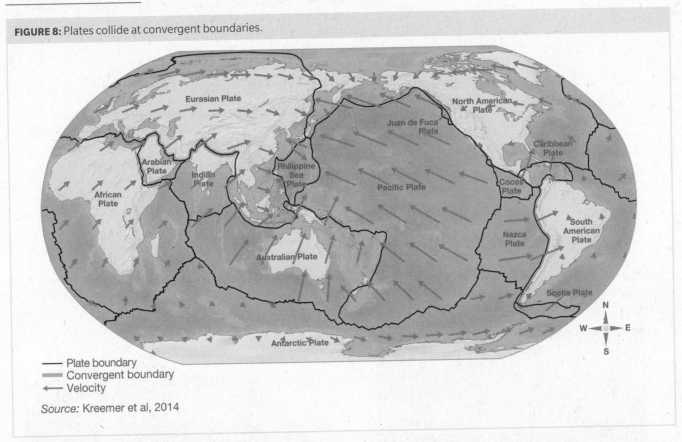

- —— Plate boundary
- —— Convergent boundary
- ←— Velocity

Source: Kreemer et al, 2014

Recall that there are only two types of divergent plate boundaries (continent-continent and ocean-ocean). There are three types of convergent plate boundaries. The types are defined by the types of lithosphere found along the boundary.

Continent-continent: At a continent-continent convergent boundary, both plates consist of continental lithosphere. For example, at Location A in Figure 8, the Himalayas are forming where the continental part of the Indian plate is colliding with the continental part of the Eurasian plate.

Ocean-ocean: At an ocean-ocean convergent boundary, both plates consist of oceanic lithosphere. For example, at Location B in Figure 8, the Aleutian Island chain is forming along the boundary between the Pacific oceanic plate and an oceanic part of the North American plate.

Collaborate Describe the relative motion and the types of lithosphere that are interacting along each of the labeled boundaries.

Continent-ocean: At a continent-ocean convergent boundary, one plate consists of continental lithosphere while the other is oceanic. For example, at Location C in Figure 8, the Andes are forming along the boundary between the Nazca oceanic plate and the continental part of the South American plate.

At a convergent boundary, you find one of two possibilities: (1) The two plates are moving in opposite directions and toward each other. This is occurring between the Nazca and South American plates in the Andes. (2) The two plates are moving in the same direction, but at different speeds, with the plate "behind" (the "trailing" plate) moving faster than the plate "ahead" (the "leading" plate). This is the case with the Indian and Eurasian plates in the Himalayas.

 Predict Think about the density of continental lithosphere versus oceanic lithosphere. How do you think the density of each plate affects what happens at each type of convergent boundary?

Continent-Continent Collision

When two continental plates collide, the continental crust crumples. Layers of rock are folded, metamorphosed, broken, and thrust on top of each other. The crust thickens, forming high mountain belts with deep roots underground. While some of these mountain belts are the result of present-day collisions, others, like the Appalachian Mountains, are scars left over from collisions that occurred hundreds of millions of years ago. Ancient collision zones more than one billion years old have been eroded down to flat plains, but evidence for the collisions is seen in the folds and faults in the eroded rock.

FIGURE 9: About 40 million years ago, the continental lithosphere of the Indian plate began to collide with the continental lithosphere of the Eurasian plate, and the Himalaya Mountains began to form. The crust thickened as the rocks were folded, faulted, and thrust on top of each other.

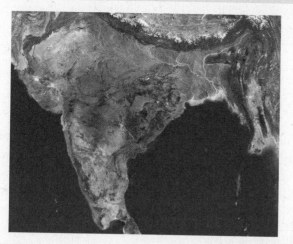

The most dramatic example of continental collision occurring today is seen in the Himalayas, where the Indian and Eurasian plates are colliding. The Himalayas are now the tallest and deepest mountains in the world, rising nearly 9 km above sea level, with a thick continental crust extending 70 km underground. The mountains are still growing at a rate of about 1 cm/year. Some of the most devastating earthquakes on Earth occur along the faults in the Himalayas.

One set of features that is not common along continental collision zones is active volcanoes. Although there is melting of the mantle and crustal rocks, continental crust is too thick and the magma formed by melting is too viscous to travel up to the surface. Instead, magma cools underground to form large bodies of igneous rock, such as granite.

Ocean-Continent Collisions

FIGURE 10: Ocean-continent convergence zones have deep underwater trenches, folded and faulted sediment, explosive volcanoes on the continent, and powerful earthquakes. The Andes Mountains are the result of convergence between the oceanic Nazca plate and the continental part of the South American plate.

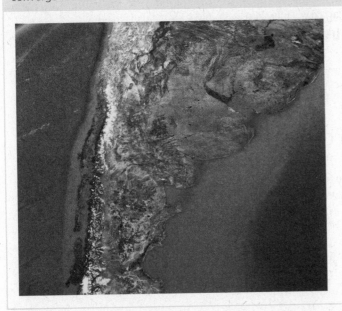
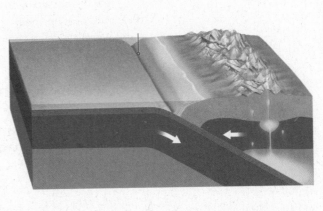

Where oceanic lithosphere and continental lithosphere converge, the denser oceanic lithosphere subducts. That is, the oceanic plate is pushed down under the continental plate. This type of convergent margin is called a subduction zone. At the subduction zone found along the western coast of South America, the oceanic Nazca plate is being subducted beneath the continental part of the South American plate.

Landforms and processes that are characteristic of a convergent boundary with subduction include trenches, wedges of folded and faulted sedimentary rock, earthquakes, and volcanoes.

Underwater Trenches

A deep, arc-shaped underwater valley known as an oceanic trench marks the boundary between the two plates. Trenches can be thousands of kilometers long, tens of kilometers wide, and more than 10 kilometers deep. The Peru-Chile trench along the west coast of South America is 5900 km long, 60 km wide, and 8 km deep.

Wedges of Sedimentary Rock

As plates converge, continental sediments get faulted and folded and layers of oceanic sediments are scraped off oceanic lithosphere as it subducts. These rocks may become part of the continent. The Andes Mountains include many folded and faulted layers of sedimentary rock.

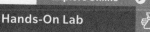
Earthquakes

A zone of earthquakes extends from the trench down along the subducting plate and beneath the continent, as deep as 670 km. These earthquakes occur as plates scrape against each other and as the subducting plate fractures as it bends downward. Subduction earthquakes can be extremely powerful and destructive. The earthquakes that have occurred off the coast of Chile include some of the most powerful ever recorded.

Continental Arc Volcanism

An arc-shaped zone of explosive volcanoes forms along the edge of a continent, roughly parallel to the trench. These volcanoes are thought to form as a result of the addition of water to the mantle rocks beneath the continent. As the subducting plate moves down into the mantle, it heats up. Water in the oceanic crust becomes water vapor and moves into the mantle above. This causes the melting temperature of the mantle rocks to decrease, which causes them to partially melt. The magma, or molten rock, rises up, melting and mixing with parts of the continental crust. The magma eventually erupts on the surface. The Andes Mountains contain numerous volcanoes.

Ocean-Ocean Collisions

The collision between two oceanic plates also results in subduction. As two oceanic plates converge, one plate subducts beneath the other. The landforms and processes that result are similar to those of ocean-continent subduction zones.

FIGURE 11: Ocean-ocean convergence zones have deep underwater trenches, folded and faulted rocks, powerful earthquakes, and an arc-shaped line of explosive volcanoes known as an island arc. The Aleutian Islands are an island arc in the northern Pacific Ocean that is caused by subduction of the Pacific plate beneath the oceanic part of the North American plate.

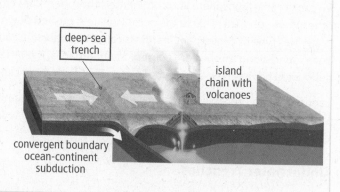

A long, deep, and narrow underwater trench marks the boundary between the two plates. A zone of earthquakes extends from the trench down along the subducting plate. Volcanoes form an island arc, an arc-shaped line of volcanic islands parallel to the trench. The process of volcano formation is similar to that of ocean-continent collisions. Convergence causes folding and faulting of ocean sediments between the trench and the volcanoes. Many of the island chains in the northern and western Pacific lie along ocean-ocean convergent boundaries.

Comparing Convergent Boundaries

Continental convergence results in the crumpling and piling up of two continental plates. Oceanic convergence results in one plate descending deep into the mantle.

No one knows exactly what causes subduction to start in the first place. However, one property that we know allows subduction to occur is density. The oceanic lithosphere is almost as dense as the mantle below and much denser than continental lithosphere, so oceanic crust tends to sink. Other forces may also push or pull the plate down. The continental lithosphere, on the other hand, is significantly less dense than the mantle below. Although the continental crust can be pushed downward as weight is added from above, it does not sink downward on its own.

FIGURE 12: Subduction results in the recycling of oceanic crust back into the mantle. At the same time, it also results in the construction of new crust through volcanism.

Explore Online ▶

a Subduction of an oceanic plate

b Melting of the subducting plate

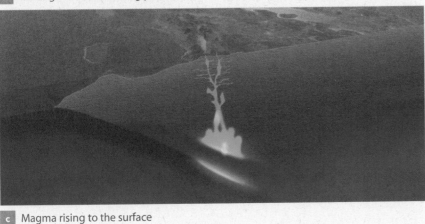

c Magma rising to the surface

Explain How do the landforms and processes that occur along each type of convergent boundary compare? Which ones occur in all three types of convergent boundaries?

Collaborate What do you think determines which of the two oceanic plates subducts? Why does one plate subduct at all? Why do the two plates not simply crumple and pile up to form extremely thick oceanic lithosphere?

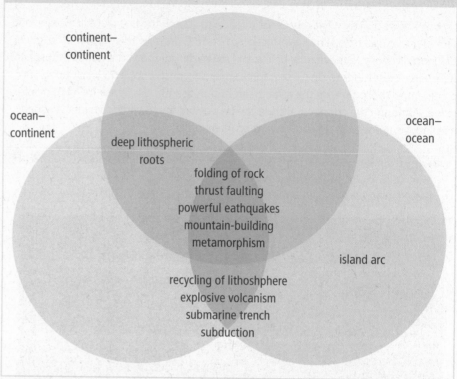

FIGURE 13: Some of the features and processes that occur along convergent boundaries are unique to one type of convergent boundary, while others are common to two or all three types.

continent–
continent

ocean–
continent

ocean–
ocean

deep lithospheric
roots

folding of rock
thrust faulting
powerful eathquakes
mountain-building
metamorphism

island arc

recycling of lithoshphere
explosive volcanism
submarine trench
subduction

Predict There is an ocean-continent boundary in the Mediterranean Sea between the African plate and the Eurasian plate. How might this boundary change over time?

Collaborate Research a convergent plate boundary that you have not already read about here. Identify and describe specific landforms and geological events that have occurred. Explain how they are related to convergent plate motion.

Although the three types of convergent boundaries are distinct, all are characterized by active faulting and resulting seismic activity, folding of sediment and rock layers, and mountain-building. All three involve the shortening of at least one plate, but also the construction of new crust or thickening of the edge of the other plate.

Over time, as two plates converge, the characteristics of the convergent boundary can change. Subduction along a continent can lead to a collision between two continents. Most plates consist of both oceanic and continental lithosphere. As the oceanic part of a plate subducts, it carries continental lithosphere toward the subduction zone. When the continental lithosphere reaches the subduction zone, it collides with the other continental plate. (Before the Himalayas were a continent-continent boundary, they were an ocean-continent boundary.)

Subduction can lead to the expansion of a continent. If subduction causes a volcanic island arc to collide with a continent, the arc can become part of the continent. Subduction can also lead to the growth of a new continent, and an ocean-ocean boundary can evolve into an ocean-continent boundary. The lavas that erupt on the ocean floor to form island arc volcanoes are a mixture of basaltic lavas and less dense "continental" types of lavas. Over time, the eruption of these lavas along with the addition of sediments scraped off the subducting plate can result in the formation of a small continental landmass. This landmass can grow through volcanism or become part of another piece of continental lithosphere.

Explain Explain how the processes that occur along convergent plate boundaries change Earth's surface over time.

Transform Boundaries

FIGURE 14: Tectonic plates slide past one another at transform boundaries.

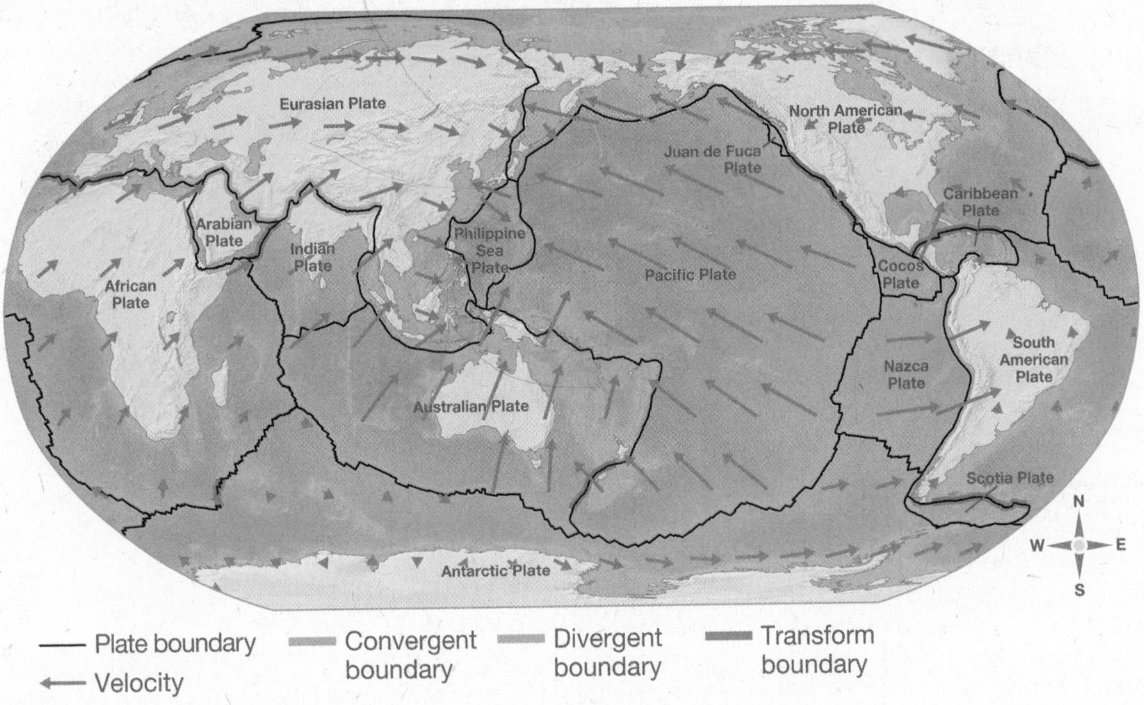

Source: Kreemer et al, 2014

Collaborate Look at the map of plate boundaries. With a partner, follow a convergent boundary from one end to the other. Do the same for a divergent boundary. Do all of the convergent and divergent boundaries connect to each other seamlessly? Do the plate boundaries end abruptly and disappear?

If you look carefully, you should notice that in many places, segments of convergent and divergent boundaries are connected to each other by a third type of boundary known as a transform boundary.

Sliding Plates

As we have seen, as plates move relative to each other, they are moving apart and growing along divergent boundaries and moving toward each other and shrinking along convergent boundaries. But because Earth is not growing, shrinking, or changing shape significantly, it is not possible for all boundaries to be divergent or convergent. There must also be boundaries where the plates slide past each other without moving into or away from each other. Transform boundaries allow for motion between two convergent boundaries, two divergent boundaries, or a convergent and divergent boundary.

FIGURE 15: Transform boundaries occur on both continental and oceanic lithosphere. Some transform boundaries, like the Alpine fault in New Zealand, connect two convergent boundaries. Some, like those along the mid-ocean ridges, connect separate segments of long divergent boundaries. The Dead Sea transform boundary connects convergent boundaries to divergent boundaries.

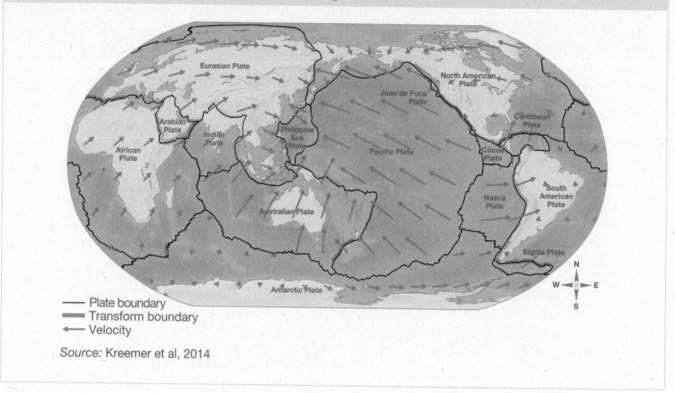

—— Plate boundary
—— Transform boundary
←— Velocity

Source: Kreemer et al, 2014

Predict A transform boundary connects subduction zones on the eastern and western boundaries of the Caribbean plate. What features and processes would you expect to observe along this transform boundary?

Many transform faults that occur in continental lithosphere on land are well known because of the earthquakes that occur along them. The motion along transforms like the San Andreas fault in California, the Anatolian fault in Turkey, and the Alpine fault in New Zealand can result in powerful earthquakes. Earthquakes along these faults can be so powerful because the motion along the fault is not even or continuous. Stress builds up along the fault over time and enormous energy is released suddenly when the rocks break.

Most transforms are much shorter faults that occur along the mid-ocean ridges. We often model seafloor spreading centers as continuous, unbroken rifts, however, because Earth is a sphere, it is not actually possible for a rift to be continuous. If you look carefully, you will see that the mid-ocean ridge is actually a series of segments offset from each other. Transform faults connect these segments and allow the plates to separate and move over Earth's curved surface. The motion along seafloor transforms is generally more continuous than the motion along continental transforms. As a result, the earthquakes along these faults are generally more frequent and much less powerful.

The general direction of motion of the plates along a transform is parallel to the boundary. Along some transforms, the plates are moving in opposite directions. Along others, they are moving in the same direction, but at different speeds.

FIGURE 16: Transform faults between mid-ocean ridge segments allow for movement between segments of sea floor spreading. The regions shown by dashed lines, extending beyond each end of the transform, are known as fracture zones.

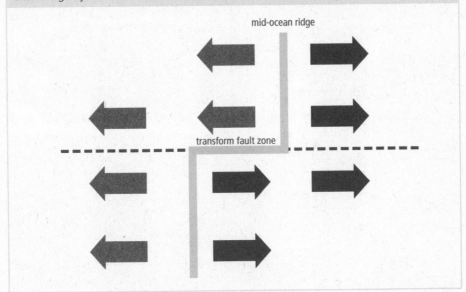

mid-ocean ridge

transform fault zone

In the idealized model of a transform fault zone in Figure 16, the two plates grind past each other in opposite directions along the fault that is parallel to the plate motion. As a result, the plates move past, but not toward or away from each other. In reality, transform faults, and the boundaries they make, are jagged and not parallel to plate motion in all places. As a result, there are places along transform zones where there are valleys formed by divergence and mountains formed by convergence.

FIGURE 17: The San Andreas is a 1300-km-long major transform fault that connects a divergent boundary in the Gulf of California to a convergent boundary off the coast of Oregon and Washington. The motion along the fault is not continuous. Stress builds up over many years, bending rocks along the fault until they break, spring back, and move suddenly, causing an earthquake that sends out powerful seismic waves in all directions.

In addition to earthquakes, transform motion can also result in a number of physical features: cliffs, narrow valleys, rugged hills and mountains, and low basins. Many transforms can be interpreted on satellite and *sonar* image by sudden linear changes in landforms. Rock formations and landforms that cross a transform are broken and displaced along the fault, and the rocks along transforms are generally faulted rather than folded. Unlike divergent and convergent boundaries, however, there is almost no volcanic activity associated with transform boundaries.

A Model of Plate Boundaries

FIGURE 18: This map is a model that illustrates the complexity of plate boundaries.

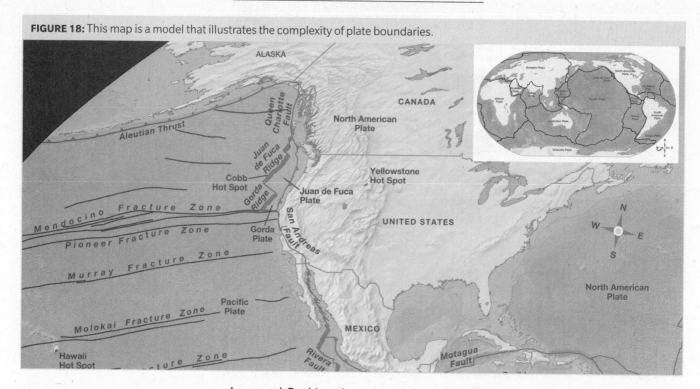

In general, Earth's major mountain belts, sites of active volcanism, and seismic activity occur along plate boundaries. Maps that display this information can be used to infer the locations of plate boundaries in general. In addition, each type of plate boundary has a specific set of landforms and processes. Thus by examining where landforms and processes occur relative to each other, we can infer where each type of boundary is present. For example, the presence of a long, narrow, arc-shaped, underwater valley, along with an arc of volcanoes, indicates a convergent boundary. A long undersea mountain with a valley and active volcanism in the center of the ridge indicates a divergent boundary. The presence of narrow valleys with seismic activity but no volcanism may be evidence for a transform boundary.

It is important to note that the global map of plate boundaries is very simplified and idealized. It is easy to infer from these models that the plate boundaries are smooth and continuous. Other inferences may include that the motion along any plate boundary is either convergent, divergent, or transform and that the motion is either perpendicular or parallel to the plate boundary.

In reality, plate boundaries are not smooth, continuous faults. They are zones of many different faults oriented in slightly different directions. If you look carefully at the maps, you will see that the motion along a boundary is rarely exactly perpendicular or parallel to the boundary. Because of variations in relative motion along the boundary, all plate boundaries include components of divergent, convergent, and transform motion. Transform boundaries in particular are very complex. They can include areas of thrust faulting and mountain-building where the plates converge, and normal faulting and valley formation where the plates diverge, as well as strike-slip faulting where the plates slip past each other.

 Explain What can a model like the diagram in Figure 18 be used for? What can it not be used for? Why do we say that it is a "simplified" model?

Causes of Plate Motion

One of the most important questions about plate motion is what causes plates to move. What force or forces can rip a 100 km thick plate in two or carry an enormous mass of rock over Earth's surface? What causes a plate to move in one direction rather than another? Why haven't continental collisions and friction along transforms stopped plate motion?

Geologists are currently considering a number of possible causes of plate motion, including mantle convection, slab pull, and ridge push.

Mantle Convection and Plate Motion

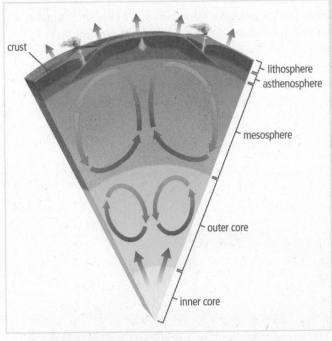

FIGURE 19: In a simplified model, buoyant hot rock rises toward the surface beneath mid-ocean ridges, moves laterally under a plate, and sinks back down at subduction zones.

Evidence from seismic waves, heat-flow measurements, and physical models shows that the solid rock of the mantle beneath plates moves slowly at a rate of a few centimeters per year. Convection occurs because of variations in temperature and density of rocks within the mantle. Cool, dense material sinks, pushing warmer, less dense material upward. The motion is called mantle convection Convection continues as the rising material cools off enough to sink again, and the sinking material heats up enough to rise again. Convection seems to occur in large convection cells. There are areas in the mantle where most of the material is colder and denser and so it is sinking, and other areas where most of the material is warmer and lighter and so it is rising. Convection in the mantle is similar to convection of water in Earth's oceans and convection of air in the atmosphere. Convection redistributes thermal energy within Earth's systems.

Gather Evidence
Examine the model of convection. Identify the matter involved in convection, the energy transfers that occur during convection, and the force or forces that drive convection.

It is likely that mantle convection is related to the motion of plates. What is not clear is whether mantle convection causes plate motion or is a result of plate motion, or some combination. In the basic model of convection-driven plate motion the mantle convects and the plates ride on top like people on a moving walkway. Hot mantle material moving upward from below and then spreading out beneath the plate causes the plate to heat up, weaken, thin, and rift apart. The convecting mantle material then moves horizontally, carrying the plate along. When the mantle rock cools enough, it descends, dragging the edge of the plate with it.

One problem with this model is that the location and motion of the convection cells do not perfectly match the location and motion of the plates. For example, there seems to be a number of cells under the Pacific plate that would be pulling the plate in different directions. Geologists also wonder if convection can really provide enough force to rip apart a plate, make it start moving, or keep it moving against friction.

Slab Pull

Gather Evidence How might slab pull affect the plate that is not subducting?

Another force that contributes to plate motion is the gravitational force on the plate—the weight of the plate. The weight of the subducting edge of the plate (the "slab") produces a force, called slab pull, that pulls the rest of the plate along over the mantle. (Think of the edge of a tablecloth dragging the rest off a table). Some geologists think that this is the main driver of plate motion. This idea is supported by the fact that the speed of the plate is directly correlated to how much of the plate is subducting.

FIGURE 20: In the slab-pull model, the weight of the subducting edge of the plate pulls the rest of the plate over the upper mantle.

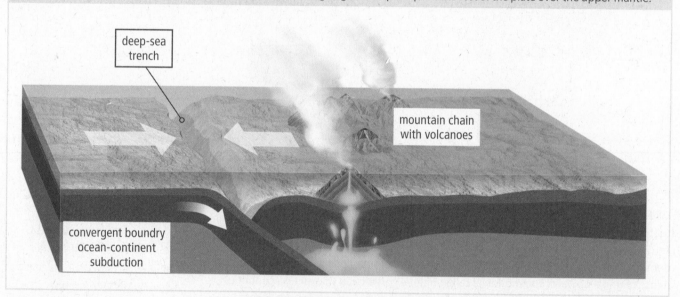

deep-sea trench

mountain chain with volcanoes

convergent boundry ocean-continent subduction

Collaborate What properties of the plate and underlying upper mantle are necessary for the slab pull mechanism to work? Think about properties such as density, flexibility, and roughness.

Geologists also think that the subducting plate can indirectly exert a force on the other plate, the overriding plate. This is known as trench suction or slab suction. As the subducting slab descends, it pulls the overriding plate toward the subducting plate.

One problem with the slab-pull/trench-suction mechanism is that it does not directly explain the absolute motion of plates like the Antarctic plate that have no significant subduction zone boundarie, or the motion of a plate that has subduction zones on opposite sides.

Ridge Push

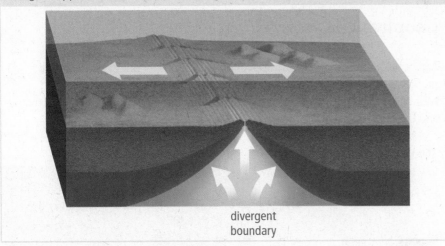

FIGURE 21: In the ridge-push model, the high lithosphere along the ridge slides down along the upper mantle under the force of gravity, pushing the rest of the plate ahead of it.

divergent
boundary

Mid-ocean ridges found along seafloor-spreading centers are mountain ranges that can be thousands of meters higher than the seafloor on either side. Gravity pulls the ridges downhill, which produces an outward force, called *ridge push*, on the rest of the plate.

How Plates Continue to Move

Once a plate is moving, the motion of the plate itself can set up a positive feedback loop that keeps it moving. There are a number of possible positive feedback mechanisms at work in plate motion.

1. **Slab pull:** As a plate subducts, the amount of plate that is subducting increases. The weight of the slab increases, which increases the force pulling the rest of the plate.

2. **Ridge push:** As the high underwater ridge slides downward under the force of gravity, pressure decreases and space opens up. This causes more mantle rock below to melt, rise, fill the gap, and maintain the presence of the mid-ocean ridge. The lithosphere at the ridge, rebuilt by new magma, continues to slide down under the force of gravity, pushing the plate ahead of it.

3. **Slab pull and ridge push:** Slab pull and ridge push can exert positive feedback on each other. Once a plate begins to subduct, slab pull can add to the forces that have been pulling the plates apart at the mid-ocean ridge. At the same time, ridge push provides force to cause more of the plate to subduct.

4. **Slab pull, ridge push, and mantle convection:** As a plate subducts, because it is realtively cool, it can reinforce downward convection of the upper mantle below. As the plate is pushed by the force of the ridge, it can reinforce the motion of the upper mantle away from the ridge.

Gather Evidence What force causes the plate to move in the ridge-push model?

Collaborate With a partner, discuss how plates move relative to other plates, the processes that occur along plate boundaries, and the possible forces that drive the plates. Describe one possible example of positive feedback in the system.

 Explain Compare the interactions between gravity and matter in each of the three main mechanisms that are thought to drive plate motion.

Careers in Science

Geophysicist

A geophysicist is a scientist who applies physics to answer questions and solve problems related to geology. Geophysicists study gravity, magnetic fields, and seismic (earthquake) waves to better understand Earth's composition and structure and the processes that shape it.

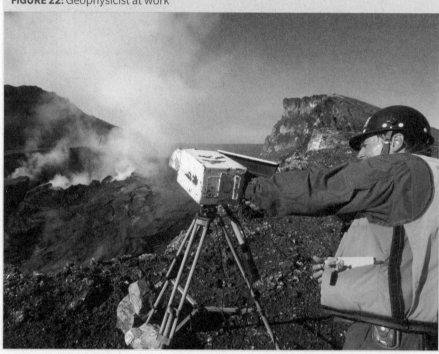

FIGURE 22: Geophysicist at work

Some geophysicists apply physics to better understand plate boundaries. For example, geophysicists can use magnetometers to measure the strength and direction of Earth's magnetic field over the ocean floor. They use this information to map the magnetic striping of the seafloor and calculate how fast two plates have been moving away from each other at a divergent boundary. Some geophysicists use seismometers to measure vibrations from earthquakes. They can use this information to figure out the direction that a plate is moving along a plate boundary. Geophysicists can also use seismic data to calculate the density of different areas of Earth's mantle. They can then use this information to infer how mantle convection works.

Collaborate Research some of the tools that geophysicists use to study plate interactions and boundaries. How do these tools work? What types of data do they help geophysicists collect? How do geophysicists use the data? What types of questions can they help answer?

DESIGN A PLATE BOUNDARY   **RIFTING RESEARCH**   Go online to choose one of these other paths.

Image Credits: ©Douglas Peebles/Science Source

Lesson Self-Check

CAN YOU EXPLAIN IT?

FIGURE 23: *Sonar* image of the seafloor in the central eastern Pacific Ocean

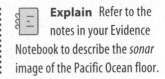

Explain Refer to the notes in your Evidence Notebook to describe the *sonar* image of the Pacific Ocean floor.

The East Pacific Rise is a mid-ocean ridge that marks the divergent boundary between the Cocos plate, which is moving toward the east, and the Pacific plate moving toward the west.

The ridge is not continuous, but is separated into segments. Between the segments are transform faults that make up a transform boundary. Along the transform faults, the plates grind past each other, parallel to the boundary.

Because Earth is a sphere, it is not possible to have a single continuous, straight divergent boundary. The transform boundaries connect segments of the mid-ocean ridge and allow for motion between the two ridge segments.

 Analyze Look carefully at the structures revealed by the *sonar* data. Consider features and boundaries that are visible in the image. What evidence does each feature provide for relative plate motion?

CHECKPOINTS

Check Your Understanding

1. The arrows on the map below show the direction of plate motion. Indicate whether each point labeled is located on a convergent or a divergent boundary.

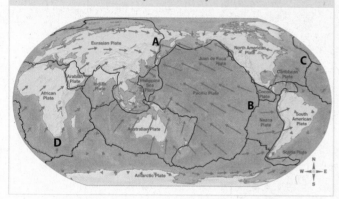

FIGURE 24: Plate boundary and velocity

2. A geologist is trying to identify plate boundary types based on physical features. Match each set of features to the boundary type that it most likely represents.

a. Normal faults, valleys, domes, volcanic eruptions

b. Normal faults, underwater ridge, underwater volcanic eruptions

c. Strike-slip faults, shallow, powerful earthquakes, no volcanic eruptions

d. Thrust faults, folded rocks, powerful earthquakes, high continental mountain range, no volcanic eruptions

e. Thrust faults, folded rocks, deep underwater trench, explosive volcanic eruptions, deep powerful earthquakes, volcanic islands

f. Thrust faults, folded rocks, deep underwater

trench, explosive volcanic eruptions, deep, powerful earthquakes, continental mountain range

1. Transform boundary

2. Oceanic divergent boundary

3. Continental divergent boundary

4. Ocean-ocean convergent boundary

5. Ocean-continent convergent boundary

6. Continent-continent convergent boundary

3. A geologist is developing an animation that models the rifting of a continent. The animation is almost complete. All of the steps are animated, but the captions are out of order. Put the captions in the correct order.

a. Divergent horizontal forces cause the lithosphere to stretch and thin.

b. Magma rises up, filling the gap between the plates and forming more oceanic crust.

c. Hot, buoyant rock exerts an upward force on the continent, causing it to dome upward. The heat from the bouyant rock thins and weakens the lithosphere.

d. As the plates diverge, the continents move farther apart and the ocean floor and oceanic lithosphere continue to grow.

e. The lithosphere is so thin that partial melting of the mantle results in the eruption of basaltic lavas. A denser oceanic crust begins to form.

4. Earth scientists who study plate boundaries often begin investigations with a specific scientific question about a particular boundary or boundaries that they want to answer. A scientific question is one that can be answered objectively with evidence and reasoning based on observations, measurements, experiments, scientific laws, and scientific principles. Scientific questions must be very clear and well defined because they are used to design and guide the scientific investigations. Analyze the questions below. Which questions are considered to be valid and well-defined scientific questions?

a. Where are divergent boundaries located on Earth?

b. Which divergent boundary has the most interesting landforms associated with it?

c. What causes landforms?

d. Which divergent boundary would Galileo have chosen to study if he were alive in the 21st century?

e. What types of landforms are associated with divergent boundaries?

f. How and why are divergent boundaries on the ocean floor different from divergent boundaries on the continents?

g. What is the value of a divergent boundary to society?

5. Explain why each question in #4 is or is not considered to be a valid and well-defined scientific question.

6. Explain why convergent boundaries are often called "destructive boundaries" and divergent boundaries are often called "constructive boundaries." Why might these labels be misleading?

7. A team of Earth scientists collects data to make a map showing the magnetic anomalies on the seafloor. They analyze the map and discover that they will be able to use it as evidence for seafloor spreading. Make a sketch to show what the pattern of magnetism could look like. Be sure to label the mid-ocean ridge and the magnetic pattern.

8. Identify three pieces of evidence for seafloor spreading. Briefly explain how each is evidence for seafloor spreading.

9. Geologists have proposed several possible mechanisms to drive plate motion. Match each driver to its description. (Some descriptions might match to more than one mechanism and some might not match to any.)

a. Gravity is the driving force in this mechanism.

b. Lithosphere is carried along by the motion of the upper mantle below.

c. Cool, dense lithosphere sinks into the mantle at subduction zones, dragging the rest of the lithosphere behind it.

d. Buoyant mantle rock rises up and pushes lithosphere away from the central submarine mountain range.

e. Gravity pulls the high central underwater mountain range downward, forcing the entire plate away from the range.

f. Cool, dense solid rock sinks under the force of gravity, pushing warmer, more buoyant rock up toward the surface.

1. Slab pull

2. Ridge push

3. Mantle convection

MAKE YOUR OWN STUDY GUIDE

In your Evidence Notebook, design a study guide that supports the main ideas in this lesson:

Earth's surface is divided into about a dozen major plates, each of which moves slowly relative to the plates around it. At divergent plate boundaries, plates move apart; at convergent boundaries, plates move toward each other; and at transform boundaries, plates grind past each other. The landforms and processes found along a plate boundary are related to the properties of the two plates and the relative motion between the two plates. Plate motion is thought to be driven by gravity and heat.

Remember to include the following information in your study guide:

- Use examples that model main ideas.
- Record explanations for the phenomena you investigated.
- Use evidence to support your explanations. Your support can include drawings, data, graphs, laboratory conclusions, and other evidence recorded throughout the lesson.

Natural Hazards

A lava fountain shoots from Kilauea, one of the world's most active volcanoes.

CAN YOU EXPLAIN IT?

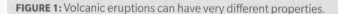

FIGURE 1: Volcanic eruptions can have very different properties.

a Kilauea, Hawaii

b Mount St. Helens, Washington

Gather Evidence: As you explore the lesson, gather evidence about how the characteristics of the Kilauea and Mount St. Helens eruptions differ.

More than 50 volcanoes have been observed erupting in the United States in the past 230 years. Two of the most famous are Mount St. Helens in Washington state, and Kilauea in Hawaii.

Mount St. Helens is a steep-sided, cone-shaped stratovolcano located on the continental crust of the North American plate. Mount St. Helens does not erupt very often—in human terms—but when it has erupted, it was very explosive.

Kilauea, on the other hand, is a low shield volcano, one of three active volcanoes on the Big Island of Hawaii. Kilauea is located on the oceanic crust of the Pacific plate. Eruptions occur relatively frequently at Kilauea, but they are much less dramatic than at Mount St. Helens.

Predict The two volcanoes shown in the images exhibited very different behaviors. In what ways did the eruptions differ? Why do you think Kilauea and Mount St. Helens are different? Predict how each volcano poses a threat to the human populations and the environment that surrounds it.

Mount St. Helens

On May 18, 1980, a powerful earthquake triggered a series of events on Mount St. Helens in Washington State. A volcanic blast tore away the north face of the mountain, flattening a forest, and causing the largest recorded avalanche in United States history.

Causes of the Eruption

In March 1980, a series of small earthquakes was the first sign of the volcanic activity to come. By May, more than 10 000 earthquakes had shaken the mountain, and the north slope had grown outward about 450 feet (140 m) to form a bulge.

FIGURE 2: A dome bulges out of the north face of Mount St. Helens.

In the weeks prior to the eruption, geologists witnessed multiple steam eruptions near the summit of the volcano, which loosened and fractured rock near the summit. Geologists predicted that loose rock near the newly formed dome could cause a massive landslide that could, in turn, trigger an explosive eruption.

Analyze What change do you notice in the seismic activity near Mount St. Helens on the morning of May 18?

FIGURE 3: This seismogram is a record of the volcanic earthquake activity over time on the morning of May 18, 1980. The horizontal lines are spaced every 15 minutes.

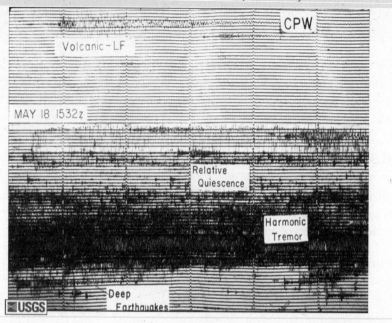

Explain What caused the bulge on the north slope of Mount St. Helens?

Factors Affecting the Eruption

Mount St. Helens is located along a boundary between two tectonic plates. As the Juan de Fuca Plate subducts beneath the North American Plate, the temperature and pressure on the rocks in the subducting plate increase. This causes water in the subducting ocean sediments and water molecules locked in the minerals of solid rock to escape. The water vapor rises above the subducting plate into the mantle. The addition of water to the mantle rock decreases the melting temperature of the rock. As a result, the mantle partially melts, forming basaltic magma that is less dense than the surrounding rock.

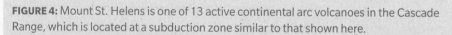

FIGURE 4: Mount St. Helens is one of 13 active continental arc volcanoes in the Cascade Range, which is located at a subduction zone similar to that shown here.

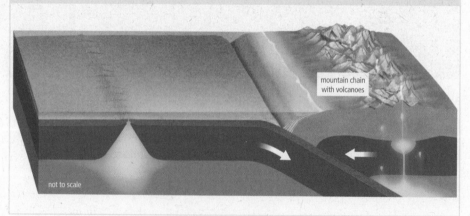

mountain chain with volcanoes

not to scale

This buoyant magma rises toward the Earth's surface. On its way to the surface, the magma melts some of the continental crust and mixes with it, becoming rich in silica (SiO_2). Eventually, some of the magma makes its way to the surface, where it is called *lava*. It erupts violently, forming steep-sided stratovolcanoes such as Mount St. Helens.

The amount of silica in magma affects the way that the magma flows and how violently it erupts. The more silica-rich the magma, the more viscous, or thick and sticky, it is. The magmas that erupt at Mount St. Helens and other volcanoes in the Cascades are intermediate to silica-rich in composition. They are generally richer in silica than the mantle and ocean crust, but poorer in silica than the continental crust.

Unlike more silica-poor lavas, which flow easily into thin layers, silica-rich lavas tend to build up without flowing far. As a result, they tend to form thick, blocky lava flows or steep-sided lava domes, like the bulge at Mount St. Helens.

Intermediate and silica-rich lavas also tend to erupt much more violently than silica-poor lavas. Magmas are mixtures of mineral crystals, liquid rock, and dissolved gases. As magma rises toward the surface, gases bubble out of the magma. In a very fluid magma, the gases can travel easily through the magma and escape to the surface like the bubbles of water vapor that you see moving up through boiling water. But if the magma is too viscous, the gas cannot move as easily. Intermediate and silica-rich lavas are both very viscous and also have a high gas content. The gas pressure builds up until it has enough force to overcome the viscosity of the magma and the pressure of the rocks above. The volcano erupts explosively. Tall columns of gas, dust, and cinders stretch up into the atmosphere from the volcano. This type of volcano also gives rise to pyroclastic flows—searing hot mixtures of gas, dust, cinders, and small particles of rock that flow down the sides of the volcano at rates as fast as 700 km/hr.

Effects on Human Activity

Mount St. Helens is a stratovolcano, the product of silica-rich magmas. The cone-shaped volcano has steep slopes topped by a glacier-capped summit. It's constructed of alternating layers of lava flows, cinder, and ash.

FIGURE 6: In the explosion, Mount St. Helen's volcanic cone was completely blasted away. The peak was reduced by 400 m (1,300 ft), leaving a deep caldera in its place.

FIGURE 5: The major volcanic rock types found at Mount St. Helens are intermediate to silica-rich rocks like andesite and dacite.

a Andesites have an intermediate silica content of around 60%.

b Dacites have a slightly higher silica content of around 65%.

Explain What process takes place during the subduction of the Juan de Fuca Plate that explains the volcanic activity in the Cascade Rage?

Explain How is the explosivity of a volcano like Mount St. Helens related to the composition of the magma?

Scale, Proportion, and Quantity

Magnitude The moment magnitude scale is used to measure the energy of earthquakes. Some units are linear—6 km is twice as great as 3 km. But the scale for earthquakes is not linear. A magnitude 3.0 earthquake is too small to be noticed by most people, while a magnitude 6.0 earthquake will cause major damage to structures. A difference of 1 on the magnitude scale indicates a factor of 32 in energy

FIGURE 7: Volcanic mudflows called *lahars* resulting from the Mount St. Helens eruption flattened forests and destroyed roads, buildings, and bridges in the area.

Shaken by a magnitude 5.1 earthquake, the north face of Mount St. Helens collapsed in an avalanche. The avalanche rapidly released pressurized gases within the volcano. A tremendous explosion ripped through the side of Mount St. Helens and the avalanche. Within minutes, nearly 600 square km (230 square mi) of forest were blown over. Large pyroclastic flows of hot volcanic gases, ash, and pumice swept down the slopes. A mushroom-shaped column of ash rose 25 km (15 mi) high, turning day into night in eastern Washington. The cloud drifted east across the United States in three days.

The eruption resulted in scores of injuries and the loss of 57 lives, including scientists and others studying the volcano. Nearly 7,000 deer, elk, bear, and most small mammals and birds perished within the 230-square-mile blast area. Economic losses, repair and cleanup costs were estimated at $1.2 billion.

In 1982, the Mount St. Helens National Volcanic Monument was created. It has become a natural laboratory where scientists study how plants and animals returned to the area around the mountain. Today, the volcano has the best seismic monitoring network of all volcanoes in the Cascade Range.

Explain Describe how the Mount St. Helens eruption affected the human population and surrounding environment.

Hawaiian Islands and Hotspots

FIGURE 8: This satellite photo shows the Hawaiian Islands, which are located in the Pacific Ocean.

Explore Online ▶

Hands-On Lab

Explore Volcanoes Develop and design your own method to explore and model a volcano.

The Hawaiian Islands are located on the Pacific Plate, far from its edges. They aren't forming at a subduction zone, like Mount St. Helens, where an ocean plate slides below a continental plate.

Most volcanoes on Earth are found along the boundaries between tectonic plates. Arc volcanoes, like Mount St. Helens, are explained by hydration melting of the mantle at subduction zones. Arc volcanoes form at convergent boundaries while mid-ocean ridge volcanoes form at divergent boundaries. The volcanoes of Hawaii, however, are located in the middle of the Pacific plate, far from boundaries with other tectonic plates.

Formation of the Hawaiian Islands

FIGURE 9: Columns of dark gray basalt along the shoreline of the Island of Hawaii, also called "the Big Island"

Predict: The basaltic rock that makes up the Hawaiian islands originated in the mantle. How do you think it came to be on the surface?

Image Credits: (t) ©Jacques Descloitres/MODIS Rapid Response Team/NASA Goddard Space Flight Center; (b) ©Birdiegal/Shutterstock

Among the Hawaiian islands are underwater, cone-shaped mountains called seamounts. The islands and seamounts are made of basalt, a volcanic rock that is poor in silica and rich in iron and magnesium. Basaltic magma forms from the partial melting of the mantle beneath the crust. Basalt is the most common type of rock in Earth's crust: All of the rock beneath the sediment on the ocean floor is basalt.

FIGURE 10: The Lōʻihi Seamount is a new volcano forming in the Pacific Ocean southeast of Hawaii.

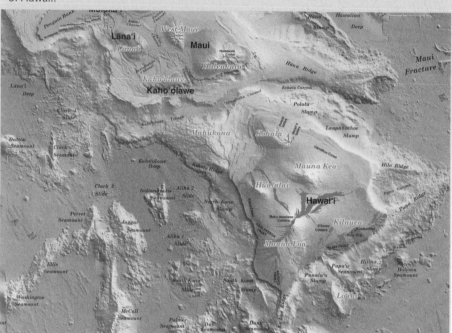

Image Credits:(t) ©U.S. Geological Survey Geologic Investigations Series Map I-2809, "Hawai'i's Volcanoes Revealed.; (b) ©Jacques Descloitres/MODIS Rapid Response Team/NASA Goddard Space Flight Center

 Explain: Based on what you learned about the Lōʻihi seamount, how do you think the islands of the Hawaiian chain formed?

 Gather Evidence Based on what you have learned so far, how is Hawaii similar to and different from the Cascades volcanoes?

Lōʻihi Seamount is an active volcano that rises roughly 4000 m above the ocean floor, with a peak about 1000 m below the ocean surface. Although it is located about 35 km off the southeast coast of the island of Hawaii, it is located on the flanks of Mauna Loa, the largest volcano not only in Hawaii, but the largest volcano on Earth.

Although Lōʻihi looks small compared to Mauna Loa, Lōʻihi if measured from the ocean floor is actually taller than Mount St. Helens was before the 1980 eruption. Continued volcanic activity is expected to eventually build a new island, but it might take about 10 000 to 100 000 years before the summit will reach the ocean surface.

FIGURE 11: The Hawaiian island chain

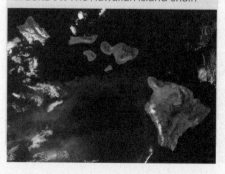

A Line of Islands

The Hawaiian island chain includes eight main islands, many small islands, and many seamounts. Together, they form a line more than 3600 km long.

The ages of the Hawaiian volcanoes show a distinct pattern: They increase steadily in age with distance away from the Big Island. In fact, the only active volcanoes are Lōʻihi, and Mauna Loa, Kilauea and Hualalai, which are on the Big Island. Some of the other volcanoes on or close to the Big Island are dormant and could erupt again, but those farther away are extinct. This is very different from the pattern in the Cascade range of the United States: all of the 13 main volcanoes in the Cascade range have erupted in the past 5000 years.

Predict If the Pacific plate stopped moving, what might happen to the island of Hawaii? Explain your prediction.

FIGURE 12: Hawaii is located on the Pacific plate. The portion of the plate that includes the Hawaiian Islands is moving toward the northwest at a rate of about 6.8 cm per year.

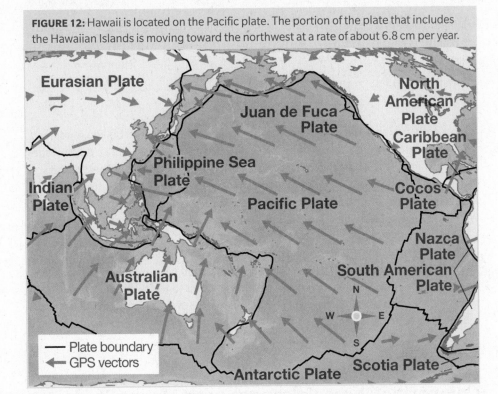

Although Hawaii is not located along a plate boundary, its pattern of ages can be explained by plate tectonics. A volcanically active region that can occur in the middle of a tectonic plate is called a *hot spot*. Scientists think that hot spots are caused by mantle plumes: hot mantle rock that wells up from deep in the mantle, perhaps as deep as the core-mantle boundary. When the rock of these plumes melts near the surface, the magma moves through cracks in the crust to form volcanoes. Although the mantle plume may stay in the same place for tens of millions of years, a volcano above a hot spot does not continue erupting forever because it is attached to the tectonic plate, and is eventually moved away from the hot spot. The pattern of volcanoes is evidence that the motion of the Pacific plate in this region is toward the northwest.

Scientists think that the magma that forms and feeds the Hawaiian volcanoes is the result of a mantle plume below the Pacific Plate. Kauai was once located where Hawaii is situated today. As the plate moved, Kauai moved away from the hot spot and became dormant. As the Pacific Plate continued to move, the islands of Oahu, Molokai, Maui, and Hawaii were formed.

Gather Evidence
Compare the pattern of volcanoes near Yellowstone to that of the Hawaiian island chain. What can you infer about the origin of the volcanoes?

FIGURE 15: Yellowstone is the youngest and eastern-most part of a line of volcanic calderas that runs for more than 700 km from Oregon to Wyoming.

1.2 mya
6 mya
11 mya
0.6 mya
4 mya
10 mya
14 mya
12 mya

mya = millions of years ago
km 0   200
mi 0   200

Yellowstone National Park is well known for its geysers, hot springs, boiling muds, and volcanic rocks. Although Yellowstone is not erupting today, volcanism at Yellowstone has occurred over the past two million years and could happen again. The park now sits in a caldera, a large, circular depression in a volcano. This one is roughly 60 km across that formed about 640 000 years ago during a massive super eruption, when so much magma erupted that the ground above the magma chamber collapsed.

Yellowstone is just one of ten major calderas in the northwestern United States. Like the islands and seamounts of Hawaii, these calderas form a line, and as in Hawaii, the ages of the calderas form a pattern, increasing from east to west. This pattern, along with the fact that the calderas are located in the middle of the North American plate, is evidence that Yellowstone is also a hot spot. The pattern of volcanoes is evidence that the motion of the North American plate in this region is toward the southwest.

Comparing These Volcanoes with Mount St. Helens

Analyze Describe the ways in which the eruptions of Mount St. Helens and Kilauea are different.

Many of the differences between Mount St. Helens and Kilauea are explained by the chemical composition of the magmas produced by each volcano. The basalt magma at Kilauea contains about 52% silica and 0.5% water, while the dacite magma at Mount St. Helens contained about 64% silica and 4% water.

FIGURE 16: The eruptions of Kilauea and Mount St. Helens differ greatly in explosivity.

a Kilauea, Hawaii

b Mount St. Helens, Washington

Analyze Describe the damage that can be caused by basaltic lava flows.

Explain How can you determine whether or not a series of volcanoes is the result of a hotspot?

Effects on Human Activity

Although they erupt more often, the Hawaiian volcanoes are not considered to be as dangerous as the Cascades volcanoes because the eruptions are generally not explosive and they don't affect large areas over a very short period of time. However, they are hazardous. Kilauea and other Hawaiian volcanoes emit gases that can harm human and ecosystem health. High concentrations of sulfur dioxide produce volcanic smog (VOG), irritating respiratory problems and damaging crops. Lava flows can be hotter than 900 °C. Although a person could outrun most of the flows, buildings and fields cannot.

FIGURE 15: Molten lava destruction from Kilauea Volcano near the village of Pahoa on Hawaii's Big Island in 2014.

Since 1983, eruptions from Kilauea have destroyed more than 214 structures and buried 14 km (9 mi) of highway under lava as thick as 34 m (115 ft). During that time, Kilauea lava flows have also added about 500 acres of new land to the Big Island of Hawaii.

 Collaborate In what ways do you think people can benefit from volcanic activity?

 Explain In what ways are basaltic shield volcanoes such as those on Hawaii different from other types of volcanoes?

1816: The Year Without a Summer

The summer of 1816 was unlike any summer people could remember. It was cold, stormy, and dark. Snow fell in New York and Maine and in Quebec City, Canada. Ice formed on lakes and rivers as far south as Pennsylvania. Cold, heavy rains fell in western Europe. Brown snow fell in Hungary, and red snow fell in Italy. Wheat, oats, potatoes, and other crops failed. Livestock died. Food prices rose sharply. In China, rice crops suffered as a result of unusually low temperatures. Poor harvests led to famine and disease in the Northern Hemisphere.

Global Temperature Drop in 1816

FIGURE 16: The summer of 1816 was one of the coldest on record.

Analyze Based on the historical evidence, what are some possible causes of the year without a summer? Describe the evidence that led to your conclusion.

The year without a summer was the result of global climate abnormalities. There was so much ash and sulfuric gas in the atmosphere that it dimmed the sun's effects and caused global temperature to drop by about 0.4–0.7 °C (0.7–1.3 °F). The northeastern United States was cloaked in what seemed to be a never-ending dry fog. Wind or rain wouldn't make it go away. The fog reddened daylight and made it possible for people to see sunspots with the naked eye. Spectacular sunsets were seen in London, England from summer through the fall that year.

Causes of Global Temperature Drop

FIGURE 17: Eruption of Mount St. Helens in 1980

When Mount St. Helens erupted in 1980, a column of ash and gas rose more than 24 km (15 mi) into the atmosphere in less than 15 minutes. The cloud of ash spread across the United States in three days and it circled the Earth in 15 days. Ash fell over 22 000 square miles, an area about the size of the states of Connecticut, Delaware, Hawaii, New Jersey, and Rhode Island combined. Although the ash plume was substantial across the United States, life continued as normal throughout most of the Northern Hemisphere.

Analyze Based on what you know about the size of the 1980 Mount St. Helens eruption, what do you think caused the unusual atmospheric conditions in 1816?

FIGURE 18: Mount Tambora's explosion left a caldera measuring about 6 km (4 mi) across.

On April 10, 1815, the catastrophic explosion of Mount Tambora in Indonesia could be heard 2000 km (1200 mi) away. It is the largest known explosive eruption in recorded history. The volcanic blast was one hundred times more powerful and ejected about 30 to 80 times more ash than did Mount St. Helens in 1980. A column of ash and gas rose to an altitude of more than 43 km (27 mi). Pyroclastic flows came hurtling down the mountainside, and pumice ash and uprooted trees washed into the sea forming rafts of debris up to 5 km (3 mi) wide. One raft was found in the Indian Ocean six months later. All vegetation on the island was destroyed, and 10,000 people lost their lives during the eruption, most likely due to the lava flows.

Predict The eruptions at Yellowstone produced rhyolitic rock. Based on the information from the table, describe the type of activity you would expect a rhyolite volcano to have.

Collaborate Complete the table to compare the chemical and physical characteristics of different types of lava.

Basalt	Andesite	Rhyolite
	Moderate Silica Content	
Low Viscosity		High Viscosity
Not Usually Explosive		
	Moderate Gas Content	High Gas Content

Effects on Human Activity

Analyze What type of magma do you think erupted from the Tambora volcano? What evidence do you have for this?

FIGURE 19: Forest destroyed by the eruption of Mount St. Helens in 1980

Analyze Compare the local effects of the 1815 eruption of Tambora to the global effects. Why were they different?

The 1815 Mount Tambora and the 1980 Mount St. Helens eruptions were both explosive in nature. However, the Tambora blast was one hundred times more powerful, and ejected about 30 to 80 times more ash, than Mount St. Helens. Fifty-seven people lost their lives during the Mount St. Helens eruption. By comparison, the village and culture of Tambora was buried in ash and lava flows, and 10 000 village residents lost their lives. More than 60 000 people are estimated to have lost their lives due to starvation and disease after volcanic fallout from the eruption destroyed agriculture production in the region.

Collaborate Although the 1980 Mount St. Helens eruption pales in comparison to the 1815 Tambora eruption, there have been even larger prehistoric eruptions. Two million years ago, a rhyolite eruption at Yellowstone released 50 times more material than Tambora. Discuss with a partner what the local and global effects of a "supereruption" like this might be.

Explain Compare the effects of the three types of magma (basalt, andesite, and rhyolite) and their associated volcanic eruptions on human populations.

Earthquake Hazards

FIGURE 20: A giant pendulum hangs in the skyscraper Taipei 101.

Explore Online ▶

Hands-On Lab

Earthquake-Safe Buildings
Create a simple model and consider the construction of damage-resistant buildings.

Taipai 101 is a super tall skyscraper in Taipai, Taiwan. Inside the building, suspended from the 92nd to the 87th floor, is a gigantic steel sphere measuring 5.4 m (18 ft) across and weighing 728 tons. Four steel cables form a sling to support the sphere, while eight dampers protect it when the sphere shifts. The sphere, which acts like a pendulum, can move 1.5 m (5 ft) in any direction.

The Role of Seismic Dampers

Earthquakes radiate seismic energy as body waves and surface waves. Body waves—P- and S-waves—travel through Earth's interior, while surface waves only travel in the crust and upper mantle, along Earth's surface. Surface waves cause the most destruction during an earthquake, causing the ground to roll up and down and shake back and forth as they pass through.

Collaborate Work with a partner to come up with an explanation for how the movable steel sphere might be used to protect the building.

Like water waves, seismic waves can be described by their amplitude and frequency. The amplitude is a measure of how far the ground moves when a wave passes through. The frequency is a measure of how quickly it moves up and down or back and forth. The greater the amplitude, the farther the ground—and all the buildings on the ground—moves up and down or from side to side. The greater the frequency, the faster the shaking occurs.

Damping devices act like shock absorbers. Different types work in different ways to reduce the amplitude of the shaking. They help to stabilize a building and decrease the impact of violent motion from surface waves during an earthquake.

FIGURE 21: Brick walls are generally designed to bear gravitational stress— the stress of the weight of the building above, typical winds, and everyday motion of people inside and outside the building.

Engineering

The Taipei 101 mass damper was designed to stabilize the skyscraper during strong earthquakes and high winds. Taiwan is located in the western Pacific Ocean in an area that is frequently hit by powerful typhoons (hurricanes). It is also located on a seismically active convergent boundary. When a gust of wind or an earthquake causes the building to move, it begins to vibrate, swaying back and forth. The steel ball in the damper is designed to sway in the opposite direction, counteracting the motion of the building. As a result, the building sways about 40% less than it would without the damper.

Damage Caused by Earthquakes

Powerful earthquakes can cause fires, landslides, and tsunamis. Fire is a major hazard following an earthquake, usually because gas pipes burst and electric lines fall down. Urban fires following an earthquake can be challenging if fire-fighting equipment and access to fire-fighting water supplies are damaged.

Landslides are the movement of rock, earth, or debris down a sloped section of land. Landslides triggered by earthquakes can destroy homes, highways, towns and villages and displace people.

Earthquakes can trigger flooding by tsunamis thousands of kilometers away if there is a substantial and sudden displacement of a massive amount of water. Tsunamis can travel up to 800 km (500 mi) an hour across an ocean. As a tsunami approaches shore, the water at the front of the wave moves slower than the water at the back of the wave, causing a piling-up effect of the water. The sea level at the shore can rise vertically to more than 30 m (100 ft). The enormous energy of a tsunami can lift boulders, flip vehicles, and demolish houses.

Collaborate With a partner, recall any recent earthquakes you have heard about or experienced. Discuss the ways in which the quake had an effect on nearby bodies of water, mountains, and cities or towns and the people who live in them.

Image Credits: ©anankml/Fotolia

Detecting Earthquakes

The motion of the ground is measured by an instrument called a *seismograph*, or sometimes a seismometer. The recording is a seismogram. Seismographs are designed to record, accurately and precisely, the motion of the ground during and between earthquakes. Compared with the examples shown here, modern seismometers used technologically advanced sensors, recording and transmitting data digitally.

FIGURE 22: A seismograph that measures seismic waves from earthquakes using a drum of paper and a pendulum with a pen attached. Each instrument records waves in only one direction.

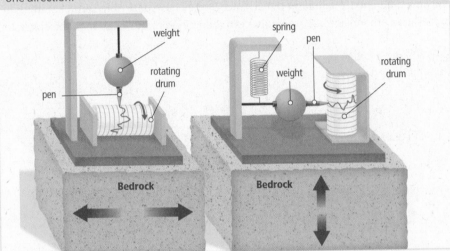

A seismograph consists of a rotating drum of paper and a stationary weight or pendulum suspended by a wire from a fixed point within the frame. A pen is attached to the weight. A single seismograph weight works only in one direction and cannot give a complete picture of wave motions from other directions. Therefore seismograph stations have three separate instruments, one to record north-south horizontal waves, another to record east-west horizontal waves, and a vertical one in which a weight rests on a spring to record vertical ground motions. Clocks are also an important part of a seismograph system and are used to record time of day and the synchronization of events.

Analyze Which seismic event seems to have the greatest magnitude? Which would you expect to have the most devastating impact on human activity? Support your claim with reasoning.

FIGURE 23: A seismograph records the motion of the ground.

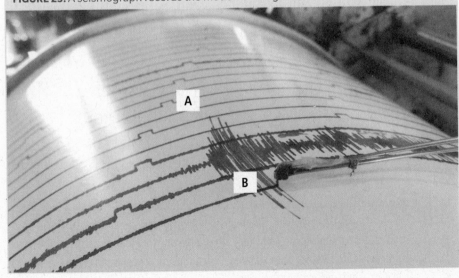

Image Credits: (b) ©Budi Selamat/EyeEm/Getty Images.

Most of the ground motion that is recorded on a seismograph is background motion. These vibrations can be caused by the wind, waves crashing on shore, or heavy traffic near the seismograph. Scientists can infer that an earthquake has occurred when the pattern of motion changes in a certain way.

When an earthquake occurs, seismic waves travel through Earth and along the surface. The fastest waves, the first ones to arrive, are the P-waves or primary waves. The next set of waves are S-waves, or secondary waves. The surface waves arrive later, but result in the greatest ground motion.

Scientists can use the time between the first P-waves and the first S-waves to calculate the distance from the recording station to the epicenter of an earthquake. The greater the time difference, the greater the distance. If they have data from seismic stations in at least two other places, seismologists can then pinpoint the location of the epicenter.

Explore Online ▶

Hands-On Lab

Finding an Epicenter Analyze P-waves and S-waves detected in three cities to determine the location of an earthquake's epicenter.

FIGURE 24: Scientists use the arrival times of seismic waves at various locations to locate earthquake epicenters.

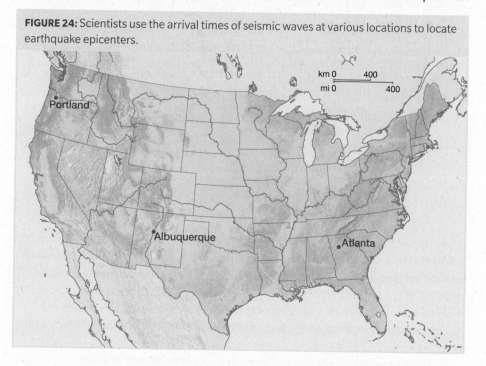

Collaborate Scientists use the time between the arrival of P-waves and S-waves to calculate the distance to the epicenter of an earthquake. They find that the earthquake occurred 560 km from Atlanta, GA, 1550 km from Albuquerque, NM, and 2930 km from Portland, OR. Where did the earthquake occur? How can you figure it out?

Explain Unlike volcanic eruptions, earthquakes provide very little warning. However, scientists can make earthquake hazard maps based on what they understand about what causes earthquakes and how they affect different types of materials. Describe how earthquakes are detected and measured. How do you think people can protect themselves and each other from earthquakes?

Careers in Science

Volcanologist

Volcanology is the study of volcanoes: volcanic landforms, volcanic rocks, and eruption processes. Many volcanologists are employed by federal and state governments to monitor active volcanoes. Others work as researchers and professors at universities.

Like other scientists, volcanologists ask questions, like *How does magma move underground? When will Yellowstone erupt again?* They plan and carry out investigations to make observations and collect data about active and extinct volcanoes in the field and in the lab, and analyze and interpret data collected using tools like temperature probes, gas meters, and seismographs. Volcanologists make and use models of volcanoes to describe the physical structure of the interior of a volcano and use math to analyze their data and make predictions about eruptions. Finally and very importantly, volcanologists communicate their observations, analyses, and conclusions in volcano alert notifications, government reports, scientific journals, conferences, books, webpages, films, and classes.

There are several different fields of volcanology. Physical volcanologists use simple tools like compasses and rock hammers as well as more complicated tools like gas samplers and thermal imaging cameras to map volcanic landforms and understand the processes that form them.

Geophysicists who work in volcanology use seismometers to understand how magma is moving underground and to predict when a volcano will erupt, gravity-meters to map structures underground, and magnetometers to identify and date different lava flows.

FIGURE 25: Volcanologists observe the eruption of Alaid, a volcano in eastern Russia.

Collaborate With a partner, write a scientific question that a volcanologist might try to answer. What fields of volcanology would be involved? What tools would he or she need in an investigation to try to answer this question?

Language Arts Connection Choose a phenomenon related to volcanoes that you would like to investigate. Construct a plan for how you could investigate the phenomenon as well as how you would communicate your findings.

Image Credits: ©ITAR-TASS Photo Agency/Alamy

HUMAN BOTTLENECK EVENT

HUMAN RESPONSE TO DISASTERS

Go online to choose one of these other paths.

Lesson Self-Check

CAN YOU EXPLAIN IT?

Image Credits: (l) ©Charles Douglas Peebles/Alamy; (r) ©Robert Krimmel/USGS

Analyze Refer to the notes in your Evidence Notebook to explain the eruptions of Kilauea and Mount St. Helens.

FIGURE 26: Kilauea and Mount St. Helens display very different types of eruptions.

a   Kilauea, Hawaii

b   Mount St. Helens, Washington

Explain Why are Mount St. Helens and Kilauea different? What would you predict the effects of these volcanoes—and volcanoes like them—to be on people in the future?

Mount St. Helens and Kilauea represent two very different types of volcanoes and styles of volcanism. While Mount St. Helens is a steep stratovolcano made of alternating layers of andesitic lavas, pyroclastic flows, and volcanic ash, Kilauea is a low shield volcano composed of layers of basaltic lava. Mount St. Helens erupts explosively, sending pyroclastic flows speeding down the mountain and volcanic ash high up into the air. Kilauea erupts more slowly and steadily, with lava flows that flow down valleys in a matter of weeks and months rather than seconds or minutes. Because of the difference in eruption styles, they also have very different effects on human populations living nearby. An eruption of Kilauea can engulf a town in lava over a few weeks, but it is rare for anyone to be killed. An eruption of a volcano like Mount St. Helens, however, can not only destroy a nearby town almost instantly, but is very likely to kill many people in the area.

The differences between the volcanoes can be explained by their magma composition. Andesitic magma is viscous and gas-rich, while basaltic magma is more fluid and gas-poor. As a result, andesitic magma erupts much more explosively than basaltic magma. The difference in magma composition can be explained partly by the difference in geologic setting. Mount St. Helens lies above a subduction zone where the addition of water causes mantle rock to melt and then move up through the continental crust before erupting. Kilauea is located on a hot spot where thermal energy causes mantle rock to partially melt and then move up through basaltic oceanic crust before it erupts.

Check Your Understanding

1. Complete the paragraph:

   Partial melting of the mantle results in the formation of basaltic magma. Partial melting of the mantle can be caused by a number of processes. A(n) _____ in pressure, such as that experienced along continental rifts and _____ oceanic boundaries can cause the mantle to melt. The addition of _____ to the mantle causes the melting temperature of upper mantle rock to _____, which causes the it to melt. This type of melting is called hydration melting and it occurs along _____ boundaries, specifically those that involve the _____ of oceanic lithosphere. Melting can also occur where plumes of anomalously _____ mantle rock rise up toward the surface. Volcanoes that form above mantle plumes are known as _____ volcanoes.

2. Olympus Mons is an enormous shield volcano on Mars. It is a hotspot volcano and is the largest known volcano in the solar system. Assuming that Mars's mantle is similar in composition to Earth's, and assuming processes on Mars are similar to those on Earth, which is the most likely composition of the rock that makes up Olympus Mons?

   a. Basalt

   b. Rhyolite

   c. Andesite

3. Plate tectonics do not operate on Mars today, and there is no evidence that they operated while Olympus Mons was forming. How do you think Olympus Mons would be different if there were plate tectonics while it was forming? (Assume the volcano was located in the middle of a plate.)

   a. Olympus Mons would be even larger.

   b. Olympus Mons would be a steep stratovolcano rather than a low shield volcano.

   c. Olympus Mons would be a giant caldera like Yellowstone instead of a shield volcano.

   d. Olympus Mons would consist of a line of many smaller shield volcanoes rather than one large shield volcano.

4. What can scientists calculate from the P-wave and S-wave interval?

   a. The cause of the earthquake

   b. How strong the earthquake was

   c. The distance to the earthquake epicenter

   d. The effects of the earthquake on structures

5. A salesperson has just started a new job selling "Earthquake-Proof," a seismic damper technology, to construction companies. Where is she likely to make the most sales?

   a. In the Midwest because it is located in the middle of a plate

   b. In the Northeast because many large cities are located there

   c. On the West Coast because it is located along plate boundaries

   d. On the East Coast because it is located along the boundary between the ocean and continent

6. Potential customers ask the salesperson how the technology works. Which explanation is most accurate?

   a. The technology bolts the two sides of a fault beneath a building together, preventing motion along the fault.

   b. The technology helps absorb vibrations from the ground or counteract motion of a building, stabilizing the building.

   c. When the technology senses seismic waves, it creates another set of seismic waves that partially cancel out those of the earthquake.

   d. The technology strengthens the vertical beams in the building, preventing them from moving at all during an earthquake.

MAKE YOUR OWN STUDY GUIDE

 In your Evidence Notebook, design a study guide that supports the main ideas in this lesson.

Remember to include the following information in your study guide:

• Use examples that model main ideas.

• Record explanations for the phenomena you investigated.

• Use evidence to support your explanations. Your support can include drawings, data, graphs, laboratory conclusions, and other evidence recorded throughout the lesson.

A BOOK EXPLAINING COMPLEX IDEAS USING ONLY THE 1,000 MOST COMMON WORDS

RANDALL MUNROE
XKCD.COM

BIG FLAT ROCKS WE LIVE ON

How the ground under your feet is always on the move

Huge, moving slabs of rock called tectonic plates constantly reshape Earth's surface. Here's how it happens.

THE STORY OF ROCKS THAT MOVE

THE SURFACE OF THE EARTH IS MADE UP OF BIG FLAT ROCKS MOVING AROUND. THE ROCKS UNDER LAND AREAS ARE USUALLY THICK, SLOW-MOVING, AND LAST FOR A LONG TIME, AND THE ONES UNDER SEAS ARE THIN, HEAVY, AND MOVE FAST.

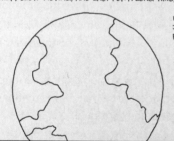

HARD TO BELIEVE IT'S JUST A BIG PILE OF ROCKS DOWN THERE . . .

YOU COULDN'T JUST ENJOY THE MOMENT, COULD YOU?

(FAST FOR A ROCK, THAT IS. THEY MOVE ABOUT AS FAST AS THE THINGS ON THE ENDS OF YOUR FINGERS GROW.)

WHAT EXACTLY ARE YOU DOING?

COME ON— FASTER, FASTER!

IT'S CLOSE, BUT I THINK I CAN BEAT THIS ROCK!

WHEN A SEA ROCK HITS A LAND ROCK, THE SEA ROCK IS USUALLY PUSHED UNDER IT, DOWN INTO THE EARTH. AREAS WHERE THIS HAPPENS OFTEN HAVE DEEP SEAS RIGHT NEAR LAND, LINES OF MOUNTAINS, SHAKING GROUND, AND BIG WAVES.

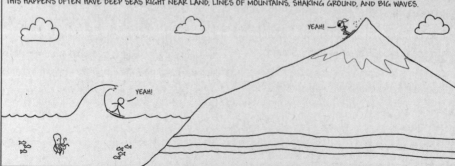

YEAH!

YEAH!

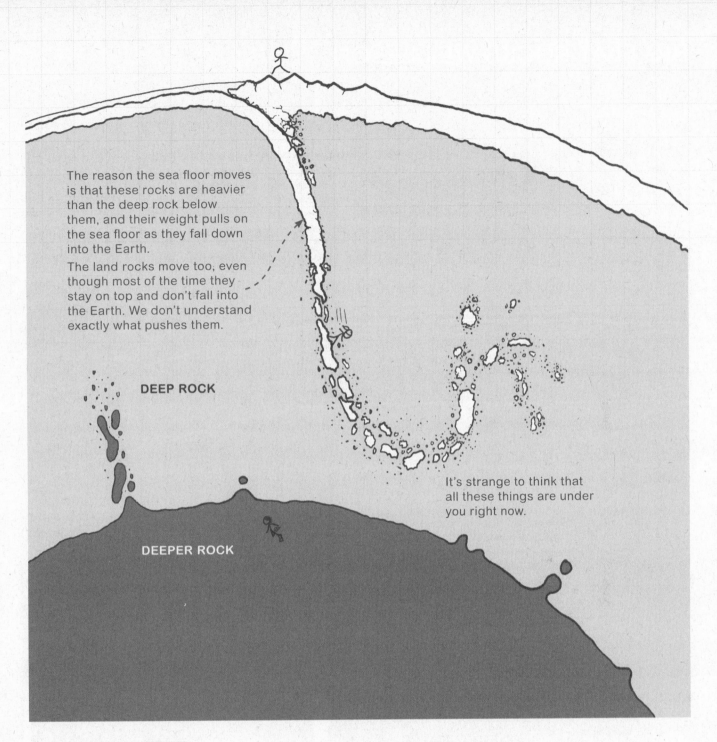

The reason the sea floor moves is that these rocks are heavier than the deep rock below them, and their weight pulls on the sea floor as they fall down into the Earth.

The land rocks move too, even though most of the time they stay on top and don't fall into the Earth. We don't understand exactly what pushes them.

DEEP ROCK

DEEPER ROCK

It's strange to think that all these things are under you right now.

...WHAT ARE YOU DOING?

STOP IT! STOP IT!

AUGH!

WHERE DO ROCKS GO AFTER THEY DIE?

We used to think that when rocks fell into the Earth, they broke up right away from the heat. And even if they stayed together for a little while, it didn't really matter, since they were hidden away forever. That part of our history was gone.

But it turns out they're not quite gone. When the world shakes, we can listen to the sound go around and through the world. By listening very carefully, we can hear the sound hitting things inside the Earth, and learn what it's like in there.

By listening to the Earth, we've learned that the rocks don't all turn to water right away. We can keep track of them, even when they're out of reach of our eyes, as they fall down, down, down into the Earth.

I think that's really cool.

BIG FLAT ROCKS WE LIVE ON

DEEP PART
The sea floor is deeper here
because the sea rocks are getting
pushed down as they run into the
land rocks.

**SEA
FLOOR**

LAND FLOOR

SEA ROCKS
Sea rocks are heavy. They slide along
like a moving road, and they move fast!
Not as fast as a person, but faster than
most kinds of land.

When sea rocks hit land rocks, the sea
rocks usually get pushed back down
under the land rocks, down into the
Earth, where they break down. Because
most sea rocks run into land and disappear
after a while, most parts of the sea floor
aren't as old as the land floor.

WATER-CARRYING ROCKS
Sea water gets carried inside the
Earth here. The water changes
the rocks in a way that helps the
rock go back up through the rocks
above it and come out of holes in
the ground.

DEEP ROCK
This part of the world can be hard to understand.
Sometimes people talk about it like it's watery, but
sometimes they talk about it like it's hard.

The real truth is that it's very hard. If you touched
a piece of it, it would feel very hard. (You shouldn't
touch it, though, because it would also set your hand
on fire.) It's harder than the hardest metal, glass,
or even stones in a marriage ring. That makes it sound
a lot like rock, not water.

But in some ways, it also acts like water. It's sort of
like the big rivers of ice that slide slowly down from
mountains. The ice is hard up close, and you can walk
on it and break pieces off. But if you look at it from
far away, and wait a very long time, you'll see that it
moves like water.

© Giles Harvey/Shutterstock

LOW AREA

These low areas between mountains sometimes have water in them, and the ground there is usually good for growing things, so people like to live there. Sometimes hot rocks come out of the mountains and cover everyone's houses. But that doesn't happen very often, so people try not to worry about it too much.

Small Soft, the company that makes Windows®, is in a city like this.

HOT ROCK MOUNTAIN

The rocks that get pushed into the Earth get hot and watery, and some of them come up through holes in the rock above them. They come out of those holes and cool down and turn into mountains.

Go online for more about *Thing Explainer*.

LAND ROCKS

These are like big rock boats that drive around on top of the hotter rocks under them.

ROCK MOUNTAIN

Not all the mountains in this kind of place are made from hot rock. When a sea plate goes under a land plate, it can make mountains by pushing up on the land plate.

If two land plates hit, it can make very big mountains. The biggest mountains on Earth right now were made this way.

WHEN THE EARTH SHAKES, SOMETIMES THERE ARE BIG WAVES. THIS IS THE KIND OF SHAKING THAT MAKES THE BIGGEST WAVES:

There's a place in my country on the edge of the sea. (They once made a game for kids about trying to get to this place. You had to cross rivers and shoot animals for food and sometimes people in your family died. It was supposed to teach you about the past, but I just played the shooting part and never learned very much.)

Right by the water, there's something very strange: dead trees in the sea. There are lots of dead trees in the sea. But what's strange about these trees is that they're not lying down. They're sticking up from the sea floor, like they grew there. That shouldn't be possible, because those trees can't grow in sea water. The sea rises and falls, but the trees only died 300 years ago, and the sea hasn't risen enough to explain how these trees grew there.

The answer is that the sea didn't rise. The land fell.

On the other side of the sea, 300 years ago, there was a big wave. People who saw it wrote about it. They also wrote that they didn't feel the ground shake before the wave.

The reason they didn't feel the ground shake is that the shaking didn't happen near them. It happened far away, across the sea, in the place from the kids' game. And by the edge of the water, the ground went down a little bit, and the sea came in and covered the trees.

Engineering Connection

Exploring Deep-Sea Vents More than two kilometers below the ocean surface, scorching water jets out of the seafloor along the mid-ocean ridge. A rich ecosystem of bacteria, tubeworms, crabs, and a variety of other organisms survive on the warmth and chemicals provided by these hot springs. Exploring the submarine hot springs is challenging. Scientists and engineers have had to design vehicles that can travel deep underwater and navigate through rugged terrain without sunlight. They have had to build equipment to withstand the extreme pressure from the water above as well as the temperatures ranging from 4°C to greater than 350°C.

> Using library and Internet resources, research the challenges of conducting investigations in the dark at high pressures and temperatures. Develop a model of a piece of technology that is used to investigate submarine hot springs and vent communities, and explain how the technology is designed to deal with these challenges.

FIGURE 1: Robotic vehicles like JASON are used to explore the deep ocean floor.

Literature Connection

Earthquakes and Volcanic Eruptions in Folklore People have tried to explain natural events such as earthquakes and volcanic eruptions for thousands of years. Many of these explanations are in the form of myths and legends, or folklore. Native Hawaiians, for example, believed that volcanic eruptions were caused by Pele, the goddess of fire, lightning, dance, wind, and volcanoes. People in Siberia told a story of a god named Tuli, who drove a dogsled over the earth. When the dogs stopped to scratch fleas, the ground would shake.

> Use library or Internet resources to research myths and legends about earthquakes and volcanic eruptions. Compare stories from different regions and cultures, such Greek, Roman, Hawaiian, Native American, Maori, and Japanese. How are they similar and different? What do the stories say about both the culture and the geography of the region?

FIGURE 2: In Japan, people traditionally attributed earthquakes to the movement of a giant catfish called Namazu.

Biology Connection

Using Earth's Magnetic Field People use Earth's magnetic field for navigation using compass needles, which point toward Earth's magnetic poles. Scientists have discovered that many other organisms—including certain types of birds, bats, fish, worms, and bacteria—also navigate or orient themselves using Earth's magnetic field. The ability to sense a magnetic field is known as *magnetoreception*. Since the strength and direction of the magnetic field depends on location, organisms with magnetoreception can use it to orient themselves.

> Use library and Internet resources to find out more about magnetoreception. Find out what types of organisms have this ability, how they use it, and exactly how they sense magnetic fields. As you conduct your research, make a list of questions you have. What questions do scientists still have about magnetoreception?

FIGURE 3: Homing pigeons can use Earth's magnetic field to find their way back to their nests from hundreds of kilometers away.

SYNTHESIZE THE UNIT

In your Evidence Notebook, create a concept map, graphic organizer, or outline using the Study Guides you created for each lesson in this unit. Be sure to use evidence to support your claims.

When synthesizing individual information, remember to follow these general steps:

- Find the central idea of each piece of information.
- Think about the relationships among the central ideas.
- Combine the ideas to come up with a new understanding.

Go online to access detailed lesson summaries for this unit.

DRIVING QUESTIONS

Look back to the Driving Questions from the opening section of this unit. In your Evidence Notebook, review and revise your previous answers to those questions. Use the evidence you gathered and other observations you made throughout the unit to support your claims.

PRACTICE AND REVIEW

1. The diagram below shows a basic model of Earth's interior. Identify each layer and describe its basic composition (metal or silicate rock) and physical properties (solid, liquid, gas, convecting, or nonconvecting).

FIGURE 4: Layers of Earth

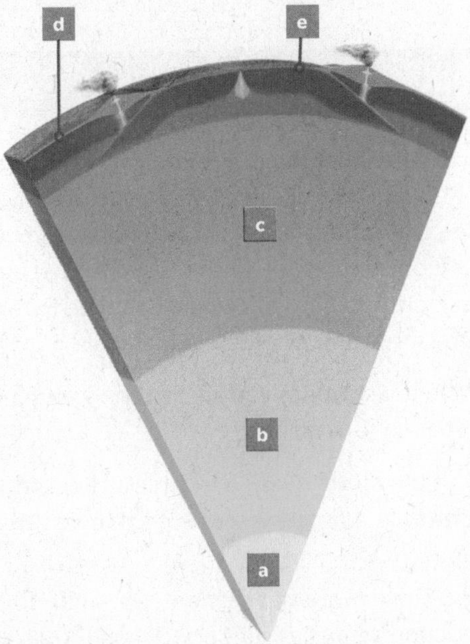

2. Explain how the outward transfer of energy as heat from inside Earth drives the movement of tectonic plates.

3. Our understanding of the structure and composition of Earth and the processes that affect it are based on scientific evidence. Match each type of investigation or evidence to the scientific claims that it supports.

   a. Earth's inner core is solid metal.

   b. Earth's outer core is convecting liquid iron metal.

   c. A plate boundary lies along the western coast of South America.

   d. New ocean crust forms through a process known as seafloor spreading.

   1. Studies of Earth's magnetic field.

   2. Analysis of seismic waves and calculations of Earth's bulk density

   3. Analysis of landforms, patterns of earthquakes, volcanic eruptions, and velocity vectors

   4. Measurements of the age and magnetic orientation of rocks and the thickness of sediment on the ocean floor

4. At which of the following locations do most of Earth's earthquakes and volcanoes occur?

   a. Over hotspots

   b. In the center of continents

   c. At plate boundaries

   d. In the center of oceanic plates

5. Which of the following statements about plate tectonics are true? Choose all correct responses.

   a. Earth's gravity is a driving force for plate tectonics.

   b. Plate tectonics is just a theory that has not yet been proven.

   c. Volcanoes and earthquakes occur only along the boundaries of tectonic plates.

   d. Earth goes through periods of increases and decreases in volume as a result of plate tectonics.

   e. Seafloor spreading would not occur if convection in the core did not generate a magnetic field.

   f. The energy that drives plate motions comes primarily from sunlight that is absorbed into Earth's interior.

   g. The processes that occur along a plate boundary depend on the type of crust that is found along the boundary.

   h. People who live along the boundaries between tectonic plates are more likely to be directly affected by plate tectonics than those who live in the middle of a plate.

6. Suppose you had to build a physical, 3D model of Earth, showing its layers. What materials would you use, and how would you arrange them? Explain your choices.

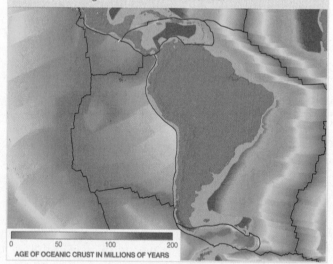

FIGURE 5: The ages of rocks on the seafloor

0   50   100   200
AGE OF OCEANIC CRUST IN MILLIONS OF YEARS

7. The map above shows the ages of rocks on the seafloor.

   a. In general, where are the areas with the oldest seafloor?

   b. Where do you find the areas with the newest seafloor on the map?

   c. How does what you have learned about plate tectonics help to explain the patterns you observed in parts **a** and **b**?

8. Scientists look for patterns to understand the natural world. Give three examples of patterns that can be used to understand plates and plate motions. Briefly describe how each is related to plates and plate motion.

9. Suppose Earth's mantle and outer core did not convect. How would Earth be different?

10. What properties of seismic waves make them useful for studying Earth's deep interior?

11. In 1999, planetary scientists announced that there was evidence for magnetic anomalies—parallel strips of rock magnetized in opposite directions—on the surface of Mars.

   a. How could this evidence support the idea that there may have once been some form of plate tectonics on Mars?

   b. Why would it be important to have information about the ages of the magnetized rocks?

UNIT PROJECT

Return to your unit project. Finalize your model so that it clearly shows how ocean crust is being destroyed at the particular subduction zone you chose. In your final presentation, explain how the model changed as you learned more and how you would continue to revise it if you had more time or different materials.

Remember these tips as you are finalizing your model and preparing to present it:

- Look at the model. Does it include all relevant landforms and processes? Is everything clearly labeled?

- Does it show processes that are related to subduction as well as subduction itself?

- How well does the model explain subduction? What does it not show?

- If you had more time and more materials, how would you improve the model?

Analyzing Evidence About the Atlantic

The Atlantic Ocean currently separates North and South America from Europe and Africa. Millions of years ago, however, these continents were part of one larger supercontinent and the Atlantic Ocean did not exist. When did the Atlantic start to open? There are several types of data that can be used to answer this question, including (1) the age of the seafloor, (2) the current velocity of the continents, and (3) the age of fossils or matching rock formations on either side of the Atlantic.

When scientists try to answer a question like, "When did the Atlantic Ocean begin to open?" they approach it in different ways with different types of data. If the results are consistent, scientists are more confident that their conclusions are valid.

Use each of the three types of data to determine when the Atlantic Ocean began to open in a particular place. Are the results consistent? If not, what could explain the differences?

FIGURE 6: North and South America are moving slowly away from Europe and Africa as the Atlantic Ocean grows wider.

With your team, plot each data point on a map of the Atlantic region. Use a different color or symbol for each type of data. Each member of the team should plot his or her own data.

1. PLAN THE INVESTIGATION

With your team, plan how to go about using each type of data to work out when the Atlantic began to open in a certain area.

- How can the age of the seafloor be used to estimate when the Atlantic began to open?

- How can you use current plate velocity to calculate when the Atlantic began to open? What equation can you use? What other information will you need? What assumption will you need to make?

- How can you use the age of a rock formation found on both sides of the Atlantic to estimate when the Atlantic began to open?

- Where will you find all of the information you need?

2. CONDUCT RESEARCH

On your own, choose a particular part of the Atlantic. Use library and Internet resources and the information in the text and images in this unit to find out the age of the oldest seafloor. Then calculate how long the continents have been moving apart. Finally, find out the age of a rock formation or a set of fossils that was separated as the Atlantic formed.

3. ANALYZE DATA

On your own, analyze your data. What does each type of data tell you about the minimum or maximum age of the seafloor in the area you studied?

4. DRAW CONCLUSIONS

Based on your results, when do you think the Atlantic started to open in the area you studied? Share your conclusions with your team. Are your conclusions consistent with those of others on your team? What might explain any differences?

5. COMMUNICATE

Post your team's map along with each of your conclusions about when the Atlantic opened. Your conclusion should include not only your claim, but also the evidence and reasoning that support your claim. Compare your data and conclusions to those of other groups. Are they consistent?

 CHECK YOUR WORK

Once you have completed this task, you should have the following:

- A map showing the locations on the seafloor and continents that the data you used come from
- The data you collected
- Inferences made from each type of data
- A full conclusion, supported by the data and by scientific reasoning
- Comparison of your conclusions with those of others, along with a possible explanation for any differences

Earth's Changing Surface

This striking geologic feature in northern Arizona is known as the Wave.

Image Credits: ©Katrina Brown/Fotolia

FIGURE 1: This landslide swept away dozens of houses near Rio de Janeiro, Brazil, in 2010.

Earth's surface is constantly changing. Some rapid changes such as landslides can alter landscapes in dramatic ways that may endanger lives and property. In contrast, other forces shape Earth's surface features gradually over long periods of time.

 Predict What are some of the forces that may have worked to produce a landform like the Wave?

DRIVING QUESTIONS

As you move through the unit, gather evidence to help you answer the following questions. In your Evidence Notebook, record what you already know about these topics and any questions you have about them.

1. What processes lead to the development of different landscape features, such as valleys, mountains, and plateaus?

2. What factors on Earth's surface affect how landscapes evolve?

3. How do Earth's internal processes affect features on Earth's surface?

UNIT PROJECT

Altering Landscapes

 Go online to download the Unit Project Worksheet to help plan your project.

How can you simulate how landforms are produced? How can you alter a landform? How do different types of sediment affect the types of landforms produced? During this activity you will develop a model based on evidence to describe how loss of groundcover can accentuate erosion in landscapes.

Surface Processes

Small, smooth holes in rock, called *tafoni*

CAN YOU EXPLAIN IT?

FIGURE 1: The Remarkable Rocks on Kangaroo Island, Australia

Sometimes rock can be seen in shapes that suggest growth. The Remarkable Rocks, shown in Figure 1, may even remind you of broken eggshells. These unusual shapes are found on top of a dome of solid granite. Recall from the rock cycle that granite is a type of igneous rock that forms slowly within Earth's crust. Think about other things you know about how rock forms. For example, think about the connections between pebbles, larger pieces of rock, and bedrock—the solid rock beneath the pebbles and other material.

 Gather Evidence
Record evidence about processes that shape rock at and near Earth's surface. As you explore the lesson, gather evidence to help you explain unusual formations, such as the Remarkable Rocks.

Predict Does rock "grow" from smaller pieces to larger pieces? If rock can grow, is this process usual?

Agents of Change

Earth's internal energy drives plate tectonics and some of the changes between igneous, sedimentary, and metamorphic rock. Internal energy heats and changes rock within the crust. It can melt rock into magma that may form new rock.

Earth's external energy comes mostly from sunlight. It drives weather, waves, most of the water cycle and similar cycles, most of the biosphere, and even some of the geosphere. Surface processes begin with external energy and affect the geosphere at or near Earth's solid surface, including the sea floor. They can be active for short distances underground, such as at the top of bedrock that is covered by sediment. Surface processes tend to break rock into particles of many sizes, or clasts, that may become sediment. They also move rock and change it in other ways.

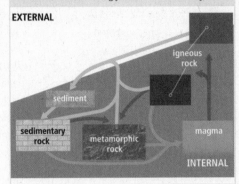

FIGURE 2: Energy from Earth's interior and external solar energy drive the rock cycle.

Gravity and Other Agents

Gravity causes rock to move downward and to compress, so it contributes to surface processes. Rock at or near Earth's surface also changes in response to wind, water, and variations of temperature and pressure. Organisms also change rock. These agents of change cause rock to break down and to move across Earth's surface.

FIGURE 3: Some surface processes and agents of change

a Gravity causes rock to break off, slide, and tumble downhill.

b Waves smash pebbles against each other and against solid rock.

c Wind hurls sand against rock and other grains of sand.

d Plants push roots into cracks and sometimes dissolve rock.

Daily and seasonal changes in temperature cause rock to expand and contract, which often causes cracks to form. Gravity can cause large or small particles to break away from the rock surface at cracks. The particles may abrade, or wear away, rock surfaces and other particles as they fall, slide, and tumble downhill. Plants can enlarge cracks as their roots grow into the cracks. Plants and other organisms can produce chemicals that dissolve rock. Water, especially when slightly acidic, also dissolves some rock. Water and wind can move particles, which can abrade solid rock. The moving particles also abrade each other. They get smaller and may become rounded.

Geologists often classify surface processes by three patterns. Weathering is the breakdown of rock into smaller pieces. Erosion is the removal and transport of material, such as sand and other particles. Deposition is the dropping of material, such as sediment. Rock is also deposited when it forms out of materials that were dissolved in water. Both types of deposits can become sedimentary rock.

Gather Evidence
List examples of how the geosphere interacts with Earth's other spheres through surface processes.

Image Credits: (l) ©Ammit/Fotolia; (cl) ©RandyAndy101/iStock/Getty Images Plus/Getty Images; (cr) ©David Parker/Science Source; (r) ©9photos/Fotolia

When scientists talk about rock or soil eroding, they usually mean transport away from a place. Sometimes, however, erosion is used as a quick way to refer to the breakdown, transport, and deposition of rock.

Cause and Effect

Gather Evidence
Preview the lesson by looking at the headings and the images. Decide on a way to keep your notes organized. Graphic organizers, such as charts and concept maps, may help you see different patterns in surface processes.

Sometimes surface processes are classified by their effects: weathering, erosion, and deposition. This classification is useful when several processes act together, such as when temperature changes and roots both crack rock. Sometimes surface processes are grouped by the agent of change, such as water. This classification is useful when one agent of change or cause produces many different features of a landscape. As a result of these different classifications, it can be a challenge to learn about surface processes. Think about how you might use one or both classifications to keep your notes organized. You might devise a way to note the agents of change, the effects, and the scales of space and time.

Surface processes result in some overall patterns. Rock that is exposed to air, and especially to changing weather, tends to break down more quickly than rock that is covered. Rock at the top of mountains and other high elevations is usually the most exposed, or least protected. Rivers and other water, wind, and gravity move rock from higher elevations to lower elevations such as valleys, plains, and the ocean floor. The particles tend to break down into smaller pieces as they are transported downhill and across Earth's surface. Particles are deposited and become sediment. The sediment often covers bedrock at low elevations and protects it from further weathering. The sediment may erode many times and be deposited at lower and lower elevations. When enough mass is deposited, the lower layers may be compressed and form sedimentary rock. Chemical deposition can also form rock or can glue sediments into rock.

Explain Why is so little of Earth's surface found far above sea level?

As you explore this unit, look for these patterns in the ways surface processes generally affect the geosphere. You will find some exceptions to the patterns.

Earth's Solid Surface

FIGURE 4: Surface processes move rock from high places to low places.

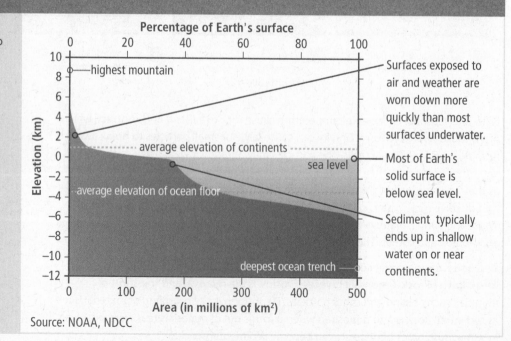

Source: NOAA, NDCC

FIGURE 5: Water breaks down and transports rock.

weathering

erosion

deposition

Scale and Rates

Surface processes work over different scales—a wide range of distance, area, or amount of time. They also work at different speeds—different rates. For example, rock can break off a cliff in tiny flakes or building-sized pieces. You can look at the unit of measure to get an idea of scale. The flakes might be measured in millimeters while large pieces of rock can be meters across. Mountains would be described on a scale of kilometers. Processes may take seconds, hours, years, or centuries.

Processes at very different scales may be related. For example, slow erosion at the base of a cliff may lead to a large collapse that takes place in a few seconds. More generally, small or slow effects can build up or trigger feedback that results in large or fast effects.

An agent of change can produce effects at different scales. The effects depend on the strength or amount of the agent and how long it acts. For example, a gentle rain may cause less erosion than a downpour (strength), but several days of gentle rain may cause more erosion than a brief downpour (quantity of water). Think about whether you would expect more erosion from water in a rain forest or a desert.

One agent of change can be more important than another in a particular situation. Wind and water both cause erosion in a rain forest and in a desert. Wind is usually more of a factor in a desert: The proportion, or relative amount, of wind erosion is greater than the amount of water erosion.

FIGURE 6: The effects of water depend in part on its quantity.

a **Rain forest** 2 000–10 000 mm of rain per year

b **Desert** About 250 mm of rain per year

Characterizing Scales

You can use different methods to describe scales such as size. You can use the unit that is closest to the size, such as millimeters or kilometers. You can use comparison objects, such as sand grains or houses, to identify the scale. You can use other terms that describe a scale, such as *local*, *regional*, and *global*. You might even use relative categories, such as labeling sizes from 1 to 5 or from tiny to gigantic. In a similar way, you can use scales that describe speed or amount of time—a faster process takes less time than a slower process. But to make comparisons, it helps to describe scales in a consistent way. As you take notes, choose a method that works well for you. You may need to understand your notes long after you write them.

 Scale, Proportion, and Quantity

Analyze Of the methods described, which will you use to describe scales of time and size? Can you find ways to use them consistently?

 Explain On what scales might erosion occur?

Weathering

Surface processes have been breaking down rock for more than 4 billion years. Weathering wears down mountains, develops sediment and minerals, and helps shape features of all scales. Weathering leads to soil, one of Earth's most valuable resources.

Mechanical Weathering

Mechanical weathering occurs through physical means such as abrasion or changes in temperature. Weathering often speeds up when rock is exposed at Earth's surface. However, weathering can also affect covered rock, such as when plant roots or water moves through sediment and breaks down the underlying bedrock.

Changing Pressure

Rock in Earth's crust is under pressure from material above the rock. Forces within Earth's crust can move rock upward and reduce the amount of material covering the rock. Pressure on the rock is reduced and the rock may expand. Higher parts of the rock are under less pressure and may expand more. The difference in expansion can cause cracks in the rock. Sheets of rock can peel away in a process called *exfoliation*.

Changing Weather

Temperature changes cause rock to expand and contract. When the changes are extreme and fast, such as the day-night changes in a desert, cracks may develop quickly. Temperature changes may also cause water to freeze and melt. Liquid water flows into cracks and other spaces in rock. Then the water freezes and expands, acting as a wedge that splits rock a tiny bit more with each cycle. This process of ice wedging causes potholes in roads as well as Earth's natural surface.

Rock can contain minerals, sometimes called *clay minerals*, that swell as they become wet and shrink as they dry. Cycles of wetting and drying of these minerals can have an effect similar to ice wedging. Wet/dry cycles can occur from temperature changes and other weather as water from air wets the minerals and then evaporates. This type of weathering is very common at shorelines, because waves and tides contribute to wet/dry cycles and because the rock is often sedimentary and contains clay minerals.

FIGURE 7: Broken sheets of rock, often curved, show exfoliation.

Explore Online ▶

Hands-On Lab

Weathering of Rock Materials Observe and measure the effects of weathering on rock samples.

Explain Use Figure 8 to explain how water and changing temperatures cause the weathering of rock.

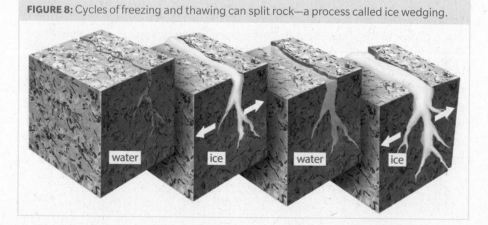

FIGURE 8: Cycles of freezing and thawing can split rock—a process called ice wedging.

water   ice   water   ice

Image Credits: ©C. Matthew Bonhamgregory/EyeEm/Getty Images

Moving Water, Air, and Ice

Wind, rain, hail, streams, and other moving water and air can break rock fragments from a surface. Water and wind can also break a surface of sediment, freeing the particles to move. The smaller particles may scrape and bump, abrading solid rock by causing scratches or pits. Abrasion on a small scale can leave a surface very smooth. Abrasion on a large scale can shape geological features on land and underwater. Particles also hit each other and break down further, often becoming smooth and rounded.

Abrasion can be a fast form of weathering when there are many particles, when particles move quickly, or when they scrape with great force. For example, waves can smash particles of sand hard against a rock surface, over and over again. Loose particles in a windy desert can carve rock into interesting shapes. Glaciers are large masses of moving ice that carry rock fragments of all sizes. Even though a glacier moves slowly, the many fragments scrape along a rock surface with great force.

Analyze Compare the ways air and water break down rock. How are they different?

FIGURE 9: Agents from Earth's other spheres break rock at different rates.

a Wind abrasion weathers rock quickly.

b Roots break rock slowly as they grow.

Organisms

Mechanical weathering also can be caused by living things. Rock can split as plant roots grow into cracks. A network of roots can break down particles further. The resulting sediment, including the material added by organisms, is called soil. Some animals dig tunnels through soil, which exposes new particle and rock surfaces to air and water that may flow through the tunnels. Animals may break the surface of a sediment and free particles to move.

Additional Agents of Change

Particles from space can also cause weathering. They usually hit a surface with great force and produce a pit, called a *crater*, much larger than the size of the particle. When the particle is large, the crater can be dramatic. Examples exist on Earth's surface as well as on most other solid surfaces in the solar system. Particles the size of dust or sand grains burn up in Earth's atmosphere but cause tiny craters on the moon and other airless places. Very tiny charged particles from the sun and electromagnetic radiation also hit and weather surfaces. The process is called *radiation weathering* and may produce a color change as well as a weakening of the surface material.

These types of weathering, along with temperature changes and gravity, shape many bodies in space. The processes are generally slower than weathering by air and water.

 Explain Many of the craters on Earth are difficult to find. How might weathering affect a large crater on Earth differently than a similar crater on the moon?

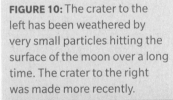
FIGURE 10: The crater to the left has been weathered by very small particles hitting the surface of the moon over a long time. The crater to the right was made more recently.

Chemical Weathering

Chemical weathering occurs through chemical reactions. The minerals that make up the rock may be affected differently. Chemical bonds, or connections, may be broken. Some minerals may become softer or break. Some minerals may be removed, leaving cracks or gaps in the rock. One mineral may change into another with different properties. Even when the new mineral is strong, the change can produce areas of weakness in the rock. For example, if the new mineral takes more space, the effect can be similar to a cycle of ice wedging.

Organisms break down soil as they remove nutrients. They add chemicals that weather particles of rock and even the bedrock below the soil.

FIGURE 12: Lichens produce an acid that dissolves minerals.

FIGURE 11: Chemical weathering breaks the bonds that hold particles together in rock.

Water and Acid

Many chemical reactions take place because of water. Water can react with minerals and can even become part of some minerals. Water dissolves some materials. As it moves, it brings these dissolved materials into contact with rock. Water within bedrock may move near magma and become heated. Heated water then moves faster. The extra energy also increases the rate of many chemical reactions.

Water can gain acids as it seeps through soil and rock. Acids react with minerals. The resulting new minerals are often weaker than the original minerals, so the affected rock may crumble. Acids also increase water's ability to dissolve many materials. For example, calcium carbonate is a mineral found in limestone. It often forms the cement between particles in rock. Water with even small amounts of acid can dissolve calcium carbonate. Over time, large amounts of rock can be removed from an area.

Plants called *mosses* and organisms called *lichens* (Figure 12) can grow on rock surfaces. These organisms produce acids that weather rock. Decaying organisms in soil can also produce acids.

The atmosphere contains carbon dioxide, sulfur dioxide, and nitrogen gases, which react with water in the atmosphere. The water falls as acid precipitation and hits many surfaces, such as the columns in Figure 13. When fossil fuels are burned, more of the gases are released. Acid precipitation and the rate of chemical weathering increase.

Oxygen and Air

About 20% of air is oxygen gas. Oxygen reacts with other substances and may combine with them in a process often called *oxidation*. Oxygen and iron produce rust, an orange-colored material. Rock that contains minerals rich in iron, such as hematite, break down as oxygen reacts with the iron to form new substances. This reaction is responsible for much of the red color observed in rock.

Gather Evidence
Compare the new and old columns in Figure 12. How fast can acid precipitation break down rocklike material?

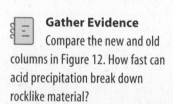

FIGURE 13: The column on the right shows weathering by acid precipitation since the 1800s.

Image Credits: (t) ©Monica Schroeder/Science Source; (b) ©Pavel Klimenko/Fotolia

Rates of Weathering

Many factors can affect the rate of weathering. You already know that different types of weathering act at different scales and rates. Particle size and surface, composition, and environment are also factors that affect the rate of weathering.

Surface Area and Particle Size

Most weathering acts on the exposed surface of rock. When the area of the surface is greater, the rate of weathering is greater. A rough surface has more area than a smooth surface, and so it may weather faster. It may also have more places for water to collect.

Weathering breaks rock into smaller pieces. Each break exposes new surface. For example, Figure 14 shows the surface area of a cube as if it were spread flat. As the cube is cut into smaller pieces, each cut adds two new surfaces to the total area. The total surface area of the smaller pieces is greater than the surface area of the solid cube, even though both have the same amount of material. The rate of weathering increases as rock breaks into smaller pieces. Some material dissolves, which reduces the amount of material, but the overall rate typically increases as rock weathers.

Analyze Does the change in surface area produce positive or negative feedback?

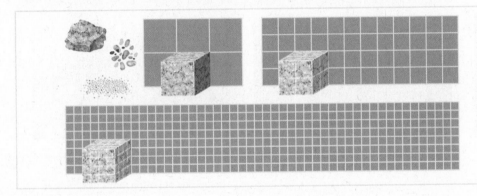

FIGURE 14: As rock breaks into smaller pieces, the amount of surface increases.

Composition

Some minerals weather more slowly than others. The rate may depend on the type of weathering. For example, rock that contains quartz (silicon dioxide), such as sandstone, resists weathering by water better than limestone. But in some conditions, limestone may weather more slowly than sandstone. A change in the color or texture of rock may indicate a change in the properties that affect weathering.

Environment

Different types of weathering may work together. Water affects many types of weathering, such as ice wedging. Places with a lot of moisture usually have high rates of weathering. Water also supports organisms, which can further increase weathering. However, some types of weathering are faster in dry areas. Wind is more likely to pick up particles that are dry. Temperature changes are usually more extreme in dry areas.

As rock weathers, the particles—sediment—may cover the rock surface. Sediment can act as a barrier that protects the rock surface from agents of weathering. But sediment can also help water reach the surface, so it may increase the rate of weathering.

FIGURE 15: Balancing rocks form more often than you might expect.

Explain How did the balancing rock in Figure 15 form? Provide evidence to support your claim.

Analyze Select one example of chemical or physical weathering. Describe how it is affected by temperature or moisture.

Transport of Material

Weathered particles are transported—eroded—by water, wind, ice, and gravity. The sediment is deposited and in layers and can become rock if it is not eroded away by the same processes that deposited it.

Downhill Motion

Gravity causes weathered rock fragments to move downhill. The process is called *mass wasting*. One large fragment of rock may fall suddenly, or many tiny particles may fall over a long period of time. The fragments move downward without being transported much across Earth's surface. They often leave behind a newly exposed surface.

FIGURE 16: Sediment moves downhill under the influence of gravity. Mass wasting and its effects have many special names.

a **Creep** occurs when rock particles move downhill slowly, producing bulges or wrinkles.

b **Landslides** occur when a large amount of material moves quickly.

c **Talus or Scree** is the collected rock fragments below a cliff. It can form quickly but often forms over time.

Collaborate With a partner, search online for *talus, scree, landslide, creep, slump, earthflow, mudflow,* and *lahar* to learn more about mass wasting and its effects.

Several factors can affect the speed of downhill motion. You can infer from Figure 16 that steep slopes result in faster downhill motion, while gentle slopes result in slower motion. Sediment that is saturated with water is heavier and moves downhill faster. The speed of downhill flow can also be affected by the cause of the motion, such as when a lot of motion is triggered by an earthquake.

Erosion and Deposition

FIGURE 17: Try to estimate the rock shape before erosion.

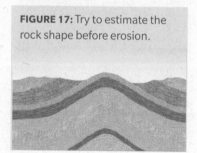

Weathered material erodes away from the location of the original rock. The original rock becomes smaller. Grooves and other features may develop. But over a long time, the peaks wear away and the rock erodes into a flatter and lower shape. The remaining shape may still have clues to its original form. The eroded material may be transported across Earth's surface by wind, liquid water, and ice. It may be deposited and eroded again many times but generally moves downhill and fills in low elevations.

Wind and flowing water move particles long distances. A faster flow allows larger, heavier particles to be transported. Small, light particles are carried easily and move with the water or wind. Larger or more dense particles are lifted and fall repeatedly, seeming to hop across the surface. The heaviest particles are dragged or rolled without being lifted very high. The particles may dig out pits or build up into piles, which can change the flow.

You can use stream tables and other models, including computer models, to study the effects of different agents, slopes, particle sizes, and other factors. Look for common patterns due to surface processes. Near a surface, wind or water speeds up and slows down as it moves over and around objects. It may move particles smoothly up a slope but then drop them after the peak. A small ripple or a large dune may wear away on one side and build up on the other, gradually moving in the direction of the flow. A ripple may also cause a change in the flow that produces another ripple downstream.

As water or wind slows down, it drops the heaviest particles first. Then it drops the medium and the lightest particles. As a result, particles of different materials or sizes may be deposited in different places, or sorted. Pebbles may become separated from smaller and smaller particles, which are called *sand*, *silt*, and *clay*.

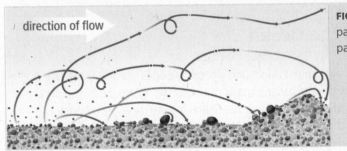

direction of flow

FIGURE 18: The size of particles affects their patterns of motion.

Analyze How might a large particle become a "seed" for a dune?

Glaciers can transport and mix together particles of all sizes, even very large boulders. Waves can transport particles back and forth, sorting them or mixing them up. The slower motion of tides can have a similar effect but over a larger distance. Currents in the ocean can transport material in ways similar to rivers on land.

Over thousands of years, sea level changes. When sea level falls, rock and sediment at the edges of continents and islands become exposed. The patterns of erosion and deposition in these locations are affected by such changes.

Sea Level Changes

FIGURE 19: Sea level changes over time, which changes the weathering and erosion patterns at the edges of continents.

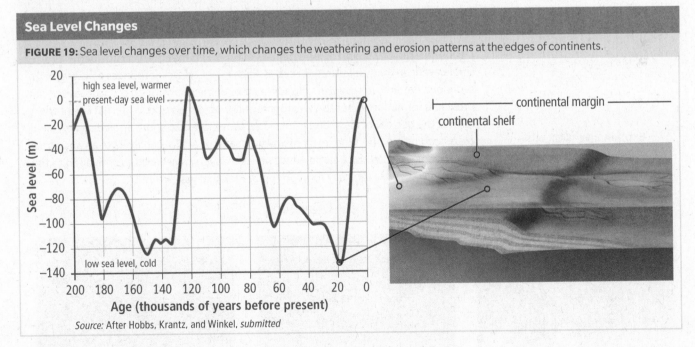

Source: After Hobbs, Krantz, and Winkel, *submitted*

Explain Why do humid regions tend to have less jagged topography than dry regions?

Sediment and Soil

FIGURE 20: Diatoms produce oozes on the ocean floor.

Recall that erosion can sort particles by size or composition. Weathering can sort particles as it breaks down different materials at different speeds. Quartz, a material that resists many types of weathering, is often the main or only rocky material remaining in a sediment. But materials from organisms can also become part of sediments. The same organisms that break down rock can produce waste material. The remains of organisms can also become part of a sediment.

Deposition in the Ocean

Much of the sediment from land is deposited along the edges of continents. Ocean water can carry the sediment to other parts of the ocean floor. Wind can also drop particles of rock or volcanic ash from land over water, where it can settle to the ocean floor. However, the rock of the ocean floor does not weather as quickly as rock exposed on land. Material from organisms has a larger effect. For example, corals can grow into very large structures on the ocean floor.

Explore Online ▶

Hands-On Lab 🧪

Soil Chemistry
Test and identify the composition of soil samples.

Microscopic organisms live in the surface water of the ocean. When they die, their remains settle on the ocean floor. Tiny shells build up thick layers over time. The shells can be composed of silicon dioxide (a glassy material, including quartz) or calcium carbonate (a material found in many larger, more familiar seashells). When sediment contains a large proportion of shells, it is called *ooze*.

Patterns of Sediment

Deposition can be steady for long periods of time. Sediment can also be deposited in a single event, in many events, or in cycles. Each event or cycle produces a new layer of sediment. Patterns in the layers of sediment, or in the rock formed of those layers, can provide information about the environment during deposition. Wide, flat layers often form at the bottom of large bodies of water. Wavy layers or short, angled layers called *cross-bedding* are often the result of flowing water or air. Larger layers at an angle may have been deposited on a slope. However, such layers may have become tilted as the rock moved. New layers may form on top of rock that was eroded.

 Explain How might each of the patterns in Figure 21 have formed?

FIGURE 21: Some patterns often seen in layers of sediment and sedimentary rock

a Flat layers with gradual or sharp changes

b Ripples or cross-bedding

c Layers tilted and partly removed

Development and Characteristics of Soil

Sediment that consists only of broken rock, such as that found on the moon, is called *regolith*. As plants and other organisms grow, they contribute material—organic matter. The enriched sand, silt, and clay develop into soil. Soil also contains water and air. It supports plants; animals, such as worms and ants; fungi; and microscopic organisms such as bacteria. The organisms contribute organic matter, which helps the soil support more organisms.

Layers of soil, called horizons, develop over time. Organisms are in the uppermost layer—the topsoil or A horizon. Organic matter is found mostly in this layer. Some organic matter, weathered particles, and other material wash downward into the rocky sediment. The result is the subsoil, or B horizon. The layer below contains only rocky sediment, the regolith or C horizon. At the bottom of the C horizon, bedrock continues to break down. Places with particular patterns of precipitation and temperature changes—climates—tend to develop soil of different thicknesses, as shown in Figure 22.

Collaborate Soil is full of nutrients that help support life. Sometimes nutrients can become contaminants. With a partner, discuss ways that a nutrient, which is helpful, could become a contaminant, which is harmful.

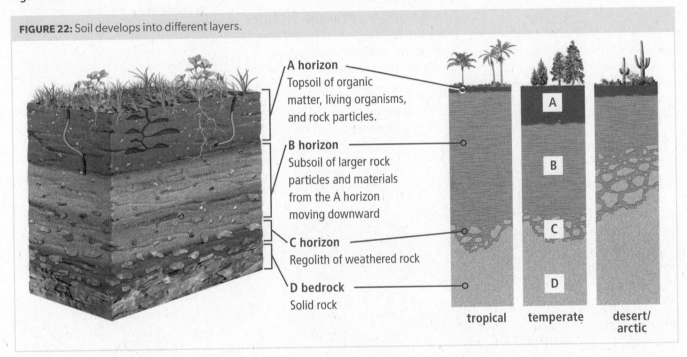

FIGURE 22: Soil develops into different layers.

A horizon
Topsoil of organic matter, living organisms, and rock particles.

B horizon
Subsoil of larger rock particles and materials from the A horizon moving downward

C horizon
Regolith of weathered rock

D bedrock
Solid rock

tropical   temperate   desert/arctic

Characteristics of Soil

Soil is a valuable resource for agriculture—the growing of organisms for food and other uses. It varies in characteristics and in the types of plants and other organisms it can support. Characteristics of soil include the size and composition of rock particles, the amount and types of organic matter, and the color and texture of soil. The amount of air space—the looseness or compactness of the soil—affects how organisms and water can move. If water moves too quickly through soil, it can wash away nutrients. The roots of plants can hold soil in place, increasing the stability of the soil.

Explain Horizon A is also called *topsoil*. Explain why topsoil is thicker in temperate areas than in tropical and desert areas.

Explain Think about how weathering, erosion, deposition, and soil are related. What processes might result in the loss of soil?

Careers in Science

Cartographer

People who make maps are called *cartographers*. They research, plan, draft, print, edit, and preserve maps. Cartographers find jobs with the government, private businesses, and universities.

Maps contain many different types of information and are used for many different purposes. For example, the map in Figure 23 shows regions in which water collects—watersheds—combined with the rate of deposition of sediments into the ocean. The combination of two or more types of information on a map can help people see patterns and relationships that

are hard to notice in other displays of information.

Cartographers design maps to communicate information effectively. They consider the area a map should depict, the map projection, the scale, and the possible ways to represent different types of information. For example, they might represent elevations as different colors. But if they want to use color to depict other data, they might use patterns of light and shadow to show mountains and plains.

Cartographers often use computers to organize information and produce maps. The data they put on the maps

may combine locations from the global positioning system (GPS) with other measurements. Data may also come from satellite images. The maps may be kept in a digital form so that different types of information can be displayed or hidden, and different amounts of area can be selected for display.

Language Arts Connection
Use Figure 23 to find a large area that produces little sediment and a smaller area that produces a lot of sediment. Use what you know about weathering and erosion to propose an explanation for the difference. Support your claim with evidence and reasoning.

FIGURE 23: A map can show two sets of information, such as the areas defined by the way water moves (watersheds) and the rates of deposition into the ocean.

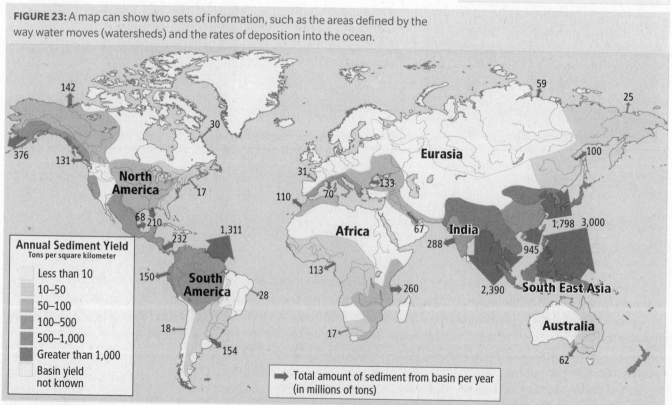

Annual Sediment Yield
Tons per square kilometer

- Less than 10
- 10–50
- 50–100
- 100–500
- 500–1,000
- Greater than 1,000
- Basin yield not known

➡ Total amount of sediment from basin per year (in millions of tons)

| DIATOMACEOUS EARTH | MODELING SURFACE PROCESSES | STUDYING TRANSPORT | Go online to choose one of these other three paths. |

Lesson Self-Check

CAN YOU EXPLAIN IT?

FIGURE 24: The Remarkable Rocks in Flinders Chase National Park, Australia

Analyze Refer to the notes in your Evidence Notebook to help you explain how the processes that shape rock at and near Earth's surface can lead to unusual formations.

Look again at these Remarkable Rocks in Flinders Chase National Park, Australia. Despite their appearance, you probably dismissed the idea that something hatched from a shell of rock. But a more reasonable explanation must exist.

You have learned about minerals, about the rock cycle, plate tectonics, and surface processes. When you see an unusual formation, such as a balancing stone or the Remarkable Rocks, put these ideas together. Think through a sequence of processes that might produce the formation you see.

To answer the questions below, consider a wide range of possibilities, but also think about the most common processes affecting the geosphere. Whether you argue for or against the idea of rock "growing," provide evidence to support your view. Include one or more examples of when someone might think of rock growing, and then explain what happens. Compare that explanation with the most common processes that produce large and small pieces of rock. You may wish to work with a partner to refine your claim, evidence, and reasoning.

Explain Does rock "grow" from smaller pieces to larger pieces? If it can grow, is this process usual?

CHECKPOINTS

Check Your Understanding

1. In what order (first to last) are particles of different sizes—such as clay, sand, and silt—deposited as water flows from the continental crust into the oceans? How are they deposited as wind blows over the top of a dune? Are the two patterns the same or different?

2. Suppose there is a hill behind your home that is starting to erode. Some of the soil from the near side of the hill has been transported and is beginning to build up near your back door. Which of these actions would reduce the erosion of the hill? *Select all that apply.*
   a. Add a layer of shredded bark to the eroding area.
   b. Add more soil to the hill in the eroding area.
   c. Build a wall between the hill and your door.
   d. Compact the side of the hill.
   e. Grow plants on the side of the hill.
   f. Use a leaf blower to remove lose material from the hill.

3. Dams are constructed across rivers. They block most of the water, which backs up and forms a lake. Most of the time, a small amount of water flows over or through the dam. How would the construction of a dam change the rate of weathering and erosion? *Select all that apply.*
   a. The lake formed by the dam increases the rate at which rock is dissolved because more rock is covered by water.
   b. The lake reduces the rates of weathering by wind and by changing air temperature where its water covers rock.
   c. The calmer water of the lake decreases erosion and increases deposition.
   d. The calmer water of the lake increases erosion and decreases deposition.

4. Suppose that you find shallow soil that appears to have no horizons. You consider the possibilities below. Which can you rule out? If two or more remain, what information might help you determine what had happened?
   a. The soil has been acted upon by rainfall. Material was washed downward, eliminating the differences between horizons.
   b. The upper layers of soil have been eroded by a dust storm.
   c. Small particles have formed from the rock below, but the sediment has not yet developed into soil.
   d. The soil was affected by an earthquake, so the horizons sank into the ground.

5. Suppose you find a boulder in a dry streambed. You want to know which way the water will flow after a storm. To the left of the boulder is a mound of sediment. To the right of the boulder is exposed bedrock. What can you infer about the direction of flow?

6. Suppose you see a rock cliff that is made of many different minerals, light and dark. A beach below the cliff has only light-colored quartz sand. How might the beach have formed from the rock of the cliff?

7. Compare the temperature and precipitation in Miami, Florida, and Great Basin National Park, Nevada.

Place	Annual High Temp (°F)	Average Annual Precipitation (in)
Miami, Florida	84.2	61.93
Great Basin National Park, Nevada	58.8	13.59

Which place most likely has deeper soil?

 In your Evidence Notebook, design a study guide that supports the main ideas from this lesson:
- Sunlight and gravity drive surface processes—weathering, erosion, and deposition—which act at different scales of time and space.
- Physical and chemical weathering break rock down into smaller particles, which become sediment.
- Sediment is transported downhill—eroded from higher elevations and deposited at lower elevations.

Remember to include the following in your study guide:
- Support main ideas with details and examples.
- Apply any observations from using stream tables to support explanations for phenomena.
- Consider how the significance of a phenomenon is dependent on the scale, proportion, and quantity at which it occurs.

Earth's Surface

Delicate Arch at Arches National Park near Moab, Utah, is a 20-m tall sandstone arch.

CAN YOU EXPLAIN IT?

FIGURE 1: A meander in the Colorado River produced a dramatic landform called Horseshoe Bend.

Gather Evidence
As you explore the lesson, gather evidence about different processes that change Earth's landscape.

Explore the different forces that transform our planet's landscape. For example, moving water can exert a very powerful force. It is responsible for altering Earth's landscape and can produce beautiful landforms and dramatic vistas.

Horseshoe Bend is a meander in the Colorado River located in north-central Arizona. This curve began to form millions of years ago at a time when the river flowed over a flat sandstone plateau. The Colorado River slowly moved back and forth in a winding pattern, eroding the sedimentary rock beneath it. This carving of rock by moving water became more rapid when, around 5 million years ago, gradual uplift occurred along the Colorado Plateau. Instead of continuing to wind across the sandstone plateau, the river began to cut rapidly downward into the underlying sandstone. Over time, the banks of the river grew steeper and steeper. The river became trapped in its bed, and the horseshoe-shaped bend seen in Figure 1 formed.

 Predict What forces might be responsible for carving the deep meander in the Colorado River that produced Horseshoe Bend?

Features Shaped by Flowing Water

Moving water exerts a powerful force that carves new features into landscapes. Flowing water in river systems, as well as in other natural settings, weathers and erodes rocks and transports and deposits sediment.

Drainage Basins

A drainage basin is an area of land where surface water, rain, and snowmelt flow from higher elevations to a single body of water at a lower elevation. The drainage basin acts like a funnel, collecting water within an area and channeling it to a collection point, such as a river, lake, wetland, or ocean. Factors that affect the type of drainage found in an area include regional topography, or shape of the land; the underlying soil and rock; and the speed of the water flowing over the land surface.

Explain Why is it important to understand the formation of the drainage basins that flow into the Colorado River basin?

FIGURE 2: The Colorado River basin is divided into two drainage basins, the upper basin and the lower basin, as shown in the map.

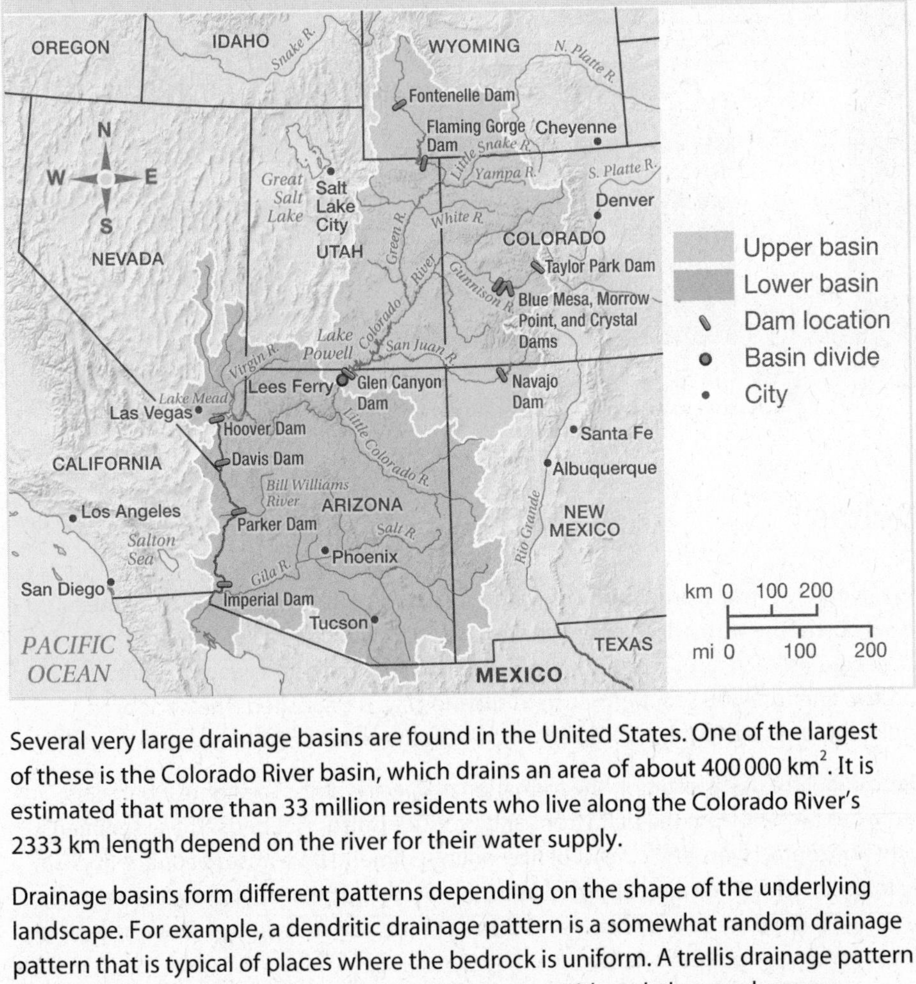

Several very large drainage basins are found in the United States. One of the largest of these is the Colorado River basin, which drains an area of about 400 000 km². It is estimated that more than 33 million residents who live along the Colorado River's 2333 km length depend on the river for their water supply.

Drainage basins form different patterns depending on the shape of the underlying landscape. For example, a dendritic drainage pattern is a somewhat random drainage pattern that is typical of places where the bedrock is uniform. A trellis drainage pattern forms where rock resistant to weathering alternates with rock that erodes more rapidly. A rectangular drainage pattern forms when small streams flow along faults or joints at right angles.

Analyze How does topography affect the type of drainage basin found in a region?

Channel Patterns

As a river flows over gently sloping land, it does not have the energy needed to cut deeply into the underlying rocks. Instead, the water in rivers flows back and forth across the landscape, producing an S-shaped pattern. This shape is produced by the way water flows in the stream. As a result of a kind of flow set up by the stream, sediment is swept toward the inside of a bend in the stream and is deposited. It is eroded from the outside of the bend. Over time, the build-up of sediment on the inside of the stream along with the removal from the outside results in a greater and greater curvature. Along the inner curve, sediment is deposited and produces features such as sandbars. As erosion and deposition occur over time, the shape of the river changes, from straight, to a little curve, to having wide, swooping curves.

 Explain How do meanders in a river form?

FIGURE 3: A meandering stream forms as the slope of the land decreases. Water flowing through the inner river channel deposits clay, silt, and sand in sandbars, while water erodes the outer side of the river channel. The difference in erosion and deposition eventually causes the river channel to produce a pronounced S shape.

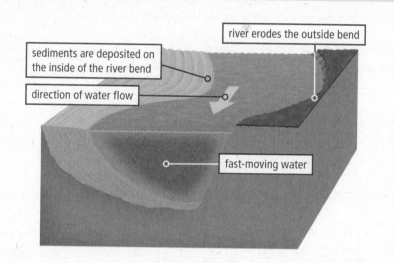

sediments are deposited on the inside of the river bend

direction of water flow

river erodes the outside bend

fast-moving water

a A meandering stream

b A cross section of a meandering stream

Deltas

As a river flows into a larger body of water, such as an estuary or ocean, the water slows down. The water does not have enough energy to carry all of the sediment. Larger grains, such as gravel and sand, are deposited first. As the water continues to slow, finer-grained sediment, such as silt and clay, is deposited. The deposited sediment forms a roughly triangular structure at the mouth of the river called a delta.

Deposition in a delta results in the formation of specific beds. The lightest particles settle out farthest from the delta front and produce bottomset beds. These sediments form horizontal layers and consist of fine-grain sediment. Bottomset beds are overlain by foreset beds, which are deposited as inclined layers. The overlying topset beds are once again deposited horizontally and consist of the coarse sediment that forms along the advancing edge of the delta.

If a river channel changes position over time, the delta will change shape as a result. Sandbars form in the middle of a stream channel, and water is routed around a bar. When this happens, a fan-shaped delta is formed.

FIGURE 4: A satellite view of the Mississippi River delta

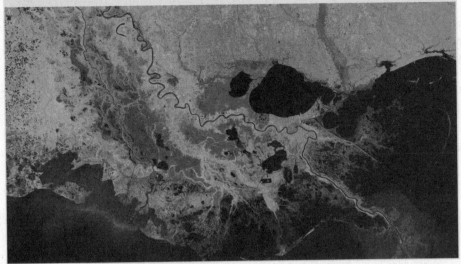

Explain How does a knowledge of modern delta formation help one understand the ancient flow patterns of a river?

The largest river delta on the planet is the Ganges-Brahmaputra delta, which lies on the border between India and Bangladesh and empties into the Bay of Bengal. The triangle-shaped delta covers an area of slightly more than 105 000 km^2. The Mississippi River delta is the largest river delta in North America. It covers an area of about 33 000 km^2 south of New Orleans, where the river empties into the Gulf of Mexico. The current delta of the Mississippi River has been forming over the past 7000 to 8000 years. However, every 1000 to 2000 years during this time period, the river's path to the Gulf of Mexico changed. This happens when so much sediment accumulates that the river's route to the Gulf becomes longer and it cuts a shorter path.

Alluvial Fans

When a stream descends a steep slope and reaches a flat plain, the speed of the stream suddenly decreases. As a result, the stream deposits some of the sediment on the level plain at the base of the slope. A fan-shaped deposit called an *alluvial fan* forms on the land, and its tip points upstream. In arid and semi-arid regions, temporary streams that form during a wet season commonly deposit alluvial fans.

Analyze How is an alluvial fan like a delta?

FIGURE 5: Alluvial fan As water flows down a steep slope and reaches a flat plain, it slows, depositing sediment that forms a fan-shaped deposit.

Caves, Caverns, and Sinkholes

Some landscape features form as rock is dissolved. Limestone, gypsum, and rock salt are all types of rock that can be easily eroded when water dissolves them. Even when a limestone layer is not porous, vertical and horizontal cracks commonly cut through limestone layers. As groundwater flows through these cracks, carbonic acid, which forms when carbon dioxide in the air combines with rainwater, slowly dissolves the limestone and enlarges the cracks. Eventually, a cave or cavern may form.

FIGURE 6: A cave is a feature that forms when water dissolves limestone, forming voids in the rock.

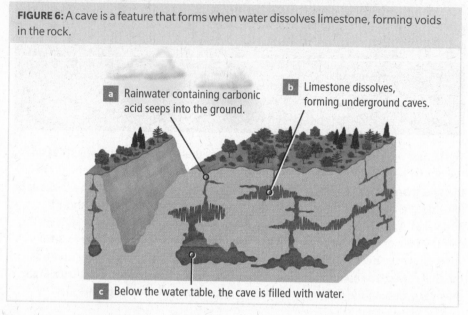

a Rainwater containing carbonic acid seeps into the ground.

b Limestone dissolves, forming underground caves.

c Below the water table, the cave is filled with water.

 Explain How do caves form?

Many caves are open spaces in rock that form as limestone dissolves. A network of rooms form in the cave as groundwater dissolves rock along joints and faults. A cavern is a large cave that may consist of many smaller connecting chambers. Within these chambers, a variety of interesting and often beautiful mineral deposits form. Two of the most common mineral deposits found in caves are stalactites and stalagmites. Water seeping through the rock into a cave slowly drips from the cave ceiling, forming stalactites that extend downward from the cave roof toward the floor. The water flows down the stalactite and drips onto the cave floor, forming stalagmites that grow upward toward the ceiling.

Approximately 17 000 caves have been reported in the United States. The largest cave system in the country—and in the world—is Mammoth Cave in south-central Kentucky, the chambers of which extend almost 460 km through the subsurface.

Another feature that may form as a result of water dissolving rock is a sinkhole. A sinkhole is a circular depression that forms at the land surface when the rock beneath collapses. One type of sinkhole, known as a collapse sinkhole, may form during dry periods when the water table is low and caves are not completely filled with water. Because there is no water to support the roof of the cave, the roof may collapse. Collapse sinkholes may develop suddenly and cause extensive damage at the surface, including damage to homes, buildings, and automobiles, and even lead to loss of life. In the United States, sinkholes are common in Texas, Alabama, Missouri, Kentucky, Tennessee, and Pennsylvania, and especially common in Florida.

Explain How can an erosional feature lead to a depositional feature?

Features Shaped by Waves

The coastline marks the transition from land to ocean. This area is in a constant state of change. Rivers that drain inland water transport sediment from rocks farther upstream down to the coast. Waves lap and crash on the shore and, as they do so, move sediment up and down beaches. Currents erode and deposit sediment along the coastline. As a result of these processes, the region is marked by many unique erosional and depositional landforms that are constantly changing.

Beaches

A beach is a narrow strip of sediment that separates ocean from dry land. Most commonly, beaches are composed of loose sediment that originates from rocks on land and shell fragments from organisms living in shallow water. Sand on the beach collects around objects such as vegetation or rocks or flat, moist areas, forming small hills called *dunes*. Dunes vary in size and location along a beach.

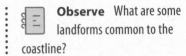

Observe What are some landforms common to the coastline?

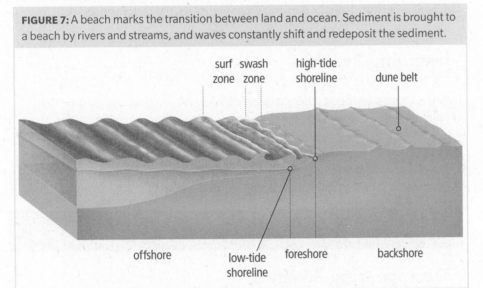

FIGURE 7: A beach marks the transition between land and ocean. Sediment is brought to a beach by rivers and streams, and waves constantly shift and redeposit the sediment.

Beaches can be divided into different zones: offshore, foreshore, and backshore. The offshore is the area close to dry land but, even at low tide, is always underwater. The foreshore, also called the intertidal zone, is the zone that is above water at low tide and below water at high tide. The backshore zone is the generally dry zone that lies behind the foreshore. The backshore is only submerged during storms or very high tides.

Moving Beach Sand

Waves break on a beach at an angle. The water flows back into the ocean perpendicular to the shoreline under the pull of gravity. The resulting movement of water produces a zigzag motion along the shoreline. This motion of water along the shoreline is called the longshore current. The longshore current is responsible for moving sediment along the beach in one direction.

Analyze How does sand move along a beach?

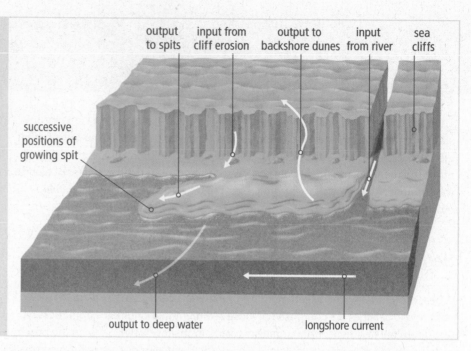

FIGURE 8: The sand on a beach is constantly in motion. The sand is transported to the beach by rivers. Waves move the sediment back and forth up and down the beach.

output to spits input from cliff erosion output to backshore dunes input from river sea cliffs

successive positions of growing spit

output to deep water longshore current

If sediment input to the beach from rivers is greater that the output carried away by the longshore current, the beach will grow. If the longshore current carries more sediment away from a beach than is replaced by rivers, the beach will shrink.

Preserving Beaches

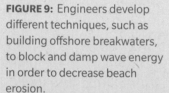

Explain What techniques have engineers developed to prevent the movement of sediment along a beach?

Engineers have developed different techniques to stabilize beaches and limit the amount of sediment moved by the longshore current. A seawall is designed to break incoming waves and reduce the velocity of water that is approaching the shore. A jetty is a pair of parallel breakwaters that are built perpendicular from the shoreline along either side of a navigable waterway. Jetties are built to stop the waterway from filling with sand that is being transported by the longshore current.

Stability and Change

Disappearing Beaches

FIGURE 9: Engineers develop different techniques, such as building offshore breakwaters, to block and damp wave energy in order to decrease beach erosion.

In an effort to protect property and lives, authorities have spent millions of dollars attempting to save beaches from erosion. Some of these measures have involved the construction of seawalls. Seawalls temporarily stop storm waves from reaching homes but do not save beaches. In fact, the findings suggest that seawalls may actually speed erosion. Waves crashing against a seawall carry away more sand than they would if they spent their energy gently rolling onto a beach. Some towns have built jetties, structures in the sea that trap sand carried by longshore currents. However, jetties often trap the sand needed at other beaches farther down the coast, causing those beaches to erode more swiftly. Recent "beach nourishment" efforts, in which offshore sand is dredged up and redeposited on a beach, have been somewhat successful. A drawback of beach nourishment is that eventually the sand washes back out to sea. For this reason, nourishment, which is costly, must be ongoing.

Erosional Coastal Landforms

A number of different types of landforms can result from erosion of rock by ocean waves. For example, when waves strike rocks along a coastline, the waves slowly erode the base of the rock. As the waves erode the base of the rock, an overhang is produced. When this overhanging rock collapses, a steep sea cliff forms. The rate at which sea cliffs erode depends on the amount of wave energy and on the resistance of the rock along the shoreline to erosion. Resistant rocks that project out from the shore are called headlands. When waves cut completely through a headland, a sea arch forms. Offshore columns of rock that were once connected to a sea cliff or headland are called sea stacks. A wave-cut terrace forms when a sea cliff is worn, producing a nearly level platform. It usually remains beneath the water at the base of the cliff.

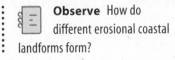

Observe How do different erosional coastal landforms form?

FIGURE 10: Different erosional landforms can form along a rocky shoreline because of erosion of less resistant sedimentary rock, such as shale, by wave action.

sea arch

sea cave

sea stack

Depositional Coastal Landforms

In addition to erosional features, the movement of sediment along the coastline by a longshore current produces a variety of depositional features. In fact, some shorelines may be dominated by depositional features.

Sediment carried by a longshore current cannot follow a shoreline that curves more than 30 degrees. Instead, the sediments continue to be deposited as a straight extension from the shoreline. This process produces features such as a sand spit. A sand spit is a beach landform composed of sediment with one end attached to the shoreline and the opposite end terminating in open water, where deposition occurs. Sand spits often form at the entrances to bays. Over time, a sand spit may extend across an open body of water, such as a bay, to the adjacent shoreline, producing a feature called a bay mouth bar. Bay mouth bars may dam up most of the water in a bay, leaving only a channel for water to flow into and out of a bay. A narrow piece of land that extends perpendicular to the shoreline and connects a barrier island or sand spit with the mainland is called a tombolo. Tombolos occasionally form parallel to the shoreline.

FIGURE 11: The movement of sand along a coastline by a longshore current can produce many depositional features, such as sand spits, sand bars, barrier islands, and tombolos.

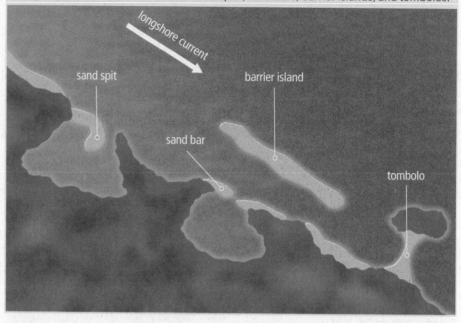

Most barrier islands in North America are located along the Atlantic seaboard and the Gulf of Mexico. Because of their location, barrier islands help protect the mainland from erosion caused by wind and ocean waves, especially large waves that are produced by tropical storms and hurricanes. Barrier islands are also coastal habitats for both plants and animals. But barrier islands are constantly being reshaped, and they are under increasing threat from rising global sea level. This makes building on barrier islands potentially dangerous.

Stability and Change

FIGURE 12: Green Island

Coral Reef Islands

The Great Barrier Reef is located in the Coral Sea off of the northeastern coast of Australia. It is the world's largest coral reef system, covering an area of 344 400 km² and is composed of more than 2900 individual reefs and 900 islands. Many of these islands are made up of the remains of reef organisms. Though these islands are young in terms of geologic time, their sediment provides important evidence of the organisms that have inhabited the reef and the processes of cementation and rock formation that provide island stability. In addition, they record the history of major environmental events, including cyclones and delivery of sediment to the island.

Analyze Describe the major erosional and depositional features that are produced along a coastline and how they form. What determines whether a part of a coastline will have mostly erosional and depositional features?

Features Shaped by Ice

Today, about 10 percent of Earth's land surface is covered by ice. In the recent past, much more of the land surface was encased in ice. Ice has a powerful effect on Earth's surface. It can erode rock more efficiently than liquid water or wind can. Large areas of ice on land are called glaciers. In areas of Earth's surface where they have been present, glaciers have altered Earth's landforms by both the processes of erosion and deposition.

Glaciers and Glacial Flow

An ice sheet, also known as a continental glacier, is a massive sheet of ice that covers the land surface. Today, two ice sheets are found on Earth—one covers much of the land surface in Greenland, and the other covers Antarctica. The Greenland ice sheet covers 1.7 million km² of land and has a maximum thickness of more than 3000 m. The larger Antarctic ice sheet covers an area of more than 13 million km² and in some places is more than 4000 m thick. Ice that flows off land and into the ocean forms ice shelves. Ice shelves are found only in Antarctica, Greenland, and Canada. An ice shelf loses mass when sections calve, or break off, and fall into the ocean, forming icebergs. An icecap is smaller than an ice sheet—less than 50 000 km². Ice caps are found at high elevations on mountains and flow downhill in all directions.

A glacier can be divided into two parts. The upper part of a glacier is called the accumulation zone. In the accumulation zone, more snow falls than melts. The lower part of a glacier is called the ablation zone, where more snow melts than falls. A glacier in a state of equilibrium will not change in steepness or size, because the gain of ice in the accumulation zone and the loss of ice in the ablation zone are precisely balanced.

FIGURE 13: The Greater Aletsch Glacier, the largest glacier in the Alps, has a length of about 23 km.

Explain What is the difference between an icecap and an ice sheet?

FIGURE 14: Glaciers move most rapidly at their surface and at their center.

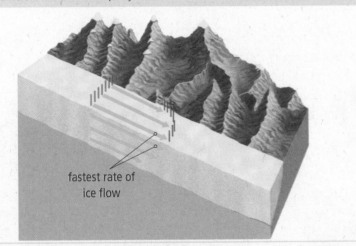

fastest rate of ice flow

Two processes cause glaciers to move. A glacier can slip over a thin layer of water and sediment that lies between the ice and the ground. This process reduces friction at a glacier's base, causing the glacier to slide forward. In the interior of a glacier, ice grains change shape under the pressure of overlying snow and ice. The change in shape of ice grains causes them to slip past each other, producing forward movement.

Image Credits: ©Paolo Koch/Science Source

Slipping Ice

MATERIALS

· snow or shaved ice

· tray

· weight, heavy

PROCEDURE

1. Squeeze a handful of snow or shaved ice flat until you notice a change in the particles.

2. Place the squeezed ice on a tray. Place a heavy weight on the squeezed ice.

3. Lift one end of the tray to a 30° incline, and record your observations.

ANALYSIS

1. What is the effect of squeezing the particles of snow or ice?

2. How is squeezing the snow or ice similar to the formation of a glacier?

3. What did you observe when you placed the squeezed ice on the tray? Which glacial movement process is modeled here?

Erosional Glacial Landforms

Predict What are some erosional landforms formed by glacial ice?

A narrow, wedge-shaped mass of ice that forms in a mountainous area and is confined by a steep-walled valley is a valley glacier. Valley glaciers produce unique landforms by erosive processes. As a valley glacier moves down a mountain, it typically moves through a V-shaped river valley. As it does, the rock from the valley wall breaks off, and blocks of rock are pulled from the valley floor. This changes the cross section of the valley into a U shape. Small glaciers in adjacent valleys may flow into the main valley glacier. When the ice melts, the adjacent valleys, called h*anging valleys,* are suspended above the main valley floor. A bowl-shaped depression eroded into the head or side of a valley glacier is called a *cirque*. Between cirques, a narrow, jagged ridge—an arête— forms. When several arêtes join, they form a sharp, pyramid-like peak called a *horn*.

FIGURE 15: A valley glacier can produce many erosional features, such as a horn, arête, cirque, and U-shaped valley.

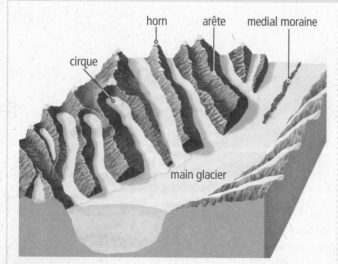

a When glaciers erode mountainous regions, characteristic landforms develop.

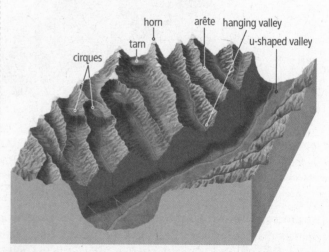

b These landforms can be identified after the glaciers retreat.

Deposition by Glaciers

As a glacier moves across the landscape, the ice plucks rock debris from the valley walls and floor. Unlike wind or liquid water, ice can carry sediment grains of different sizes. The sediment ranges in size from clay (very fine particles) to boulders. Over time, this material will work its way toward the lower part of the glacier, where melting exceeds the addition of new ice. When the ice melts, the sediments flow from the base of the glacier in melt-water streams called *outwash*. As the water in the outwash slows, the sediments in the water are deposited in a large mass of poorly sorted sediments called *drift*. Sediment deposited directly from melting ice is called *till*.

Observe How are sediments carried from the lower part of a glacier to their sites of deposition?

FIGURE 16: A creek flows out of the terminal moraine of this glacier in the Swiss Alps.

Ice can carry large boulders hundreds of kilometers from their place of origin. When the ice melts, the rock is left in an area in which it is different from the surrounding rock. These unusual rocks that do not fit in with the landscape are called *erratics*. Glacial erratics can be very large, sometimes greater than 1 km² in area. Erratics are important because they provide evidence for the direction of flow of a prehistoric glacier.

Landforms that result when a glacier deposits till are called *moraines*. Moraines are ridges of unsorted sediment on the ground or on the glacier itself. There are several types of moraines. A lateral moraine is a ridge of sediment that is located on a glacier's surface adjacent to the valley walls. It extends down to the leading edge of the glacier. A lateral moraine forms by the accumulation of rock material that falls onto the glacier from the valley wall. Medial moraines are ridges of sediment that form when two glaciers merge and the adjacent lateral moraines combine. Terminal, or end, moraines are small ridges of till that are deposited at the leading edge of a melting glacier. These moraines have many depressions in which water may be contained in lakes and ponds.

FIGURE 17: Glacial ice can move large boulders, called *erratics*.

Explain How do lateral, medial, and terminal moraines form?

FIGURE 18: Glaciers form moraines—deposits that consist of poorly sorted sediment.

lateral moraines

medial moraines

end moraines

outwash

Explain Describe how the following glacial depositional features form: eskers, kames, and kettles.

FIGURE 19: Glacial depositional features include eskers, kames, and kettles.

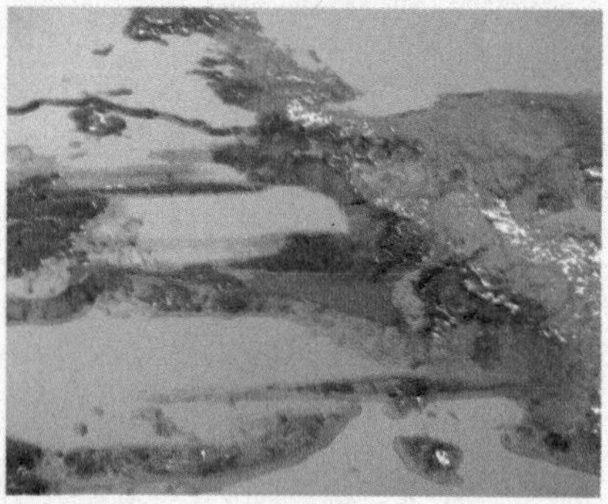

a Eskers and kames

b Kettles

Not all glacial deposits are poorly sorted. Streams that flow over the leading edge of a glacier often deposit sediment in their channels. This sediment is sorted, or deposited, into layers similar to the way that sediment is deposited in rivers.

Long, winding, steep-sided ridges of gravel and sand that are left behind when a glacier melts are called *eskers*. These landforms are thought to have been formed by streams that flowed through ice-walled tunnels within and under glaciers.

Kames are rounded mounds or hills of sand and gravel that are deposited along the front of a slowly melting or stationary glacier. Kames are thought to form when depressions on the surface of a melting glacier filled with sediment and then gradually sank to lower levels as the ice melted, forming a mound on the ground surface.

An outwash plain is a wide, flat region of sediment deposited by water that flows from the base of a melting glacier. Most outwash plains are pitted with depressions called *kettles*. Kettles form when a large block of ice is buried in sediment, or drift. As the ice melts, a cavity forms in the drift. The drift collapses into the cavity. This produces a depression that often fills with water to form a kettle lake.

 Observe What are some erosional and depositional features produced by glaciers?

Features Shaped by Wind

Like water, wind can pick up and move sediment. And just like water, wind can produce a variety of erosional and depositional landforms.

Wind as an Agent of Weathering and Erosion

Erosion by wind is most effective in areas where a large supply of loose sediment is available and there is little plant life and/or soil. Except under unusual circumstances, wind is seldom strong enough to transport particles larger than sand-sized grains.

Like water, wind is capable of eroding, transporting, and depositing sediments based on changes in wind energy. Wind transports sediment by two main processes— suspension and saltation. Suspension occurs when fine particles of sand and dust are lifted and carried away by a light wind. All that is required to put these particles in motion is a wind speed of about 16 km/h (10 mi/h). Saltation is a process by which larger sand grains are picked up by the wind and repeatedly bounced across the land surface. Saltating grains reach heights of less than 5 cm and move horizontally around 5 to 10 cm during each bounce, or saltation.

 Observe How does wind sculpt the landscape?

FIGURE 20: Desert landforms produced by wind abrasion include (a) ventifacts, such as this one found in Death Valley, California, and (b) yardangs, such as these found in the Gobi Desert, China.

a Ventifact

b Yardang

Wind not only moves fine-grained sediments, but it can also smooth other features by abrasion. Abrasion is the wearing away of rock surfaces through the mechanical action of other rock or sand particles. Ventifacts are rocks that have been pitted, grooved, or polished by the abrasive action of wind. Ventifacts are useful in determining the direction of the prevailing wind in areas where they are found.

Yardangs are another desert landform that are formed by abrasion. Yardangs form parallel to desert winds and have a tall, steep side that faces the prevailing wind and then slopes gently downward. Yardangs can be up to tens of meters high and kilometers long.

Monument Valley

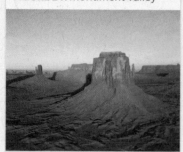

FIGURE 21: Monument Valley

Monument Valley is a tribal park located on the Navajo Indian Reservation along the Arizona-Utah border. The striking features in Monument Valley formed from the slow erosional processes of water and wind. The area was once covered by several thousand feet of sedimentary rocks. These rocks were regionally uplifted and have been eroded by water and wind up to the present day. The landforms in Monument Valley—mesas and buttes—have steep-sided erosional cliffs that are capped by resistant rock that erodes more slowly.

Wind as a Depositional Agent

Explain How does wind affect the shape of different dunes?

A feature in which sand or other loose sediment is deposited in mounds or ridges is called a *dune*. Dunes form most commonly in areas where there is an abundant supply of sand, wind speeds are high enough to move sand grains, little plant life exists, and places exist for sand grains to accumulate. Desert and coastal environments most often fulfill these conditions.

FIGURE 22: Dunes are depositional features. The shape of the dune depends on the direction of the prevailing wind and local topography.

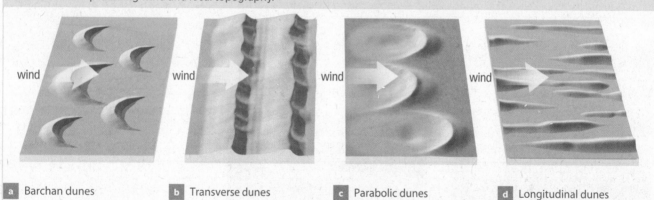

a Barchan dunes **b** Transverse dunes **c** Parabolic dunes **d** Longitudinal dunes

Dunes form when the wind blows sand grains behind an obstacle and the sand grains begin to pile up. The wind causes sand to pile up in dunes when sand grains are moved upslope by the wind to the top, or crest, of the dune. Once sand grains reach the crest of the dune, they then fall or slip down the face of the dune. When the angle of the sand at the crest of the dune becomes too steep, the dune will collapse. This repeating cycle of sand grains being moved to the crest of the dune and then slipping down the face causes dunes to migrate in the direction of the wind.

Modeling Desert Winds

PROCEDURE

1. Spread a mixture of dust, sand, and gravel on a table placed outdoors.

2. Set up an electric fan at one end of the table.

3. Wear safety goggles and a filter mask. Aim the fan across the sediment on the table. Start the fan on the lowest speed. Record your observations.

4. Increase the fan speed to medium, and record your observations. Then turn the fan to its highest speed to imitate a desert windstorm. Record your observations.

MATERIALS
- dust
- fan, electric
- mask, filter
- gravel
- sand

ANALYSIS

1. In what direction did the sediment move?

2. What was the relationship between the wind speed and the sediment size that was moved?

3. How did the sand move in this activity? How do your observations relate to dune migration?

4. Using the same materials, how would you model dune migration? How would you model the formation of different types of dunes?

Desert Landforms Formed by Wind and Water

A large flat area of land that is higher than other areas of land that surround it is called a plateau. Plateaus generally have one or more sides with steep slopes and little vegetation. The Colorado Plateau is the largest plateau in the southwestern desert, covering an area of 337 000 km^2 at an average elevation of 2450 m above sea level.

A mesa is a table-like landform with steep-sided cliffs that is smaller than a plateau. A mesa begins as a flat-topped plain. Rivers and streams then wear away the surrounding landscape, leaving a flat-topped mountain, or mesa. Differences in the ability of rock to resist weathering and erosion cause the weaker rocks at lower elevations to erode away. More resistant rocks cap the top of mesas. The largest mesa in the world is Grand Mesa, located in Colorado. It has an area of about 1300 km^2.

Mesas can be eroded to form buttes. A butte is a small, isolated hill with steep vertical sides and a small flat top. As a general rule, mesas are wider than tall, whereas buttes are taller than wide. Just like mesas, buttes are typically capped by resistant rock that erodes slowly.

 Predict How do wind and water produce mesas and buttes?

 Explain Describe the erosional and depositional features formed by wind. Explain how they form. Describe what might be the best conditions for each to form.

Guided Research

The Channeled Scablands

The eastern portion of Oregon and Washington in the Pacific Northwest of the United States is a landscape unlike most other places on Earth. The region is relatively barren, lacking even soil. But this region is littered with large, parallel gravel bars and ridges that extend about 115 m from crest to crest and are 10 m high. Scientists coined the term *scablands* to describe this foreign terrain. The formation of these bizarre features was a mystery that puzzled scientists for decades. The answer came from an unexpected process.

To understand how the strange gravel bars and ridges that scar the landscape formed requires turning back time thousands of years. About 14 000 years ago, the planet was a very different place than today. Large ice sheets covered present-day Canada and the northern United States. A portion of the ice sheet dammed the Clark Fork River in modern-day Montana. The ice dam produced Lake Missoula, a glacial lake as big as Lake Erie and Lake Ontario combined. Scientists estimate that the dam held about 2100 km³ of water. Scientists think that the ice dam broke several times during the last cold period. As the ice dam broke, it unleashed a cataclysmic wave of water 650 m high. The water swept across the landscape at 90 km/h, scouring eastern Washington and Oregon and emptying the lake in only two days. In addition, the region is littered with large boulders called glacial erratics. The boulders were carried in icebergs ripped from the ice sheet when the ice dam burst.

FIGURE 23: Giant ripple marks formed by the powerful currents that flowed across Markle Pass in the vicinity of Camas Hot Springs, Montana

To gather evidence to support these claims, scientists turned to aerial photography of the region. They showed that the gravel ridges are giant ripple marks that formed as a huge amount of water poured across the land. Scientists had observed similar ripples created by the movement of flowing water in rivers and on beaches, but no one had ever seen ripples this size. Scientists estimate that the planet experienced 44 glacial cycles during the past 2.58 million years. During each glacial cycle, they suggest that there could have been a dozen or more cataclysmic floods that scoured the region known today as the Channeled Scablands. The actual number of floods is difficult to tell because each flood washes away some of the evidence of earlier floods.

Language Arts Connection
Gather evidence to construct an explanation of whether beach nourishment is an effective solution for preventing the problem of beach erosion. Gather evidence from more than one source to construct your explanation. As you do research, be sure to make notes about your sources. As you conduct your research, evaluate your sources carefully to make sure they are reliable. Is there enough evidence to show that reported successes are viable? Develop a presentation to explain whether beach nourishment is an effective solution for preventing beach erosion. Include a list of sources that you need to develop your explanation. Write a summary of what you learned from your research. What were some of the differing viewpoints? How did these influence your view on this issue?

GLACIOLOGIST

BEACH NOURISHMENT PROJECTS

Go online to choose one of these other paths.

Lesson Self-Check

CAN YOU EXPLAIN IT NOW?

FIGURE 24: Horseshoe Bend

The rocks exposed along the canyon that surrounds Horseshoe Bend include the Navajo Sandstone. The Navajo Sandstone is a white- to pink-colored, cross-bedded sandstone that stretches from Arizona to Wyoming and is more than 600 m thick in some areas. This ancient rock was thought to have been deposited by wind during the Jurassic Period, about 200 million years ago. (The exact date of the sandstone is difficult to establish given that there are few fossils found in the rock.) At that time, the region was covered by large sand dunes, similar to the seas of sand in the Sahara desert today. The sand grains that made up these dunes were cemented together by calcite over about a 20-million-year period into the cross-bedded Navajo Sandstone. The presence of iron minerals in the sandstone gives the formation the range of colors that are visible today.

 What caused this deep meander (Horseshoe Bend) to form in the Colorado River? Consider the following questions:

- What are the rocks exposed along the cliff by the meander in the river?
- Why is it important to examine ancient rocks to understand past climate conditions on the planet?
- Why is the surrounding canyon carved out around the curve in the river?
- What might this region look like if it was more humid in Arizona?

CHECKPOINTS

Check Your Understanding

1. Compare and contrast dunes and moraines.

2. Which of the following is a depositional feature found along a coastline?
   a. sea arch
   b. wave-cut terrace
   c. sea cave
   d. sand spit

3. Sediments that are deposited in subglacial streams produce sinuous mounds of stratified sediment called
   a. dunes.
   b. arêtes.
   c. moraines.
   d. eskers.

4. Choose all that apply. A terminal moraine is
   a. composed of stratified sediment.
   b. found at the snout of a glacier.
   c. composed of poorly sorted sediment.
   d. deposited by glacial outwash.

5. A mesa is
   a. an eroded plateau.
   b. smaller than a butte.
   c. a precursor to an arch.
   d. eroded by glaciers.

6. What kind of drainage pattern forms where rock that is resistant to weathering alternates with rock that erodes more rapidly?
   a. trellis drainage pattern
   b. dendritic drainage pattern
   c. radial drainage pattern
   d. rectangular drainage pattern

7. If sediment input to a beach from rivers is greater than the output carried by the longshore current, will a beach grow or shrink? Explain your answer.

8. When is a glacier in a steady state?

9. The largest ice sheet on Earth is located in
   a. Canada.
   b. Greenland.
   c. Antarctica.
   d. Russia.

10. Which sediments are deposited farthest from the mouth of a river?
    a. silt grains
    b. pebbles
    c. sand grains
    d. cobbles

11. The size and the shape of a dune are a result of
    a. wind speed
    b. wind direction
    c. wind speed and direction
    d. shifts in sediment size

12. Which of the following statements about meandering streams are true? Choose all that apply.
    a. Water in the river channel flows at different speeds.
    b. Meanders grow smaller over time.
    c. Streams flow in S-shaped patterns.
    d. Streams cut deeply into underlying rocks.

13. Why have seawalls and jetties proven to be of little value against beach erosion?

14. Which of the following statements about buttes are true? Choose all that apply.
    a. A butte is a landform that is taller than wide.
    b. A butte is a table-like landform with steep-sided cliffs.
    c. A butte is a small, isolated hill with steep sides and a small flat top.
    d. A butte is a flat area of land that is higher than other areas that surround it.

15. What is a process by which sinkholes can form?

16. What is the difference between suspension and saltation?

17. Which of the following statements about barrier islands are true? Choose all that apply.

   a. Barrier islands are constanly being reshaped.

   b. Barrier islands are common along the U.S. Pacific Coast.

   c. Barrier islands are good places to build homes.

   d. Barrier islands form parallel to the coastline.

18. Which of the following landforms form by deposition along a coastline? Choose all that apply.

   a. sand spits

   b. wave-cut terraces

   c. bay mouth bars

   d. tombolos

19. Which of the following landforms are produced by the process of abrasion? Choose all that apply.

   a. yardangs

   b. ventifacts

   c. dunes

   d. buttes

20. Valley glaciers produce which of the following erosional landforms? Choose all that apply.

   a. V-shaped valleys

   b. horns

   c. glacial erratics

   d. arêtes

21. Which factors affect the type of drainage basin that forms in an area? Choose all that apply.

   a. speed of the water flowing over the land surface

   b. collection point to which water is channeled

   c. regional topography

   d. underlying soil and rock

22. Which of the following statements about caves and caverns are true? Choose all that apply.

   a. Caves form when rock collapses to form a circular depression.

   b. A cavern consists of many connecting chambers.

   c. Caves are formed as rock is dissolved.

   d. Caves are depositional landforms.

23. Describe two processes that cause glaciers to move.

24. Describe the process by which dunes migrate.

25. Which of the following statements about the Mississippi River and the Mississippi River delta are true? Choose all that apply.

   a. The path of the Mississippi River to the ocean changes over time.

   b. The Mississippi River delta is the largest river delta in the world.

   c. The Mississippi River empties into the Gulf of Mexico.

   d. The shape of the Mississippi River delta will not change over time.

26. Which of the following statements about the ablation zone of a glacier are true? Choose all that apply.

   a. The ablation zone of a glacier is located in the upper part of a glacier.

   b. The ablation zone of a glacier is located in the lower part of a glacier.

   c. In the ablation zone, more snow falls than melts.

   d. In the ablation zone, more snow melts than falls.

27. Which of the following statements about coral-reef islands are true? Choose all that apply.

   a. Coral-reef islands record a history of major environmental events.

   b. Coral-reef islands form parallel to the coastline.

   c. Coral-reef islands are common off northwest Australia.

   d. Coral-reef islands provide important evidence of organisms that have inhabited a reef.

MAKE YOUR OWN STUDY GUIDE

 In your Evidence Notebook, design a study guide that supports the main ideas in this lesson:

Water, wind, and ice are important erosional and depositional forces that change the landscape.

Remember to include the following information in your study guide:
- Use examples that model main ideas.
- Record explanations for the phenomena you investigated.
- Use evidence to support your explanations. Your support can include drawings, data, graphs, laboratory conclusions, and other evidence recorded throughout the lesson.

Development of Features

Canyonlands National Park, Utah, shows several stages of erosion.

Gather Evidence

Record evidence about the Zhangye Danxia mountains. As you explore the lesson, gather evidence about how surface processes and plate tectonics might form mountains such as these.

CAN YOU EXPLAIN IT?

FIGURE 1: Colorful stripes in the Zhangye Danxia mountains, China

The mountains in Figure 1 are a part of the Zhangye National Geopark in China. This type of landscape is also called a Danxia landform. The photograph shows details that you can observe. You might infer some possible reasons for the patterns you see. As you work through this lesson, you may want to know a few more details about these mountains: They are a part of a large mountain range along the northern edge of a large raised region called the Tibetan plateau. The mountains are far from the nearest coastline. Red sandstone and conglomerates make up the colored stripes.

Predict: How might the striped Zhangye Danxia mountains have formed? Start by thinking about the processes of plate tectonics that you have already learned.

Image Credits: (t) ©Zack Frank/Fotolia; (c) ©dinozzaver/Fotolia

Constructive and Destructive Processes

FIGURE 2: North America has mountain ranges in the west and east. The western mountains include the Cascades. The eastern mountains include the Appalachians.

a Mountains in the Cascade range

b Mountains in the Appalachian range

Constructive processes build up features, such as mountains. Destructive processes erode, reduce, or remove some features, which often results in other features.

Analyze Observe the two mountain ranges. What differences are visible in the photographs?

Coastal Mountains

You can use an understanding of plate tectonics and surface processes to understand the mountain ranges in North America. In Figure 2, observe differences in the shapes (sharp or rounded) and the slopes of the mountains. You might also notice a difference in the plants. Where the slopes are gentler, plants may hold the soil better. As a result, the soil in the Appalachians is deeper and has developed more than the soil in the Cascades. The map in Figure 3 gives you more information about the two mountain ranges, such as their relationships to other features.

FIGURE 3: The map shows some features of North America, which include the Cascade and Appalachian mountain ranges. Observe the distance of each range to the nearest coast and to the nearest plate boundary.

One of the mountain ranges is much older than the other—surface processes have been acting on it for a much longer time. Older mountains tend to be rounder and less steep because they have been worn down by erosion and other surface processes. With age, deposition builds up the shoreline and the continental shelf. More clues can be found in the distance and type of the nearest plate boundary.

Collaborate With a partner, organize and compare evidence about the ages of the two mountain ranges.

Explain Based on the evidence, which of the two ranges shows more of the effects of surface processes?

Edges of Continents

 Analyze Look through your notes to review the different effects of plate tectonics and surface processes. Can you classify them as constructive or destructive?

Apply the idea of constructive and destructive processes to help you think through how mountain ranges build up and wear down. Where plates converge, whether oceanic or continental, they tend to build up islands, mountains, and wedges of sediment and other material—constructive processes. If subduction occurs, one plate is pushed down and an oceanic trench forms. Molten rock may rise and build up new rock at or below the surface. Where oceanic crust subducts under continental crust, the result is an active continental margin, or active margin. Overall, the edge of continental crust is being built up by active plate tectonics.

Predict Do you expect mountains near an active margin to be sharp or rounded, steep or gently sloping, close to the shore or far from it, and close to the boundary or far from it?

FIGURE 4: Look for constructive processes in the active margin shown. (a) Mountains build up as the plates converge and as volcanoes add new material. (b) Sediment is scraped up and compressed, building up the edge of the continent.

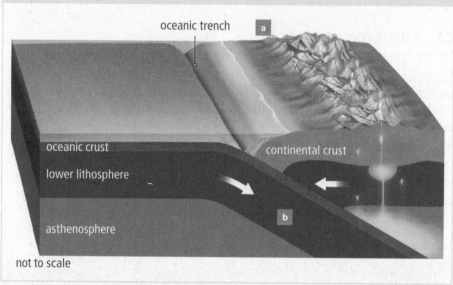

The Cascades are made of rock layers that formed and changed through many different processes, starting about 400 million years ago. The rock includes volcanic island arcs, deep ocean sediments, basalt from the ocean floor, and pieces of the mantle. But the present-day mountains began to rise only about 40 million years ago as an oceanic plate subducted below the North American plate. Material from the subducting plate was added to the edge of the continental crust. Convergence pushed up mountains. Rising magma formed a line of volcanoes. The subducting Juan de Fuca plate is still producing active volcanoes—evidence that the process is ongoing.

New mountains expose new surfaces of rock, which weather and erode. These destructive processes tend to act most strongly where the surface is high and steep. The eroded material is eventually deposited in lower-lying areas. No deep trench is located near the Cascades, in part because sediment fills it in quickly.

In contrast, a passive continental margin (Figure 5), or passive margin, begins at a divergent plate boundary. As new oceanic crust is added to the edge of the plate, the continent gets farther from the boundary. The edge of the continent becomes less active. Destructive surface processes round and wear down any mountains or other high regions. Soil develops above rock. Sediments build up the coastline, continental shelf, and other low-lying regions. As different materials are eroded and then deposited, they can form wide, flat layers of sediment. These layers may be altered as further constructive and destructive processes shape new features.

The Appalachian mountains are very old. The nearby continental margin is now passive, with a mid-ocean ridge far from the continent. But the plate boundaries have changed several times.

Long ago, sedimentary layers formed at a passive margin. The sediment was raised into mountains starting about 480 million years ago, as the region became an active margin with a subducting oceanic plate. The plates and plate boundaries continued to move and change through several more events. Island arcs and crust from other continents were added to the edge of the continent. The mountains were pushed up—again—as the continental crust was repeatedly compressed.

 Explain How are the two types of margins related to the two example mountain ranges?

FIGURE 5: At a passive margin, look for destructive processes in the high regions and constructive processes in the low regions. Notice (a) erosion of high regions, (b) sediment in low regions, (c) rifts from the divergent boundary, and (d) new oceanic crust pushing the continent farther away.

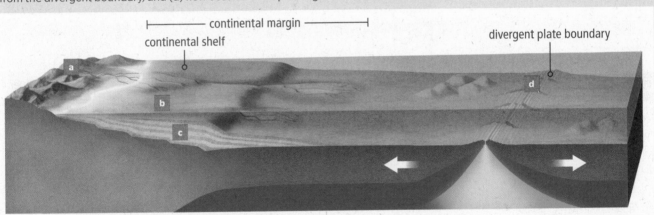

Surface processes are always at work and have been eroding the higher elevations and building up the lowlands for a very long time. At one time, the mountains were worn almost flat. The region was pushed up again, but slowly. Some rivers had time to erode through the rock as the mountains rose, cutting gaps through the long ridges.

 Gather Evidence Record examples of observations of the Cascades and the Appalachians to help you explain your observations of the Zhangye Danxia mountains.

Uplift and Subsidence

Explore Online ▶

Hands-On Lab 🧪

Model Rising and Sinking
Add and then remove mass from a floating wooden block to model what happens as mountains form and erode.

As features are built up and worn down, rock and sediment are moved across Earth's surface. Regions of the lithosphere can also move up and down.

Equilibrium of Plates

Earth's lithosphere—made of huge plates—floats on the asthenosphere below. An area of lithosphere sinks lower into the asthenosphere when it becomes heavier. It floats higher when lighter. The balance is called isostatic equilibrium.

FIGURE 7: As mountains erode, weight is removed and the lithosphere floats higher, restoring some of the mountains' height.

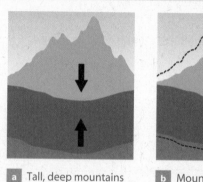
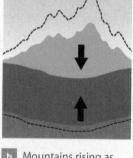
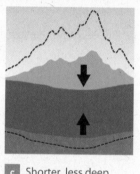

a Tall, deep mountains   b Mountains rising as they erode   c Shorter, less deep mountains

As mountains form, the crust gets thicker. That part of the tectonic plate sinks lower. As mountains erode, mass is removed and the lithosphere floats higher—it rebounds. Rebound occurs whenever mass is removed, such as when glaciers melt. Gravity acts faster on higher, steeper features. As a region becomes flatter, erosion slows.

Stability and Change ⊶

Explain As mountains wear down, they become less steep. Erosion continues more and more slowly until the surface is flat. Would you say that isostatic equilibrium is the result of a positive or a negative feedback loop?

Analyze Compare the features of the two areas shown in Figure 8 to help you apply the ideas of uplift and subsidence.

Compare Two Landscapes

The top and bottom of the lithosphere can move in opposite directions as a plate gets thinner or thicker. Scientists use the top of the lithosphere to define uplift and subsidence—motion up and down, respectively.

FIGURE 8: The Colorado Plateau is much higher than the sinking Mississippi Delta.

a The Colorado Plateau   b The Mississippi Delta

Uplift

Upward motion can occur across a wide range of scales. Convergent plate boundaries often lift large, flat areas called plateaus. Convergence can lift individual mountains or long mountain ranges. Upward convection in the mantle can lift a region of continent or the ocean floor. Rebound can occur at a large scale as a continental glacier retreats or mountains erode. It can also occur at a smaller scale, such as when a lake dries up.

Molten rock tends to move upward through the crust. A mass of salt that is under pressure can also move through the crust. Either can push upward on the rock above, forming a dome. The dome may cover a large region or form a small, isolated hill. The height and shape of a surface or the curve of rock layers can be evidence for uplift. Shoreline features higher than the current water level may also be evidence of uplift.

Predict What would happen if the peat bog dried out? What if magma pushed upward under the bog?

FIGURE 9: Examples of uplift and subsidence

a A dome

b A peat bog

Subsidence

As rock moves away from a mid-ocean ridge, it cools, contracts, and becomes more dense. Large-scale subsidence occurs. Rock under water is pushed down by the mass of water above it. Water also fills spaces in the rock and makes it more dense. Glaciers and inland seas can weigh down large regions within continents. Large amounts of sediment can also cause the lithosphere to sink. Even organic matter can add mass, such as at a peat bog. At a smaller scale, areas can sink when material below the surface is removed. Often, limestone below the surface dissolves and is replaced by water. Areas of the surface may subside or sinkholes may form. Subsidence may also occur where people remove material below ground, such as water, oil, or gas. Even decomposing organic matter can cause subsidence as it becomes more compact.

FIGURE 10: As plate boundaries change, a once-passive margin (not shown) can become an active margin. Continents collide, adding new mountains to an existing range.

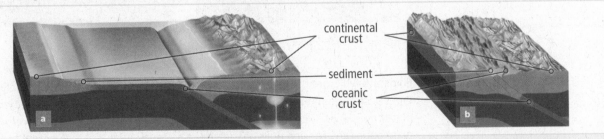

continental crust

sediment

oceanic crust

Explain How can seashells end up in the rock at a mountain's peak? Use Figure 10 to infer how deposition, subduction, convergence, uplift, and erosion can be related.

Folding and Faulting

 Hands-On Lab

FIGURE 11: Apply forces to putty

MATERIALS

· insulated gloves

· frozen plastic play putty

· warm plastic play putty

Model Forces

PROCEDURE

1. Put on insulated gloves and pick up a small square of frozen plastic play putty. Hold one edge in each hand.

2. Model each of the three directions of force (see Figure 13). You may have to reshape the putty between steps.

3. Repeat with the warm play putty.

 Analyze

1. What happened as you applied each type of force?
2. What differences did you notice between the warm and the frozen play putty?
3. In which ways do you think this model accurately represents rock?

Compare Two Features in Rock

Rock can be deformed by forces from plate tectonics as well as from changes of mass due to surface processes. The changes can occur at a wide range of scales and a range of speeds. When rock is layered, the deformation may be easy to see. Rock can wrinkle up in folds. It can break, forming flat or curved faults, and then slide along the faults.

 Predict If rock is stretched, can folds form?

FIGURE 12: Rock can form folds, faults, or both together. Think about the forces that might produce folds and those that might produce faults.

a Folds

b Faults

Folds and faults are the result of forces. Scientists classify the directions of force, or types of stress, as compression, tension, and shear stress. Think of the three types of plate boundaries. Compression pushes material together, such as at a convergent plate boundary. Tension pulls or stretches a material, such as at a divergent boundary. Shear stress occurs when forces are not aligned, such as at a transform plate boundary. Stresses can deform rock far from a plate boundary, often at a much smaller scale.

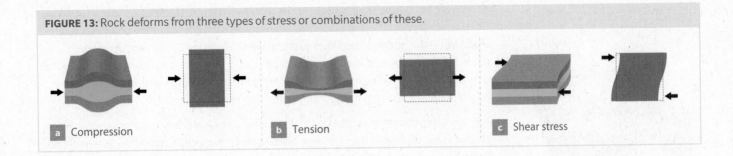

FIGURE 13: Rock deforms from three types of stress or combinations of these.

a Compression

b Tension

c Shear stress

Folding

Deep in the lithosphere, high pressure and temperature can make rock more likely to bend than break. When plates push together, rock can be compressed into folds. The folds can be as large as mountains and deep-sea trenches or as small as the wavy patterns within a sample of metamorphic rock.

When you see layers of rock that maintain the same thickness over a long distance, think of horizontal layers of sediment forming at the bottom of a large body of water. The curved layers you see in Figure 14 began this way. The layers are visible in a roadcut—a place where rock was removed so that a road could pass through. Each layer may have different properties. Folding can also change the properties of the rock—unevenly. It compresses and stretches the rock, hardening some parts and weakening other parts. The weaker rock erodes faster. The harder rock may protect rock beneath it. The layers in Figure 14 once continued up into high mountains.

Predict Would you expect to see a pattern like Figure 14 in the Cascades? Explain

FIGURE 14: Compare the curve of the layers to the curve of the surface of Sideling Hill, Maryland, in the Appalachians.

Faulting

Faults are breaks in the rock along which sections of rock can move. They occur near Earth's surface where temperature and pressure are relatively low.

Many faults occur at an angle. The side that sits above the fault is called a hanging wall. In some faults (Figure 15b), the hanging wall sticks out above the footwall—the side below the fault. Compression can produce such an overhang. You can use these patterns to infer whether the rock has been pushed together or pulled apart.

Collaborate With a partner, discuss ways to model the different types of faults. What materials would you use? What would be the strengths and limitations of your top two choices of model?

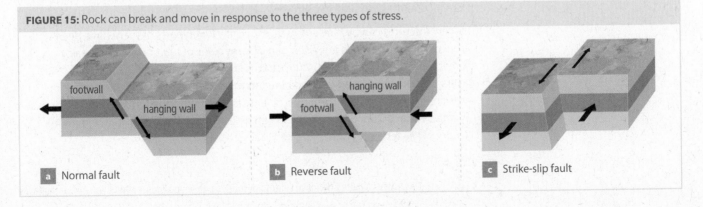

FIGURE 15: Rock can break and move in response to the three types of stress.

a Normal fault   footwall   hanging wall

b Reverse fault   hanging wall   footwall

c Strike-slip fault

Explain Use the layers shown in Figure 17 to make inferences. How many faults are visible? What do you think happened?

At convergent boundaries, reverse faults can cause the crust to pile up into mountains. Deep strike-slip faults often occur near mid-ocean rifts. But faults are often much shallower—the upper part of the crust can break while the lower part bends or stretches. Forces from plate interactions can cause faults far from plate boundaries. For example, a region called the Basin-and-Range Province in the western United States has long mountains that formed due to tension within a plate.

Tension often causes the upper part of the crust to break into large blocks, called fault blocks. The fault blocks may become tilted and slide against each other, as when a rift valley forms. Some blocks may drop down relative to the blocks around them, most often when the faults are angled in a V shape. The part that drops is called a graben, while the parts that remain higher are called horsts.

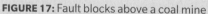

FIGURE 17: Fault blocks above a coal mine

Recognizing Faulting and Folding

Faulting can sometimes be seen as an offset at Earth's surface. A sharp change in elevation or in the location of a stream or other feature can be evidence of a fault. Scraped, polished lines on rock can be evidence of faulting in the area, though they can also be due to other processes. Folds may be seen as rolling hills or mountains, although erosion can produce similar features.

Faults and folds are easiest to see where layers of rock are exposed in a rock face, such as at a fault or a road cut. Faults are visible where layers seem to stop and start, as in Figure 17. Small folds look like bends in the layers, as in Figure 12a.

Larger structures can be harder to see, especially when parts of them have been eroded. Tilted rock layers are often part of large folds or fault blocks. You may sometimes see widths of different rock crossing a horizontal surface. It is likely that layers of rock continue downward beneath the surface at an angle. Differences in erosion may help you see the angle. Scientists read faults and folds as a record of past events. Features from different places can be compared to determine the geologic history of the tectonic plates.

Explain What evidence of folding or faulting have you found where you live or in places you have visited or seen in photographs?

Cycles of Mountains and Sediment

Tectonic plate boundaries change over time. Think about how the changes can produce mountain ranges made of sedimentary layers of rock.

A Sequence of Processes

Oceanic crust tends to be melted and formed from magma as plates move and change. Continental crust tends to be eroded and recycled into sedimentary rock.

FIGURE 18: Plate interactions and surface processes form different patterns of geologic features.

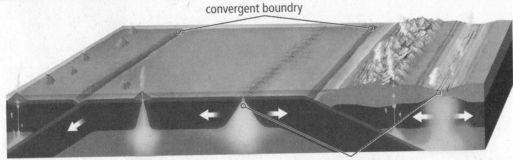

convergent boundry

divergent boundry

a Oceanic plate boundaries and a continental rift (a new divergent boundary)

b Passive margin and a mid-ocean ridge (an old divergent boundary)

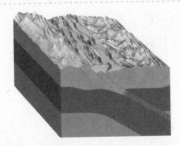

c Continent-continent convergence

Use the following simplified sequence to understand how plates change over time and interact with surface processes. Suppose Earth started with just two tectonic plates: one with a large continent and the other with oceanic crust. Mantle convection causes a rift in the continent. The resulting two plates—call them A and B—move apart, and new oceanic crust forms and grows at the rift. At the same time, the original oceanic plate subducts under the continents on both sides. Eventually, plates A and B meet on the other side of Earth. The oceanic part of plate B splits and the oceanic piece subducts, producing new islands. Subduction overtakes the oceanic ridge, and so plates A and B are pulled apart again. The islands become part of one continent. The pieces of continental crust meet again.

Collaborate With a partner, work through the sequence of plate interactions using sketches or other materials. How many times do each of the boundaries in Figure 18 form?

Analyze In the sequence, how long does the original oceanic crust last? Identify the stage where the last of it is destroyed. Compare it with the original continental crust.

Data Analysis

Forces in New Zealand

FIGURE 19: Maps showing New Zealand, tectonic plates, and data about changes in the rock

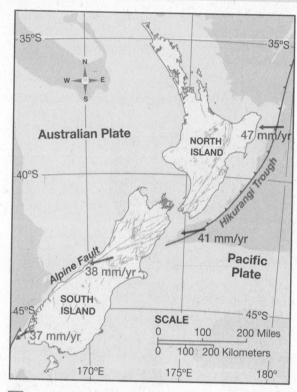

a The map shows tectonic plates affecting New Zealand. Triangles on blue lines point in the direction of plate movement.

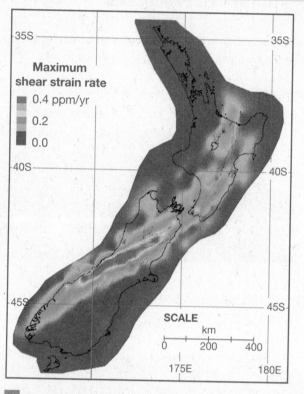

b Rate of deformation (strain)

The plate boundary along New Zealand is where the Australian plate is moving north and the Pacific plate is moving west. The plate movements produce areas of tension, compression, and shear stress, which deform the rock. A change in the shape or volume of rock, called strain, can be measured in parts per million (ppm). Map b shows how quickly this deformation occurs. A rate of 2 parts per million per year would mean that each meter of rock changes by 2 millionths of a meter in a year.

Data Analysis

1. What is the greatest rate of change shown?

2. Describe the location of the area that has the highest amount of shear strain.

3. What is the approximate length of the area of maximum shear strain?

4. Interpret the shear strain rate for a location in the area of maximum shear strain. How much would a 1-km length of rock change in a year?

5. What type of plate boundary occurs along the east coast of the North Island? Summarize the evidence.

6. What area is likely affected by compression?

7. What type of stress are you likely to find at the Alpine Fault? Explain your reasoning.

 LOCAL FEATURES | **MODEL FAULTING AND FOLDING** | **CONTRAST RIVER DELTAS** | Go online to choose one of these other paths.

Lesson Self-Check

CAN YOU EXPLAIN IT?

FIGURE 20: Colorful stripes in the Zhangye Danxia mountains, China

> **Analyze** Refer to the notes in your Evidence Notebook to find examples and processes to help you explain the phenomenon.

Take another look at the mountains in the Zhangye Danxia mountains. Think about the ways that features are shaped by both constructive and destructive processes. Apply what you have learned about surface processes and plate tectonics to explain the mountains. Recall that the stripes are made of different compositions of rock, such as red sandstone and conglomerate.

Your explanation should include how the stripes formed, their angle, and how the stripes are related from one ridge to another. You may be able to find a single event or process that formed the mountains into this shape, or you may need to propose a sequence of several events or processes. Show how your proposed event or sequence explains the evidence.

> **Explain** Based on what you know now, how might the striped Zhangye Danxia mountains have formed?

CHECKPOINTS

Check Your Understanding

1. Suppose you are standing next to a hanging wall that slopes upward and over you. This reverse fault would have formed when
   a. tension pulled two blocks apart
   b. blocks slid past each other
   c. compression pushed two blocks together

2. Which of these features indicates a passive continental margin? List all that apply.
   a. a range of folded mountains
   b. a chain of active volcanoes
   c. a deep trench
   d. deep soil and sediments

3. A salt dome is an example of _____.
   a. equilibrium
   b. subsidence
   c. uplift
   d. faulting

4. What characteristics tell you that you are on a boundary where subduction is taking place?
   a. a salt dome near an area of subsidence
   b. a volcano and mountains made of rock from islands and the ocean floor
   c. wide, flat layers of sediment on the continental shelf
   d. matching patterns of rock on the two sides of a boundary

5. Which surface processes can be both destructive and constructive?
   a. floods, landslides, wind-carried particles
   b. weathering, deposition, subduction
   c. rift formation, volcanoes
   d. earthquakes

6. Which of these would lead you to think that a mountain range is still being uplifted? Select all that apply.
   a. many fault blocks
   b. active volcanoes
   c. deep soil
   d. sharp, bare peaks

7. In a horst and graben region, tension produces a series of faults. Some of the resulting fault blocks _____ and produce _____ overhangs.
   a. rise, no
   b. rise, large
   c. drop, no
   d. drop, large

8. Features that show little evidence of surface processes may lead you to infer that
   a. the region is part of a stable plate
   b. plates are interacting in the region
   c. surface processes in the region have stopped
   d. constructive and destructive processes are balanced

9. As continents collide and produce uplift, the weather patterns change and the erosion rate increases. Explain how this is part of a positive or negative feedback loop.

10. Do you expect weathering and erosion to be faster or slower at a fault, compared with the rates nearby?

11. Plate tectonics can produce each of the following changes. Explain which, if any, can be a result of surface processes.
    a. uplift
    b. subsidence
    c. compression
    d. tension
    e. shear stress

12. Which of these represents the largest scale?
    a. a rift that has been spreading for millions of years
    b. subsidence
    c. compression
    d. tension

13. The soil in older mountains, such as the Appalachians, is generally _____ than the soil in younger mountains, such as the Rocky Mountains.
    a. deeper and more developed
    b. shallower or absent

14. Which of the following most likely formed deep in the lithosphere?
    a. large, flat layers of rock
    b. breaks cutting across rock layers
    c. curves in rock layers

15. Mountains in a region show matching horizontal layers. Which of these is not part of the sequence of events that formed them?
    a. Sedimentary layers form at the bottom of a large body of water.
    b. Compression produces folded mountains.
    c. Uplift produces a plateau.
    d. Rock erodes.

16. A mountain range is parallel to a passive margin. The rock forming the mountains is of several very different ages. It includes some basalt similar to the ocean floor, as well as volcanic mountains. Which of these is most likely part of the past history of the region? Select all that are justified by the given evidence.
    a. a mid-ocean rift
    b. an active continental margin
    c. convergence between two continents
    d. subduction

 In your Evidence Notebook, design a study guide that supports the main ideas from this lesson:
- Constructive and destructive processes shape features.
- Plate tectonics, driven by internal energy, is responsible for the formation of many of the features on continental and oceanic crust.
- Surface processes, driven mostly by external energy, tend to flatten Earth's surface by wearing down mountains and filling in low regions.
- Three types of stress produce faults and folds.

Remember to include the following in your study guide:
- Support main ideas with details and examples.
- Record explanations for the phenomena you investigated.
- Record examples of positive or negative feedback.
- Consider how evidence of plate tectonics and surface processes can help you make inferences about the stability of a region.

A BOOK EXPLAINING COMPLEX IDEAS USING ONLY THE 1,000 MOST COMMON WORDS

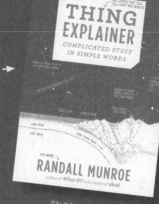

RANDALL MUNROE
XKCD.COM

EARTH'S SURFACE
All about Earth and what happens at its surface

Transferring a curved surface to a flat map results in a distorted image of the curved surface, so cartographers have developed several ways to do it. On the following pages are cylindrical projections of Earth.

THE STORY OF MAPPING OUR ROUND EARTH

THE EARTH'S SURFACE IS SPECIAL, AS FAR AS WE KNOW. IT'S THE ONLY PLACE WHERE WE'VE FOUND SEAS OF WATER, AND THE ONLY PLACE WHERE THE LAND IS MADE OF SHEETS OF ROCK THAT MOVE AROUND.

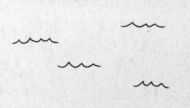

THERE ARE A LOT OF INTERESTING THINGS HERE.

MAPS OF EARTH'S SURFACE SHOW WHERE SOME OF THEM ARE.

EARTH IS A ROUND BALL, SO TO FIT ITS SURFACE ON A PAGE, IT HAS TO BE STRETCHED OUT.

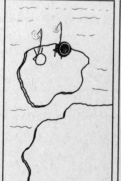
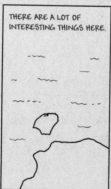
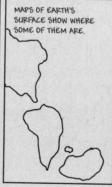

HEY, DID YOU KNOW THAT STRETCHING IS REALLY GOOD FOR YOU?

THIS CHANGES THE SHAPES AND SIZES OF SOME AREAS.

VERY FUNNY.

ON THIS MAP, IT MAKES THE LAND AT THE TOP AND THE BOTTOM LOOK MUCH BIGGER THAN IT REALLY IS, AND SOME OF THE PLACES NEAR THE SIDES LOOK STRETCHED OUT.

???

There's no way around this problem. Every paper map of a round world is wrong about size, shape, or the direction from one place to another. The shape chosen for this map tries to keep all these things in mind, not stretching any one part too much or making any area look too wrong.

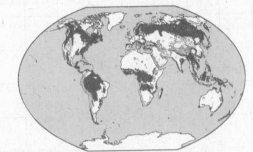

PLACES WHERE THERE ARE A LOT OF TREES

PLACES WHERE THE ROCKS ARE OLD

■ As old as the first big animals   ■ As old as the earliest life

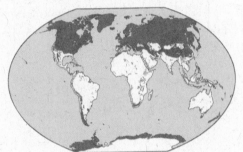

PLACES WHERE IT SNOWS

PLACES WHERE A LOT OF PEOPLE LIVE

PLACES WHERE THE EARTH SHAKES A LOT

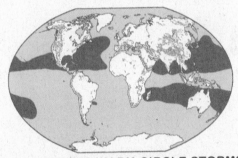

SEAS WITH BIG WARM CIRCLE STORMS

PLACES WITH LOTS OF FLASHING SKY LIGHTS

PLACES WHERE LONG SPINNING CLOUDS REACH DOWN FROM STORMS AND BLOW AWAY HOUSES

 Sometimes   ■ A lot

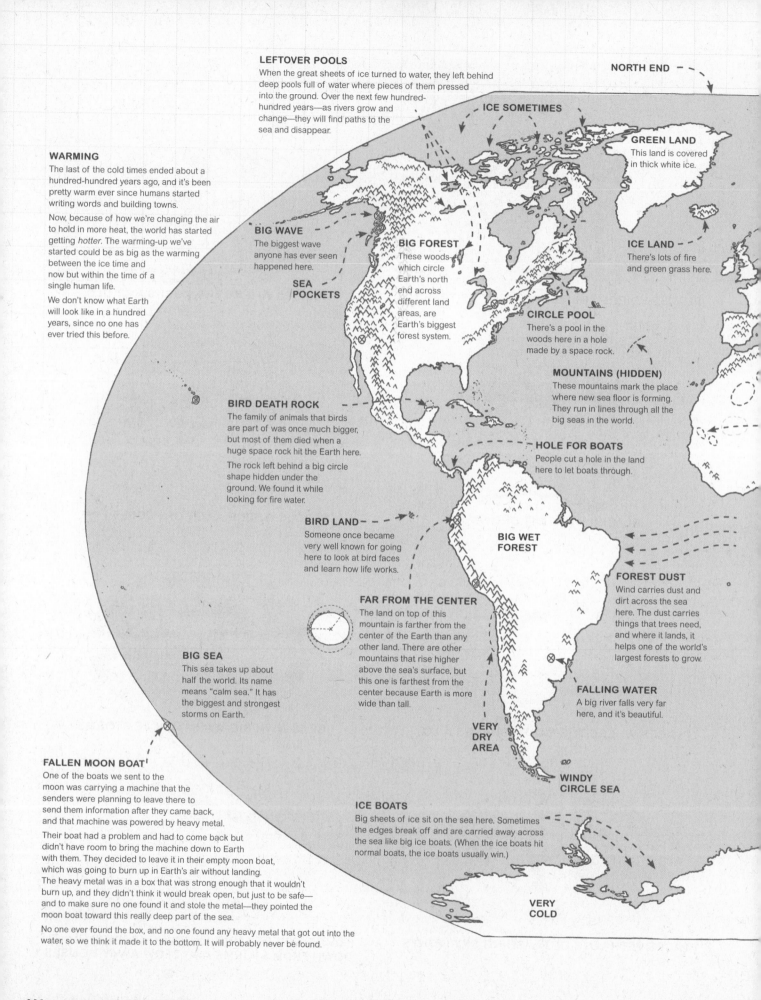

LEFTOVER POOLS
When the great sheets of ice turned to water, they left behind deep pools full of water where pieces of them pressed into the ground. Over the next few hundred-hundred years—as rivers grow and change—they will find paths to the sea and disappear.

NORTH END

ICE SOMETIMES

GREEN LAND
This land is covered in thick white ice.

WARMING
The last of the cold times ended about a hundred-hundred years ago, and it's been pretty warm ever since humans started writing words and building towns.

Now, because of how we're changing the air to hold in more heat, the world has started getting *hotter*. The warming-up we've started could be as big as the warming between the ice time and now but within the time of a single human life.

We don't know what Earth will look like in a hundred years, since no one has ever tried this before.

BIG WAVE
The biggest wave anyone has ever seen happened here.

SEA POCKETS

BIG FOREST
These woods, which circle Earth's north end across different land areas, are Earth's biggest forest system.

ICE LAND
There's lots of fire and green grass here.

CIRCLE POOL
There's a pool in the woods here in a hole made by a space rock.

MOUNTAINS (HIDDEN)
These mountains mark the place where new sea floor is forming. They run in lines through all the big seas in the world.

BIRD DEATH ROCK
The family of animals that birds are part of was once much bigger, but most of them died when a huge space rock hit the Earth here.

The rock left behind a big circle shape hidden under the ground. We found it while looking for fire water.

HOLE FOR BOATS
People cut a hole in the land here to let boats through.

BIRD LAND
Someone once became very well known for going here to look at bird faces and learn how life works.

BIG WET FOREST

FOREST DUST
Wind carries dust and dirt across the sea here. The dust carries things that trees need, and where it lands, it helps one of the world's largest forests to grow.

FAR FROM THE CENTER
The land on top of this mountain is farther from the center of the Earth than any other land. There are other mountains that rise higher above the sea's surface, but this one is farthest from the center because Earth is more wide than tall.

BIG SEA
This sea takes up about half the world. Its name means "calm sea." It has the biggest and strongest storms on Earth.

FALLING WATER
A big river falls very far here, and it's beautiful.

VERY DRY AREA

FALLEN MOON BOAT
One of the boats we sent to the moon was carrying a machine that the senders were planning to leave there to send them information after they came back, and that machine was powered by heavy metal.

Their boat had a problem and had to come back but didn't have room to bring the machine down to Earth with them. They decided to leave it in their empty moon boat, which was going to burn up in Earth's air without landing. The heavy metal was in a box that was strong enough that it wouldn't burn up, and they didn't think it would break open, but just to be safe—and to make sure no one found it and stole the metal—they pointed the moon boat toward this really deep part of the sea.

No one ever found the box, and no one found any heavy metal that got out into the water, so we think it made it to the bottom. It will probably never be found.

WINDY CIRCLE SEA

ICE BOATS
Big sheets of ice sit on the sea here. Sometimes the edges break off and are carried away across the sea like big ice boats. (When the ice boats hit normal boats, the ice boats usually win.)

VERY COLD

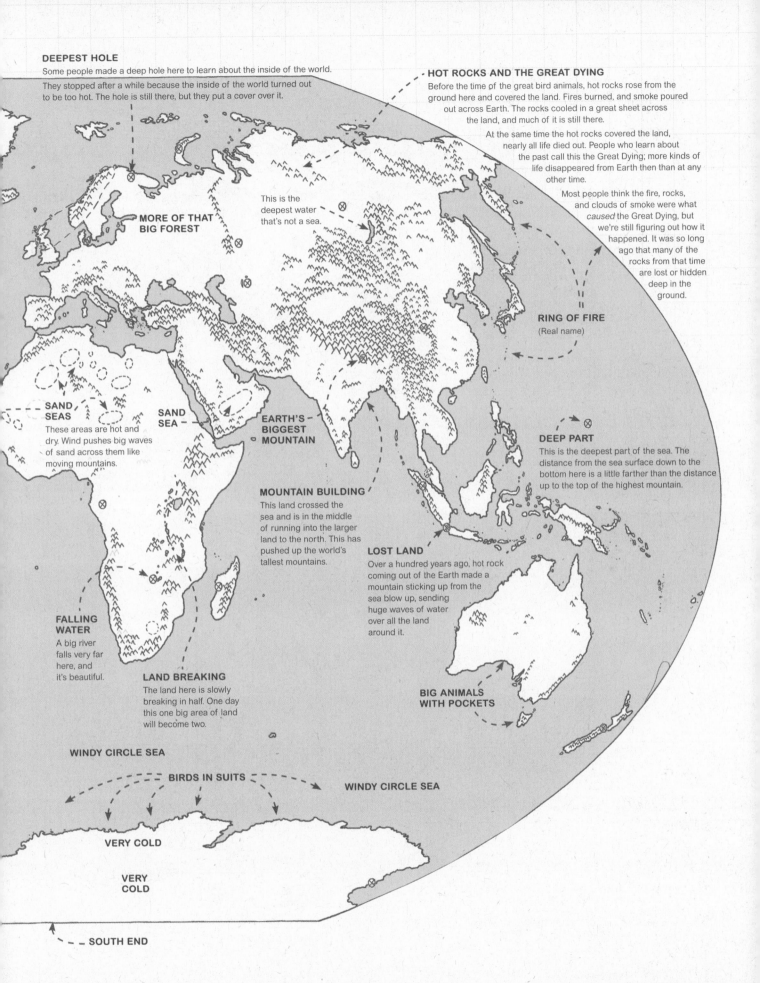

DEEPEST HOLE

Some people made a deep hole here to learn about the inside of the world.

They stopped after a while because the inside of the world turned out to be too hot. The hole is still there, but they put a cover over it.

HOT ROCKS AND THE GREAT DYING

Before the time of the great bird animals, hot rocks rose from the ground here and covered the land. Fires burned, and smoke poured out across Earth. The rocks cooled in a great sheet across the land, and much of it is still there.

At the same time the hot rocks covered the land, nearly all life died out. People who learn about the past call this the Great Dying; more kinds of life disappeared from Earth then than at any other time.

Most people think the fire, rocks, and clouds of smoke were what *caused* the Great Dying, but we're still figuring out how it happened. It was so long ago that many of the rocks from that time are lost or hidden deep in the ground.

This is the deepest water that's not a sea.

MORE OF THAT BIG FOREST

RING OF FIRE
(Real name)

SAND SEAS

These areas are hot and dry. Wind pushes big waves of sand across them like moving mountains.

SAND SEA

EARTH'S BIGGEST MOUNTAIN

DEEP PART

This is the deepest part of the sea. The distance from the sea surface down to the bottom here is a little farther than the distance up to the top of the highest mountain.

MOUNTAIN BUILDING

This land crossed the sea and is in the middle of running into the larger land to the north. This has pushed up the world's tallest mountains.

LOST LAND

Over a hundred years ago, hot rock coming out of the Earth made a mountain sticking up from the sea blow up, sending huge waves of water over all the land around it.

FALLING WATER

A big river falls very far here, and it's beautiful.

LAND BREAKING

The land here is slowly breaking in half. One day this one big area of land will become two.

BIG ANIMALS WITH POCKETS

WINDY CIRCLE SEA

BIRDS IN SUITS

WINDY CIRCLE SEA

VERY COLD

VERY COLD

SOUTH END

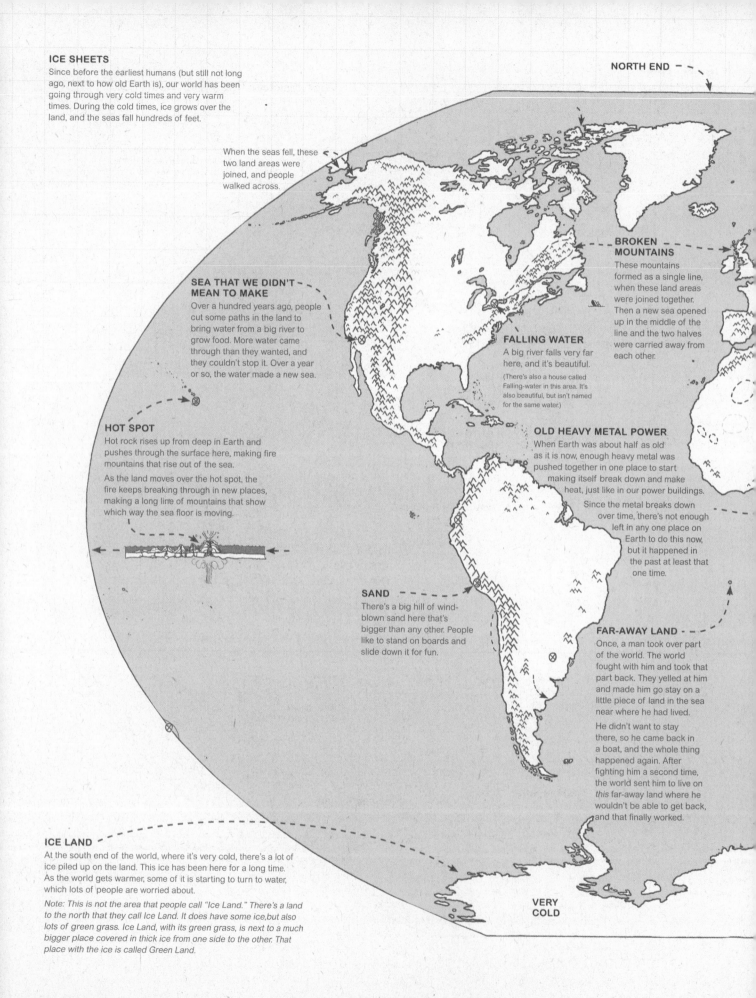

ICE SHEETS

Since before the earliest humans (but still not long ago, next to how old Earth is), our world has been going through very cold times and very warm times. During the cold times, ice grows over the land, and the seas fall hundreds of feet.

When the seas fell, these two land areas were joined, and people walked across.

NORTH END

SEA THAT WE DIDN'T MEAN TO MAKE

Over a hundred years ago, people cut some paths in the land to bring water from a big river to grow food. More water came through than they wanted, and they couldn't stop it. Over a year or so, the water made a new sea.

BROKEN MOUNTAINS

These mountains formed as a single line, when these land areas were joined together. Then a new sea opened up in the middle of the line and the two halves were carried away from each other.

FALLING WATER

A big river falls very far here, and it's beautiful.

(There's also a house called Falling-water in this area. It's also beautiful, but isn't named for the same water.)

HOT SPOT

Hot rock rises up from deep in Earth and pushes through the surface here, making fire mountains that rise out of the sea.

As the land moves over the hot spot, the fire keeps breaking through in new places, making a long line of mountains that show which way the sea floor is moving.

OLD HEAVY METAL POWER

When Earth was about half as old as it is now, enough heavy metal was pushed together in one place to start making itself break down and make heat, just like in our power buildings.

Since the metal breaks down over time, there's not enough left in any one place on Earth to do this now, but it happened in the past at least that one time.

SAND

There's a big hill of wind-blown sand here that's bigger than any other. People like to stand on boards and slide down it for fun.

FAR-AWAY LAND

Once, a man took over part of the world. The world fought with him and took that part back. They yelled at him and made him go stay on a little piece of land in the sea near where he had lived.

He didn't want to stay there, so he came back in a boat, and the whole thing happened again. After fighting him a second time, the world sent him to live on *this* far-away land where he wouldn't be able to get back, and that finally worked.

ICE LAND

At the south end of the world, where it's very cold, there's a lot of ice piled up on the land. This ice has been here for a long time. As the world gets warmer, some of it is starting to turn to water, which lots of people are worried about.

Note: This is not the area that people call "Ice Land." There's a land to the north that they call Ice Land. It does have some ice, but also lots of green grass. Ice Land, with its green grass, is next to a much bigger place covered in thick ice from one side to the other. That place with the ice is called Green Land.

VERY COLD

446 Unit 7 Earth's Changing Surface

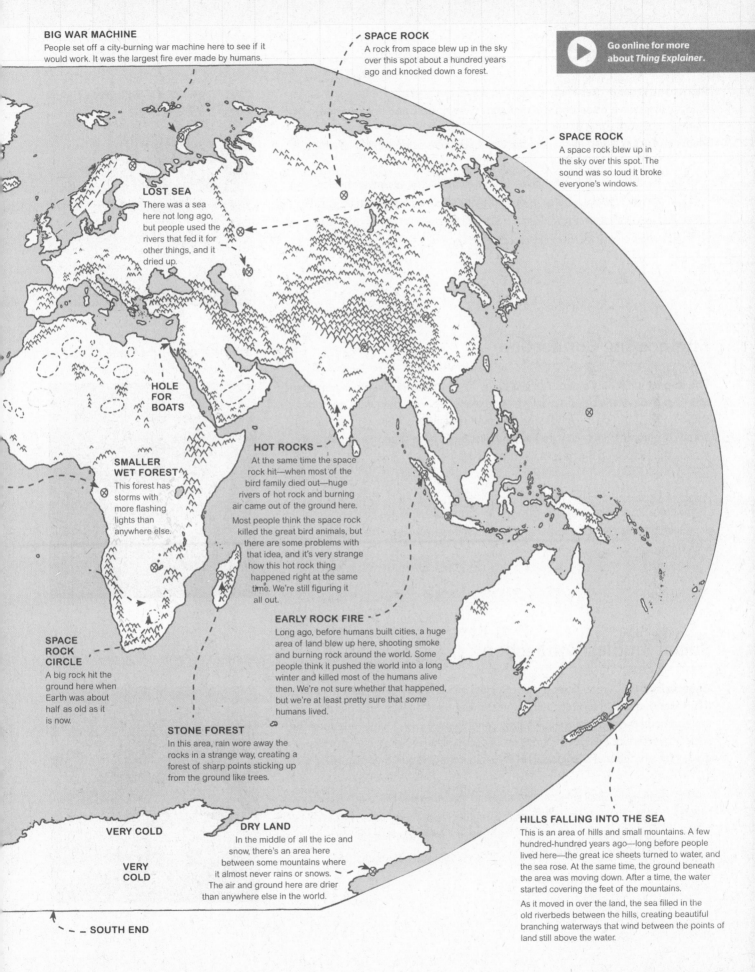

BIG WAR MACHINE
People set off a city-burning war machine here to see if it would work. It was the largest fire ever made by humans.

SPACE ROCK
A rock from space blew up in the sky over this spot about a hundred years ago and knocked down a forest.

Go online for more about *Thing Explainer*.

SPACE ROCK
A space rock blew up in the sky over this spot. The sound was so loud it broke everyone's windows.

LOST SEA
There was a sea here not long ago, but people used the rivers that fed it for other things, and it dried up.

HOLE FOR BOATS

SMALLER WET FOREST
This forest has storms with more flashing lights than anywhere else.

HOT ROCKS
At the same time the space rock hit—when most of the bird family died out—huge rivers of hot rock and burning air came out of the ground here.

Most people think the space rock killed the great bird animals, but there are some problems with that idea, and it's very strange how this hot rock thing happened right at the same time. We're still figuring it all out.

EARLY ROCK FIRE
Long ago, before humans built cities, a huge area of land blew up here, shooting smoke and burning rock around the world. Some people think it pushed the world into a long winter and killed most of the humans alive then. We're not sure whether that happened, but we're at least pretty sure that *some* humans lived.

SPACE ROCK CIRCLE
A big rock hit the ground here when Earth was about half as old as it is now.

STONE FOREST
In this area, rain wore away the rocks in a strange way, creating a forest of sharp points sticking up from the ground like trees.

VERY COLD

VERY COLD

DRY LAND
In the middle of all the ice and snow, there's an area here between some mountains where it almost never rains or snows. The air and ground here are drier than anywhere else in the world.

SOUTH END

HILLS FALLING INTO THE SEA
This is an area of hills and small mountains. A few hundred-hundred years ago—long before people lived here—the great ice sheets turned to water, and the sea rose. At the same time, the ground beneath the area was moving down. After a time, the water started covering the feet of the mountains.

As it moved in over the land, the sea filled in the old riverbeds between the hills, creating beautiful branching waterways that wind between the points of land still above the water.

Biology Connection

Plants and Erosion Heavy rains and high winds can lead to extensive soil erosion. Plants can lessen erosion because their root systems grab and hold the soil in place. Plants can absorb some of the water in soils as well, so it is harder to wash away. Plants also act as a break lessening the impact of the erosional effect of wind.

> Use library and Internet resources to learn more about how plants are used to prevent erosion in different environments. Develop a short presentation about specific types of plants that are especially effective in preventing or reducing the effects of soil erosion.

FIGURE 1: Plants have extensive root systems.

Engineering Connection

The Impact of Flood Control Technologies The Mississippi River is an important route for trade. Many cities have developed along the river, but rivers are not stationary features on the landscape. The river channel and delta migrate over time. Some communities located in or near the river basin have spent a great deal of money trying to keep the river in its current position.

> Using library and Internet resources, research levees and other technologies that have been put in place to control flooding along the Mississippi River. Examine the unintended negative consequences that these technologies have had on the Mississippi Delta.

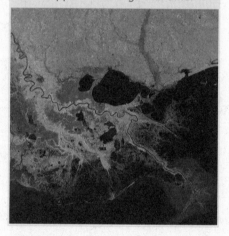

FIGURE 2: The size and location of the Mississippi Delta change over time.

Social Studies Connection

Geotourism The National Geographic Society defines geotourism as tourism that sustains or enhances the geographical character of a place, including its environment, culture, aesthetics, heritage, and the well-being of its residents. The society has developed a set of principles of geotourism and produced geotourism guides for a number of scenic areas in the United States and other countries.

> Work with a small group to select a national park you would like to visit. Use library and Internet resources to learn more about the features in the park as well as about the principles of geotourism. With your group, develop a geotourism guide for the national park that you selected.

FIGURE 3: Striped rock formations in Badlands National Park, South Dakota

SYNTHESIZE THE UNIT

In your Evidence Notebook, create a concept map, graphic organizer, or outline using the Study Guides you created for each lesson in this unit. Be sure to use evidence to support your claims.

When synthesizing individual information, remember to follow these general steps:

- Find the central idea of each piece of information.
- Think about the relationships among the central ideas.
- Combine the ideas to come up with a new understanding.

Go online to access detailed lesson summaries for this unit

DRIVING QUESTIONS

Look back to the Driving Questions from the opening section of this unit. In your Evidence Notebook, review and revise your previous answers to those questions. Use the evidence you gathered and other observations you made throughout the unit to support your claims.

PRACTICE AND REVIEW

1. How does the rock cycle create greater diversity of rocks on Earth's surface?

2. Which of the following statements are true about weathering? Select all correct statements.
   a. It describes the break down of rocks into smaller pieces.
   b. It describes the transport of smaller pieces of rocks to another location.
   c. It alters the chemical surface of rocks.
   d. It weakens rock through changes in pressure that allow the rock to expand and crack.

3. How are an alluvial fan and a delta similar and different?

4. Which statements are true about longshore current? Select all correct statements.
   a. It causes beaches to shrink when supply equals demand.
   b. It produces features, such as spits, barrier islands, and tombolos.
   c. It moves sediment along the coast in a back and forth motion.
   d. It is halted by human-made constructions like seawalls, riprap, and jetties.

5. Create a model in your Evidence Notebook to show the steps that occur in the formation of a sinkhole.

6. How can a volcanic eruption be both a constructive and destructive process?

7. Which statements accurately describe mid-ocean ridge systems? Select all correct statements.
   a. Age of crust increases with distance from the ridge system.
   b. Alternate anomalies of magnetic polarity show similar patterns on either side of the ridge system.
   c. Ridge systems around the world spread at the same rate.
   d. The ridge towers above the ocean floor because the basalt accumulates at the spreading center.

Use Figure 4 to answer Questions 8 and 9.

8. Which of the following is a correct statement about the distribution of land on Earth?

a. Most land on Earth is found above 2000 meters.

b. About 40 percent of Earth's surface is found below sea level.

c. The average elevation of continents is about 1000 meters above sea level.

d. The highest mountains rise to about 6000 meters above sea level.

9. Place the following in order from smallest to largest in terms of difference in elevation.

a. The average elevation of the ocean floor and the deepest ocean trench

b. The highest mountain and the average elevation of the continents

c. The average elevation of continents and the average elevation of the ocean floor

d. Sea level and the average elevation of the ocean floor

10. The summit of Mauna Kea on the island of Hawaii rises about 4.2 kilometers above sea level. However, measured from its base on the ocean floor, Mauna Kea's total elevation is more than 10 kilometers. Based on that information, is the base of Mauna Kea above or below the average elevation of the ocean floor? Explain your reasoning.

11. What process describes the movement of continental crust when a glacier melts?

a. Interglacial episode

b. Isostatic rebound

c. Continental depression

d. Buoyancy

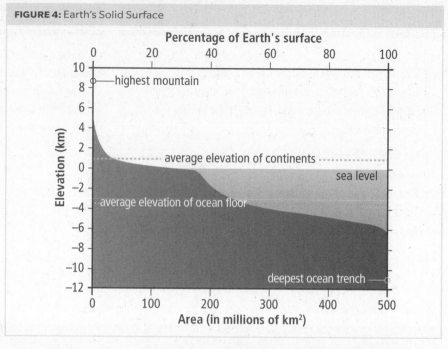

FIGURE 4: Earth's Solid Surface

12. Compare and contrast features that form along ocean-ocean convergent plate boundaries with features that form along ocean-continent convergent plate boundaries.

13. Why is topsoil less well developed in areas with cold, arid climates?

UNIT PROJECT

Altering Landscapes

Return to your unit project. Finalize your model so that it clearly shows how loss of groundcover can accentuate erosion in landscapes. In your final presentation, explain how the model changed as you learned more and how you would continue to revise it if you had more time or different materials.

Remember these tips as you are finalizing your model and preparing to present it:

· Look at the model. Does it show processes that are related to the erosion of different types of landforms?

· Does it include all relevent types of sediment? Is everything clearly labeled?

· How well does the model explain erosion? What does it not show?

Modeling a Sandy Shoreline

In this activity, you will explore the evolution of a shoreline through normal coastal sediment movement by longshore drift. Use knowledge about geologic processes in the coastal area to explain how these features form and change, including spits, barrier islands, tombolos, etc.

1. Place sand of uniform size along one side of a box.
2. Fill the remainder of the box with water.
3. Set up a fan to blow across the water, producing waves and a current that moves the sand grains. Alternatively, move a block in one direction in the water to simulate waves on the shoreline.
4. Observe and record how the sand moves and how the features form through time.
5. Repeat the activity, but place one or two barriers either perpendicular or parallel to the shoreline.

1. DEFINE THE PROBLEM

With your team, write a statement outlining the problem of placing barriers along the coastline. Record any questions you have on the problem and the information you need to solve it.

2. CONDUCT RESEARCH

With your team, investigate the cause-and-effect relationship between placing barriers along the coastline and longshore current. Select two coastlines to compare and contrast.

3. ANALYZE DATA

On your own, analyze the problem you have defined along with your research. Use your research to develop a plan to alleviate the effects of barriers on longshore current.

4. IDENTIFY AND RECOMMEND A SOLUTION

Develop a short white paper to outline the consequences of placing barriers along a coastline. Develop options available to a community to alleviate the effects of barriers on the shape of the coastline.

5. COMMUNICATE

Present your findings to the class in a six-minute PowerPoint presentation, or write a short report with an abstract, introduction, methods, results, conclusions, and discussion section.

FIGURE 5: Longshore current moves sand grains along the coastline.

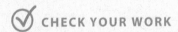 CHECK YOUR WORK

A complete presentation should include the following information:

- A clearly defined problem with supporting questions that are answered in the final presentation
- A model of longshore current
- A recommendation that explains how to alleviate the problem of erosion when barriers are placed along the coastline and uses evidence to support the solution
- Images and data that further support your solution

Earth's Water

Iguazu Falls on the border of Argentina and Brazil

Image Credits: ©Jorisvo/Fotolia

FIGURE 1: Fog-collection system in the Atacama Desert of Chile

Water is a vital resource for people all over the world. In deserts and other areas that receive very little rainfall, people must rely on surface water or groundwater for their daily needs. But water vapor is also available in the atmosphere. Many species of plants and animals have evolved specialized means of capturing moisture from the air. Today, humans are engineering technologies to capture water vapor as well. For example, the fog-collection system shown above uses large pieces of canvas that cause the fog to condense into water droplets and flow down into a trough.

 Explain What technologies are used to supply water to homes and businesses in your community?

DRIVING QUESTIONS

As you move through the unit, gather evidence to help you answer the following questions. In your Evidence Notebook, record what you already know about these topics and any questions you have about them.

1. How are the unique properties of water related to the roles it plays in Earth's systems?

2. How does water cycle through different phases at Earth's surface?

3. What are some major challenges in managing water resources?

UNIT PROJECT

Engineering: Harvesting Water through Biomimicry

 Go online to download the Unit Project Worksheet to help plan your project.

Biomimicry is an approach to designing sustainable solutions to human problems through copying patterns and strategies found in nature. In this project, you will research adaptations of living things that enable them to capture water from their environment. Then you will work with a group to use what you've learned to design and test a simple water-collection system.

Properties of Water

Oil and water interact in a beaker.

CAN YOU EXPLAIN IT?

FIGURE 1: Potholes are troublesome and dangerous road hazards that seem to reappear every year.

 Gather Evidence As you explore the lesson, gather evidence about the different properties of water.

Driving down the road can be a challenge, especially when the road is pitted with holes. Potholes are dangerous to drivers and a nuisance to repair, since they seem to multiply every year despite our attempts to fill them. To road-repair crews, keeping up with potholes is a constant struggle.

Potholes begin as harmless cracks in the pavement but slowly grow to become large holes in the road surface that can damage vehicles and cause accidents. Potholes are not only dangerous, they also are expensive. In the United States, road and vehicle repairs resulting from potholes cost citizens billions of dollars every year.

Predict What factors lead to the formation of potholes? What role does water play in their formation?

Image Credits: (t) ©Jitka Volfova/Shutterstock; (c) ©Vadim Lukin/Shutterstock

The Strength of Water

Caves are large empty spaces underground that form as a result of natural weathering. They can range from sea caves to magnificent cathedral-like spaces like the Luray Caverns in Virginia, as seen in Figure 2. The features in Luray Caverns are made of limestone shaped by interactions with water.

Explain What is the role of water in making cave formations?

FIGURE 2: These features in the Luray Caverns in Virginia are primarily made of limestone.

Water: The Great Dissolver

Limestone deposits that cling to the ceiling of a cave are called *stalactites,* while those that reach up from the cave floor are called *stalagmites*. Both of these features grow slowly over the course of thousands of years. Because stalactites slowly grow toward the ground and stalagmites grow toward the ceiling, they sometimes join in the middle to form a new structure called a *column*.

FIGURE 3: The slow drip of water through the cave leads to unique formations.

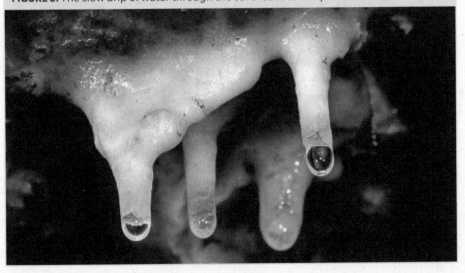

Collaborate Caves are generally very wet places, and it is often possible to see water dripping from stalactites and landing on stalagmites. With a partner, come up with a hypothesis for how water helps them grow.

Image Credits: (t) ©Vanessa Vick/Science Source; (b) ©Marko König/imageBROKER/Alamy

MATERIALS

- beakers, 600 mL (4)
- flour
- salt
- sand
- stir rod
- sugar
- water, 1.2 L, room temperature

Water Solubility

Dissolving is the process in which a solid becomes incorporated into a liquid. The liquid that does the dissolving is called the solvent. The substance being dissolved is called the *solute*. Solubility is a measure of how much solute will dissolve in a given amount of solvent under given conditions. Water incorporates certain types of solutes better than others. Salt and sugar are considered polar solutes, while flour and sand are considered nonpolar.

PROCEDURE

1. Label each beaker with the name of one of the solutes.
2. Pour 300 mL of water into each beaker.
3. Measure 30 g of each solute (sugar, flour, salt, and sand) and place into separate beakers.
4. Use the stir rod to stir each beaker for two minutes.
5. Observe what happens to each solute. Record whether the solute is polar or nonpolar and whether it dissolves or does not dissolve in water.

ANALYZE

From what you observed in your experiment, does water more easily dissolve polar or nonpolar substances?

Compared to most other liquids, water is excellent at dissolving things and is often referred to as the *universal solvent*. Water's three atoms are not quite in a line. The positive and negative charges are centered in slightly different places, or poles, so water is said to be polar. Water is very effective at dissolving other polar molecules.

The caves discussed earlier in the lesson are composed of a rock called limestone, which itself is made up of a polar mineral called calcite. Because calcite is polar, it easily dissolves in water. This property is responsible for the formation of caves as well as the features within them. Limestone on Earth's surface is dissolved in water, which flows downward through Earth's crust until it reaches the cave roof. When this calcite-rich water drips from the cave roof, it deposits some of the calcite on the roof, forming a stalactite. When it lands on the cave floor, it deposits more calcite, forming stalagmites.

FIGURE 4: A water molecule has a unique structure. It consists of one oxygen atom and two hydrogen atoms that are joined together to form a shape something like the letter *v*.

FIGURE 5: The Dead Sea is many times saltier than Earth's oceans.

Image Credits: ©agphotos/Fotolia

Water's ability to dissolve many substances, especially polar substances, produces amazing features like those found in caves. Water also dissolves components of other rocks on Earth's surface, which can then be redistributed by moving water. In the ocean, many of these molecules remain dissolved in water for thousands, even millions of years. The concentration of dissolved molecules in ocean water is much higher than in fresh water, such as rivers and lakes, and is the reason that ocean water tastes salty.

The characteristic of water as the universal solvent also makes it ideal to transport nutrients and minerals in plants and animals. Water can pass through the different membranes in the body. The nutrients dissolved in water are carried into the bloodstream to cells. Waste also is carried away from the cells in the bloodstream and expelled from the body in water.

The Nature of Liquids

Though water also occurs in nature as ice and water vapor, it is most common in its liquid form. Liquid water is a fluid, which means that it is cohesive and capable of flowing. Anyone who has witnessed an ocean wave crashing on the beach can tell you that moving water has energy. All flowing water has energy, and over long periods of time, even the smallest stream is capable of wearing down materials in its path. The smaller particles weathered from rocks, called *sediments,* are removed from the original location of the parent rock by erosion. Over long periods, the constant flow of water can carve a path through a landscape.

FIGURE 6: Flowing water can produce features like this landscape in the southwestern United States.

Explain With a partner, consider the role that water plays in producing the the Grand Canyon, seen in Figure 6.

Image Credits: ©Nature/UIG/Universal Images Group/Getty Images

Water Density Analyze the effects of temperature and salinity on the density of water.

👥 **Collaborate** Examine Figure 7. As a group, develop an explanation to describe how the feature forms. Think about what materials make up the feature and the properties of water in the river and the ocean that contribute to forming the feature.

FIGURE 7: This fan-like image is not biological. It is a depositional feature, produced when fast-moving water from a river enters calm water in a sea, bay, or ocean.

Flowing water has energy that allows a river to transport sediments of different sizes for great distances across land. As river water flows into another body of water, like an ocean or bay, the water slows and its energy decreases. The water is no longer able to carry the same volume of sediment, especially sediment with a larger particle size. The sediment falls out of the flowing water and is deposited on the riverbed. Over time, the accumulation of sediment produces a feature called a delta. Deltas come in many forms and varieties, but each is a unique environment where water from a river merges with water in a still body.

📝 **Explain** How do the properties of water as a solvent and its ability to flow work together to shape Earth's surface?

The Strength of Ice

Rocks seem like indestructible objects, but many rocks exposed at Earth's surface are riddled with cracks and fissures. Though the rocks in Figure 8 may look as though they were pulled apart by some catastrophic event, their current condition is actually due to the action of water.

FIGURE 8: The Castell y Gwynt in Wales is a fractured rock that is a popular destination for mountain climbers.

The Unique Nature of Ice

It can be frustrating when you put bottles or cups of water in the freezer only to have them shatter when they freeze. Though this is often inconvenient, the same principle that causes water bottles to rupture in the fridge is responsible for a wide range of surface processes on Earth.

FIGURE 9: A bottle of water ruptures in the freezer.

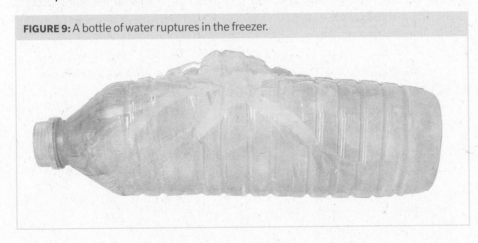

Collaborate Why do you think that liquids often break their containers when left in the freezer? What must be happening to the liquid?

Image Credits: (t) ©James Grant/Alamy; (b) ©James Stevenson/Dorling Kindersley/Getty Images

Water is not only special because of its abilities to dissolve minerals and flow with enough kinetic energy to weather and erode rocks, it also has an unusual property—it expands when it freezes. Most materials contract, or get smaller, when they freeze, but when water freezes, it expands.

FIGURE 10: As water freezes, it expands.

As water temperature dips below 39 °F (4 °C), something unusual happens. The water molecules move farther apart. Then as water reaches its freezing point, the water molecules reconfigure themselves to form a crystal, which forces the molecules farther apart. The frozen water expands to become 9% larger than the original volume of the liquid water. Water's ability to expand when it freezes is the reason that ice floats on liquid water (ice has a lower density than liquid water).

Ice as an Agent of Weathering

Similar to the scenario in Figure 10, water expands when it seeps into cracks in rocks. It enters the rock in its liquid form and freezes when temperatures dip below 0 °C. As the ice expands, it forces the crack in the rock apart in a process called frost wedging. When the temperature increases, the ice thaws, returning to the liquid state. The thawing exposes the widened crack in the rock to nature. The repetition of this process over many years can cause wide openings in rocks and ultimately break them down into sediments.

 Predict What would happen if you placed water in a crack in a rock and placed the rock in the freezer? What if you repeated this every day for a month?

FIGURE 11: As water freezes in cracks in the rock, the ice expands, pushing the rock apart.

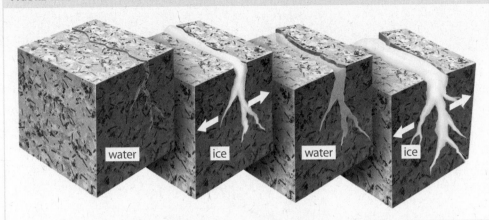

water   ice   water   ice

Many features in nature are the result of frost wedging. Bryce Canyon National Park is known for unusual spires of rock that fill the canyon. The sandstone spires are primarily formed by frost wedging. The rocks are exposed to more than 200 freeze-thaw cycles every year. The process wedges the rocks apart forming the unique, finger-like spires of rock. Unfortunately, the same process that creates these remarkable features is also the cause of their destruction. Once the rock is broken by ice, it is carried away by liquid water. It is estimated that the average rate of erosion at Bryce Canyon National Park is 2–4 feet every 100 years. The rapid rate of erosion will eventually erase any evidence of these unique features from the region.

FIGURE 12: Freezing and thawing cracks concrete.

Frost wedging is not only destructive to rocks, it also is destructive to manufactured structures. Water can seep into any porous structure, like concrete sidewalks or asphalt. Water expands as it freezes, resulting in frost wedging just like in rocks. As more surface area is exposed to the environment, water can continue to break down the structure by freeze thawing, as well as by dissolving the substance. Communities must continuously replace and repair sidewalks and roads to avoid dangerous pavement conditions.

Explain How do the properties of water as a liquid and a solid affect rocks and human-made structures?

Unique Properties of Water

Predict What property of water allows it to produce lake-effect snow?

Some regions of the country experience unusually large and frequent snowstorms. Many of these areas are nestled close to large bodies of water, like lakes. Cities on the shores of lakes receive some of the heaviest snowfalls in all of the United States. Some cities like Cleveland, Ohio, have been known to experience snowfalls as large as 178 cm from a single winter storm.

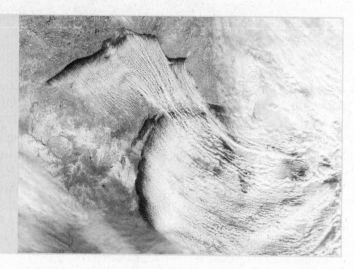

FIGURE 13: Winter winds move across Lakes Superior and Michigan.

Water Retains Heat

Though Chicago and Lake Michigan experienced nearly the same atmospheric temperatures in 2015, their temperatures changed at different speeds. As can be seen in Figure 14, Chicago warms up and cools down faster than Lake Michigan. This results from the difference between water and land in the way they store energy. Specific heat is a property of a substance that describes the amount of energy required to raise its temperature. Water requires more energy to change its temperature than land does, so we would say that it has a higher specific heat.

Analyze Using the graph, how does water temperature change compared to air temperature?

Mean Monthly Temperature

FIGURE 14: The water of Lake Michigan takes longer to heat up and cool down than the land surrounding it. As a result, it doesn't get as hot in the summer or as cold in the winter.

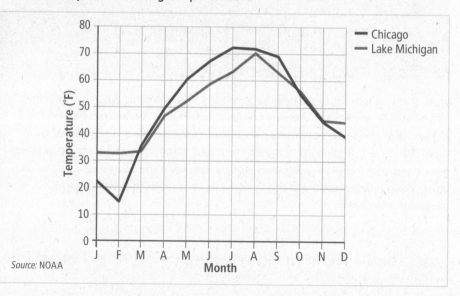

Source: NOAA

As a result of water warming and cooling more slowly than air or land, oceans and lakes modify the temperature of a region by slowing its rate of change. Water surrounding or near cities takes longer to heat up and longer to cool down than do land masses, so cities near large bodies of water tend to have less change and less extreme temperatures than inland cities. This is why, even though Chicago's temperature changed faster than Lake Michigan's, it changed more slowly than cities farther from the water. This property of water is one reason why states on the coast and in the center of the United States can differ so much in temperature patterns. A midwestern state, such as Nebraska, will have colder winters and hotter summers than Oregon, which is located at a higher latitude but is situated next to the Pacific Ocean.

The Water Cycle

Water is a unique molecule on the planet because it can exist in the three phases of matter—solid, liquid, or gas—at the temperature and pressure conditions of the planet's surface. The water cycle describes how water transitions through the three phases of matter at or close to the planet's surface. At Earth's surface, water evaporates, transitioning from liquid water to water vapor. As water evaporates from the planet's surface, it increases the humidity of the surrounding air. When the concentration of water vapor in the air is high enough, the water will condense, transitioning from water vapor to tiny droplets of liquid water or ice. The water falls from the atmosphere as precipitation, primarily as rain, snow, or hail, back to the planet's surface. The precipitation recharges oceans, rivers, and lakes, as well as percolates through the rocks and soil, recharging aquifers.

FIGURE 15: As temperature cools, water vapor condenses to form tiny liquid water droplets that hang in the air as fog.

FIGURE 16: The water cycle shows the movement of water between different spheres on the planet.

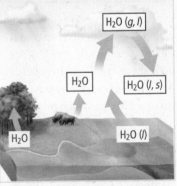

Predict How do warm water molecules change the temperature of cool air molecules?

As water moves through the water cycle, it absorbs and transfers heat as water undergoes phase changes. Returning to a previous example, lake-effect snow forms when a cold air mass passes over a large body of water, like an ocean or lake. The water has a higher specific heat capacity than the overlying air. The air warms as it passes over the lake. Warm air can hold more water vapor than cold air. Water evaporates from the lake surface into the overlying air mass. As the air moves away from the body of water, it cools. Cool air cannot hold as much water vapor as warm air. The water vapor begins to condense, producing precipitation that falls to Earth's surface as snow, rain, hail, or sleet.

Explain Why is the specific heat of water an important property, especially for communities living close to the ocean?

Guided Research

Hypersaline Environments

FIGURE 16: Stromatolites in Shark Bay, Australia

Recall that water is a universal solvent. It can easily dissolve compounds, commonly called salts. Salinity is the measure of all the salts dissolved in water. It is measured in parts per thousand (ppt). Salinity is used to differentiate fresh water from ocean water. Fresh water has an average salinity of less than 10 ppt, whereas ocean water has an average salinity of 35 ppt. This means every kilogram (1000 grams) of ocean water contains 35 grams of dissolved salt. Not all ocean water is the same, however. A hypersaline environment is an example of extremely salty water. It can have a salinity of up to a 350 ppt, which means a kilogram of water contains 350 grams of dissolved salt!

Hypersaline environments are typically found where restricted water flow allows a high concentration of dissolved salts to develop. Some organisms survive in these harsh environments because there are few organisms around to eat them.. For example, in Shark Bay on the western coast of Australia, hypersaline conditions result from a combination of restricted water flow and high rates of evaporation due to the arid climate. The bay contains structures called stromatolites that have been part of the fossil record for more than three billion years. A stromatolite consists of layers of microorganisms (cyanobacteria) that trap sediment. Then a new layer of organisms grows on the sediment layer. Over time these layers build up into a mound. These mound-like structures dot the shallow coastline of Shark Bay.

 Language Arts Connection Research where hypersaline environments form today. What kind of ecosystems form in this extreme environment?

 WATER AND ENERGY | **OCEAN SURFACE TEMPERATURES** | Go online to choose one of these other paths.

Lesson Self-Check

CAN YOU EXPLAIN IT?

FIGURE 17: Potholes are troublesome and dangerous road hazards that seem to reappear every year.

While there are many misconceptions about how potholes form, the role of water is clear. Water occurs naturally in all three phases of matter—solid, liquid, and gas—at Earth's surface. Liquid water can enter cracks in surfaces and freeze to form ice. As water freezes, its volume expands by 9%. Water expands when it freezes, whether it's in cracks in a rock or in a road surface. The ice acts like a wedge, forcing the crack farther apart.

As a result of frost wedging and heavy use from passing traffic, roads sustain a great deal of wear and tear every year. As weathering increases, potholes get larger. As potholes get larger, traffic slows, not only to avoid the large chasms opening in the road, but also to wait as road crews patch and repair the road every year.

Predict What factors lead to the formation of potholes in areas of cold climate? What role does water play in their formation?

CHECKPOINTS

Check Your Understanding

1. What are some fundamental properties of water? Choose all that apply.
   a. It is a universal solvent.
   b. It can hold a large amount of heat.
   c. It has the ability to corrode rocks.
   d. It expands when it transitions to a solid.

2. How do the properties of water lead to erosion of rock features on land?

3. How does the structure of the water molecule lead to its ability to dissolve polar compounds?
   a. It is a polar compound.
   b. It is a bent compound.
   c It exists in all three phases on Earth's surface.
   d. It expands when it freezes.

4. How do the properties of water produce the features seen in caves?

5. How do the properties of water break down rocks?

6. What factors affect lake-effect snow?

7. How does the structure of the water molecule make it a good solvent?

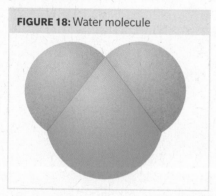

FIGURE 18: Water molecule

   a. It can be found in all three phases of matter at Earth's surface.
   b. It is polar.
   c. It has a partial neutral charge.
   d. It can dissolve organic compounds.

8. Why should a community in Maine set aside additional revenue to repair roads in the spring, but this may not be necessary in Texas?

9. Predict how the climate of an island might be affected by the surrounding ocean.

10. What might be a reason for the difference in the climate conditions between a city on the coast and one far from the coast?
    a. The ocean has a moderating effect on the climate of the city near the coast.
    b. The land has a moderating effect on the climate of the city far from the coast.
    c. The city on the coast receives more sunlight.
    d. The city far from the coast is drier.

11. What process is responsible for forming spires of rock like those in Bryce Canyon?

12. Describe the water cycle, being sure to include all three phases of water.

13. How might the climate differ on the planet if large amounts of water were trapped in glaciers (blocks of ice) on land?

14. Why might a city spend money patching cracks in a road rather than laying out a new road?

15. Caves primarily form in rocks made of limestone. Why is limestone a particularly good cave-forming rock?
    a. It breaks apart very easily by frost wedging.
    b. It is made of the mineral silica, which easily breaks down in the presence of water.
    c. It is not dissolved by water.
    d. It is made of the mineral calcite, which easily breaks down in the presence of water.

16. If substance A has a higher specific heat capacity than substance B, which of the following is true?

    a. Substance A dissolves polar molecules better than substance B.

    b. Substance B freezes at a higher temperature than substance A.

    c. Substance A requires more energy to change its temperature than substance B.

    d. Substance B changes temperature more slowly than substance A.

17. Why do containers sometimes break in the freezer?

    a. They dissolve in water as their temperatures decrease.

    b. Water's volume increases as it freezes.

    c. Water contracts as it freezes.

    d. Water creates small cracks in containers as it freezes.

18. What is the relationship between solvents and solutes?

    a. Solutes are polar, solvents are nonpolar

    b. Solutes dissolve solvents

    c. Solvents are polar, solutes are nonpolar

    d. Solvents dissolve solutes.

 In your Evidence Notebook, design a study guide that supports the main ideas in this lesson.

Remember to include the following information in your study guide:

- Use examples that model main ideas.
- Record explanations for the phenomena you investigated.
- Use evidence to support your explanations. Your support can include drawings, data, graphs, laboratory conclusions, and other evidence recorded throughout the lesson.

Water Resources

Water pours over Niagara Falls on the United States/ Canada border.

CAN YOU EXPLAIN IT?

FIGURE 1: Workers release shade balls into a Los Angeles freshwater reservoir.

 Gather Evidence
As you explore the lesson, gather evidence to help explain how the availability of water resources influences activities in your community.

See the "bathtub rings" around this freshwater reservoir? What do you think caused the water level to drop? Safe and accessible fresh water is a vital resource, yet its availability can be threatened by natural and human activities.

Around the world, scientists, politicians, community activists, and industry leaders often collaborate and develop ideas for how to conserve and protect freshwater resources. In Figure 1, workers are seen dumping specially designed plastic balls into the main water reservoir for the city of Los Angeles. The balls are intended to shade the water in order to prevent chemical reactions that can produce harmful chemicals in the water and to limit algae and bacterial growth, but they also reduce evaporation.

Explain How do you think people can help conserve and protect freshwater resources?

The Water Supply

Earth's freshwater supply is unevenly distributed. In California, rain and snow in the northern part of the state are an important water source. Through elaborate delivery systems and complex water-sharing agreements between local agencies, water from the north is delivered to places like Los Angeles in the drier, southern part of the state.

Water on Earth

The hydrosphere is the system that contains all of the water on Earth in all of its forms. This includes water in the oceans and all the fresh water on land and in the air.

FIGURE 2: The world's oceans, lakes, rivers, and groundwater are some of Earth's natural water reservoirs.

a lakes

b rivers

c groundwater

d ocean

Anything that stores water on Earth is called a *reservoir*. The salty oceans are Earth's largest near-surface water reservoir. They contain 97% of Earth's total water. Fresh water in ice sheets and glaciers, in soil and underground rock, in lakes and rivers, in living things, and in the atmosphere makes up the balance of Earth's total water.

Only a small fraction of all fresh water is easily accessible to meet people's needs. The majority of Earth's fresh water is in ice sheets and glaciers. These reservoirs are mostly in sparsely populated regions of the planet—near the poles or at very high elevations.

Groundwater—water held underground—is the second largest freshwater reservoir in the hydrosphere. Groundwater is stored in rock layers called aquifers. The Ogallala, Floridan, and Central Valley aquifers are among the most used in the United States. Water drawn from these and other aquifers help supply water and food to millions of people in cities across the country.

Explain A resource is accessible when people can get to it with relative ease to meet their needs. What makes groundwater more accessible than water stored in ice sheets?

Infer Examine the illustration in Figure 3 showing the distribution of near-surface water on Earth. Is the relative size of a freshwater reservoir a good measure of its importance as a resource? Use logic and reasoning to support your claim.

Collaborate Research the most important water resource in your city or county. Why is it important? Is it fresh water or salt water? Does any other community have access to it? If so, how does it impact water availability in your state?

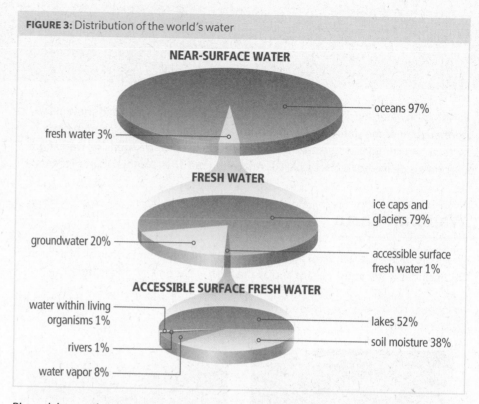

FIGURE 3: Distribution of the world's water

NEAR-SURFACE WATER

oceans 97%

fresh water 3%

FRESH WATER

ice caps and glaciers 79%

groundwater 20%

accessible surface fresh water 1%

ACCESSIBLE SURFACE FRESH WATER

water within living organisms 1%

rivers 1%

water vapor 8%

lakes 52%

soil moisture 38%

Rivers, lakes, and swamps make up the balance of the freshwater reservoirs. Although these reservoirs are the most accessible, they also make up the smallest fraction of Earth's freshwater storage.

The amount of water stored in reservoirs can vary significantly over time. Over thousands of years, for example, cooling and warming cycles in the atmosphere cause ice reservoirs to grow during cold periods and melt during warm periods. As result of these changes, sea levels fall during cold periods and rise during warm periods.

Connected Water Reservoirs

Besides the lake, what other water reservoirs are shown in Figure 4? How do you think water moves between them? Through matter and energy interactions, water moves between the different reservoirs in the hydrosphere through a process called the water cycle—also known as the *hydrologic cycle*.

FIGURE 4: Water in different Earth systems

In Figure 4, you can see liquid water in the lake and in the air as fog—water vapor is also present, but it is an invisible gas. In this setting, an increase in energy—such as an increase in air and surface water temperatures—will cause the fog and some of the lake's surface water to evaporate. Water then changes form and moves from the lake reservoir to the atmosphere.

Solar energy facilitates the movement of water through the water cycle. When water absorbs or releases energy, it can change form. Water changes form when it moves from reservoirs such as oceans, glaciers, rivers, and lakes to the atmosphere. Once in the atmosphere, water changes form again before it returns to Earth's surface.

FIGURE 5: The water cycle model

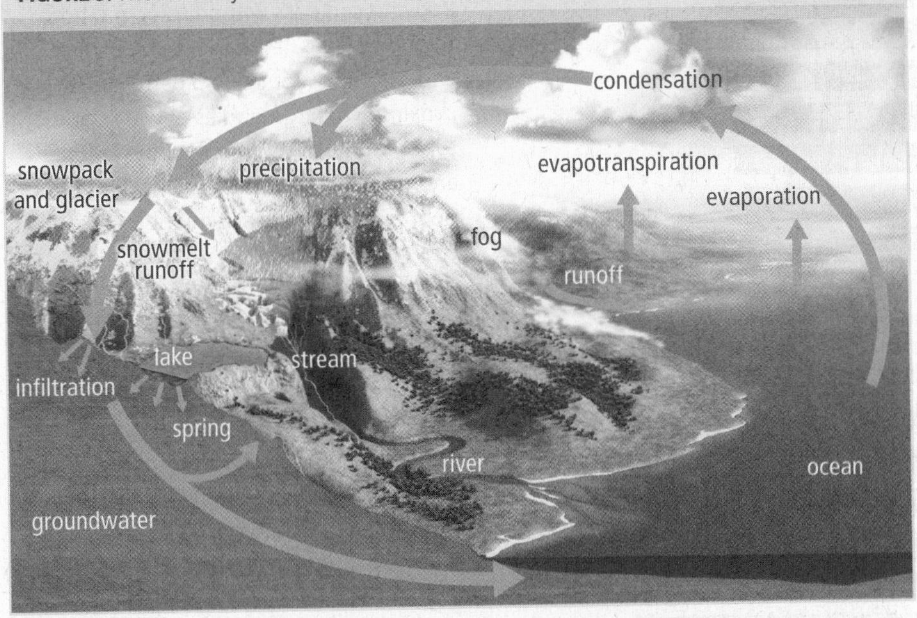

condensation

precipitation

evapotranspiration

evaporation

snowpack and glacier

fog

snowmelt runoff

runoff

lake

stream

infiltration

spring

river

ocean

groundwater

Collaborate On this page, we described a path water might take through the water cycle. In your group, discuss alternative paths water might take as it moves between Earth's surface reservoirs and the atmosphere. Develop a model to describe and share with the class one of the paths discussed in your group.

Explore Online ▶

Hands-On Lab

Water and CO_2 Experiment with the CO_2 in soda and consider the exchange of gases between the ocean and the atmosphere.

Water absorbs energy and evaporates into the atmosphere constantly. In the atmosphere, water vapor may release energy and condense—change from a gas to a liquid—to form water droplets. However, if the air temperature is below freezing (0 °C), water vapor may skip the liquid phase and form ice crystal instead.

Water droplets and ice crystals form clouds that can produce precipitation—water that falls back to Earth as rain, snow, sleet, or hail. If water precipitates as snow in a place that is cold for most of the year, it can form glaciers. Precipitation and meltwater from snowpacks and glaciers may infiltrate, or seep, into the land and become groundwater. They may also flow over the land as runoff. Runoff flows downhill and often merges with water in streams and rivers. Rivers may flow into lakes, aquifers, or they may return water to the oceans.

Water moves through the reservoirs in the water cycle over different time scales. Water in the atmosphere, for example, has the shortest average residence time—only about 9 days. Residence time is the time matter is estimated to remain within a reservoir. The average residence time of water in ice sheets is 20 000 years. Groundwater can have a residence time from 100 years for aquifers near the surface to 10 000 years for those deep underground.

The water cycle is an example of a biogeochemical cycle. Recall that in a biogeochemical cycle, matter and energy move through Earth's living and nonliving systems. The movement of water in various forms is important to living things in the biosphere, weathering and erosion in the lithosphere, and the formation of storms in the atmosphere. For example, through transpiration, plants return water that they extract from soil back to the atmosphere as water vapor.

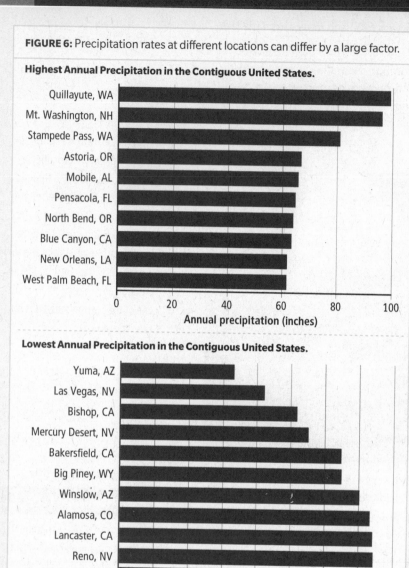

FIGURE 6: Precipitation rates at different locations can differ by a large factor.

Highest Annual Precipitation in the Contiguous United States.

Quillayute, WA
Mt. Washington, NH
Stampede Pass, WA
Astoria, OR
Mobile, AL
Pensacola, FL
North Bend, OR
Blue Canyon, CA
New Orleans, LA
West Palm Beach, FL

Annual precipitation (inches)

Lowest Annual Precipitation in the Contiguous United States.

Yuma, AZ
Las Vegas, NV
Bishop, CA
Mercury Desert, NV
Bakersfield, CA
Big Piney, WY
Winslow, AZ
Alamosa, CO
Lancaster, CA
Reno, NV

Annual precipitation (inches)

Source: NOAA

Uneven Precipitation

What factors affect the amount of annual precipitation that a place receives? Precipitation redistributes fresh water over Earth's surface, but it does so unevenly. In some places, decades can pass without precipitation. In other places, it is easier to track days without rain. Global wind patterns, proximity to large bodies of water, and topography, or the shape of the land, are some factors that affect the amount of precipitation a place might receive over time.

Materials

Precipitation data, maps of the North America, reference books or access to the Internet

Analysis

Examine the precipitation charts. Select a location from each chart. Research these locations to describe how they differ in terms of wind patterns, proximity to large bodies of water, and topography. Then use evidence to explain how the factors listed above may affect the precipitation rates of your chosen locations.

Precipitation and the Freshwater Supply

Explain Some of the world's highest precipitation rates are observed near the equator. Use evidence and reasoning to explain this observation.

Whether precipitation produces water that is accessible to meet people's needs depends on many factors. The majority of the world's precipitation takes place over the oceans and is immediately inaccessible to people. Of the precipitation that falls on land, that which falls in cities is largely lost as it quickly turns into runoff over paved streets and mixes with oil and other pollutants. Precipitation that falls in rural, undeveloped areas has the greatest potential of being available to meet people's needs.

Predict Think about the distribution of water on Earth's surface. Make a prediction about how Earth's water reservoirs might be affected by the observed pattern of increasing average global temperatures.

Freshwater Resources

Surface water is fresh water that is available for people and organisms to use. Humans have been drawn to areas where surface water is abundant.

Surface Water

Lakes, swamps, and rivers are examples of surface water resources. Lakes store the largest share of surface water. The majority of the world's large lakes, such as the Great Lakes, have glacial origins—they formed in places where ice sheets and glaciers once stood. Other large lakes, such as the great lakes of East Africa and Siberia, formed as surface runoff filled in rift valleys formed by plate tectonics.

Swamps and rivers make up a very small but important fraction of the surface fresh water. The water in these reservoirs may come from several sources such as precipitation, runoff, and groundwater that reaches Earth's surface. Natural and human activities can affect the water levels in these reservoirs. For example, water flow in the Everglades, a massive tropical freshwater swamp in South Florida, increases during the state's wet season. The water flow drops significantly during the dry season, during droughts, and during periods of heavy human use.

FIGURE 7: The Florida Everglades

Analyze Consider the natural variations the Everglades's water levels. What can you infer about the rates of evaporation and precipitation over a period of a year in the Everglades?

The Florida Everglades is a significant freshwater resource, and the area is home to many different plant and animal species. In a relatively short period of time, people have had a large impact on this resource. Beginning in the 1880s, canals, dams, and levees were built to control flooding and to develop the land. Today, millions of people in South Florida get their drinking water from the Everglades, and only half of the original 11 000 square miles that once made up the Everglades is preserved.

In the drier southwestern United States, people have used the Colorado River as a main source of fresh water. As many as 40 million people get their drinking water from this river, and in California and Arizona, the water is also used to irrigate crops. However, in recent years, severe droughts and increased water demands have diminished the Colorado River's water levels. In early 2017, Lake Mead, the river's largest artificial water reservoir, held just 39% of the water it was designed to hold.

FIGURE 8: Map of surface waters

Gulf of Mexico

Tracking Surface Water

The map shows the network of rivers, lakes, and streams found in the eastern United States. The Everglades in Florida is a small part of this network. The Comprehensive Everglades Restoration Plan (CERP) is a multi–year, large-scale effort to reverse the damage done to this ecosystem by human activity. To understand this project, it is useful to think of the Everglades as a system with defined boundaries and a set of current or initial conditions. Do research about CERP. Identify the system's current boundaries and initial conditions (components, processes, inputs, and outputs). Explain, using systems language, the goals, or desired final conditions, of the restoration work.

Groundwater

Evaluate Glacial till is a type of sediment made up grains of different sizes. Would glacial till be more or less permeable than sand- and clay-rich sediments? Use evidence and reasoning to support your claims.

Soil particles can attract and hold water, but when there is more water than soil can hold, gravity pulls it down into the rock layers below. Water that fills in spaces in rock and sediment is called *groundwater*.

The ability of a material to allow water to pass through is called permeability. Rock that has a high porosity, or open spaces in between grains, is permeable if these spaces are interconnected. Permeability increases with grain size and sorting. Water moves more easily through soil and rock made up of grains of roughly the same size such as sand and sandstones. A permeable rock or sediment layer that stores groundwater and allows its movement is called an aquifer. The small grains in clay-rich soils and rock makes them nearly impermeable. Impermeable rock and sediment layers are known as *aquitards*.

FIGURE 9: An aquifer model shows surface and subsurface features.

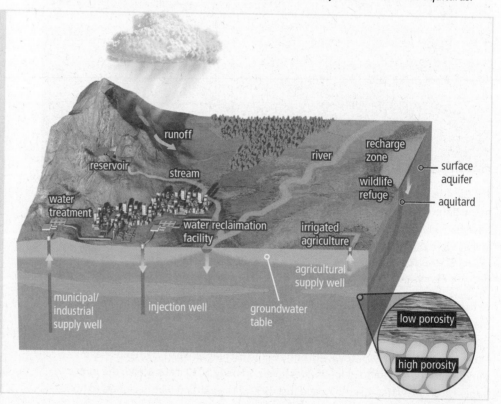

Often, alternating layers of permeable and impermeable rock produce complex aquifer systems. The Floridan aquifer, which spans the entire state of Florida and parts of Mississippi, Alabama, Georgia, and South Carolina, is a complex aquifer system. It consists of a shallow upper aquifer just a few feet below the soil, separated from a deep aquifer hundreds of feet below the surface by impermeable rock layers. Precipitation and runoff can add water to, or recharge, shallow aquifers. Usually, water can only seep into deep aquifers at recharge zones, or areas where permeable layers reach the surface and allow water to flow deep into the ground.

 Collaborate Research information about the permeability of different rock types. Then construct a two-dimensional model to show your data.

 Explore Online ▶

Hands-On Lab

Porosity, Permeability, and Capillarity Measure and identify the significance of different sediment properties.

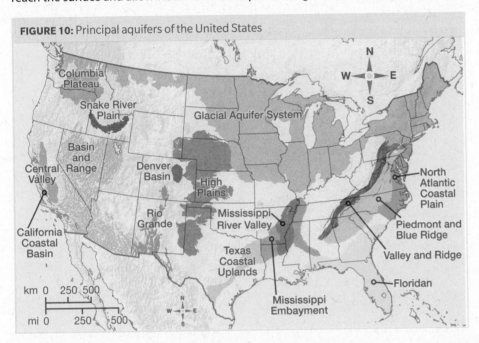

FIGURE 10: Principal aquifers of the United States

Accounting for about 20% of Earth's fresh water, groundwater is an important freshwater source. About 50% of all Americans use groundwater for drinking and household use. Located in the northern United States, the Glacial aquifer system is a principal aquifer—a large aquifer system that can be a fresh water source for drinking, household, and agricultural use. According to the United States Geological Survey, water withdrawals from this aquifer system for public use are the largest in the nation and play a key role in the economic development of parts of 26 states.

Getting to the groundwater often requires operating and maintaining expensive drilling and pumping equipment. In California's Central Valley, agriculture thrives because growers have for decades pumped water from the Central Valley aquifer system. However, increased water withdrawals, long and frequent droughts, and a naturally slow recharge rate have caused the water levels in the aquifer to drop. New deeper, more expensive wells have been dug to get to the water. Yet subsidence, the sinking of the land, is another problem associated with groundwater overuse. Lacking the support of the water, the weight of the rock layers above the aquifer causes the land to sink. The land in the San Joaquin Valley has sunk nearly 30 feet since the 1920s.

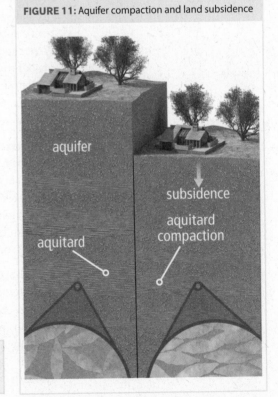

FIGURE 11: Aquifer compaction and land subsidence

Explain Recharge and discharge are balanced in a stable aquifer. What factors can complicate recharge?

Watersheds

You have learned that precipitation can be stored on land as ice sheets and glaciers, surface water, and groundwater. But how do the characteristics of the landscape affect what happens to precipitation? Precipitation that falls on high mountains may form glaciers. Soil and rock permeability in part determine whether precipitation seeps into the ground or runs off along the surface. The place where all these things happen is called the *watershed*.

Analyze Identify your local watershed. How does it compare to other watersheds in the United States?

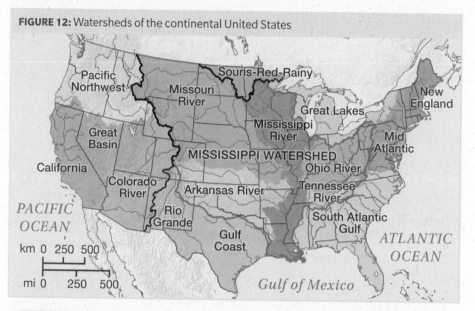

FIGURE 12: Watersheds of the continental United States

A watershed is the area of land that drains all precipitation into a common place. All of the surface water—lakes, streams, reservoirs, and wetlands—and all the underlying groundwater makes up the watershed. A watershed could be a small area, such as a ravine and a small stream, or a much larger area, such as the Mississippi watershed. Watersheds are separated by a divide—a mountain or ridge of high ground that divides the flow of water into the different watersheds. Watersheds are characterized by their size, shape, land use, geology, soils, vegetation, and discharge—the amount of water it drains. These variables affect each other and the movement of water of a region.

As one example, the Santa Clara River watershed is located in southern California, near Los Angeles. It covers an area of about 1634 square miles and is bounded by mountain ranges on nearly all sides. The region has a moderate climate, with warm and wet winters and calm, hot, and dry summers. Precipitation rates vary widely over time. Extended periods of little or no rain are common. During El Niño years, increased precipitation can cause substantial flooding in the watershed. Overall, the watershed gets just enough precipitation over time to avoid being classified as semi-arid.

The Santa Clara River, the largest in southern California, drains the Santa Clara River watershed. The river supports a variety of plant and animal life, but some species are threatened by human use and pollution. People use the water of the watershed for drinking, farming, and recreation. Food growers in the area benefit from the regular flooding that deposits rich sediment on the valley floor, fertilizing the soil. Citrus, avocados, strawberries, and other crops are grown in the fertile land nourished by floods.

FIGURE 13: The Santa Clara watershed

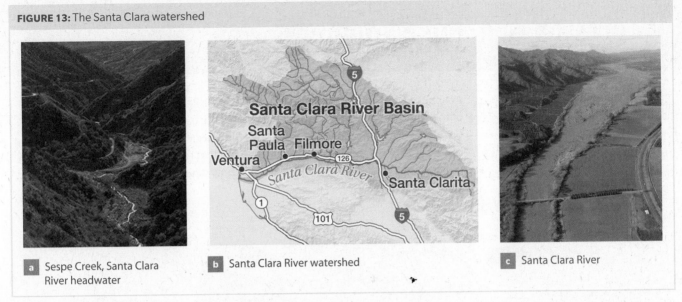

a   Sespe Creek, Santa Clara River headwater

b   Santa Clara River watershed

c   Santa Clara River

Although the watershed and the Santa Clara River have been modified through farming, mining, and flood control systems, there is awareness in the community that further development puts both people and the environment at risk. In recent years, proposals to build thousands of housing and commercial units in the area have been challenged in court and delayed. Opponents of these projects cite environmental studies indicating that human activity can severely impact ecosystems in the watershed, threatening plant and animal species unique to the region. Opponents of development are also concerned that building on floodplains in the watershed will put people in danger during floods. They reason that further damage to the watershed might be caused as new flood control systems would be proposed and likely built in the watershed to protect any new developments.

Identify What are some natural and human activities that can affect water in a watershed?

Watersheds and the Water Cycle

It is in the watersheds that all of Earth's systems interact through the water cycle. Precipitation formed in the atmosphere falls on the lithosphere within a watershed. Precipitation and runoff reshape the land through weathering and erosion. Surface runoff breaks down and carries rock and sediment in rivers and streams. During floods, rivers deposit large quantities of sediment in valleys, building up the land.

As rivers wind their way toward the ocean, they carve channels on the landscape. In some places, over millions of years these channels have developed into canyons. Along coastal areas, rivers return water back to the ocean and drop their sediment loads. Living things benefit from Earth's systems interactions in the watershed. Water that pools on the lithosphere in lakes, rivers, and swamps, for example, provides homes for aquatic organisms and a reservoir of drinking water for animals and people. Plants specialize to take advantage of the ability of different types of soils to retain water. Some plants, for example, have root systems that enable them to draw water from relatively dry soils.

Explain How are Earth's systems connected throughout the watershed?

Water Use and Management

Gather Evidence

The map in Figure 14 shows world populations in coastal areas. Why did people settle along the coasts?

At about 11 000 meters, the Mariana Trench in the Pacific Ocean is the deepest part of the world's ocean. At such great depths, scientists envisioned an environment unspoiled by human activity. This idea was challenged when a study found that marine organisms there had levels of pollution that rivaled those found in the world's most polluted surface water environments. How did pollution reach this far?

FIGURE 14: Populations living in world coastal areas

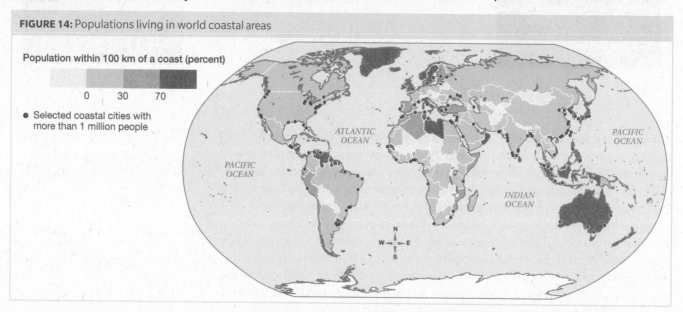

Population within 100 km of a coast (percent)

0   30   70

● Selected coastal cities with more than 1 million people

ATLANTIC OCEAN

PACIFIC OCEAN

PACIFIC OCEAN

INDIAN OCEAN

You learned that the oceans are the world's largest water reservoir and the atmosphere's main source of water vapor. For thousands of years, the oceans have also been a source of food and salt and a means to connect distant lands for exploration and trade. By some estimates, nearly 60% of the world population lives on a coast, near the ocean. Humans cannot drink salt water, but through desalination technology, people in coastal regions around the world, including here in the United States, are getting fresh water from the seawater.

Our use of water resources has an impact on all of Earth's waters. For example, water used in agriculture can be contaminated by fertilizers and pesticides used to grow crops. If not carefully contained within the agricultural fields, this water can contaminate surface water resources. And as the contaminated water travels through parts of the water cycle, it might reach the deepest parts of the world's oceans.

Water Use

An important first step for efficient water management planning is to make an accounting of all uses of water. The graph in Figure 15 shows the trend in water used over several decades in five different categories. In the graph, *public supply* refers to water supplied by a public agency for use in residential, business, and public service such as firefighting and maintaining community pools. *Rural domestic* is water that is largely self-supplied from wells and used to meet household and livestock needs in rural communities. The *other* category in the chart also refers to self-supplied water, but the water in this category is used for industrial activities such as mining.

Water Use Trends in the United States

FIGURE 15: Trends in water use for different activities in the United States

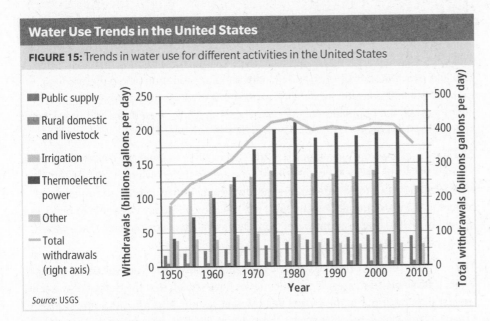

Legend:
- Public supply
- Rural domestic and livestock
- Irrigation
- Thermoelectric power
- Other
- Total withdrawals (right axis)

Source: USGS

Infer Analyze the graph showing water use trends (Figure 15). What might explain the decrease in water withdrawals observed in the mid 2000s? Use evidence to support your claims.

Irrigation is essentially water used to sustain plant growth in agriculture. Water is lost in agriculture when it evaporates or runs off before it irrigates crops. Technological innovations, such as drip irrigation systems that deliver water more efficiently to plants, have been developed to minimize these losses. In the United States, water used for irrigation has decreased since 2005.

Industrial uses of water include product manufacturing and energy generation. In recent decades, environmental regulations and advances in reuse and recycling practices have helped reduce industrial water use. For example, thermoelectric energy stations use steam-driven machines, called *turbines,* to generate electricity. Engineered systems in these facilities recirculate the steam in order to use less water.

FIGURE 16: Industrial water use

World Water Use by Category

FIGURE 17: Comparison of water use across continents

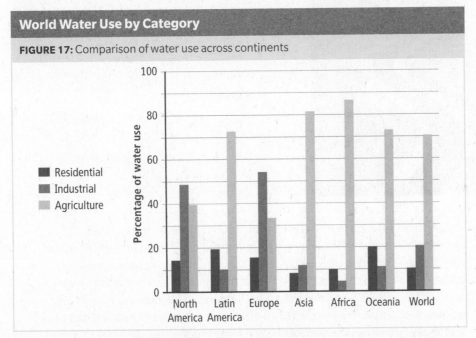

Legend:
- Residential
- Industrial
- Agriculture

What can we learn from comparing water use by category across different continents? Knowing how water is used in different parts of the world provides an opportunity for global collaboration in managing this finite resource. For example, people may choose to share water-conserving technology such as drip irrigation systems to prevent waste.

Analyze Examine Figure 17. Which water use category worldwide might yield the greatest potential savings as a result of water conservation strategies? Use evidence and reasoning to support your claim.

Image Credits: ©chinaface/Vetta/Getty Images

Water and Human Activity

Analyze How does the Los Angeles aqueduct support human activity and influence freshwater availability?

Freshwater availability is one of the most important factors affecting human activity. Conflicts over water use, rights, and management are common where there is high demand but limited water availability. An example involves the early part of the 20th century, when the population of the city of Los Angeles increased and additional water sources were needed.

City leaders at the time looked north to the Owens River to meet the city's water needs. Farmers in Owens Valley knew that diverting water to the growing city would threaten their livelihood, but they were unable to stop the city from purchasing farmland and acquiring the water rights. Los Angeles's city officials eventually were able to build an aqueduct system that brought water from Owens Valley to Los Angeles. Once water was available, the city could grow.

The long-term effects of the Los Angeles aqueduct construction are still being studied. Water is available to city residents, but studies have shown that the output of water is greater than the input to the Owens Valley water system. According to some studies, Owens Valley will eventually become more desert-like. This will impact the people, agriculture, and industry in the region.

FIGURE 18: The Los Angeles aqueduct and a map of Owens Valley

Los Angeles's solution to its water needs is not unique. Even today, other municipalities across the country are planning and developing projects to secure water for their growing populations. New York City, for example, has invested billions of dollars to construct a new tunnel that will deliver water to the city from reservoirs in upstate New York. The tunnel, under construction since the 1970s, is scheduled to be completed in 2020. Once in operation, it will become part of a system of existing tunnels, aqueducts, and reservoirs that deliver water to more than eight million New York citizens.

On a larger scale, the federal government has also used its resources to manage and control the flow of fresh water. During the early 1900s, for example, the federal government built hundreds of dams and canals in western states. The goal was to divert water from places where it was abundant to semi-arid regions where it was needed for irrigation. This initiative, known as the Reclamation Act of 1902, used vast amounts of diverted water to make western, semi-arid lands, hardly suitable for farming and raising livestock, among the most productive in the nation.

The success of the Reclamation Act was not limited to farming. Because water falling from the dams could be used to generate electricity, the Reclamation Act is directly responsible for the construction of hundreds of hydroelectric generating stations. In a hydroelectric generating station, water turbines convert the energy of motion of water into electrical energy. The Hoover Dam is one of the most famous dams constructed under the Reclamation Act. It harnesses part of the Colorado River to provide water and electricity for cities such as Phoenix, Tucson, and Las Vegas.

FIGURE 19: Water diversion programs make farming possible in semi-arid regions.

FIGURE 20: Dams are flood controls systems and enable farming and energy production.

Collaborate Identify and research an example of human activity influenced by the availability of fresh water not described on these pages. Develop a presentation to communicate your findings to your classmates.

The ability of water to flow and be pressurized has made it a valuable tool in resource extraction. Some mining operations would be difficult without the use of water. High-pressure water cannons are sometimes used to break rock and to extract mineral ores. In some oil and gas extraction processes, water is also used to break rock and release the fossil fuels trapped in it.

The supply of fresh water and open space can also determine where aquaculture— the breeding, rearing, and harvesting of aquatic plants and animals—can take place. Freshwater aquaculture takes place primarily in ponds. Aquaculture can be used for raising animals and plants for food, for ecosystem restoration and conservation work, or for recreational activities. In the United States, this industry produces catfish, trout, tilapia, and bass for human consumption.

FIGURE 21: Water used in mining

Water Resource Management

Explain Identify a problem that illustrates the need for water management. Explain.

Managing freshwater resources is important to maintain their availability for human use. Because water pollution can be difficult to manage and clean up, conservation and pollution prevention are very important strategies.

Dams, canals, aqueducts, and levees are important engineering-designed structures used to manage fresh water resources. They are often large-scale projects that significantly impact water resources and the ecosystems that rely on them. In the past, people paid little attention to the environmental costs associated with these designed structures. For example, in the early part of the 1800s, people built the Erie Canal system to connect New York City—and cities along the Hudson River—to the Great Lakes, western New York, and the Midwest.

FIGURE 22: The Erie Canal

Data Analysis

Water Use and the United States Economy

FIGURE 23: Until recently, water use increased with economic activity.

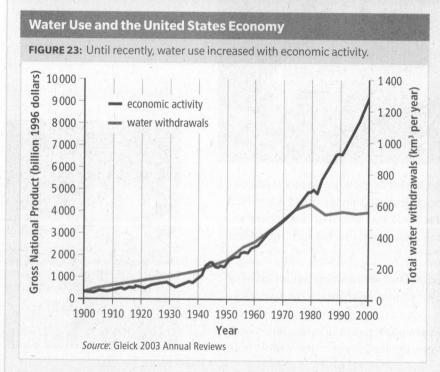

Source: Gleick 2003 Annual Reviews

Water Use Predictions

Until recently, there was an assumption that demand for water would increase with population and economic growth. This makes sense; a growing population would use more water to produce food items and other products and services. However, data for the United States seem to suggest that less water is being used. In the graph, economic growth is represented as a dollar amount by the economic activity line, and water usage is shown by the water withdrawals line. How do the rates of economic growth and water withdrawals compare over time? What changes might be responsible for the pattern shown after the late 1970s?

The natural flow of rivers and streams in several of New York state's watersheds were changed during construction. Miles of swamp and low-lying land were either drained or flooded. The economy of the area benefited from the project; however, it negatively impacted ecosystems. Changing the course of the water increased erosion and the sediment deposition in river and lake ecosystems. It also facilitated the movement of plant and animal species that until then had been separated by natural barriers.

Today there is a greater awareness of the need to protect and carefully manage our freshwater resources. Before a dam, levee, or aqueduct is constructed, upgraded, or just maintained, it is common for the environmental and social costs to be carefully evaluated and debated. Scientific, political, business, and community leaders carefully evaluate the benefits and drawbacks of projects before they are approved.

Water Quality and Conservation

Clean, fresh water is a finite resource. As water sources become depleted, water becomes more expensive. Cost increases because wells must be dug deeper, water must be piped greater distances, and polluted water must be treated before it can be used. Across the nation, water utility companies and environmental conservation agencies are responsible for assessing the quality of water resources. Scientists and field technicians from these private and public agencies collect and analyze surface and groundwater samples. Their work becomes ever more complicated as sources of water pollution are often difficult to identify and regulate. Wastewater from agricultural, industrial, and residential uses are major sources of water pollution.

FIGURE 24: Scientists sample water to test for pollutants.

Evaluate Suppose a series or levees and dam are proposed in your local watershed. What are some of the factors that should be considered during the approval process?

Explore Online ▶

🧪 **Hands-On Lab**

Quality of Water Examine important qualities of water and how the properties of water affect them.

Following strict pollution prevention and water conservation strategies is important if we are to ensure clean water availability. Some national and local policies encourage recycling of wastewater into industrial, energy generation, and agricultural uses, which can drastically decrease the need for fresh surface water or groundwater. Another strategy with great potential is the use of wastewater to fertilize algae used for biofuel—an alternative energy source made from living organisms that can be used instead of fossil fuels. The algae crops could soak up nutrients and purify wastewater, thereby reducing wastewater treatment costs and fresh water use.

 Explain Consider the allocation of limited freshwater resources. What requires clean water and must be done first? What secondary uses of wastewater are possible?

Guided Research

Freshwater Reservoirs

There are many threats to the public freshwater supply. From contamination and pollution, to overuse and drought, water managers have to anticipate challenges and find solutions to keep the water flowing into people's homes.

In semi-arid regions like Southern California, lack of precipitation and high rates of evaporation can be big problems for water managers to address. Precipitation rates can vary significantly from one year to the next, and repeating cycles of above-and below-average rates of precipitation are common.

Open-air water reservoirs are susceptible to evaporation. In Los Angeles, the region's hot and dry climate makes evaporation an even more crucial concern. In addition to affecting rates of evaporation, sunlight also reacts with bromite, a naturally occurring chemical, and the chlorine used to sanitize the water to form bromate, a chemical suspected to cause cancer.

In less-arid climates, there is a more balanced relationship between rates of evaporation and precipitation. However, more precipitation can cause higher rates of runoff. Runoff can increase the rates of soil erosion and sediment deposition. Sediments in reservoirs can be a real concern.

The Rocky Gorge reservoir between Baltimore and Washington, DC, for example, is a watershed reservoir for two metropolitan areas. The reservoir

FIGURE 25: Water reservoirs are a key component of the public water supply.

was constructed by damming and flooding an existing streambed and part of the floodplain. Because the area experiences considerable rainfall, sediment goes into the reservoir.

Sediment deposition into the reservoir can affect water quality and area available for water retention. While the sediment eventually settles, because it is uncemented, it can be stirred back up into the water and previously buried pollutants can be released. Some of these pollutants are trace metals such as lead and mercury, which are known to cause long-term illness in people.

Explain The Rocky Gorge reservoir is in the mid-Atlantic region of the country. Research the area's climate characteristics and recent history of land use. Explain how one or both of these factors can affect the reservoir's water level and quality.

Language Arts Connection Do research to compare and contrast Los Angeles with another local or regional city not facing the same water concerns. What inferences can you make about these two locations?

Image Credits: ©Andriy Prokopenko/Moment/Getty Images

AMERICA'S GROUNDWATER — MODEL RIVER DISCHARGE — WHO PAYS FOR POLLUTION — Go online to choose one of these other paths.

Lesson Self-Check

CAN YOU EXPLAIN IT?

FIGURE 26: Los Angeles's main water reservoir

Explain Think of the problem the balls were designed to solve. Plan and design an engineering solution that would address one or more of the problems affecting the reservoir.

Take another look at this freshwater reservoir. The bathtub rings around it suggest that the water level has changed over time. Now supposed that you are the person responsible for managing this reservoir. How would you apply what you have learned in this lesson to communicate with your fellow citizens about the challenges and opportunities that your community will be facing with regard to the water supply?

As you get ready to address your fellow citizens, you will likely think about the distribution of water on Earth's surface. You will recall that although most of the planet is covered in water, only a small fraction of it is available to meet people's needs. You would undoubtedly think of the Earth system and how interactions of matter and energy within it enable the movement of water through Earth's different spheres.

Finally, after working through this lesson, you have learned that water is a finite resource. As you communicate with your fellow citizens, you are likely to emphasize the need to understand how water is used and managed in the community.

Explain What do you think are the most important elements of a successful water management plan? Use evidence and reasoning to support your claims.

Image Credits: ©Los Angeles Times/Irfan Khan/Contributor/Getty Images

CHECKPOINTS

Check Your Understanding

1. Which of the following statements best describes salt water?

   a. Salt water redistributes solar energy and moderates weather and climate.

   b. Salt water is used for crop irrigation when freshwater resources are not accessible.

   c. During ice ages the percentage of salt water increases as the water cycle is off balance.

   d. Given its large quantity, the world's saltwater reservoir does not have a problem with pollution.

2. In which of the following reservoirs does water have the longest residence time?

   a. atmosphere

   b. groundwater

   c. glaciers

   d. oceans

3. In the water cycle, surface water evaporation exchanges energy between which two spheres of Earth's system?

   a. atmosphere and asthenosphere

   b. hydrosphere and atmosphere

   c. lithosphere and hydrosphere

   d. lithosphere and atmosphere

4. In the early 1900s, the city of Los Angeles managed to secure water rights from the Owens Valley to the north and expand its water supply. Which of the following concepts does this historical fact best illustrate?

   a. Cities have more of a right to water than rural areas.

   b. Freshwater availability influences human activity.

   c. Valleys store large amounts of freshwater resources.

   d. Precipitation and runoff are higher in northern areas.

5. Which of the following statements best describes how the attitude toward large-scale water projects has changed since the Erie Canal was built?

   a. People are less interested in nature conservation.

   b. Decision-makers often debate the benefits and drawbacks of large-scale water projects.

   c. Scientists generally oppose any large-scale construction project having to do with water.

   d. Communities generally think that water resources will always be replenished via the water cycle.

6. Use the following words to complete this statement:

groundwater	*recharge zones*
runoff	*withdrawals*
aquifer	*permeable*.

   Nearly 20 percent of fresh water is _____, which is stored in the pore spaces of _____ rock called an_____. Precipitation that isn't_____ into may seep into the ground at _____ and replenish the groundwater in an aquifer. Groundwater _____ in places like the San Joaquin Valley in California have cause the ground to sink.

7. Explain how the water cycle connects all of Earth's systems.

8. In the Everglades, _____ and _____ were constructed to harness _____ and _____resources. The Everglades Restoration project aims to reverse the damage done to this _____ ecosystem.

   a. dams, levees, land, water, wetland

   b. farms, homes, plant, animal, lake

   c. wells, reservoirs, land, water, wetland

   d. ranches, factories, plant, animal, valley

9. Describe two ways human activity can impact freshwater availability.

10. The graph in Figure 27 shows water withdrawals in the United States. Describe how water conservation, reuse, and recycle strategies may account in part for the observed water withdrawals trend.

FIGURE 27: Water use and the United States economy

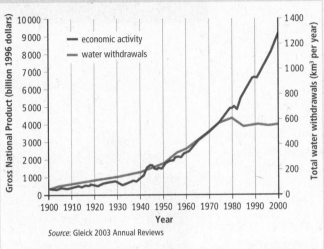

Source: Gleick 2003 Annual Reviews

MAKE YOUR OWN STUDY GUIDE

 In your Evidence Notebook, design a study guide that supports the main ideas from this lesson (water cycle, watershed, water resources, water management):

Remember to include the following in your study guide:
- Support main ideas with details and examples.
- Record explanations for the phenomena you investigated.
- Use empirical evidence to differentiate between cause and correlation and make claims about specific causes and effects.

Biology Connection

Water in Living Systems Just as in Earth's systems, the special properties of water make it a vital part of living systems, from cells to tissues to organisms. For example, the chemical processes that take place within cells can only occur when molecules and ions are dissolved in water.

Research how living things depend on the special properties of water, such as its high heat capacity or its ability to dissolve many substances. Make a poster or other presentation to illustrate a variety of ways in which the property you researched is important in living systems.

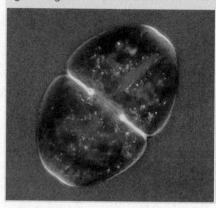

FIGURE 1: *Cosmarium*, a single-celled green algae

Social Science Connection

The Social Cost of Water Water is a scarce resource for many communities in the western United States. Communities in Arizona, Nevada, and California share water in the Colorado River system for drinking water and agriculture. Between 2011 and 2016, California experienced a severe drought. Conditions improved in 2017, but the effective management of water remains vital.

Use library and Internet resources to learn about the recent drought affecting California. Examine different ways the state is working to conserve water and how water is allocated between agriculture and the public.

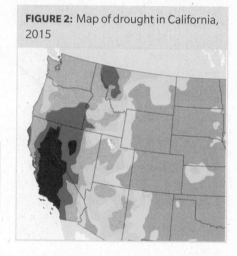

FIGURE 2: Map of drought in California, 2015

Engineering Connection

Safe Drinking Water In the United States and other developed nations, civil engineers design sophisticated systems to deliver safe drinking water to homes and businesses. However, access to clean, safe drinking water is a major challenge in many areas of the developing world. In recent years, engineers have worked to design simple, low-cost water filtration devices that can be used effectively in areas where people have limited resources.

Use the Internet to learn more about how simple water-filtration technologies are used in the developing world. Choose one specific example of a water filter and develop a presentation to explain how it operates as well as how it works within local constraints to deliver safe drinking water.

FIGURE 3: A simple water-filtration device in use in Kenya

SYNTHESIZE THE UNIT

In your Evidence Notebook, create a concept map, graphic organizer, or outline using the Study Guides you created for each lesson in this unit. Be sure to use evidence to support your claims.

When synthesizing individual information, remember to follow these general steps:
- Find the central idea of each piece of information.
- Think about the relationships among the central ideas.
- Combine the ideas to come up with a new understanding.

Go online to access detailed lesson summaries for this unit.

DRIVING QUESTIONS

Look back to the Driving Questions from the opening section of this unit. In your Evidence Notebook, review and revise your previous answers to those questions. Use the evidence you gathered and other observations you made throughout the unit to support your claims.

PRACTICE AND REVIEW

1. In your Evidence Notebook, draw a model of the structure of a water molecule and explain how this structure relates to some of the unique properties of water.

2. Which of the following statements are true about water as a compound? Choose all that apply.
   a. It consists of polar molecules.
   b. It has a high specific heat.
   c. It is an oxidizing compound.
   d. It expands when it freezes.

FIGURE 4: Freeze-thaw cycle

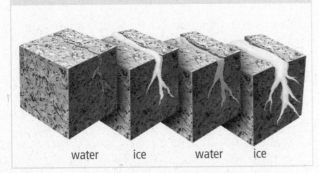

water   ice   water   ice

3. Select the statements that are true about the role of water in weathering. Choose all that apply.
   a. As water freezes, it contracts, aiding in weathering.
   b. Water is the universal solvent that breaks down rocks.
   c. Ice expands and pushes cracks apart.
   d. As ice melts, water seeps deeper into cracks and dissolves rocks.

4. Identify the properties of water that lead to erosion of rock features on land, and explain how this happens.

5. Which statements are true about caves? Choose all that apply.
   a. Caves primarily form in volcanic rocks
   b. Caves can form by the dissolution of rocks on land.
   c. Caves only form in the eastern United States.
   d. When a cave ceiling collapses, a sinkhole forms.

6. In your Evidence Notebook, draw a model of the water cycle. Identify the inputs and outputs of the system. Where is water stored within the system?

7. Describe the sources of fresh water on the planet, and explain how fresh water compares with salt water.

8. What conditions make aquifers in the northeastern United States vulnerable to contamination?

9. How does the depletion of groundwater leave an aquifer vulnerable to the encroaching ocean?
   a. It increases the cone of depression.
   b. It increases land subsidence.
   c. It raises the water table.
   d. It allows salt water to intrude, which taints the fresh water with salt.

10. Figure 5 shows changes in the water level in the Arapahoe aquifer in the Denver area between 1890 and 1990. Use information from the table to answer Questions 10 and 11.

FIGURE 5: Water Level in the Arapahoe Aquifer

Year	Water level (ft above sea level)
1890	5200
1910	5000
1940	4950
1960	4900
1990	4980

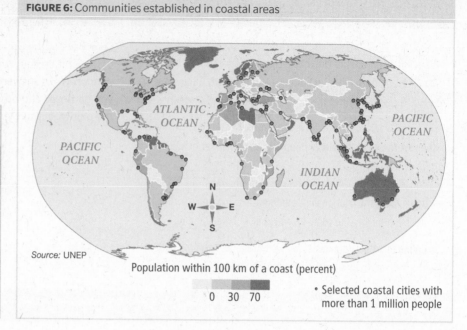

FIGURE 6: Communities established in coastal areas

Source: UNEP

Population within 100 km of a coast (percent)

0   30   70

• Selected coastal cities with more than 1 million people

Match each time period with the appropriate description of the change in water level.

a. 1890 to 1910
b. 1910 to 1940
c. 1940 to 1960
d. 1960 to 1990

1. Water level increased during this period.

2. Water level decreased gradually during this period.

3. Water level decreased rapidly during this period.

11. Between 1960 and 1990, population increased and annual rainfall remained relatively constant in the Denver area. What other factors might explain the pattern of change in the water level during that period?

12. The map in Figure 6 shows communities established along coastal areas. What is true about the reasons people built communities near the coasts? Choose all that apply.

a. Conditions were safer near the coast.
b. The coast provided food for the community.
c. Coastal areas often have milder climates.
d. The ocean provides a means of transportation.

13. Match each process from the water cycle with the correct description of that process.

a. evaporation
b. condensation
c. sublimation
d. runoff

1. The transition from a solid to a vapor

2. The movement of liquid water on Earth's surface

3. The transition from a liquid to a vapor

3. The transition from a vapor to a liquid

UNIT PROJECT

Return to your unit project. Prepare your research and materials into a presentation to share with the class. In your final presentation, evaluate the strength of your collection device. What could be done to improve it? How might you use ideas from other groups to change or improve your own device? If you were making these devices to distribute to water-poor areas, what might be some of the constraints you would have to consider?

Modeling an Aquifer

In this activity, you will explore how water flows through an aquifer. You will use different types of sediment, including sand, gravel, silt, or clay. You will determine unique combinations of sediment layers to examine how quickly and efficiently water flows through the model aquifer. Separate into small groups to determine the type of aquifer you want to make. Share with the class to limit the number of repeated types of aquifers.

1. Place sediment in a shoebox following the layering selected by your group (e.g., sand, clay, sand).
2. Punch a hole in the bottom of the shoebox, and insert half of a drinking straw.
3. Place the shoebox in an aluminum pan. Place the edge of the shoebox/pan with a straw on the side of a table. Place a bowl on the floor under the straw.
4. Begin by slowly pouring one cup of water on the opposite side of the shoebox as the straw. Wait. Repeat until water begins to flow through the straw. Once water flows, stop adding water. Record how much water you poured into the box.
5. Wait one hour. Record how much water was collected in the bowl under the shoebox. How does this volume differ from the amount poured into the model aquifer?

1. DEFINE THE PROBLEM

With your team, write a statement outlining what factors affect how water flows through an aquifer.

2. CONDUCT RESEARCH

With your team, investigate the cause-and-effect relationship between sediment type and water movement.

3. ANALYZE DATA

On your own, analyze the problem you have defined along with your research. Use your research to explain why some areas of the country have more efficient aquifers than other regions.

FIGURE 7: Groundwater well pumping water into a holding pond

4. IDENTIFY AND RECOMMEND A SOLUTION

Develop a short white paper to outline the limitations of your aquifer—how water flows through it (quickly, slowly), the rate of recharge (how water infiltrates into the aquifer), and any consequences that you found with this type of aquifer in terms of pumping or contamination.

5. COMMUNICATE

Present your findings to the class in a six-minute PowerPoint presentation, or write a short report with an abstract, introduction, methods, results, and conclusions/ discussion section.

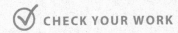 CHECK YOUR WORK

A complete presentation should include the following information:

- A clearly defined problem with supporting questions that are answered in the final presentation
- A model of the aquifer
- A recommendation that explains how to deal with water use or contamination for a community with this type of aquifer
- Images and data that further support your solution

The Atmosphere

Around 100 cloud-to-ground lightning bolts strike Earth's surface every second.

Image Credits ©krasyuk/Fotolia

FIGURE 1: This image of Hurricane Felix over the Grand Cayman Islands was taken from the International Space Station on September 3, 2007.

Hurricane Felix, a strong Category 5 hurricane that hit the Caribbean and Central America in 2007, was caused by interactions between Earth's atmosphere and oceans. Although extreme weather events like hurricanes, as well as everyday weather, occur within the atmosphere, they have an important influence on Earth's biosphere, geosphere, and hydrosphere.

 Predict How would the biosphere, geosphere, and hydrosphere be different without the thin layer of gases surrounding Earth?

DRIVING QUESTIONS

As you move through the unit, gather evidence to help you answer the following questions. In your Evidence Notebook, record what you already know about these topics and any questions you have about them.

1. How does solar energy flow from the sun to Earth, within Earth's spheres, and between Earth's spheres?

2. How have natural processes and human activities changed Earth's atmosphere and climate over time?

3. What evidence supports the claim that Earth's climate is being affected by human activities?

4. How do changes in Earth's atmosphere, weather, and climate affect other systems on Earth?

UNIT PROJECT

Design a Weather Instrument

 Go online to download the Unit Project Worksheet to help plan your project.

Weather is defined as the conditions of the atmosphere at a particular place and time. How do scientists measure the conditions of the atmosphere? How do they use these measurements to predict the weather? Design, build, and test your own weather instrument and then use it to make your own measurements and predictions. How do they compare to official measurements and weather forecasts?

The Atmosphere

Different clouds form at different altitudes within the troposphere.

CAN YOU EXPLAIN IT?

FIGURE 1: The glow of Earth's atmosphere as seen from the International Space Station (ISS) as it circled the globe

Gather Evidence
Record observations about Earth's atmosphere, the layers of the atmosphere, and what occurs in each. As you explore the lesson, gather evidence to help explain the structure of the atmosphere, what occurs in each layer and how the atmosphere interacts with other earth spheres.

The layer of gases that surrounds Earth is called the *atmosphere.* The atmosphere is made up of air, a mixture of chemical elements and compounds. The atmosphere protects Earth's surface from the sun's radiation, helps regulate the temperature of Earth's surface, and redistributes the energy absorbed from the sun.

The atmosphere is constantly changing. Weather systems form, move across Earth's surface, and dissipate. Weather systems do not move randomly but follow patterns. Although such patterns can make the weather predictable, there is still much that we do not know about this important sphere of Earth.

Explain From the ISS view, the atmosphere appears to be made of several layers. Why do you think the atmosphere has different layers? What roles might each layer have?

The Structure of the Atmosphere

How do scientists gather information about the structure of Earth's atmosphere? One way of doing this involves attaching instruments to a weather balloon. As the balloon rises, onboard instruments take various measurements at different altitudes, such as gas compositions, temperatures, pressures, and wind directions. The instrument package relays the information to the ground by radio.

Composition of the Atmosphere

Air is composed of different gases. These gases include elements and compounds. Air is mainly composed of the elements nitrogen, oxygen, and argon. The two most abundant compounds in air are the gases water vapor, H_2O, and carbon dioxide, CO_2. In addition to containing gaseous elements and compounds, the atmosphere commonly carries various kinds of tiny solid particles called *particulates*. Particulates in the atmosphere can include dust, pollen, and pollution, such as smoke.

FIGURE 3: The atmosphere is constantly interacting with Earth's other spheres.

a Plant photosynthesis and respiration

b Animal respiration

c Clouds

d An industrial smokestack

 Predict What elements and compounds make up the gases in the atmosphere?

FIGURE 2: As a weather balloon rises, its instruments gather important data about the atmosphere.

 Predict Atmospheric scientists use weather balloons to take measurements continuously as they rise through the atmosphere. However, weather balloons are only useful up to an altitude of about 40 km. Above this altitude, the balloons break. Why do you think this happens?

Gases in the atmosphere can cycle from the atmosphere to other Earth spheres (hydrosphere, biosphere, lithosphere, etc.). For example, the process of photosynthesis cycles oxygen, carbon dioxide, and water vapor between the biosphere and the atmosphere. Similarly, certain bacteria absorb nitrogen from the atmosphere while others release it. Water vapor enters the atmosphere when water evaporates and returns to Earth's surface as it condenses and falls as precipitation.

These cycles can cause the concentrations of some gases to fluctuate. For example, in arid environments, the concentration of water vapor in the air can be less than 1%, while in wet climates, it can be as high as 4%.

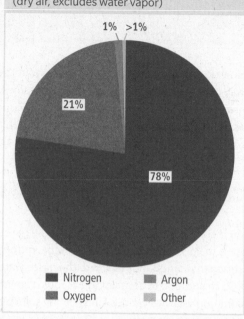

FIGURE 4: Composition of Earth's atmosphere (dry air, excludes water vapor)

- Nitrogen
- Oxygen
- Argon
- Other

Atmospheric scientists have studied the composition of Earth's atmosphere with weather balloons, sounding rockets, aircraft, and spacecraft. Their data indicate that the composition of dry air is nearly the same everywhere on Earth's surface up to an altitude of about 80 km.

> **Explain** How do local fluctuations in the gas composition of the atmosphere relate to biogeochemical cycles that you have learned?

Hands-On Activity

Temperature Trends In Figure 5, does the temperature stay the same at all altitudes? Are there specific altitudes where the changes in temperature trends occur? In your Evidence Notebook, copy this graph and draw horizontal lines where the temperature changes occur.

Layers of the Atmosphere

Is the atmosphere the same at all altitudes? When traveling up a mountain road to a high altitude, you may have noticed that your ears "pop" somewhere along the way. Perhaps you noticed that at higher altitudes, it is often colder than near sea level. These observations indicate that the atmosphere is not the same at all altitudes.

Because of the force of gravity, the air molecules are compressed together and exert a force on everything near Earth's surface. The pressure exerted on a surface by the atmosphere is called *atmospheric pressure*. Atmospheric pressure is exerted equally in all directions—up, down, and sideways. Earth's gravity keeps 99% of the total mass of the atmosphere within 32 km of Earth's surface. The remaining 1% extends upward for hundreds of kilometers but gets increasingly thinner at high altitudes. Because there is less weight pressing down from above at higher altitudes, the air molecules are farther apart and exert less pressure on each other. Thus, atmospheric pressure decreases as altitude increases.

Levels in the Atmosphere

FIGURE 5: Graph of altitude versus temperature for Earth's atmosphere

The Troposphere

Earth's atmosphere has a distinctive pattern of temperature changes that occur with increasing altitude. The temperature differences mainly result from how solar energy is absorbed as it moves through the atmosphere. Scientists identify four main layers of the atmosphere based on these differences.

The atmospheric layer that is closest to Earth's surface is called the troposphere. Almost all the water vapor in the atmosphere is found in this layer where nearly all weather occurs. Most sunlight passes through the atmosphere and warms Earth's surface, which in turn heats the lower part of the troposphere by evaporation, thermal radiation, and conduction. The combination of these factors creates a heat gradient in which temperature decreases as altitude increases. The temperature decreases at an average rate of 6.5 °C per kilometer from Earth's surface. However, at an average altitude of 12 km, the temperature stops decreasing. This zone is called the tropopause and represents the upper boundary of the *troposphere*. The altitude of the tropopause varies with latitude and season.

The Stratosphere

The layer of the atmosphere called the stratosphere extends from the tropopause to an altitude of nearly 50 km. Almost all the ozone in the atmosphere is concentrated in this layer. In the lower stratosphere, the temperature is almost −60 °C. In the upper stratosphere, the temperature increases with altitude because air in the stratosphere is heated as ozone absorbs solar radiation. The temperature of the air rises steadily to a temperature of about 0 °C at an altitude of about 50 km above Earth's surface. This zone, called the *stratopause,* marks the upper boundary of the stratosphere.

The Mesosphere

Located above the stratopause is the *mesosphere* where temperature decreases as altitude increases. The mesosphere extends to roughly 80 km, though the exact altitude changes with the seasons. The upper boundary of the mesosphere is called the *mesopause*. It has an average temperature of nearly −90 °C, which is the coldest temperature in the atmosphere. Above this boundary, temperatures again begin to increase.

In the mesosphere, atmospheric pressure becomes so low that weather balloons expand to many times their original size before rupturing.

Temperature Change with Altitude

FIGURE 6: Trends in temperature change reverse at the various pauses of Earth's atmosphere.

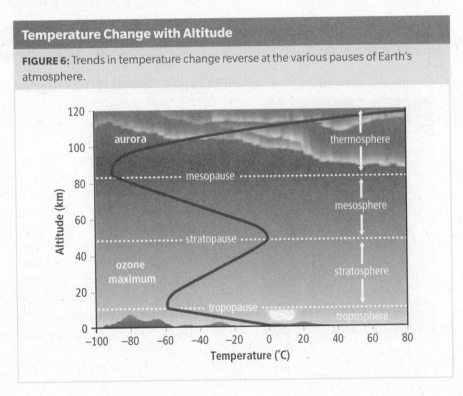

The Thermosphere

The atmospheric layer above the mesopause is called the *thermosphere*. In the thermosphere, temperature increases steadily as altitude increases because nitrogen and oxygen atoms absorb solar radiation. Because air particles in the thermosphere are very far apart, they do not strike a thermometer often enough to produce an accurate temperature reading. Therefore, special instruments are needed. These instruments have recorded temperatures of more than 1000 °C in the thermosphere.

FIGURE 7: An aurora as seen from space

The lower region of the thermosphere, at an altitude of 80 to 400 km, is commonly called the *ionosphere*. In the ionosphere, solar radiation that is absorbed by atmospheric gases causes the atoms of gas molecules to lose electrons and to produce ions and free electrons. Interactions between solar radiation and the ionosphere cause the phenomena known as *auroras*. The upper limit of the thermosphere varies through time from 500 km to 1000 km. However, above the thermosphere is the region where Earth's atmosphere blends into the almost complete vacuum of space. This zone of indefinite altitude, called the *exosphere,* extends for thousands of kilometers above the ionosphere. The exosphere is rich in hydrogen and helium gases, which are light enough to escape Earth's gravity into outer space.

Technology and Engineering

FIGURE 8: Weather balloon

Studying the Atmosphere

The atmosphere has many layers at different altitudes. So, how can scientists gather data from the entire height of the atmosphere? They must use an array of technologies and instruments. These technologies include aircraft, weather balloons, sounding rockets, and orbiting spacecraft. Each technology can carry instruments to a different altitude within the atmosphere. For example, planes can fly at different levels up to about 21 km, the upper limit of the troposphere. Weather balloons can travel through the troposphere, stratosphere, and mesosphere to about 80 km, the limit of the mesosphere. Sounding rockets can travel into the thermosphere to an altitude of about 200 km. Finally, spacecraft like low-Earth orbit satellites and the International Space Station orbit Earth at altitudes of 300–600 km. By combining the data from instruments aboard all of these technologies, atmospheric scientists form a vertical profile of Earth's atmosphere with information on temperature, pressure, and gas composition.

Explain A group of students wants to construct a balloon containing a camera and instruments to travel through the atmosphere. Describe the changes that occur with altitude as the balloon travels through the atmosphere. What conditions will the students have to design their camera and instrument package to withstand?

Interaction with Earth's Other Spheres

What does an atmosphere do for a planet? How does it interact with the planet? Consider the atmosphere of the moon. It is very thin, about as dense as Earth's exosphere. It is made of potassium and sodium, which were liberated from the lunar soil by frequent collisions with solar wind particles, micrometeorites, and comets. Would such an atmosphere be able to support or protect life?

Predict The thickness of Earth's atmosphere causes most incoming meteors to burn up, which we see as "shooting stars." What do you think Earth would look like without an atmosphere?

FIGURE 9: The surface of Earth's moon

Interaction with the Hydrosphere

Most of Earth's surface is covered with liquid water. When that water absorbs energy, it evaporates into the atmosphere. When the air can hold no more water vapor, the water vapor condenses onto particulates in the air and clouds form. The clouds grow as more water vapor condenses. The amount of water air can hold depends on temperature. A given volume of warm air cools to the point where it can hold no more water vapor, than the same volume of cold air. When the air can hold no more water vapor, the vapor condenses and falls back to the surface as precipitation. This interaction between the hydrosphere and the atmosphere is one aspect of the water cycle.

Gather Evidence In Figure 10, you see mist. Where did it come from? What processes change water between liquid and gaseous forms?

FIGURE 10: A misty sunrise over a lake

Interaction with the Biosphere

Think about how you interact with the atmosphere. You inhale air containing nitrogen, oxygen, water vapor, carbon dioxide, and other gases. Your body uses the oxygen in metabolism and generates carbon dioxide. When you exhale, the gases are nitrogen, less oxygen, more water vapor and carbon dioxide, and other gases. In another example, certain bacteria take in nitrogen from the atmosphere and convert it into nitrates and nitrites, while other bacteria do the reverse and release nitrogen to the atmosphere. As a result of respiration, the atmosphere and living things are connected by their exchange of gases.

 Collaborate How has the composition of Earth's atmosphere changed over time?

FIGURE 11: Clouds form over a mountaintop forest.

You've learned how the atmosphere can influence the metabolism of living things. But can living things influence the atmosphere? Let's consider the history of the composition of Earth's atmosphere.

Earth's early atmosphere was radically different than it is at present. It consisted chiefly of a mixture of carbon dioxide (CO_2), molecular nitrogen (N_2), water vapor (H_2O), with only small amounts of carbon monoxide (CO), molecular hydrogen (H_2), and methane (CH_4). These gases were probably extruded from Earth's interior by volcanic processes. About 2.7 billion years ago, cyanobacteria started to remove CO_2 from the atmosphere and released O_2 into it through the process of photosynthesis. Later, photosynthesis from other organisms continued the process. Overall, the buildup of O_2 in the atmosphere from less than 1% to today's levels of 20% took approximately 2.4 billion years.

Carbon dioxide did not disappear from the atmosphere entirely, but rather stabilized at low levels because of volcanic activity which releases carbon dioxide into the atmosphere.

In the past century, human activities (most notably burning fossil fuels and eliminating large areas of forest) have been adding carbon dioxide to the atmosphere.

Analyze How does the atmosphere play a role in the carbon, oxygen, nitrogen, and phosphorus cycles?

Interaction with the Geosphere

As noted in the previous section, volcanos can spew gases, such as methane, water vapor, carbon dioxide, and hydrogen sulfide, into the atmosphere. Volcanoes also throw ash high into the atmosphere. Besides volcanoes, sand and dust can be blown into the atmosphere by winds blowing over a desert.

While the geosphere can influence the atmosphere, the atmosphere can also shape the geosphere. Blowing winds cause weathering and erosion of rocks on Earth's surface. Wind erosion creates landforms such as sand dunes.

Explore Online ▶

Hands-On Lab

Measuring Particulates
Measure the particulates deposited in your area, and determine their sources.

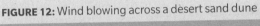
FIGURE 12: Wind blowing across a desert sand dune

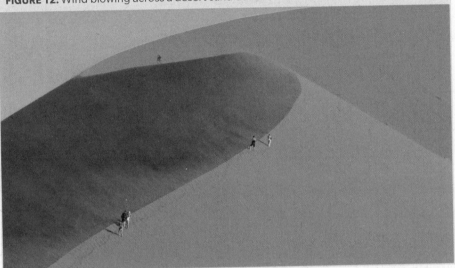

Earth's atmosphere shapes Earth's surface by weathering and erosion. Early Earth looked much like the moon with vast craters. However, over time, wind and rain from the atmosphere weathered the rocks away and smoothed out the craters so that we do not see them anymore.

FIGURE 13: The moon and Earth

a The moon

b Earth

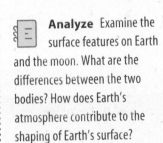
Analyze Examine the surface features on Earth and the moon. What are the differences between the two bodies? How does Earth's atmosphere contribute to the shaping of Earth's surface?

Plate movements produce mountain ranges that push high into the sky. Over time, wind and rain from the atmosphere weather and erode them, which reduces their height.

Explain How does the atmosphere interact with other spheres? What would Earth be like if it didn't have an atmosphere?

Image Credits: (t) ©anni94/Fotolia; (bl) ©John Chumack/Science Source; (br) ©Corbis

The Atmosphere in Motion

The atmosphere is not stagnant but constantly in motion. You see it in the winds and weather. In this exploration, you will learn the causes and patterns of motion within the atmosphere.

Analyze During the Age of Exploration, explorers navigated the globe in wooden sailing ships. These ships relied on wind energy to move. Analyze the map from this period, and describe any trends that you see. How do winds vary with latitude? Are the patterns the same in both hemispheres?

FIGURE 14: Historic map of trade winds

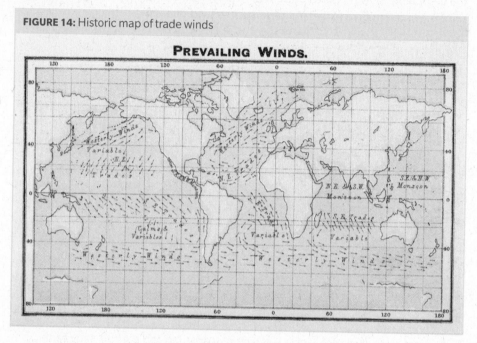

Unequal Heating of Earth's Surface

Earth's surface absorbs radiation from the sun, which heats the surface. However, radiation from the sun does not heat Earth equally at all places. Because Earth is spherical, the sun's rays do not strike all areas at the same angle. The rays of the sun strike the ground near the equator at an angle near 90°. At the poles, sunlight strikes the ground at a much smaller angle. When sunlight hits Earth's surface at an angle smaller than 90°, the energy is spread out over a larger area and is less intense. Thus, the energy that reaches the equator is more intense than the energy received at the poles, so average temperatures are higher near the equator than near the poles.

Because most of the atmosphere's heat comes from Earth's surface, the parts of Earth's surface that receive

FIGURE 15: Earth's surface does not heat equally.

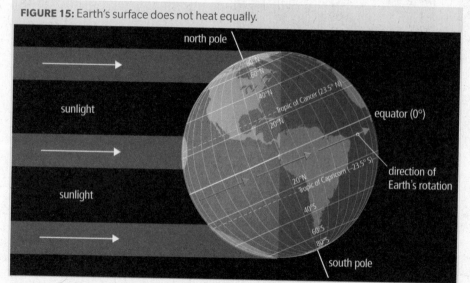

the most energy tend to heat the local atmosphere more. The heat causes the air to expand, which lowers the air pressure. Cooling air has the opposite effect: it contracts, and the air pressure increases.

As air is heated by radiation or conduction, it becomes less dense, rises, and is replaced by nearby cooler, denser air. In turn, this cooler air absorbs heat from Earth's surface, and the cycle repeats. Because warm air is less dense than cool air, warm air exerts less pressure than the same volume of cooler air does. So, the atmospheric pressure is lower beneath a mass of warm air. In contrast, cool air is denser than warm air and sinks. So, the atmospheric pressure beneath a mass of cool air is higher than beneath a mass of warm air.

FIGURE 16: Movement of air in high- and low-pressure systems

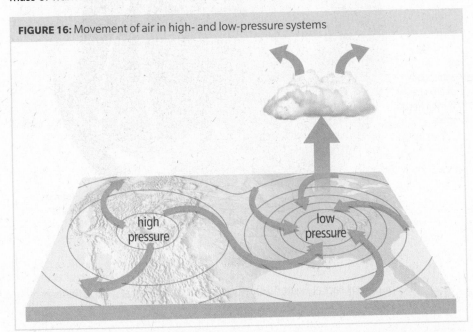

Analyze Does air flow from areas of high pressure to areas of low pressure, or does air flow in the opposite direction?

Where there is a pressure difference, air will flow. As air is pushed from high pressure to low pressure, the air comes together in the lower pressure air and rises. These pressure differences, which are the result of the unequal heating, cause convection, thereby causing winds. So, winds flow from areas of high pressure to areas of low pressure.

The Coriolis Effect

Earth does not stand still but rather rotates on its axis. Because each point on Earth makes one complete rotation every day, points near the equator travel farther and faster in a day than points closer to the poles do. When air moves from the poles toward the equator, air travels east slower than the land beneath it does. As a result, moving air in the Northern Hemisphere has a tendency to veer to the right. The opposite happens to moving air in the Southern Hemisphere. The tendency of a moving object to follow a curved path rather than a straight path because of the rotation of Earth is called the Coriolis effect. The Coriolis effect is strongest near the poles and weakest near the equator. The Coriolis effect has a strong influence on the course of global wind belts.

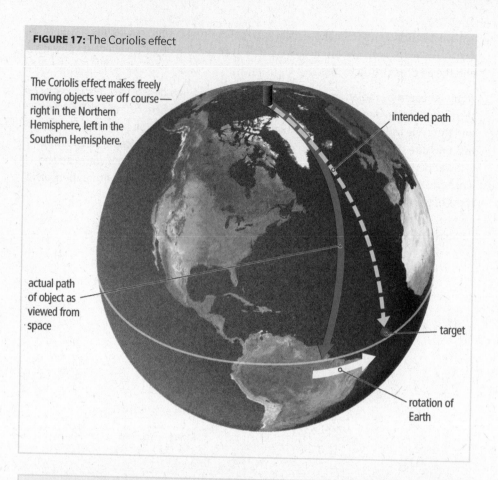

FIGURE 17: The Coriolis effect

The Coriolis effect makes freely moving objects veer off course— right in the Northern Hemisphere, left in the Southern Hemisphere.

intended path

actual path of object as viewed from space

target

rotation of Earth

 Explain Look back at Figure 16. Does this pattern of air flow occur in the Northern or Southern Hemisphere? Explain your answer.

 Hands-On Activity

FIGURE 18: A marble is rolled across a lazy Susan.

MATERIALS
- lazy Susan
- a marble
- masking tape

Curved Motion

Do the following:

1. Apply a thick piece of masking tap or duct tape so that one side of the tape lines up with the center of the lazy Susan.

2. With the lazy Susan stationary, roll the marble along the edge of the tape. Try it from the center to the outside of the lazy Susan.

3. Now spin the lazy Susan. Attempt to roll the marble along the edge of the tape from the outside toward the center. Then, try to roll it from the center to the outside of the lazy Susan.

4. Compare the motions of the marble when the lazy Susan is stationary with when it is moving.

5. When the lazy Susan is spinning, compare the motions of the marble when it is rolled from the center to the outside with when it is rolled from the outside to the center.

Global Winds

You have learned about the causes of winds (differences in solar heating, temperature, and pressure) and how they are influenced by the Coriolis effect. As you will see, these factors combine to yield global patterns of air circulation. Also, these patterns not only affect air movements in the atmosphere but also water movements in the hydrosphere.

FIGURE 19: Global wind currents affect regional climates.

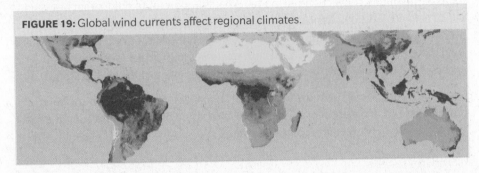

 Collaborate Assuming that the equator is heated more by the sun than other latitudes, would it be a high-pressure or low-pressure area? As a result, how would the winds north and south of the equator flow?

Energy from the sun heats the equator. The warm air rises, thereby creating a low-pressure system below. Cooler, high-pressure air from areas north and south of the equator flow toward the equator, creating winds. The Coriolis effect causes these winds to curve slightly as they travel.

Analyze How might the existence of low-pressure bands at the equator and 60° and high-pressure bands at 30° and the poles affect the types of biomes in those areas?

FIGURE 20: Air circulation and major wind belts across the globe

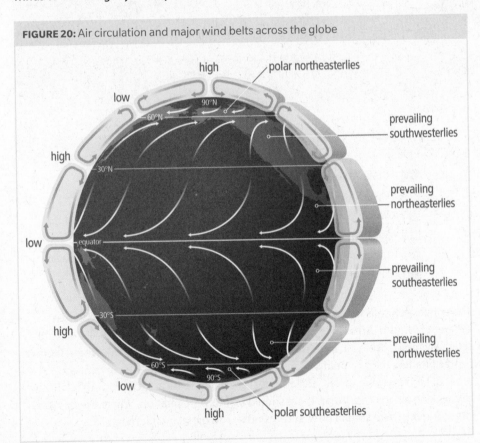

Image Credits: ©NASA Goddard Space Flight Center

The warm air at the equator rises and spreads north and south at high altitudes. As the air travels away from the equator, it begins to cool and sink at about 30°N and 30°S. The sinking air is dense and creates a high-pressure area, which causes winds to flow toward the low pressure at the equator. The winds are curved by the Coriolis effect. This sets up a convection cell between the equator and the 30° latitudes that sustains a wind belt (the trade winds).

The processes that drive the global wind belts are too complex to be described in terms of the simple convection cell model. What is important to note is that between the 30° and 60° latitudes, atmospheric processes set up a pattern that results in an overall westward movement of winds that curve because of the Coriolis effect. This wind pattern is called the westerlies. These westerlies help explain why weather systems tend to move from west toward the east over much of the United States.

Finally, between the 60° latitudes and the poles, convection cells and atmospheric processes set up another set of wind patterns that curve because of the Coriolis effect. This wind pattern is called the polar easterlies.

FIGURE 21: Earth's biomes are affected by global wind patterns.

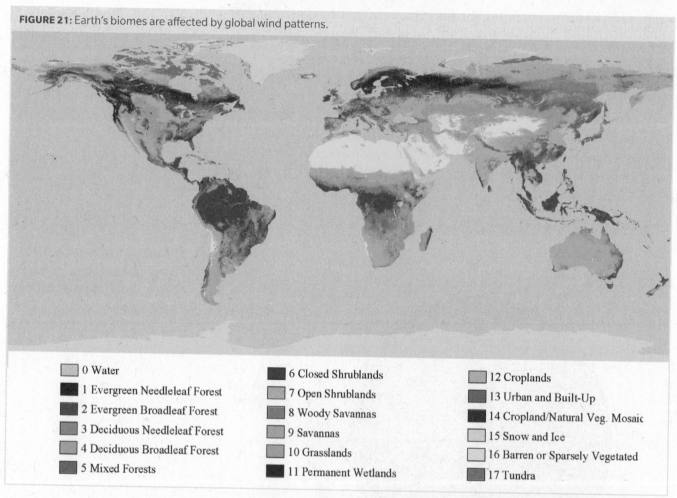

0 Water	
1 Evergreen Needleleaf Forest	6 Closed Shrublands
2 Evergreen Broadleaf Forest	7 Open Shrublands
3 Deciduous Needleleaf Forest	8 Woody Savannas
4 Deciduous Broadleaf Forest	9 Savannas
5 Mixed Forests	10 Grasslands
	11 Permanent Wetlands

12 Croplands
13 Urban and Built-Up
14 Cropland/Natural Veg. Mosaic
15 Snow and Ice
16 Barren or Sparsely Vegetated
17 Tundra

The convection cells in the atmosphere set up bands of low and high pressure at different latitudes. Areas of low pressure (equator, 60° latitudes) are associated with relatively moist, rising air. In these areas, there should be precipitation. Where there is precipitation, there should be forest biomes (tropical, temperate). In contrast, areas of high pressure (poles, 30° latitudes) are going to be associated with relatively dry, sinking air. In these areas, there should be less precipitation. Where there is less precipitation, there should be deserts, tundra, and grassland biomes.

Image Credits: ©NASA Goddard Space Flight Center

FIGURE 23: Global winds and ocean surface currents

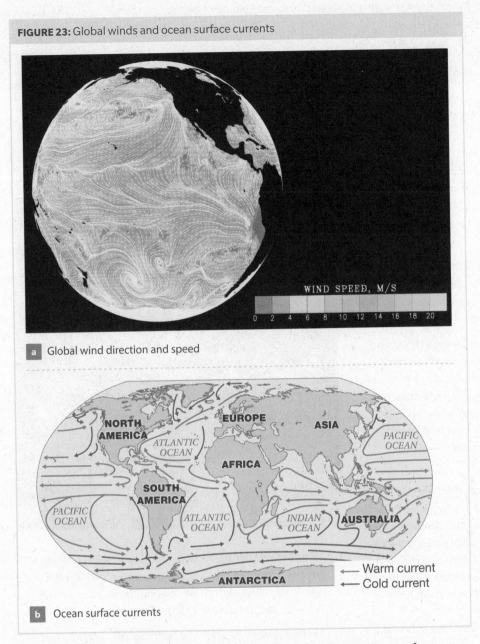

WIND SPEED, M/S

0 2 4 6 8 10 12 14 16 18 20

a Global wind direction and speed

b Ocean surface currents

← Warm current
← Cold current

Analyze the images of winds, ocean temperatures, and ocean currents. Develop a hypothesis of how these parameters might be related.

The data show that the directions of the prevailing winds and the ocean surface currents are similar. Winds blow along the ocean surface. Friction (drag) between the moving air and the water pushes the water in the direction of the wind. The global winds curve because of the Coriolis effect and so do the surface currents.

For example, look in the North Atlantic ocean between 20°N and 40°N where the winds blow from the northeast and water in this area flows from northeast to southwest. In the area of the North Atlantic between 40°N and 60°N, the winds blow from the southwest to the northeast and the water follows. Between these two sets of wind, the ocean currents set up a circular, clockwise pattern of flow in the North Atlantic.

Explain How are winds generated by differential heating of Earth's surface?

Guided Research

Studying the Atmosphere from Space

For many atmospheric studies, Earth orbit provides the best vantage point for making observations of the atmosphere. One of the many difficulties in studying Earth from space is the tremendous cost associated with putting equipment and researchers in orbit. Currently, it costs about $10 000 to put a pound of instruments into outer space.

So, how do instruments and people get into outer space? In the 1950s, rocket planes like the X-15 tried to enter outer space; although they could reach the edge of space, they did not have enough velocity to enter orbit.

Rockets burn chemical fuels to generate enough thrust and velocity to reach outer space. Early rockets like the German V-2 and Mercury Redstone could reach outer space but not enter orbit. More powerful single-stage and multi-staged rockets such as the Atlas, Titan, and Saturn rockets could generate enough thrust and velocity to send payload into orbit, to the moon, and beyond. All of these rockets were single-use, expendable rockets.

In the 1970s and 1980s, the United States developed a reusable space shuttle that was capable of reaching low Earth orbit and returning to Earth. The shuttle used chemically propelled rocket engines as well. Chemically propelled rockets are explosive and expensive. NASA has been researching alternate ways to put scientific equipment and researchers into outer space. These ideas include some of the following:

- **Space elevator**—A strong cable is tethered between the ground and a satellite in geosynchronous orbit, an orbit of 22 500 miles (35 786 km). An elevator can be attached to the cable to take payloads into space. The idea was tested on a shuttle flight with a tethered satellite in 1992.

- **Sky hook**—A tethered system similar to the space elevator. One end is attached to a satellite in high orbit. The other end is in a lower position. A payload could be lifted to the lower end of the hook. The two ends would spin and switch positions, thereby lifting the payload to the higher orbit.

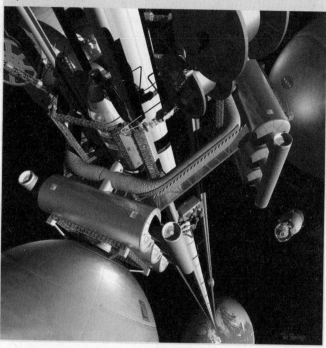

FIGURE 24: Future travel to Earth orbit may involve a space elevator.

- **Magnetic rail gun**—A large track containing a series of superconducting magnets generates force on the payload vehicle, which has no engine, and accelerates it to velocities capable of reaching orbit.

- **Space cannon**—Similar to the magnetic rail gun, but it uses explosives like an artillery cannon to launch a payload into space.

None of these ideas has yet been tested fully on the scale required for actual use.

 Language Arts Connection Choose one of the ideas for getting people into outer space. Research the idea, and write a proposal on how that idea has the potential to be developed. In your proposal, defend your idea with costs and benefits.

THE CORIOLIS EFFECT — BUILDING WITH WIND — Go online to choose one of these other paths.

Lesson Self-Check

CAN YOU EXPLAIN IT?

FIGURE 25: The glow of Earth's atmosphere as seen from the International Space Station (ISS) as it circled the globe

The thin orange layer near the horizon is the troposphere. It is the layer closest to the surface. (You can also see clouds in it.) The blue layer is likely the stratosphere as it is the next layer up. The layer where the blue fades to a deep purple occurs is most likely the thermosphere. It is where the International Space Station travels and where ionized particles from the sun interact with atmospheric gases to produce glows like the auroras (the orange glow).

 Explain Refer to your notes in your Evidence Notebook to explain how the atmosphere is layered. From the ISS view, the atmosphere appears to be made of several layers. Why do you think the atmosphere has different layers? What roles might each layer have?

Image Credits: ©NASA

CHECKPOINTS

Check Your Understanding

1. Which major gas in today's atmosphere was introduced by living organisms about 2.7 billion years ago?
   a. oxygen
   b. carbon dioxide
   c. nitrogen
   d. argon

2. How does the atmosphere protect us from harmful ultraviolet radiation?

3. Which statement correctly characterizes the relationship between water vapor and air?
   a. Warmer air can hold more water vapor.
   b. Colder air can hold more water vapor.
   c. Warmer and colder air can hold the same amount of water vapor.
   d. Water vapor condenses when air temperature increases.

4. In the Northern Hemisphere, what effect does the Coreolis effect have on winds?
   a. It causes them to flow north.
   b. It causes them to flow south.
   c. It causes them to veer to the right.
   d. It causes them to veer to the left.

5. Explain how and where auroras occur in the atmosphere.

6. In which layer of the atmosphere is the maximum altitude to which weather balloons can travel?
   a. troposphere
   b. stratosphere
   c. mesosphere
   d. thermosphere

7. Describe the interaction between the atmosphere and the hydrosphere.

8. Explain how the atmosphere shapes the geosphere.

9. What causes high-pressure belts in the atmosphere?

10. Explain the relationship between global winds and ocean surface currents.

11. Which types of biomes would you expect to find along the high-pressure belts of Earth's atmosphere?
    a. snow and ice
    b. deserts
    c. rainforests

12. Which sentence correctly characterizes the relationship between air pressure and wind movement?
    a. Winds tend to flow from areas of low pressure to areas of high pressure.
    b. Winds tend to flow north from high-pressure systems.
    c. Winds tend to flow from areas of high pressure to areas of low pressure.
    d. Winds tend to flow south from high-pressure systems.

13. Which layer of the atmosphere contains a protective layer of ozone?
    a. troposphere
    b. stratosphere
    c. mesosphere
    d. thermosphere

14. Weathering and erosion occur when which two Earth system spheres interact?
    a. geosphere and biosphere
    b. atmosphere and hydrosphere
    c. biosphere and atmosphere
    d. geosphere and atmosphere

15. Which global wind pattern did explorers use to travel to the New World?

a. polar northeasterlies

b. prevailing northwesterlies

c. prevailing northeasterlies

d. polar southeasterlies

16. Explain the difference between the formation of the atmospheres of Earth and the moon.

17. Which of the following is a cause of wind?

a. differences in gravity

b. differences in solar heating

c. Coriolis effect

d. Earth's curvature

 In your Evidence Notebook, design a study guide that supports the main ideas in this lesson:

Earth's atmosphere is composed mainly of nitrogen, oxygen, water vapor, and argon; other gases comprise less than 1% and include water vapor, carbon dioxide, methane, and others. The atmosphere consists of four layers from the ground up: the troposphere, stratosphere, mesosphere, and thermosphere; each layer has different properties with respect to temperature, pressure, gas composition, and interactions with particles from the sun. The atmosphere interacts with other spheres, including the hydrosphere, biosphere, and geosphere, through various biogeochemical cycles.

Differential heating of the atmosphere creates areas of rising warm air (low pressure) and falling colder air (high pressure) at different latitudes. Air flows from the high-pressure areas to the low-pressure areas, creating winds. The rotation of Earth causes these winds to follow curved paths (Coriolis effect). The winds drag across the oceans, forming surface currents that also follow curved paths.

Remember to include the following information in your study guide:

- Use examples that model main ideas.
- Record explanations for the phenomena you investigated.
- Use evidence to support your explanations. Your support can include drawings, data, graphs, laboratory conclusions, and other evidence recorded throughout the lesson.

Weather Prediction and Modeling

Satellite images show how weather systems move across the world.

CAN YOU EXPLAIN IT?

FIGURE 1: The weather affects what we can and choose to do outdoors every day.

Gather Evidence
Record observations about weather and the factors that influence weather. As you explore the lesson, gather evidence to help explain how interactions between Earth's systems affect weather.

Think about an outdoor activity that you enjoy. Maybe it is a sport such as soccer, skateboarding, or skiing. Maybe you enjoy hiking, swimming in the ocean, or walking around the city. Now imagine the perfect weather for that activity. Can you pick a specific day next year that would be best for that activity? What about a specific time during that day?

Most of us would probably be able to predict which season would be best for a given outdoor activity. However, accurately predicting months in advance which particular day or time the weather will be suitable for an event is nearly impossible in many parts of the world.

Explain Most of us have planned an outdoor activity or event, only to have it spoiled by the weather. Why isn't it possible to schedule outdoor events far in advance without the risk of having to postpone or move the event indoors?

Weather

How much do weather predictions affect your daily choices? We often decide what to wear and what to do outdoors based on the weather report for our area. Suppose that we did not have the technology to predict the weather as we do today. How would this affect your daily routine?

Weather Conditions

If you have ever traveled by airplane or seen a weather report for a large region of the country, you are probably aware that weather varies from place to place. While it is hot, cloudy, humid, and calm in one part of the country, it is cool, sunny, windy, and dry in another. If a storm is moving across a region, it can even be hailing in one part of town while it is sunny and warm just a few miles away.

FIGURE 2: The atmospheric conditions of an area can change quickly as a storm approaches.

Explore Online ▶

a Increasing cloudiness

b Overcast skies and precipitation

Analyze The two images show the changes in weather over the course of one day. How do you think the changes shown in the images affect weather conditions on the surface? Use evidence and reasoning to support your claims.

Weather is defined as the condition of the atmosphere at a given time and place. These conditions—air temperature, precipitation, cloud cover, humidity, air pressure, and wind speed and direction—differ from place to place at any given time. They also change over time at any given place.

A variety of instruments are used to measure weather, including barometers to measure air pressure; hygrometers or psychrometers to measure the amount of water vapor in the air, or humidity; anemometers to measure wind speed; and thermometers to measure air temperature.

Weather influences our behavior and activity. It affects what we wear and what we can do outdoors from one day to another and even within a single day. We are comfortable in a relatively narrow range of temperatures. People tend to stay indoors more when the weather is too cold, too hot, too rainy, or too windy. We are generally more active when it is cool and dry and less so when it is very hot and humid.

When the weather is outside the comfortable range of temperature and humidity, the indoor air can quickly become uncomfortable as well. In many parts of the world, air-conditioning and heating systems are used to adjust the indoor air to solve this problem. People use fossil fuels and other energy resources for heating, cooling, and adjusting the humidity inside buildings and vehicles when the weather outside is too hot, cold, humid, or dry.

FIGURE 3: The satellite image shows cloudy conditions over different parts of North America.

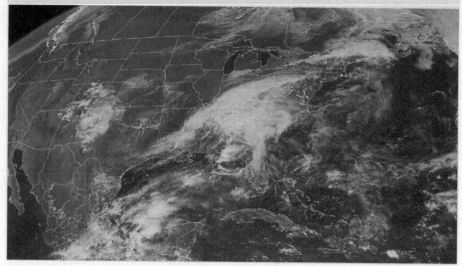

Cloud cover can also affect what we do—even if the temperature is suitable for being outside, people tend to stay in more when it is cloudy. Weather affects people's moods—people can feel gloomy and depressed when the weather is too cloudy, rainy, hot, or cold and then brighten up when the weather changes.

 Hands-On Activity

FIGURE 4: Cloud cover can be described by the portion of the sky that is covered in clouds.

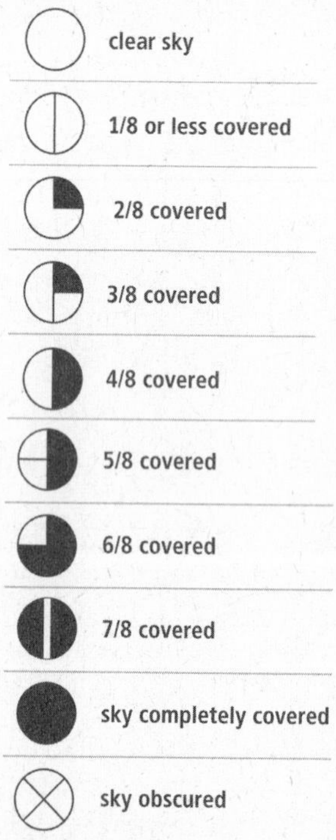

clear sky

1/8 or less covered

2/8 covered

3/8 covered

4/8 covered

5/8 covered

6/8 covered

7/8 covered

sky completely covered

sky obscured

Measuring Cloud Cover

You have likely observed that clouds come in different shapes. Some are thin, gray, and wispy. Others are white and puffy. Yet others cover the sky in a sheetlike layer, while gray, puffy ones often produce rain. Clouds are also classified by their height above the ground. Thin, gray, and wispy clouds tend to form high in the sky, while sheetlike clouds can be much lower to the ground. Puffy clouds can rise from low to high altitudes.

Clouds are visible masses of water droplets and/or ice crystals suspended above the ground. Most of us can accurately describe cloud cover in relative terms such as *clear* or *cloudy*. Determining the percentage of sky covered by clouds requires more careful observation. One way to measure cloud cover is by looking up at the sky and imagining that it covers a large circle. Suppose that the circle is divided into eight equal wedges. Each wedge is equivalent to 1 *okta*, one-eighth of the sky. Now count the number of wedges that are covered in clouds. If three of the eight wedges are covered, we say that the cloud coverage is 3 oktas. No cloud coverage is 0 oktas, while a completely overcast sky would be 8 oktas.

Use Figure 4 to estimate cloud cover on your own using this method. Compare your estimate to your classmates'. Did you have any problems? How precise do you think this method is? Work with your group to develop a more precise method. (Hint: Think about how you could use supplies like graph paper, a mirror, a ruler, and a crayon.)

Air Masses

In summertime, during a heat wave, air temperatures in parts of the country are significantly higher than the average for several days. With air temperatures often surpassing 100 °F, people are advised to stay indoors and drink plenty of fluids when outdoors. Although weather can vary dramatically from place to place, it can also be the same over hundreds to thousands of square kilometers and can last for several days or weeks. Large-scale weather, such as a heat wave, is the result of an air mass. An air mass is a large body of air with roughly the same temperature and moisture conditions throughout.

How does an air mass acquire its distinct characteristics? Specifically, what determines whether an air mass is cold or hot, dry or moist? Recall that Earth's atmosphere is heated primarily by Earth's surface. The sun heats up land and water, which then transmit this energy back out to the atmosphere. As a result, air masses take on the temperature of the part of Earth's surface that they spend time over. Air masses from polar regions are therefore colder than those from the tropics, which receive more direct sunlight. The humidity of an air mass is also determined by Earth's surface—air masses that form over oceans become humid with evaporated ocean water. In essence, air masses owe their characteristics to interactions between Earth's systems.

FIGURE 6: The temperature and moisture content of an air mass depend on the source region of the air mass.

Air masses can be classified according to their source region, or where they form. There are four major classifications. Continental (c) air masses form over large land masses and are dry. Maritime (m) air masses form over oceans and are moist. Polar (P) air masses form at high latitudes—between 60° and the poles—and are cool. Tropical (T) air masses form at low latitudes—between the equator and 30°—and are warm.

Air masses are further classified based on whether they form over land or ocean and whether they form at low latitudes near the equator or high latitudes closer to the poles. There are four main classifications: continental polar (cP), maritime polar (mP), continental tropical (cT), and maritime tropical (mT). Sometimes, extremely cold air masses originate in the arctic and are known as *continental arctic masses* (cA).

FIGURE 5: The characteristics of these locations affect the properties of their air.

a Hot desert

b Tropical island

c Polar desert

Analyze Use prior knowledge of solar energy in Earth's systems to infer the properties of the air above each location in Figure 5. Use evidence and reasoning to support your claim.

Predict The city of New Orleans is located on the Gulf of Mexico. What type of weather will be typical of the area?

Fronts

Model Make a sketch to illustrate the interaction between air masses that forms the arc of clouds shown in the satellite image in Figure 7.

FIGURE 7: The arc of clouds is the result of a front.

What happens when an air mass is replaced by another? Specifically, what happens at the boundary between air masses? If you ever watch a weather report, you may have noticed forecasters refer to a "front" moving in. A front is a boundary or transition zone between two air masses with different properties, such as temperature and humidity. The weather along a front depends on the properties of the two air masses and is often different from the weather within each air mass. Fronts are classified into four types.

Cold Front

Cold fronts occur where cooler, often drier air moves into a region, replacing warmer, usually moister air. Because the cool, dry air is denser, it moves along the ground, forcing the less dense, warm, moist air upward. The warm air mass cools as it rises, which causes the water vapor to condense, forming clouds. Strong winds, heavy precipitation, lightning, and thunder are common along cold fronts. Cold fronts are particularly noticeable in the summertime, when a tropical air mass is replaced by a polar continental air mass.

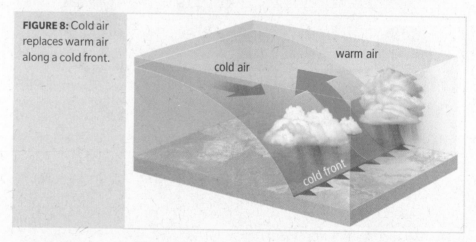

FIGURE 8: Cold air replaces warm air along a cold front.

cold air

warm air

cold front

Warm Front

A warm front forms where a warm air mass is replacing a cool air mass. Because the warm air is less dense, it rides up over the cool air mass. The warm air cools as it rises, causing the water vapor in it to condense and form clouds. The weather that occurs along warm fronts is generally less severe than the weather along cold fronts. The air temperature tends to change gradually rather than suddenly, and precipitation is generally not as heavy.

Notice that the terms *cold* and *warm* are relative. A cold front brings cooler weather but not necessarily cold weather; a warm front brings warmer weather but not necessarily hot weather.

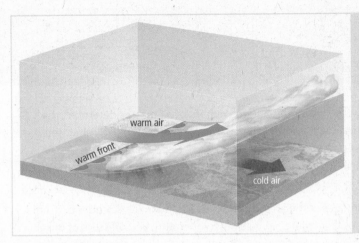

FIGURE 9: Warm air replaces cooler air at a warm front.

Stationary Front

Sometimes there is little or no surface movement at the boundary between two air masses. These are known as *stationary fronts*. On either side of a stationary front, winds are usually blowing parallel to the front and in opposite directions, as a result neither air mass moves. Weather along a stationary front depends on the properties of the two masses. If both are cold and dry, the weather is likely to be clear. But if one is warm while the other is cold, the weather can be very cloudy with much precipitation.

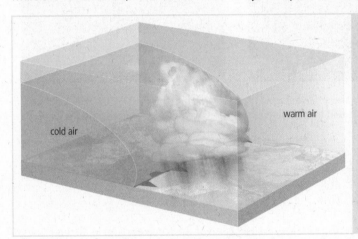

FIGURE 10: At a stationary front, two air masses are pushing against each other resulting in little to no movement.

Occluded Front

Fronts can be hundreds of miles apart, but the distance between them changes as air masses move. If a cold front overtakes a warm front, a complex situation called an *occluded front* can form. During an occluded front, a faster-moving cold air mass pushes an entire slower-moving warm air mass upward. As a result, none of the warm air is in contact with the ground, and the occluded front separates two cold air masses. At an occluded front, cloud formation and precipitation patterns similar to those observed at a cold front prevail. As an occluded front passes your area, you would notice a decrease in temperature and drier weather conditions.

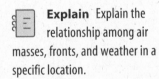

Explain Explain the relationship among air masses, fronts, and weather in a specific location.

Predict Choose one of the four types of fronts, and explain how the weather might change before and after it passes a location. How could it affect activities and home energy use?

Weather in Motion

Gather Evidence
During the day, the air over Lake Michigan has different properties from the air over land. How do you think the properties are different? What evidence do you see for this in Figure 11?

You have learned that the properties and movement of air masses determine the weather of a place. But how exactly do these large parcels of air move? What sets weather in motion? In part, global wind patterns in the upper atmosphere set air masses and the weather in motion. At a regional scale, local wind has the same effect on the movement of local air parcels and local weather conditions.

Look at the satellite images of the area around Lake Michigan. As day goes on from early morning to noon, solar energy affects the temperature and pressure of the air over the land and lake. To a meteorologist, observing clear skies over a lake might indicate a local high air pressure system. Clouds around the edges of the same lake might be a sign of a local low air pressure system. What is air pressure? How is it related to air temperature, wind, and weather?

FIGURE 11: Satellite images of Lake Michigan during a summer day.

a Just after sunrise, the sky over Lake Michigan and the land surrounding it are clear.

b By mid-afternoon, clouds have formed over the land surrounding the lake, while the lake remains clear.

Analyze The cabin of an airplane must be pressurized—that is, air must be pumped into the cabin to ensure there is enough for passengers to breathe. How is the air pressure inside an airplane cabin different from the pressure outside during flight? Why is it different?

Air Pressure

Air pressure, or barometric pressure, is a measure of the force exerted in all directions by the air. It can also be thought of as the weight of the air. Air pressure is affected by

FIGURE 12: Air pressure decreases with elevation.

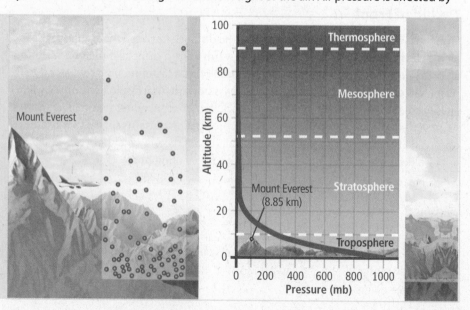

Mount Everest

Thermosphere

Mesosphere

Mount Everest
(8.85 km)

Stratosphere

Troposphere

Altitude (km)

Pressure (mb)

the density of air. The denser the air—the more mass there is per unit of volume—the greater the pressure it exerts. This makes sense—a cubic meter of air is heavier if it is more tightly packed with air particles and has more mass. Two main factors affect air density near the ground: temperature and moisture content.

As air warms up, the gas particles are free to move farther apart. Fewer air particles per unit area results in lower air density and lower air pressure. A cool air mass is denser than a warm air mass because the gas particles are closer together.

The amount of water vapor, or humidity, in air varies. When air becomes humid, water molecules displace oxygen and nitrogen molecules. Dry air is denser than humid air because oxygen and nitrogen molecules have more mass than water molecules, which are made of oxygen and hydrogen, the lightest known element.

Math Connection

Calculate Different units can be used to measure air pressure, including inches of mercury (inHg), millimeters of mercury (mmHg), pounds per square inch (psi), atmospheres (atm), kilopascals (kPa), and millibars (mb). Standard pressure at sea level is 1 atm, which is equal to 1013.25 mb, 29.92 inHg, 760 mmHg, and 14.7 psi.

One of the lowest air pressures ever recorded was 25.69 inHg in a storm in the Pacific Ocean. If 1 inHg = 33.86 mb, what was the pressure in millibars?

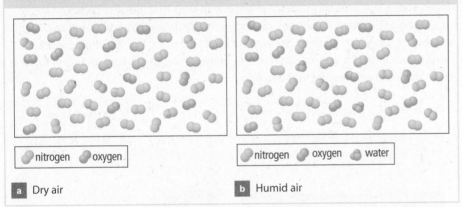

FIGURE 13: Humid air is not as dense as dry air at the same temperature. In humid air, water molecules take the place of some of the oxygen and nitrogen molecules.

nitrogen   oxygen

nitrogen   oxygen   water

a Dry air

b Humid air

Air Pressure and Winds

If you have ever spent time at the ocean or on the shore of one of the Great Lakes, you may have noticed that a cool breeze often comes off the water during the day. These are local winds known as *sea* or *lake breezes*. At night, there is often a warmer land breeze moving off the land toward the water. What causes local winds?

Explain Look again at the satellite images of Lake Michigan. Based on the satellite images and what you already know about the relationship between air pressure and global wind systems, what do you think explains daytime lake breezes?

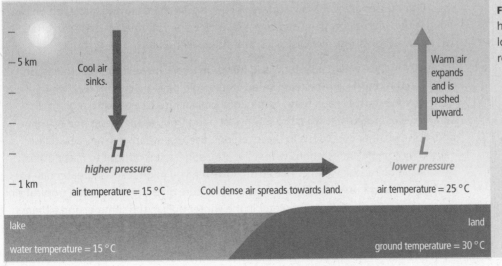

FIGURE 14: During the day, land heats up faster than water. A local lake or sea breeze is the result of this unequal heating.

— 5 km

Cool air sinks.

Warm air expands and is pushed upward.

H

higher pressure

air temperature = 15 °C

L

lower pressure

air temperature = 25 °C

Cool dense air spreads towards land.

— 1 km

lake

land

water temperature = 15 °C

ground temperature = 30 °C

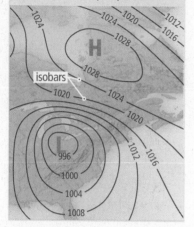

FIGURE 15: On a map used to describe weather, isobar lines show areas of equal pressure.

Analyze What does the distance between isobars on the weather map indicate about the change in pressure from place to place on the map?

Global winds are driven by differences in air pressure, which are a result of the unequal heating of Earth's surface. Lake breezes are a smaller-scale example of the same effect. The land heats up more quickly than the water, and as a result, the air above the land heats up more quickly. The difference in air temperature causes a difference in pressure, which causes the denser, cooler air over the water to sink and then move horizontally along the ground, pushing the warmer air over land upward. The cool breeze is the horizontal movement of cool air off the water. Air moves from a region of high pressure over the lake toward a region of lower pressure over land.

Air Pressure Systems and Weather

You have probably heard weather forecasters refer to the movement of high- and low-pressure weather systems. This information is important because changes in air pressure signal changes in weather conditions. If you look at a weather map of the United States, you are likely to see it marked with lines that look like contour lines on a topographic map. These lines are known as *isobars*, and they are used to depict air pressure. Each isobar connects points of equal pressure. Isobars often consist of roughly concentric circles with an *H* or an *L* in the center to mark the points of highest (H) or lowest (L) air pressure in the region.

FIGURE 16: Different pressure systems are associated with different weather conditions.

a High-pressure systems are generally associated with clear, dry weather.

b Low-pressure systems are often associated with stormy weather.

Surface air pressure systems are associated with air masses and their distinct characteristics. Global wind patterns—which are related to global pressure systems—"push" air masses across Earth's surface. A cool, dry air mass moving into a region can bring with it high air pressure and clear weather; a warm, humid air mass can bring with it low air pressure, overcast skies, and stormy conditions.

In North America, weather systems and fronts generally move from west to east. In winter, in the central and eastern United States, cold days are common, as winds from northwestern Canada bring continental polar air masses to these regions. In summer, winds generally from the southwest bring tropical air masses and warm and moist weather conditions to these regions. Because weather in any season is caused by complex interactions within the atmosphere, it is difficult to make useful generalizations about weather patterns. However, you might expect greater day-to-day variability in the winter because the temperature differences between tropical air masses and polar air masses is greater in the winter than in the summer and air mass transitions are less common in the summer than in other seasons.

FIGURE 17: Low-pressure areas are associated with front boundaries and stormy weather.

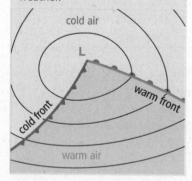

Predict What would the weather conditions be like along the cold and warm fronts?

 Explain What is the relationship between air temperature, humidity, air pressure, and weather?

Weather Forecasting and Technology

If you think about all of the variables involved in weather and the many ways that air masses can move and interact, it becomes clear that lots of data is needed to accurately predict the weather. The seemingly simple, clear weather forecasts that we are used to are based on millions of daily measurements around the globe, on the surface, in the air, and from space.

Weather Safety

The ability to forecast weather accurately and precisely is not only useful for scheduling events and determining what to wear, but it is also extremely important for safety.

While unpredicted drizzle may be just an inconvenience, severe weather can injure or kill. Lightning can result in electrocution and fires; strong winds can rip roofs off of houses; flash floods can submerge entire neighborhoods; and hail can damage property. During a heat wave, people can suffer heat stroke if exposed for too long, while hypothermia is a risk to those exposed to cold temperatures.

As methods of gathering and analyzing atmospheric data improve, weather forecasts become more accurate, giving people the warning they need to prepare for severe weather. While some types of severe weather, such as hurricanes, heat waves, and cold spells can now be predicted many days in advance, others still cannot. Slight differences in temperature and humidity can determine whether severe weather will form in one location and not another. The time between the beginning of storm formation and severe weather development can be short, giving weather forecasters only a few minutes to warn the public. For example, although forecasters issue a tornado watch for a region when they observe certain storm conditions forming, they cannot predict exactly where or when a tornado will form more than about 15 minutes in advance.

FIGURE 18: Weather alert technology.

a A ground-based lightning sensor detects pulses of radio waves that travel out from a lightning bolt.

b Tornado sirens are activated when meteorologists observe tornadoes or tornado-forming conditions.

Collaborate In a small group, research which parts of the country are likely to have a specific type of severe weather, such as lightning, tornadoes, or flash floods. Use what you have learned about weather to explain why some areas experience more of a certain type of severe weather than others.

FIGURE 19: Satellite imagery combined with ground-based measurements enable meteorologists to predict and track severe storm systems.

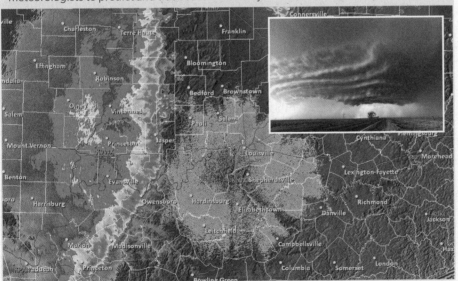

Gathering Weather Data

Evaluate Make a chart comparing the advantages and disadvantages of each technology used to collect weather data. Think about the data they can collect and the relative cost and ease of using each.

Accurate weather predictions require the collection of data such as air temperature and pressure, humidity, wind velocity, cloud cover, and precipitation over both land and large bodies of water. Scientists use instruments on the ground, at sea, floating or flying in the air, and orbiting Earth from space to gather data.

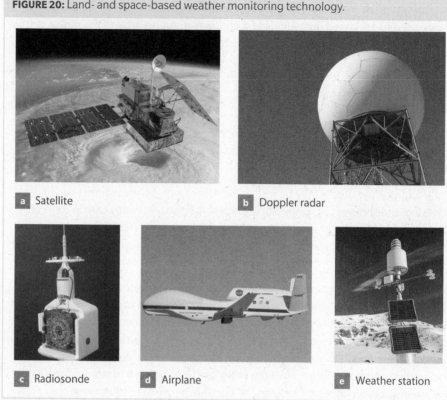

FIGURE 20: Land- and space-based weather monitoring technology.

a   Satellite

b   Doppler radar

c   Radiosonde

d   Airplane

e   Weather station

A weather station is a site on the ground where instruments are used to gather weather data. If you look at a local weather report on a weather application or on the Internet, you are likely to see the weather conditions as reported from a specific weather station. The data from thousands of these stations on land, as well as stations on ships and buoys at sea, are used to develop surface weather maps. Another form of ground-based monitoring technology is Doppler radar, which is used to detect precipitation and measure the motion of the precipitation system.

Instruments near the ground help monitor weather that develops from the interactions of the troposphere and the hydrosphere and lithosphere. But because weather is influenced by all of the air in the troposphere, adequately measuring atmospheric conditions above the ground is also important. Weather instruments are sent into the sky using weather balloons. Planes are also used to collect data, particularly in storm systems like hurricanes that are difficult to measure in other ways.

One of the most important tools we have today for predicting and tracking large-scale weather systems is satellites. During the day, satellites can monitor visible aspects of the atmosphere such as clouds and storms. Using infrared detectors, they can also monitor invisible aspects of Earth such as air and sea surface temperatures. Although satellites cannot be used for direct measurements of properties like air pressure, they provide a global view of the atmosphere, which is crucial for long-range weather forecasting.

Explore Online ▶

Hands-On Lab

Correlating Weather Variables Measure and record weather variables twice every day, and make predictions for future weather conditions.

Modeling Weather

While a weather report describes current weather conditions in an area, a weather forecast is a prediction based on current conditions along with an understanding of physical laws and processes. Weather forecasts are also based on past experience. If particular conditions often resulted in a particular type of weather in the past, they are likely to result in similar conditions in the future.

Image Credits: ©HWRF/National Oceanic And Atmospheric Administration (NOAA)

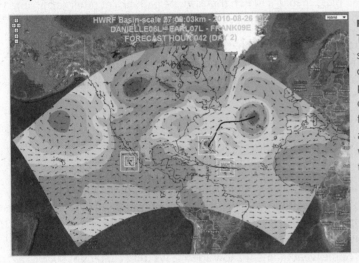

FIGURE 21: This computer simulation compares the predicted tracks of three hurricanes five days in advance (in gray) with their actual tracks (in black).

Analyze Look at the computer simulation models used to predict the track of hurricanes and to evaluate the accuracy of models. Of the two hurricanes in the Atlantic, which was predicted more accurately?

Because interactions between various parts or "parcels" of air are influenced by so many different changing variables, including temperature, water vapor, air pressure, and wind velocity, meteorologists now rely on complex computer models for predictions.

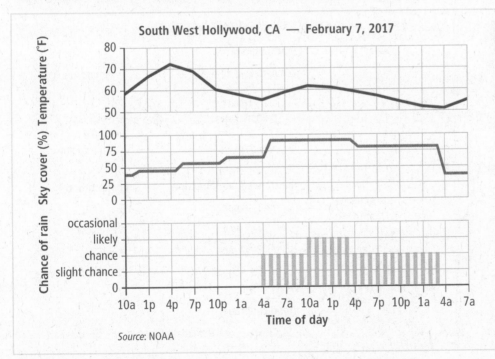

Hourly Weather Forecast Graph

FIGURE 22: This multiple-day weather forecast is based on data from weather stations around the region.

It is important to understand, however, that because weather is so complex, even the most sophisticated models based on millions of data points cannot be expected to be 100% accurate. A small, unobserved change in one condition can cause a ripple effect that magnifies over time. In general, short-term forecasts are more accurate than long-term forecasts because there is less time for unpredicted effects to occur and multiply.

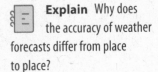

Explain Why does the accuracy of weather forecasts differ from place to place?

Weather Forecasting
Observe and record locations of weather fronts, and predict weather conditions based on data you collected.

There are several other factors that affect the accuracy of weather forecasts. The lack of ground-based data can reduce the accuracy of forecasts in remote areas. Some regions are characterized by weather that is more stable and/or predictable, while others are more changeable or unpredictable. For example, the weather in Southern California is about the same every day, while the weather in England changes quickly in relatively unpredictable ways. The large-scale atmospheric conditions also affect forecast accuracy. It is much easier to predict the weather in a region in the middle of a large, slow-moving air mass than in a region that is in the path of a number of possibly interacting fronts.

The accuracy of a forecast also depends on the scale of the forecast— a general forecast for tomorrow's weather may be accurate, while the hour-by-hour forecast a day ahead of time is not. The forecast might be accurate for a region as a whole but not for a specific location in that region.

Weather Maps and Weather Predictions

Analyze Describe the weather in Houston. What is the weather like offshore, in the Gulf of Mexico south of New Orleans? Use evidence from the map to support your claims.

What is the easiest way to find out the current weather conditions in different parts of your state? You could look at tables of data from weather stations in different locations, but a much more useful way would be to look at a weather map. Weather maps are two-dimensional models of the weather conditions over a particular area at a certain point in time. Some weather maps show specific weather conditions such as air temperature, precipitation, or wind speed and direction. A surface weather map uses symbols to show all of these weather conditions and others such as air pressure, cloud cover, and the location of fronts.

FIGURE 23: A surface weather map provides detailed weather conditions at a specific location on the ground.

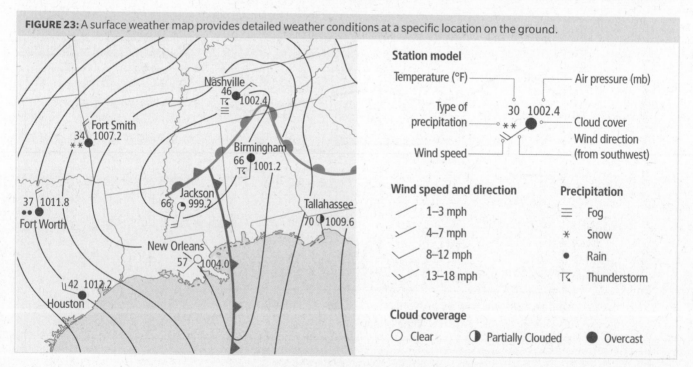

Surface weather maps are useful tools that enable us to understand weather systems and predict how weather is likely to change over time. Surface weather maps not only include the conditions at specific weather locations, but they also enable us to infer what the weather is between stations where it is not actually measured.

The weather map in Figure 24 shows conditions in the Southeastern United States. Notice that the map includes detailed information at specific locations. These are known as *station models*. The key shows the measurement that each number refers to. Notice also that the map includes isobars to show air pressure and symbols to show where fronts are. A map like this allows you to infer what the weather is like at any point in the region.

 Stability and Change

Forecast Weather Maps

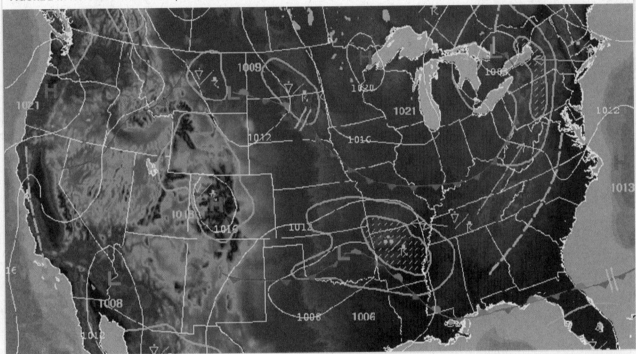

FIGURE 24: A forecast weather map shows concise weather data.

Look at the forecast weather map. What is the weather like in the Great Lakes region? A forecast weather map uses some of the same symbols found on a surface weather map. If you understand how to read a forecast weather map and you know what weather is associated with different types of fronts and pressure systems, you can use the map to describe the current weather and predict how it is likely to change over the short term. In the forecast weather map shown, the cold front located south of the Great Lakes region shows that cooler air is moving south from the northwest. The isobars show a region of high air pressure behind the cold front, and the orange dashed lines ahead of the front represent a region of relative low air pressure. For the northeast region of the country, a reasonable prediction would be that rain would move eastward across the region, followed by a cold front and a transition to clear, cooler weather.

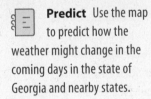 **Predict** Use the map to predict how the weather might change in the coming days in the state of Georgia and nearby states.

 Explain Explain how technology used to collect, analyze, and display weather data helps people understand current weather conditions and forecast future conditions.

Hands-On Lab

FIGURE 25: Seven day forecasts are typically the longest.

Forecast Limitations

How accurate is the weather forecast? It depends on many variables, including where you are and how far in advance the forecast is given. Do you think it is possible to accurately predict the weather 90 days in advance where you live?

Before trying to answer that question, analyze how accurate forecasts are in your area.

PROCEDURE

Collect and Record Data

1. Find a weather forecast for your area that you can access every day.

2. Use the Weather Forecast data table to track the 5-, 10-, or 15-day forecast each day for at least 10 days.

3. Each day, observe and record the current weather conditions.

4. Each day, summarize the weather from the previous day.

ANALYZE DATA

5. Compare each forecast with the conditions reported by the weather service that day (the 0-day forecast) and your own observations of weather conditions.

6. Consider how accurate each forecasted condition is. Come up with a set of criteria for assessing the relative accuracy of each forecasted condition.

7. Color code each forecasted condition as green for relatively accurate, yellow for somewhat accurate, and red for relatively inaccurate.

8. Compare the accuracies of the forecasts 1 day in advance to those 5, 10, and 15 days in advance. Is there a difference? Is there a pattern?

Explain and Apply the Results

9. In general, does the accuracy of the forecast for a particular day change over time? If so, how? Why?

10. What do your results say about the predictability of weather in your area?

11. Based on your results, how accurate do you think a 90-day forecast could be for your area? Use evidence and reasoning to support your claim.

Evaluate the Study Methods

12. Why is it important to collect forecast data for as many days as possible?

13. Evaluate your system for observing and recording daily weather. What tools did you use? How reproducible do you think your observations are? How could you improve your methods?

Language Arts Connection

If you are asked to show quantitative or technical information (such as the results of a lab activity) in a visual format, keep these tips in mind: Use the rows and columns of a table to show how facts are related to one another. Use a graph to compare the data.

| FIND THE LOCATION OF A LOW-PRESSURE SYSTEM | LAKE EFFECT | Go online to choose one of these other paths. |

Image Credits: ©James Thew/Fotolia

Lesson Self-Check

CAN YOU EXPLAIN IT?

FIGURE 26: Weather can affect whether an event occurs and how comfortable the audience for the event will be.

Describe If you were to measure the weather conditions on this field, what might some reasonable values for conditions like temperature, pressure, humidity, and wind velocity be? What might the weather map for this area look like?

How much does weather influence the choices you make throughout the day? How does it affect your daily activities? Have you ever had a game rained out, had to reschedule a hike, or had to move an outdoor event indoors? If you live in a place where the weather is similar every day, you may not notice its effect, but if you live where it is less predictable or more changeable, you are probably more aware of the problems weather can cause when you are not prepared for it. Our ability to predict the weather is, of course, much better today than it was 100 years ago.

Developments in technology used to collect and communicate weather data, improvements in our understanding of how different variables affect air, and advances in our ability to analyze data and model weather systems continually improve our ability to forecast accurately but do not guarantee it.

Explain Why is it not possible to schedule outdoor events far in advance without the risk of having to postpone or move the event inside?

CHECKPOINTS

Check Your Understanding

1. Which of the following statements about weather are accurate? *Select all that apply.*

   a. Wind direction is given in terms of the direction the wind is blowing from.

   b. Weather is a description of the average temperature and precipitation range of a region over time.

   c. With the right tools, weather can be predicted with 100% accuracy five days ahead of time.

   d. Humidity is a measure of the amount of water molecules in the atmosphere.

   e. Weather can be described in terms of characteristics such as air temperature, air pressure, wind velocity, and rainfall.

2. Identify which types of air mass each description can refer to.

Description	Air Mass Type
Warm	
Cool	
Dry	
Humid	
Forms over large landmasses	
Forms over oceans	
Forms at high latitudes	
Forms at low latitudes	

3. What is the relationship between the source region of an air mass and the properties of the air mass?

4. Weather forecasting and severe weather warning systems rely on data collection, data analysis, and computer modeling. They also rely on fast communication systems. Explain why communication is an important part of forecasting and warning systems.

5. Identify the statements on the right that best describe each front.

   a. cold front
   b. warm front
   c. stationary front
   d. occluded front

   1. Most likely to result in severe weather and rapid change in temperature.
   2. Warm air replaces cold air.
   3. Warm air is found above two cool air masses that are in contact along the ground.
   4. Denser air moves along the ground forcing less dense air to rise.
   5. Cold air replaces warm air.
   6. There is little to no movement between air masses and weather conditions hold steady.

6. What is likely to occur in a location where warm, humid air meets cool, dry air? Explain why this happens.

7. Identify the technology best suited to help answer each question.

   a. What is temperature at the top of the troposphere?
   b. What are the humidity and barometric pressure at city hall?
   c. How fast is the hurricane in the Atlantic Ocean moving toward land?
   d. At what speed and in which direction is a rainstorm moving across the state?

   1. satellite
   2. radiosonde
   3. Doppler radar
   4. ground-based weather station

8. Compare the predicted and the actual paths of a hurricane in the northern Atlantic Ocean in Figure 21. The two paths are the same for the first two days and then they diverge. What aspect of weather forecasting explains this difference?

Use Figure 27 to answer Questions 9–12.

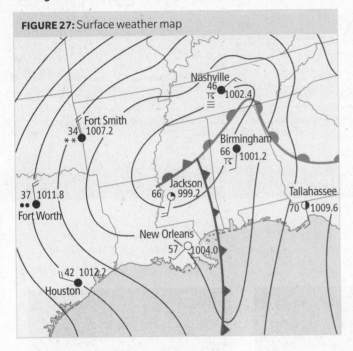

FIGURE 27: Surface weather map

9. In which city is air pressure lowest?
   a. Birmingham, AL
   b. Fort Worth, TX
   c. Jackson, MS
   d. New Orleans, LA

10. In general, which best describes the way the wind is blowing?
    a. from west to east
    b. from ocean onto land
    c. clockwise around the area of low pressure
    d. counterclockwise toward the area of low pressure

11. A cold front intersects an isobar east of Jackson, Mississippi. Which is the best estimate of the air pressure at the point the fronts intersect?
    a. 10 mb
    b. 900 mb
    c. 1000 mb
    d. 9900 mb

12. As the cold front continues to move, which two cities would experience a significant change in weather? Use evidence and reasoning to support your claim.

MAKE YOUR OWN STUDY GUIDE

In your Evidence Notebook, design a study guide that supports the main ideas from this lesson:

- Weather is defined as the conditions of the atmosphere in a specific time and place, including temperature, air pressure, wind velocity, humidity, and precipitation.
- Weather changes as air masses move and interact with each other.
- Technology used to collect, analyze, and communicate weather data, models, and predictions is essential to modern life.

Remember to include the following in your study guide:

- Support main ideas about the causes and effects of weather with details and examples.
- Record explanations for the weather-related patterns and phenomena you investigated.
- Describe the flow of matter and energy related to stability and change in weather experienced on Earth's surface.

Climate and Climate Change

A rainstorm in the Namib Desert in southwestern Africa

CAN YOU EXPLAIN IT?

FIGURE 1: Between 1984 and 2016, both the total area covered by sea ice and the portion of sea ice that was more than a year old decreased significantly. The images show the sea ice in September, when it covers the smallest area.

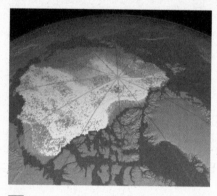

a Arctic sea ice cover in September 1984

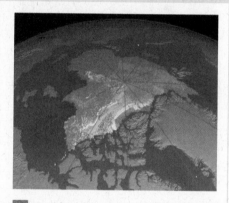

b Arctic sea ice cover in September 2016

 Gather Evidence

Record observations about Earth's global and regional climate today and how climate has changed in the past. As you explore the lesson, gather evidence to help explain the factors that influence climate, why climate has changed in the past, and why it is changing today.

The North Pole is located not on land, but on sea ice floating on the Arctic Ocean. The sea ice grows during the fall and winter months as seawater freezes, and it shrinks during the spring and summer as it thaws. The ice that forms in the winter and melts during the summer is called *seasonal ice*. Ice that lasts through the summers is known as *multiyear ice*, or *perennial ice*. Perennial ice gets thicker from year to year, and it is more resistant to melting than seasonal ice.

Over the past three decades, scientists have noticed that the total area covered by Arctic sea ice has been steadily shrinking. For example, in September 1984, the ice covered 6.43 million square kilometers, but in September 2016, it covered only 4.14 million square kilometers. In addition, the portion of ice that is more than a year old has decreased. In the 1980s, about 45% of the ice was perennial ice. In 2016, only about 20% of the ice was perennial. This is a sign that the ice is not just covering a smaller area but is also becoming thinner.

Explain What could be the cause of the gradual decrease in sea ice coverage and thickness in the Arctic? What effects could this change have on the land and sea in the Arctic, the ecosystems in the Arctic, or even on the rest of the globe?

Climate

Earth's average surface temperature is about 15 °C, or 60 °F. The average annual precipitation on Earth is about 100 cm, or 40 in. Overall, Earth has a climate that can be described as mild, or temperate. If this were all you knew about Earth, you might expect the average weather, seasonal weather changes, and even the plant and animal life on land to be similar everywhere on Earth.

FIGURE 2: These photographs show vegetation and landscape that are typical of each region.

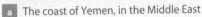

a The coast of Yemen, in the Middle East

b The Congo River Basin in the Democratic Republic of the Congo, Central Africa

Analyze The average annual temperature is about 25 °C in both Yemen and the Democratic Republic of Congo. Why do the two places look so different?

In fact, at any given location on Earth, you are unlikely to find these average conditions. The day-to-day weather conditions may be much warmer, colder, wetter, or drier than this. While conditions average out to about 15 °C and 100 cm of precipitation in some places on Earth, this is not the case everywhere. For example, the average temperature in Dallol, Ethiopia, is about 34 °C, while the average temperature in Eureka in northern Canada is nearly –20 °C. The average annual rainfall in Mawsynram, India, is nearly 1200 cm, while Arica, Chile, receives on average less than 1 mm of rain each year. Scientists estimate that in the dry valleys of Antarctica, there has been no rain for the past 2 million years.

Look at the photographs in Figure 2. What can you tell about the climate of the two areas based only on the photographs? It might be surprising to find that the two have the same average annual temperature of around 25 °C. However, based on the vegetation, it should be unsurprising that the average rainfall in that part of Yemen is only a few centimeters per year, while the rainfall in the Congo River Basin is around 150 cm per year. The combination of high rainfall and high temperatures in the Democratic Republic of the Congo support the growth of a dense, diverse rainforest, while the low rainfall and high temperatures in Yemen result in fewer, hardier organisms in that region. The differences in ecosystems from place to place on Earth are heavily influenced by the regional climate factors, including average humidity, cloud cover, and wind speed, as well as temperature and precipitation.

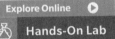

Explore Online ▶

Hands-On Lab

Microclimates Compare weather conditions from three different areas, and relate differences in the plants and animals you observe to the microclimates of the areas.

Climate versus Weather

Analyze Compare the climates shown in the four photos in Figure 3. Make a table that compares each location in terms of temperature, precipitation, vegetation or biome, and climate zone.

Explore Online ▶

Hands-On Lab 🧪

Comparing Climate Features Record, graph, and analyze temperature and precipitation data for multiple regions.

Imagine taking a hike on a warm day in March. It is 17.5 °C (63.5 °F) and sunny. Can you imagine seeing penguins, icebergs, and glaciers on this hike? When we think of dressing for a hike in Antarctica, most of us probably imagine wearing several layers of clothing, including a warm hat and gloves. But on March 24, 2015, jeans and a short-sleeved shirt would have been more appropriate. Now think about what you would wear on a trip to the Atacama Desert in Chile. Would you bother taking a raincoat to a place that receives less than 15 mm of rain per year? If your hike was on March 25, 2015, when a low-pressure system poured several years' worth of rain on the desert, that raincoat would have been useful.

In spite of Antarctica's extremely warm day and the Atacama's extremely wet day in March 2015, it would be hard to argue that Antarctica has a temperate climate or that the Atacama is rainy. The weather experienced on those days was not typical of either region. Recall that weather is defined as the current state of the atmosphere. Climate, on the other hand, is defined as the average weather patterns over a long period of time. A description of a region's climate includes average temperature and total precipitation as well as ranges of temperature and precipitation: the maximum and minimum that are typically experienced. Because many parts of the world experience seasonal variations, complete descriptions of climate also include monthly averages. At any given time, the weather in a region can be typical of the region and season or it can be extreme—outside the "normal" range. These extreme weather events in Antarctica and the Atacama were remarkable, but on their own, they provide little indication about the climate of the region.

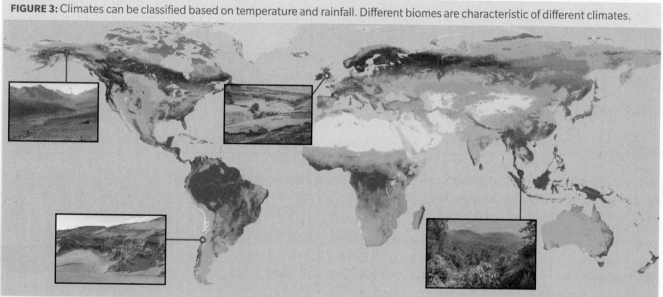

FIGURE 3: Climates can be classified based on temperature and rainfall. Different biomes are characteristic of different climates.

Analyze Look at the location of each photograph in Figure 3. What is the relationship between the climate of the region and its location?

Scientists use a number of systems for classifying regional climates. One of the most common systems includes five major climate types based on temperature and precipitation: tropical, dry, temperate, continental, and polar. Each of these can be divided into more specific climate zones. Tropical climates are warm to hot year-round and can be wet part or all of the year. Dry climates include hot and cold regions with low rainfall. Temperate climates are warm to hot in the summer and cool in the winter, with moderate rainfall. Continental climates are cool to warm in the summer and cold in the winter, with precipitation in the summer or year-round. Polar climates are cold year-round.

Factors that Influence Climate

Although Earth has a temperate climate overall, there are many regional climates, which differ from each other primarily in terms of temperature and precipitation. Why isn't climate about the same everywhere on Earth?

Latitude

In general, hot climates are found near the equator, very cold climates are found near the poles, and temperate climates are in the mid-latitudes. The correlation between climate and latitude occurs because Earth is a sphere. Because Earth's surface is curved, each point faces in a slightly different direction relative to the sun. Over a 24-hour period, every point along a single line of latitude receives the same amount of energy from the sun, but low latitudes closer to the equator receive more than high latitudes closer to the poles. As a result, tropical regions are warmer than polar regions.

Recall that this unequal heating of Earth's surface, along with the Coriolis effect, drives the global wind systems, which also influence climate. Climates tend to be wetter along the equator, where hot air rises and cools, causing the moisture in the air to condense and fall as rain. Desert climates are common at latitudes around 30°N and 30°S, where cool, dry air sinks from a high altitude.

Heat Absorption

Because land and water heat up and cool down at different rates, climates near large bodies of water may be very different from those inland. Water takes longer to heat up, and it retains energy longer. As a result, coastal regions tend to be more moderate with more stable temperatures than those inland, which can experience much greater fluctuations. The effects of ocean water on climate are also related to the wind systems, which push warm water from the equator toward the poles and cold water from the poles toward the equator. The reflectivity, or albedo, of surface materials also affects climate. Dark-colored materials like water and soil absorb more sunlight than light-colored materials like ice. Therefore, dark surfaces heat up more than light surfaces, warming the air above them. Albedo affects not only regional climates, but also Earth's climate as a whole. Earth reflects more sunlight when there is more ice and absorbs more when there is less.

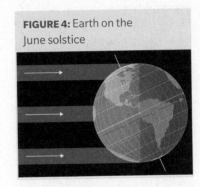

FIGURE 4: Earth on the June solstice

Factors that Affect Climate Determine whether land or water absorbs heat faster, and explain how the properties of land and water affect climate.

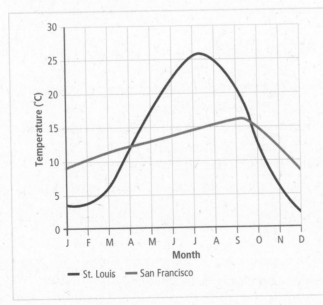

Average Monthly Temperatures

FIGURE 5: Although the average temperature in San Francisco and St. Louis are about the same, about 13.5 °C, the climates are not. Temperature varies more throughout the year in St. Louis than in San Francisco.

FIGURE 6: The climate of the Sierra Nevada Mountains is cooler than areas at lower elevation. The Great Basin region east of the Sierras is dry in part because of the rain shadow created by the mountains.

Surface Features

If you compare a climate map to a topographic map, you will probably notice a strong correlation between temperature, precipitation, and surface features. Regions at high elevation, for example, tend to have cooler climates than those at low elevation. This effect occurs in part because air temperature decreases with altitude: air expands as it rises and cools as it expands. Mountains can also affect climate by redirecting air currents by channeling or blocking winds. Precipitation patterns are also affected by mountains. When warm, humid air reaches a mountain range, it rises and cools, resulting in high precipitation on one side of the range. In some cases, so much moisture is lost from the air that by the time it reaches the other side of the mountains, the air is dry. This effect can result in extremely wet climates on one side of a mountain range and extremely dry climates, or rain shadows, on the other.

Math Connection

Sioux Falls, South Dakota, Climate Graph (Altitude: 435 m)

FIGURE 7: Average temperature and average total precipitation per month

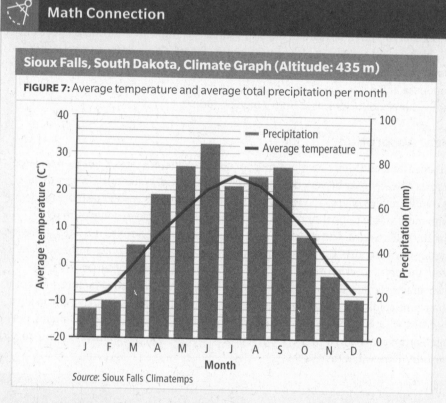

Source: Sioux Falls Climatemps

Look carefully at the graph.

1. Write a brief description of the climate of Sioux Falls, based on the information in the graph.
2. Describe the relationship between temperature and precipitation in Sioux Falls.
3. Can you tell from the graph what the weather would be like in Sioux Falls on July 4 of this coming year? If so, what is your prediction? If not, why not?
4. Look back to the information on climate classifications. How do you think Sioux Falls's climate is classified?

 Explain What is the relationship between climate and weather?

Earth's Changing Climate

Evidence from rocks, sediments, fossils, ice cores, and climate monitoring instruments show that Earth's global and regional climates have changed continuously since Earth formed more than 4.5 billion years ago and are still changing today. Both global and regional climates have changed with fluctuations in solar radiation, cyclical patterns of Earth's motion in space, changes in atmospheric composition, and the formation, motion, and destruction of continents and ocean basins.

Studying Climate Change

Because climate is defined by average weather conditions over a period of years, climate change is measured over long periods. Climate change is a change in Earth's climates, usually due to a change in Earth's energy. The term especially refers to the recent overall warming trend. Understanding how global and regional climates are changing today requires many measurements around the globe over many years. In order to understand how climate change today is similar to and different from climate change in the past, we also need to study past climates.

Explain Why must scientists study historical records to understand how Earth's climate is changing?

FIGURE 8: Scientists remove an ice core from a core barrel in Antarctica.

Some of the most useful tools for studying how global climate has changed are cores of ice from Greenland and Antarctica. When snow falls and transforms into glacial ice, bubbles of atmosphere are trapped in the ice. By analyzing the composition of oxygen in the bubbles, scientists can calculate air temperature at the time that the snow fell. Ice builds up in annual layers, giving scientists a clear record of temperature change from year to year. Ice cores have the added advantage of recording other important information about the atmosphere, including the presence of volcanic ash and the concentration of gases such as carbon dioxide and methane. This allows scientists to analyze correlations between temperature changes and other changes in the atmosphere.

Ice cores provide a record of climate going back as far as 800 000 years, the age of the oldest ice yet found. To understand more-ancient climates, scientists study sedimentary rocks, seafloor sediments, and fossils. Coal, for example, is made of the remains of plants that lived in warm, swampy environments and is therefore evidence for a warm, humid climate. Fossils of tiny marine animals can provide extremely precise information about seawater temperature when the animals were alive.

Image Credits: ©Arctic-Images/Corbis Documentary/Getty Images

FIGURE 9: This image from the GEOS-5 computer model shows the concentration of carbon dioxide in the atmosphere on January 1, 2006. Areas in orange are relatively high in CO_2, while those in gray are low.

Scientists use a variety of instruments and methods to monitor climate change today. On the ground, thousands of measurements of air temperature, humidity, precipitation, and other weather conditions are taken each day and averaged over time. Similar measurements of sea surface temperature are made from buoys and satellites, which can be used to monitor air and ocean circulation patterns as well.

Climate change is also monitored indirectly through its effects. Long-term changes in the volume of sea ice in the Arctic and glacial ice in Antarctica, changes in sea level, and changes in vegetation are all signs of changes in global and/or regional climate.

Causes of Climate Change

Earth's climate changes on different scales of space and time. It can change slowly, over the course of millions of years, or almost instantly, over the course of a few days. Climate change can involve a small portion of Earth's surface or the entire globe.

Volcanism

Early in Earth's history, volcanoes erupted around the world, emitting gases like water vapor, carbon dioxide, nitrogen oxide, and sulfur dioxide, forming Earth's early atmosphere. Gases like water vapor and carbon dioxide are greenhouse gases, which trap thermal energy and are crucial for keeping Earth's atmosphere warm enough for life as we know it today. Scientists calculate that without greenhouse gases, Earth's average surface temperature would be −18 °C (0 °F) rather than the +15 °C (59 °F) it is today.

Today, volcanoes still emit some carbon dioxide and water vapor into the atmosphere, but the overall effect of volcanism is to cool the planet. This occurs because volcanoes also erupt small particles and gases that condense to form tiny liquid droplets that reflect sunlight. If the eruption is large enough, these particles and droplets spread out around the globe, affecting not only the regional climate near the volcano, but also the entire Earth. A single massive eruption like that of Tambora in 1815, Krakatau in 1883, or Pinatubo in 1991 can have a global cooling effect that lasts several years. Once the particles and droplets settle, the climate eventually returns to its previous conditions.

FIGURE 10: Eruptions of Kilauea, in Hawaii, send particles and liquid droplets into the air that can affect the amount of sunlight that reaches the surface. Small eruptions may also affect local air circulation and precipitation patterns.

Image Credits: (t) ©NASA Goddard Space Flight Center; (b) ©Charles Douglas Peebles/Alamy

Orbital Changes

Based on evidence from rocks, fossils, and ice cores, we know that Earth's global climate has gone through much cooler periods, in which much more of Earth's surface was covered in ice, and much warmer periods, in which the surface was virtually free of ice. For the most part, these long-term patterns can be explained by patterns of change in Earth's motion in space. Over thousands of years, the eccentricity of Earth's orbit changes, the tilt of its axis increases and decreases, and the direction that its axis points in space changes. The combination of these changes causes fluctuations in the total amount of solar energy that reaches Earth's surface near the poles during summer.

Another factor that affects the amount of solar energy reaching Earth is the amount of energy emitted by the sun. For example, over a period of 11 years, the energy emitted by the sun increases and decreases. This causes slight changes in global temperatures.

Plate Tectonics

Regional climates change over millions of years as landmasses move toward or away from the equator. Mountain building caused by plate collisions can affect local air temperature and air circulation, increasing precipitation in some areas and decreasing it in others. As oceans grow and shrink, continents move, and mountains form and erode. Global air and ocean circulation patterns also change, altering the cycling of energy through Earth's systems and affecting global climate. Periods of mountain building can also affect global climate by increasing rates of weathering, which removes carbon dioxide from the atmosphere.

Changes in Atmospheric Composition

Recall that one of the most important factors influencing Earth's global climate is the composition of its atmosphere. Although gases like carbon dioxide (CO_2) and methane (CH_4) make up less than 0.05% of the atmosphere, they, along with water vapor (H_2O), have a significant effect on air temperature.

Earth's atmosphere, oceans, and land surface are heated almost entirely by sunlight. (Although thermal energy does move out from Earth's interior, it accounts for very little of the energy we feel on the surface.) When sunlight strikes Earth, some is absorbed by the oceans, soil, and other surface materials. The surface then heats up and transmits energy back out into the atmosphere. Without greenhouse gases, most of this energy would be emitted out into space. Instead, greenhouse gases like CO_2, CH_4, and H_2O absorb much of this energy. When the concentration of greenhouse gases increases, the amount of energy the atmosphere can absorb before radiating it out to space increases. The air temperature increases until it reaches a new equilibrium.

Many factors can influence the concentration of greenhouse gases in the atmosphere. The growth of plants removes CO_2 from the atmosphere through photosynthesis, while respiration and decomposition release CO_2 back into the atmosphere. When ocean water temperature increases, more CO_2 moves out of ocean water and into the atmosphere. When water temperature decreases, more CO_2 moves from the atmosphere into the oceans. Very small amounts of CO_2 move from Earth's interior into the atmosphere during volcanic eruptions. During weathering, CO_2 reacts with rocks and is removed from the atmosphere. Human activities like burning fossil fuels and making cement also release carbon dioxide—nearly 100 times as much as volcanoes. Figure 9 shows a computer model used to visualize the changes in concentration of carbon dioxide in the atmosphere over the course of a year. It helps scientists identify sources of CO_2 and understand how it moves around the globe.

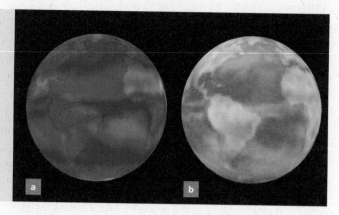

FIGURE 11: Instruments on NASA's Terra satellite measure (a) the amount of terrestrial radiation being emitted and (b) the amount of sunlight being reflected to space by Earth.

If the amount of CO_2 and other greenhouse gases moving into and out of Earth's atmosphere annually is balanced, there is no overall change. But if it is not balanced, the total concentration in the atmosphere changes over time, causing global climate change.

FIGURE 12: Solar energy is reflected and absorbed by Earth's atmosphere and surface materials. Energy that is absorbed causes materials to heat up. They then reradiate that energy out as terrestrial radiation. Greenhouse gases absorb terrestrial radiation, causing the atmosphere to heat up.

reflected by air and clouds

absorbed by air and clouds

absorbed by surface

reflected by surface

Earth's global climate changes for various reasons and on many different scales of time. It changes over millions of years as a result of plate tectonics,; tens of thousands of years as a result of orbital changes, and over several years as a result of major volcanic eruptions and sunspot cycles.

Many different independent lines of evidence show that global climate has been changing over the past 100 years for another reason: a rapid increase in concentration of CO_2 and other greenhouse gases. Since 1960, the concentration of CO_2 has increased more than 25%. At the same time, global temperatures have been rising at a rate of 1 °C to 1.5 °C per century. Similar increases in CO_2 and corresponding increases in temperature have occurred before in Earth's past, but not at such a fast pace. The current rate may not seem fast to us, but it is 10 times as fast as any other time in the last 66 million years.

 Explain Compare the different causes of climate change and the timescales over which they affect Earth's climate.

Our Role in Climate Change

Earth's population is now 10 times greater than it was 250 years ago, while the amount of energy people use today is 20 times greater. With the quickly increasing population and increasing use of resources associated with modern life, the impact of humans on Earth is greater now than at any time in the past.

Effects of Human Civilization

Earth's climate changes continuously between periods of relatively warm and cool global temperatures. Currently, we are in a relatively cool period of geologic history.

> **Collaborate** With a partner, look carefully at the models of CO_2 and CO in the atmosphere. Why do the concentrations of CO_2 and CO differ from place to place? Why do they change over time?

Because we are in a relatively cold period, it seems reasonable that global temperatures would be rising. In the past, temperatures have risen much higher as a result of natural causes. The issue today is the rate of temperature increase. Compared with the temperature changes shown in Figure 14, the warming we are experiencing today is at least 40 times faster than any other event in Earth's geologic history.

To understand the causes of today's temperature increase, scientists model the effects of various factors like volcanism, solar intensity and burning fossil fuels on climate. Because so many factors are interacting, climate models can be very complicated. But with the help of powerful computers, it is now possible to make models that accurately simulate real conditions and that help predict future conditions.

Explore Online ▶

FIGURE 13: The GEOS-5 computer model of CO_2 (blue to violet) and CO (grayscale)

a January 14, 2006

b February 16, 2006

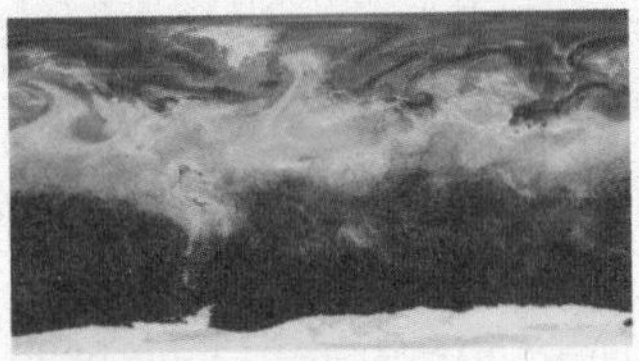

c April 17, 2006

Global Temperature Changes

FIGURE 14: Average global temperature has changed over geologic history.

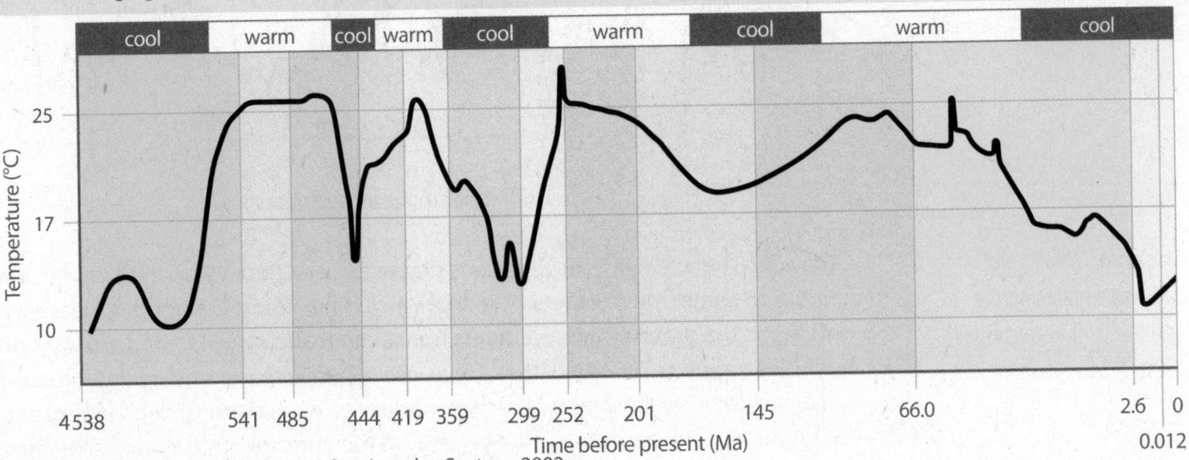

| cool | warm | cool | warm | cool | warm | cool | warm | cool |

Temperature (°C)

25

17

10

4538   541 485   444 419 359   299 252   201   145   66.0   2.6   0
                                                                                        0.012
Time before present (Ma)

Source: International Commission on Stratigraphy; Scotese, 2002

> **Explain** What is the reasoning behind the statement that we are currently in a relatively cool period of geologic history?

Climate Models

FIGURE 15: Climate models help us understand the causes of climate change.

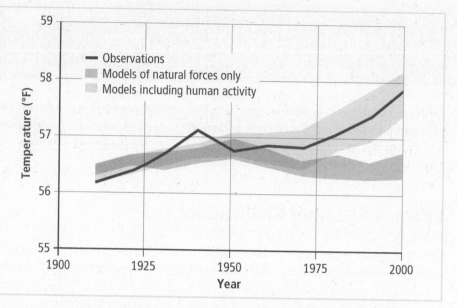

Analyze How do the models in Figure 15 support the claim that climate change between 1906 and 2000 is a result of a combination of natural and human factors?

The models in Figure 15 show that global temperatures are currently rising much faster than they would if climate were influenced only by natural factors. Based on many lines of evidence, our understanding of scientific laws and principles, and scientific reasoning, most scientists have concluded that the current increase in average global temperature is primarily a result of greenhouse gas emission caused by human activities since the Industrial Revolution began around 1750. These activities include burning fossil fuels such as coal, oil, and gas; making concrete; and agriculture.

Historical Carbon Dioxide Levels

FIGURE 16: Data from ice cores show how carbon dioxide levels in the atmosphere have changed over the past 400 000 years as compared to the current increase. They also show a clear correlation between CO_2 and air temperature.

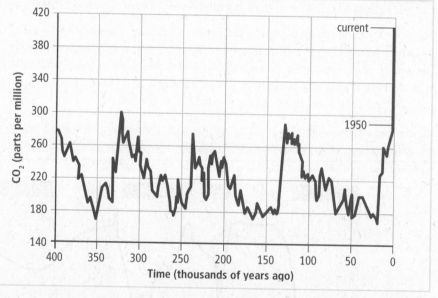

Analyze What is the evidence supporting the statement that CO_2 concentrations are rising faster today than in the past?

The actual data of CO_2 concentrations that were used to develop the models shown in Figure 16 come from a variety of sources, including almost continuous measurements of CO_2 on the ground, measurements from aircraft and satellites, and analyses of air bubbles trapped in ice. All of these data, combined with our understanding of current and past sources of CO_2 and other greenhouse gases and our understanding of the ways that greenhouse gases affect energy in the atmosphere, have led scientists to conclude that the increase in human activities like burning coal, oil, and gas since 1750 is the main cause of the rapid climate change that we observe today.

Effects of Global Climate Change

The most obvious effect of global climate change is an increase in average annual global surface temperature. Because current climate change involves an increase in average global temperatures, it is often referred to as *global warming*. However, this does not mean that every region will get warmer or will experience the same increase in average temperature. Some regions may warm more rapidly than others. Some may not change significantly at all. Because so many factors affecting regional climates interact with each other, some regions may become cooler.

Changing Weather Patterns

With climate change comes changes in the weather in general, and not just in terms of temperature. With an increase in temperature, evaporation rates will increase, changing precipitation patterns. Current models show, for example, that the tropical rainforests are likely to be wetter, with the subtropical dry areas becoming even drier. Scientists also predict that with an increase in ocean temperatures, there will likely be an increase in the maximum wind speeds and rainfall rates of hurricanes.

However, the fact that global climate is warming does not mean that every winter will be warmer and every summer will be hotter. A cold day, an extremely cold winter, or a cool summer are not evidence that climate is not warming overall. Any individual weather event or short-term pattern of events is a result of many interacting factors.

FIGURE 17: As sea ice melts, Earth becomes less reflective and absorbs more solar energy.

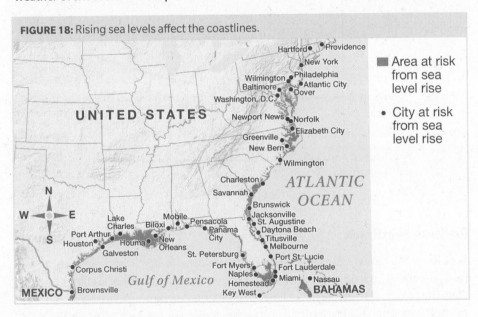

FIGURE 18: Rising sea levels affect the coastlines.

Sea-Level Changes

One of the most dramatic effects of global climate change is sea-level rise. Measurements from tide gauges show that over the past 100 years, global mean sea level has been rising at a rate of about 1.3–1.7 mm/y. Satellite and tide gauge measurements show that since 1993, the rate has doubled to about 2.6–3.5 mm/y. Current climate change models suggest that sea level could rise another 1 to 2 meters by 2100.

One meter over 100 years might not seem like a lot, but keep in mind that many coastlines consist of gently sloping land, not sheer cliffs. An increase in sea level of 1 meter can flood many kilometers inland. In addition, sea-level rise increases the frequency of flooding during extreme weather events like hurricanes.

A major cause of sea-level rise today is the addition of water to the oceans as glaciers and ice sheets melt. However, even when no water is being added to oceans through melting, increasing temperature causes sea levels to rise. This happens because water expands as it warms. As ocean water increases in temperature, the water molecules move apart. The water becomes less dense and takes up more space. Melting and thermal expansion have played major roles in sea-level rise in the past and today.

The exact rate of sea-level change varies from place to place as a result of local and regional factors. Some areas of the ocean are warming up and expanding faster. Wind systems can push water from one part of the ocean to another. Earth's gravitational pull varies across the oceans. Land itself can rise or fall. For example, land that was once covered in ice can slowly rise upward as weight is released from above.

Specific Volume and Temperature

FIGURE 19: As seawater heats up, it expands, causing sea levels to rise.

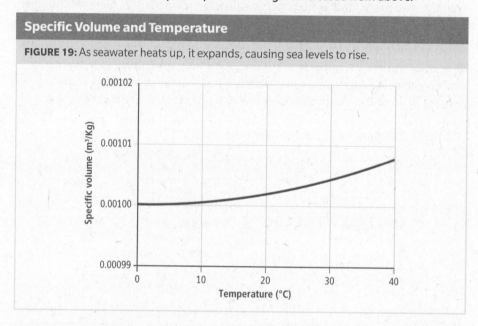

Positive Feedback

The effects of a global increase in temperature are complicated in part because of feedback effects. Scientists are most concerned with positive feedback: effects of temperature increase that result in an even greater temperature increase. For example, when snow and ice melt, leaving bare ground or seawater, the overall albedo, or reflectivity, of Earth's surface decreases. As a result, more solar energy is absorbed, causing the surface and atmosphere to heat up more. Another important feedback effect is related to evaporation. When air and water temperature increase, rates of evaporation increase, moving more water vapor into the atmosphere. Water vapor is a very powerful greenhouse gas and thus causes air temperature to rise even further. A positive feedback effect that scientists are particularly concerned about now involves methane (CH_4). Methane constitutes a much smaller portion of the atmosphere than CO_2, but it is a much more potent greenhouse gas. As rising temperatures cause permafrost to melt in polar regions, methane and carbon dioxide trapped underground are released into the atmosphere, causing temperatures to increase even more.

Stability and Change

Feedback Feedback is a special situation of cause and effect in which the cause and the effect are intertwined. Positive feedback, if large enough, can destabilize a system. Negative feedback helps keep systems stable. An important example of negative feedback related to climate has to do with plant growth: An increase in carbon dioxide in the atmosphere can lead to an increase in plant growth, which removes carbon dioxide from the atmosphere.

What We Can Do

Nearly 10 gigatons of carbon atoms, mainly in the form of CO_2 molecules, are released into the atmosphere each year through human activities like burning fossil fuels and making cement, and only about half of that is taken up by plants or absorbed by the oceans. The rest is accumulating in the atmosphere and contributing to the current increase in temperature and related effects we are experiencing. There are several things that scientists, engineers, and individual citizens can do to mitigate the problem.

Refine Our Energy Production

The majority of human CO_2 emissions come from burning fossil fuels like oil, gas, and coal. Fossil fuels are a major source of energy for powering cars, trucks, trains, planes, and ships; for heating homes and cooking food; and for generating electricity. One way to reduce these emissions is to replace fossil fuels with other energy resources like solar, wind, water, geothermal, and nuclear power.

FIGURE 20: A solar panel array in Nevada generates electricity from sunlight.

Increase Efficiency

Another way to reduce emissions of CO_2 is to use less energy. Effective methods include turning off lights when they are not needed; turning down the heating in the winter and the air-conditioning in the summer; and walking, biking, or using public transportation instead of driving. We can also use less energy by developing and using technology that is more energy efficient. Proper insulation in buildings can drastically reduce the amount of energy required for heating and cooling. Smaller, more aerodynamic cars require less gasoline. Technologies such as LED bulbs and hybrid car engines require less energy than traditional models.

FIGURE 21: Replacing traditional incandescent lightbulbs with compact fluorescent (CFL) or light-emitting diode (LED) bulbs can reduce energy use by more than 75%.

Remove Carbon from the Atmosphere

Scientists and engineers are also developing methods for removing excess carbon that is already in the atmosphere. The most obvious way is to encourage the growth of other organisms, like trees and phytoplankton, that remove CO_2 from the air through photosynthesis. Scientists are also developing machines, sometimes referred to as "artificial trees," that suck up CO_2. Similar devices can capture CO_2 on its way out of a pollution source like a coal-fired power plant before it even enters the atmosphere.

Explain How have people contributed to climate change? What can individuals do to decrease their impact on climate?

Guided Research

Iron Solutions or Iron Problems?

Could dumping iron into the oceans solve our CO_2 problem? Some scientists and engineers think so. Others are less optimistic.

In a stable, balanced system, the amount of CO_2 moving into the atmosphere each year is offset by the amount being removed. However, this is not happening right now. Only about half of the extra CO_2 that people emit into the atmosphere is being removed by natural processes like photosynthesis and dissolving into the oceans. Scientists estimate that as a result, more than 4 gigatons of carbon are added to the atmosphere every year.

One possible solution to this problem is to increase the amount of CO_2 that is removed from the air by photosynthesis. This, of course, means figuring out how to increase rates of photosynthesis. Most of us tend to think only about land plants when we think about photosynthesis, but in fact, the oceans are teeming with tiny photosynthetic organisms called *phytoplankton*. Increasing the number of phytoplankton in the oceans could help remove CO_2 from the atmosphere. The question is how to do this.

It turns out that one important factor limiting the growth of phytoplankton is iron. Scientists think that iron can act as a fertilizer to spur the growth of phytoplankton. Some scientists estimate that if enough iron were added, the concentration of CO_2 could drop so much that we would not only stop global warming, but we would

FIGURE 22: Blooms of phytoplankton form in the cool, nutrient-rich waters of the Barents Sea in August 2011. Could dumping iron in the oceans increase the growth of phytoplankton? Is stimulating the growth of phytoplankton this way a good idea?

be plunged back into another ice age. They suggest that fertilizing just a small portion of the oceans could be useful.

But would it work? CO_2 does not just disappear when it is removed from the air. It is converted into compounds that make up phytoplankton. Unless they fall to the seafloor, when the phytoplankton die and decompose, CO_2 is released back into the water and eventually into the air. Some scientists think fertilizing the oceans is a very short-term solution that could backfire later.

Even if it did work, would a decrease in CO_2 in the atmosphere be the only effect? Probably not. Adding iron to the oceans could increase levels of other greenhouse gases. Blooms of phytoplankton can release other compounds that can be toxic to animals

or harm the ozone layer. An increase in phytoplankton could provide more food for fish and other marine animals, which could be helpful in some ways but harmful in others. If large numbers of phytoplankton die off at once, their decomposition can remove oxygen from the water, leading to a die-off of fish and other marine animals.

Language Arts Connection

Scientists and engineers must take many factors into account when deciding how to solve problems like climate change. What do you think? Is fertilizing the oceans with iron a good idea or not? Should the ocean be a testing ground for the method? Support your opinion with evidence and reasoning.

| TIDAL ENERGY | | CALCULATE YOUR CARBON FOOTPRINT | Go online to choose one of these other paths. |

Lesson Self-Check

CAN YOU EXPLAIN IT NOW?

FIGURE 23: Between 1984 and 2016, the total area covered by sea ice in the Arctic decreased by 35%.

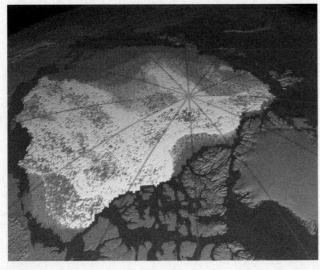

a September 1984

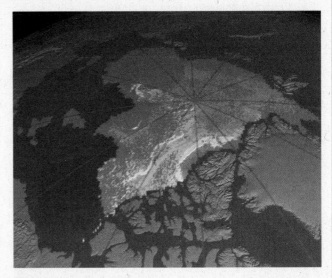

b September 2016

Over the past three decades, the total area covered by Arctic sea ice has been shrinking. In addition, the portion of perennial ice—ice that remains through the summer and is more than a year old—has also decreased; this is a sign that the ice is not only covering a smaller area but is also becoming thinner. The amount of ice on Greenland has also been declining.

Melting of sea ice, ice sheets, and alpine glaciers can have far-reaching effects. Melting ice contributes to an increase in sea level, which causes flooding of coastlines and destruction of coastal habitats. Melting also affects the habitats of animals such as polar bears that use the ice and may disrupt ocean circulation patterns, which can further affect global and regional climates. In addition, the positive feedback associated with the decrease in Earth's albedo can lead to additional warming. Melting sea ice may even have geopolitical effects. For example, new oceanic trade routes between countries may open up, while older ones may become unusable.

 Explain What could be the cause of the gradual decrease in sea ice coverage and thickness in the Arctic? What effects could this change have on the land and sea in the Arctic, on the ecosystems in the Arctic, or even on the rest of the globe?

CHECKPOINTS

Check Your Understanding

1 What is the difference between regional and global climate? Identify whether each description, term, or measurement is related to global climate, regional climate, both, or neither.

   a. 1 mm average annual precipitation

   b. 100 cm average annual precipitation

   c. 1200 cm average annual precipitation

   d. 15 °C and sunny

   e. average annual temperature of 15 °C

   f. average annual temperature of –18 °C

   g. average annual temperature of 34 °C

   h. average weather conditions over a specific part of Earth over many years

   i. average weather conditions over the entire Earth over many years

   j. temperate

   k. polar

2. On March 24, 2015, it was 63 °F and sunny at the Esperanza Base on the northern tip of Antarctica. On March 25, 2015, several centimeters of rain fell in the Atacama Desert, one of the driest places on Earth. Use these two examples to explain the difference between weather and climate.

3. Regional climates can be categorized as tropical, dry, temperate, continental, and polar. The distinction between these climates is based on which of the following?

   a. average wind speed and direction

   b. latitude and proximity to the oceans

   c. temperature and precipitation patterns

   d. how similar they are to average global climate at the time

4. Which of the following statements about studying climate change is true? Choose all that apply.

   a. With modern technology, it is possible to measure climate change almost instantly.

   b. Ground-based weather stations are no longer useful for studying climate change.

   c. Air bubbles trapped in ice cores help scientists estimate the temperature of the air hundreds of thousands of years ago.

   d. Most fossils do not provide any information about past climates.

   e. Scientists assume that rocks that form only in warm tropical places today must have formed in warm tropical places in the past.

   f. Satellites are useful for studying weather but not climate.

5. What is a greenhouse gas? What are the main greenhouse gases in Earth's atmosphere? How are they related to climate change?

FIGURE 24: Past trends in temperature

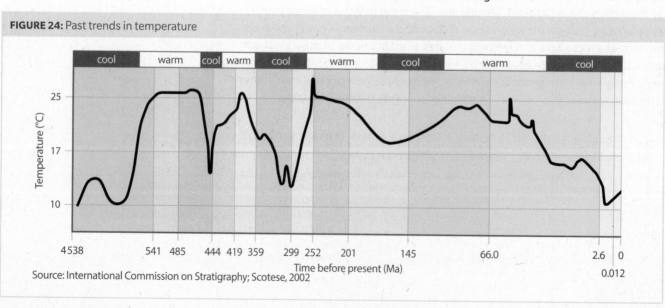

Source: International Commission on Stratigraphy; Scotese, 2002

6. Some people argue that the current warming that Earth is experiencing is just part of the natural cycle of warming and cooling that Earth goes through over geologic time. Use the diagram in Figure 24, along with what you have learned in this chapter, to support or refute this claim.

7. How do scientists interpret the graph in Figure 25?

   a. Natural factors have played no role in climate change since 1906.

   b. There is actually no evidence that climate change is occurring.

   c. Climate change since 1906 can be explained by natural factors alone.

   d. Climate change since 1906 can be explained better by human and natural factors combined than by natural factors alone.

8. Describe one example of positive feedback in the climate system that scientists are concerned about, and explain why they are concerned.

9. Briefly explain how changes in technology and changes in behavior can affect climate change. Give specific examples to support your claims.

 In your Evidence Notebook, design a study guide that supports the main ideas in this lesson:

- Regional climates are affected by a number of interacting factors, including latitude, topography, and ocean circulation patterns.
- Global climates are affected by a number of interacting factors, including Earth's motion in space, solar output, plate tectonics, and atmospheric composition.
- Earth's climate changes on various scales of time and space.
- Earth's climate is currently changing at a very fast rate, which is thought to be a result of an increase in greenhouse gas concentration caused by human activities.

Remember to include the following information in your study guide:

- Use examples that model main ideas about climate and climate change.
- Record explanations for the climate phenomena you investigated.
- Use evidence to support your explanations about the causes of climate change. Your support can include drawings, data, graphs, and other evidence recorded throughout the lesson.

Consider how the models for equilibrium you have developed in this lesson can be used to analyze the stability and change of many different types of systems.

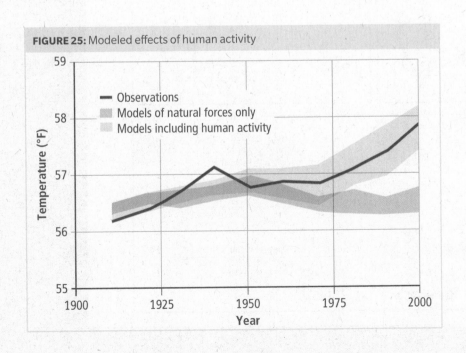

FIGURE 25: Modeled effects of human activity

— Observations
■ Models of natural forces only
■ Models including human activity

A BOOK EXPLAINING
COMPLEX IDEAS USING
ONLY THE 1,000 MOST
COMMON WORDS

CLOUD MAPS
How maps that help us guess the future are put together

You've seen weather maps on TV or online. Scientists use weather data and weather patterns to help predict and forecast the weather. How are all these data gathered?

RANDALL MUNROE
XKCD.COM

THE STORY OF MAPS THAT SHOW RAIN, WIND, AND STORMS

THE AIR CHANGES EVERY DAY.

EVERY . . .

EVERY DAY, CLOUDS MOVE AROUND, RAIN COMES AND GOES, AND WINDS CHANGE.

SINGLE . . .

. . . TIME.

AND EVERY DAY, PEOPLE ALL OVER THE WORLD TRY TO FIGURE OUT WHAT THE AIR IS DOING AND WHERE THE RAIN WILL GO NEXT.

IT'S SUCH A NICE DAY. NOT A CLOUD IN THE SKY!

TO MAKE MAPS OF THE SKY, WE USE SPACE BOATS LOOKING AT CLOUDS FROM ABOVE, RADIO WAVES LOOKING AT CLOUDS FROM THE SIDE, AND PEOPLE ALL OVER THE WORLD LOOKING AT CLOUDS FROM BELOW.

HEY, THAT ONE KIND OF LOOKS LIKE A BIRD!

IT JUST LOOKS LIKE RAIN TO ME.

HIGHS AND LOWS

These lines show how hard the air is pressing down on different areas of the map—which is sort of a strange idea, but important for understanding rain and wind.

These maps are a lot like maps used to show the shape of mountains. The lines join areas where the air is pressing down with the same weight, and the middles of circles are areas where air is especially heavy or light. They're marked "Heavy" and "Light" (or "High" and "Low") to help you know which is which.

LOWS (RAIN MAKERS)

Areas with lighter air over them are called "lows." Air moves across the ground toward those areas, and—just like water moving toward a hole in the bottom of a pool—it goes faster and starts moving in a circle.

Air usually rises up in these "light" areas, which makes rain. As the air rises, the water in the air cools down and turns into little drops, just like water on the side of a glass with a cold drink in it.

This area will have heavy rain (or snow, if it's cold enough).

COLD AIR

This area will be cold and clear.

This area will have strong, cold winds and heavy rain.

COOL AIR

This area will be cool.

The dark areas on this map show where it will rain.

This area may see flashes of light in the sky and winds strong enough to blow away a house.

Low

WARM AIR

This area will have light wind and light rain.

COOL AIR

This area will be clear and warm for now.

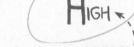

HIGHS (CLEAR AREAS)

In a "heavy" (or "high") area, air is pressing down hard, which keeps wet air from rising and keeps clouds and rain from forming. These areas usually have clear skies and not very much wind.

Low

GREAT CIRCLE STORMS

These storms are a kind of "low" powered by the heat carried by sea-water as it turns to air and rises from the surface when warmed by the sun. They have very strong winds in a circle near the center, but right *in* the center it's calm—and can even be clear. People call this clear area the "eye" of the storm.

When these storms come in from the sea, they bring the sea with them. Their winds push water ahead of them, and it can make the sea come up onto the land and cover whole cities. They can also make so much rain that rivers rise and wash away people, cars, and houses.

Thanks to computers, we've gotten a lot better at guessing where circle storms are going to go, which helps us to tell people to get out of the way.

CLOUD MAPS

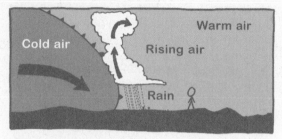

COLD AIR COMING IN

This line shows where cold air is coming in. This can mean there will be wind and then flashes of light, sounds from the clouds, and very, very heavy rain, but it doesn't last long.

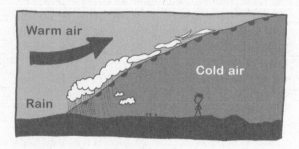

WARM AIR COMING IN

This line means warm air will be moving into an area. This can mean there will be clouds ahead of the warm air, sometimes a few days before it gets there, and rain as it moves in.

Around here, the air stops getting colder as you go higher, so warm air stops rising.

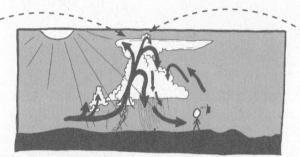

This piece of cloud sticking up means warm air is rising so fast that it shoots up above where it would normally stop. It means the storm is very strong.

VERY BIG SUMMER STORMS

Sometimes, on hot days, air heated by the sun rises up very fast, then cools and pours down rain. These storms can make spinning wind that blows away houses.

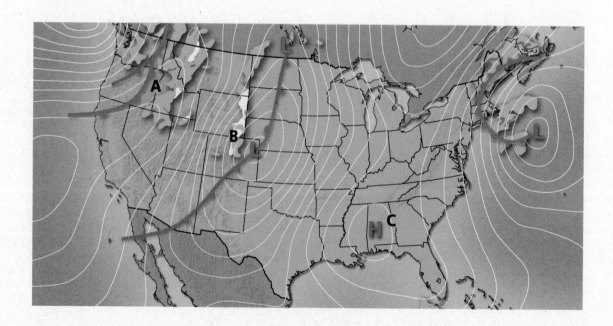

THINGS YOU SEE ON RADIO MAPS AND WHAT THEY MEAN

Sky-watching stations point radio waves at clouds. If there are big drops of water in the clouds, the radio waves hit them and come back. By pointing the radio in different directions, the people in the stations can make a map of all the rain and snow in clouds around them.

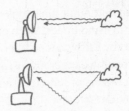

Here's how to understand some of the shapes you see on those maps:

RAIN

Big shapes like this mean rain. It will probably last a while and be light sometimes and heavy other times.

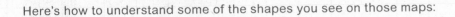

SOUND STORM

This shape means a storm is coming, which may bring light, sound, and strong wind.

WIND STORM

This shape means a storm with lights and sound is coming, and the wind ahead of it might be even stronger than normal.

SPINNING WIND

This shape, like a bent finger, means a spinning cloud is touching the ground, and may be tearing up trees and houses.

Sometimes, if you look at the shapes made by the radio, you can see the stuff the storm has picked up. It looks like a small ball in the middle of the bent finger shape.

SKIN BIRDS

This circle shape isn't rain—it's hundreds and hundreds of little skin birds all flying out of a big hole to eat flies when the sun sets.

Sometimes other animals, like normal birds or flies, show up on these maps too.

TREES

When there's no rain to see, sometimes the map shows little lines of noise from the radio waves hitting the tops of trees and houses.

GROUND

This shape happens when the radio waves hit clouds, then a pool of water on the ground, then come back. That makes them take longer, so it looks like there's rain far away.

Engineering Connection

Testing Sunscreen Although sunlight is vital to life on Earth, ultraviolet radiation can be dangerous to living things. Much of the UV radiation from the sun, but not all of it, is absorbed by Earth's ozone layer. Sunscreens are lotions designed to protect the skin from the dangerous UV rays that make it to Earth's surface. There are many different brands of sunscreen, and each bottle contains lotion with a specific sun protection factor (SPF).

Begin by conducting some background research on sunscreens and SPF using library or Internet resources. Then design an experiment to compare the effectiveness of different brands or different SPFs of sunscreen. Think about the materials you will need, how you will measure the sunscreen effectiveness, what variables you will change and which you will keep constant, and how you will record your data. Prepare a list of materials, a list of procedures, and a labeled sketch showing how you would set up the experiment.

FIGURE 1: Skiers apply sunscreen because UV rays are reflected by snow.

Social Studies Connection

Clothing and Climate In what way is the clothing you wear affected by the climate of the region you live in? Clothing is designed to protect the body from the weather. One reason that clothing styles and materials differ from place to place throughout the world is because climates differ.

Using library and Internet resources, research an article of clothing from a particular part of the world. Find out how the clothing is related to the climate of the region in terms of its ability to protect people from the weather. How does climate influence the availability of plant and animal resources used to make the clothing? Prepare a small poster that includes a labeled photograph or illustration of the clothing, a description of what it is made of, and an explanation of how the materials and design are influenced by the climate.

FIGURE 2: People who live in a polar climate must wear warm clothing throughout the year.

Health Connection

Climate Change and Infectious Diseases Many infectious diseases are carried by organisms that thrive in particular climates. For example, malaria is a deadly disease that is transmitted by mosquitoes that live in tropical climates. Scientists are worried that climate change will make it possible for disease-carrying organisms to spread to other parts of the world, potentially increasing the number of people who might be affected by these diseases.

Use library and Internet resources to research an infectious disease such as malaria, cholera, dengue fever, or hantavirus. Where is the disease found today? How does it spread? How is it related to climate? How do scientists think climate change will affect where the disease is found in the future? Prepare a brief report about the disease, including how it is spread, how it is affected by climate, and how people can protect themselves from it. Include a map that shows where the disease affects people today and where it might affect people in the future.

FIGURE 3: Malaria is transmitted by mosquitos and is most prevalent in tropical climates.

SYNTHESIZE THE UNIT

In your Evidence Notebook, create a concept map, graphic organizer, or outline using the Study Guides you created for each lesson in this unit. Be sure to use evidence to support your claims.

When synthesizing individual information, remember to follow these general steps:
- Find the central idea of each piece of information.
- Think about the relationships among the central ideas.
- Combine the ideas to come up with a new understanding.

Go online to access detailed lesson summaries for this unit.

DRIVING QUESTIONS

Look back to the Driving Questions from the opening section of this unit. In your Evidence Notebook, review and revise your previous answers to those questions. Use the evidence you gathered and other observations you made throughout the unit to support your claims.

PRACTICE AND REVIEW

1. Earth's atmosphere is divided into troposphere, stratosphere, mesosphere, and thermosphere based on
   a. altitude
   b. air composition
   c. the way pressure changes with altitude
   d. the way temperature changes with altitude

2. Which of the following are causes of motion within the atmosphere? Choose all that apply.
   a. Earth's rotation, which causes air to veer east or west
   b. gravity, which causes dense air to sink and push up warmer air
   c. unequal heating of Earth's surface, which creates differences in temperature, density, and air pressure
   d. the solar system's orbit around the galaxy, which causes friction between the atmosphere and other matter in space

3. Weather and climate are influenced by interactions between the atmosphere, geosphere, biosphere, and hydrosphere. Give an example of each of the following:
   a. interaction between the atmosphere and geosphere that affects global climate
   b. interaction between the atmosphere and hydrosphere that affects weather
   c. interaction between the atmosphere and biosphere that affects the composition of the atmosphere
   d. interaction between the atmosphere and geosphere that affects regional climate

FIGURE 4: The Sierra Nevada Mountains run along the eastern edge of California.

4. Describe the difference in air pressure and temperature at the top of the Sierra Nevada as compared to the base of the mountains. Explain your answer.

5. The land to the east of the Sierra Nevada is part of a region known as the Great Basin. Why is the Great Basin brown while the land on the western side of the mountains is green? Explain the difference in terms of the effects of the mountains on air masses.

6. The climate of the Great Basin is characterized by hot, dry summers, and cold, snowy winters. The Sierra Nevada mountain range is one factor that affects Great Basin climate. Describe two other factors that affect the climate of the Great Basin.

7. Winters in the Sierra Nevada tend to be snowy. How might the increase in concentration of CO_2, CH_4, and other greenhouse gases in Earth's atmosphere affect snowfall in the Sierras? Explain your answer.

FIGURE 5: Concentration of CO_2 and CO in Earth's Atmosphere (January 2006)

8. What are the sources of CO_2 shown in Figure 5

9. Use Figure 6 to answer the question. Which of the following are factors that could have contributed to the changes in temperature shown? Choose all that apply.

a. volcanism

b. increases and decreases in ice cover

c. fluctuations in energy output from the sun

d. natural variations in Earth's motion in space

e. fluctuations in the temperature of Earth's core

f. inputs of energy from powerful star explosions

g. changes in the amount of radiation received from other stars as the solar system moves through the galaxy

h. changes in the position of the continents and oceans over time

10. Why are scientists particularly worried about the climate change that is occurring today?

a. Earth's climate has generally been stable over the past 4.5 billion years.

b. No one knows what is causing temperatures to rise or how to stop them.

c. Temperatures are much higher today than they have ever been in the past.

d. Temperatures are currently increasing at a much faster rate than is known to have occurred in the geologic past.

UNIT PROJECT

Design a Weather Instrument

Return to your unit project. Share your instrument along with the data you collected with the class. Be prepared to explain how the instrument works, describe any problems you had building it or getting it to work properly, and evaluate how well it worked based on the data you collected and forecasts you made with it.

Remember these tips as you are preparing your presentation:

· Look at the instrument. How is it similar to and different from instruments used by professionals?

· Think about how you collected data. Were there variables that you were not able to control? How accurate and precise were your data?

· Think about the design of the instrument. How would you build it differently if you had more time or different materials?

FIGURE 6: Average Global Air Temperature over Geologic Time.

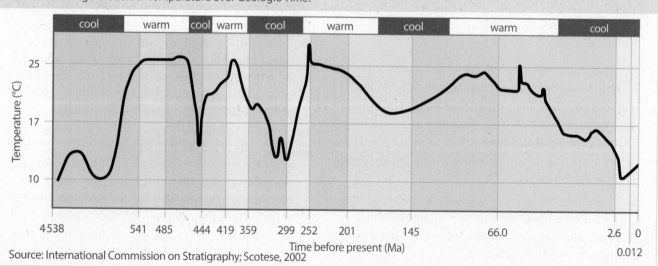

Source: International Commission on Stratigraphy; Scotese, 2002

Image Credits: ©NASA Goddard Space Flight Center

Making Predictions Based on Patterns

The carbon dioxide concentration in Earth's atmosphere has increased by more than 30% since 1880. At the same time, Earth's average global surface temperature has also increased.

A number of solutions have been proposed to slow climate change and/or reduce its effects on other parts of Earth's systems.

1. ANALYZE DATA

With your team, analyze the relationship between carbon dioxide concentrations and global average temperature shown on the graph in Figure 7. If the pattern continues, what do you predict the values will be in the year 2050? 2100? Do you think it is reasonable to assume that the trends will continue exactly as they have in the past?

2. DEFINE THE PROBLEM

With your team, brainstorm and discuss the effects of the changing global temperature on other aspects of Earth, such as regional climates, volume of sea ice, and sea level.

3. CONDUCT RESEARCH

On your own, research how the change in Earth's average global air temperature is affecting one of the aspects of Earth that you discussed. You may focus on a specific regional climate, sea ice, sea level, or another aspect approved by your teacher. Find out what scientists predict will happen if temperatures continue to increase. Find information in the form of data tables, graphs, images and/or maps that illustrates what is happening or what scientists predict will happen.

4. IDENTIFY AND EVALUATE SOLUTIONS

Come back together as a team to brainstorm and discuss possible solutions to the problem of increasing CO_2 levels. Solutions could involve technology, environmental regulations, or changes in human activities and behaviors. If these solutions were put in place, how might the trends shown on the graph in Figure 7 change over time?

Global Temperature and Carbon Dioxide

FIGURE 7: Graphs of the change in CO_2 concentration in the atmosphere and average global surface temperature.

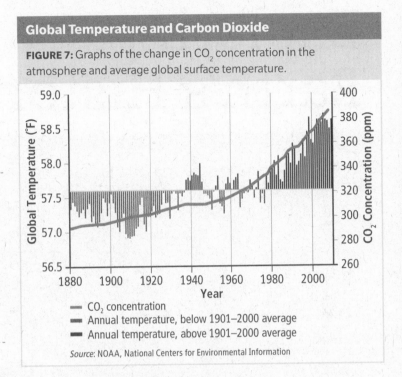

- CO$_2$ concentration
- Annual temperature, below 1901–2000 average
- Annual temperature, above 1901–2000 average

Source: NOAA, National Centers for Environmental Information

5. MAKE A PREDICTION

Choose one solution that you think could be effective in addressing the problem of increasing CO_2 concentrations in the atmosphere. If the solution were successful, how would the particular aspect of Earth you researched be affected?

6. COMMUNICATE

Create a poster or infographic that describes the problem caused by climate change, predictions for how the problem will get worse over time if trends continue, and predictions for how the problem could be solved or lessened by an effective solution for reducing the increasing CO_2. Include labeled graphs, charts, maps, and/or images to illustrate your points.

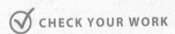 CHECK YOUR WORK

Once you have completed this task, you should have the following:

- A prediction of future atmospheric conditions based on historical data.
- An explanation of how a possible method for reducing the increase in CO_2 in the atmosphere could solve or lessen the problem.
- Graphs, charts, maps, or images illustrating the problem.

Exploring Earth's History

The Little Atlas Mountains in Morocco formed approximately 300 million years ago when Africa collided with North America to form the supercontinent Pangaea. The Appalachian Mountains in North America formed during the same mountain-building event.

Image Credits: ©Hermes Images/AGF Srl/Alamy

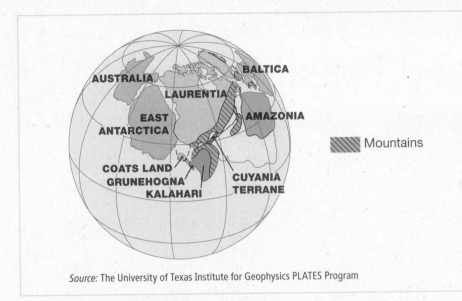

FIGURE 1: Rodinia was a supercontinent that formed about 1.1 billion years ago and broke apart about 750 million years ago. Continent locations shown are approximations.

Source: The University of Texas Institute for Geophysics PLATES Program

A supercontinent is a single massive continent that forms by the collision of continents along convergent boundaries. The formation and breakup of supercontinents follows an approximately 300–500 million-year cycle. The movement of continents affects climate conditions, sea level, and the distribution of plants and animals on land and in the ocean.

 Explain Why is it important to understand the formation and breakup of past supercontinents?

DRIVING QUESTIONS

As you move through the unit, gather evidence to help you answer the following questions. In your Evidence Notebook, record what you already know about these topics and any questions you have about them.

1. How have the shape and configuration of continents and ocean basins changed through time?
2. How do we use the rock record to construct an account of species that lived on Earth in the past?
3. What evidence can we use to reconstruct Earth's recent past?

UNIT PROJECT

Go online to download the Unit Project Worksheet to help plan your project.

Exploring Pangaea

In this activity, you will investigate the formation and breakup of the supercontinent Pangaea. Use the theory of plate tectonics to help you explain how the supercontinent formed and rifted apart, and how landmasses drifted to their current positions. Gather different lines of evidence to support the presence of the planet's most recent supercontinent.

The Rock and Fossil Record

Jurassic dinosaur bones are preserved in rock at Dinosaur National Monument in Colorado and Utah.

CAN YOU EXPLAIN IT?

FIGURE 1: Billions of years of Earth history are revealed in the layers of rock exposed in the Grand Canyon, Arizona.

Over millions of years, the Colorado River has cut a deep gorge approximately 450 km long, 15 km wide, and more than 1.5 km deep. Nearly 40 separate layers of rock are exposed in the canyon walls, from igneous and metamorphic rocks more than 1.8 billion years old on the canyon floor to 270 million-year-old limestone at the top. In between are shales full of trilobite fossils; mudstones with ferns, reptiles, and dragonfly fossils; and sandstones with fossilized dunes, reptiles, and scorpions.

 Explain How do the rocks and fossils exposed in the walls of the Grand Canyon provide evidence for Earth's geologic history?

Gather Evidence
Record observations about the different types of fossils, how they are preserved, and the various ways of determining the age of a rock layer. As you explore the lesson, gather evidence to help explain how geologists use fossils and rocks to infer ancient environments, climates, and the geologic history of a region.

Image Credits: (t) ©Lowell Georgia/National Geographic/Getty Images; (c) ©Larry Geddis/Alamy

Fossil Formation and Types of Fossils

A fossil is evidence of an ancient organism that is preserved in rock or sediment. Fossils are not only physical remains such as bones and teeth, but also casts and molds, tracks, burrows, and other signs of life. Fossils include the huge skeletons of dinosaurs such as *Apatosaurus,* as well as smaller shells, plants, and microscopic bacteria.

Fossilization

Very few of the uncountable number of organisms that have lived on Earth are fossilized. Their bodies have been broken down and transported elsewhere, and their footprints and burrows have been washed away. Specific conditions must exist and certain processes must occur for an organism or its traces to become fossilized.

FIGURE 2: Bones, teeth, footprints, and other signs of life can be fossilized when they are buried in sediment.

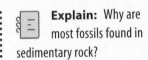
Explain: Why are most fossils found in sedimentary rock?

Flesh rots away; bones remain.

Water level rises; sediment buries the bones and footprints.

Dinosaur collapses and dies.

Footprints are left in the mud.

Erosion exposes the layers of strata containing the bones and footprints.

A thick sequence of sediments accumulates over the bones; gradually the bones fossilize.

This bed contains the dinosaur bones.

When an organism dies, it immediately begins to decay. If a dead animal is not buried soon, scavengers and decomposers feed on the flesh, while microbes break down carbon-rich molecules in the animal. Eventually, the soft tissues are gone, and all that remains are hard parts such as bones, teeth, shells, and cellulose—the plant material that makes stems and branches strong. Bone, teeth, and shells are made of materials such as calcium carbonate, calcium phosphate, and silica, which are not easily broken down by microorganisms. Remaining hard parts may be buried, eventually resulting in the fossilization of an intact skeleton that can provide important information about the original animal. This is rare, however. More often, the hard parts are broken, separated, and transported to new locations. Bones, shells, and teeth are weathered and eroded by wind, running water, and moving ice in the same way as rock.

Types of Fossils

Fossils can be classified based on how they form and what they represent. For example, some fossils are the actual parts of the organisms that have remained relatively unchanged. Others, however, have been replaced by mineral crystals or are simply imprints or casts. Still others are not pieces of the organism at all, but rather are signs of its existence.

Explain Why are body fossils such as those shown in Figure 3 so rare?

Body Fossils

Body fossils are actual remains of ancient organisms. Body fossils generally consist of the hard parts of organisms, such as shells, bones, teeth, and cellulose. In rare cases, soft parts such as muscles are also preserved.

FIGURE 3: Body fossils are physical remains of ancient organisms.

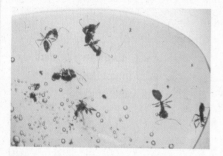

a Ants preserved in amber

b Beetle preserved in asphalt

c Mammoth preserved in frozen soil

Explain How are fossils formed by replacement different from the original organism?

Body fossils provide direct evidence of the physical size and shape of an organism. By comparing the structures of a body fossil to those of a living organism, scientists can use the fossils to infer the type of plant, animal, or other living thing the fossil belonged to and how the organism functioned.

Figure 3 shows three examples of body fossils that are extremely well preserved. The ants were trapped in tree resin that then hardened, separating the animal from the air and from organisms that could break it down. Beetles were trapped and preserved with many other animals in the sticky natural asphalt of the La Brea Tar Pits. The mammoth was preserved in frozen soil at temperatures too low for most bacteria. Organisms can also be well preserved in arid climates, where they dry out and become mummified. Some of the best preserved ice age fossils are found in dry caves.

Such complete and well-preserved fossils are rare. More commonly, body fossils consist of parts of organisms, such as individual teeth or bones, broken or abraded bones and shells, or small fragments of wood.

Replacement

FIGURE 4: Wood has been replaced with silica to form petrified wood seen at Petrified Forest National Park, Arizona.

If you pick up a fossil, you may find that it feels dense and hard. This may be because the fossil is no longer made of the same material that made up the original organism. The material has been replaced by other minerals, such as quartz or pyrite. This process is called *petrification* or *replacement*. Replacement can happen as the sediment that the organism is buried in turns into sedimentary rock. Fluids flow through the sediment and through the fossils, replacing organic material with mineral crystals. Under ideal conditions, replacement preserves the detailed structure of the interior of the organism, including features such as cells and growth rings.

Casts, Molds, and Imprints

Some types of body fossils are not actually body parts, but instead are molds, casts, or imprints of the original body part.

FIGURE 5: Casts and imprints provide evidence for the shape and size of an organism.

a A cast (left) and a mold (right) of an ammonite

b Compression has preserved the delicate structures of this leaf.

Model If you were to model how a mold of a fossil forms, what materials could you use?

A mold is a three-dimensional impression of an organism. Molds form when the body of the organism decays or dissolves after it has been buried. Although molds do not preserve the organism itself, important surface features such as shell striations, fish scales, and bark textures can be preserved. Once a hollow mold forms, fluids may flow through it, slowly filling it with minerals such as calcite, silica, and pyrite, forming a cast. Casts can also be made of fine sediments that have filled the mold. Like molds, casts can provide information about the overall shape and surface features of an organism, but not the internal structure, because internal soft parts are not preserved.

Sometimes all that remains of an organism is a dark imprint covered in a thin carbon-rich film. These two-dimensional fossils form when soft material and organisms such as leaves and insects are squeezed or compressed between layers of sediment. Over time most of the organic material decomposes and is removed. The carbon that remains can reveal detailed structures such as veins in leaves and insect wings.

Soft-Part Preservation

FIGURE 6: These are examples of exceptional preservation in which the soft body parts of organisms were mineralized before they decayed.

a Partial cast of a dinosaur brain fossil

b *Tullimonstrum gregarium*

Explain Why are oxygen-poor, acidic environments ideal for preserving organisms?

Soft parts like skin, muscle, and internal organs are rarely fossilized because they are easily decomposed by microbes. However, exceptional preservation—preservation of soft tissues—can occur when the organism is buried quickly, for example by a submarine landslide. It can also occur when the organism settles in a very oxygen-poor or acidic environment such as a bog, where scavengers, bacteria, and fungi are not active. For soft parts to be preserved, they must be mineralized before they decay. The Tully Monster fossil in Figure 6b is just one of many soft-bodied animals found at Mazon Creek in Illinois. These fossils are found inside ironstone concretions that formed around the organisms, protecting them from decay and compaction.

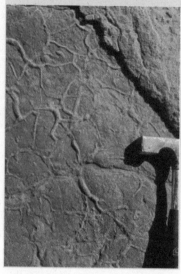

FIGURE 7: *Chondrites* looks like plant roots or coral, but it is actually fossilized burrows.

Trace Fossils

Unlike body fossils, trace fossils are not actual pieces, molds, or impressions of organisms. Instead, they are preserved signs of the activity or behavior of an organism.

There are a wide variety of trace fossils. Some, such as dinosaur tracks and worm trails, provide evidence for how an organism moved. The size and depth of dinosaur tracks can be used to estimate the animal's size, while the spacing between footprints can be used to infer how fast the animal walked or ran. Coprolites, which are pieces or pellets of fossilized dung, can provide information about the diet of ancient organisms. Fossilized burrows are evidence for where and how an organism lived. In addition, like other trace fossils, they can also provide information about the sedimentary environment where they formed. The presence of a fossilized burrow shows that the sediment was still loose and soft when the organism was living. The existence of some organisms can be inferred only from tracks and other trace fossils.

Trace fossils are different from body fossils in a few ways. Although they are given scientific names, the names refer only to the physical characteristics of the trace, not the organism that made it. A single organism can leave a variety of traces, and a single type of trace fossil can be formed by a variety or organisms. A crab, for example, could leave tracks on the sediment surface, burrows under the surface, pellets of sand excavating a burrow, and fecal pellets that become coprolites.

 Explain Dinosaur eggs are sometimes classified as body fossils and sometimes classified as trace fossils. What do you think the reasoning is behind classifying eggs in each way?

 Cause and Effect

Identifying Trace Fossils

If you come across a set of animal prints in sand, mud, or snow, it is usually relatively easy to figure out what animal made them and how the animal caused them. By comparing the tracks to known tracks, you should be able to identify the animal. By observing an animal make the tracks, you can figure out if it hopped, walked, ran, or slithered. Working out the exact cause of a trace fossil can be more challenging, because the organisms that formed them may no longer be alive on Earth. However, scientists can learn a lot by comparing fossilized tracks and burrows to those that form today. Scientists reason that tracks and burrows in the past were caused by the same behavior and similar types of organisms as tracks and burrows today.

 Explain A set of dinosaur footprints could be classified in a number of different ways. Identify two ways that they could be classified, and explain the reasoning behind the classification. What evidence can a set of dinosaur footprints provide about the physical characteristics and behavior of the animal?

Evidence Provided by Fossils

Fossils can provide information about ancient life, how living things evolved on Earth, and extinction. Fossils are also important scientifically, because they can be used to unravel Earth history. They can be used to estimate the age of rock layers, work out the connection between rock layers that are separated by vast distances, and infer the environment and climate in the region and time they existed.

Principle of Faunal Succession

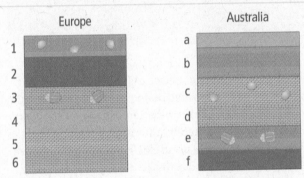

European Stratum 1 is the same age as Australian stratum c.
European Stratum 3 is the same age as Australian stratum e.

FIGURE 8: Scientists can use the specific combinations of fossils in rock layers to correlate layers in different parts of the world.

In the early 1800s, scientists studying layers of rock in Europe noticed that different layers contain very distinct assemblages, or combinations, of fossils. For example, one layer of rock contained trilobite molds and clam-like shells, while another contained reptile and fish bones.

They noticed two important things: (1) In a set of sedimentary layers, the assemblage of fossils—the combination of plants and animals in a layer—changes vertically, from layer to layer. (2) The groupings of fossils and the order of assemblages are consistent from place to place. That is, a group of fossils in a layer in England is the same as a group in France.

The observation that there is a clear pattern in the arrangement of fossilized plants and animals in rock layers gave rise to the principle of faunal succession. Scientists soon recognized that they could use this principle to connect layers of rock that are separated by long distances. For example, in Figure 8, Layers c and e in Australia formed at the same time as Layers 1 and 3 in Europe.

Scientists also recognized that sedimentary rock layers are generally in order by age. The oldest layers are at the bottom, and the youngest are at the top. They began to recognize that they could also use the principle of faunal succession to organize rock layers into broad groups by age. For example, the lowest and oldest layers, rich with trilobites, were classified as *Paleozoic* ("ancient life"). The middle layers containing ammonites and dinosaur bones were called *Mesozoic* ("middle life"). And the top and youngest layers, with mammal fossils, were called *Cenozoic* ("new life").

Explore Online ▶

🧪 **Hands-On Lab**

History in the Rock Apply information from throughout this lesson to demonstrate the use of index fossils for determining relative and absolute ages.

Explain Scientists can use the principle of faunal succession to connect rock layers that are separated by long distances. What is the reasoning behind this?

Index Fossils

Explain Why wouldn't a fossil of an organism that lived on Earth for hundreds of millions of years be very useful as an index fossil?

If you find a sedimentary layer with the fossils of a species of *Tropites* (Figure 9) in it, you can infer that the layer must have been deposited during the Mesozoic, sometime between 230 and 208 million years ago. As scientists were correlating and classifying layers based on faunal succession, they also noticed that some fossils, such as species of ammonites of the genus *Tropites,* were particularly useful for inferring the relative age of a rock layer. These species are known as index fossils.

To typically be useful as an index fossil, a fossil must meet a few important requirements: (1) The organism must have lived over a relatively short period of geologic time—hundreds of thousands to a few million years. (2) The organism must have been widespread on Earth, not just in one small area. (3) The fossil must be easy to identify and distinguish from similar fossils. (4) The fossil should be abundant in rock layers. (5) The organism must have become extinct.

Ammonites such as *Tropites* are particularly good index fossils because they were so widespread, evolved, and thus changed quickly over time, and are very distinctive. There are many other important organisms in the fossil record that can be used as index fossils.

Fossil Evidence for Past Environments

Gather Evidence How can microfossils provide evidence for Earth's history?

In 1987, a fossil collector in Gloucester, England, came across the bones of *Cetiosaurus,* a plant-eating dinosaur that lived approximately 165 million years ago. Further exploration revealed that the site was also rich with the bones and teeth of turtles, lizards, crocodiles, fish, mammals, and the feather-like coverings of the flying reptile known as *pterosaur.* Gloucester is now rolling farmland in a cool, temperate climate. But the fossils and rocks found there reveal that 165 million years ago, it was more like the warm, swampy Everglades of Florida.

We know that plants and animals alive today have specific features that make them adapted to particular environments. We can assume that the same was true for ancient organisms. Not only are fossils useful for correlating and estimating the ages of rock layers, they can also provide information about environments in which ancient organisms lived.

Evidence from Microfossils

Fossils of microscopic bacteria, single-celled protists, invertebrate animals, and plant spores and pollen are known as microfossils. Like larger fossils, microfossils can provide information about environments and climates. For example, spores and pollen found in pond sediments are used to figure out whether an area was covered in forest or grassland and whether the climate was warm and humid or cool and dry. The oceans in particular are full of microscopic organisms that live in the water and on the seafloor. When these organisms die, they accumulate on the bottom, building up the seafloor sediments. In fact, these organisms have been very important in identifying the age of deep-sea sediments recovered through scientific ocean drilling.

One way scientists can study ancient climates is by drilling into sediments and carefully examining the microfossils. After classifying the fossils, they can analyze the shells and skeletons. For example, foram shells are made of calcium carbonate ($CaCO_3$). The oxygen in the calcium carbonate comes from the ocean water. Oxygen in seawater is present in two forms: light oxygen (oxygen-16) and heavy oxygen (oxygen-18). When the global climate is relatively warm—ocean water is warm and less ice covers Earth's surface—seawater is richer in light oxygen. When the climate is cooler, seawater has a greater abundance of heavy oxygen. Scientists can measure the ratio of heavy oxygen to light oxygen in the shells to estimate how warm or cool Earth's climate was.

FIGURE 10: *Globorotalia* is one of many genera of microscopic marine organisms known as foraminifera, or forams for short. Finding a particular species of foram in a sample helps a scientist infer the age of the sediment and the temperature, depth, and salinity of the water they lived in.

Evidence from Coral

Corals are simple marine animals that live in shallow tropical and subtropical oceans. Many corals live in vast colonies, forming coral reefs. Because corals are very sensitive to changes in water temperature and other factors, they are also useful for inferring what Earth was like in the past.

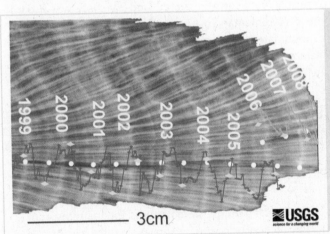

FIGURE 11: An x-ray image that shows the light- and dark-colored annual bands in a coral that was living in the late 20th and early 21st centuries.

Like the shells of forams, the skeleton of corals is made of calcium carbonate ($CaCO_3$). As a coral grows, it lays down layers of calcium carbonate, forming a pattern of bands. Light-colored bands form during the summer, while darker bands form during the winter. Scientists can analyze the growth patterns to gather information about the temperature, salinity, depth, and clarity of the water. As in foram shells, the oxygen in the calcite comes from the seawater. By analyzing the ratio of oxygen-18 to oxygen-16 in the water, scientists can gather evidence about Earth's global climate. Analyses of ancient corals can also provide evidence about other aspects of Earth history, such as the positions of the continents, the frequency of tides, and even Earth's rotation.

Explain In what way is it useful that corals add visible layers of calcite to their skeletons with each season or year?

Evidence from Plants

Gather Evidence
Would it be possible to infer the exact temperature of a region based on a single leaf? Why or why not?

FIGURE 12: The shape of a leaf margin can be related to climate.

 Hosta sieboldiana is a flowering plant with smooth-edged leaves that is found in Japan and Korea.

b Stinging nettles, *Urtica dioica*, have serrated leaves and are native to Europe, Asia, northern Africa, and western North America.

If you find a fossil of a plant that still exists today, you can assume that it lived in the same environment and the same climate that it does today. But what if the species is extinct? One method of inferring climate from fossils of extinct plants involves looking carefully at their leaves. In ecosystems today, there is a strong correlation between temperature and the proportion of plants with smooth leaf edges versus serrated leaf edges. In warm tropical climates, a higher percentage of species have smooth leaf edges, while in cooler temperate climates, a higher percentage have serrated leaf edges. Since plants are adapted to certain climates, and leaf shape is an adaptation, we can assume that the correlation between temperature and leaf shape was also true for ancient plants. Therefore, if a sedimentary rock has leaf fossils of enough different species, scientists can get an estimate of the temperature of the region when the plants were alive. Other characteristics of fossil plants can also be used to estimate temperature, rainfall, and whether or not an area experienced seasonal changes.

Patterns

Patterns in Plants

Plants have numerous patterns: leaf patterns, stem patterns, root patterns, and flower patterns. Whether you recognize it or not, when you identify a plant, you are comparing physical patterns that you see to those that you remember from other plants. The same is true for fossilized plants. Even when only part of the plant is fossilized—part of a leaf or some of the bark—it is identified by its recognizable patterns. In some cases, fossils are also identified based on the rocks they are found in or the other fossils that they are associated with. Identifying fossils in this way also involves analyzing patterns.

Evidence from Pollen

The powdery substance that is found on flowers and fills the air during the spring and fall is made of microscopic grains of pollen, which are produced by seed plants. Pollen is particularly useful, because each type of pollen is unique to a specific species of plant. When pollen is released, it is carried by wind and water and is deposited within fine sediments. A core of sediment from a lake or marsh can reveal a very detailed record of the particular species of plants that have lived in an area. If we know the environment and climate that the plants grew in, pollen collected by coring through the sediments can be used to reconstruct the climate history of a region.

Pollen is often more useful than fossils, such as leaves, because it is much more widespread and abundant. Pollen grains are resistant to abrasion, corrosion, and decay and are easily dispersed over a wide area. As a result, pollen can be preserved in different types of sediment, including ice cores. But its resistance can also be a drawback. Pollen is carried by the wind and can be deposited far from the plants that it came from. Therefore, scientists must be careful when making interpretations about an area based on a small sample.

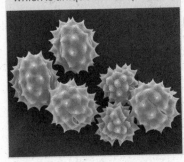

FIGURE 13: A scanning electron microscope image of pollen grains reveals their structure, which is unique to each plant.

 Explain What is it about pollen that makes it especially useful to scientists in reconstructing the past climate history of a region?

Fossil Evidence for Environmental Change

Organisms can also provide evidence for past environments and environmental change. As mentioned earlier, the fossil site in Gloucester, England, contained the bones and teeth of turtles, lizards, crocodiles, dinosaurs, fish, mammals, and the feather-like coverings of pterosaurs. This indicated that the climate in the area some 165 million years ago was more like the Everglades in southern Florida than rolling farmland in southwestern England. Another example is that fossils of whales, sharks, and crocodiles can be found today in the Egyptian desert, which shows show that the climate has changed significantly since the time when the animals were alive 35–40 million years ago.

Insects are particularly useful indicators of paleoclimate. Because they live for a short time, reproduce very quickly, and can move quickly from one place to another, insects respond very quickly and dramatically to small environmental changes. A small change in temperature, water availability, and even air composition can affect insects. We can assume that ancient insects responded to environmental changes in the same way that they do today. By identifying fossil species, counting the numbers of different types of species in a rock layer, and comparing numbers from layer to layer, we can build a detailed record of environmental change in an area. Insect fossils can reveal changes that occur over a time period as short as a few decades.

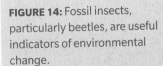

FIGURE 14: Fossil insects, particularly beetles, are useful indicators of environmental change.

 Explain What makes insects useful indicators of environmental change?

 Explain Ecology is the study of interactions between living things and their environment. Why is it important for a paleoclimatologist, a scientist who studies past climates, to have a strong understanding of ecology?

The Relative Ages of Rocks

We have seen how fossils can be used to correlate rock layers in different places, estimate the exact age of a rock layer, and infer how environments have changed over time. Our ability to use fossils in this way is based on some fundamental principles about the way that rocks form and the way that rock layers change over time.

The Present Is the Key to the Past

When scientists use fossils to describe ancient life and past climates, they are basing their conclusions on what is known about life and climate today. In order to make inferences from fossils, we must assume that Earth's systems worked in much the same way in the past as they do today.

The concept that Earth worked in the same way in the past as it does today is known as the principle of uniformitarianism: the present is the key to the past. The principle may seem obvious, but when it was first promoted by scientists in the 18th and 19th centuries, it was revolutionary. Prior to that time, most people believed Earth's history to be the result of a series of catastrophic events that occurred over a relatively short period of time.

In contrast, uniformitarians looked to current processes to try to understand the past. They reasoned that the landforms and layers of rock and sediment were formed by the same processes as they are today: gradual wearing down by wind and rain and slow deposition by rivers. Uniformitarians reasoned that an incredible amount of time must have been required to deposit thick layers of rock, uplift mountains, and erode the plains.

The idea that we can use what we know about fossils and Earth systems today to interpret the past is fundamental to our understanding of Earth history.

FIGURE 15: According to the principle of uniformitarianism, the processes that formed, transformed, broke down, and reformed rock in the past were the same as those that act on Earth's surface and interior today.

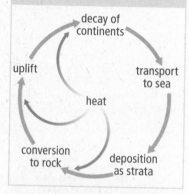

Explain Why is the principle of uniformitarianism important for our ability to interpret the rock record?

Stability and Change

Catastrophes

In the 18th and 19th centuries, scientists debated whether Earth's surface was a result of gradual changes, as argued by uniformitarians, or of a series of catastrophic events, as argued by the catastrophists. Ultimately, uniformitarianism was accepted over catastrophism by scientists, because it was based on direct observations and reasoning. However, since the 19th century, scientists have come to recognize that not all processes are gradual. Earth's surface is, in fact, shaped by very rapid events such as earthquakes, landslides, floods, and volcanic eruptions. While many of these events are catastrophic on only a small scale, events such as massive eruptions can affect large regions of Earth. In addition, there is now abundant evidence for globally catastrophic events, such as super-eruptions and giant asteroid impacts that have occurred in Earth's past but that humans have not experienced.

Relative Age

If you were sorting through a box of family photographs, you might not be able to figure out the exact date and time that each picture was taken. However, you could probably use clues to put them in chronological order. We can do the same thing with rock formations. By looking at how the formations are arranged relative to each other, we can infer the order in which they formed—their relative ages.

FIGURE 16: These layers of sedimentary rock are at Grand Staircase Escalante National Monument, Utah. The oldest layers are at the bottom.

Once we know the order in which a set of layers formed, we can determine their relative ages. On a small scale, relative age is described simply in terms of which layers are older and which are younger. In Figure 16, for example, the layers on the bottom are older than those on the top. Using fossils, we can describe the relative age more precisely in terms of rocks in distant locations. The rock shown in Figure 16 is Mesozoic. It is younger than Paleozoic formations and older than Cenozoic. Knowing the relative ages of rock formations is important because it allows us to determine the sequence of events that shaped the local area, a larger region, and even Earth as a whole.

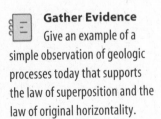

Gather Evidence What conclusions can you make about Earth history if you know the relative ages of rock formations, even if you don't know their actual ages in years?

How Rocks Are Deposited

There are several geological principles, or laws, that we can use to determine the relative age of rock formations. The most fundamental of these principles is the law of superposition, which states that sedimentary layers are deposited on top of each other. Unless the layers have been overturned, the oldest rocks are at the bottom and the youngest are at the top. Another key principle is the law of original horizontality: Sediments are deposited in relatively flat layers. This is also based on observation and reasoning. We see that when a river floods, mud, sand, and gravel are deposited in horizontal layers. We can also reason that it is impossible to deposit layers vertically, because gravity pulls loose sediments downward. The principles of superposition and original horizontality were well established by the 18th century. Geologists who were developing ideas about fossils and faunal succession relied on these basic ideas.

Gather Evidence Give an example of a simple observation of geologic processes today that supports the law of superposition and the law of original horizontality.

Apparent Exceptions to the Rules

If you look carefully at a lot of different rock formations, at some point you will come across layers of rock that are vertical, not horizontal. These observations require us to come up with other explanations.

FIGURE 17: Not all sedimentary layers are horizontal.

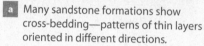

a Many sandstone formations show cross-bedding—patterns of thin layers oriented in different directions.

b At Siccar Point, Scotland, rock layers that were originally horizontal were tilted vertically, eroded, and overlain by other horizontal layers.

If you were to cut a trench through a sand dune and look at it from the side, you would see that the thin layers of sand are not horizontal, but are instead oriented at a steep slope. This feature is known as cross-bedding (Figure 17a), and it is one explanation for layers that appear to violate the rule of original horizontality.

The angle of the thick vertical layers in Figure 17b indicates that some force tilted them after they formed. The tilted layers were then eroded, and new horizontal layers of sediment were deposited on top. The younger layers are also not horizontal, showing that the whole region was tilted again.

The Law of Crosscutting Relationships

Look at the block diagram in Figure 18. Can you figure out the order of events based on relationships between the different rocks and other features?

Gather Evidence How do we know that the fault in Figure 18 formed after the horizontal layers were deposited?

FIGURE 18: The law of crosscutting relationships can be used to infer the relative ages of rocks, faults, and other features.

The law of crosscutting relationships states that if a feature such as an igneous intrusion cuts through another rock, the feature that cuts through must be younger. If a fault displaces a rock layer, the rock layer must have been there first.

Explain In chronological order, describe the events that formed the scene in Figure 18. Support your interpretations with evidence and reasoning.

The Absolute Ages of Rocks

Index fossils and geological principles, such as the law of superposition and the law of crosscutting relationships, can be used to determine the relative age of a rock formation. But what about determining the approximate age in years or millions of years? We can say that a rock with dinosaur bones in it formed during the Mesozoic era, but when was that exactly? How many millions of years ago? Scientists use absolute dating methods to work out the precise timeline of Earth history.

Counting Time

Some methods of absolute dating are relatively simple. These methods of dating are called numerical dating. For example, recall that corals form annual layers of calcite. One set of light and dark layers represents one year. If you drill into a coral reef, you can count backward, starting from today, to figure out how long ago each layer formed. The same is true for some types of sediments and sedimentary rocks.

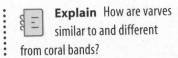

Explain How are varves similar to and different from coral bands?

FIGURE 19: Varves Each pair of light and dark layers represents one year.

Varves are sedimentary layers that can be counted similarly to bands of coral. Varves form in lakes at the edges of glaciers. During the summer, glacial ice melts and carries heavy loads of sediment into the lakes, where it is deposited as coarse, light-colored silt and sand. During the winter, the lake is ice covered, so the sediments that settle to the bottom are much finer clay particles that form a thinner, darker layer. Each varve is a pair of layers that represents one year. One drawback of counting sedimentary layers in the rock record is that we don't always know the exact year that they began to form or stopped forming. We might be able to count the number of years they were forming, but not exactly when they were forming.

Another method of numerical dating is the science of using tree rings, or growth rings, to determine climate change over time. Trees that live in temperate zones will grow a visible ring every year. Therefore, over the lifetime of a tree, an annual record is formed that can be used, along with the growth rings of other surrounding trees, to determine the environmental conditions in a specific area during a specific period of time.

Radioactive Isotopes

Determining absolute time involves making measurements and calculations that are based on changes and rates of change in natural systems. However, the most accurate and precise method for measuring time relies on changes that happen to individual atoms. This method of measuring time is called *radiometric dating*.

Explain Describe how the atom of carbon-14 in Figure 20 is changing as it decays.

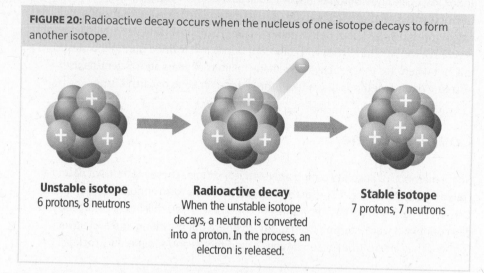

FIGURE 20: Radioactive decay occurs when the nucleus of one isotope decays to form another isotope.

Unstable isotope
6 protons, 8 neutrons

Radioactive decay
When the unstable isotope decays, a neutron is converted into a proton. In the process, an electron is released.

Stable isotope
7 protons, 7 neutrons

Many elements exist in several different forms, known as *isotopes*. Some of these isotopes are unstable. That is, over time, they decay to become isotopes of other elements. For example, carbon-14 decays to form nitrogen-14, and uranium-238 decays to make lead-206. The rate that a specific parent isotope decays to form a daughter isotope is unique to each isotope and does not change over time or vary from place to place. For example, every 5730 years, half of the carbon-14 in a sample decays to form nitrogen-14. Every 4.468 billion years, half of the uranium-238 in a sample decays to form lead-206. The half-life of an isotope is the time it takes for half of the atoms of that isotope in any sample to decay.

Radiometric Dating

Predict Because atoms are too small to see with the naked eye, and because there are millions of atoms in even the smallest sample, radiometric dating requires specialized equipment. How do you think our ability to date rocks and fossils using radiometric dating will change as technology improves?

The fact that radioactive isotopes decay at a constant rate means that we can use them to measure time. For example, suppose that a sample of wood starts out with 100 million carbon-14 atoms. In 5730 years, half will have decayed, leaving 50 million carbon-14 atoms. In another 5730 years, half of the remaining 50 million carbon-14 atoms will have decayed, leaving 25 million. Scientists can use this pattern. By knowing the original number of parent carbon-14 isotopes in the sample and measuring the remaining carbon-14 parent atoms in the sample, they can work backward to figure out how long the parent has been decaying.

Different isotopes are useful for different types and ages of materials. Carbon-14 is useful for young samples of wood and bone because they are carbon-rich. It is not useful for old samples because it decays too quickly. Samples older than about 75 000 years don't have enough carbon-14 left to measure. Uranium-lead dating, however, is useful for older igneous and metamorphic rocks that have uranium-rich minerals. It is not useful for very young rocks, because uranium decays so slowly. If a sample is too young, there are not enough lead atoms to measure.

Math Connection

There are a number of common radiometric dating methods. Use the table to answer each question.

1. How much of the parent uranium-238 is left in a sample after one half-life?

2. Assuming the system is closed (nothing leaves or enters), how much potassium-40 is left in a sample that is 2.5 billion years old?

3. How much carbon-14 is left after a period of 17 190 years?

Parent	Half-Life	Daughter
Carbon-14	5730 years	Nitrogen-14
Potassium-40	1.25 billion years	Argon-40
Uranium-238	4.47 billion years	Lead-206
Rubidium-87	48.8 billion years	Strontium-87

Absolute Age

We have seen that we can determine the relative age of a rock formation based on fossils within it and nearby rocks and based on its relationship to other formations. The absolute age, or actual numeric age of a formation, can be determined by methods such as counting varves and radiometric dating.

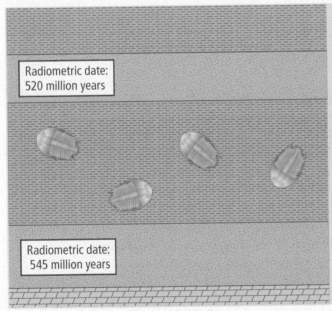

Radiometric date:
520 million years

Radiometric date:
545 million years

FIGURE 21: Combining relative dating methods with absolute dating methods allows us to work out the age of a rock layer in thousands or millions of years before the present. For example, based on the ages of the layers above and below it, we can infer that the trilobite layer must have formed between 545 and 520 million years ago. We can use this information to construct a precise timeline of events in Earth history.

Even if we don't measure the radiometric age of each layer, by measuring a few key layers, we can constrain the ages of the others layers. If we find the radiometric age of a layer with index fossils, we can then assume that any layer that contains those fossils is the same age. For example, we know from radiometric dating that a layer of rock with *Tropites* fossils in it formed between 230 and 208 milllion years ago. Using absolute dating methods, we can now say that a rock layer is not just "Mesozoic," but that it is approximately 210 million years old.

Explain How can absolute dating methods and relative dating methods be used together to infer the age of the trilobite layer in Figure 21?

Explain Given that we now have the ability to determine the absolute ages of rocks using radiometric dating, why are the principles of relative dating and the use of index fossils still important? Think about how they might be used in oil or mineral exploration.

Hands-On Activity

Modeling Molds and Casts

MATERIALS

- clay, modeling
- container, plastic
- hard objects, such as a shell, key, paper clip, or coin
- leaf
- newspaper
- paper, carbon, soft
- paper, wax
- paper, white (one sheet)
- pencil (or wooden dowel)
- plaster of Paris
- spoon, plastic
- tweezers
- water

Language Arts Connection Research a specific type of trace fossil. Gather evidence to explain the type of information that is provided by the fossil. Be sure to cite specific text evidence to support your claims. Finally, present your findings in the form of a poster or video. Submit a list of resources with your final presentation. Follow the format specified by your instructor.

PROCEDURE

1. Place a ball of modeling clay on a flat surface that is covered with wax paper.

2. Press the clay down to form a flat disk about 8 cm in diameter. Turn the clay over so that the smooth, flat surface is facing up.

3. Choose a small, hard object. Place the object onto the clay carefully so that you do not distrub the indentation. Is the indentation left by the object a mold or a cast? What features of the object are best shown in the indentation? Sketch the indentation.

4. On a second piece of smooth, flat clay, make a shallow imprint to represent the burrow or footprint of an animal. Sketch your fossil imprint.

5. Fill a plastic container with water to a depth of 1 to 2 cm. Stir in enough plaster of Paris (or, instead, a mixture of white glue and sand) to make a paste that has the consistency of whipped cream.

6. Using the plastic spoon, fill both indentations with plaster. Allow excess plaster to run over the edges of the imprints. Let the plaster set for about 15 minutes until it hardens.

7. After the plaster has hardened, remove both pieces of plaster from the clay. Do the pieces of hardened plaster represent molds or casts?

8. Place the carbon paper on a flat surface with the carbon facing up. Gently place the leaf on the carbon paper, and cover it with several sheets of newspaper. Roll the pencil or wooden dowel back and forth across the surface of the newspaper several times, and press firmly to bring the leaf into full contact with the carbon paper.

9. Remove the newspaper. Lift the leaf by using the tweezers, and place it on a clean sheet of paper with the carbon-coated side facing down. Cover the leaf with clean wax paper, and roll your pencil across the surface of the wax paper.

10. Remove the wax paper and leaf. Observe and describe the carbon print left by the leaf.

ANALYSIS

1. Look at molds and casts made by others in your class. Identify as many of the objects used to make molds and casts as you can.

2. How does the carbon print you made differ from an actual carbonized imprint?

3. Trace fossils are evidence of the movement of an animal on or within soft sediment. Why are imprints, molds, and casts not considered trace fossils?

| NATURAL HISTORY MUSEUM CURATOR | WILLIAM SMITH | Go online to choose one of these other paths. |

Evaluate

CAN YOU EXPLAIN IT NOW?

FIGURE 22: Layers of rock exposed at the Grand Canyon, Arizona

The Colorado River has carved a gorge more than 1500 m deep into the layers of sedimentary, igneous, and metamorphic rock that make up the Colorado Plateau. The rocks and fossils exposed in the Grand Canyon reveal hundreds of millions of years of Earth history in the region. For example, the 1800 million-year-old metamorphic rocks exposed on the floor of the Grand Canyon reveal evidence for ancient mountain building and the early growth of the North American continent. The unconformity that separates these basement rocks from the rocks above, a mixture of sedimentary and igneous rocks that began forming 1200 million years ago, is evidence for millions of years of erosion. The steep angle of this bottom group of sedimentary layers is evidence that the region was tilted by some tectonic force after the sediments were deposited, while the sharp boundary between these tilted layers and flat layers above is evidence for more erosion. The thick sequence of flat sedimentary layers reveals evidence for changing geologic environments, from sandy beaches preserved in sandstone, to deeper marine muds preserved in limestone, to continental stream environments preserved in shales. While body fossils of animals like ammonites provide evidence that the region was under ocean water, trace fossils of reptiles are evidence that it was at other times part of a sandy desert. With the help of index fossils like trilobites, which allow scientists to determine the relative age of each layer, and radiometric ages from minerals in layers of volcanic rock and crosscutting igneous intrusions, scientists have been able to construct a detailed timeline of events and unravel the complex geologic history of the region.

Explain How do the rocks and fossils exposed in the walls of the Grand Canyon provide evidence for Earth's geologic history?

CHECKPOINTS

Check Your Understanding

1 A geologist gets a call from a friend who is visiting a national park. The friend is looking at a rock layer and wants to know how old it is. Which question would be most useful for the geologist to ask her friend?

   a. What fossils are in the rock layer?

   b. What species of pollen are in the rock layer?

   c. Is the rock layer high in the mountains or low in a valley?

   d. What is the uranium-lead ratio of the minerals in the rock layer?

2. Trace fossils are also referred to as ichnofossils, from the Greek root *ikhnos*, which means footprint or track. Do you think this term is appropriate? Support your argument with evidence and reasoning.

3. Why is rock type alone not a good basis for correlating rock layers or determining the age of a rock layer?

4. A museum curator is organizing the fossils in a collection. There are two cabinets: body fossils and trace fossils. Which cabinet should each fossil be placed in?

   a. bird nest

   b. coprolite

   c. leaf imprint

   d. pyritized ammonite

   e. shark tooth

   f. trilobite cast

   g. trilobite tracks

   h. worm burrow

5. The curator has been asked to put the fossils on exhibit. Which label goes with which fossil?

   a. coprolite
   b. leaf imprint
   c. pyritized ammonite
   d. trilobite cast
   e. worm burrow

   1. a thin carbon film
   2. provides evidence for the animal's diet
   3. evidence for the lifestyle of an organism
   4. formed when minerals filled a mold left by the body of the animal
   5. formed when minerals replaced the original material in the animal's body

6. Which of the following statements about the principle of faunal succession is true? Choose all that apply.

   a. It relies on radiometric dating techniques.

   b. It assumes that rock layers are deposited on top of each other.

   c. It can be used to correlate metamorphic rocks that occurred in different parts of the world.

   d. It has been used to show that different continents were once connected as one landmass.

   e. It assumes that specific combinations of organisms were living only at a certain time in Earth history.

7. Why is an ammonite found in place more useful to a scientist than one found in a fossil shop?

8. Which of the following is the best analogy for the principle of superposition?

   a. the order of songs on a playlist

   b. the order of pages in a printer tray

   c. the arrangement of buildings in a neighborhood

   d. the arrangement of different types of cereal in the grocery store

9. A proxy is a person who represents someone else, or a thing that represents something else. Why certain fossils, such as forams, corals, leaves, and pollen are referred to as "climate proxies"?

10. In the 1950s, scientists found hard evidence that Meteor Crater in Arizona was formed by an impact. Before this evidence was found, geologists generally rejected the idea because it seemed to violate a fundamental principle of geology. Which principle did the impact interpretation seem to violate?

   a. Crosscutting relationships, because the sediments inside the crater are younger than the crater itself.

   b. Uniformitarianism, because no one had ever seen an impact before.

   c. Original horizontality, because the crater was originally bowl shaped.

   d. Superposition, because the impact blasted old rocks out on top of younger rocks.

11. Identify the method or principle of geology that is best used to determine each of the following.

  a. the age of the fault relative to the intrusion and sediments

  b. the age of the igneous intrusion in years

  c. the age of layer B relative to layers A and C

  d. the age of layer D relative to a layer in another part of the country

  e. the age of the intrusion relative to Layer B

12. Why is it important for radiometric dating that isotopes decay at a specific rate that does not change over time and does not vary from place to place?

13. The half-life of a particular radioactive isotope is 500 million years. If the parent:daughter ratio in a rock is 1:3, how old is the rock?

Geologic Time

An artist's conception of the ancient ocean floor

CAN YOU EXPLAIN IT?

FIGURE 1: An asteroid impact near the Yucatán Peninsula in southeastern Mexico may have been one of the chief causes of the mass extinction at the end of the Mesozoic era.

Gather Evidence
Gather evidence about how scientists define a geologic timescale and what has happened to Earth through time.

Scientists need a way to talk about the events of Earth's history and divide geologic time so that these discussions can proceed without confusion. They separate units of geologic time using the appearance and disappearance of fossil organisms in the geologic record. Geologic time is separated into different segments based on significant changes in the numbers and kinds of fossils found. The boundaries of some time periods are marked by huge extinction events that wiped out a majority of the living organisms of the time. One of these that most people are aware of is the extinction of the dinosaurs about 66 million years ago. At that time other groups of animals, such as flying and marine reptiles and ammonites, also became extinct. Other boundaries in the geologic timescale are based on smaller events that may have affected only a small group of animals, but all boundaries are marked by a change in the fossil record. Scientists use the geologic timescale to talk about events in Earth history: mountain building, formation and breakup of supercontinents, and major volcanic eruptions.

Predict What major events might a scientist studying Earth history be interested in? What information might a geologist need to be able to talk about these events?

Early Earth

Over the 4.6 billion years of Earth's existence, its surface and the organisms that live on land and in the oceans have changed dramatically. The movements of tectonic plates have altered the configuration of landmasses and ocean basins and have had a considerable effect on the organisms that have lived on the planet.

Explain. How have scientists used changes in the organisms living on the planet to create the geologic time scale?

The Geologic Timescale

The geologic time scale divides Earth's history into intervals based on evidence found in layers of rock and the appearance and extinctions of organisms. Discoveries around the world enable us to reconstruct the slow changes and sudden events that led to the present world.

FIGURE 2: Scientists use the geologic time scale to understand Earth's long history.

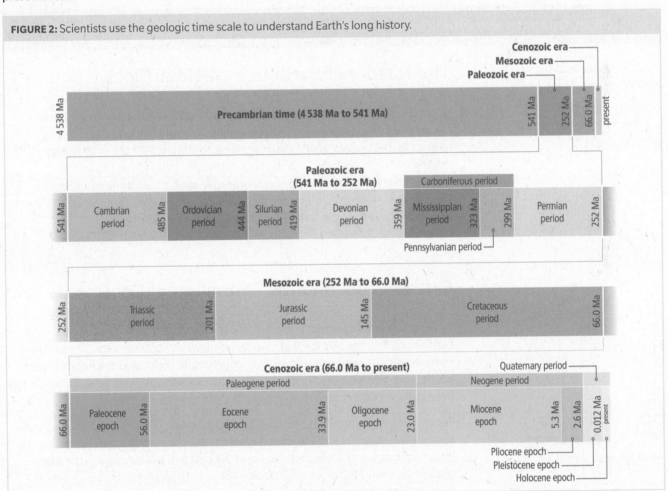

Geologists have interpreted the rock and fossil record to show that Earth's history can be organized, like a calendar, into time divisions of different lengths. The largest divisions of geologic time are eons, and the first three eons are sometimes referred to as the Precambrian. Eons are divided into smaller time segments called *eras*: the Paleozoic era, the Mesozoic era, and the Cenozoic era. The three eras are divided into periods, and periods may be further divided into smaller time periods called *epochs*.

Explain How has the Quaternary period been subdivided into epochs? Why might the Quaternary period be an important time to study?

The Precambrian

The Precambrian is the span of time between Earth's formation approximately 4.6 billion years ago through 541 million years ago and accounts for almost 90% of Earth's history. Many of the rocks that remain from the Precambrian have been so heavily metamorphosed at a later time that much of the evidence about early Earth contained in them has been lost. Also, because Precambrian fossils are rare, scientists have had a difficult time interpreting events that occurred during this period of time. As a result, evidence of Earth events preserved in Precambrian rocks is relatively rare compared with later time periods.

FIGURE 3: The Precambrian spans almost 90% of Earth's history, yet relatively little evidence from this period remains.

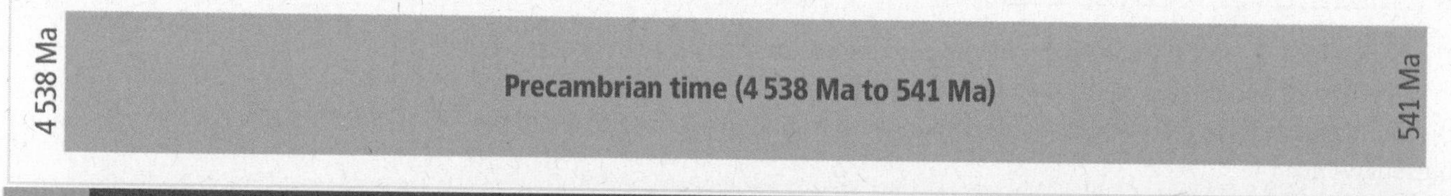

4 538 Ma	Precambrian time (4 538 Ma to 541 Ma)	541 Ma

Scale, Quantity, and Proportion

 Explain If the Precambrian makes up almost 90% of Earth's history, why is this period so poorly understood?

The History of Earth in a 24-Hour Clock

Scientists often explain geologic time in terms of a clock. Using this analogy, the Precambrian would make up 10.6 hours on the 12-hour clock face. Another way to describe the Precambrian is that it accounts for almost 90% of Earth's history. Use the scale of a clock face and the information you gather from this lesson or other sources to calculate what proportions of the face the three eras of the Phanerozoic—Paleozoic, Mesozoic, and Cenozoic—comprise. About which of these eras do we have the most information? Explain your reasoning.

Earth's Crust and the Formation of Continents

By 2.5 billion years ago, approximately 50% to 60% of Earth's continental crust had formed. Yet, few of these rocks are found today on Earth's surface. The earliest continental crust known to still exist is a metamorphic rock called the Acasta Gneiss, which is exposed on a single isolated island in the Northwest Territories, Canada. It has been radiometrically dated to about 4 billion years before the present.

Predict Why might scientists be interested in studying supercontinents?

Recall that Earth's crust is fragmented into tectonic plates of different sizes that move slowly across its surface as a reaction to motion and pressure deep within the planet. Plate tectonics transformed Earth's crust in the past and will continue to gradually change the configuration of landmasses and ocean basins in the future. At several times in Earth's history, all of the landmasses have converged to form one massive continent, which scientists call a supercontinent. One of these early supercontinents, Rodinia, formed in a global collision event during the Precambrian between 1.3 billion and 900 million years ago. It is challenging for scientists to attempt to reenact plate movements from the distant past, because new oceans and continents have since formed or split apart. But scientists study rocks and other data to approximate the location, size, and shape of ancient supercontinents.

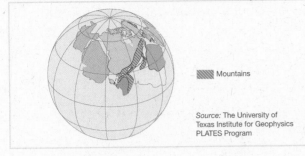

Mountains

Source: The University of Texas Institute for Geophysics PLATES Program

FIGURE 4: Rodinia formed between 1.3 billion and 900 million years ago during the Precambrian.

Earth's Early Atmosphere and Oceans

Two of the most distinguishing components of the Earth system are water and oxygen, but early Earth lacked both. Scientists propose two different possible sources for Earth's water. Water could have arrived with asteroids during early collisions with the planet. It also could have condensed from gases expelled during volcanic eruptions. It is probable that both sources contributed to the enormous amount of water on Earth. As Earth's molten surface cooled, the water slowly condensed and filled Earth's basins, forming the earliest oceans by at least 4 billion years ago.

The early atmosphere contained very little oxygen. Single-celled, photosynthetic organisms called cyanobacteria started to transform the atmosphere. They used carbon dioxide and produced oxygen during photosynthesis. By about 2.3 billion years ago they had produced enough oxygen to cause the Great Oxidation Event. After a gap of almost a billion years, cyanobacteria and other photosynthetic organisms caused another spike in oxygen production. This spike produced enough oxygen to support the evolution of multicellular organisms.

Banded iron formations are important indicators of ancient atmospheric composition. They formed about 3.0 to 1.8 billion years ago, with a peak at about the same time as the Great Oxidation Event. Banded iron formations consist of gray, silver, or black iron-oxide layers that alternate with red, iron-poor silica layers.

FIGURE 5: The banded iron shown formed when oxygen-producing bacteria released free oxygen in amounts plentiful enough to combine with dissolved iron in ocean water to produce bands of iron-rich minerals.

Earth's Early Climate

Considering how long the Precambrian is, there is relatively little direct evidence about climate during the time. It is likely that soon after Earth's formation, temperatures were quite high with a slow cooling throughout much of the time period.

Evidence from rock formations and isotopes suggests three periods of very cold temperatures that resulted in glaciers forming over much of Earth. These periods have been referred to as "snowball Earth," because sea-ice covered most or all of the ocean and glaciers covered much of the land. The first, relatively brief period may have been about 3 billion years ago. The second occurred around the time banded-ironstones formed about 2.3 billion years ago and may have been related to oxygenation of the atmosphere at that time. This later glacial event may have lasted for hundreds of millions of years.

The third period includes two snowball Earth events near the end of Precambrian time (800 to 600 million years ago), possibly related to the second major rise in oxygen in the atmosphere. As photosynthesis removed carbon dioxide from the atmosphere, temperatures cooled, glaciers formed, and albedo increased. The higher albedo caused a positive feedback loop that produced glacial cycles lasting 4 million to 30 million years. Evidence for this massive glaciation includes glacial deposits found even in areas that would have been close to the position of the equator during that time.

Predict Why are scientists curious about the origin of water on Earth?

FIGURE 6: Locations on Earth where evidence of a glaciation that occurred about 650 million years ago is found.

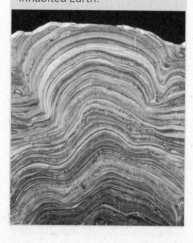

FIGURE 7: Cyanobacteria, which form structures called *stromatolites*, are among the oldest organisms to have inhabited Earth.

Earth's Earliest Life

Although other organisms evolved before them, cyanobacteria are the ancient organisms that had the most profound influence on the early evolution of Earth's spheres. These organisms formed unique mounds, called *stromatolites*, in shallow oceans. Stromatolites formed when layers of bacteria populated the surface of a mound. The layer of bacteria would trap sediment, and a new layer of cyanobacteria would populate the sedimentary layer. Over time, layers of cyanobacteria built up on top of each other (as seen in the fossil example in Figure 7). This process occurred over and over again, and the mounds grew. Stromatolite formation can be observed in stromatolites living today in Australia and the Bahamas. The first cyanobacteria are thought to have lived in an oxygen-poor environment, where they photosynthesized, releasing oxygen into the ocean water.

Until the late Precambrian, all organisms were prokaryotes, which are single-celled organisms, such as cyanobacteria, with a cell that has genetic material but does not have a nucleus or other membrane-enclosed organelles. The first eukaryotes (organisms with cells that have an organized nucleus and organelles) appeared in the late Precambrian after the second big oxygenation event. This led to the evolution of multicellular organisms. Fossils of the first multicellular animals (metazoans) were discovered in the Ediacara Hills of southern Australia. These soft-bodied organisms did not have any hard parts, so preservation of a complete animal fossil is somewhat rare.

FIGURE 8: Ediacaran fossils are from organisms that lived 600 to 545 million years ago.

a *Dickinsonia*

b sea pen

  Summarize Describe the importance of the rise of eukaryotes.

Image Credits: (t) ©Francois Gohier/Science Source; (bl) ©De Agostini Picture Library/Getty Images; (br) ©Sinclair Stammers/Science Source

Earth During the Paleozoic Era

As you can see in Figure 9, the Paleozoic era spanned almost 300 million years of Earth's history from 541 million years ago to 252 million years ago. It was a time of very important change on the planet, as the supercontinent Rodinia broke up and the supercontinent Pangaea formed. Life on Earth experienced a dramatic period of evolution. The "Cambrian Explosion" describes a relatively brief time span that lasted from about 541 to 485 million years ago. During this time in the planet's history, life forms evolved from simple unicellular organisms to more complex organisms.

FIGURE 9: The Paleozoic era spanned from 541 to 252 million years ago and encompassed six periods.

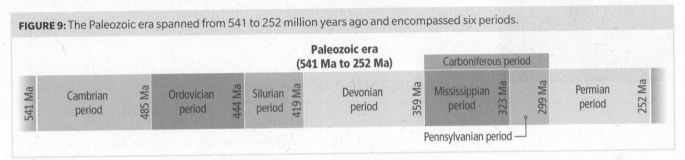

The Breakup of Rodinia

The supercontinent Rodinia had begun to rift apart about 750 million years ago during the Precambrian. Lava flows from this time are found on most of the continents, providing evidence for this breakup. Around 650 million years ago, the Iapetus Ocean formed, as shown in Figure 10. The eastern part of the ocean formed between the continents of Baltica and Laurentia. The western part of the ocean formed between Amazonia and Laurentia. Continued plate tectonic processes formed a growing region of shallow ocean between the separating parts of the former supercontinent.

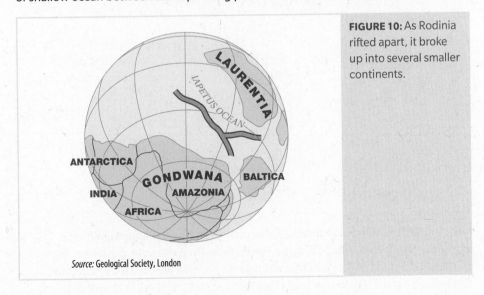

Source: Geological Society, London

FIGURE 10: As Rodinia rifted apart, it broke up into several smaller continents.

Explain What is the consequence of supercontinent rifting in terms of the reconfiguration of continents?

FIGURE 11: The Appalachian Mountains are an ancient mountain range that began to form 480 million years ago.

Laurentia and Gondwana

Laurentia and Gondwana were separated by the Iapetus Ocean. About 480 million years ago, a subduction zone formed along the eastern margin of the continent Laurentia. (Laurentia would become the continent of North America.) During the next 250 million years, more collisions caused other mountain-building events along the continent's eastern margin. Around 300 million years ago, the collision of what are now the continents of North America and Africa caused the Appalachian Mountains to grow to a height that may have approximated that of today's Himalaya Mountains. The formation of Gondwana was also caused by a series of mountain-building events. Two events in particular, involving Africa and Arabia, and Africa and India, led to the consolidation of Gondwana.

 Predict What type of rock would you expect to find making up the Appalachian Mountains?

The Formation of Pangaea

Earth's most recent supercontinent, Pangaea, began forming about 300 million years ago. The continental collisions that formed the Appalachian Mountains sutured the continents together to form the supercontinent. Pangaea extended from about the current North Pole to the South Pole. This vast landmass incorporated almost all the smaller landmasses on Earth and covered nearly one-third of the planet—thus, its name comes from the Greek words *pan-* and *gaia*, meaning "all the earth."

FIGURE 12: The supercontinent Pangaea began forming about 300 million years ago. The map shows the configuration of Pangaea during the Permian period, approximately 252 million years ago.

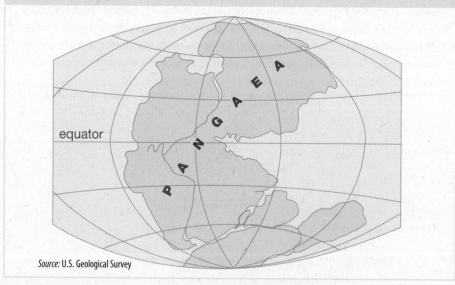

Source: U.S. Geological Survey

 Explain How did the climatic conditions in Pangaea affect the formation and distribution of the coal that is used to produce energy today?

The climate of Pangaea was zoned. Glacial centers shifted as Pangaea migrated across the South Pole. When Pangaea moved away from the pole, glaciation ceased. The portion of Pangaea that contained Laurentia was located in a warm, tropical, equatorial region that contained lush vegetation. Recall that over time, the accumulation of plant debris under elevated temperature and pressure produces coal. In fact, the coal deposits found in the eastern United States and Europe formed in the lush, tropical forests that grew along the equatorial region of Pangaea.

Paleozoic Climate

Laurentia's tropical climate was warm and humid during the Cambrian. By the late Ordovician, a mass extinction caused by a decrease in global temperature greatly reduced the number of marine species. The Silurian and Devonian periods were warm, producing evaporite deposits and rich layers of fossiliferous carbonate rocks. During the Carboniferous period, climate returned to being humid and tropical. At this time, Laurentia was covered with evaporite and sand-dune deposits, suggesting arid desert conditions in the western region of Pangaea. In Permian time, temperatures had once again cooled enough to cause glaciation.

Observe Why do evaporite deposits and fossiliferous carbonate rocks indicate that global temperature was warm?

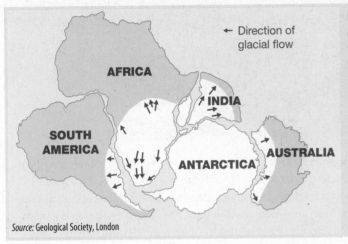

← Direction of glacial flow

AFRICA

INDIA

SOUTH AMERICA

ANTARCTICA

AUSTRALIA

Source: Geological Society, London

FIGURE 13: Glacial deposits that formed during the late Paleozoic glaciation can be found on modern-day continents based on their configuration in the supercontinent Pangaea.

Cambrian Life

During the late Cambrian period, perhaps the greatest evolutionary change in life forms in Earth history took place. Within about a 40 million-year period, most complex organisms with mineralized skeletons developed, and almost all major animal groups present on Earth today appeared. In rare instances, soft-bodied fossils were preserved; however, scientists have found these fossils to be difficult to identify with certainty, as they are unlike organisms living today. The first complex trace fossils are also found in the fossil record from Cambrian sediments. Some of these trace fossils provide evidence that organisms were developing new ecological interactions, such as burrowing into soft sediment and predation. At the end of the Cambrian period, one of Earth's major mass extinction events changed everything.

Stability and Change

Coevolution in the Fossil Record

FIGURE 14: Trilobites are a diverse group that developed a variety of adaptations to avoid predation.

Following the Cambrian–Ordovician extinction event, life became dramatically different. During the Ordovician, marine ecosystems expanded in a uniform climate, and high sea levels produced shallow seas all over Earth. These conditions favored Paleozoic marine invertebrates. Ecological diversity was expanded by the evolution of large predators. This evolution affected trilobites, arthropods which developed spines and other features that allowed them to avoid predation. This is an example of coevolution in the fossil record.

Land Plants and Animals Appear

Explain Why are the coal deposits that exist today considered a nonrenewable resource?

FIGURE 15: Early forests consisted of club mosses, ferns, and horsetails.

The first land plants appeared during the late Ordovician. By the Devonian, forests of club mosses, horsetails, and ferns covered the land. Land plants diversified further, and by the Carboniferous, vegetation accumulated in coastal swamps. When this vegetation was buried in an anaerobic environment, the organic matter in the plant material was converted into the rich coal deposits that are still being mined today.

By the Silurian, the first land animals, including spiders, scorpions, and primitive insects, inhabited the young forests. By the late Devonian, amphibians evolved from lobe-finned fish that crawled onto land for the first time.

The End-Permian Extinction

The most catastrophic mass extinction event in Earth's history occurred at the end of the Permian period, approximately 252 million years ago. Although it is still under debate, many scientists now attribute the end-Permian mass extinction event to the volcanic eruptions that produced a massive outpouring of basaltic rock called the Siberian Traps, located in present-day Russia. It is thought that the extinction resulted in the death of 81% to 96% of marine organisms and 70% of land organisms. Clues to the greatest mass extinction of all time are elusive, because sediments with fossils from the latest Permian are scarce.

The Siberian Traps formed around the time of the end-Permian extinction. Eruptions of glowing magma from numerous volcanoes lasted for about 900 000 years, creating a massive lava field. Computer modeling shows that these eruptions could have released more than 1.2 billion tons of methane and 4 billion tons of sulfur dioxide into the atmosphere. Tremendous amounts of CO_2 were also released into the skies during the eruptions. As all that CO_2 dissolved in the ocean, it caused the pH in the world's oceans to rapidly fall, causing acidification and the loss of species that could cause the food web to crash.

FIGURE 16: The Siberian Traps in Russia are the remains of volcanic activity on a massive scale that is thought to have caused the end-Permian extinction.

 Predict How might massive volcanic eruptions lead to a global mass extinction?

Earth During the Mesozoic Era

The Mesozoic era, also called the *Age of Reptiles,* ranged from 252 million years ago to 66 million years ago. At the beginning of the era, the supercontinent Pangaea began to break apart, which again dramatically affected climate and the evolution of life on Earth. The Mesozoic was characterized by the rise and fall of the dinosaurs and the rise of flowering plants.

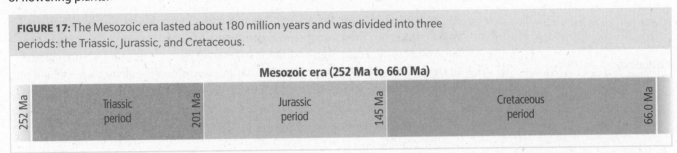

FIGURE 17: The Mesozoic era lasted about 180 million years and was divided into three periods: the Triassic, Jurassic, and Cretaceous.

Mesozoic era (252 Ma to 66.0 Ma)					
252 Ma	Triassic period	201 Ma	Jurassic period	145 Ma	Cretaceous period	66.0 Ma

The Breakup of Pangaea Begins

During the late Triassic, approximately 215 million years ago, the supercontinent Pangaea began to break apart. This rifting began the formation of the Atlantic Ocean. As the Atlantic opened, the proto–North American continent moved westward on a collision course with small island arcs. The collisions produced mountains on the western margin of the continent.

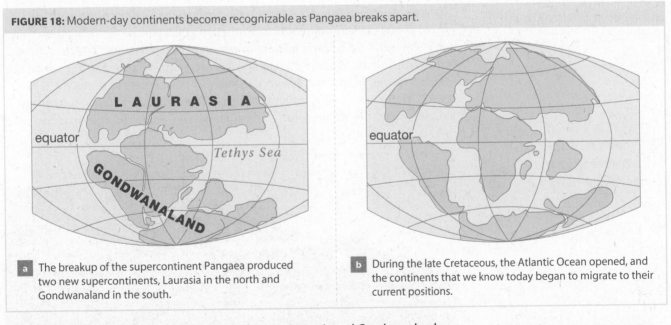

FIGURE 18: Modern-day continents become recognizable as Pangaea breaks apart.

a The breakup of the supercontinent Pangaea produced two new supercontinents, Laurasia in the north and Gondwanaland in the south.

b During the late Cretaceous, the Atlantic Ocean opened, and the continents that we know today began to migrate to their current positions.

Pangaea separated to form two new supercontinents, Laurasia and Gondwanaland. Laurasia consisted of the present-day continents of Europe, North America, and Asia. Gondwanaland was made up of South America, Africa, Antarctica, Australia, and the Indian subcontinent.

Observe What was the first event in the breakup of the supercontinent Pangaea?

The Breakup Continues

During the Mesozoic, the continents began to migrate toward their current positions. The southern margin of North America began separating from South America during the Jurassic period, forming the Gulf of Mexico. India separated from Africa and Australia. By the middle of the Cretaceous period, South America had rifted from Africa. North America had separated from Greenland and Europe, and by the end of the Cretaceous, Australia had separated from Antarctica.

The Opening of the Atlantic

As Pangaea rifted apart, the Atlantic Ocean began to grow along the newly formed spreading center. The rapid spreading produced a large midocean ridge system. The large ridge system displaced enormous volumes of water, producing a higher global sea level. During the Mesozoic, North America was divided in half by a large inland sea, which extended from the Arctic Ocean to the Gulf of Mexico.

Observation What evidence exists to help scientists reconstruct the opening of the Atlantic Ocean?

Mesozoic Climate

During the late Mesozoic, when a larger area of Earth's surface was covered by water, more incoming solar radiation was absorbed by water, and heat was transported toward the poles by ocean currents. This created an overall warm, mild climate with the poles being ice free.

Scientists use several lines of evidence to understand the climate conditions that existed during the Mesozoic era. Plant fossils imply mild temperature conditions consistent with subtropical conditions over most of the continents. Cretaceous fossils from North America, Western Europe, and Russia confirm mild temperatures along the middle latitudes. In addition, evidence reveals that polar waters were around 10 °C to 15 °C. North America was mainly subtropical. The uniformity of Cretaceous plants indicates that the North American continent lacked any sharp climatic variations.

Observe In what order did the continents break apart from Pangaea?

FIGURE 19: The first major phase of the breakup of Pangaea took place during the Jurassic as Africa and North America separated, forming the North Atlantic Ocean.

NORTH AMERICA

AFRICA

Explore Online ▶

Hands-On Lab

Matching Lines of Evidence Model the lines of evidence for the age of the Atlantic Ocean.

Analyze What lines of evidence are used to interpret Mesozoic climate?

FIGURE 20: *Acrocanthosaurus* was a predatory dinosaur that lived approximately 115 million to 108 million years ago in the subtropical temperatures of North America.

Image Credits: ©Stocktrek Images/Getty Images

The Rise of Flowering Plants

The Mesozoic era also witnessed the rise of flowering plants, called angiosperms. The presence of angiosperms increased biological diversity on the planet.

Gymnosperms are seed-bearing plants that include modern-day pines and similar cone-bearing plants. These evolved during the late Carboniferous, about 300 million years ago. Wind carried pollen from plant to plant for pollination and reproduction. Angiosperms developed about 125 million years ago during the Cretaceous. Unlike gymnosperms, angiosperms have flowers that attract insects and birds. Birds and insects act as the primary pollinators of the flowering plants. In addition, in angiosperms the ovary of the flower is fertilized by one pollen grain, and a second pollen grain causes the growth of a nut or fruit. Animals eat the nuts or fruit and spread the seeds over a large area.

The success of angiosperms lies in the coevolution of insects. Insects went through an evolutionary explosion in response to the development of angiosperms. As a result, insect diversification caused more types of flowering plants to evolve. This is an example of a relationship in which a plant and a pollinator place evolutionary pressure on each other that leads to changes in both the plant and the animal.

FIGURE 21: A fossil impression of a Mesozoic angiosperm, *Glossopteris browniana.*

Analyze What advantages do angiosperms have over gymnosperms?"

The Age of Reptiles

Reptiles entered the fossil record 310 million years ago during the Carboniferous period. As the Paleozoic transitioned into the Mesozoic, reptiles rose to become the dominant animals on the planet.

Explain Why is the Mesozoic era commonly known as the "Age of the Dinosaurs"?

FIGURE 22: Dinosaurs dominated the planet during the Mesozoic era.

During the early Mesozoic, mammal-like reptiles were the dominant terrestrial vertebrates. However, by the late Triassic, dinosaurs and their relatives had replaced mammal-like reptiles as the principal animals on the planet. Reptiles continued to evolve and diversify through the Mesozoic, expanding their range to include marine environments and the air. The first true birds emerged from birdlike dinosaurs during the Jurassic, though their fossils are comparatively rare. Although primitive mammals evolved in the late Triassic, they appear to not have changed much throughout the Mesozoic era.

Image Credits: (t) ©Natural History Museum, London/Alamy; (d) ©De Agostini Picture Library/De Agostini Editorial/Getty Images; (cr) ©MasPix/Alamy; (bl) ©Natural History Museum, London/Alamy

FIGURE 23: Two groups of marine mollusks that were abundant during the Mesozoic era were rudists and ammonites. During the Paleozoic, brachiopods were abundant; by the Mesozoic, they were few.

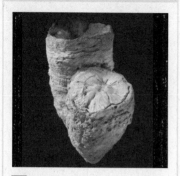

a rudist

b ammonite

c brachiopod

 Gather Evidence
What direct evidence is there for the Cretaceous-Tertiary mass extinction?

Marine Life During the Mesozoic

The immense Permian extinction removed about 81% to 96% of marine organisms and 70% of land organisms, opening niches for new organisms to inhabit and become diversified. By the Mesozoic, the ocean floor was no longer covered by Paleozoic marine invertebrate fauna. Mollusks fared well after the extinction; they had stronger shells and the ability to burrow to withstand predation. During the Mesozoic era, reef-building corals were displaced by reef-building mollusks—rudists—that had the ability to anchor to the ocean floor. Today, Mesozoic rudist reefs found in rocks in areas such as Saudi Arabia are good indicators for locating petroleum.

Explain Why did mollusks fare better in Mesozoic oceans than brachiopods?

The Cretaceous-Paleogene Mass Extinction

The Cretaceous period ended with another mass extinction, during which dinosaurs disappeared from the planet, as did marine reptiles and dominant invertebrates such as ammonites and rudists.

FIGURE 24: The image is an artist's conception of what the world may have been like at the end of the Cretaceous period.

Scientists have developed two hypotheses to explain the end-Mesozoic mass extinction. The first hypothesis proposes that the extinction was the result of an asteroid that impacted the planet about 66 million years ago. Evidence for the impact includes a 10-km-diameter crater on the seafloor and land surface of the Yucatán Peninsula in southeastern Mexico. The impact would have greatly heated the global atmosphere and produced a dust cloud that encircled the planet, limiting incoming solar radiation. A decrease in incoming solar radiation would have caused plants to die, which would have triggered a collapse of global ecosystems.

A second hypothesis is that giant volcanic eruptions in India and Pakistan around 66 million years ago released enormous amounts of volcanic ash and carbon dioxide into the atmosphere. The ash would have produced global cooling by limiting incoming solar radiation, which would affect plant growth and the food chain. Today, scientists think that the mass extinction resulted from a combination of both events.

 Summarize What are some of the important changes that took place in life forms during the Mesozoic era?

Earth During the Cenozoic Era

The Cenozoic era, called the *Age of Mammals,* is the era from 66 million years through today. During the Cenozoic, the continents moved to their present positions. The Himalayas, Andes, Alps, and Rocky Mountains rose. The planet experienced multiple episodes of glaciation. The glaciation of Antarctica began about 30 million years ago. Finally, mammals, including *Homo sapiens,* became dominant life forms on the planet.

FIGURE 25: The Cenozoic era covers 66 million years of Earth's history and continues to the present day.

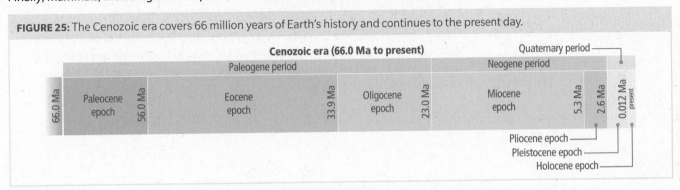

Cenozoic Changes in the Worldwide Landscape

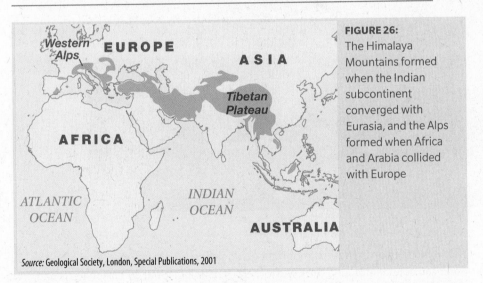

FIGURE 26: The Himalaya Mountains formed when the Indian subcontinent converged with Eurasia, and the Alps formed when Africa and Arabia collided with Europe

Source: Geological Society, London, Special Publications, 2001

During the Cenozoic era, important mountain-building events took place. The Alpine-Himalayan mountain chain arose about 55 million years ago when Africa and Arabia collided with Europe and India collided with Asia.

Approximately 85 million years ago, Australia began to separate from Antarctica. The separation was complete around 30 million years ago. Rifting opened a new ocean basin that allowed a current to flow around Antarctica. Warm water was no longer able to reach the South Pole, which triggered the first Antarctic glaciation.

As Africa and India traveled northward, South America also was on the move and began to separate from Antarctica about 21 million years ago. As the continent moved northward, the Drake Passage opened. This passage is a place where ocean water circulates between South America and Antarctica.

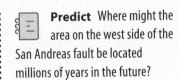

Predict Where might the area on the west side of the San Andreas fault be located millions of years in the future?

Changes in Landscape in North America

Explain What role did collision at a convergent plate boundary play in the formation of the Basin and Range Province?

The Rocky Mountains formed between 80 and 55 million years ago when a volcanic arc collided with the North American plate along a convergent plate boundary. The collision transferred stress inland to the basement of the Rocky Mountains. About 17 million years ago, the Basin and Range Province that extends north-south along Utah, Nevada, Arizona, and eastern California formed. The Basin and Range Province is heavily faulted because of the thinning and cracking of the crust as it was being pulled apart. Mountains formed on the upthrown side of these faults, and valleys have formed on the downthrown sides. There is considerable debate in the scientific community about what caused the formation of the Basin and Range.

From 17 to 15.5 million years ago, flood basalts erupted from fissures along eastern Washington and Oregon. These flood basalts formed the Columbia River Plateau, which covers an area of approximately 164 000 kilometers between the Cascade Mountains and the Rocky Mountains.

FIGURE 27: The Rocky Mountains formed above a shallow-angle subducting plate, which caused the mountains to form far inland.

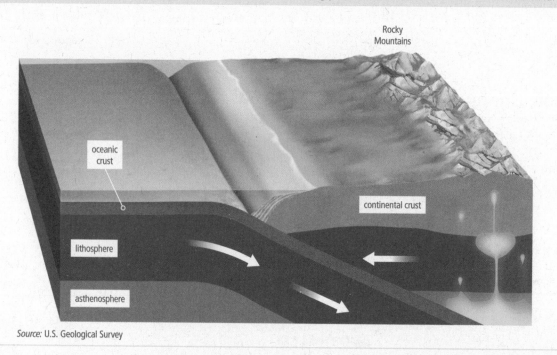

Source: U.S. Geological Survey

The Grand Canyon is another important geologic feature that formed on the North American continent during the Cenozoic era. Beginning about 20 million years ago, during the Miocene epoch, the Colorado Plateau was uplifted as much as 3 kilometers. Beginning about 5 to 6 million years ago, the Colorado River began to carve into the plateau. Today, the Grand Canyon of the Colorado River is approximately 446 km long, up to 29 km wide, and has a depth of more than 1850 m.

Coastal California converted from being a convergent boundary with a subduction zone to a transform boundary that includes the San Andreas fault. During the past 5 million years, Baja, California has pulled away from mainland Mexico and migrated northward.

About 4 to 5 million years ago, the Sierra Nevada Mountains of California began to rise along a system of faults. The eastern slope of the Sierras was uplifted steeply, whereas the western slope of the Sierras was downdropped and slopes gently westward into the Central Valley.

Cenozoic Climate

Throughout Earth's history, global climate has fluctuated from warm to cold periods. During the Paleocene and Eocene epochs, the planet experienced unusually warm conditions. In fact, crocodiles and temperate-zone plants lived near the Arctic. However, since the temperature peak at the Eocene thermal maximum slightly more than 50 million years ago, global temperature has trended downward.

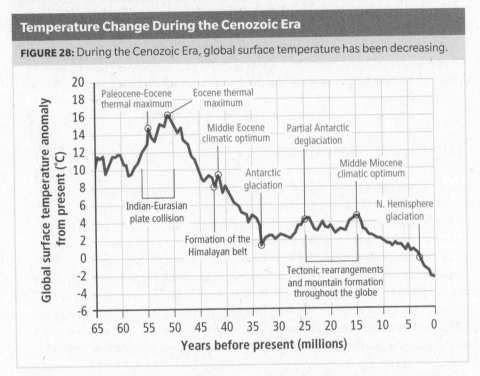

Temperature Change During the Cenozoic Era

FIGURE 28: During the Cenozoic Era, global surface temperature has been decreasing.

During the Eocene-Oligocene transition, Earth underwent a rapid shift in climate. Cooling destroyed the warm, tropical Eocene forests and caused the extinction of many mammals adapted to living in the forests and warmer climate conditions. This cooling began following the rifting of Australia from Antarctica.

Since the Miocene, Antarctica has become permanently glaciated. By the Pliocene epoch, cold climates prevailed in the Northern Hemisphere, forming the Arctic ice cap. However, northern Africa was fertile grassland only about 6000 years ago. Today, because of changes in Earth's tilt, this area has dried up and become the Sahara Desert.

Predict How might plate tectonics have affected global temperature during the Cenozoic era?

The Coming of the Ice Ages

The Pleistocene marked the end of a long Cenozoic cooling trend. During the Pleistocene, rapid transitions between cold (glacial) and warm episodes occurred. For the first million years, these cycles were about 40 000 years long. The current 100 000-year cycle of cooling and slight warming, called an 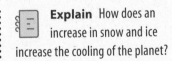 ice age, began about 1 million years ago and has continued to the present.

During the cold episodes, large sections of the planet were covered in snow and ice. Both snow and ice increased the planet's albedo, which reflected more incoming solar radiation, leading to further cooling. As more water was trapped on land as ice, sea levels dropped.

Explain How does an increase in snow and ice increase the cooling of the planet?

The Age of Mammals

After the mass extinction at the end of the Mesozoic era, the surviving mammals underwent adaptive diversification, dominating the terrestrial and marine environments. By the early Eocene, most of the major groups of mammals living today had evolved.

After Australia separated from Antarctica, mammals called *marsupials* evolved to fill ecological niches in Australia. Marsupials, such as kangaroos and koalas, give birth to live young, which continue to develop while living in the mother's pouch close to her body for warmth and nourishment. Marsupials still thrive in Australia today. The Pleistocene epoch is notable for its megafauna—large mammals of a particular region or habitat. Some examples are mammoths and giant ground sloths, but most of these large mammals became extinct at the end of the ice age because of climatic change and/or hunting by humans.

Gather Evidence How could climate change have caused the extinction of most Pleistocene megafauna?

The Rise of Hominins

Hominins—a generic term that groups humans and our extinct ancestors—are commonly placed in two genera: *Homo* and *Australopithecus*. *Australopithecus afarensis* lived 4 million to 3 million years ago in Africa. *Homo habilis*, which lived in Africa 2.4 to 1.5 million years ago, is the earliest known hominin to make stone tools. One of the most recent hominin relatives to modern humans was *Homo neanderthalensis,* which lived from 430 000 to about 40 000 years ago in Europe and the Middle East. Some evidence suggests that *Homo neanderthalensis* coexisted with modern *Homo sapiens*. Fossil evidence reveals that *Homo sapiens* evolved between 200 000 and 100 000 years ago in what is now Ethiopia in Africa. However, many of their features were different than those of modern humans, *Homo sapiens sapiens*.

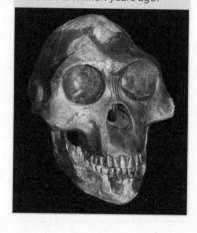
FIGURE 30: The hominin "Lucy" is a female *Australopithecus afarensis* that lived in Africa about 3.2 million years ago.

FIGURE 29: This artist's rendition shows different mammals that lived in North America during the Paleocene and Eocene epochs of the early Cenozoic era.

Summarize What are some of the changes that took place in life forms and climate during the Cenozoic era?

Hands-On Activity

Build Your Own Timescale

Earth's early history was complex. For example, approximately 4.1 to 3.8 billion years ago, the planet experienced a period of intense bombardment by asteroids and comets, which may have originated in the outer region of the solar system. This bombardment may have disrupted primitive life on Earth or, instead, may have carried the molecules important to the emergence of life to the planet. Capturing Earth's 4.6 billion years of history may seem daunting. The goal of this activity is to attempt to conceptualize this vast amount of time and place events in the context of when they occurred.

MATERIALS
- colored pencils (4)
- meter stick
- receipt tape (5 m)

PROCEDURE

1. Roll out the receipt tape.

2. Starting on the left side of the tape, measure 5 cm to the right and draw a vertical line. Annotate as **Present.**

3. Next to **Present**, note that 1 cm = 10 million years and 1 m = 1000 my.

4. From the vertical line, mark off four 1 m sections and annotate each with vertical lines.

5. Measure 60 cm past the final vertical line.

6. Determine when the following events occurred:
   - Rodinia forms/Pangaea forms.
   - Appalachian Mountains form/Himalaya Mountains form.
   - End Precambrian glaciation/Antarctic glaciation
   - Unicellular organisms appear on Earth.
   - Trilobites appear on Earth/fish appear on Earth.
   - Permian/Cretaceous-Tertiary mass extinction events
   - Gymnosperms appear on Earth/angiosperms appear on Earth.
   - Dinosaurs appear on Earth/mammals appear on Earth.
   - Hominins appear on Earth.

7. Use the time for each event and determine the correct location on the receipt tape. Use a separate color to represent events during each era: Paleozoic and earlier, Mesozoic, and Cenozoic.

 Analyze In your Evidence Notebook, analyze how scientists divide geologic time, and explain why, as scientists collect and analyze more information, the names and the dates of different periods change.

Language Arts Connection
Conduct an investigation into how analyses of rock formations and the fossils they contain are used to establish relative ages of major events in Earth's history.

- Gather relevant information from multiple print and digital sources, and condense your findings into a single paragraph.

- Assume your reader has a basic understanding of the fossil record. Avoid plagiarism, and follow a standard format for citation.

THE LATE HEAVY BOMBARDMENT   **THE "SNOWBALL EARTH"**   Go online to choose one of these other paths.

Lesson Self-Check

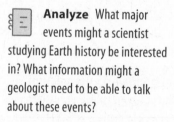

Review the notes in your Evidence Notebook and identify what evidence scientists use to divide geologic time and what kinds of events they record in each time period.

Analyze What major events might a scientist studying Earth history be interested in? What information might a geologist need to be able to talk about these events?

CAN YOU EXPLAIN IT?

FIGURE 31: An artist's conception of a possible asteroid impact with Earth.

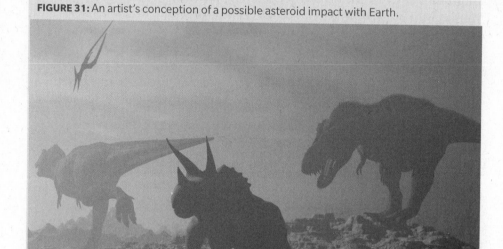

Scientists have attributed catastrophic events, such as an asteroid impact or massive volcanic eruptions, and long-term events, such as climate change and rising or lowering sea level, as causes of mass extinctions. However, another underlying cause of mass extinction can be attributed to the motion of Earth's tectonic plates.

At several times in Earth history, tectonic plate motion has caused the global landmasses to converge and form supercontinents. When supercontinents form, the total area of the world's continental shelves is reduced, primarily by drops in sea level. A continental shelf is the area of shallow seabed around a continent that extends from the shoreline out to the continental slope. The reduction of continental shelves is of major importance, because even though continental shelves make up only about 10% of Earth's oceans at present, they are areas where marine life flourishes. This is due to the fact that water on the shelves is shallow, averaging about 60 m in depth, so sunlight illuminates the entire depth of the shelf waters, which enables producers, such as algae and phytoplankton, to capture and use solar energy via photosynthesis. Producers play an important role in ecosystems because they supply most of the energy, or food, that other species need to survive.

During supercontinent formation, collisions of landmasses cause mountain ranges to rise. Mountain-building reduces the volume of the continents that can displace the oceans, so sea level falls further, and more continental shelf is lost. Supercontinent formation also results in widespread glaciation. This causes even more lowering of sea level and a further reduction of room on continental shelves. This reduction of the continental shelves decreases the favorable environmental niches that are habitable by shelf dwellers and leads to the extinction of some organisms.

1. Which factors about the Pleistocene glaciation are true? Choose all that apply.

   a. Episodes occur in cycles of 10 000 years.

   b. Ice increased Earth's albedo.

   c. Glaciation was due to changes in Earth's orbit.

   d. Antarctica experienced episodes of intensified glaciation.

2. Which is the correct order in which organisms first appeared on Earth?

   a. cyanobacteria-reptiles-fish-hominins

   b. ediacaran fauna-angiosperms-reptiles-mammals

   c. cyanobacteria-angiosperms-mammals-gymnosperms

   d. ediacaran fauna-gymnosperms-reptiles-mammals

3. Explain how mountains act to suture together a supercontinent. Use Pangaea as an example.

4. What is true about climate conditions during the Cenozoic? Choose all that apply.

   a. Global temperature has progressively warmed since the beginning of the Cenozoic.

   b. Global temperature reached a maximum for the Cenozoic during the Paleocene and Eocene epochs.

   c. Climate fluctuated between cold and warm episodes in 100 000 year cycles during the Miocene.

   d. Climate has progressively cooled since the Eocene.

5. Which of the following is a geologic feature that did not form during the Cenozoic era? Choose all that apply.

   a. Grand Canyon

   b. Himalaya Mountains

   c. Siberian Traps

   d. San Andreas fault

6. Which of the following is the largest division of time on the geologic time scale?

   a. period

   b. era

   c. epoch

   d. eon

7. Explain how volcanic eruptions on a massive scale could cause a mass-extinction event.

8. Explain how the opening of the Atlantic Ocean affected Mesozoic climate.

9. Which of the following statements about the "Cambrian explosion" are true? Choose all that apply.

   a. Life forms evolved from unicellular organisms to more complex organisms.

   b. Photosynthesizing organisms first appeared on Earth.

   c. Most major groups of animals first appeared during this time period.

   d. The "Cambrian explosion" occurred over a very long span of time.

10. Describe the formation of three important geologic features in North America during the Cenozoic era.

11. Explain competing theories about the formation of Earth's oceans.

12. Explain the evolution of angiosperms and insects in terms of coevolution.

MAKE YOUR OWN STUDY GUIDE

 In your Evidence Notebook, design a study guide that supports the main ideas in this lesson:

Over the past 4.6 billion years, the configuration of land and ocean basins has changed.

Plate tectonics have led to the formation of several supercontinents and the opening and closing of ocean basins.

During the Paleozoic, the earliest life-forms were simple, unicellular organisms. Through time, organisms evolved and became more complex.

Remember to include the following information in your study guide:

- Use examples that model main ideas.
- Record explanations for the phenomena you investigated.
- Use evidence to support your explanations. Your support can include drawings, data, graphs, laboratory conclusions, and other evidence recorded throughout the lesson.

Earth: Past, Present, and Future

The woolly rhinoceros lived in the cold climates of the Pleistocene epoch— different from the warm-climate rhinoceros of today.

CAN YOU EXPLAIN IT?

FIGURE 1: The Great Lakes can be seen from space in this combination of satellite images. Left to right, the lakes are Superior, Michigan, Huron, Erie, and Ontario.

 Gather Evidence
Record evidence about the Great Lakes. As you explore the lesson, gather evidence to help you explain the formation of these lakes.

The Great Lakes are part of the border between the United States and Canada. Each is among the largest freshwater lakes in the world—so large that they are easily visible in images taken from space. Like inland seas, they lie on top of continental crust, rather than oceanic crust. However, they are bodies of fresh water rather than saltwater.

Clues to the formation of the lakes lie in the history of the region and in features around the lakes. Scientists have also mapped the surface beneath the lakes and found more clues. For example, there is a winding riverbed and waterfall beneath present-day Lake Michigan and Lake Huron. Long, winding ridges of sediment stretch across the bottoms of Lake Erie and southern Lake Michigan. Some of these ridges continue from the lakebed onto dry land.

Analyze What characteristics of the lakes can you infer from the photograph? What might this imply about how the lakes formed?

Evidence of Earth's Recent Past

Scientists use evidence to construct an explanation of Earth's past. However, evidence of Earth's rock, climates, and organisms is destroyed over time. The evidence from Precambrian time—Earth's first few billion years—is very limited. Many more forms of evidence are available for Earth's recent past, especially for the past few million years. For example, evidence from ice in the Paleozoic era (hundreds of millions of years ago) was lost when the ice melted. But some of the ice from 10 000 years ago is still frozen.

 Gather Evidence As you study this lesson, review your Evidence Notebook from earlier lessons. Bring together observations about Earth's spheres—such as plate motion and climate change—that you can use as evidence of Earth's recent past.

Synthesizing Evidence of the Past

Remember that layers of rock show relative ages. Radioactive isotopes, magnetized minerals, and other evidence are used to determine the absolute ages of layers. Some layers are tied to events, while some layers are regular in occurrence, such as annual layers of sediment in lakes. Rock also contains evidence of past plate interactions, uplift, erosion, deposition, and other geologic activity. Some evidence is lost, such as when rock erodes, but much of the evidence in rock lasts for long periods of time.

FIGURE 2: Recall the sources of evidence of the history of Earth's four spheres.

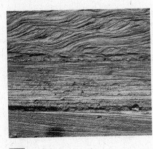  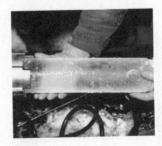 

a layers of rock   b fossils   c ice cores   d tree rings

In contrast, past climates are not recorded directly. Scientists use information in features such as layers of sediment, plant and animal fossils, ice cores, tree rings, and corals. These measurements are proxies—data sets that can represent past climates.

Fossils provide evidence of past organisms and are also part of the evidence of the geosphere's past. The types of organisms, along with the nature of erosion and deposition patterns, can show how past climates were hot, cold, dry, or wet. Growth patterns, such as coral bands, stromatolite layers, and tree rings, can show details of changes over relatively short times. Fossilized shells and ice cores also provide evidence of the past conditions of the ocean and atmosphere. However, most of the detailed climate evidence shows only relatively recent times. For example, ice cores extend back only about 800 000 years.

FIGURE 3: Because of the amount of evidence, scientists can divide recent geologic time into smaller pieces.

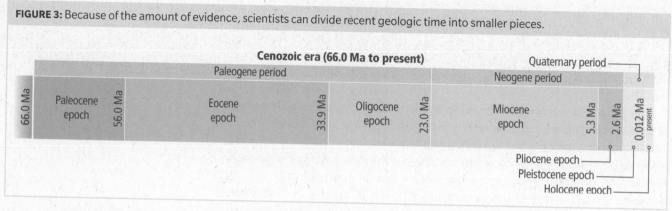

Cenozoic era (66.0 Ma to present)

| Paleogene period | | | | | Neogene period | | | Quaternary period |

66.0 Ma | Paleocene epoch | 56.0 Ma | Eocene epoch | 33.9 Ma | Oligocene epoch | 23.0 Ma | Miocene epoch | 5.3 Ma | 2.6 Ma | 0.012 Ma present

Pliocene epoch
Pleistocene epoch
Holocene epoch

Collaborate With a partner, make a scale diagram or digital model to show how far back in time each type of evidence can be used. How do the types and amount of data compare between the most recent epochs and earlier times?

Sources of evidence have different strengths and limitations. For example, evidence from tree rings gives temperature and precipitation patterns for hundreds, sometimes thousands, of years. But the evidence is limited to temperate zones, where tree growth is tied to seasons. Corals provide evidence of annual changes in ocean water chemistry that can extend back thousands of years but only for warm, shallow regions of the ocean. The older ice from the bottom of the Antarctic ice sheet (800 000 Ma) has been distorted from the weight of the ice above and from the motion of the ice. Most radioactive isotopes take so long to decay that they are best used for dating igneous rock and give little detail about recent times. In contrast, carbon dating is used on the remains of organisms—often in sedimentary rock—and is limited to more recent times.

When different types of evidence overlap, they can be used together. Many types of evidence together produce a more complete picture of recent times than is possible for earlier times. As a result, scientists have been able to describe events in Earth's recent history more precisely.

Using Current Observations and Models

Scientists use what is known about modern Earth to understand the past. They study the relationships among such things as mountains, volcanoes, and earthquakes; rivers and deltas; the sea floor; and also the rocks tied to these features and events. The modern studies help scientists understand the evidence preserved in rock.

Scientists use modern organisms to make inferences about extinct organisms. They study relationships of bone to muscle, of teeth to diet, and of the shapes of stems and leaves to climate. The modern studies help scientists interpret evidence from fossils. Scientists also analyze DNA from fossils, such as bone fragments. The results are compared to modern DNA to determine how organisms are related.

Models help scientists connect the different lines of evidence. For example, scientists may use current plate velocities to infer past positions of continents. Then they might use climate evidence to confirm or challenge the results. Scientists may base a climate model on one proxy and then compare the result to other climate proxies to test the accuracy of the model. A model that works well for the past may be used to predict the future, including possible effects of human activities.

FIGURE 4: The bones and teeth of a saber-toothed cat from the Pleistocene epoch can be understood by comparing them with related structures in modern cats.

Explain What type of modern study might a scientist use to help interpret the fossilized tracks of an animal?

 Explain Choose a type of evidence that is available only for recent times. Describe how it might be combined with a second type of evidence to understand Earth's recent past.

Earth's Recent Past

Recall that Earth's geologic time spans 4.6 billion years. Billions of years of Precambrian time was followed by hundreds of millions of years of the Paleozoic and Mesozoic eras. The current era is the Cenozoic, which started just 66 million years ago.

The Cenozoic Era

By the start of the Cenozoic era, the last supercontinent had split into most of the current continents, increasing the number of coastal regions. The Mediterranean Sea was larger. The Atlantic Ocean was smaller, but it was growing. Some of the major mountain chains of today were starting to rise. The planet was warm and wet, with no polar ice. Flowering plants had become widespread, along with the birds and insects that interact with them. Dinosaurs and marine reptiles had just died out in one of Earth's major mass extinctions.

Scale, Proportion, and Quantity

Scales of Time

Use orders of magnitude—factors of ten—to help you distinguish between thousands, millions, and hundreds of millions of years.

The divisions of geologic time are based on observed changes rather than a standard length of time, such as 100 million years. As evidence builds up, scientists can define more divisions. Precambrian time has been divided into eras and periods. Epochs have been divided into ages. Some divisions were changed in the early 21st century as understanding grew.

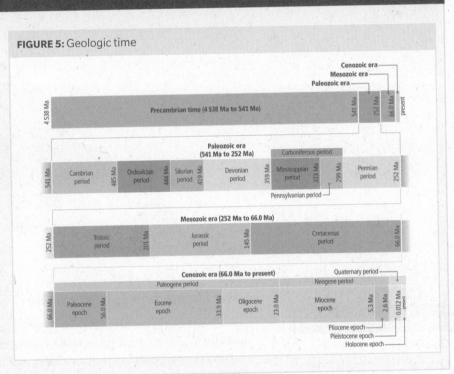

FIGURE 5: Geologic time

The Early Cenozoic Era (66 Ma)

During the first part of the Cenozoic era, Earth continued to warm. Plates continued to move. The patterns of continents then caused a change in the ocean circulation around Antarctica. Ice started to form, which changed Earth's albedo. About 50 million years ago, a cooling trend started, which enabled new mammal species to develop.

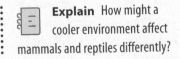

Explain How might a cooler environment affect mammals and reptiles differently?

The Miocene Epoch (23 Ma)

During the Miocene, plate movement closed the body of water that would become the Mediterranean Sea. A hot, dry climate in the area helped to shrink the sea. In other regions, high mountain ranges developed. They blocked moist air from the ocean, producing rain shadows and cooler, drier climates. As a result, forests shrank in size. In their place, large grasslands, similar to the modern savannah in Africa, developed. Some mammals developed teeth that helped them graze on (eat) the grasses. The number of species of birds increased greatly, and in North America, so did the number of snake species. The new species took advantage of the open spaces of the grasslands. Many new species also developed in the many regions of shallow ocean along the continents. Fast-growing kelp supported ecosystems that were like underwater forests.

The Pliocene Epoch (5.3 Ma)

Cooling continued during the Pliocene epoch. The North and South American continents converged, uplifting land between them (now the Isthmus of Panama). The new land bridge enabled species to expand north or south into an additional continent. The South American continent gained animals such as dogs, wolves, mastodons, and cats, while the northern continent gained armadillos, giant ground sloths, and porcupines. As a result of the changes, some species became extinct.

Analyze How did Earth's spheres affect one another during the Miocene epoch?

FIGURE 7: Large mammals were common in the Pliocene. The glyptodon, an animal of the Pliocene epoch similar to a large armadillo, spread from South America into North America as the continents were joined by a bridge of land.

armadillo   glyptodon

Explore Online ▶

Hands-On Lab

Glaciers and Sea Level Change Model the melting of an ice sheet and analyze the effects of melting ice on sea level.

Explain Think about the reservoirs that make up the hydrosphere. Sea level drops during an ice age. Where does the water go?

The Pleistocene Epoch (2.6 Ma)

An ice age marks the beginning of the Pleistocene epoch. Earth experienced cold glacials in which ice sheets expanded across continents. In between were brief, slightly warmer interglacials in which ice sheets shrank or melted and the land rebounded. During these cycles, smaller glaciers in mountainous regions also developed and then shrank or melted. Continents were in roughly their current positions, but coastlines changed as sea level rose and fell. At times, areas of the continental margin became dry land. Connections formed among islands and the continents. For example, modern-day Alaska and Siberia became connected by a wide region of dry land. Organisms moved into new areas of land or sea when locations were joined, but were sometimes isolated by the changes. The last glacial episode of the Pleistocene reached its maximum extent around 26 500 years ago. Ice covered about 30% of Earth's surface, and sea level was lower by 120 meters.

FIGURE 8: Glacial ice and lower sea level affected North America 18 000 years ago.

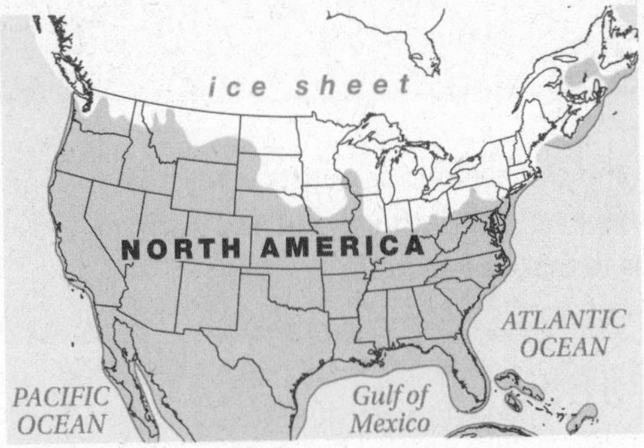

ice sheet

NORTH AMERICA

ATLANTIC OCEAN

PACIFIC OCEAN

Gulf of Mexico

km 0 500 1,000

mi 0 500 1 000

Source: Oak Ridge National Labratory

Analyze How might the events of past epochs help explain current features and observations?

The Holocene Epoch (0.012 Ma)

The Holocene is the name of the current interglacial episode. As it began, ice sheets retreated, sea level rose, and land areas became less connected. The rising ocean separated Alaska from Siberia. With the warmth, some of the regions that had been cold, dry grasslands—called *steppes*—shrank and forests grew farther north. Many of the giant mammals became extinct, such as the woolly rhinoceros and the saber-toothed cat. Horses and camels died out in North America but survived in other places.

The Age of Humans

All of recorded history is within the Holocene epoch. Human history adds to the amount of information available, such as records of individual volcanoes, earthquakes, and regional shifts in climate. Humans have also influenced the environment. Hunting has affected the survival of species, while farming has affected the interactions of soil, water, air, and organisms. Greenhouse gases released over the past 200 years have led to a significant increase in Earth's temperature.

Explain How might evidence left by prehistoric humans also provide information about Earth's past?

Engineering

Designing Survival

People have designed ways to restore endangered species. For example, California condors are a species of large birds dating from the Pleistocene epoch. Human activities had reduced the number of these birds to fewer than 30 by the 1980s. Then zoos, government agencies, and other organizations developed a solution of taking the remaining birds into captivity. By the early 1990s, there were enough birds to release some back into the wild. Similarly, people designed ways to restore the American bison (buffalo). In turn, herds of bison may help restore grasslands.

Analyze How might you use engineering to help reduce the impact of human activity on local species?

Gather Evidence Examine how geologists define different epochs. Do you think there is enough evidence to define a new epoch—the Anthropocene, or age of humans?

Models of the Future

Models of plate tectonics, Earth's orbit, and climate help scientists study how changes in land distribution and solar radiation have helped produce cold and warm periods on Earth. Scientists can also use the models to make predictions.

The Geosphere in the Future

FIGURE 9: Supercontinents form and break up as tectonic plates move. Models include the convecting mantle below.

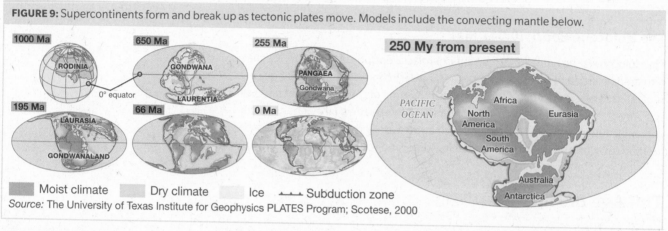

Moist climate   Dry climate   Ice   ⌁ Subduction zone

Source: The University of Texas Institute for Geophysics PLATES Program; Scotese, 2000

Predict Do you think the Atlantic ocean will close again, as shown in Figure 9? Support your prediction with evidence and reasoning.

As tectonic plates continue to move, the patterns of subduction and mountain building change. Sometime in the future, the Himalayas will stop rising and erode. The rift zone in Africa may develop more fully into a divergent plate boundary and perhaps passive continental margins. Subducting plates, such as the Juan de Fuca plate, may disappear entirely. Predictions of the long-term motion of plates vary. The prediction shown in Figure 9 includes the closing up of the Atlantic.

Climate in the Future

FIGURE 10: Magnetic field reversals (a) show changes in Earth's core, while overall temperature (b) reflects changes in Earth's orbit and energy feedbacks.

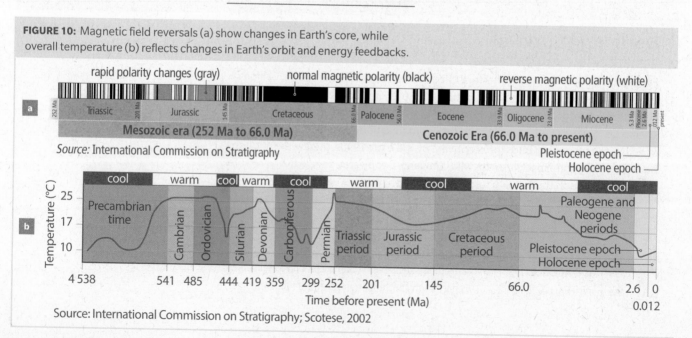

Source: International Commission on Stratigraphy; Scotese, 2002

FIGURE 11: Solar radiation changes due to Earth's orbit, past and future

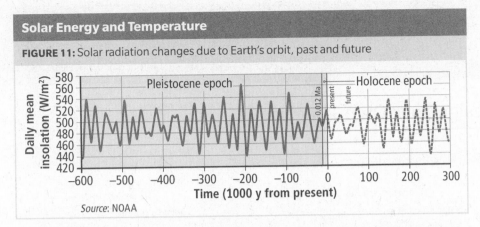

Source: NOAA

Figure 10 shows Earth's overall temperature in the past, including the cooling trend of the Cenozoic era. To predict whether the cooling will continue, scientists look at the expected changes in solar radiation (Figure 11). The positions of continents (Figure 9) help scientists include energy absorption, ice cover, and Earth's future albedo in their predictions. These factors help scientists model the natural cycles of climate.

However, human activities have introduced very rapid changes. These changes affect the models of changing climates and their consequences. Scientists have developed models to explore many different factors of future climate. They compare the different results and combine models to make climate predictions.

The Biosphere in the Future

Life responds to changing geologic features and climate patterns. As supercontinents form and break up, the amount of coastal area shrinks and grows. Changes in climate and sea level also change the amount of shallow water. Circulation patterns in the ocean and atmosphere also change. Species are affected by these changes and, in turn, affect the cycling of materials and energy. But when a region changes quickly, it is more difficult for species to adapt fast enough to survive.

Human activities have caused very rapid changes in some regions as well as globally. As human populations grow, more resources are needed. To help feed the growing population, forests are cut down and replaced by grazing land and farms, as you can see in Figure 12. The ground is mined for fossil fuels and mineral resources. The pace of change, like the human population, has been increasing.

Stability and Change

Recall that greater ice cover means a higher albedo—more sunlight is reflected. A loss of ice means lower albedo and more sunlight absorbed. In both cases, the feedback is positive, as it increases the rate of change.

Explain Evaluate how the current changes in solar energy would affect climate in the near future if it were the only input affecting climate change.

FIGURE 12: Satellite images show how forests (dark green) have been replaced by farmland (pink) in Bolivia over time.

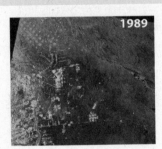

Explain Given the changes in the other spheres, what changes would you expect in the biosphere in the future?

Hands-On Lab

Design Your Own Timeline

FIGURE 13: Include details about the Cenozoic era in your timeline.

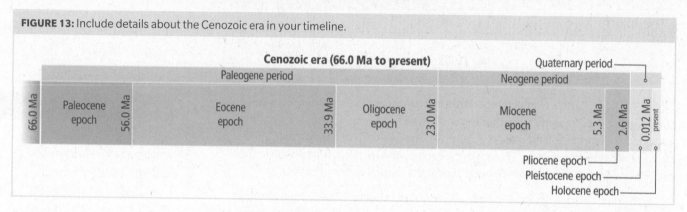

MATERIALS
(optional)

- meter stick or tape measure
- paper, roll
- pencils or markers, colored
- slideshow application
- spreadsheet application

Design a timeline for the Cenozoic era—or longer—and extend it into the future. You may wish to start with a timeline you have already made and add details. You may prefer to start fresh with a different medium or different scale to better hold the large amount of information available for this era. A spreadsheet application can help you sort your data or graph the data. It can help you make calculations for a scale model, such as a scale that represents 1 million years as 1 mm, 1 m, 1 city block, 1 hallway tile, 1 s, or 1 slide.

PROCEDURE

1. Use a table or a computer spreadsheet application to organize information about the different epochs. Put the entries in order so that it is easy to place them on a timeline.

2. Include the epochs, an indication of time, and the main changes in Earth's spheres.

3. Show predictions of the future in a way that differs from the way you show observations.

4. Communicate the information for your timeline as a scale model, a graphical display, or a live or recorded presentation.

 Language Arts Connection Once you have a table of data, select a medium and a type of timeline through which you can communicate the information effectively.

- Decide whether to graph time to a uniform scale (such as 1 tile = 10 Ma) or to use more space or time for epochs that have more entries.
- Decide how to represent epochs and other information. Decide how much detail to include for other information. You may wish to indicate the ranges of different types of information, such as ice cores.
- Share your timeline and your data table. As you explore timelines from other students, identify ways you might improve your own work.

| EXPLORE PROXY DATA | MIGRATION ROUTES | FUTURE SUPERCONTINENTS | Go online to choose one of these other paths. |

Lesson Self-Check

CAN YOU EXPLAIN IT?

FIGURE 14: The Great Lakes are (from left to right) Lakes Superior, Michigan, Huron, Erie, and Ontario.

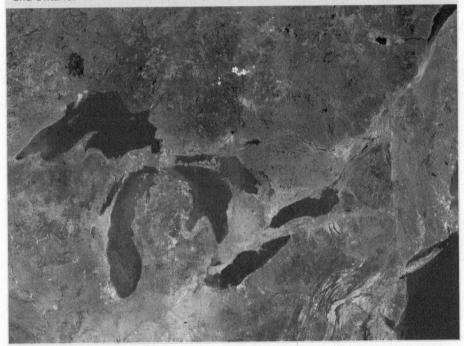

Analyze Refer to the notes in your Evidence Notebook to help you explain when and how the Great Lakes formed.

Recall that the Great Lakes form part of the northern border of the present-day United States. They are enormous bodies of fresh water—the system is comparable in size to an inland sea. Beneath the lakes are long, winding ridges of sediment, some of which stretch onto dry land.

Use observations of the Great Lakes and your knowledge about Earth's recent past to make a claim about how the Great Lakes formed. Think about the history of the geosphere, the biosphere, and the climate that involved the atmosphere and hydrosphere. Remember that many features are formed through a series of events that can include both plate tectonics and surface processes. If you don't yet have an explanation, review the types of plate interactions and the main agents of change.

Describe how you think the Great Lakes formed. List the evidence, and then explain how the evidence supports your claim. For example, the ridges of sediment should be part of your explanation. In your claim, include an estimate of how long ago the lakes formed. Your estimate might be roughly 200 Ma if you think the lakes were part of the rift that formed the Atlantic (Mesozoic era) or less than 0.01 Ma if you think they formed because of human activity.

Explain How did the Great Lakes form? Use evidence to support your explanation.

CHECKPOINTS

Check Your Understanding

1. How long is the Cenozoic era compared with Earth's entire history?

   a. It is less than 2% of Earth's history.

   b. It is about one quarter (25%) of Earth's history.

   c. It is more than 90% of Earth's history.

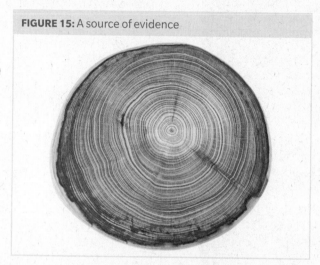

FIGURE 15: A source of evidence

2. Describe how the evidence shown in Figure 15 is used to determine Earth's history. Which of the spheres is most clearly represented? Explain your choice.

3. Give another example of a type of evidence that exists only for recent epochs. Explain how it provides evidence of the history of one or more of Earth's spheres.

4. How does albedo affect climate? Give an example of a change in ice cover and the resulting effect on climate.

5. Suppose Earth became much warmer and wetter, leading to dark green forests covering much of the continents. How would the tree growth and change in color produce a positive or negative feedback?

Use Figure 16 to answer questions 6 and 7.

6. Draw a diagram to show how the collision of the North and South American continents affected the biosphere.

7. Identify the false statement(s) about what the graph in Figure 16 shows. Then revise each false statement to make it true.

   a. The scale of time changes from left to right (the scale is uneven, not linear).

   b. Earth was relatively cool for billions of years.

   c. Earth's cool episodes since the Cambrian period have lasted much longer than Earth's warmer episodes.

   d. Changes between warm and cool episodes are sometimes very fast and sometimes very slow.

8. Use Figure 16 to identify any true statement(s) below.

   a. Earth was warmest at the transition between the Permian and Triassic.

   b. Earth was coolest during the middle of the Cambrian period.

   c. Temperatures during the Pleistocene epoch were similar to temperatures during the Jurassic period.

   d. A general cooling trend has occurred during the Cenozoic era.

FIGURE 16: The history of Earth's overall climate

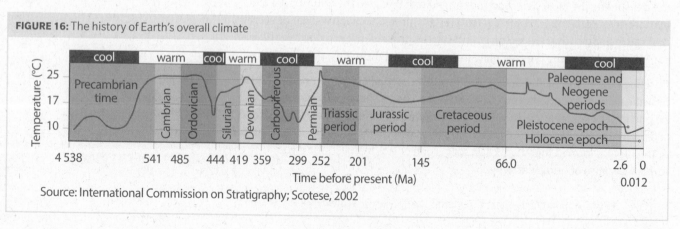

Source: International Commission on Stratigraphy; Scotese, 2002

9. During the Cenozoic era, the continents broke apart enough for ocean water to circulate completely around Antarctica. The continent became cooler because it was cut off from warmer ocean water. The continent's air masses became cooler. Explain how a change such as this can trigger a cooling trend for all of Earth.

10. During most of the Cenozoic era, the input of solar energy in the Northern Hemisphere has influenced Earth's average temperature more than the input of solar energy in the Southern Hemisphere. Based on Figure 9, do you think the same was true in the past, for example at 1000 Ma or 650 Ma?

11. Preserved examples of very large mammals, called *megafauna*, have been found frozen in ice. How does this fact help explain why the woolly rhinoceros was woolly, unlike today's species of rhinoceros?

12. Which of the following items are true about tree rings?
    a. They are only useful in tropical climates.
    b. The records extend back hundreds to thousands of years.
    c. They produce an annual record.
    d. Their thicknesses record the effects of temperature and precipitation.

13. Why might scientists combine data from rings of living trees together with data from layers of lake sediment?

14. Suppose high mountains stand between the ocean and a region of grassland. What changes would you expect as the mountains erode?

15. Suppose rising sea levels again separate the continents of North and South America. Choose one of Earth's spheres, and explain how it might interact differently with another of Earth's spheres because of this change.

16. Review the changes between forest and grassland in the Miocene and Holocene epochs. Compare the human activity of cutting down forests to produce grazing land and fields of wheat and other grasses. Choose one important similarity and one important difference. Explain each.

MAKE YOUR OWN STUDY GUIDE

In your Evidence Notebook, design a study guide that helps you explain the related changes in Earth's spheres in the recent geologic past and the present.

Remember to include the following in your study guide:
- Support main ideas with details and examples.
- Record explanations for the phenomena you investigated.
- Include the scale or order of magnitude of phenomena.

Consider how feedback has affected either the stability or the changes through Earth's recent history and how it will affect Earth's likely future.

A BOOK EXPLAINING COMPLEX IDEAS USING ONLY THE 1,000 MOST COMMON WORDS

EARTH'S PAST
Everything* that has happened here so far

The geologic time scale provides a framework for understanding the processes that shape our planet. Here's a look at Earth's geological history, layer by layer.

*NOT QUITE EVERYTHING

THING EXPLAINER
COMPLICATED STUFF IN SIMPLE WORDS

RANDALL MUNROE
author of *What If?* and creator of *xkcd*

RANDALL MUNROE
XKCD.COM

THE STORY OF EARTH, ONE LAYER AT A TIME

WE LEARN ABOUT THE HISTORY OF THE EARTH FROM ROCKS.

SO, DOES ANYONE HAVE ANY QUESTIONS?

ROCKS ARE LAID DOWN IN LAYERS, AND BY LOOKING AT THE LAYERS FROM DIFFERENT PARTS OF THE WORLD, WHICH ARE ALL DIFFERENT AGES, WE CAN PIECE TOGETHER A SINGLE HISTORY THAT GOES BACK ALMOST TO THE START OF THE WORLD.

THIS PICTURE SHOWS WHAT IT WOULD LOOK LIKE IF YOU COULD SEE THE WHOLE HISTORY OF EARTH IN A SINGLE SET OF LAYERS, WITH EVERY YEAR AS THICK AS EVERY OTHER. IN REAL LIFE, NO SINGLE PLACE HAS ALL THESE LAYERS TOGETHER, AND THERE ARE NO LAYERS AT ALL FROM THE OLDEST PART OF EARTH'S HISTORY.

I WONDER IF WE CAN FIND WHEN THAT SPACE ROCK HIT EARTH!

COOL! CHECK OUT THESE BIG STRANGE ANIMALS!

WHERE ON EARTH DID THESE LAYERS GO?

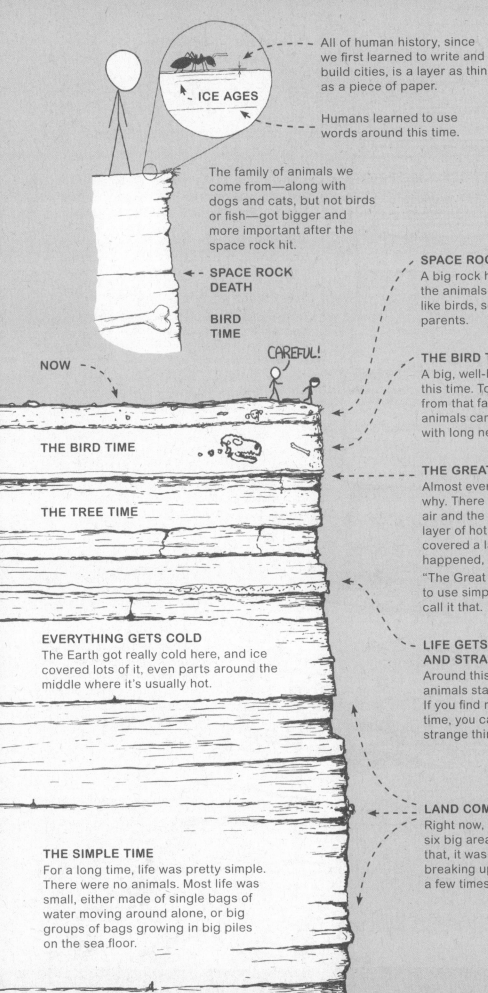

All of human history, since we first learned to write and build cities, is a layer as thin as a piece of paper.

ICE AGES

Humans learned to use words around this time.

The family of animals we come from—along with dogs and cats, but not birds or fish—got bigger and more important after the space rock hit.

← SPACE ROCK DEATH

BIRD TIME

NOW

CAREFUL!

THE BIRD TIME

THE TREE TIME

EVERYTHING GETS COLD
The Earth got really cold here, and ice covered lots of it, even parts around the middle where it's usually hot.

THE SIMPLE TIME
For a long time, life was pretty simple. There were no animals. Most life was small, either made of single bags of water moving around alone, or big groups of bags growing in big piles on the sea floor.

YOU ARE HERE
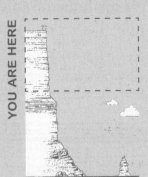

SPACE ROCK HITS THE EARTH
A big rock hit the Earth, and lots of the animals died. Some groups lived, like birds, some kinds of fish, and our parents.

THE BIRD TIME
A big, well-known group of animals lived during this time. Today's birds are the only animals from that family alive now, but many other animals came from it in the past—like big ones with long necks and bitey ones with huge teeth.

THE GREAT DYING
Almost everything died here, and we're not sure why. There were lots of strange changes in the air and the sea, and around that time a huge layer of hot rock came up out of the Earth and covered a large part of the land. So whatever happened, it was pretty bad.

"The Great Dying" sounds like a name made up to use simple words, but it's not; serious people call it that.

LIFE GETS BIG AND STRANGE
Around this time, big animals started to appear. If you find rocks from this time, you can see lots of strange things in them.

LAND COMES TOGETHER AND BREAKS UP
Right now, Earth's land is broken up into five or six big areas with water in between, but before that, it was pushed together. We think this breaking up and pushing together happened a few times, although it's hard to tell how many.

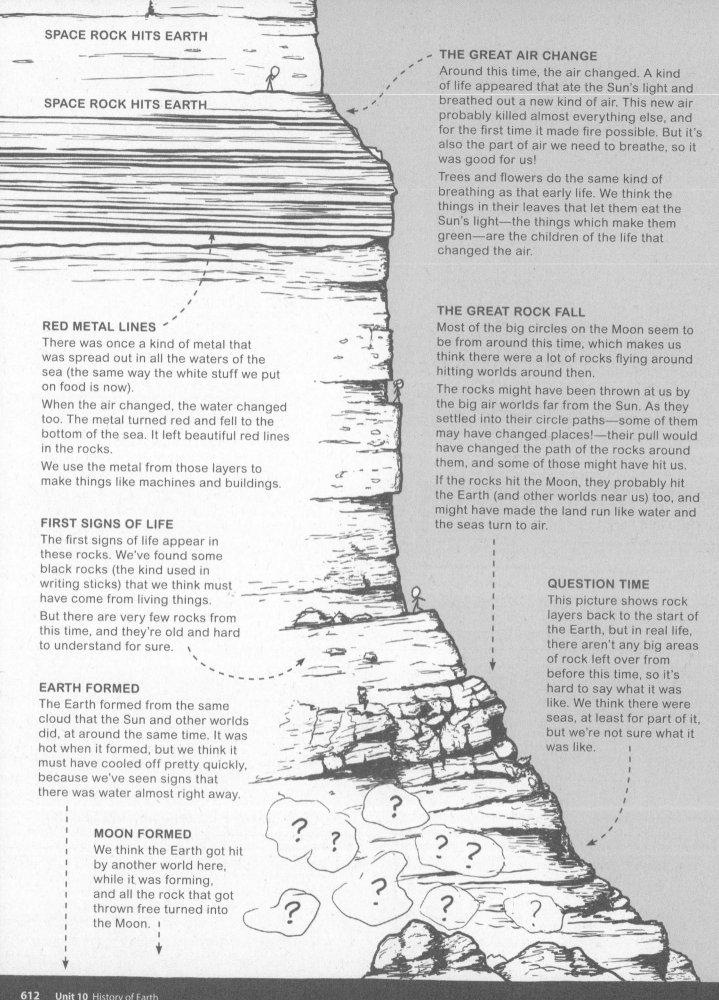

SPACE ROCK HITS EARTH

SPACE ROCK HITS EARTH

THE GREAT AIR CHANGE

Around this time, the air changed. A kind of life appeared that ate the Sun's light and breathed out a new kind of air. This new air probably killed almost everything else, and for the first time it made fire possible. But it's also the part of air we need to breathe, so it was good for us!

Trees and flowers do the same kind of breathing as that early life. We think the things in their leaves that let them eat the Sun's light—the things which make them green—are the children of the life that changed the air.

RED METAL LINES

There was once a kind of metal that was spread out in all the waters of the sea (the same way the white stuff we put on food is now).

When the air changed, the water changed too. The metal turned red and fell to the bottom of the sea. It left beautiful red lines in the rocks.

We use the metal from those layers to make things like machines and buildings.

FIRST SIGNS OF LIFE

The first signs of life appear in these rocks. We've found some black rocks (the kind used in writing sticks) that we think must have come from living things.

But there are very few rocks from this time, and they're old and hard to understand for sure.

EARTH FORMED

The Earth formed from the same cloud that the Sun and other worlds did, at around the same time. It was hot when it formed, but we think it must have cooled off pretty quickly, because we've seen signs that there was water almost right away.

MOON FORMED

We think the Earth got hit by another world here, while it was forming, and all the rock that got thrown free turned into the Moon.

THE GREAT ROCK FALL

Most of the big circles on the Moon seem to be from around this time, which makes us think there were a lot of rocks flying around hitting worlds around then.

The rocks might have been thrown at us by the big air worlds far from the Sun. As they settled into their circle paths—some of them may have changed places!—their pull would have changed the path of the rocks around them, and some of those might have hit us.

If the rocks hit the Moon, they probably hit the Earth (and other worlds near us) too, and might have made the land run like water and the seas turn to air.

QUESTION TIME

This picture shows rock layers back to the start of the Earth, but in real life, there aren't any big areas of rock left over from before this time, so it's hard to say what it was like. We think there were seas, at least for part of it, but we're not sure what it was like.

▶ Go online for more about *Thing Explainer*.

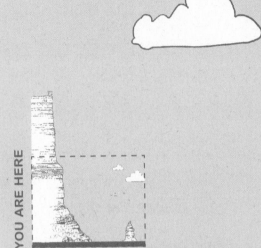

YOU ARE HERE

OLDER LIFE?

All life is part of one family, and the information stored in our water bags changes over time, as animals have children and those children have children. By looking at the information stored in the water bags of living things, doctors can figure out how long ago their shared parents lived.

When people have tried to work out how old life's shared parent is, they sometimes come up with a number that's a little *older* than the great rock fall.

But we think the seas turned to air and the rocks to fire, and it's hard to understand how anything could have lived through that.

Engineering Connection

Pangaea Pangaea was the most recent supercontinent to form on Earth. It began forming approximately 300 million years ago during the late Paleozoic when smaller continents collided. Pangaea began breaking apart in the early Mesozoic, roughly 200 million years ago. The continents that we know today are pieces of that ancient supercontinent.

Use library and Internet resources to learn more about different lines of evidence that scientists used to develop a model of Pangaea. Identify at least three lines of scientific evidence and explain how scientists used each one to support the idea of the formation and/or breakup of Pangaea.

FIGURE 1: The configuration of the supercontinent Pangaea approximately 225 million years ago

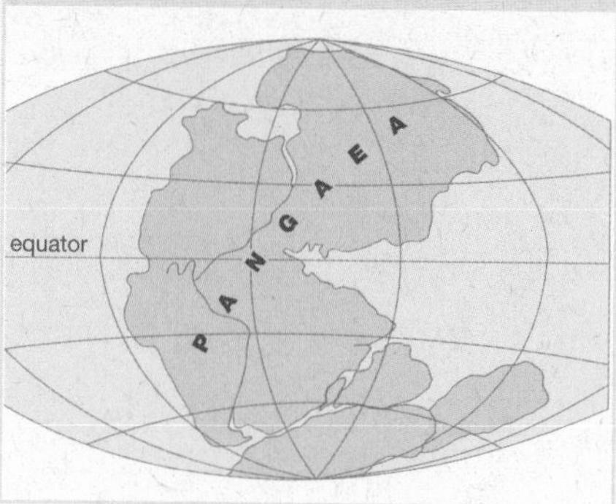

Art Connection

Artistic License Artists sometimes modify reality when creating a scene, but how much liberty do they take when re-creating organisms from Earth's past? In this activity, you will identify one piece of art displaying an extinct species or, instead, a diorama and critique it in terms of the scientific thought that existed at the time it was created and the scientific thought that exists today.

Using library and Internet resources, identify a piece of art that illustrates an extinct species of plant or animal. Another option is to find a diorama of a particular episode in Earth's history, such as the "Age of Dinosaurs" or the "Age of Mammals." Identify when the art was created and what the prevailing scientific thought was at that time. Explore the accuracy of the art using scientific information that is available today. Prepare a poster with the image and several facts about what you learned, and present your findings to the class.

FIGURE 2: An artist's rendition of the asteroid impact that caused the Cretaceous-Tertiary mass extinction

Computer Science Connection

Mapping Fossils Separate into small groups and identify a fossil of interest. The fossil can be from any period during Earth's history. Try not to pick a fossil type that spans too large a period of geologic time, such as stromatolites, which have inhabited Earth for billions of years. Once your group has identified a particular fossil to study, share the idea with your teacher before you begin your investigation.

Use library and Internet resources to find information about the fossil, and create a list of all of the locations that you can find where the fossil has been found around the world. Use a mapping program, such as ArcGIS, to map the locations. Take note of the time when the organism lived, and provide a reference map of the configuration of land/ocean at the time that the organism was living. As a group, develop a six-minute presentation, including images of the fossil, an artist's representation of the organism when it was living, a map of the fossil finds, and a map of the land/ocean configuration at the time when the organism was living. Present your findings to the class in a poster presentation.

FIGURE 3: *Stegosaurus* lived on the planet from approximately 159 to 144 million years ago.

SYNTHESIZE THE UNIT

In your Evidence Notebook, create a concept map, graphic organizer, or outline using the Study Guides you created for each lesson in this unit. Be sure to use evidence to support your claims.

When synthesizing individual information, remember to follow these general steps:
- Find the central idea of each piece of information.
- Think about the relationships among the central ideas.
- Combine the ideas to come up with a new understanding.

Go online to access detailed lesson summaries for this unit.

DRIVING QUESTIONS

Look back to the Driving Questions from the opening section of this unit. In your Evidence Notebook, review and revise your previous answers to those questions. Use the evidence you gathered and other observations you made throughout the unit to support your claims.

PRACTICE AND REVIEW

1. Why are most fossils found in sedimentary rock?

2. What was the last process to happen in the sequence in Figure 4?
   a. Faulting
   b. Deposition of Layer B
   c. Emplacement of the igneous intrusion
   d. Deposition of Layer A

FIGURE 4: This block diagram illustrates the law of cross-cutting relationships, which can be used to infer the relative ages of rocks, faults, and other features.

igneous intrusion   fault

3. Which of the following statements about the principle of superposition are true? Choose all that apply.
   a. Older rock layers are found on top of younger rock layers.
   b. Rocks that are cut by a fault or intrusion are younger than the fault or intrusion.
   c. Layers of sediment, lava, and ash are deposited on top of each other.
   d. Older rock layers are found below younger rock layers.

4. How do scientists use half-lives to find the absolute age of an object using radiometric dating?

5. Which of the following statements about mass extinctions are true?
   a. Mass extinctions are relatively rare on Earth.
   b. A mass extinction is defined as the disappearance of a large percentage of organisms from the land and the ocean.
   c. Scientists used mass extinctions to develop the geologic timescale.
   d. Mass extinctions are only defined for organisms on land.

6. Explain why scientists are curious about the origin of water.

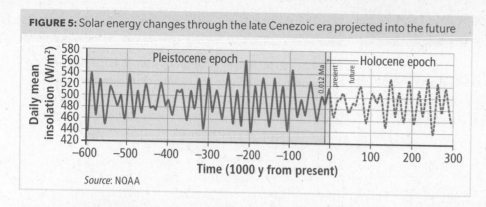

FIGURE 5: Solar energy changes through the late Cenezoic era projected into the future

Source: NOAA

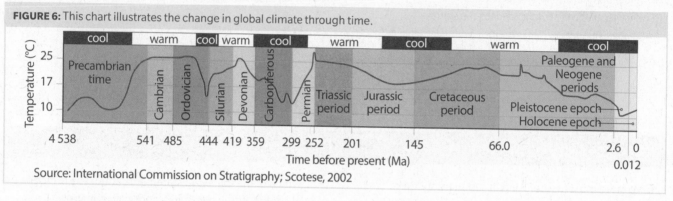

FIGURE 6: This chart illustrates the change in global climate through time.

Source: International Commission on Stratigraphy; Scotese, 2002

7. Which of the following shows the correct progression of organisms on the planet?

a. reptiles–fish–hominins

b. ediacaran fauna–reptiles–mammals

c. stromatolites–angiosperms–gymnosperms

d. ediacaran fauna–mammals–fish

8. Explain the process that determines the direction in which continents move.

9. Which of the following statements explain processes that can affect the global climate? Choose all that apply.

a. When a continent passes over one of the poles, an increase in ice formation may occur, which will increase planetary albedo.

b. A substantial increase in lava expelled at Earth's surface may cause the planet to cool.

c. Methane hydrates that are found along the edges of continents could be released and cause planetary cooling.

d. Changes in ocean and atmospheric circulation patterns can alter the global climate.

10. Use Figure 5 to help you draw a model to explain how the solar energy Earth receives has changed through time and how this affects the planet's climate.

11. Refer to Figure 6, and explain the global temperature trend during the Mesozoic Era.

12. To get the longest, most continuous global picture of climate conditions in the past, scientists might examine

a. fossil coral

d. ocean sediment

c. tree rings

d. fossil megafauna

UNIT PROJECT

Return to your unit project. Prepare your research and organize your materials to share with the class. In your final presentation, evaluate the strength of your hypothesis, data, analysis, and conclusions.

Remember these tips while evaluating:

- Look at the empirical evidence—evidence based on observations and data. Does the evidence support the explanation?

- Consider if the explanation is logical. Does it contradict any evidence you have seen?

- Think of tests you could do to support and contradict the ideas.

Evolution of Dinosaurs

FIGURE 7: Theropods are an extinct group of dinosaurs that are the ancestors of birds.

In this activity, you will explore how birds are descendants of theropod dinosaurs.

1. Use the Internet to investigate the relationship between dinosaurs and birds.
2. Research should focus on theropod dinosaurs.
   a) What did theropod dinosaurs look like?
   b) When did theropod dinosaurs inhabit Earth?
3. Draw several evolutionary links from certain theropod dinosaurs to birds.
4. What forms of evidence are available to support the idea that birds are descendants of theropod dinosaurs?

1. DEFINE THE PROBLEM

With your team, write a statement outlining the facts you need to investigate to support the claim that certain theropod dinosaurs are the ancestors of birds.

2. CONDUCT RESEARCH

With your team, investigate the evolutionary links between theropods and modern birds. What lines of evidence are available to support this claim?

3. ANALYZE DATA

Research and analyze the changes in anatomical features of bird ancestors over time that are recorded in the fossil record.

4. IDENTIFY AND RECOMMEND A SOLUTION

Develop a short paper to outline the natural history of the theropod dinosaurs during the Mesozoic, how they gave rise to birds, and the different lines of evidence you have discovered to support this claim.

5. COMMUNICATE

Present your findings to the class in a six-minute presentation, or write a short scientific report with an abstract, introduction, methods, results, and conclusions/discussion section.

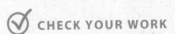 CHECK YOUR WORK

A complete presentation should include the following information:

- A clearly defined problem with supporting questions that are answered in the final presentation.
- A model showing the evolution of theropod dinosaurs into birds. An explanation of evidence used to support this claim.
- Images and data that further support your claim.

Image Credits: ©Spencer Sutton/Science Source

Human Activity and Earth

The Las Vegas Valley is one of the most
rapidly growing areas in the United
States, nearly tripling its population
from 1990 to 2016.

Image Credit: ©abit75_fot/Fotolia

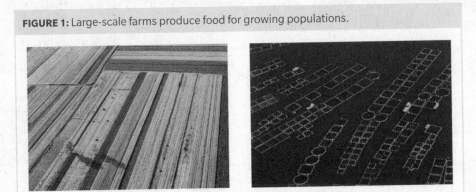

FIGURE 1: Large-scale farms produce food for growing populations.

a Agricultural farm

b Fish farm

People depend on Earth's natural resources for their survival. Human activities such as agriculture and industry have affected and sometimes changed Earth's spheres. As the human population continues to grow, some scientists predict that the impact of humans on Earth's spheres will increase as well. More people will require more natural resources, such as food, land, and water. The relationship between human population size and resource availability prompts questions about how people should manage and distribute resources now and in the future.

 Predict What are some ways in which food production affects Earth's spheres?

DRIVING QUESTIONS

As you move through the unit, gather evidence to help you answer the following questions. In your Evidence Notebook, record what you already know about these topics and any questions you have about them.

1. How do human societies use Earth's resources?
2. How do natural hazards affect individuals and societies?
3. How do human activities change the planet?

UNIT PROJECT

 Go online to download the Unit Project Worksheet to help plan your project.

Meeting Future Water Demands

How is water managed where you live? How is water used? Research water treatment facilities in your community. Evaluate the system in terms of how well it serves the community and how well it can meet future water demands. Write a proposal to the local government for improving the system. Your proposal should describe the existing system, describe one or more changes you think should be made, and provide reasoning for these changes.

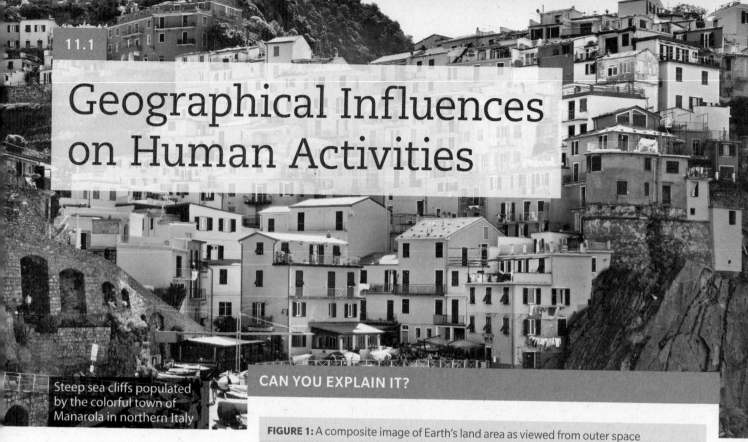

Geographical Influences on Human Activities

Steep sea cliffs populated by the colorful town of Manarola in northern Italy

CAN YOU EXPLAIN IT?

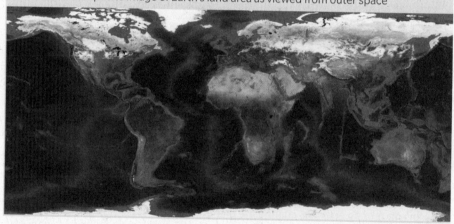

FIGURE 1: A composite image of Earth's land area as viewed from outer space

Gather Evidence As you explore the lesson, gather evidence to help you explain why Earth's population is not evenly spread over the continents.

The image of Earth shows that the world is not uniform. The climate, vegetation, and landforms of each region are different. For example, the areas near the North Pole are covered in snow and ice. In contrast, desert areas in places like North Africa, Australia, and the Middle East receive less than 10 inches of water per year. Besides climate, landforms vary across the globe. There are mountain ranges along the west coasts of the American continents and plains and flatlands as one travels east. Accessibility to water differs across the globe. Water is abundant on the coasts and inland areas near well-established rivers.

Similarly, people are not evenly spread across the globe but rather are concentrated in specific areas. With such diverse conditions across Earth, people weigh a variety of factors when deciding where to live.

Predict Why are humans spread unevenly across the globe? What factors influence the distribution of people?

Image Credits:(t) ©pavlobaliukh/Fotolia; (c) ©Reto Stöckli/NASA Earth Observatory

Human Dependency on Earth's Resources

Humans have always depended on natural resources to meet their needs. Early civilizations centered around major rivers. Rivers supplied some of the requirements for these early societies, including fish and water fowl for food, water for irrigating crops, and a means of transportation for trade. Though industry and technology have changed the way people interact with their natural surroundings, people continue to rely on natural resources to provide the basic necessities of life.

Collaborate With a partner, brainstorm what you need to live. Then discuss where these things that you need ultimately come from.

Requirements for Survival

At the most basic level, all humans need clean air, water, food, living space, and shelter. Some of these necessities are found directly in the environment, such as air, food, and water. Other needs, such as shelter, must be constructed from wood, stone, and metals obtained from the environment. Provisions that come from the environment and can be used by people are called natural resources. Some natural resources, such as air and water, are easy to get from the environment. Others, such as minerals and fossil fuels, are much harder to get. Because people require natural resources to meet their most basic needs, access to natural resources is an important factor in how groups of people determine where to settle and live.

Analyze How can urban dwellers use the natural resources available in their area to meet their needs?

FIGURE 2: Urban dwellers interested in producing food locally use farming methods that take advantage of limited space, such as rooftop gardening.

Image Credits:©Alison Hancock/Shutterstock

Resource Distribution

When you examine the image of Earth from space in Figure 1, you see that vegetation, climate, and landforms differ from region to region. Similarly, Figure 3 shows that minerals and fossil fuels are not evenly distributed but are located as a result of Earth's processes.

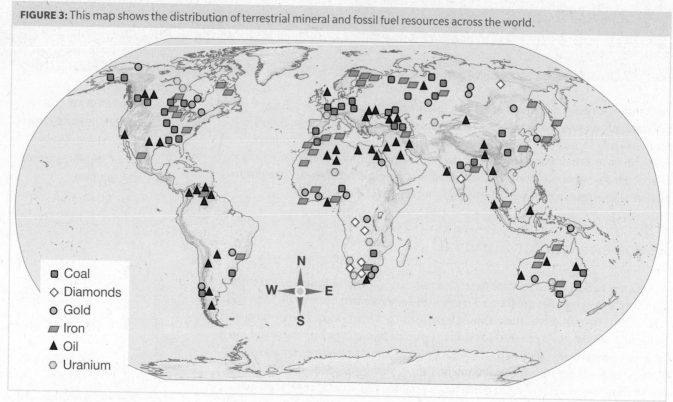

FIGURE 3: This map shows the distribution of terrestrial mineral and fossil fuel resources across the world.

Legend:
- □ Coal
- ◇ Diamonds
- ○ Gold
- ▱ Iron
- ▲ Oil
- ○ Uranium

N
W · E
S

Predict Look at the worldwide distribution of minerals and fossil fuels. Based on the uneven distribution of these resources, where do you think the population density will be highest?

Throughout this book, you have explored various resources including minerals, fossil fuels, water, air and climate, and land. Where are each of these resources found?

Rock and Mineral Resources

Mineral ores and precious metals crystallize from magma as it rises through the crust to the surface and cools. Places where magma rises to the surface include volcanic areas along plate boundaries such as subduction zones, spreading centers, and hotspots. These ores and metals are common along the western edges of North and South America, the eastern edge of Asia, and central and southern Europe.

Energy Resources

Fossil fuels such as coal, oil, and natural gas come from plants that lived in ancient inland seas and continental shelves. These resources are found in areas where those seas were or where they have moved because of continental drift. For example, the remnants of ancient seas are found in the Middle East, along the southern end of the Mediterranean Sea, the Gulf Coast of North America, and the northern portion of South America.

Water Resources

Fresh water is found on Earth's surface where there are rivers, lakes, and swamps. Fresh water is also found seasonally in areas where there is ground ice and permafrost. Besides in surface waters, fresh water is located in glaciers, ice caps, and large areas of groundwater aquifers.

Air and Climate Resources

People tend to live in areas of moderate temperatures. Moderate temperatures, seasonal rainfall, and mild weather patterns are good for agriculture. Most moderate temperatures are found near large bodies of water, such as oceans, seas, and large lakes.

Research Conduct research on the natural resources available in your state. Describe how access to natural resources affects the economic and social activities of people in your state.

Land Resources

Agriculture requires fertile soils, which can come from areas rich in organic materials and minerals. The organic materials found in river sediment nourish the soil along rivers and coastal areas where river deltas occur. The minerals deposited from volcanic ash nourish areas near plate boundaries. Furthermore, fertile soil tends to be in areas of moderate climate. Examples of fertile areas include the central plains of the United States (along surface waters), deltas such as those of the Nile, Rhine, and Ganges rivers, and plate boundaries such as those found in California, Peru, and Italy

 Analyze Discuss possible reasons why natural resources are not distributed uniformly across Earth.

Patterns

Patterns in Human Settlement

Use the three distribution maps to compare the location of rainfall and cropland with the settlement patterns of people around the world. Where do people tend to settle? Do you think this was true in ancient times as well?

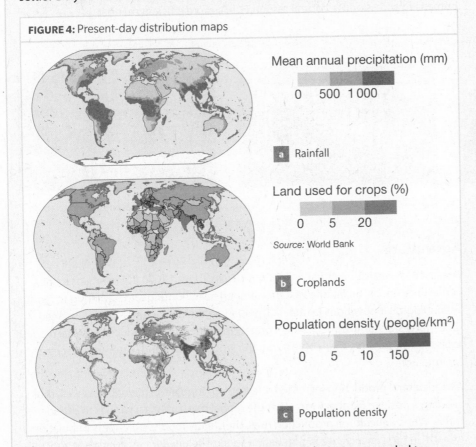

FIGURE 4: Present-day distribution maps

Mean annual precipitation (mm)

0   500 1 000

a Rainfall

Land used for crops (%)

0   5   20

Source: World Bank

b Croplands

Population density (people/km²)

0   5   10   150

c Population density

 Analyze What other natural resources might affect human settlement patterns? Compare these resources with other maps you have seen throughout this book, such as maps of minerals resources, plate tectonics, surface waters, and climate.

People tend to settle in areas that are rich in the natural resources needed to survive, have moderate temperatures and abundant rainfall, and have easy access to transportation and commerce. Natural resources are often found near plate boundaries where earthquakes and volcanic eruptions also occur. As a result, areas where people choose to live often have increased levels of natural hazards.

 Explain Describe the relationship between the location of natural resources and the distribution of human populations.

Natural Resources and Human Activity

When early agricultural societies learned to cultivate farmland and produce a reliable source of food, the human population grew. The resulting increase in demand for food and other resources pushed societies to acquire more resources and develop new technologies to increase productivity. This relationship between population growth and resource availability has been an important factor in the development of human societies.

Resource Supply

There have been several revolutions—periods of advancement—in human history. Each revolution was sparked by the development of new technologies that allowed humans to access or use natural resources in a more efficient manner.

FIGURE 5: Modern versions of revolutionary technology that increased the availability and usability of natural resources

a Soil cultivator

b Cargo ship

c Automated manufacturing

Analyze How might a change in the availability of a natural resource affect human activities?

Agriculture

The first of several agricultural revolutions began about 10 000 BCE. Humans in the Fertile Crescent of the Middle East transitioned from hunting and gathering to farming. Technological innovations in metallurgy sparked the development of plows, seed drills, harvesters, and reapers, which greatly increased food production. Metal digging tools made it possible for people to dig the long trenches and waterways necessary for irrigation.

As agricultural production increased, the human population increased as well, thus creating a positive feedback loop that the global population continues to experience today. When agricultural production rises, the steady food supply spurs population growth. In turn, an increase in population sparks the need for innovation in agriculture and possible expansion of farmlands.

Trade

Innovations such as saddles, wagons, trains, and ships revolutionized transportation. As a result, agricultural products and minerals—coal, iron, and copper—were traded, permitting people to settle almost every part of the globe. Additionally, trade became a way to overcome the uneven distribution of natural resources. The ability to trade drives the global economy and affects the geopolitical relationships that nations have with one another.

Industry

During the Industrial Revolution, human and animal labor were replaced in part by machines that produced goods more efficiently. These machines used energy from steam, which required burning coal to provide the energy necessary to convert water to steam. Because coal had to be extracted from the ground, the increased demand for coal spurred many innovations in mining technology. Advances in mining technology allowed humans to extract, or remove, a wide range of minerals.

With the invention of the steam engine to drive trains and ships, people could more easily access and remove resources from around the globe. Railroads made it easier and faster to cross the interiors of continents and extract available resources. Ships with steam engines made it easier and faster to cross oceans for trade and exploration.

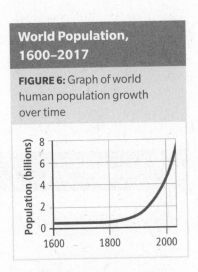

Explain While steam technology revolutionized manufacturing processes, it also generated large amounts of pollution. Describe a modern technology that has both positive and negative effects on humans.

Resource Demand

Human populations tend to show growth characteristics similar to other species. When a population initially settles an area, resources such as food, water, and living space are plentiful. As the population grows, resources dwindle. Eventually the population size is limited by the availability of resources, stops growing, and reaches a stable number.

The human population differs from this pattern because it has not stopped growing. Humans have been able to continually find new resources to meet their needs and therefore have not yet experienced a resource shortage. Scientists disagree about the maximum number of people Earth can support.

World Population, 1600–2017

FIGURE 6: Graph of world human population growth over time

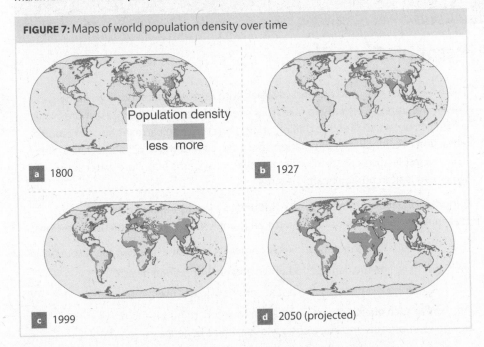

FIGURE 7: Maps of world population density over time

Population density
less more

a 1800

b 1927

c 1999

d 2050 (projected)

Although the human population is rapidly growing, the size of Earth stays the same. As of August 2016, the world population was estimated at 7.4 billion people. Some forecasts predict there will be 9.7 billion people on the planet by 2050. With more people, the demand for natural resources increases. For example, in some areas, the demand for living spaces with mild climates and clean air has led to the expansion of residential areas into prime agricultural lands. This reduces the land available to grow food. A larger population also creates more pollution and waste. Together, an increase in both the demand for and the contamination of natural resources may lead to resource shortages in the future.

Cause and Effect

Predict Based on the population trends shown in the Figure 7 maps, where do you think people will choose to live in the future? What natural resources will they prioritize when deciding where to live?

Collaborate With a partner, discuss how the resource requirements of societies have changed throughout history.

FIGURE 8: Growing populations require more land for living space, which in turn reduces the land available for agriculture.

Resource scarcity challenges scientists, engineers, and entrepreneurs to find new ways to meet the needs of future generations. Solutions to resource availability issues often use one of two strategies: either increasing the supply of or decreasing the demand for natural resources.

Engineering

Analyze Make a list of the criteria that various stakeholders—local residents, government officials, business owners—might specify for an acceptable design solution to extract resources. On a scale of 1 to 5, how might each stakeholder group weigh each criterion?

Resource Extraction

There are costs, risks, and benefits involved with resource extraction and land use. Fresh water is relatively easy to take from rivers or lakes. Oil and coal are more difficult to obtain and require drilling or digging deep into Earth. Although resource extraction can benefit the population, there can be hazards or risks associated with it. For example, the process may disrupt local ecosystems or pollute water supplies, which can lead to human health hazards.

Suppose a valuable natural resource is found in a locally inhabited area. Stakeholders rely on scientific and economic analysis to answer particular questions:

- What are the monetary and environmental costs of extracting the resource?
- What will be the damage to human and environmental health?
- How long will the resource last at current usage? Future usage?

Answers to such questions can provide a framework to guide engineers as they design solutions that minimize costs and maximize benefits.

Explain Describe some of the problems people face as the global population increases. What criteria and constraints should engineers prioritize when developing solutions to these problems?

Natural Hazards and Human Activity

Throughout human history, people have lived in areas where natural hazards abound. For example, Italian farmers live and farm along the slopes of active volcanoes because of the rich, fertile volcanic soil. Similarly, people across the world farm on floodplains because the sediments deposited when the river floods enriches the soil for farming. Despite such hazards, people often choose to live in these areas because they consider the benefits to outweigh the risks.

Natural Hazards

Many areas of Earth are prone to natural hazards—effects of specific Earth processes that can cause harm to people and property. Earthquakes and volcanic eruptions occur along plate boundaries. Tsunamis occur in coastal regions near offshore plate boundaries. Natural hazards occur as a result of natural processes, which cannot be controlled by humans. As a result, they will always be a part of life on Earth.

Natural hazards can be classified by the Earth processes that cause them. Geophysical hazards result from Earth's interior processes and include volcanoes and earthquakes. Hydrological hazards result from changes in Earth's water and include floods and tsunamis. Climatological hazards result from severe weather and include droughts, extreme temperatures, and wildfires. Some natural hazards have more than one origin and can be classified into multiple categories. For example, landslides are often hydrological in origin but can also occur as a side effect of an earthquake.

Analyze What arguments might a scientist use to classify floods into more than one category? What other natural hazards could be classified into more than one category?

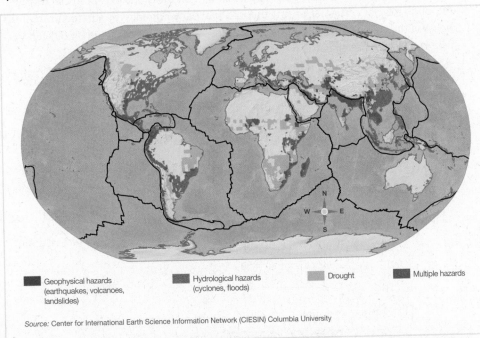

FIGURE 9: Map of natural hazard hot spots, which are areas with a particularly high risk of natural disasters

Geophysical hazards (earthquakes, volcanoes, landslides)　　Hydrological hazards (cyclones, floods)　　Drought　　Multiple hazards

Source: Center for International Earth Science Information Network (CIESIN) Columbia University

Collaborate With a partner, discuss how an increased likelihood of natural hazards might influence human activities.

Classifying Natural Hazards

Natural hazards can be classified on the basis of their time of onset, duration, and impact. Natural hazards occur over different timescales. Some occur rapidly (earthquakes, tornadoes), yet others have a slow onset (hurricanes). Natural hazards also vary in duration. Tornadoes are short-lived, whereas droughts can last for years. The impact of any particular natural disaster, or extreme event, is usually based on the number of people affected, damage costs, and geographical impact (local, regional, global).

		Impact		
		Local	Regional	Global
Timescale	Short	Wildfires	Earthquakes	Volcanic eruption
	Medium			
	Long			

Analyze Copy the table into your notes and classify as many natural hazards as possible in the table. What types of natural hazards might be classified in more than one place in the table? Use evidence to support your claim.

Effects on Human Activities

Natural hazards have the potential to bring about changes in climate, vegetation, and landforms that can create conditions unfavorable to human life. Such events have shaped human history, causing changes in the size and location of human populations.

The first humans lived in East Africa about 2.5 million years ago. Since then, there have been various waves of human migration out of Africa spreading into Arabia and the Middle East and eventually to every continent on the globe except Antarctica. Although it is not certain, scientists theorize that early hominins emigrated from Africa because the climate cooled, resulting in colder temperatures that made it difficult to find food. When the climate improved, the population expanded.

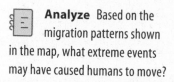 **Analyze** Based on the migration patterns shown in the map, what extreme events may have caused humans to move?

FIGURE 10: One model of human migration based on mitochondrial DNA

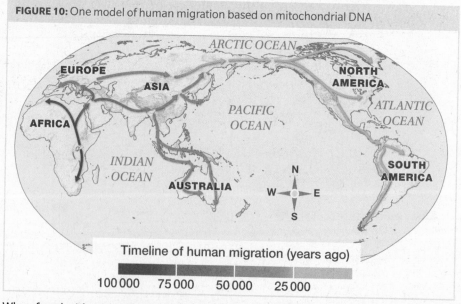

Timeline of human migration (years ago)

100 000   75 000   50 000   25 000

When faced with natural hazards, people tend to migrate in search of safer regions. For example, during an ice age about 16 000 years ago, water froze in glaciers and polar ice caps. The resulting lower sea levels exposed a land bridge from Asia to the

Americas across the Bering Sea. Humans migrated across the land bridge and spread throughout North and South America.

Other natural process, such as desertification, can degrade land and impede people's ability to survive. The Sahara Desert was once a thriving grassland. About 8000 years ago, the tilt of Earth's orbit changed from about 24° to the present-day 23.5°, causing more sunlight to fall upon North Africa. As a result, the Sahara became a desert over about a 300-year period, making it uninhabitable. Today, the Sahara is expanding and encroaching on farmlands.

Effects of Population Growth

Natural hazards affect humans, but humans also influence natural hazards. Expanding human populations will infiltrate areas prone to natural hazards—volcanic eruptions, earthquakes, floods, hurricanes, and tsunamis. When these disasters strike, the impact is magnified by the increased population.

Explore Online ▶

Hands-On Lab

Tsunami Model the movement of a tsunami and compare the impact of a tsunami on different types of shorelines.

FIGURE 11: Earthquakes cause damage directly and indirectly.

a In 2011, an offshore earthquake generated a tsunami that devastated Fukushima, Japan.

b In 2015, an earthquake in Nepal caused extensive damage.

Human activities can increase the frequency and intensity of natural hazards. Scientists agree that centuries of burning fossil fuels has increased greenhouse gases in the atmosphere, leading to global climate changes, rising sea levels, and weather instability. More recently, scientists have inferred that increased earthquake activity is a result of hydraulic fracturing. In Oklahoma, about 21 magnitude 3+ earthquakes occurred between 1973 and 2008, but more than 600 such earthquakes have occurred annually from 2014 to 2016.

Analyze What are some of the risk tradeoffs that people make when choosing where to live?

Increases in natural disasters have unequal effects on human populations. Generally, wealthier areas exhibit more property loss, while impoverished areas experience more loss of human life. In 2011, floods hit both Queensland, Australia, and Pakistan. The Queensland flood spread across 1 851 841 sq km, impacted 200 000 people, killed 9 people, and cost billions of dollars. The Pakistan flood spread across 160 580 sq km, impacted 20 million people, killed 2000 people, and cost $10 billion. Queensland sustained less damage than Pakistan for reasons largely related to its relative wealth, including the superior quality of housing in Australia and the ability of the government to respond to disasters.

Explain How do natural hazards affect human activities? Cite multiple examples to support your answer.

Reducing the Impact of Natural Hazards

Because natural hazards are a result of Earth's processes such as plate tectonics, climate, and weather, humans cannot eliminate or control them. However, technology helps warn populations of the onset of natural hazards and minimizes damage and loss of life from them.

Predicting Natural Hazards

Technological advances have allowed scientists to gather precise information about when and where natural hazards will occur.

Explore Online ▶

Hands-On Lab 🧪

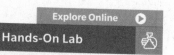

Building a Weather Station Build a weather station, observe and record information, and make predictions based on your data.

FIGURE 12: Technologies help scientists understand and predict natural hazards.

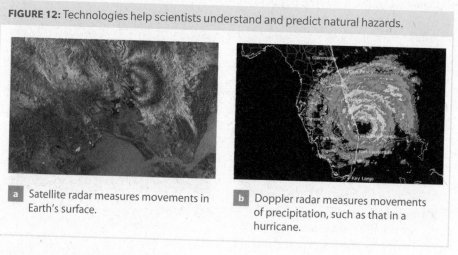

a Satellite radar measures movements in Earth's surface.

b Doppler radar measures movements of precipitation, such as that in a hurricane.

Indirect Prediction

Predicting natural hazards most often involves analyzing data from past events for patterns that can be used to predict future occurrences. Tools that scientists use for these early predictions include geographic information systems that allow scientists to correlate and map many types of information, such as temperature changes and seismic activity. The United States Geological Survey (USGS) has a network of seismometers to continuously monitor and analyze seismic activity due to plate movements. Radar technology on orbiting satellites monitors changes in electromagnetic fields and small movements associated with plate tectonic shifts.

Explain Because many people live in disaster-prone regions, how do scientists and meteorologists attempt to keep the people safe?

Direct Prediction

Scientists directly predict other types of natural hazards from patterns. For example, meteorologists know that hurricanes develop from tropical depressions in the ocean, which progress into tropical storms and then into hurricanes. In addition, volcanoes show increases in seismic activity and emissions of specific gases prior to eruptions.

Forecasting

Scientists forecast some natural hazards in the short term for areas of high risk. This happens most frequently with weather-related hazards such as tornadoes and hurricanes. Hurricane forecasts involve gathering data about wind speeds, wind directions, and barometric pressure from the storm using Doppler radar, satellite imagery, and aircraft. They track the movements of the storm, determine the intensity, and predict the most likely path. Meteorologists also use Doppler radar, along with ground observations, to monitor thunderstorm activity for the development of tornadoes.

Preparing for Natural Hazards

After a natural disaster, the damage to buildings and structures, such as gas lines or water treatment facilities, can be much more dangerous than the actual event. Engineers have a key role in designing solutions to reduce damages that occur as a result of natural disasters.

FIGURE 13: Technologies help prepare for natural disasters.

a Flexible bases help buildings withstand earthquakes.

b Mortars prevent large-scale avalanches.

c Flood tunnels divert water to prevent flooding.

One way that engineers minimize the impact natural hazards have on buildings and structures is to construct systems that lessen the physical effects of a disaster. To withstand earthquakes, the bases of buildings are made flexible. As a result, the building's foundation moves with the shaking ground, but the building above does not move. In addition, walls can be braced with crossbeams to make them stronger so that they do not shake apart.

Engineers sometimes design ways to initiate natural hazards under controlled circumstances. Avalanches occur when the weight of snow and ice builds up on mountaintops, causing the underlying snow to loosen and eventually give way. The upper layers slide down the mountain and bury everything in their path. By using cannons or mortars to fire charges into developing areas of snow and ice sheets, scientists can trigger smaller avalanches that do relatively little harm compared to a full-sized avalanche.

Engineers also plan infrastructure solutions that manage the impact of natural disasters. Tsunamis and floods impact many coastal cities. In Tokyo, Japan, engineers have constructed a network of flood tunnels that redirect incoming floodwaters underground and to the Edo River. This redirection of water spares the city's surface from damage.

FIGURE 14: After Hurricane Andrew hit South Florida in 1992, new building codes required buildings to better withstand high-velocity winds.

Analyze Give examples of engineering advances or building codes that could reduce the impact of natural hazards.

FIGURE 15: A seawall

Preparing for Climate Change

Scientists predict that sea levels could rise more than six feet by the end of this century as a result of global climate change. Higher sea levels coincide with severe flooding, land erosion, and subsidence. For businesses like shipyards that are located along inland rivers and shorelines, these changes will require solutions that protect costly equipment from damage and ensure the structural integrity of buildings.

 Analyze Conduct research on the extent of the problem and on some of the current solutions being proposed to fix the problem. Then develop a short-term and long-term plan to recommend how coastal communities can prepare for the increase in sea level and reduce damage to the area. When developing your plan, be sure to address the following:

1. Define the engineering problem.
2. Describe the major consequences to society, the environment, and the economy if this problem is not solved.
3. List some critical criteria and constraints of acceptable solutions to this problem.

Pushing the Boundaries of Technology

Technological advances increase humanity's ability to change and shape the environment. As technology improves and people use natural resources more efficiently, humans may continue to exploit those resources. The increased capacity to manipulate the natural world poses the risk of rapidly diminishing, even completely exhausting, common resources. Similarly, technological improvements can help reduce the danger of residing in disaster-prone areas. Advances in predicting and preparing for natural hazards may encourage larger population growth in those areas, which can make the impact of a hazard more severe.

These same technologies can give us a better understanding of how Earth's systems are interconnected and how they are affected by human activities. Scientists have a dual role to play, pushing the frontiers of scientific understanding today while providing the data that people need to responsibly make choices for tomorrow.

 Explain How can new technology help reduce the impact of natural hazards and other geologic events on human populations?

Careers in Science

Civil Engineer

Civil engineering is a branch of engineering concerned with the design, construction, and maintenance of the built environment. Civil engineers study how to build structures such as dams, roads, buildings, and bridges. They also design and build infrastructure systems such as waterways, sewage systems, and other systems that are important for cities and towns.

Civil engineers prepare for natural disasters by designing systems that will reduce their impacts. You have explored solutions to floods, such as the Tokyo flood tunnels, and solutions to earthquakes, such as flexible building bases. Another natural disaster that affects towns and cities is high winds from hurricanes and tornadoes. Along coasts, many new buildings are required by building codes to withstand wind speeds of up to 130 mph. The same could be done for buildings in tornado-prone areas because the wind speeds of tornadoes are about the same as major hurricanes. Here are some solutions that civil engineers have implemented:

- High winds can tear the roofs off buildings. Civil engineers replace simple nails with metal connectors designed to enable roofs to withstand winds of up to135 mph.
- High winds can also weaken the edges of roofs. Civil engineers utilize a roof with four sloping sides rather than the traditional two sloping sides to reduce wind resistance.
- High winds can cause buildings to fall down or cave in. Civil engineers

FIGURE 16: Civil engineers design, build, and maintain the buildings and infrastructure that can withstand natural hazards.

build shelters and safe rooms where occupants can go to survive a building collapse.

- Wind-borne projectiles can endanger people inside buildings. Civil engineers install storm shutters and multipane windows that can absorb the impact.

Concerning floods, civil engineers have learned that concrete structures absorb little water. Concrete walls extending from the foundation to the roof can prevent a flooded house from coming loose from its foundation and floating away as happened in the aftermath of Hurricane Katrina in New Orleans.

Civil engineers are involved in the planning of city infrastructure such as buildings, roads, bridges, and dams. They gather data to monitor the health of these systems, which is important for predicting if or when they might fail during a natural disaster. They

often gather data about stresses on these structures with wireless probes. Besides monitoring the structures, civil engineers can use the data to simulate how these structures and new designs will behave under the conditions of various natural disasters.

These activities by civil engineers help reduce the impact of a natural disaster, speed recovery, and improve quality of life of those people living in disaster-prone areas.

Language Arts Connection
Research some of the tools civil engineers use to test the ability of a building to withstand natural disasters. How do these tools work? What types of data do they help civil engineers collect? How do civil engineers use the data? What types of questions can they help answer?

THE COST OF AN OIL SPILL   BUILDING THE IKE DIKE   Go online to choose one of these other paths.

Lesson Self-Check

Explain Examine the area in which you live. Explain the factors that your family considered in the decision to live there. What natural resources and natural hazards exist in your area?

FIGURE 17: Climate, landforms, and vegetation vary across the world.

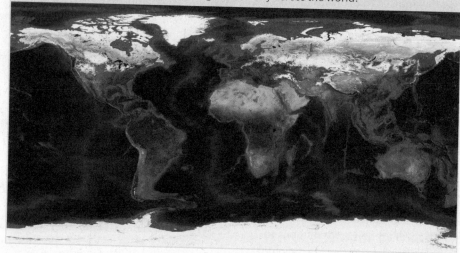

Prior to the Industrial Revolution, society was based on agriculture. People's primary concerns were to grow food, protect themselves from attack, and survive the weather. They sought out fertile river valleys for growing crops and raising livestock or coastal regions for the proximity to fishing, trade, and exploration. Now, with the advent of modern heating and cooling technology and easier distribution of goods, humans can live almost anywhere.

Available work is often the single most important factor in deciding where to live. A job might take one to the heart of a business or political center in a bustling city. Workers in the lumber, petroleum, and mineral mining industries need to live near the source of their occupations. Other workers, such as barbers, teachers, medical personnel, and attorneys, are needed everywhere.

Other factors are climate preferences, aesthetics, and the preferred size of town. Often, natural beauty drives what is considered valuable real estate. Coastal areas, mountains, or tropical areas appeal to many. Sometimes, however, those are the areas with an above-average potential for natural hazards such as hurricanes, tornadoes, earthquakes, volcanoes, avalanches, and floods. People continue to live there anyway, relying on advanced warning systems to reduce the effects of a disaster.

Nature and the elements have impacted where people live throughout most of human history. Now more than ever, people have options regarding where to live. The technological advances brought about by human ingenuity and innovation have the potential to keep people comfortable and well-fed no matter where they live.

 Explain Why are humans spread unevenly across the globe? What factors influence the distribution of people?

Check Your Understanding

1. Where do the majority of people live across the globe?
   a. polar regions
   b. inland regions with poor vegetation
   c. coastlines of continents
   d. inland mountainous regions

2. Explain the Earth processes that determine where the majority of Earth's mineral resources are located.

3. Explain in general how one might weigh the costs and benefits of extracting a particular resource.

4. Predict how the human population growth curve will most likely look in the future.
   a. It will continue to curve upward.
   b. It will curve upward for a while and then drop abruptly.
   c. It will curve upward for a while and then level out.
   d. It will curve downward.

5. What resource(s) are in short supply in a desert environment along the sea, like the Arabian Peninsula, and how might technology help a population live in that environment?

6. What are the impacts of tornadoes, and what technologies can help buildings survive them?

7. Which technologies are used to monitor and predict earthquakes?

8. How does technology make buildings better able to withstand earthquakes?

9. Croplands tend to have a distribution pattern similar to which of the following?
   a. temperature
   b. plate tectonic boundaries
   c. wind patterns
   d. rainfall

10. Which of the following was the first innovation in the Agricultural Revolution?
    a. metal digging tools
    b. domestication of wild plants
    c. irrigation
    d. genetic modification

11. Which of the following has the longest duration?
    a. earthquake
    b. drought
    c. tornado
    d. hurricane

MAKE YOUR OWN STUDY GUIDE

 In your Evidence Notebook, design a study guide that supports the main ideas in this lesson:

When selecting a place to live, people need to consider the availability of resources and the proximity to natural hazards. Human population growth can be limited by available resources. Therefore selecting a place to live involves a tradeoff between available resources and hazards.

Remember to include the following information in your study guide:
- Use examples that model main ideas.
- Record explanations for the phenomena you investigated.
- Use evidence to support your explanations. Your support can include drawings, data, graphs, laboratory conclusions, and other evidence recorded throughout the lesson.

Sustainability of Human Activities

A hydroponic system allows plants to be grown without requiring farmland.

CAN YOU EXPLAIN IT?

FIGURE 1: An artist's concept design for a city of the future

 Gather Evidence As you explore the lesson, gather evidence to help you explain how resources can be managed sustainably, how human activities affect Earth systems both intentionally and unintentionally, and how technology can be used to reduce the negative impacts of human activities on Earth's spheres.

The human population continues to increase steadily. As it does, more people are moving into cities to pursue economic opportunities. By 2050, it is projected that two-thirds of the world's population will live in cities. While this reduces the impact of land use by individuals, it creates problems of its own. City populations put stress on the environment, such as additional pollution and increased demands for space and natural resources. Civil engineers, urban planners, and policymakers must meet these challenges to design cities that serve the needs of growing populations, yet are less wasteful, more efficient, and better positioned to work with the environment.

Predict What are some criteria that civil engineers and urban planners might use to design cities that reduce the impact of human activities on the environment?

Defining Sustainability

The concept of sustainability arose from a growing concern for humanity's ability to exist in the near and distant future. Given current trends in population growth and human consumption, some scientists predict that essential resources will become too depleted to support modern societies. While most people agree on the importance of sustainability, there is much debate about how to achieve it.

The Sustainability of Human Activities

When the planet's population was much smaller, human activities such as farming, fishing, and mining had a much smaller impact. The resources consumed and the wastes produced could be replenished easily and disposed of without doing much harm to the environment. As the human population grew, Earth's capacity to accommodate the increased demand placed on its resources became ever more strained.

> **Collaborate** With a partner, discuss ways in which humans have impacted Earth.

> **Analyze** Look at the graph of Earth Overshoot Day. What do the data tell you about the impact of human activities on Earth?

Earth Overshoot Day

FIGURE 2: In a given year, the date when humanity's demand for Earth's resources and ecosystem services exceeds what Earth can replenish in that year, called *Earth Overshoot Day*, is one way to measure sustainability.

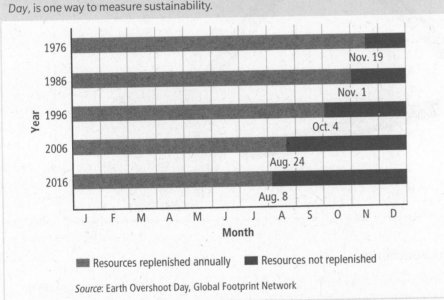

Source: Earth Overshoot Day, Global Footprint Network

Sustainability is the ability for natural systems and human needs to remain in balance indefinitely. There is concern that many human activities are unsustainable and that a limit may one day be reached. As you can see in Figure 2, the rate at which humans require Earth's resources and services increases each year. Resources once considered renewable, such as fresh water and timber, can become nonrenewable when used at a rate faster than they form. Likewise, through pollution and overuse, human activities can weaken many important natural processes. These ecosystem services are functions or processes that help sustain life or contribute to other important resources. Some of the services ecosystems naturally perform that benefit humans include supplying food for organisms, filtering water, and forming soil.

The impact of human activities on Earth's resources and services continues to grow. Sometimes scientists find it useful to look at human influence as a separate sphere, called the *anthroposphere*. The anthroposphere is the part of the environment made or modified by humans and used for their activities. Because the anthroposphere interacts with all of Earth's spheres, it can be difficult to identify the exact cause of changes to the environment. However, changes caused by human activities often occur much more rapidly than those caused by natural processes.

Planet, People, and Profits

Sustainability can be measured by the ability to balance the sometimes-competing needs of three key dimensions: environmental, social, and economic dimensions—or planet, people, and profits.

FIGURE 3: Sustainability occurs when the interactions between all three dimension are balanced.

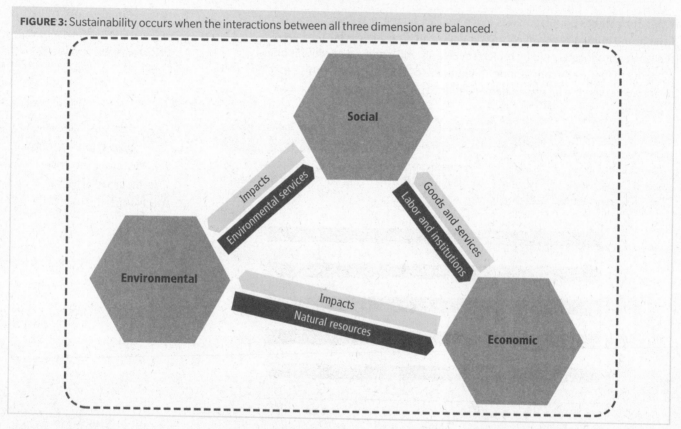

Collaborate

Brainstorm several human activities common in urban areas. Rank the activities from most to least sustainable. Use the three dimensions to defend your rankings.

Environmental

Environmental sustainability is the ability to maintain levels of renewable resource consumption, nonrenewable resource depletion, and pollution creation that can be continued for a long time. Sustainable measures allow for acceptable rates of resource use while generating tolerable amounts of pollution, and thus, they work within Earth's ecological capacity.

Social

Social sustainability is the ability of a social system—a population, culture, family, or social organization—to function at a defined level of social well-being indefinitely. Wars, poverty, and other injustices all place stresses on a system that threaten social sustainability.

Economic

Economic sustainability is the ability to support a defined level of economic production indefinitely in the areas of agriculture, households, industry, transportation, services, and technology. Sustainable economies strive to make life better for all people and reduce poverty. Resources are distributed fairly and efficiently.

More-sustainable actions balance all three dimensions, and less sustainable actions favor one dimension over the others. Societies and economies rely on the environment for resources and ecosystem services. In turn, the environment is impacted by how economies value it and how societies interact with it. Because of the interactions among all three dimensions, no one dimension is more important than any other.

 Hands-On Activity

Simulation of Natural Resource Management

SETUP

- Work in groups of four. Each member controls one lettered area.
- In each round, group members may take beans from the center to place in their area.
- Once a bean is taken, it cannot be replaced.
- At the end of each round, the number of beans left in the center is doubled.
- The maximum number of beans that can be in the center at any time is 20.
- If no beans are left in the center, the simulation is over.

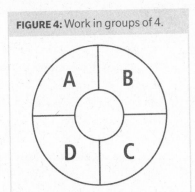

FIGURE 4: Work in groups of 4.

PROCEDURE

1. Place 20 beans in the center of the circle.
2. Without talking, run the simulation for 5 rounds.
3. With talking allowed, run the simulation for 5 more rounds.

EXTENSION

Divide each member's area in half. Run the simulation for 5 more rounds.

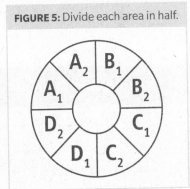

FIGURE 5: Divide each area in half.

ANALYZE

1. What do the beans represent?
2. How do your group's strategies compare to how different countries share natural resources?
3. What changed once your group was able to talk?
4. What changed when each group member's area was divided in half?
5. Based on the simulation, how can sustainablility be attained and maintained? How might this apply in the real world?

FIGURE 6: Extraction of natural resources from the oceans can disrupt marine life.

a Off-shore oil rig

b Deep-sea robotic arm

Sustainable Development

Analyze What strategies could a community use to influence individuals to act for the common good?

To ensure that Earth can continue to support a growing human population, it is important to use and manage Earth's resources in a way that meets current needs without hurting future generations. This way of thinking is known as sustainable development. Unfortunately, there is no set course of action to achieve sustainable development. Each society has to make decisions about the tradeoffs available within its particular context. For example, a town in need of more local jobs may prioritize the economic dimension and relax environmental regulations in order to attract businesses to the area.

Tradeoff decisions are more complicated when resources must be shared internationally. Some people today see oceans and the atmosphere as unlimited resources. Practices such as dumping toxic materials, emitting large amounts of carbon dioxide, and mining in the deep ocean may benefit individual communities in the short term but can cause environmental damage that affects the global community in the long term. There is growing recognition that damages to Earth's resources can have global consequences. However, because no one nation owns these resources, it is unclear how to manage and protect them. Defining the common good is not within the realm of science, but rather in that of public policy. Scientific data and research can help communities propose solutions as well as provide information on the sustainability of different plans.

Stability and Change

Tragedy of the Commons

Analyze Who should be responsible for managing common resources?

In 1968, biologist Garrett Hardin wrote an essay called "The Tragedy of the Commons" to describe how societies decide to share common resources. Hardin argued that the main difficulty in managing natural resources is the conflict between the short-term interests of individuals and the long-term welfare of society. Hardin thought that people would continue to deplete natural resources by acting in their own self-interest to the point of society's collapse.

Explain Crop rotation is a sustainable practice of agriculture where different crops are successively planted on the same land to improve soil fertility and reduce pests and diseases. How is this practice sustainable across the three dimensions?

Image Credits: (l) ©Georg Lehnerer/Fotolia (r) ©IFE, URI-IAO, UW, Lost City Science Party; NOAA/OAR/OER; The Lost City 2005 Expedition

Human Impacts on Earth's Systems

Unexpected changes in one of Earth's spheres can happen because of changes in another sphere. Scientists measure changes in each of Earth's systems and put the data into models to look at the relationships among Earth's spheres and quantify the impact of human activities on these relationships. Scientific research has a critical role to play in helping people to better define challenges as well as develop more sustainable solutions.

Beyond the Limits of Sustainability

The system of all the living and nonliving things in an area is called an *ecosystem*. Because of the size of their population and the scale of their activities, humans represent a key part of Earth's ecosystems. As a result, the sustainability of societies and the ecosystem with which they interact are intricately tied together.

FIGURE 7: Many of Earth's spheres interact to generate climate.

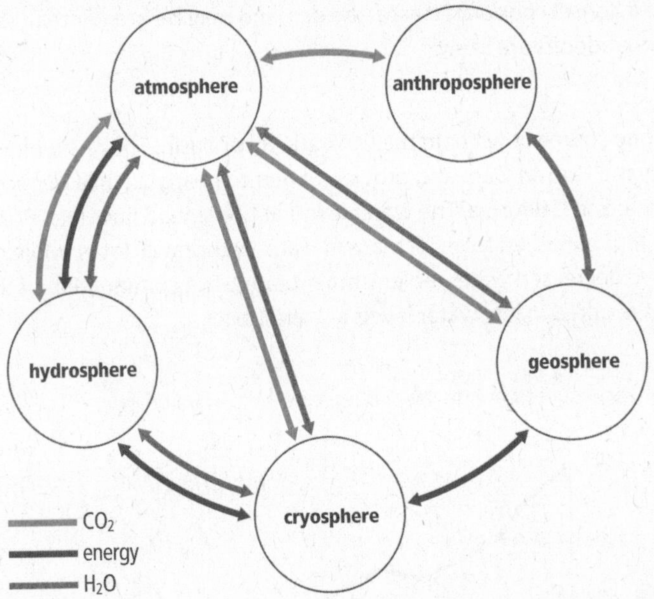

atmosphere

anthroposphere

hydrosphere

geosphere

cryosphere

— CO₂
— energy
— H₂O

Collaborate The arrows in Figure 7 show some of the interactions between Earth's spheres that generate climate. With a partner, discuss another set of arrows to model interactions that occur as a result of a human activity, such as adding carbon dioxide to the atmosphere.

FIGURE 8: Japan's forests are carefully planned and managed to make them sustainable.

Adopting sustainable practices can better help societies maintain their ecosystems. However, when societies do not make efforts to reverse unsustainable practices, there can be long-term consequences. For centuries, forests supplied timber for fuel and construction. People extracted timber at a rate much faster than it could be naturally replenished. This led to widespread deforestation in many nations. For example, England depleted many of its forests because of shipbuilding and industrialization. Forested areas reached an all-time low in the early 1900s and have not yet recovered. In contrast, Japan conteracted deforestation with government intervention. In the 1900s, Japan managed its forests and developed sustainable tree plantations that continue to this day.

Explain What happens when societies achieve sustainability? What happens when they do not?

Water

Collaborate Average water use across the globe is not uniform, but is increasing with time. With a partner, brainstorm ways a city might sustain its freshwater supply.

The hydrosphere is all of the water on Earth's surface and includes oceans, streams lakes, rivers, and groundwater. Liquid fresh water is only a small part—about 3%—of Earth's water supply. It is considered a limiting factor for human population growth. In many places, people withdraw water faster than it can naturally be replenished. When the population grows to a point that the available water supply cannot support the population, water becomes a limiting factor.

One estimate of the minimum amount of water people require in a year is 1700 m^3 per person. When an area has less than this amount available per person, the United Nations classifies the area as water stressed. Scientists predict that approximately 48% of the world's population will be water stressed by the year 2025.

Engineering

Analyze When analyzing a water crisis, how might the criteria and constraints an engineer specifies in a dry area differ from those in an overpopulated area?

Water Crisis

Engineers analyze the details of a water crisis when developing design solutions. A dry environment may provide an important constraint on the amount of water available. A criterion for a solution might be the desired amount of water per person. In a densely populated area, the demand may be greater than the constraint, and tradeoffs are likely.

Predict At a lake level of 895 feet, water does not flow downstream from Lake Mead. How might a decrease in Lake Mead's water levels drive changes in Earth's other spheres?

Lake Mead is one source of water in the Colorado River basin. The reservoir is impounded by the Hoover Dam and provides water to nearly 22 million people across Nevada, Arizona, and California. The water levels at Lake Mead fluctuate. Population growth in the region has led to an increase in water withdrawal rates, while drought conditions have decreased water replenishment rates. The combination of these two conditions has resulted in low water levels at Lake Mead.

FIGURE 9: Water levels of Lake Mead fluctuate. This graph represents water levels during a period of decline.

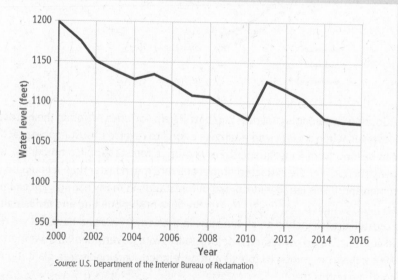

Source: U.S. Department of the Interior Bureau of Reclamation

a A white "bathtub ring" marks the decrease in water levels at Lake Mead.

b Graph of the change in water levels of Lake Mead over time

Image Credits: ©stock_alexfamous/Fotolia

Hands-On Activity

Lake Mead Water Simulation

PROCEDURE

1. On paper, mark four areas: Lake Mead, California, Nevada, and Arizona.

2. Place 26 pennies in the Lake Mead reservoir.

3. Distribute some of the pennies as follows: 5 pennies to California, 2 pennies to Nevada, and 3 pennies to Arizona.

4. Remove any pennies distributed to the states. Add 8 pennies to Lake Mead, and then repeat Step 3.

5. Continue until you reach a steady state or cannot proceed.

MATERIALS

- piece of paper, large
- pennies or other small objects

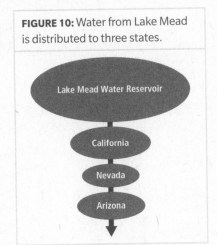

FIGURE 10: Water from Lake Mead is distributed to three states.

ANALYZE

1. How did the initial conditions affect the amount of water in Lake Mead over time?

2. How sustainable is the current rate of water usage? Use evidence from the simulation to support your claim.

 Collaborate Do research on water use in one of the states that receives water from Lake Mead and adjust the model accordingly. For example, if drought conditions increased California's water withdrawal, how would you model this?

Land

The geosphere is the mostly solid, rocky part of Earth that includes the soil and organic matter near Earth's surface. It includes the land people inhabit and depend on for agriculture. As more people move to cities, more land is converted for urban use.

Land Usage in the United States

FIGURE 11: Changes in urban land in the United States over time

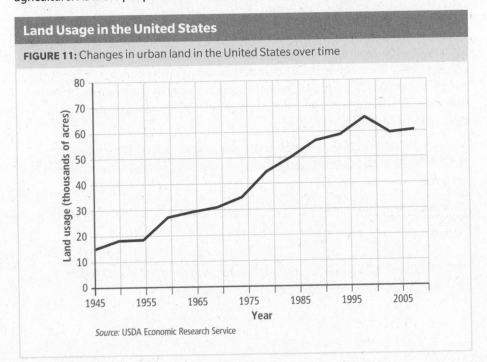

Source: USDA Economic Research Service

Both urban and agricultural land use requires the clearing of land. When the native vegetation in an area is removed, it becomes more vulnerable to erosion. Trees and plants slow the flow of water by increasing the infiltration rate—the rate of vertical water movement. The roots of these plants also hold soil together. Both of these functions prevent large-scale erosion, reducing water evaporation in dry areas and lessening the impact of floods in wet areas. When land is cleared, soil is less protected from wind and water erosion.

Although erosion is a naturally occurring process, the rate of erosion due to human activities is depleting the world's topsoil at a much faster rate than it can be naturally replenished. Topsoil is the nutrient-rich layer of soil in which plants grow. A loss of topsoil negatively impacts the world's food supply. As topsoil levels decrease, the soil becomes less fertile and the amount of crops that can be produced on the land declines.

 Analyze How does increased land use for cities affect changes in Earth's systems? What strategies might cities use to promote healthy soil?

Urban construction impacts how the geosphere interacts with Earth's spheres. Building materials such as concrete and asphalt do not allow water to seep into the ground. As rain runs down these hard surfaces, it collects chemicals, sediment, and other waste products that make their way into water supplies. This polluted water, called *runoff*, can contaminate drinking water and destabilize freshwater ecosystems. For example, the nutrients in freshwater pollution can accelerate plant and algae growth. After an algae bloom peaks and begins to die, oxygen levels decline during the decomposition process. Low oxygen areas, called dead zones, do not have enough oxygen to support life and have led to fish kills.

 Math Connection

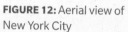 **FIGURE 12:** Aerial view of New York City

Population Density

In 1900, there were less than 2 billion people on the planet. In 2000, there were 6 billion people. Some people estimate there will be 11 billion people on the planet by the year 2100. More and more people are living in urban areas, which can support higher levels of population density. You can calculate population density to compare cities. Divide the total number of people in a city by the land area in which they live. Copy the table into your notes and calculate the population density of some of the world's largest cities.

City	Population	Land Area (km²)	Density (people per km²)
New York	8 550 405	783.8	10 908
Shanghai	24 256 800	6340.5	
Mumbai	12 442 373	603.4	

 Analyze At the population density of New York, how much land would 11 billion people need? How does it compare to the size of your state?

Air

Human activities are placing ever greater stresses on the natural balance of Earth's atmosphere. Because humans and human activities are concentrated in urban areas, the air there is often more polluted than in rural areas. Exhaust from automobiles includes harmful gases (such as carbon monoxide and sulfur dioxide). Higher concentrations of these gases can make breathing difficult, especially for children and older adults. The burning of fossil fuels for heat and energy also adds gases harmful to human health. Places with greater industrialization—large-scale manufacturing—contribute a lot more of these pollutants.

Because air pollution can threaten public health, government agencies in the United States and other countries monitor the levels of air pollution and alert residents when these levels rise. For example, the United States Environmental Protection Agency calculates the level of air pollution, called the air quality index (AQI), based on five major air pollutants: ground-level ozone, particulates, carbon monoxide, sulfur dioxide, and nitrogen dioxide. Other countries calculate AQI in various ways, and the map in Figure 13 shows global air quality based on the World Air Quality Index.

Predict How could poor air quality affect Earth's other systems?

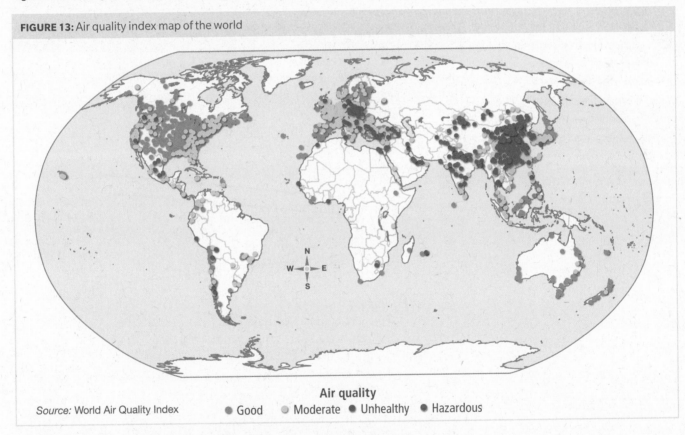

FIGURE 13: Air quality index map of the world

Source: World Air Quality Index

Air quality

● Good ● Moderate ● Unhealthy ● Hazardous

Increased levels of pollutants in the air affect a number of Earth's systems. For example, the atmosphere and the hydrosphere are connected through the water cycle. Carbon dioxide in the atmosphere is dissolved into the oceans, rivers, and lakes. When this occurs, some of it undergoes a chemical reaction with water to form an acid called carbonic acid. As a result, the acidity of the water increases.

Ocean Acidification

MATERIALS
- indicator solution, 50 mL
- straw and beaker, 200 mL

Test if a change in carbon dioxide can change the pH of sea water.

PROCEDURE

1. Pour 50 mL of indicator solution into the beaker. Make note of its color.

2. Exhale into the straw to add the carbon dioxide from your breath to the beaker.

3. Stop exhaling once a color change has occurred. Colors will range from yellow to blue—yellow indicates a lower pH and blue a higher pH.

 Analyze Based on what you have learned, what would happen if the temperature of the water changed?

 Explain How does the amount of carbon dioxide in the atmosphere relate to the amount of carbon dioxide in sea water? How does the amount of carbon dioxide dissolved in seawater relate to its pH?

Carbon Dioxide and pH

FIGURE 14: This graph shows changes in atmospheric carbon dioxide concentrations, seawater carbon dioxide concentrations (pCO$_2$), and seawater pH over time. A decrease in the pH of water indicates an increase in acidity.

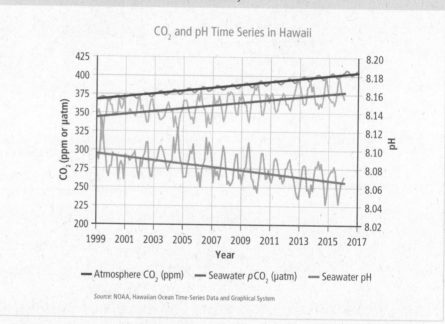

As carbon dioxide levels in the atmosphere increase, the amount of carbonic acid in the hydrosphere also increases. This rise in acidification is particularly problematic for marine animals, such as coral and oysters, that build their shells using carbonate molecules found in seawater. Increasing carbon in the ocean produces a higher quantity of bicarbonate molecules, which the marine life can no longer use for building shells. Large increases in carbonic acid can even break down part of an animal's existing shell. Because ocean acidification can cause environmental changes at rates much faster than aquatic life can adapt, marine life and existing ecosystems are increasingly vulnerable.

Life

The biosphere includes all living things and extends from genes on the molecular level to ecosystems on the macro level. Recall that ecosystems provide numerous essential ecosystem services—or functions on which humans rely—such as nutrient cycling, water filtration, and soil formation.

Human activities such as polluting, farming, and fishing can impair the ability of ecosystems to provide ecosystem services. Such activities can also contribute to habitat loss and change the distribution of plants and animals on the planet. Scientists have measured extraordinary decreases in biodiversity—the variety of organisms often associated with the health of an ecosystem—and increases in extinction rates. Approximately 25 percent of mammals and 42 percent of amphibians are estimated to be in threat of extinction. As the biodiversity of an ecosystem decreases, it becomes less stable and less able to recover when disturbances, such as pollution or fire, occur. The current rate at which species are becoming extinct has prompted some scientists to declare the current period as the Sixth Mass Extinction.

Commercial fishing has had a huge impact on the collapse of many species of fish. For example, North Atlantic cod are found in bays and ocean water as far out as the continental shelf. They feed on small invertebrates, have few natural predators, and are prized seafood. Centuries of overfishing, development of more efficient fishing methods, warmer waters, and habitat destruction have led to the decline of cod populations. This decline in a top predator like cod, along with declines in other top predator fish populations, has complex, often negative impacts on ocean food webs.

FIGURE 15: Some commercial fishing methods catch or harm non-targeted fish and animals, called bycatch.

 Explain How have human activities affected North Atlantic cod populations? What strategies might promote the long-term sustainability of fish populations?

FIGURE 16: Regulation of fishing and the development of marine preserves can help restore and maintain fish populations.

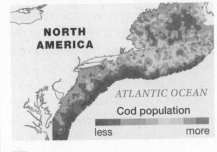

a Cod population, 1968–1972

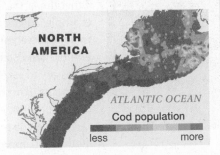

b Cod population, 2003–2008

By harvesting species of fish at a rate faster than they can naturally reproduce, overfishing poses a serious threat to marine life. Some contributing factors to the problem are giant factory ships, use of sonar to locate large schools of fish, illegal and unregulated fishing, and increased demand for fish. Declining fish populations have disproportionate effects on nations that are economically dependent on fishing.

Collaborate How can fishing practices be unsustainable? How can a city promote fishing practices that are more sustainable?

 Explain How can human activities that affect one of Earth's systems drive changes in another? Use evidence to support your claim.

Sustainability Today and Tomorrow

Analyze Select and research a sustainability challenge of your choice. How will meeting this goal impact the long-term welfare of humans and the environment?

To achieve sustainability now and in the future, there are many opportunities and challenges that humans face. Sustainability goals can help to focus international efforts on increasing the well-being of both humans and the environment. Several organizations have drafted plans to address some of the most pressing challenges, which include issues such as providing access to clean water, making renewable energy more affordable, and improving urban infrastructure.

Challenges to Sustainability

FIGURE 17: Global organizations, such as the United Nations, work to highlight sustainability issues.

Sustainability is inherently complex and occurs at the intersection of many factors. Sustainable solutions must balance interconnected needs and avoid advancing one dimension at the expense of another. Some of the major challenges to sustainability include scalability, externalities, and unintended consequences.

Scalability

Sustainability can be attempted on all levels: personal, municipal, national, and global. Sometimes a local sustainable solution can be modified to address a larger problem. Other times, the solution is not viable on a larger scale. For example, advances in solar technology have made it possible to generate enough energy to fulfill the energy needs of the entire United States population. However, the infrastructure necessary to store and distribute this energy does not yet exist and in some cases, may not even be possible to construct with current technology. Plans to use kelp to offset carbon dioxide emissions or use wastewater treatment methods to improve water quality are often not scalable.

Externalities

Sustainable practices are sometimes costly and often require a large investment of time and labor. As such, goods that are produced by sustainable methods are often more expensive than those produced by unsustainable methods. Because global producers use common resources, the price a consumer pays at the register does not always include certain costs, or externalities, associated with their use. Examples of externalities include environmental degradation, climate change, and international insecurity. When these externalities are not accounted for, prices are typically lower. Many people disagree about whether the benefits of sustainability outweigh these costs.

 Collaborate Consider all of the costs involved in the production of an item made in your area. What costs are not calculated in the price consumers pay at the store? Who pays for these additional costs?

Unintended Consequences

Science does not, and may never, have complete knowledge of the relationships between Earth's systems. As a result, some solutions to sustainability problems may have unintended consequences or outcomes that run counter to our initial intentions. For example, in China, an improved power grid led to large increases in air pollution. When more electricity became available, people used more electricity, particularly for air conditioners. This required burning more fossil fuels and led to large increases in carbon dioxide emissions. Because unintended consequences are difficult to predict, scientists disagree about the long-term impacts of many new technologies.

Working Towards Sustainability Today

Many solutions to sustainability challenges either reduce the inputs necessary to meet human needs or recycle the outputs of human activities as inputs for other activities. Because traditional agriculture and energy production use so many natural resources, engineers improve old ways and design new ways of accomplishing these tasks.

FIGURE 18: Sustainable methods for producing food and energy

a Commercial aquaponics sustainably provides fish.

b A large network of solar panels sustainably produces energy.

Explore Online ▶

Hands-On Lab

Energy Absorption Test materials to determine how much energy they absorb and decide which material would work best to keep the inside of a house cool.

Agriculture

Agriculture requires a large percentage of energy, land, and water—about 70% of the freshwater supply is used for agricultural purposes. Farming within a closed system can minimize some of the resource demands required by traditional farming.

Hydroponic farming is the process of growing food without the use of soil. Some farmers have started to use a combination of hydroponic systems and sensors to farm indoors. Specially calibrated lights provide the exact spectrum of light waves needed for each plant to maximize growth. This method of farming happens in an enclosed indoor environment. Because water condenses and recycles into the system, it is not lost to evaporation and much less is needed.

Aquaponics is an adaptation of an ancient farming method that has grown in popularity. Aquaponics combines fish farming and hydroponics into an integrated system. Vegetable grow beds filled with gravel or some other media are set on top of fish tanks. Water is pumped from the fish tank into the grow bed and then trickles down back to the tank. The fish provide nitrogen and organic wastes that fertilize growing plants, while the plants filter the water for the fish. This system is very effective at recirculating water and only requires about 10% of the water needed to grow vegetables on land.

Energy

Most energy today is generated by burning nonrenewable fossil fuels such as coal, natural gas, and crude oil. There is motivation to develop renewable energy sources—solar, wind, and geothermal energy—because the use of fossil fuels has a negative impact on human health and the environment.

FIGURE 19: Generating capacity of alternative fuel sources

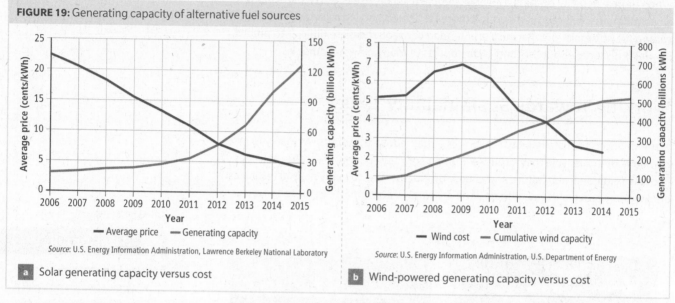

a Solar generating capacity versus cost

Source: U.S. Energy Information Administration, Lawrence Berkeley National Laboratory

b Wind-powered generating capacity versus cost

Source: U.S. Energy Information Administration, U.S. Department of Energy

FIGURE 20: Primary energy sources for the U.S. in 2016

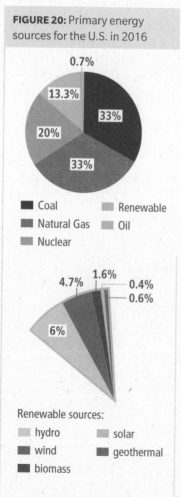

Analyze How might urban planners help cities transition to more renewable energy sources?

The transition from fossil fuels to renewable energy sources will take time and will require a decrease in the cost of renewable energy sources. The cost of generating electricity from solar cells is approaching that of fossil fuels. However, new battery technology is needed to achieve its full potential, for example, as an energy source for long-range electric cars. Additionally, researchers are developing hydrogen fuel cells that harness the energy in hydrogen and convert it into usable electricity. The only by-products of this process are pure water and heat. Though this technology is not yet as cost-competitive or reliable as fossil fuels, prospects for this renewable energy source are promising.

Every energy source currently available poses some degree of threat to the environment. In response, engineers develop new technologies to increase the efficiency of energy use and reduce people's energy demands. For example, electronically switchable glass and roof tiles transition from black to white, absorbing heat when outdoor temperatures are cool and reflecting heat when temperatures are warm. On hot summer days, this mechanism keeps heat from entering buildings and decreases the need for air conditioning. Design solutions can also harness untapped naturally existing energy sources to heat buildings and homes. In Paris, the movement of subway riders heats large tanks of water that is then piped into nearby homes.

Planning for a Sustainable Future

Because biodiversity and technology are key factors that influence the sustainability of the human population, many plans for achieving sustainability in the future involve one or a combination of these factors.

Biodiversity

Future sustainability efforts will aim to create a more symbiotic, or mutually supporting, relationship between human-created landscapes and natural ecosystems. Civil engineers and urban planners will design cities that support biodiversity. Healthy urban ecosystems will provide habitats for a diversity of species and allow ecosystems to function efficiently. When disturbances occur, ecosystems will be better able to recover. These cities will increasingly blur the line between industrial, residential, and natural spaces.

Scientist are now beginning to plan for sustained biodiversity. The Svalbard Global Seed Vault stores seeds from across the world so that species of plants are not permanently lost because of natural disasters or other large-scale crises. A similar world vault exists to protect animal diversity. The Frozen Ark project stores frozen samples of DNA from endangered animals around the world.

 Engineering

Solutions Inspired by Nature

When developing solutions to problems, engineers look for solutions that already exist. Biomimicry is the practice of adopting patterns and models found in nature to solve human sustainability problems. The bumps found on the *Stenocara* beetle's back collect water from fog and redirect it to the beetle's mouth, keeping it hydrated in dry desert conditions. Engineers have developed coatings with similar structures so that buildings gather water from fog and are less dependent on local surface and groundwater resources.

 Collaborate Research other sustainable solutions that engineers have adapted from nature. With a partner, list some of the advantages and disadvantages of each solution; consider cost, safety, and reliability.

FIGURE 21: *Stenocara* beetle

Technology

Future sustainable cities will use a variety of local renewable energy sources to meet the energy needs of a growing population. Current power grid systems consist of one-way paths that allow electricity to flow from a small number of generators to a large number of users. Solar panels and other technologies will allow a larger number of individuals to generate more electricity than they need at a given time. To manage this exchange, future power grids, sometimes called smart grids, will need to permit a two-way flow of electricity and information. A diversified smart grid is necessary to coordinate the storage of excess electricity and redistribute it to areas of high demand. Progress in developing this technological solution may ultimately determine whether humanity will be able to stop using fossil fuels.

 Explain How do we currently use technology to reduce the negative impacts of human activities on Earth's natural systems?

Hands-On Lab

Design a Water Filtration System

MATERIALS

- charcoal (optional)
- cloth or screen (optional)
- containers
- other materials as desired and available
- sand, pebbles, or similar materials (optional)
- water

FIGURE 22: Filters often include layers of material that serve different functions.

Use the engineering design process to develop a water filtration system.

DEFINE

As a class, select a community that is facing a water crisis. Identify the community's main challenge in securing freshwater resources. Collaborate with your classmates to define the criteria and constraints of an acceptable water filtration system. In what ways does the water need to be cleaned to make it usable? Are there requirements that the cleaning be done at the community level (such as before the water flows through pipes) or at the individual level (such as when campers collect water from a river)?

DESIGN

With a small group, think of several possible solutions. You may wish to research existing solutions. Use the criteria and constraints to choose one or more possibilities to develop. Build a prototype or a model and test it. Iterate until you have a design that stays within the constraints and addresses the criteria.

OPTIMIZE

Compare the solutions of different groups. What are the tradeoffs? Choose the best solution or combine solutions.

Language Arts Connection

Summarize the problem, your group's solution, and the class's solution in a short report. Include a drawing of your design. How did your view of the criteria and constraints change as you developed possible solutions? Would you be willing to drink water from the community after it passed through your filtration system? Would you be willing to have an infant drink it?

| CAPTURING CARBON | 21ST CENTURY ENGINEERING CHALLENGES | Go online to choose one of these other paths. |

Lesson Self-Check

CAN YOU EXPLAIN IT?

FIGURE 23: A futuristic city

Many cities have developed over time from original layouts in ancient and medieval times (e.g., Paris, London, Rome). The streets were planned for foot or horse traffic. Business sectors were located near major water routes. Residential districts were separated from business districts. These layouts made sense at the time. However, as human civilzations have changed over time, some of these layouts have become inefficient.

All cities can be made more sustainable. Urban planners, along with scientists and engineers, can build urban ecosystems that support high population densities and work with local ecosystems. Sustainable cities can also use integrative designs that include

- compact buildings that leave room for parks and natural habitats
- multi-use buildings and spaces to decrease the per-person floor-area ratio
- city layouts that integrate life, work, and transportation needs

These types of changes in urban planning can reduce land use and thus reduce urban sprawl. By integrating residential and business areas, the need for transportation decreases, which will reduce fossil fuel use and pollution. Overall, all cities can benefit by adapting sustainable design practices.

> **Explain** What are some criteria that civil engineers and urban planners might use to design cities that reduce the impact of human activities on the environment?

Collaborate Design a model of a future city system, including the city and the agricultural lands that will support it. Label the parts of the plan that will ensure it is sustainable.

CHECKPOINTS

Check Your Understanding

1. What is the most general description of sustainability?
   a. the ability to continue a defined behavior for an extended, but limited, time
   b. the ability to continue a defined behavior indefinitely
   c. the ability to maintain the environment indefinitely
   d. the ability to benefit economically indefinitely

2. Which dimension(s) of sustainability benefits from industrial pollution? Choose all that apply.
   a. social sustainability
   b. economic sustainability
   c. environmental sustainability
   d. political sustainability

3. How does the "Tragedy of the Commons" concept apply to logging on federal lands?

4. Which human activity uses the most water?
   a. transportation
   b. irrigation
   c. drinking
   d. mining

5. Urban sprawl uses much land for housing. The distances between sprawling residential areas and downtown economic areas require the use of automobiles, which pollute the environment and increase traffic. People who cannot afford automobile transportation are disproportionately affected, as they are shut out from either the economic areas or desirable living spaces in the residential areas. Explain how this situation is unsustainable across all three dimensions of sustainability.

6. Spraying sulfate into the stratosphere has been proposed as a possible solution to reduce global warming. When sulfates are sprayed into the stratosphere, sulfates form aerosol particles that reflect sunlight back into space. When sunlight is reduced, global temperatures will reduce. How might this solution impact Earth's spheres?

7. What is a disadvantage of sustainably produced goods compared to those produced by unsustainable methods?
   a. poorly made
   b. more expensive
   c. less labor-intensive
   d. less durable

8. A new technology uses chemical reactions to lock carbon emissions into basalt rock. Some scientists are concerned that the carbon may leak out of the rock over time. They are unsure how carbon leaks might impact air and water quality. This situation is an example of which of the following challenges to sustainability?
   a. scalability
   b. externalities
   c. unintended consequences
   d. increased demand

9. Though kelp has the capacity to offset stores of carbon dioxide found in water, some researchers are skeptical about farming kelp to reduce ocean acidification. They believe the oceans are too large for kelp to make much of a difference. This situation is an example of which of the following challenges to sustainability?
   a. scalability
   b. externalities
   c. unintended consequences
   d. increased demand

10. Aquaponics combines fish farming and hydroponics. The fish provide nitrogen and organic wastes that fertilize the growing plants, while the plants filter the water for the fish. How is an aquaponics system a sustainable solution?

   a. It reuses wastes, while providing food.
   b. It saves water, while providing food.
   c. It reclaims polluted water, while providing food.
   d. It recycles water, while providing food.

11. In what ways are farming methods such as hydroponics and aquaponics more sustainable than traditional farming methods? In what ways might these methods be less sustainable than traditional farming methods?

12. Evaluate the following statement:

   The benefits of sustainability outweigh the costs.

   Do you agree or disagree with this statement? Use evidence and reasoning to support your answer.

 In your Evidence Notebook, design a study guide that supports the main ideas from this lesson:

Sustainability is the ability for natural systems and human needs to remain in balance indefinitely.

Sustainability can be measured by three key dimensions: environmental, social, and economic dimensions.

Some of the major challenges to sustainability include scalability, externalities, and unintended consequences.

Remember to include the following information in your study guide:
- Use examples that model main ideas.
- Record explanations for the phenomena you investigated.
- Use evidence to support your explanations. Your support can include drawings, data, graphs, laboratory conclusions, and other evidence recorded throughout the lesson.

Environmental Connection

Gone Forever Similar to animals, plant diversity can change through time. Changes to the environment are now happening faster than before because of relatively rapid changes in temperature and precipitation patterns on the planet. Some scientists believe that we are in the midst of a sixth mass extinction of plants and animals. Species are interdependent. When a species is lost, its loss affects other plants and animals in the ecosystem.

Use Internet resources to learn more about different types of plants and animals that have become extinct during the past decade. Identify one plant or animal. Explain why the organism became extinct and how the loss of this organism is affecting the surrounding ecosystem. Present your findings as a poster.

FIGURE 1: The Pyrenean Ibex became extinct in 2000.

Health Connection

Feeding the Masses As you learned, it takes a lot of space and time to grow vegetables for one person. Today, agriculture has become industrialized to efficiently produce food for a growing population. This is true for both crops and animals. Industrialized agriculture has benefits, but it also has drawbacks. Many pathogens, such as bacteria that are harmful to people, are more common today, especially in animal production.

Using library and Internet resources, identify a pathogen that has become more common in meat, poultry, or egg products. Explain how this pathogen affects people and why it is more common for a particular food commodity, like chicken or ground beef, than before. Look for solutions, such as different types of safe-food handling, that limit the chance of becoming sick from this pathogen.

FIGURE 2: Large-scale industrialized agriculture has changed the way we consume food.

Architecture Connection

Living Underground Buildings do not have to reach the sky. Some architects are now looking to build underground. One reason for this trend is that underground sheltered homes have a lower carbon footprint because they require less energy to heat and cool. Underground homes come in a variety of styles that best suit the surrounding landscape and climate.

Use the Internet to find out information about underground homes. Explore the architectural varieties of underground dwellings, the materials used in the construction, and the environmental benefits of such a dwelling.

FIGURE 3: Zero-carbon home built underground

SYNTHESIZE THE UNIT

In your Evidence Notebook, create a concept map, graphic organizer, or outline using the Study Guides you created for each lesson in this unit. Be sure to use evidence to support your claims.

When synthesizing individual information, remember to follow these general steps:
- Find the central idea of each piece of information.
- Think about the relationships among the central ideas.
- Combine the ideas to come up with a new understanding.

Go online to access detailed lesson summaries for this unit.

DRIVING QUESTIONS

Look back to the Driving Questions from the opening section of this unit. In your Evidence Notebook, review and revise your previous answers to those questions. Use the evidence you gathered and other observations you made throughout the unit to support your claims.

PRACTICE AND REVIEW

1. Which statements are true about the distribution of people across the globe? Choose all that apply.
   a. People tend to live near river and coastal areas.
   b. People tend to live in areas with easy access to transportation.
   c. People tend to settle near areas where volcanoes and earthquakes occur.
   d. People tend to settle in areas rich in natural resources.
   e. People tend to live in areas with tropical climates.
   f. People tend to adapt to extreme environments.

2. Which of the following statements describe the effects of a growing human population? Choose all that apply.
   a. The demand for living space will increase.
   b. The demand for food and fresh water will increase.
   c. Pollution will increase.
   d. Global temperatures will decrease.

Use Figure 4 to answer Questions 3 and 4.

FIGURE 4: Map of worldwide natural disaster hotspots

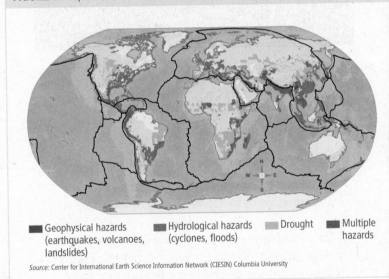

◼ Geophysical hazards (earthquakes, volcanoes, landslides)   ◼ Hydrological hazards (cyclones, floods)   ◼ Drought   ◼ Multiple hazards

Source: Center for International Earth Science Information Network (CIESIN) Columbia University

3. Where are geophysical disasters such as volcanoes and earthquakes most likely to occur?
   a. Ancient inland seas
   b. Areas of moderate temperatures
   c. Plate boundaries
   d. River deltas

4. On average, more deaths result from droughts and floods than any other natural hazards. Describe how human activities such as farming and construction might increase the impact of these hazards.

5. Evaluate the following statement:

Human activities can increase the frequency and intensity of natural hazards.

Do you agree or disagree with this statement? Use evidence and reasoning to support your answer.

Use Figure 5 to answer Questions 6 and 7.

FIGURE 5: Doppler radar shows rainbands in a hurricane.

6. What information does a Doppler radar measure?

a. Speed and direction of target objects

b. Movement of tectonic plates

c. Changes in temperature

d. Changes in electromagnetic fields

7. How might scientists use Doppler radar images to prepare residents for future weather conditions?

8. The atmosphere, oceans, and outer space are examples of natural resource shared by all societies. What factors should international organizations take into account when deciding how to manage shared natural resources? Identify at least three factors, and briefly explain how each affects the decision.

9. The city of Nayarit, Mexico lies on the western coast just north of Puerto Vallarta and relies on tourism for its income. After seeing growth and tourism degrade the natural beauty of Puerto Vallarta, developers wanted to take a different approach in Nayarit. They brought in scientists to study the landscape's natural attributes and identify sensitivities and constraints of plants, animals, the culture, and society. The developers established nature reserves, recommended land conservation and suitable improvement strategies, and created an environmental council consisting of local citizens. Explain how the developers' actions fostered sustainability.

10. For each event, identify how a change in one of Earth's spheres affects the other spheres.

a. Deforestation

b. Ocean acidification

c. Oil spill

UNIT PROJECT

Return to your unit project. Finalize your proposal so that it clearly explains how the water treatment facility works, how well it serves your community, how it needs to be improved, and what the benefits of improving the system will be to the community and to the environment.

Remember these tips while you are finalizing your proposal:

- Is the way the system works now clearly described?

- Are the problems with the current system clearly identified?

- Is the evidence and reasoning for improving the system clear?

- Are the costs and benefits of your improved system clearly outlined?

- Did you include an action plan?

Building a Dam

FIGURE 6: The Three Gorges Dam in China supplies hydroelectric energy, opens new shipping routes, and provides flood control. The dam took 17 years to build and was completed in 2008. The reservoir required the relocation of more than a million people.

A group of urban developers is planning a community near a river and needs to provide a stable water supply and energy source. The local government has approved the construction of a large-scale hydroelectric dam upstream. Some developers are concerned about the impact of the dam on the local environment. They are not sure whether the benefits of the dam will outweigh the costs and risks.

1. DEFINE THE PROBLEM

With your team, write a statement outlining the factors you need to investigate to understand how a dam might impact the community.

2. CONDUCT RESEARCH

With your team, investigate the water resources, water usage, and the effect on the surrounding landscape of the area. What lines of evidence are available?

3. ANALYZE DATA

On your own, analyze the problem you have defined along with your research. Use your research to explain the potential benefits and risks of planning a community near the dam.

4. IDENTIFY AND RECOMMEND A SOLUTION

Develop a short white paper to outline the short- and long-term effects the dam may have on the new community. Make a recommendation about whether the developers should carry out the project.

5. COMMUNICATE

Present your findings to the class in a six-minute PowerPoint presentation, or write a short report with an abstract, introduction, methods, results, and conclusions/ discussion section.

 CHECK YOUR WORK

A complete report should include the following information:

- A clear description of the problems that the developers could have if they were to build the dam in this area
- Evidence that supports the claims
- A recommendation for preventing the predicted problems
- Reasoning to support the recommendation

Resources

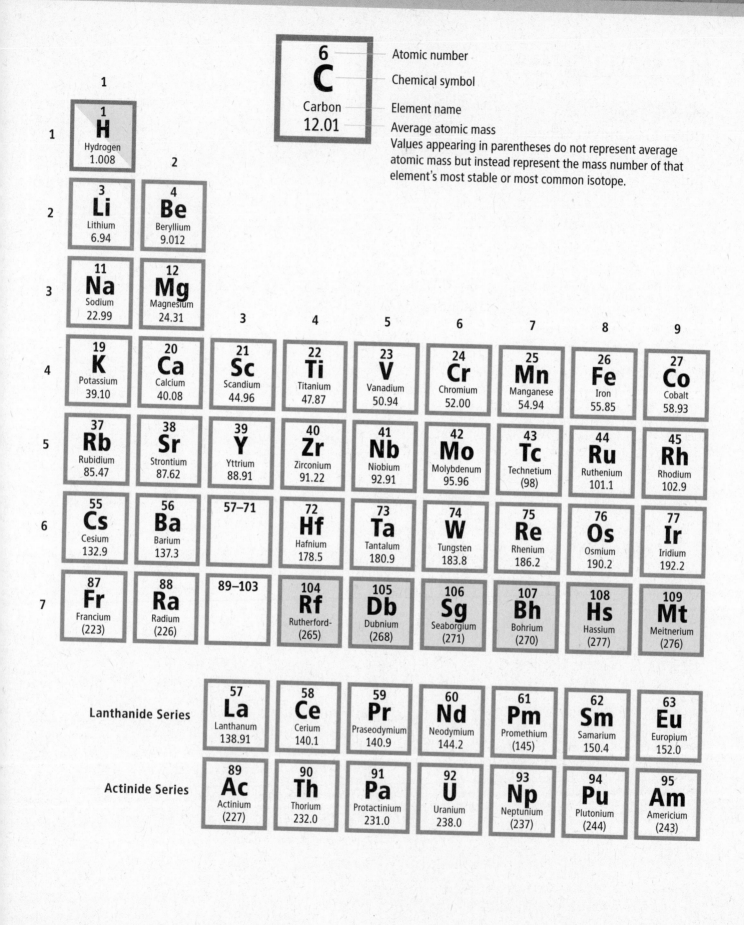

6 **C** Carbon 12.01	— Atomic number — Chemical symbol — Element name — Average atomic mass								

Values appearing in parentheses do not represent average atomic mass but instead represent the mass number of that element's most stable or most common isotope.

Group	1	2	3	4	5	6	7	8	9
1	**1** **H** Hydrogen 1.008								
2	**3** **Li** Lithium 6.94	**4** **Be** Beryllium 9.012							
3	**11** **Na** Sodium 22.99	**12** **Mg** Magnesium 24.31							
4	**19** **K** Potassium 39.10	**20** **Ca** Calcium 40.08	**21** **Sc** Scandium 44.96	**22** **Ti** Titanium 47.87	**23** **V** Vanadium 50.94	**24** **Cr** Chromium 52.00	**25** **Mn** Manganese 54.94	**26** **Fe** Iron 55.85	**27** **Co** Cobalt 58.93
5	**37** **Rb** Rubidium 85.47	**38** **Sr** Strontium 87.62	**39** **Y** Yttrium 88.91	**40** **Zr** Zirconium 91.22	**41** **Nb** Niobium 92.91	**42** **Mo** Molybdenum 95.96	**43** **Tc** Technetium (98)	**44** **Ru** Ruthenium 101.1	**45** **Rh** Rhodium 102.9
6	**55** **Cs** Cesium 132.9	**56** **Ba** Barium 137.3	57–71	**72** **Hf** Hafnium 178.5	**73** **Ta** Tantalum 180.9	**74** **W** Tungsten 183.8	**75** **Re** Rhenium 186.2	**76** **Os** Osmium 190.2	**77** **Ir** Iridium 192.2
7	**87** **Fr** Francium (223)	**88** **Ra** Radium (226)	89–103	**104** **Rf** Rutherford- (265)	**105** **Db** Dubnium (268)	**106** **Sg** Seaborgium (271)	**107** **Bh** Bohrium (270)	**108** **Hs** Hassium (277)	**109** **Mt** Meitnerium (276)

Lanthanide Series	**57** **La** Lanthanum 138.91	**58** **Ce** Cerium 140.1	**59** **Pr** Praseodymium 140.9	**60** **Nd** Neodymium 144.2	**61** **Pm** Promethium (145)	**62** **Sm** Samarium 150.4	**63** **Eu** Europium 152.0
Actinide Series	**89** **Ac** Actinium (227)	**90** **Th** Thorium 232.0	**91** **Pa** Protactinium 231.0	**92** **U** Uranium 238.0	**93** **Np** Neptunium (237)	**94** **Pu** Plutonium (244)	**95** **Am** Americium (243)

Metals Metalloids Nonmetals

State of Element at STP

☐ Solid ◨ Liquid

◨ Gas ▨ Not yet known

	13	14	15	16	17	18

18
2
He
Helium
4.003

13
5
B
Boron
10.81

14
6
C
Carbon
12.01

15
7
N
Nitrogen
14.007

16
8
O
Oxygen
15.999

17
9
F
Fluorine
19.00

10
Ne
Neon
20.18

13
Al
Aluminum
26.98

14
Si
Silicon
28.085

15
P
Phosphorus
30.97

16
S
Sulfur
32.06

17
Cl
Chlorine
35.45

18
Ar
Argon
39.95

10 11 12

28
Ni
Nickel
58.69

29
Cu
Copper
63.55

30
Zn
Zinc
65.38

31
Ga
Gallium
69.72

32
Ge
Germanium
72.63

33
As
Arsenic
74.92

34
Se
Selenium
78.96

35
Br
Bromine
79.90

36
Kr
Krypton
83.80

46
Pd
Palladium
106.4

47
Ag
Silver
107.9

48
Cd
Cadmium
112.4

49
In
Indium
114.8

50
Sn
Tin
118.7

51
Sb
Antimony
121.8

52
Te
Tellurium
127.6

53
I
Iodine
126.9

54
Xe
Xenon
131.3

78
Pt
Platinum
195.1

79
Au
Gold
197.0

80
Hg
Mercury
200.6

81
Tl
Thallium
204.38

82
Pb
Lead
207.2

83
Bi
Bismuth
209.0

84
Po
Polonium
(209)

85
At
Astatine
(210)

86
Rn
Radon
(222)

110
Ds
Darmstadtium
(281)

111
Rg
Roentgenium
(280)

112
Cn
Copernicium
(285)

113
Nh
Nihonium
(284)

114
Fl
Flerovium
(289)

115
Mc
Moscovium
(288)

116
Lv
Livermorium
(293)

117
Ts
Tennessine
(294)

118
Og
Oganesson
(294)

64
Gd
Gadolinium
157.3

65
Tb
Terbium
158.9

66
Dy
Dysprosium
162.5

67
Ho
Holmium
164.9

68
Er
Erbium
167.3

69
Tm
Thulium
168.9

70
Yb
Ytterbium
173.1

71
Lu
Lutetium
175.0

96
Cm
Curium
(247)

97
Bk
Berkelium
(247)

98
Cf
Californium
(251)

99
Es
Einsteinium
(252)

100
Fm
Fermium
(257)

101
Md
Mendelevium
(258)

102
No
Nobelium
(259)

103
Lr
Lawrencium
(262)

Elements with atomic numbers of 95 and above are not known to occur naturally, even in trace amounts. They have only been synthesized in the lab. The physical and chemical properties of elements with atomic numbers 100 and above cannot be predicted with certainty.

Guide to Common Minerals

Luster			Hardness	Cleavage	Fracture	Color/opacity
Nonmetallic; light color	glassy to pearly	Scratches glass	6	two cleavage plains at nearly right angles		various colors but often white or pink; opaque
	glassy		6	two cleavage planes at 86° and 94°		colorless, white, pink, or various colors; translucent to opaque
	glassy and waxy		7	no cleavage	conchoidal	various colors; transparent to opaque
	glassy		6.5–7	no cleavage	conchoidal to irregular	olive green; transparent to translucent
	glassy	Does not scratch glass	2.5–3	three cleavage planes at right angles		colorless to gray; transparent to opaque
	glassy		3	three cleavage planes at 75° and 105°		colorless or white and may be tinted; transparent to opaque
	glassy, pearly, or silky		1–2.5	one perfect cleavage plane	conchoidal and fibrous	white, pink, or gray to colorless; transparent to opaque
	pearly to waxy		1	one cleavage plane		white to green; opaque
	glassy or pearly		2–2.5	one cleavage plane		colorless to light gray or brown; transparent to opaque
	glassy		4	eight cleavage planes (octahedral)		green, yellow, purple, and other colors; transparent to translucent
	glassy		4.5–5	no cleavage	conchoidal to irregular	green, blue, violet, brown, or colorless; translucent to opaque
	silky		3.5–4	no cleavage	irregular, splintery	green; translucent to opaque
Nonmetallic; dark color	glassy and silky	Scratches glass	5–6	two cleavage planes at 56° and 124°		dark green, brown, or black; translucent to opaque
	resinous and glassy		6.5–7.5	no cleavage	irregular	dark red or green; transparent to opaque
	pearly and glassy	Does not scratch glass	2.5–3	one cleavage plane		black to dark brown; transparent to opaque
	metallic to earthy		1–2	one cleavage plane		black to gray; opaque
Metallic	metallic or earthy	Does not scratch glass	5.5–6.5	no cleavage	irregular	reddish brown to black; opaque
	metallic		2.5	three cleavage planes at right angles		lead gray; opaque
	metallic	Scratches glass	5–6	two cleavage planes at 56° and 124°		iron black; opaque
	metallic		6–6.5	no cleavage	conchoidal to irregular	brass yellow; opaque

Streak	Specific gravity	Other properties	Mineral name and chemical formula
white	2.6	prismatic, columnar, or tabular crystals	orthoclase, $KAlSi_3O_8$
blue-gray to white	2.6 to 2.7	striations	plagioclase, $(Na, Cl)(Al, Si)_4O_8$
white	2.65	six-sided crystals	quartz, SiO_2
white to pale green	3.2 to 3.3	stubby, prismatic crystals	olivine, $(Mg, Fe)2SiO_4$
white	2.2	cubic crystals and salty taste	halite, $NaCl$
white	2.7	may produce double image when you look through it	calcite, $CaCO_3$
white	2.2 to 2.4	thin layers and flexible	gypsum, $CaSO_4 \cdot 2H_2O$
white	2.7 to 2.8	soapy feel and thin scales	talc, $Mg_3Si_4O_{10}(OH)_2$
white	2.7 to 3	thin sheets	muscovite, $KAl_2Si_3O_{10}(OH)_2$
white	3.2	fluorescent under UV light; cubic and six-sided crystals	fluorite, CaF_2
white or pale red-brown	3.1	six-sided crystals	apatite, $Ca_5(OH, F, Cl)(PO_4)_3$
emerald green	4	fibrous, radiating aggregates or circular, banded structure	malachite, $CuCO_3 \cdot Cu(OH)_2$
pale green or white	3.2	six-sided crystals	hornblende, $(Ca, Na)_{2-3}(Mg, Fe, Al)_5$ $Si_6(Si, Al)_2O_{22}(OH)_2$
white	4.2	12- or 24-sided crystals	garnet, $Fe_3Al_2(SiO_4)_3$
white to gray	2.7 to 3.2	thin, flexible sheets	biotite, $K(Mg, Fe)_3AlSi_3O_{10}(OH)_2$
black to dark green	2.3	greasy feel, soft, and flaky	graphite, C
red to red-brown	5.25	granular masses	hematite, Fe_2O_3
lead gray to black	7.4 to 7.6	very heavy	galena, PbS
black to dark green	5.2	8- or 12-sided crystals; may be magnetic	magnetite, Fe_3O_4
greenish black	5	cubic crystals	pyrite, FeS_2

Glossary

A

abrasion (uh·BRAY·zhuhn) the grinding and wearing away of rock surfaces through the mechanical action of other rock or sand particles
abrasión proceso por el cual las superficies de las rocas se muelen o desgastan por medio de la acción mecánica de otras rocas y partículas de arena

absolute age (AB·suh·loot AYJ) the numeric age of an object or event, often stated in years before the present, as established by an absolute-dating process, such as radiometric dating
edad absoluta la edad numérica de un objeto o suceso, que suele expresarse en cantidad de años antes del presente, determinada por un proceso de datación absoluta, tal como la datación radiométrica

accretion growth or increase in size by gradual external addition, fusion, or inclusion
acreción crecimiento o aumento en tamaño por fusión, inclusión o adición externa gradual

active margin a continental margin at which an oceanic plate is subducting under a continental plate, characterized by the presence of a narrow continental shelf and a deep-sea trench
margen activo margen continental en el que una placa oceánica se subduce bajo una placa continental, caracterizado por la presencia de una plataforma continental estrecha y una fosa oceánica profunda

air mass a large body of air throughout which temperature and moisture content are similar
masa de aire un gran volumen de aire, cuya temperatura y cuyo contenido de humedad son similares en toda su extensión

albedo (al·BEE·doh) the fraction of radiation that is reflected off the surface of an object
albedo porcentaje de la radiación que la superficie de un objeto refleja

alloy a metallic solid or liquid that is composed of a homogeneous mixture of two or more metals or of metals and nonmetal or metalloid elements, usually for the purpose of imparting or increasing specific characteristics or properties
aleación sólido o líquido metálico que está compuesto de una mezcla homogénea de dos o más metales o de metales y no metales o metaloides, generalmente con el objetivo de impartir o aumentar características o propiedades específicas

alluvial fan (uh·LOO·vee·uhl FAN) a fan-shaped mass of rock material deposited by a stream when the slope of the land decreases sharply; for example, alluvial fans form when streams flow from mountains to flat land
abanico aluvial masa de materiales rocosos en forma de abanico, depositados por un arroyo cuando la pendiente del terreno disminuye bruscamente; por ejemplo, los abanicos aluviales se forman cuando los arroyos fluyen de una montaña a un terreno llano

angiosperm (AN·jee·uh·sperm) a flowering plant that produces seeds within a fruit
angiosperma una planta que da flores y que produce semillas dentro de la fruta

anthroposphere the part of Earth that has been constructed or modified by humans; sometimes considered one of the spheres of the Earth system
antropósfera parte de la Tierra que ha sido construida o modificada por los seres humanos; a veces es considerada una de las esferas del sistema de la Tierra

aquifer (AK·wuh·fer) a body of rock or sediment that stores groundwater and allows the flow of groundwater
acuífero un cuerpo rocoso o sedimento que almacena agua subterránea y permite que fluya

asthenosphere (as·THEN·uh·sfir) the solid, plastic layer of the mantle beneath the lithosphere; made of mantle rock that flows very slowly, which allows tectonic plates to move on top of it
astenosfera la capa sólida y plástica del manto, que se encuentra debajo de la litosfera; está formada por roca del manto que fluye muy lentamente, lo cual permite que las placas tectónicas se muevan en su superficie

atmosphere (AT·muhs·fir) a mixture of gases and particles that surrounds a planet, moon, or other celestial body; one of the four major spheres of the Earth system
atmósfera una mezcla de gases y partículas que rodea un planeta, una luna, u otros cuerpos celestes; una de las cuatro esferas principales del sistema terrestre

atom (AT·uhm) the smallest unit of an element that maintains the chemical properties of that element
átomo la unidad más pequeña de un elemento que conserva las propiedades químicas de ese elemento

axis a center line to which parts of a structure or body may be referred
eje línea central a la cual pueden referirse partes de una estructura o cuerpo

B

big bang theory the theory that all matter and energy in the universe was compressed into an extremely dense volume that 13.7 billion years ago suddenly expanded in all directions
teoría del big bang la teoría que establece que toda la materia y la energía del universo estaban comprimidas en un volumen extremadamente denso que hace 13.7 miles de millones de ános de repente se expandió en todas direcciones

biodiversity (by·oh·dih·VER·sih·tee) the variety of organisms in a given area, the genetic variation within a population, the variety of species in a community, or the variety of communities in an ecosystem
biodiversidad la variedad de organismos que se encuentran en un área determinada, la variación genética dentro de una población, la variedad de especies en una comunidad o la variedad de comunidades en un ecosistema

biogeochemical cycle movement of a chemical through the biological and geological, or living and nonliving, parts of an ecosystem
ciclo biogeoquímico movimiento de una sustancia químicaa través de los componentes biológicos y geológicos, o vivos einertes, de un ecosistema

biosphere (BIE·oh·sfir) the part of Earth where life exists; includes all of the living organisms on Earth; one of the four major spheres of the Earth system
biosfera la parte de la Tierra donde existe la vida; comprende todos los seres vivos de la Tierra; una de las cuatro esferas principales del sistema terrestre

C

carbon cycle the movement of carbon from the nonliving environment into living things and back
ciclo del carbono el movimiento del carbono del ambiente sin vida a los seres vivos y de los seres vivos al ambiente

Cenozoic era (sen·uh·ZOH·ik ER·uh) the current geologic era, which began 65.5 million years ago; also called the *Age of Mammals*
era Cenozoica la era geológica actual, que comenzó hace 65.5 millones de años; también llamada Edad de los Mamíferos

chemical (KEM·ih·kuhl) any substance that has a defined composition
sustancia química cualquier sustancia que tiene una composición definida

chemical sedimentary rock sedimentary rock that forms when minerals precipitate from a solution or settle from a suspension
roca sedimentaria química roca sedimentaria que se forma cuando los minerales precipitan a partir de una solución o se depositan a partir de una suspensión

clastic sedimentary rock sedimentary rock that forms when fragments of preexisting rock are compacted or cemented together
roca sedimentaria clástica roca sedimentaria que se forma cuando los fragmentos de rocas preexistentes se unen por compactación o cementación

cleavage (KLEEV·ij) in geology, the tendency of a mineral to split along specific planes of weakness to form smooth, flat surfaces
exfoliación en geología, la tendencia de un mineral a agrietarse a lo largo de planos débiles específicos y formar superficies lisas y planas

climate (KLIE·muht) the characteristic weather patterns in an area over a long period of time
clima las condiciones del tiempo en un área durante un largo período de tiempo

climate change changes in regional climates or global climate, especially the change in global climate patterns in the 20th and 21st centuries; previously called global warming
cambio climático cambios en los climas regionales o en el clima mundial, especialmente, el cambio en los patrones climáticos globales en los siglos XX y XXI; anteriormente llamado calentamiento global

compound (KAHM·pownd) a substance made of atoms of two or more different elements joined by chemical bonds
compuesto una sustancia formada por átomos de dos o más elementos diferentes unidos por enlaces químicos

conduction (kuhn·DUHK·shuhn) the transfer of heat or another form of energy from one particle of a substance directly to another
conducción la transferencia de energía en forma de calor de una partícula de una sustancia directamente a otra

constraint (kuhn·STRAYNT) a restriction or limitation; in engineering design, a limitation that a design or solution must stay within, often determined when defining a problem
restricción condicionamiento o limitación; en diseño de ingeniería, limitación dentro de la cual un diseño o solución debe mantenerse, a menudo determinada al definir un problema

continental margin (kahn·tuh·NEN·tl MAR·jin) the sea floor that is located between dry land and the deep oceanic crust, consisting of the continental shelf, slope, and rise
margen continental fondo del mar que se encuentra entre la tierra firme y la corteza oceánica profunda, que consiste en la plataforma, el talud y la emersión continenta

convection (kuhn·VEK·shuhn) the movement of matter due to differences in density; can result in the transfer of energy as heat
convección el movimiento de la materia debido a diferencias en la densidad; puede resultar en la transferencia de energía en forma de calor

convergent boundary (kuhn·VER·juhnt BOWN·duh·ree) the boundary between tectonic plates that are moving toward each other

límite convergente el límite entre placas tectónicas que se mueven una hacia la otra

core the central part of Earth below the mantle; also the center of the sun

núcleo la parte central de la Tierra, debajo del manto; también, el centro del Sol

Coriolis effect (kohr·ee·OH·lis ih·FEKT) the curving of the path of a moving object from an otherwise straight path due to Earth's or another celestial object's rotation

efecto de Coriolis la desviación de la trayectoria recta que experimentan los objetos en movimiento debido a la rotación de la Tierra

cosmic microwave background (CMB) radiation detected from every direction in space almost uniformly; considered a remnant of the big bang

radiación cósmica de fondo radiación que se detecta de manera uniforme desde todas las direcciones en el espacio; se considera un resto del big bang

criterion (kry·TIR·ee·uhn) *(plural, criteria)* a standard, rule, or test on which a judgment or decision can be based; in engineering design, a specific requirement that a design or solution should meet, often determined when defining a problem

criterio norma, regla o prueba sobre la que pueden basarse un juicio o una decisión; en el diseño de ingeniería, requisito específico que un diseño o solución debe cumplir, a menudo determinado al definir un problema

crust the thin and solid outermost layer of Earth above the mantle; continental and oceanic crust form the upper part of the lithosphere

corteza la capa externa, delgada y sólida de la Tierra, que se encuentra sobre el manto; corteza continental y oceánica forman la parte superior de la litosfera

cryosphere the part of the hydrosphere that is frozen water, often excluding ice in the atmosphere; sometimes considered one of the spheres of the Earth system

criósfera la parte de la hidrósfera que es agua congelada, en la cual generalmente se excluye el hielo de la atmósfera; a veces es considerada una de las esferas del sistema de la Tierra

crystal a solid whose atoms, ions, or molecules are arranged in a regular, repeating pattern

cristal un sólido cuyos átomos, iones o moléculas están ordenados en un patrón regular y repetitivo

cyanobacteria a bacterium that carries out photosynthesis; sometimes called a blue-green alga

cianobacteria bacteria que lleva a cabo la fotosíntesis; a veces llamada alga verde azulada

D

delta a fan-shaped mass of sediment deposited at the mouth of a stream; for example, deltas form where streams flow into the ocean at the edge of a continent

delta un depósito de sedimento en forma de abanico ubicado en la desembocadura de un río; por ejemplo, los deltas se forman en el lugar donde las corrientes fluyen al océano en el borde de un continente

density (DEN·sih·tee) the ratio of the mass of a substance to the volume of the substance; commonly expressed as grams per cubic centimeter for solids and liquids and as grams per liter for gases

densidad la relación entre la masa de una sustancia y su volumen; comúnmente se expresa en gramos por centímetro cúbico para los sólidos y líquidos, y como gramos por litro para los gases

deposition the process by which materials are dropped, such as sand or silt by a stream; also the process by which frost forms when water vapor condenses as a solid

sedimentación proceso por el cual los materiales descienden, como la arena o el cieno por una corriente

deposición proceso por el cual se forma escarcha cuando el vapor de agua se condensa como un sólido

discharge the volume of water that flows out within a given time

descarga el volumen de agua que fluye en un tiempo determinado

divergent boundary (dy·VER·juhnt BOWN·duh·ree) the boundary between two tectonic plates that are moving away from each other

límite divergente el límite entre dos placas tectónicas que se están separando una de la otra

Doppler effect (DAHP·ler ih·FEKT) an observed change in the frequency of a wave when the source or observer is moving

efecto Doppler un cambio que se observa en la frecuencia de una onda cuando la fuente o el observador está en movimiento

drainage basin the entire region draining into a river, river system, or other body of water; a watershed

cuenca de drenaje toda la región que drena hacia un río, sistema fluvial u otro cuerpo de agua; una cuenca

E

earthquake a movement or trembling of the ground that is caused by a sudden release of energy when rocks along a fault move

terremoto un movimiento o temblor del suelo causado por una liberación súbita de energía que se produce cuando las rocas ubicadas a lo largo de una falla se mueven

eccentricity the degree of elongation of an elliptical orbit (symbol, e)
excentricidad el grado de alargamiento de una órbita elíptica (símbolo: e)

ecosystem services an ecological function or process of a region that helps sustain life or contributes an important resource
servicio ecosistémico función o proceso ecológico de una región que ayuda a preservar la vida o contribuye un recurso importante

electromagnetic spectrum (ee·lek·troh·mag·NET·ik SPEK·truhm) all of the frequencies or wavelengths of electromagnetic radiation, which is the radiation associated with an electric and magnetic field, including visible light
radiación electromagnética todas las frecuencias o longitudes de onda de la radiación electromagnética, que es la radiación asociada con an campo eléctrico y magnético, incluyendo luz visible

element (EL·uh·muhnt) a substance that cannot be separated or broken down into simpler substances by chemical means; all atoms of an element have the same atomic number
elemento una sustancia que no se puede separar o descomponer en sustancias más simples por medio de métodos químicos; todos los átomos de un elemento tienen el mismo número atómico

ellipse an oval shape defined by points for which the sum of the distances to two fixed points (foci) is a constant; a circle is an ellipse of zero eccentricity
elipse forma ovalada definida por puntos en los que la suma de las distancias de dos puntos fijos (focos) es una constante; un círculo es una elipse de excentricidad cero

engineering design process the steps that engineers follow to come up with a solution to a problem
proceso de diseño de ingeniería los pasos que los ingenieros siguen para llegar a una solución de un problema

epicenter (EP·ih·sen·ter) the point on Earth's surface directly above an earthquake's starting point, or focus
epicentro el punto de la superficie de la Tierra que queda justo arriba del punto de inicio, o foco, de un terremoto

erosion (ee·ROH·zhuhn) the removal and transport of materials by natural agents such as wind and running water; sometimes used in a broader sense that includes weathering
erosión el desgaste y transporte de materiales por agentes naturales como el viento y el agua corriente; a veces, es usado en un sentido más amplio que incluye la meteorización

fault (FAWLT) a break in a body of rock along which one block slides relative to another; a form of brittle strain
falla una grieta en un cuerpo rocoso a lo largo de la cual un bloque se desliza respecto a otro; una forma de tensión quebradiza

feedback the return of a portion of the output of a process or system to the input; the process by which a system, often biological or ecological, is modulated, controlled, or changed by the product, output, or response it produces
retroalimentación respuesta de una parte del resultado de un proceso o sistema a la entrada; el proceso mediante el cual el producto, el resultado o la respuesta que produce un sistema, que generalmente es biológico o ecológico, lo modula, controla o cambia

felsic describes magma or igneous rock that is rich in feldspars and silica and that is generally light in color
félsico término que describe un tipo de magma o roca ígnea que es rica en feldespatos y sílice y generalmente tiene un color claro

focus (FOH·kuhs) the location within Earth along a fault at which the first motion of an earthquake occurs; also one of the two central defining points of an ellipse
foco el lugar dentro de la Tierra a lo largo de una falla donde ocurre el primer movimiento de un terremoto; también uno de los dos puntos definitorios de una elipse

foliation (foh·lee·AY·shuhn) the metamorphic rock texture in which mineral grains are arranged in planes or bands
foliación la textura de una roca metamórfica en la que los granos de mineral están ordenados en planos o bandas

force an action exerted on a body that tends to change the body's state of rest or motion; force has magnitude and direction
fuerza una acción ejercida sobre un objeto que tiende a cambiar el estado de reposo o movimiento del objeto; la fuerza tiene magnitud y dirección

fossil (FAHS·uhl) the trace or remains of an organism that lived long ago, most commonly preserved in sedimentary rock
fósil los indicios o los restos de un organismo que vivió hace mucho tiempo, comúnmente preservados en las rocas sedimentarias

fossil fuel (FAHS·uhl FYOO·uhl) a nonrenewable energy resource formed from the remains of organisms that lived long ago; examples include oil, coal, and natural gas
combustible fósil un recurso energético no renovable formado a partir de los restos de organismos que vivieron hace mucho tiempo; algunos ejemplos incluyen el petróleo, el carbón y el gas natural

fracture in geology, a break in a rock, which results from stress, with or without displacement, including cracks, joints, and faults; also the manner in which a mineral breaks along either curved or irregular surfaces
fractura en geología, un rompimiento en una roca, que resulta de la tensión, con o sin desplazamiento, incluyendo grietas, fisuras y fallas; también, la forma en la que se rompe un mineral a lo largo de superficies curvas o irregulares

frequency (FREE·kwuhn·see) the number of cycles or vibrations per unit of time; also the number of waves produced in a given amount of time
frecuencia el número de ciclos o vibraciones por unidad de tiempo; también, el número de ondas producidas en una cantidad de tiempo determinada

front the boundary between air masses of different densities and usually different temperatures
frente el límite entre masas de aire de diferentes densidades y, normalmente, diferentes temperaturas

G

geosphere (JEE·oh·sfir) the mostly solid, rocky part of Earth; extends from the center of the core to the surface of the crust; one of the four major spheres of the Earth system
geosfera la capa de la Tierra que es principalmente sólida y rocosa; se extiende desde el centro del núcleo hasta la superficie de la corteza terrestre; una de las cuatro esferas principales del sistema terrestre

geothermal energy (jee·oh·THER·muhl EN·er·jee) the energy produced by heat within Earth
energía geotérmica la energía producida por el calor del interior de la Tierra

glacial a time within an ice age that is dominated by the existence of glaciers
glacial en una Edad de Hielo, periodo de tiempo que está dominada por la existencia de glaciares

glacier (GLAY·sher) a large mass of moving ice
glaciar una masa grande de hielo en movimiento

gravity a force of attraction between objects that is due to their masses and that decreases as the distance between the objects increases
gravedad una fuerza de atracción entre dos objetos debida a sus masas, que disminuye a medida que la distancia entre los objetos aumenta

greenhouse gas a gas composed of molecules that absorb and radiate infrared radiation
gas de invernadero un gas compuesto de moléculas que absorben e irradian radiación infrarroja

groundwater the water that is beneath Earth's surface
agua subterránea el agua que está debajo de la superficie de la Tierra

gymnosperm (JIM·nuh·sperm) a woody, vascular seed plant whose seeds are not enclosed by an ovary or fruit
gimnosperma una planta leñosa vascular que produce semillas que no están contenidas en un ovario o fruto

H

half-life the time required for half of a sample of a radioactive isotope to break down by radioactive decay to form a daughter isotope
vida media el tiempo que se requiere para que la mitad de una muestra de un isótopo radiactivo se descomponga por desintegración radiactiva y forme un isótopo hijo

horizon a horizontal layer of soil that can be distinguished from the layers above and below it; also a boundary between two rock layers that have different physical properties
horizonte una capa horizontal de suelo que puede distinguirse de las capas que están por encima y por debajo de ella; también, un límite entre dos capas de roca que tienen propiedades físicas distintas

hot spot a volcanically active area of Earth's surface, commonly far from a tectonic plate boundary
mancha caliente un área volcánicamente activa de la superficie de la Tierra que comúnmente se encuentra lejos de un límite entre placas tectónicas

hydraulic fracturing he process of extracting oil or natural gas by injecting a mixture of water, sand or gravel, and chemicals under high pressure into well holes in dense rock to produce fractures that the sand or gravel holds open; also called fracking
fracturación hidráulica proceso de extracción de petróleo o gas natural a través de la inyección de una mezcla de agua, arena o grava y productos químicos a alta presión en unos pozos en piedra densa para producir fracturas que la arena o los huecos de grava mantienen abiertos; también llamado fracking

hydroelectric energy (hy·droh·ee·LEK·trik EN·er·jee) electrical energy produced by the flow of water
energía hidroeléctrica energía eléctrica producida por el flujo del agua

hydrosphere (HY·druh·sfir) the part of Earth that is water; one of the four major spheres of the Earth system
hidrosfera la porción de la Tierra que es agua; una de las cuatro esferas principales del sistema terrestre

I

ice age a long period of climatic cooling during which the continents are glaciated repeatedly
edad de hielo un largo período de enfriamiento del clima, durante el cual los continentes se ven repetidamente sometidos a la glaciación

igneous rock (IG·nee·uhs RAHK) rock that forms when magma cools and solidifies
roca ígnea una roca que se forma cuando el magma se enfría y se solidifica

index fossil a fossil that is used to establish the age of a rock layer because the fossil is distinct, abundant, and widespread and the species that formed that fossil existed for only a short span of geologic time
fósil guía un fósil que se usa para establecer la edad de una capa de roca debido a que puede diferenciarse bien de otros, es abundante y está extendido; la especie que formó ese fósil existió sólo por un corto período de tiempo geológico

inner core the solid innermost part of Earth, composed mostly of iron and nickel under extremely high pressure and temperature
núcleo interno radiación solar (energía del Sol) que alcanza la Tierra; índice de emisión solar por unidad de superficie horizontal

insolation the solar radiation (energy from the sun) that reaches Earth; also the rate of delivery of solar radiation per unit of horizontal surface
insolación radiación solar (energía del Sol) que alcanza la Tierra; índice de emisión solar por unidad de superficie horizontal

interglacial a comparatively short time of warmth within an ice age
interglacial tiempo comparativamente corto de calor dentro de una Edad de Hielo

interstellar medium material, mostly hydrogen gas, other gases, and dust, occupying the space between stars and providing the raw material for the formation of new stars
medio interestelar material, principalmente compuesto por gas hidrógeno, otros gases y polvo, que ocupa el espacio entre las estrellas y provee la materia prima para la formación de estrellas nuevas

isostatic equilibrium an idealized state of balance between gravitational and buoyant forces acting on Earth's lithosphere, which results in different elevations
equilibrio isostático estado idealizado de equilibrio entre las fuerzas gravitacionales y boyantes que actúan sobre la litósfera de la Tierra, lo que resulta en diferentes elevaciones

isotope (EYE·suh·tohp) one of two or more atoms that have the same number of protons (atomic number) but different numbers of neutrons (atomic mass)
isótopo uno de dos o más átomos que tienen el mismo número de protones (número atómico) pero diferente número de neutrones (masa atómica)

iterate to do again or repeat; in design testing, the results of each repetition are used to modify the next version of the design
iterar volver a hacer o repetir; en las pruebas de diseño, los resultados de cada repetición se utilizan para modificar la siguiente versión del diseño

L

lava (LAH·vuh) magma that flows onto Earth's surface; also the rock that forms when lava cools and solidifies
lava magma que fluye a la superficie terrestre; la roca que se forma cuando la lava se enfría y se solidifica

light-year the distance that light travels in a vacuum in one year; about 9.46 trillion kilometers
año luz la distancia que viaja la luz en un año; aproximadamente 9.46 trillones de kilómetros

lithosphere (LITH·uh·sfir) the solid, outer layer of Earth that consists of the crust and the rigid upper part of the mantle
litosfera la capa externa y sólida de la Tierra que está formada por la corteza y la parte superior y rígida del manto

longshore current a water current that travels near and parallel to the shoreline
corriente de ribera una corriente de agua que se desplaza cerca de la costa y paralela a ella

luster (LUHS·ter) the way in which a mineral reflects light
brillo la forma en que un mineral refleja la luz

M

mafic (MAF·ik) describes magma or igneous rock that is rich in magnesium and iron and that is generally dark in color
máfico término que describe un tipo de magma o roca ígnea que es rica en magnesio y hierro y generalmente tiene un color oscuro

magnetic field a region where a magnetic force can be detected
campo magnético una región donde puede detectarse una fuerza magnética

magnitude a measure of the strength of an earthquake
magnitud una medida de la intensidad de un terremoto

mantle the thick layer of rock between Earth's crust and core
manto la gruesa capa de roca que se encuentra entre la corteza terrestre y el núcleo

mantle convection the slow movement of matter in Earth's mantle, which transfers energy as heat from the interior of Earth to the surface
convección en el manto movimiento lento de la materia en el manto terrestre, el cual transfiere la energía en forma de calor desde el interior de la Tierra hacia la superficie

mass a measure of the amount of matter in an object; a fundamental property of an object that is not affected by the forces that act on the object, such as the gravitational force
masa una medida de la cantidad de materia que tiene un objeto; una propiedad fundamental de un objeto que no está afectada por las fuerzas que actúan sobre el objeto, como por ejemplo, la fuerza gravitacional

mass extinction an episode during which large numbers of species become extinct
extinción masiva un episodio durante el cual grandes cantidades de especies se extinguen

mass wasting the movement of soil, sediment, or rock material down a slope under the influence of gravity
remoción de masa movimiento de suelo (tierra), sedimento o material de roca cuesta abajo (que desciende) por una pendiente bajo la influencia de la gravedad

mesosphere (MEZ·uh·sfir) literally, the "middle sphere"; the strong, lower part of the mantle between the asthenosphere and the outer core; also the coldest layer of the atmosphere, between the stratosphere and the thermosphere, in which temperature decreases as altitude increases
mesosfera literalmente, la "esfera media"; la parte fuerte e inferior del manto que se encuentra entre la astenosfera y el núcleo externo; también, la capa más fría de la atmósfera que se encuentra entre la estratosfera y la termosfera, en la cual la temperatura disminuye al aumentar la altitud

Mesozoic Era the geologic era that lasted from 251 million to 65.5 million years ago; also called the Age of Reptiles
era Mesozoica la era geológica que comenzó hace 251 millones de años y terminó hace 65.5 millones de años; también llamada Edad de los Reptiles

metamorphic rock rock that has been altered in structure or composition by heat, pressure, and chemical substances, usually deep in Earth's crust
roca metamórfica roca que ha sido alterada en su estructura o composición por el calor, la presión y las sustancias químicas, generalmente se encuentran en la profundidad de la corteza terrestre

mid-ocean ridge a long, undersea mountain chain that has a steep, narrow valley at its center, forms as magma rises from the asthenosphere, and produces new oceanic lithosphere (sea floor) as tectonic plates move apart
dorsal oceánica una larga cadena submarina demontañas que tiene un valle empinado y angosto en el centro, se forma a medida que el magma se eleva a partir de la astenosfera y produce una nueva litosfera oceánica (suelo marino) a medida que las placas tectónicas se separan

mineral a natural, usually inorganic solid that has a characteristic chemical composition, an orderly internal structure, and a characteristic set of physical properties
mineral un sólido natural, normalmente inorgánico, que tiene una composición química característica, una estructura interna ordenada y propiedades físicas y químicas características

mining the process of extracting ore, minerals, and other solid materials from the ground
minería proceso de extracción de minerales y otros materiales sólidos del suelo

model a simplified representation designed to show the structure or workings of an object, system, or concept
modelo una representación simplificada cuyo objetivo es mostrar la estructura o funcionamiento de un objeto, sistema or concepto

moraine a landform that is made from unsorted sediments deposited by a glacier; the till deposited by a glacier
morrena un accidente geográfico que se forma a partir de varios tipos de sedimentos depositados por un glaciar; la arcilla glaciárica depositados por un glaciar

N

natural hazard a naturally occurring phenomenon that produces a chance of harm to humans, property, or the environment
peligro natural un fenómeno natural que produce una posibilidad de ocasionar daño a los humanos, la propiedad o al ambiente

natural resource a material or capacity, such as timber, a mineral deposit, or water power, that occurs in a natural state and has economic value
recurso natural un material o una capacidad, como la madera, un depósito mineral o la energía hidráulica, que tiene lugar en estado natural y que tiene valor económico

nebula (NEB·yuh·luh) a large cloud of gas and dust in interstellar space; a region in space where stars form
nebulosa una nube grande de gas y polvo en el espacio interestelar; una región en el espacio donde las estrellas nacen

negative feedback feedback that applies the output against the initial conditions, which tends to counteract or reduce a change and stabilize a process or system
retroalimentación negativa retroalimentación que aplica al resultado contra las condiciones iniciales y que tiende a contrarrestar o reducir un cambio y a estabilizar un proceso o sistema

nonrenewable not capable of being renewed, such as a resource that forms at a rate that is much slower than the rate at which the resource is consumed
no renovable incapaz de ser renovado, tal como un recurso que se forma a una tasa que es mucho más lenta que la tasa a la que se consume

nuclear fusion the process by which nuclei of small atoms combine to form a new, more massive nucleus; the process releases energy
fusión nuclear el proceso por medio del cual los núcleos de átomos pequeños se combinan y forman un núcleo nuevo con mayor masa; el proceso libera energía

O

oceanic trench a long, narrow, and steep depression that forms on the ocean floor as a result of subduction of a tectonic plate, that runs parallel to the trend of a chain of volcanic islands or the coastline of a continent, and that may be as deep as 11 km below sea level; also called a *trench* or a *deep-ocean trench*
fosa oceánica depresión larga, estrecha y empinada que se forma en el fondo oceánico como resultado de la subducción de una placa tectónica que corre paralela a la tendencia de una cadena de islas volcánicas o la costa de un continente y que puede tener una profundidad de hasta 11 km bajo el nivel del mar; también llamada trinchera o zanja de aguas profundas

oil shale a black, dark gray, or dark brown shale containing hydrocarbons that yield petroleum by distillation
pizarra bituminosa roca sedimentaria negra, gris oscura o marrón oscura que contiene hidrocarburos y produce petróleo por destilación

orbit the path of a body as it moves around another body due to their mutual gravitational attraction
órbita trayectoria de un cuerpo según se mueve alrededor de otro cuerpo debido a su atracción gravitacional mutua

ore a natural material whose concentration of economically valuable minerals is high enough for the material to be mined profitably
mena un material natural cuya concentración de minerales con valor económico es suficientemente alta como para que el material pueda ser explotado de manera rentable

organic sedimentary rock sedimentary rock that forms from the remains of plants or animals
roca sedimentaria orgánica roca sedimentaria que se forma a partir de los restos de plantas o animales

outer core the layer of Earth's interior located between the inner core and mantle, composed mostly of molten iron and nickel
núcleo externo capa del interior de la Tierra, ubicada entre el núcleo interno y el manto, que está compuesta principalmente de hierro fundido y níquel

ozone (OH·zohn) a gas molecule that is made up of three oxygen atoms
ozono una molécula de gas que está formada por tres átomos de oxígeno

P

Paleozoic era the geologic era that followed Precambrian time and that lasted from 542 million to 251 million years ago
era Paleozoica la era geológica que vino después del período Precámbrico; comenzó hace 542 millones de años y terminó hace 251 millones de años

parallax (PAIR·uh·laks) an apparent shift in the position of an object when viewed from different locations
paralaje un cambio aparente en la posición de un objeto cuando se ve desde lugares distintos

passive margin a continental margin that does not occur along a plate boundary
margen pasivo margen continental que no tiene lugar a lo largo de un límite de placas

phenomenon an occurrence, circumstance, or fact that is observable
fenómeno un suceso, circunstancia o hecho que es observable

photon a massless particle of electromagnetic radiation
fotón una partícula sin masa de radiación electromagnética

photosynthesis process by which light energy is converted to chemical energy by organisms such as plants; produces sugar and oxygen from carbon dioxide and water
fotosíntesis proceso mediante el cual la energía luminosa se convierte en energía química; produce azúcar y oxígeno a partir de dióxido de carbono y agua

plasma a state of matter that starts as a gas and then becomes ionized; it consists of free-moving ions and electrons, it takes on an electric charge, and its properties differ from the properties of a solid, liquid, or gas
plasma un estado de la materia que comienza como un gas y luego se vuelve ionizado; está formado por iones y electrones que se mueven libremente, tiene carga eléctrica y sus propiedades difieren de las propiedades de un sólido, líquido o gas

plateau a large, elevated, comparatively level expanse of land, which is higher than a plain and larger than a mesa
meseta gran extensión de tierra elevada y comparativamente nivelada, que es más alta que una llanura y más grande que una mesa

plate tectonics (PLAYT tek·TAHN·iks) the theory that explains how large pieces of the lithosphere, called plates, move and change shape
tectónica de placas la teoría que explica cómo las grandes partes de litosfera, denominadas placas, se mueven y cambian de forma

polar describes a molecule in which the positive and negative charges are separated
polar término que describe una molécula en la que las cargas positivas y negativas están separadas

positive feedback feedback that tends to amplify or increase a change and destabilize a process or system
retroalimentación positiva retroalimentación que tiende a amplificar o aumentar un cambio y desestabilizar un proceso o sistema

Precambrian the interval of time in the geologic time scale from Earth's formation to the beginning of the Paleozoic era, from 4.6 billion to 542 million years ago
período Precámbrico el intervalo en la escala de tiempo geológico que abarca desde la formación de la Tierra hasta el comienzo de la era Paleozoica; comenzó hace 4,600 millones de años y terminó hace 542 millones de años

precession the motion of the axis of a spinning body, such as the wobble of a spinning top, when there is an external force acting on the axis; a slow gyration of Earth's rotational axis relative to its orbit
precesión movimiento del eje de un cuerpo giratorio, como el tambaleo de un trompo, cuando hay una fuerza externa que actúa sobre el eje; un giro lento del eje de rotación de la Tierra con relación a su órbita

protoplanetary disk a disk of gas and dust particles that orbit a newly formed star, from which planets may form
disco protoplanetario disco de gas y partículas de polvo que orbita alrededor de una estrella recién formada, del cual se pueden formar planetas

P wave (PEE WAYV) a primary wave, or compression wave; a seismic wave that causes particles of rock to move in a back-and-forth direction parallel to the direction in which the wave is traveling; P waves are the fastest seismic waves and can travel through solids, liquids, and gases
onda P una onda primaria u onda de compresión; una onda sísmica que hace que las partículas de roca se muevan en una dirección de atrás hacia delante en forma paralela a la dirección en que viaja la onda; las ondas P son las ondas sísmicas más rápidas y pueden viajar a través de sólidos, líquidos y gases

R

radiation the emission and propagation of energy in the form of electromagnetic waves; also moving subatomic particles
radiación emisión y propagación de energía en forma de ondas electromagnéticas; también, partículas subatómicas en movimiento

radioactive decay (ray·dee·oh·AK·tiv dih·KAY) the disintegration of an unstable atomic nucleus into one or more different types of atoms or isotopes, accompanied by the emission of radiation, the nuclear capture or ejection of electrons, or fission
desintegración radiactiva desintegración de un núcleo atómico inestable para formar uno o más diferentes tipos de átomos o isotópos, lo cual va acompañado de emisión de radiación, captura o expulsión nuclear de electrones o fisión

rare earth element any of a group of naturally occurring metallic elements that have similar properties, consisting of scandium, yttrium, and the 15 elements with atomic numbers 57 through 71 (the lanthanides). The rare earth elements are widely used in electronics and other high-tech products.
elementos de tierras raras cualquiera de un grupo de elementos metálicos que ocurren naturalmente y que tienen propiedades similares; este grupo consiste del escandio, el itrio y los 15 elementos con números atómicos entre 57 y 71 (los lantánidos). Los elementos de tierras raras son ampliamente utilizados en electrónica y otros productos de alta tecnología.

recharge the volume of water that flows in within a given time
recarga volumen de agua que fluye dentro de un periodo de tiempo determinado

reclamation the process of bringing into or restoring to a suitable condition, such as a previous natural state
recuperación el proceso de traer a o de restaurar una condición adecuada, tal como en un estado natural previo

recycle to put or pass through a cycle again; to recover valuable or useful materials from waste or scrap or to reuse items
reciclar poner o pasar de nuevo por un ciclo; recuperar materiales valiosos o útiles de desechos o chatarra o reutilizar artículos

relative age the age of an object in relation to the ages of other objects
edad relativa la edad de un objeto en relación con la edad de otros objetos

renewable capable of being renewed, such as a resource that is inexhaustible or replaceable by new formation
renovable capaz de ser renovado, tal como un recurso que es inagotable o replicable por nueva formación

reservoir a place or part of a system in which something collects or is collected
depósito lugar o parte de un sistema en que algo se recoge o es recogido

respiration the process occurring within living cells by which the chemical energy of organic molecules is converted into usable energy, involving the consumption of oxygen and the production of carbon dioxide and water as byproducts
respiración proceso que ocurre dentro de las células vivas, mediante el cual la energía química de las moléculas orgánicas es convertida en energía utilizable; implica el consumo de oxígeno y la producción de dióxido de carbono y agua como subproductos

ridge push a force that is exerted by cooling, subsiding rock on the spreading lithospheric plates at a mid-ocean ridge
empuje de la dorsal fuerza que es ejercida por el enfriamiento y el hundimiento de la roca en la extensión de las placas litosféricas en la dorsal medio oceánica

rock cycle the series of processes in which rock forms, changes from one type to another, is destroyed, and forms again by geologic processes
ciclo de las rocas la serie de procesos por medio de los cuales una roca se forma, cambia de un tipo a otro, se destruye y se forma nuevamente por procesos geológicos

S

sediment solid particles such as weathered rock fragments, materials from organisms, or minerals that settle out of solution that are transported and deposited at or near Earth's surface
sedimento partículas sólidas, tales como fragmentos de roca erosionada, materiales de organismos o minerales, que se depositan fuera de la solución, que son transportados y depositados en o cerca de la superficie de la Tierra

sedimentary rock rock formed by the compaction and cementing of layers of sediment
roca sedimentaria roca formada por la compactación y cementación de capas de sedimento

seismic wave an elastic wave, or packet of energy, produced by an earthquake
onda sísmica onda elástica, o paquete de energía, producida por un terremoto

seismogram (SYZ·muh·gram) a tracing of earthquake motion that is recorded by a seismograph
sismograma una traza del movimiento de un terremoto registrada por un sismógrafo

silicate a mineral that contains a combination of silicon and oxygen and that may also contain one or more metals
mineral silicato un mineral que contiene una combinación de silicio y oxígeno y que también puede contener uno o más metales

sinkhole a circular depression that forms when rock dissolves, when overlying sediment fills an existing cavity, or when the roof of an underground cavern or mine collapses
depresión una depresión circular que se forma cuando la roca se funde, cuando el sedimento suprayacente llena una cavidad existente, o al colapsarse el techo de una caverna o mina subterránea

slab pull a force at a subduction boundary exerted on a subducting plate due to the weight of the sinking edge
fuerza de arrastre de placas en un límite de subducción, fuerza ejercida sobre una placa subductora debido al peso del borde que se hunde

soil a loose mixture of rock fragments and organic material that can support the growth of vegetation
suelo una mezcla suelta de fragmentos de roca y material orgánico en la que puede crecer vegetación

solar wind a stream of high-speed, ionized particles ejected primarily from the sun's corona
viento sol corriente de partículas ionizadas de alta velocidad que son principalmente expulsadas de la corona del Sol

solvent (SAHL·vuhnt) in a solution, the substance in which another substance (the solute) dissolves
solvente en una solución, la sustancia en la que se disuelve otra sustancia (el soluto)

specific heat (spih·SIF·ik HEET) the quantity of heat required to raise a unit mass of homogeneous material 1 K or 1 ºC in a specified way, given constant pressure and volume
calor específico la cantidad de calor que se requiere para aumentar una unidad de masa de un material homogéneo 1 K ó 1º C de una manera especificada, dados un volumen y una presión constantes

spectrum a pattern of radiation seen or recorded when the components making up light are separated in order of frequency, as when light passes through a prism
espectro patrón de radiación visto o registrado cuando los componentes que constituyen la luz son separados en orden de frecuencia, como cuando la luz pasa a través de un prisma

stratosphere the layer of the atmosphere that lies between the troposphere and the mesosphere and in which temperature increases as altitude increases; contains the ozone layer
estratosfera la capa de la atmósfera que se encuentra entre la troposfera y la mesosfera y en la cual la temperatura aumenta al aumentar la altitud; contiene la capa de ozono

subduction a process at a convergent boundary in which an oceanic plate is descending beneath another, overriding plate.
subducción en un límite convergente, proceso mediante el cual una placa oceánica desciende debajo de una placa obductante

subsidence the sinking or caving in of an area of ground due to geological processes
hundimiento hundimiento o desmoronamiento de un área del suelo debido a los procesos geológicos

sunspot a dark area of the photosphere of the sun that is cooler than the surrounding areas and that has a strong magnetic field
mancha solar un área oscura en la fotosfera del Sol que es más fría que las áreas que la rodean y que tiene un campo magnético fuerte

supercontinent a hypothetical land mass containing most of Earth's continental crust; according to the theory of plate tectonics, supercontinents form and break up
supercontinente masa terrestre hipotética que contiene la mayor parte de la corteza terrestre continental; según la teoría de la de las placas tectónicas, los supercontinentes se forman y se rompen

supernova the energetic event that follows the collapse of the iron core of a massive star; elements of atomic mass greater than iron are produced
supernova suceso energético que sigue al colapso del núcleo de hierro de una estrella masiva; durante una supernova se producen elementos de masa atómica mayor que el hierro

surface process a process affecting the geosphere at or near Earth's surface and driven mostly by external energy, such as weathering and erosion
proceso de la superficie proceso que afecta la geósfera en o cerca de la superficie de la Tierra y está impulsado mayormente por energía externa, tales como la meteorización y la erosión

sustainability (suh·stayn·uh·BIL·ih·tee) the condition in which human needs are met in such a way that a human population can survive indefinitely
sustentabilidad la condición en la que se cumple con las necesidades humanas de una forma tal que una población humana pueda sobrevivir indefinidamente

sustainable capable of being continued or prolonged
sostenible capaz de ser continuo o prolongado

S wave (ES WAYV) a secondary wave, or shear wave; a seismic wave that causes particles of rock to move in a side-to-side direction perpendicular to the direction in which the wave is traveling; S waves are the second-fastest seismic waves and can travel only through solids
onda S una onda secundaria u onda rotacional; una onda sísmica que hace que las partículas de roca se muevan en una dirección de lado a lado, en forma perpendicular a la dirección en la que viaja la onda; las ondas S son las segundas ondas sísmicas en cuanto a velocidad y únicamente pueden viajar a través de sólidos

system a set of particles or interacting components considered to be a distinct physical entity for the purpose of study
sistema un conjunto de partículas o componentes que interactúan unos con otros, el cual se considera una entidad física independiente para fines de estudio

T

tar sand sand or sandstone containing petroleum, from which the volatiles have escaped, leaving a hydrocarbon (asphalt) residue
arena de alquitrá arena o arenisca que contiene petróleo, de la cual los volátiles han escapado, dejando un residuo de hidrocarburo (asfalto)

tectonic plate (tek·TAHN·ik PLAYT) a block of lithosphere that consists of the crust and the rigid, outermost part of the mantle
placa tectónica un bloque de litosfera formado por la corteza y la parte rígida y más externa del manto

thermosphere (THER·muh·sfir) the uppermost layer of the atmosphere, in which temperature increases as altitude increases; includes the ionosphere
termosfera la capa más alta de la atmósfera, en la cual la temperatura aumenta a medida que la altitud aumenta; incluye la ionosfera

tidal energy energy produced because of the gravitational pull of the sun and moon on Earth's oceans
energía mareomotriz energía producida debido a la fuerza gravitatoria del Sol y la Luna sobre los océanos de la Tierra

till unsorted rock material that is deposited directly by a melting glacier
arcilla glaciárica material rocoso desordenado que deposita directamente un glaciar que se está derritiendo

topography (tuh·PAHG·ruh·fee) the size and shape of the land surface features of a region, including its relief
topografía el tamaño y la forma de las características de una superficie de terreno, incluyendo su relieve

tradeoff an exchange of one thing in return for another, especially relinquishment of one benefit or advantage for another regarded as more desirable
compensación intercambio de una cosa a cambio de otra, especialmente la cesión de un beneficio o ventaja por otro considerado como más conveniente

transform boundary (TRANS·fohrm BOWN·duh·ree) the boundary between tectonic plates that are sliding past each other horizontally
límite de transformación el límite entre placas tectónicas que se están deslizando horizontalmente una sobre otra

troposphere (TROH·puh·sfir) the lowest layer of the atmosphere, in which temperature drops at a constant rate as altitude increases; the part of the atmosphere where weather conditions exist
troposfera la capa inferior de la atmósfera, en la que la temperatura disminuye a una tasa constante a medida que la altitud aumenta; la parte de la atmósfera donde se dan las condiciones del tiempo

U

uplift to raise; the act, process, or result of raising or lifting up; an upheaval
levantamiento elevar; acto, proceso o resultado de levantar o alzar; un levantamienton

velocity the speed of an object in a particular direction
  velocidad la rapidez de un objeto en una dirección
  dada

volatile evaporating readily at normal temperatures and
  pressures; also a substance that is volatile
  volátil que se evapora fácilmente a temperaturas y
  presiones normales; una sustancia que es volátil

volcano (vahl·KAY·noh) a vent or fissure in Earth's surface
  through which magma and gases are expelled
  volcán una chimenea o fisura en la superficie de la
  Tierra a través de la cual se expulsan magma y gases

watershed the area of land that is drained by a river system
  cuenca hidrográfica el área del terreno que es drenada
  por un sistema de ríos

wavelength (WAYV·lengkth) the distance from any point on a
  wave to the corresponding point on the next wave
  longitud de onda la distancia entre cualquier punto
  de una onda y el punto correspondiente de la siguiente
  onda

weather the short-term state of the atmosphere, including
  temperature, humidity, precipitation, wind, and visibility
  tiempo el estado de la atmósfera a corto plazo que
  incluye la temperatura, la humedad, la precipitación, el
  ventor y la visibilidad

weathering (WETH·er·ing) the natural process by which
  atmospheric and environmental agents, such as wind,
  rain, and temperature changes, disintegrate and
  decompose rocks
  meteorización el proceso natural por medio del cual
  los agentes atmosféricos o ambientales, como el viento,
  la lluvia y los cambios de temperatura, desintegran y
  descomponen las rocas

Index

Page numbers for illustrations, maps, and charts are printed in *italics*.
Page numbers for definitions are printed in **boldface** type.

light and latitude, 51
mineral identification, 69
model forces, 434
modeling desert winds, 423
modeling expanding universe, 288
modeling molds and casts, 574
model water cycle, 97
monthly sea surface temperatures, 9, *9*
ratios, 102
reclamation, 141
resources, 114, *114*
slipping ice, 418
space images, 262, *262*
spectral analysis, 248
thermal spectra, 266
uneven precipitation, 472, *472*
water solubility, 456
Anatolian fault, 352
andesite, *374*
andesitic magma, 380
Andes Mountains, 326, 591
formation of, 346, 347, *347*
open-pit mining in, 140
volcanoes in, 348
anemometers, 513
angiosperms, 589
animals
in biosphere, 23
in Cenozoic, 591, 594, *594*
endangered species, 603
Frozen Ark Project, 651
in Mesozoic, *589,* 589–590, *590*
in Miocene, 602
in Pliocene, 602
Precambrian, 586
anorthosite, 86
Antarctica, 206, 583
in Cenozoic, 591
climate of, 532
formation of, 588
glaciation of, 591, 593
ice cores from, 535
ice sheets in, 219, 417, 600
ice shelves in, 417
ozone over, 20, *25,* 25–26, *26,* 27, *27,*
33, 33
polar vortex, 33
precipitation in, 531
anthracite coal, 79, 150
anthroposphere, 23, 28, *28*–29, *29,* 638.
See also **human activities**
antimony, 133
ants, fossilized, 560, *560*
Appalachian Mountains, 346, 429, *429,*
431, *435, 556, 584*
aquaculture, 481
aquaponics, 649, *649*
Aquarius Reef Base, 10, *10*
aqueducts, 482

aquifers, 469, 471, 474, *474, 475,* 491, *491*
aquitards, 474
Arabia, 584
archaea, 23
Architecture Connection
living underground, 656, *656*
Arctic ice cap, *593*
Arctic Ocean, 206, 530, *530,* 545, *545*
arc volcanoes, 367
arête, 418, *418*
argon, 22, 495, *496*
argument, 109
constructing, 125
criteria for, 305
to support opinion, 125
Arizona
Barringer Crater (Meteor Crater), 186,
186
Grand Canyon, 558, *558, 575, 575*
Horseshoe Bend, 408, *408, 425, 425*
Petrified Forest National Park, *560*
water demands in, 473
the Wave, *390*
armadillo, 602
Arp, Halton, 231
Art Connection
artistic license, 614, *614*
landscape paintings, 40, *40*
minerals and art, 106, *106*
sun in art, 226, *226*
artificial trees, 543
artistic license, 614, *614*
asbestos, 133
ash, volcanic, 373, *373,* 501
Asia
in Cenozoic, *591*
viewed from International Space
Station, *174*
asking questions, about seasonal
changes
on Mars, 229
asteroid belt, 178, 181, *181,* 184, 271
asteroids
craters from, 186
distance from sun and composition of,
181, *181*
in early Earth history, 187
impacts from, 189
mass extinction from, 578, *578,* 590
mining, 170, *170*
Vesta, *179*
asthenosphere, *310, 312,* 313, 432, *432*
astronomers, 179, 193
astronomical units (AUs), 273, 274, *274*
astronomy, 231
Atacama Desert, Chile, *453,* 532
Atlantic Ocean, 344
in Cenozoic, 601
evidence about, 389, *389*

formation of, 587, *587,* 588
mid-ocean ridge system, 588
***Atlas of Peculiar Galaxies* (Arp),** 231
atmosphere (of Earth), 21, 22, *22,*
494–509. *See also* **climate; weather**
acid precipitation and, 398, *398*
altitude and temperature in, *496,*
496–498
amount of sunlight reaching, 214
aurora, 207, *207*
carbon dioxide in, 5, *14,* 15, *94*
carbon in, 91
changes in composition of, 537
changes over time in, 14, *14*
chlorofluorocarbons in, 26, *26*
circulation within, 52
composition of, 207, *495,* 495–496, *496*
definitions of, 23
of early Earth, 581
El Niño events and, 7
end-Permian mass extinction and, 586
extreme weather, 493
fresh water in, 469
greenhouse effect in, 210
greenhouse gases in, 537
human impact on, *645,* 645–646, *646*
interaction of other spheres and, *495,*
499–501, *499–501*
interaction with electromagnetic
radiation, 236
layers of, 496–498, *496–498*
motion in, 502–507, *502–507*
nitrogen in, 99
oceans and, 6
oxygen cycling in, 100
oxygen in, 20
ozone in, 20, *20, 25,* 33, *33*
of the past, evidence of, 13
phosphorus in, 100
seen from space, *21*
solar energy in, 210
solar energy reflected/absorbed by,
538
structure of, 495–498
studying, 498, *498,* 508, *508*
thunderstorms and, 10
volcanic eruptions and composition
of, *12*
in water cycle, 471, *471*
atmosphere (of moon), 499
atmosphere (of the sun), 254
atmospheric circulation, 52, 53, *53,* 605
atmospheric pressure, 496, 497, 503
atoms
in big bang theory, 285, *285*
energy gain/loss in, 242, *242*
in minerals, 61, *61,* 87
aurora, 207, *207, 308, 316,* 319, *319,* 321,
497, 498, 498, 509

luster, *64*, 64–65

M

mafic rock, 81, *81*
magafauna, 594
magma, 393
    andesitic, 380
    basaltic, 344, 368, 370, 380
    differences in chemical composition, 370
    field reversal and, 344
    in geosphere, 21
    silica in, 364, 365
    viscosity of, 365
magnesite, *106*
magnesium, 81, *81*, 101
magnetic field(s)
    basaltic rocks and, *343*, 344
    of Earth, 207, *256*, 316, 319
    of sun's surface, 256
    temporary, 317
magnetic field reversals, *604*
magnetic poles
    of Earth, reversal of, 344
    Halley's theory of, 308
magnetic rail gun, 508
magnetic reversal, 344
magnetism, of Earth, *308*
magnetite, 13
magnetoreception, 386, *386*
magnetosphere (Earth), *256*
main-sequence stars, 259, 263, *263*
malachite, *65*, 67
malaria, 552, *552*
mammallike reptiles, 589
mammals, *589*
    Cenozoic, 591, 594, *594*
    Miocene, 602
    Pliocene, 602, *602*
mammoth, 560, *560*, 594
Mammoth Cave, Kentucky, 412
Manarola, Italy, *620*
Manicouagan crater, Québec, Canada, 189, *189*
mantle (Earth), 309, *310*, 311, 312–314, *312–314*
    convection in, *317*, 318, *318*
    density of, 312
    layers of, 312, *312*
    in lithosphere, *311*
    radiogenic heat generated in, 55
    seismic waves in, 315
    upward convection in, 433
mantle convection, 318, *318*, 355, *355–356*, 357, 437
mantle plumes, 369
map(s), 3, *35*
    of air quality index, *645*

in analyzing light difference problem, 28–29, *29*
in assessing problems, 43, *43*
of bleaching alerts, 15, *15*
cartographers and, 404
cloud, 548–551, *548–551*
of coral bleaching, *15*
of cosmic microwave background, *292*
distribution, 623, *623*
of earthquakes and volcanoes, *327, 328*
of Earth's surface, *29*, 29–30, *30*, 31, *31*, 442–447
of Earth's systems, 29–32
of El Niño events, *6, 8, 15, 18*
historical, 40
information shown on, *404*
of lithosphere motion, *326*
map projections, 32, *32*
of the Milky Way, 280, *281*
as models, 3, 29
of North American mountain ranges, *429*
of ozone concentration, *20*, 33, *33*
of ozone depletion, 27
of ozone hole, *20*, 27, *27*, 33, 34
of plate boundaries, *340, 351*
of plate motion, *339*
radar, 30
radio, 551, *551*
regional, 40, *40*
relief, 3, *3*
road, 40
scientific, 31, *31*
of social media user connections, *20*
of surface waters, 474, *474*
of tectonic plates, 329, *329*
topographic, 30
tourist, 40
of the universe, *276*
weather, *524*, 524–525, *525*, 548–551, *548–551*
of your school and grounds, 3, 42
map layers, 30
mapping
    data, 31, *31*
    Earth's systems, *29*, 29–30, *30*
    ozone hole, 27, *27*
map projections, 32, *32*
marble, *74*, 83
Mariana Trench, 478
marine animals
    Mesozoic, 590, *590*
    seawater pH and, 646
    shells of, 646
    skeletons of, in geosphere, 21
marine ecosystems, Ordovician, *585*
marine mining, 138, *138*
marine organisms
    on continental shelves, 596

in coral reefs, 4
pollution levels in, 478
maritime air masses, 515, *515*
maritime polar air masses, 515, *515*
maritime tropical air masses, 515, *515*
Mars, *179*
    apparent motion of, *179*
    distance from Earth, 197
    Jezero Crater, *232*
    mass and density of, 180, *180, 181*
    physical characteristics of, *185*, 185–186
    seasonal changes on, 229, *229*
marsupials, 594
Maryland, Sideling Hill, *435*
mass
    of Earth, 316
    gravity and, 200
    of planets, 180, *180, 181*
    of protostars, 263
    of stars, 258, *258*, 259, 263
mass bleaching, 17
mass extinctions, 578, 656, *656*
    Cretaceous-Tertiary, 590
    in current period, 647
    end-Permian, 586, 590
    evidence of, 578, *578*, 596, *596*
    late Ordovician, 585
    major, 578
    Mesozoic, 578, *578*, 590, *590*
    Paleozoic, 586, *586*
    tectonic plates and, 596
mass motion, 400
Math Connection
    calculate air pressure, 519
    calculate albedo, 210
    climate graphs, 534, *534*
    compare rock compositions, 81
    density of stars, 258
    orders of magnitude, 274
    population density, 644, *644*
    radial and tangential, 244
    radiometric dating methods, 573
    sunspots recorded, 255
mathematical model, El Niño predicted from, 14
matrix (conglomerate), 73
matter. *See also* systems of matter and energy
    carbon dioxide in atmosphere, 94, *94*
    distributed in the solar system, 180–182, *180–182*
    in Earth–sun system, 207
    El Niño events and, 7
    flow of, between Earth's systems, 40, *40*
    in space, observing, 232–249
    in stars, transformations of, 263–265, *263–265*
    system interactions through, 6

Stuff in the Earth We Can Burn,
166–169
Worlds Around the Sun, 222–225
thorium, 55
Three Gorges Dam, China, *659*
thrust faults, 340
thunderstorms, 10, *10*
Tibetan Plateau, *324,* 428
tidal power, 159–160
pros and cons of, 160, *160*
technology for, 159, *159*
tides
gravity and, *208,* 208–209, *209*
materials transported by, 401
till, 419
time
build your own timescale, 595
design your own timeline, 606
geological, 578–596
scales of, 601, *601*
tin, 143
titanium, *134,* 135
tombolos, 415, *416*
tools, stone, 129, *130*
toothpaste, 106, *106*
topographic maps, 30, *30*
topset beds, 410
topsoil, 403, *403,* 644
tornadoes, 628
damage from, 633
forecasting, 521
tornado sirens, *521*
tourist maps, 40
toxic dumping, 640
trace fossils, 562, *562,* 575, 585
trade innovations, 624, *624*
tradeoff matrix, 122
tradeoffs, 118
calculating, 122, *122*
in engineering design process, 118
for sustainable development, 640
trade winds, 6, *6, 7, 502*
tragedy of the commons, 640
transform boundaries, 340, *352,*
352–353, *353*
transit, 192, *192*
transitional crust, 331
transition zone (crust), 332, *332*
transit method, for detecting
exoplanets, 279
transparency, of minerals, *64,* 64–65
transportation revolution, 624, *624*
transport of material, 400–401
by downhill motion, 400, *400*
by erosion and deposition, *400,*
400–401, *401*
by water, 457
transverse dunes, *422*
travertine, 77, 78, 79

tree rings, 571, 600
trees, as resource, 113
trellis drainage pattern, 409
tremolite, *64,* 66
trenches, underwater, 347, *348*
trench suction, 356
Triassic period, *579,* 587, *589*
trilobites, 575, 585, *585*
tropical air masses, 515, *515*
tropical climates, 532
tropical regions, solar energy in, 213
Tropites, 564, *564*
tropopause, 497, *497*
troposphere, 497, *497*
carbon dioxide in, *94*
clouds in, *494*
ozone in, 20
as seen from space, 509, *509*
tsunami, 629, *629*
caused by earthquakes, 376
as natural hazards, 627
Tullimonstrum gregarium, 561
Tully Monster fossil, 561, *561*
tungsten, 133
Turkey, Anatolian fault, 352
turquoise, 130

ultraviolet light, *49, 209*
ultraviolet radiation, 234, 235, *235*
damage from, 20
ozone and, 20, 25, 27
underground homes, 656, *656*
underwater trenches, 347, *348*
uniformitarianism, principle of, 568, *568*
unintended consequences,
sustainability and, 649
United Nations, *648*
United States
air masses in, 520
annual precipitation in, *472*
calderas in, 370
cost of potholes in, 454
energy consumption in, *147*
energy sources for, *650*
fossil fuels used in, 146, 150
geothermal power in, 160
government water management in,
480–481
hydroelectric power in, 158
infrastructure for solar energy in, 648
land use in, *643*
net import reliance, 2008-2011, *131*
principle aquifers of, *475*
space shuttle of, 508
in summer of 1816, 372–374, *372–374*
surface waters in, 474, *474*
watersheds of, *476*

water use and economic activity in, 482
water use trends in, 479, *479*
weather map, 525, *525*
wind energy in, 157
universal laws, 238
universal solvent, water as, 456–457
the universe, 270–281
comparing size and distance in, 273,
273
detecting exoplanets, 279, *279*
Doppler shifts in, 239
expanding, 287–289, *287–289* (See also
big bang theory)
extrasolar planetary systems, 279, *279*
galaxy types, 277, *277*
light-years, 274, *274*
Local Group, 276, *276*
map of, *276*
Milky Way galaxy, 275, *275,* 280, *280*
nebulae and star clusters, 275, *275*
objects in, 233
orders of magnitude in, 276
patterns in, 277–280, *277–280*
scale of, 271–276
solar system, *271,* 271–272, *272*
uplift, 432, 432–433
uranium-lead dating, 55, 265, 572
uranium-lead decay, 55
Uranus, 178, 180, *180, 181*
urban areas. *See also* **cities**
construction and water supply in, 644
healthy ecosystems in, 651
urban heat islands, 56, *56*
urban planners, 636, 651, 653
urban planning, 653
Ursa major, *230*
Urtica dioica, 566
US Environmental Protection Agency,
645
using models, of carbon cycle, 93
Utah
Canyonlands National Park, *428*
Delicate Arch, Arches National Park,
408
Grand Staircase, Escalante National
Monument, *569*
oil shale deposits in, 152

valley glaciers, 418, *418*
value, relative, 117, 118
van Gogh, Vincent, *226*
variables, controlling, 118
variation, geographic, 27
varves, 571, *571*
vascular plants, *31*
vegetation
changes in, 536